Marketing
Communications

Marketing Communications
Contexts, Strategies and Applications

Third edition

CHRIS FILL
University of Portsmouth

An imprint of **Pearson Education**

Harlow, England · London · New York · Reading, Massachusetts · San Francisco · Toronto · Don Mills, Ontario · Sydney
Tokyo · Singapore · Hong Kong · Seoul · Taipei · Cape Town · Madrid · Mexico City · Amsterdam · Munich · Paris · Milan

Pearson Education Limited
Edinburgh Gate
Harlow
Essex CM20 2JE

and Associated Companies throughout the world

Visit us on the World Wide Web at:
www.pearsoneduc.com

First published under the Prentice Hall Europe imprint 1995
Second edition 1999
Third edition published 2002

© Prentice Hall Europe, 1995, 1999
© Pearson Education Limited 2002

ISBN 0 273 65500 0

British Library Cataloguing-in-Publication Data
A catalogue record for this book is available from the British Library

Library of Congress Cataloging-in-Publication Data
Fill, Chris.
    Marketing communications: contexts, strategies, and
applications / Chris Fill.—2nd ed.
        p. cm.
    Includes bibliographical references and index.
    ISBN 0-273-65500-0 (pbk.)
    1. Communication in marketing.   2. Marketing channels.   3. Sales
promotion.   I. Title
HF5415.123.F55 2001
658.8'02—dc21   2001034648

10 9 8 7 6 5 4 3 2 1
06 05 04 03 02

Typeset in 9pt Stone Serif by 3
Printed and bound by Rotolito in Italy

To my family and especially Karen . . .
. . . simply the best

Brief Contents

Contents

Part 2   Contexts   55

The customer's context

The business context

The internal context

The external context

Part 4   Applications and methods of marketing communications   483

Preface

Welcome to this the third edition of *Marketing Communications,* one which I hope you will enjoy, find interesting and stimulating and one which will encourage you to view the world of marketing communications in a different, inquisitive and challenging way.

A world of marketing communications

All organisations, large and small, commercial, government, charities, educational and other not-for-profit organisations, need to communicate with other organisations. This may be to get materials and services in order to undertake their business activities or to collaborate and coordinate with others to secure suitable distribution of their goods and services. In addition, there are consumers, you and me, people who are free to choose amongst the many hundreds and thousands of product offerings. Marketing communications provide a core activity so that all parties can understand the intentions of others and appreciate the value of the goods and services offered.

Traditionally there are five main marketing communication tools: advertising, sales promotion, personal selling, public relations and direct marketing. In addition, there are media through which time and space can be bought to deliver messages to target audiences. The appropriate mix of these tools and the choice of media was for a long time largely predictable. Distinct mixes could be identified for business-to-consumer (b2c) audiences and business-to-business (b2b) audiences. There were variations reflecting particular brand circumstances but essentially in the b2c market, advertising was used to build brand values, sales promotions were used to instil customer action and public relations sought to generate goodwill and interest about the company. Personal selling was regarded as the primary tool in b2b markets but also had a role to play in retail environments, for example, selling consumer durables. In the 1990s direct marketing became a more prominent tool in the mix because technology had enabled a form of communication by appealing personally and directly to the target customer. This change introduced new media formats and the subsequent development of the Internet and related digital technologies has accelerated change in the marketing communications industry. There are now a myriad of opportunities to reach audiences, with the Internet representing a new, yet challenging, form of communication channel.

At the same time as the media world has splintered into many different parts so have the audiences with whom organisations need to communicate. Consumers now have a variety of different ways to spend their reducing amount of leisure time. Some of those that chose to incorporate the media as part of their relaxation now have not just two but over a hundred television channels, all have access to an increasing number of general and specific interest magazines, a multitude of new cinema complexes and, of course, the Internet with an explosion of Web sites offering a seemingly endless source of information and increasingly a source of global entertainment. The world of marketing communications is bright, exciting, sometimes unpredictable, challenging and evolving.

Managers are now not only required to find new ways to communicate but to do so on reduced budgets and they must account for their communication spend. The development of long-term relationships with customers, whether this be in b2b or b2c markets, is now an essential aspect of marketing policy. Customer retention is crucial today and various devices, such as loyalty schemes, are used to shape long-term customer behaviour. Organisations now accept that the tools of the promotional mix are not the only way brands communicate. All parts of the marketing mix communicate: the behaviour of employees and the performance of products, the actions of competitors all serve to influence the way in which each customer perceives a brand. Corporate branding is now recognised as an integral part of the overall communication effort. Corporate reputation and the actions undertaken by organisations are perceived not only in terms of brand values and profits but also in terms of their ethics and the impact organisations have on the environment.

Marketing communication agencies are trying to adjust the way they can best serve the interests of their clients and the result is structural realignment (mergers and takeovers) which leads to consolidation. Clients themselves are fighting to generate superior value for their customers and the first year of the new millennium was witness to the greatest ever number of mergers and acquisitions. Globalisation and the development of partnerships, alliances and networks are all testimony to changing markets and expectations.

Where does this all lead? It leads to integrated marketing communications and a vision that an organisation's entire planned communications should be consistent. This word consistency applies to internal policies and strategies, to messages to and from internal and external stakeholders, consistency with the values of their customers and with the relationships they forge with key suppliers and distributors.

This book will introduce readers to this changing world of marketing communications and allow them to appreciate some of the conceptual underpinnings associated with integrated marketing communications. There are examples of the practical application of marketing communications and there are examples that demonstrate the application of theory in practice. This book does not just show how organisations use marketing communications, it also contains theoretical material to enable readers to understand why organisations use marketing communications in the way they do.

Overview of this book

Despite the misuse and often laboured understanding of the term, this book presents marketing communications from a strategic perspective. The interlinking of corporate, marketing and promotional strategy, the blend of internal and external communications, the relational aspects of network communications, and the various objectives and strategies that flow from understanding the context within which marketing communications emanates, functions and forms a part of the fabric within which audiences frame and interpret marketing messages are presented to readers for consideration.

This book has been written deliberately from an academic perspective and seeks to provide a suitably consistent appraisal of the ever-expanding world of marketing communications. This book seeks to stimulate thought and consideration about a wide range of interrelated issues, and to help achieve this aim a number of theories and models are advanced. Some of these theories reflect marketing practice, while others are offered as suggestions for moving the subject forward. Many of the theories are abstractions of actual practice, some are based on empirical research and others are pure conceptualisation. All seek to enrich the subject, but not all need carry the same weight of contribution. Readers should form their own opinions based upon their reading, experience and judgement.

There are a number of themes running through the text, but perhaps the two main ones concern relationship marketing and integrated communications. I am of the view that organisations will in the future perceive communications as a core strategic activity, central to strategic management and thought. Corporate and marketing communications will inevitably merge and integrate, the need to build and sustain relationships with a variety of stakeholders inside and outside the organisation will become paramount and communications will be a vital source in making it all work.

In this light, this text assumes relationship marketing to be essential and sees communication in the context of relational exchanges. Corporate and marketing communications are considered as important components of the total process.

The structure of this book has been revised from the previous edition. It is now in four parts and several new chapters have been included. These are:

Marketing communication strategies and planning (Chapter 12)

Branding and the role of marketing communications (Chapter 14)

Business-to-business marketing communications (Chapter 15)

Interactive communication strategy (Chapter 18)

On-line marketing communications (Chapter 25)

Exhibitions, packaging and field marketing (Chapter 30)

Two chapters, 'Media and media planning' (Chapter 22) and 'Evaluating marketing communications' (Chapter 31) have been formed by amalgamating and updating material spread across several chapters in the previous edition. In addition, all chapters have been revised, updated and refreshed.

Structure of this text

There are four main parts to this book:

Part 1 introduces readers to the subject from a general perspective and seeks to establish an understanding of communication theory that serves as an anchor for much of the material that follows.

Part 2 considers the *contexts* within which communications are developed: the situations facing those responsible for the development and implementation of marketing communication strategies.

Part 3 explores some of the *strategies* available to organisations in the light of their contextual positions. This part also examines planning, branding, interactive communications and integrated marketing communications.

Part 4 examines the individual promotional methods or *application* tools available to communicate with target audiences.

Part 1: Introduction and setting the scene

This opening part of the book serves to establish the scope of the book and provides a brief overview of the content and style adopted throughout the rest of the book. Chapter 1 provides an introductory perspective to marketing communications and sets out some key concepts. It also contains a brief overview of each of the tools of the marketing communications mix. Chapter 2 addresses issues concerning communication theory and in particular moves on from the simple linear interpretation of how communication works to one that recognises the influence of people, behaviour and interactional elements on the communication process.

Part 2: Contexts

This part considers the individual elements that underpin or contribute to marketing communications. The situations in which communications occur influence current communications and the way they are received, interpreted and used by people. Only through understanding the context in which communications are developed, conveyed and understood by receivers can effective communications evolve.

Developing a contextual perspective based upon a thorough understanding of the market and the target audience is imperative if appropriate objectives, strategies, promotional methods, applications and resources are to be determined, allocated and implemented.

A number of contexts are explored, first, in Chapters 3 and 4, the *customer's context*. By understanding how customers process information and the way they make purchasing decisions in particular situations for particular product categories and brands, is it possible to design communication strategies and messages that are relevant to members of the target audience and their needs. Only by understanding target audiences is it possible to develop appropriate marketing communication strategies and relevant messages.

By analysing the *business context* it is possible to consider market conditions, competitors communications and above all else incorporate the marketing plan already devised. This will include information about the target segments and what the marketing goals are that the communication plan seeks to deliver. There is an overlap with the customer context but by considering them as two separate areas it is possible to gain a deeper communication insight. In addition, ethical issues are considered. By examining some of the responsibilities that participants in the marketing communication process hold, it assists understanding of what could, should and often is conveyed through marketing communication messages. Chapters 5 and 6 are relevant.

Next, the *internal context* is reviewed. Chapter 7 looks at those factors that influence and are influenced by communication activities within organisations. Ideally these should blend with an organisation's external communications. Chapter 8 considers the financial resources necessary to support marketing communications. Methods of budgeting and the strategic implications of financial decisions are looked at.

The final context to be considered is the *external* situation: Chapter 9 looks at the impact that wider environmental forces can have on an organisation's marketing communications. PEST analysis is used but the focus is one 'what does this mean for communications?' Chapters 10 refers to and seeks to develop an understanding of the interrelationships between the different organisations and stakeholders who impact on an organisation's marketing communications. The networks of stakeholders are considered primarily from a 'marketing channel' perspective, with a particular emphasis upon the relationships that are of increasing importance. In Chapter 11, attention is given to the communications industry and specifically the strategic and operational issues of advertising agencies and their interaction with client organisations.

Part 3: Strategies

Part 3 of the book opens with Chapter 12. This new chapter explores the nature of communication strategy and considers the interrelationship between strategy and planning. The second section of the chapter introduces the marketing communications planning framework and works through the model highlighting issues and linkages and ends with an operational approach to devising, formulating and implementing a strategic marketing communications plan.

Chapter 13 looks at the nature of objectives and positioning in marketing communications and is followed by a new chapter on branding. This chapter is significant in that it focuses on the role marketing communications can play in the development and maintenance of brands. The branding and positioning connection is significant which is why these strategically significant elements are located next to each other.

The next chapter is also new and by popular demand tries to bring some thoughts together on business-to-business marketing communications. The following chapter on international marketing communications is followed by another new chapter, this time on interactive marketing communication strategy. This chapter considers some important issues concerning the role and deployment of interactive communications. The final chapter in this part of the book is entitled 'Integrated marketing communications' and is a core chapter in that it bridges the strategy part and the application part. Various concepts are presented and explored from a strategic perspective.

Part 4: Applications and methods of marketing communications

This part looks at the promotional methods that are available to organisations to communicate with its external and internal audiences.

First, attention is given to how advertising might work. Following a consideration of some traditional and some more contemporary explanations, a cognitive association model is offered as a means of consolidating recent research and conceptual thinking. Chapters on messages and media planning then follow.

The rest of this part of the book deals with sales promotion, public relations, sponsorship, personal selling and direct marketing. However, two further new chapters need to be highlighted. The first of these is Chapter 25. This deals with issues concerning on-line marketing communications activity and, in particular, looks at Web site related communications and the use of the tools of the promotional mix, in an on-line environment. The second new chapter looks at a portfolio of other important marketing communications methods, namely exhibitions, packaging and field marketing. The book closes with a chapter on the different methods that can be used to evaluate marketing communication campaigns, each of the tools of the promotional mix and in addition, on-line marketing communications.

Design features and presentation

In addition to the four-part structure of the book, there are a number of features that are intended to help readers navigate around the material.

Chapter objectives

Each chapter opens with both the aims of what is to be covered and a list of objectives. This helps to signal the primary topics that are covered in the chapter and so guide the learning experience.

Navigation

Important key text is extracted and presented in the margin. This helps readers to locate relevant material quickly and highlight key issues. In addition, to assist readers through the various chapters, the left-hand page is used to identify the page number and in which part of the text it is located. To complement this, the right-hand page is used to flag the page number and the chapter title.

Visual supports

Numerous colour plates, located in two main sections, exhibits (black and white pictures), figures (diagrams) and tables of information throughout the text serve to highlight, illustrate and bring life to the written word.

Summaries and mini cases

At the end of each chapter is a summary and a series of review and discussion questions. These can be used by readers to test their own understanding of the contents of the chapter. In this sense the questions support self-study. A new feature of this edition is the inclusion of a mini-case study at the end of each chapter. These have been written by marketing academics from a variety of universities and colleges and some have been written by leading marketing practitioners. These short cases can be used in class for discussion purposes and to explore some of the salient issues raised in the chapter. Students working alone can use the mini-case to test their own understanding and they can use the questions that follow to consolidate their understanding.

Support materials

Students and lecturers who adopt this text have a range of support materials and facilities to help them.

Readers are invited to visit the companion Web site for the book at <u>www. booksites.net/fill</u>. Here students have access to a range of mini-case studies, including all the recent Chartered Institute of Marketing Diploma examination cases for the Integrated Marketing Communications module.

There are various text files available for downloading including the media chapter that was in the previous edition and updated as necessary. There is also a monthly update in terms of interesting journal articles and news and events from both an academic and professional perspective.

For lecturers and tutors not only is there an Instructor's Manual containing a range of teaching schemes, slides and exercises in paper format but there is also a password-protected section of the companion web site for their use. From this site a much larger range of PowerPoint slides, teaching schemes and additional mini cases can be downloaded.

A test bank of multiple-choice questions has also been developed for use by students and lecturers. In addition, there are hyperlinks to a range of related sites.

A Companion Web Site accompanies MARKETING COMMUNICATIONS, 3rd edition by Chris Fill

Visit the *Marketing Communications* Companion Web Site at
<u>www.booksites.net/fill</u> to find valuable teaching and learning material including:

For Students:
- Study material designed to help you improve your results
- Comprehensive learning objectives detailing what you need to know
- Multiple choice questions with feedback to test your learning
- Links to relevant sites on the World Wide Web
- Link to a regularly updated site containing interesting journal articles, news and events
- A downloadable version of the updated Media chapter from the previous edition
- Extra mini case studies from recent Chartered Institute of Marketing Diploma examinations

For Lecturers:
- A secure, password-protected site with teaching material
- A downloadable version of the full Instructor's Manual
- Downloadable PowerPoint slides
- Teaching schemes
- Additional mini-case studies
- A syllabus manager that will build and host your very own course web page

Acknowledgements

This book could not have been written without the support of a wide range of people. Contributions range from providing information and permissions, to writing mini-case studies, to answering my questions and tolerating my persistent nagging, sending through photographs, answering phone calls and emails and simply liaising with others. Finally there are those who have read, reviewed drafts, made constructive comments and provided moral support and encouragement.

The list of individuals and organisations involved with this book is extensive. My thanks is offered to all of you. I have tried to list everyone but if I have omitted someone then I offer my apologies.

Mini cases contributors:

Ruth Ashford – Manchester Metropolitan University
Selina Bichard - Specsavers Opticians
Jill Brown – University of Portsmouth
Eileen Buckwald – Birds Eye Walls
Mary Carberry – Bournemouth University
Debbie Clewes – Nottingham Trent University
Clifford Conway – Brighton University
Martin Evans – Cardiff Business School
Janet Hull – Lewis Moberley
Graham Hughes – Leeds Business School
Malcolm Kirkup – University of Birmingham
Geraldine McKay – Staffordshire University
Dominic Medway – Manchester Metropolitan University

Shena Mitchell – University of Portsmouth
Mike Molesworth – Bournemouth University
Alan Moore – Regent Business School
Stuart Roper – Manchester Metropolitan University
Richard Scullion – Bournemouth University
Yasmin Sekhon – Southampton Business School
Lynn Sudbury – Liverpool John Moores University
Julie Tinson – Bristol Business School
Gary Warnaby – Salford University
Hilary Wright – Taylor Nelson Sofres

Other acknowledgements:

Vicky Allard – TBWA
Rozina Ali – Akzo Nobel
Marion Baker – Procter and Gamble
Edward Lloyd Barnes – Mindshare
Felicity Best – Gemplus
Jo Bingham – Craik Jones
Claire Burgess – Twinings
Vicky Charlesworth – Barclaycard

Richard Christy – University of Portsmouth
Caroline Clarke – Sharwood's
Paul Collier – Hewlett Packard
Lorien Coutts – B&Q
Pat Dade – The Values Company
Kelly Freeman – Inland Revenue
Chris Goard – Taylor Nelson Sofres

Kate Goodfellow – Neville McCarthy Associates

Adrian Hall – Inland Revenue

Catherine Humphries – Webber-Shandwick

Jonathan Lace – Southampton Business School

Justin Leyton – Citroen UK

Judith Johnson – JCB

Nigel Markwick – Wolff Olins

Gordon Oliver – Horndean

Roger Paice – Dennis Fire Engines

Ben Pearman – Birds Eye Walls

Steve Pike – Photographer

Nick Pringle – D'arcy

Victoria Savill – Dyson

Catherine Sharp – TBWA

Richard Tansey – D'arcy

Pat Thomas – Reebok International

Phil Toms – Meat and Livestock Commission

Sam Ullah – Gemplus

Rachel West – American Express Europe

Neil Yoxall – Y&R

And thanks to:

Adshel

Allied Domecq

APA

Audi

Charnos

Coca-Cola Great Britain

Direct Line

Fiat

Gieves and Hawkes

Hugo Boss Gmbh

J Walter Thompson

Kimberley-Clark

Le Creuset

Lever Bros

Mitsubishi

Procter and Gamble

Ralph Lauren

Rainey Kelly Campbell Roalfe

Renault

Skoda

The Automobile Association

Triumph

Virgin Atlantic

Volvo

Yellow Pages

All of these people and organisations have made significant contributions to me and the development of this book. No one, however, has impacted on me or this book more than my wife Karen who has been understanding, supportive and patient as always. To her and our boys, much love.

We would also like to thank the following for permission to reproduce copyright material:

Table 2.1 from Taylor, D. and Altman, I., Communication in interpersonal relationships: social penetration theory in *Interpersonnal Processes: New Directions in Communication Research* (eds M.E. Roloff and G.R. Miller), pp. 257–77, copyright © Sage Publications Inc. Reprinted by permission of Sage Publications; Box on p. 43 from 'Store links "taint" wine critics taste' by Maurice Chittenden © Times Newspapers Limited, 26 November 2000; Table 5.6 from 'Cooker buyers have wide range of tastes' by John Lawless © Times Newspapers Limited, 5 April 1998; Box on p. 374 from 'Keeping control of panic buying' by David Hewson © Times Newspapers Limited, 26 November 2000; Table 5.1 reprinted with permission from *Business Horizons*, May–June, Vol. 40(3). Copyright (1997) by the Board of Trustees at Indiana University, Kelley School for Business; Figure 5.4 from Changing times in retail, *Admap*, May, pp. 21–24 (Teanby, D., 1999); Figure 7.1 reprinted with permission from *Journal of Marketing*, published by the American Marketing Association, Gilly, M.C. and

Wolfinbarger, M. (1988, Vol. 62, pp. 69–88); Figure 8.3 reprinted by permission of Harvard Business School Press, from Ad spending: growing market share, *Harvard Business Review* (January/February), by J. Schroer, Boston, MA 1990, pp. 44–8, copyright © 1990 by Harvard Business School Publishing Corporation, all rights reserved; Figure 8.4 reprinted by permission of Harvard Business School Press, from Ad spending: maintaining market share, *Harvard Business Review* (January/February), by J.P. Jones, Boston, MA 1990, pp. 38–42, copyright © 1990 by Harvard Business School Publishing Corporation, all rights reserved; Table 15.2 and Figure 15.3 reprinted from *Industrial Marketing Management*, vol. 26. Gilliland, D.I. and Johnston, W.J., Towards a model of business-to-business marketing communication effects, 15–29, copyright (1997), with permission from Elsevier Science; Figure 20.4 from An all-embracing theory of how advertising works?, *Admap*, February, pp. 18–23 (Prue, T., 1988); Figure 29.5 from K. Grant and D.W. Cravens (1999) Examining the antecedents of sales organisation effectiveness: an Australian study, *European Journal of Marketing*, 33 (9/10), pp. 945–957, reprinted with permission from MCB University Press; Table 31.3 from The world wide web as an advertising medium: toward an understanding of conversion efficiency, *Journal of Advertising Research* (Berthon, P., Pitt, L. and Watson, R., 1996).

Whilst every effort has been made to trace the owners of copyright material, in a few cases this has proved impossible and we take this opportunity to offer our apologies to any copyright holders whose rights we may have unwittingly infringed.

part 1

Introduction and setting the scene

Chapters 1 and 2

Understanding the role, nature and diversity of marketing communications and associated theory

1

An introduction to marketing communications

Marketing communications is a management process through which an organisation enters into a dialogue with its various audiences. To accomplish this, the organisation develops, presents and evaluates a series of messages to identified stakeholder groups. The objective of the process is to influence the perception, understanding and actions the target audience has towards the organisation and/or its products and services.

AIMS AND OBJECTIVES

The aims of this introductory chapter are to explore some of the concepts associated with marketing communications and to develop an appreciation of the key characteristics of the main tools of the communications mix.

The objectives of this chapter are:

1. To examine the concept of exchange in the marketing context.
2. To assess the role of promotion in the context of the marketing mix.
3. To consider the range and potential impact of marketing communications.
4. To identify the key characteristics of each major tool in the communications mix.
5. To examine the effectiveness of each communication tool.
6. To establish a need for marketing communications.
7. To compare marketing communications in the consumer and business markets.

The ice-cream business – Magnum

This material was kindly written by Eileen Buckwald, Product Manager for Birds Eye Walls.

The ice-cream market has become increasingly complex as consumers' understanding and expectations improve and manufacturers provide a variety of products to meet new segment needs.

One part of the impulse market is known as the 'personal indulgence' sector. Within this sector Birds Eye Walls with Magnum is the market leader, with Mars and Galaxy the other major competitors.

The Magnum brand received heavyweight support in the early 1990s and was positioned as the intensely personal, adult indulgence ice-cream. The positioning reflected the intensity of the relationship consumers felt towards the brand. It socialised their feelings by preventing any embarrassment and provided it with universal appeal (everyone is having this affair). The main result of this campaign was that it helped widen consumption habits.

By the late 1990s, the context for the brand had changed. It was being challenged as imitations began to erode Magnum's distinctiveness and price competition reduced added values. The brand no longer represented exclusiveness, nor was it a rule breaker any more. The brand had begun to age and impulse sales were declining.

The marketing plan for 1999 required that the brand be repositioned from one based on a one-to-one relationship to one where personal sacrifices had to be made. The theme 'Life is all about priorities' was adopted, so that Magnum be perceived as a brand for which sacrifices had to be made. Personal indulgence had to be fitted into a busy lifestyle because 'Magnum is worth it, and I'm worth it . . . so as Magnum is really special – so I deserve it'. It was at this point that the Magnum Girl became an additional feature associated with the brand. See Plate 1.1.

To propel the Magnum brand to power brand status in 2000, new products were developed (e.g. Magnum After Dinner) and some were renovated (Magnum Classic (see Table 1.1). However, overall the brand range was reduced on the principle that fewer bigger brands could be more effectively supported by the media spend.

Although prices were held in 2000, the media investment of £7.5 million was designed to provide support for an integrated promotional programme across television, press, outdoor (posters) and marketing public relations. This sum represented 65% share of voice and nearly 5,000 TVRs. In addition, in-store support was increased to provide for improved visibility and to cut through the own-brand imitations. Also, at a time when ideas about brand 'experiences' were becoming central, Magnum became associated with the UK's first triple loop roller coaster 'Magnum Force'.

Table 1.1   Magnum target consumers

Kids	Teenagers	Young adults	Pre-family	Family with children	Empty nesters
	Magnum Classic	Magnum Classic	Magnum Classic	Magnum Classic	Magnum Classic
	Magnum Caramel & Nuts	Magnum Double	Magnum Double	Magnum Snack Pack	Magnum After Dinner

The public relations programme sought to build on the visibility of the brand and the coverage that the Magnum Girl gained. For example, Magnum became the first brand ever to appear on the front cover of the *Sunday Mail* magazine supplement, one which has the second highest circulation of Sunday newspapers. The Magnum Girl became the central point to the campaign, featuring on posters, television, in store and press work. Each year a competition is held to find a new Magnum Girl to front the brand, in itself a positive means of securing good public relations for the brand.

The Magnum brand grew in volume terms 147% in the multipack sector. The brand retains strong measures of awareness and research indicates that consumers perceive Magnum in terms of 'treat', 'irresistible' and 'high quality'. However, above all else it is perceived as 'indulgent'.

Comment

This brief overview of the Magnum brand, while overtly orientated to the consumer sector, describes some of the issues associated with marketing communications: the market conditions, consumer's perceptions, positioning, branding, objectives, planning and strategy plus the utilisation of the tools of the promotional mix to deliver the marketing plan.

This book explores these ideas and considers some of the concepts and ideas underpinning these activities. It looks at communications in the business-to-business sector as well and considers a range of issues that impact on marketing communications. I hope you enjoy the indulgence.

Introduction

Organisations such as Unilever, Virgin, Jardines, Oxfam, CNN, Singapore Airlines, AOL/Time Warner, First-Pacific, Daewoo and Standard Life operate across a number of sectors, markets and countries and use a variety of marketing communications tools to communicate with their various audiences. These audiences consist not only of people who buy their products and services but also of people and organisations who might be able to influence them, who might help and support them by providing, for example, labour, finance, manufacturing facilities, distribution outlets and legal advice or who are interested because of their impact on parts of society or the business sector in particular.

The organisations mentioned earlier are all well-known brand names, but there are hundreds of thousands of smaller organisations who also need and use marketing communications to convey the essence of their products and services to their audiences. Each of these organisations, large and small, is part of a network of companies, suppliers, retailers, wholesalers, value-added resellers, distributors and other retailers, who join together, often freely, so that each can achieve its own goals.

Effective communication is critically important to organisations.

Effective communication is critically important to organisations which is why they use a variety of promotional tools. Advertising, sales promotion, public relations, direct marketing, personal selling and added-value approaches such as sponsorship are the most used. To get their messages through they use traditional media such as print and broadcast, cinema and radio but increasingly new media, the Internet in particular, are used to 'talk' to and with their customers, potential customers, suppliers, financiers, distributors, communities and employees, among others.

Marketing communications – Cadbury

Cadbury is one of the best-known brands in the UK and is synonymous with chocolate. In order to communicate and develop its brand with customers and other stakeholders it uses a variety of communication methods. Some of the main ones are set out in Table 1.2.

Table 1.2   Methods of marketing communication used by Cadbury

Advertising	Point of purchase materials	Public relations	Direct marketing
Web site	Personal selling	Exhibitions and events	Packaging
Sales promotions	Café Cadbury	Sponsorship (*Coronation Street*)	Trade promotions
Product placements	Cadbury World – associated merchandise	Field Marketing	Vending machines

One recent addition to this impressive list has been the development of Café Cadbury and its entry into the expanding coffee house market. Positioned as a 'Chocolate Experience', the Cadbury cafés seek to extend the Cadbury brand even though direct sales through these outlets will be small. The objective, as reported by Mason (2000), is to keep the Cadbury brand high in the minds of the public and to maintain the quality and trust that the brand has evoked. Cadbury refers to this brand extension as part of its 'presence marketing programme'.

Marketing communications provides the means by which brands and organisations are presented to their audiences with the goal of stimulating a dialogue leading to a succession of purchases. This interaction represents an exchange between each organisation and each consumer, and, according to the quality and satisfaction of the exchange process, will or will not be repeated. It follows, therefore, that presentation is a very important and integral part of the exchange process, and it is the skill and judgement of management that determines, in most cases, success or failure.

The concept of marketing as an exchange

The concept of exchange, according to most marketing academics and practitioners, is central to our understanding of marketing. For an exchange to take place there must be two or more parties, each of whom can offer something of value to the other and who are prepared to enter freely into the exchange process, a transaction. It is possible to ident-

It is possible to identify four forms of exchange: market and relational exchanges, redistributive exchanges and reciprocal exchanges.

ify four forms of exchange: market and relational exchanges, redistributive exchanges and reciprocal exchanges (Andersson, 1992).

Market exchanges (Bagozzi, 1978; Houston and Gassenheimer, 1987) are transactions that occur independently of any previous or subsequent exchanges. They have a short-term orientation and are primarily motivated by self-interest. When a consumer buys a bar of Cadbury's chocolate which they do not buy regularly then a market exchange can be identified. In contrast to this, *relational exchanges* (Dwyer *et al.*, 1987) have a longer-term orientation and develop between parties who wish to build long-term supportive relationships. So, when a consumer buys Cadbury's chocolate on a regular basis, and even buys the same brand, on a majority of purchase occasions, relational exchanges are considered to be taking place.

Pandya and Dholkia (1992) have observed that *redistributive exchanges* can exist among parties who work as a collective unit. Members of a unit or group of organisations enter into exchanges because they wish to share resources with the other members of the group. Pandya and Dholkia offer the example of the tax system of a country as an example of this type of exchange. Here a central unit collects resources and redistributes them to 'authorized beneficiaries according to the prevailing laws'.

Reciprocal exchanges (Mauss, 1974) are essentially gift transactions. Gift-giving usually occurs between members of a unit who share a close relationship and it is the frequency of the act of giving a gift that symbolises the strength of the relationship. The act of giving suggests a need to return a gift; a sense of mutuality rather than the self-interest which characterises market exchanges. The act of giving a box of chocolates as a gift to a friend or loved one is not only a symbolic gesture of thanks, or emotion, but also represents a reciprocation of feelings.

There is, therefore, a range of exchange transactions, but in industrial societies market exchanges tend to dominate although there is a substantial movement towards relational exchanges. All four can be observed at the interpersonal level, at the organisation to individual level or between organisations. As we shall see later, these member units can form together as a network. This may take the form of a dyad, triad or larger group, in order that exchanges may take place.

The concept of relational exchanges is the basis for the ideas represented in relationship marketing. Many organisations seek to use relationship marketing principles, and they are manifest in the form of customer relationship marketing programmes. This book is developed on relationship marketing principles and marketing communications is considered to be a means by which long-term relationships between organisations and between organisations and consumers are developed.

This book is developed on relationship marketing principles.

The role of communication in exchange transactions

Bowersox and Morash (1989) demonstrated how marketing flows, including the information flow, can be represented as a network which has as its sole purpose the satisfaction of customer needs and wants. Communication plays an important role in these exchange networks. At a basic level, communication can *inform* and make potential customers aware of an organisation's offering. Communication may attempt to *persuade* current and potential customers of the desirability of entering into an exchange relationship.

Table 1.3   DRIP elements of marketing communications

DRIP element	Examples
Differentiate	Burger King differentiates itself from market leader McDonald's by stating that its burgers are flame grilled for a better taste.
Remind/reassure	Specsavers Opticians to bring back people into the eyecare market (see Mini case in Chapter 20).
Inform/make aware	The Environment Agency and Flood Action Week – to inform various organisations, such as the Met Office, National Floodline and local media, of the new flood warning codes.
Persuade	So Good milk is better for us than ordinary milk.

Communications can also *remind* people of a need they might have or remind them of the benefits of past transactions and so convince them that they should enter into a similar exchange. This *reassurance* or comfort element of marketing communications is of vital importance to organisations, as it helps to retain current customers. This approach to business is much more cost-effective than constantly striving to lure new customers. Finally, marketing communications can act as a *differentiator*, particularly in markets where there is little to separate competing products and brands. Mineral water products, such as Perrier and Highland Spring, are largely similar: it is the communications surrounding the products that have created various brand images, enabling consumers to make purchasing decisions. In these cases it is the images created by marketing communications that disassociates one brand from another and positions them so that consumers' purchasing confidence and positive attitudes are developed. Therefore, communication can inform, persuade, remind and build images to delineate a product or service (see Table 1.3).

DRIP – Dyson

Dyson manufactures a revolutionary type of vacuum cleaner and has 52% of the UK market. Its communications have needed to:

differentiate it from conventional products – use of innovative technology

remind/reassure customers that the cyclone system works better than any other and to resist the competition's attempts to gain top of mind awareness

inform and educate the market about what is wrong with conventional appliances

persuade potential customers to consider Dyson as the only option when next purchasing floor cleaning appliances.

See Plate 1.2.

At a higher level, the communication process not only supports the transaction, by informing, persuading, reminding or differentiating, but also offers a means of exchange itself, for example, communication for entertainment, for potential solutions and concepts for education and self-esteem. Communications involve intangible benefits, such as the psychological satisfactions associated with, for example, the entertainment value of television advertisements. Communications can also be seen

Exhibit 1.1   Triumph has developed Trina, a cyber woman to present its apparel. Picture kindly supplied by Triumph Ltd.

as a means of perpetuating and transferring values and culture to different parts of society or networks. For example, it is argued that the way women are portrayed in the media and stereotypical images of very thin or anorexic women are dysfunctional in that they set up inappropriate role models. Some clothing manufacturers, such as Triumph, even use cyber women to present their products; see Exhibit 1.1.

The form and characteristics of the communication process adopted by some organisations (both the deliberate and the unintentional use of signs and symbols used to convey meaning) help to provide stability and continuity.

Other examples of intangible satisfactions can be seen in the social and psychological transactions involved increasingly with the work of the National Health Service (NHS), charities, educational institutions and other not-for-profit organisations, such as housing associations. Not only do these organisations increasingly recognise the need to communicate with various audiences but also they perceive value in being seen to be 'of value' to their customers. There is also evidence that some brands are trying to meet the emerging needs of some consumers who want to know the track record of manufacturers with respect to their environmental policies and actions. For example, Typhoo tea claim on their packaging, 'care for tea and our tea pickers'.

The notion of value can be addressed in a different way. All organisations have the opportunity to develop their communications to a point where the value of their messages represents a competitive advantage. This value can be seen in the consistency, timing, volume or expression of the message.

Communication can be used for additional reasons. The tasks of informing, persuading and reminding and differentiating are, primarily, activities targeted at consumers or end users. Organisations do not exist in isolation from each other: each one is part of a wider system of corporate entities, where each enters into a series of exchanges to secure raw material inputs or resources and to discharge them as value-added outputs to other organisations in the network.

The exchanges that organisations enter into require the formation of relationships, however tenuous or strong. Andersson (1992) looks at the strength of the relationship between organisations in a network and refers to them as 'loose or tight couplings'. These couplings, or partnerships, are influenced by the communications that are transmitted and received. The role that organisations assume in a network and the manner in which they undertake and complete their tasks are, in part, shaped by the variety and complexity of the communications in transmission throughout the network. Issues of channel or even network control, leadership, subservience and conflict are implanted in the form and nature of the communications exchanged in any network.

Directive communications – the countryside

Marketing communications can be used to persuade target audiences in a variety of ways. For example, speaking on BBC Radio 4, Bob Waller (1996) claimed that publicity had been used effectively by the Peak District National Park. However, instead of using publicity to attract tourists, they had deliberated used their publicity opportunities to divert visitors away from particular areas in the Park, in order to repair, preserve and protect them for visitors in the future.

In 2001, with the foot and mouth crisis mounting, the government realised that its previous policy to restrict the public's access to the countryside was deterring tourism and threatening the economy. To correct this perception it used public relations to encourage access to particular areas that were uninfected with the disease.

Within market exchanges, communications are characterised by formality and planning. Relational exchanges are supported by more frequent communication activity. As Mohr and Nevin (1990) state, there is a bidirectional flow to communications and an informality to the nature and timing of the information flows. This notion of relational exchange has been popularised by the term 'relationship marketing' and is a central theme in this text.

Marketing communications and the process of exchange

The exchange process is developed and managed by researching consumer/stakeholder needs, identifying, selecting and targeting particular groups of consumers/stakeholders who share similar discriminatory characteristics, including needs and wants, and developing an offering that satisfies the identified needs at an acceptable price, which is available through particular sets of distribution channels. The next task is to make the target audience aware of the existence of the offering. Where competition or other impediments to positive consumer action exist, such as lack of motivation or conviction, a promotional programme is developed and used to communicate with the targeted group.

Collectively, these activities constitute the marketing mix (the 4Ps as McCarthy

(1960) originally referred to them), and the basic task of marketing is to combine these 4Ps into a marketing programme to facilitate the exchange process. The use of these 4Ps has been criticised as limiting the scope of the marketing manager. The assumption by McCarthy was that the tools of the marketing mix allow adaptation to the uncontrollable external environment. It is now seen that the external environment can be influenced and managed strategically and the rise and influence of the service sector is not easily accommodated within the original 4Ps. To do this, additional Ps such as Processes, Political Power and People have been suggested. A marketing mix of 20Ps has even been proposed by some but the essence of the mix remains the same and it is what is encompassed within the mix components that is of prime concern. Kotler (2000) advocates the use of the 4Ps, the development of multiple mixes to suit trade as well as consumer markets and the use of certain communication tools to create and frame the environments in which the organisation wishes to operate. This corporate perspective is one that is adopted in this book.

Promotion, therefore, is one of the elements of the marketing mix and is responsible for the communication of the marketing offer to the target market. While recognising that there is implicit and important communication through the other elements of the marketing mix (through a high price, for example, symbolising quality), it is the task of a planned and integrated set of communication activities to communicate effectively with each of an organisation's stakeholder groups. Marketing communications is sometimes perceived as dealing with communications that are external to the organisation. It should be recognised that good communications with internal stakeholders, such as employees, are also vital if, in the long term, successful favourable images, perceptions and attitudes are to be established. This book considers the increasing importance of suitable internal communications (Chapter 7) and their vital role in helping to form a strong and consistent corporate identity (Chapter 16).

Promotion, therefore, is one of the elements of the marketing mix and is responsible for the communication of the marketing offer to the target market.

New forms of promotion have been developed in response to changing market and environmental conditions. For example, public relations is now seen by some to have

Figure 1.1   The marketing communications mix.

a marketing and a corporate dimension (Chapters 16 and 26). Direct marketing is now recognised as an important way of developing personal relationships with buyers, both consumer and organisational (Chapters 12, 14, 15, 25 and 28), while new and innovative forms of communication through sponsorship (Chapter 27), floor advertising, video screens on supermarket trolleys and check-out coupon dispensers (Chapter 24) and the Internet and associated technologies (Chapters 18 and 25) mean that effective communication requires the selection and integration of an increasing variety of communication tools. The marketing communication mix depicted in Figure 1.1 attempts to reflect these developments and represents a new promotional configuration for organisations.

A definition of marketing communications

There is no universal definition of marketing communications and there are many interpretations of the subject. Delozier's (1976) definition is that it is:

> *The process of presenting an integrated set of stimuli to a market with the intent of evoking a desired set of responses within that market set and setting up channels to receive, interpret and act upon messages from the market for the purposes of modifying present company messages and identifying new communication opportunities.*

This is a useful perspective as it introduces the concept of feedback – two-way communication – and also the concept that the stimuli, or message set, should be integrated, if the required reaction of the target audience is to be successfully generated. What it fails to draw out is the opportunity that marketing communication provides to add value through enhanced product and organisational symbolism. It also fails to recognise that it is the context within which marketing communications flow that impacts upon the meaning and interpretation given to such messages. Its ability to frame and associate offerings with different environments is powerful:

Marketing communications is a management process through which an organisation enters into a dialogue with its various audiences.

> *Marketing communications is a management process through which an organisation enters into a dialogue with its various audiences. Based upon an understanding of the audiences communications environment, an organisation develops and presents messages for its identified stakeholder groups, and evaluates and acts upon the responses received. The objective of the process is to (re)position the organisation and/or its products and services, in the minds of members of the target market, by influencing their perception and understanding. The goal is to generate attitudinal and behavioural responses.*

This definition has three main themes. The first concerns the word *dialogue.* The use of marketing communications enables organisations to communicate with their audiences in such a way that multiway communications are stimulated (Chapter 2). Promotional messages should encourage members of target audiences to respond to the focus organisation (or product/brand). This response can be immediate through, for example, purchase behaviour or use of customer care lines, or it can be deferred as information is assimilated and considered for future use. Even if the information is discarded at a later date, the communication will have prompted attention and consideration of the message. Dialogue can also be stimulated in such a way that members of the various audiences communicate with one another, primarily by way of word-of-mouth communications.

The second theme is *positioning*, and implies that the communications of the organisation affect all offerings in the opportunity set. Positioning can only work if there are two or more offerings for the receiver to position. Communications from one organisation/offering will hold attention to the extent that competitor organisations are temporarily put aside in the mind of receiver. The length of time that this temporary position lasts is, to some degree, determined by the quality of the 'blocking' communication. Furthermore, if rivals attempt to adjust or reinforce their positions then a number of competitive offerings are also going to be automatically repositioned. Positioning, therefore, is a matter of context. This is the context in which receivers perceive and understand product-based messages relative to other products which they regard as appropriate. Management attention to positioning and marketing communications is therefore of considerable importance.

Positioning, therefore, is a matter of context.

The third theme from the definition is *cognitive response*, that is receivers are viewed as active problem solvers and they use marketing communications to help them in their purchasing and organisation-related activities. For example, brands are developed partly to help consumers and partly to assist the marketing effort of the host organisation. A brand can quickly inform consumers that, among other things, 'this brand means x quality', and through experience of similar brand purchases consumers are assured that their risk is minimised. If the problem facing a consumer is 'which new soup to select for dinner', by choosing one from a familiar family brand the consumer is able to solve it with minimal risk and great speed. As explained later (Chapter 3) individuals may or may not be aware of the cognitive processing they engage in, as it varies according to variety of factors.

It follows that a brand that provides solutions on a continuous basis for a consumer may become integral to a long-term relationship. A partnership might develop whereby the brand, among other things, reassures the consumer and the consumer supports the brand by paying the price premium that the brand demands. The huge investments made by organisations in the promotion of brands, especially in the fast-moving consumer goods (FMCG) industry, is a testimony to the potential strength of these brand partnerships and to the power of marketing communications.

The role of marketing communications

Marketing communications are about the promotion of both the organisation and its offerings. Marketing communications recognise the increasing role the organisation plays in the marketing process and the impact that organisational factors can have on the minds of consumers. As the structure, composition and sheer number of offerings in some markets proliferate, so differences between products diminish, to the extent that differentiation between products has become much more difficult. This results in a decrease in the number of available and viable positioning opportunities. One way to

Marketing communications are about the promotion of both the organisation and its offerings.

resolve this problem is to use the parent organisation as an umbrella, to provide greater support and leadership in the promotion of any offerings.

A view which is becoming increasingly popular is that corporate strategy should be supported by the organisation's key stakeholders if the strategy is to be successful. Strategy must be communicated in such a way that the messages are consistent through time and targeted accurately at appropriate stakeholder audiences. Each organisation must constantly guard against the transmission of confusing messages, whether this be through the way in which the telephone is answered, the impact of sales literature or the way salespersons approach prospective clients. These and other stakeholder issues are discussed at length in Chapter 6.

Many organisations recognise the usefulness and importance of good PR. PR's key characteristics of high credibility and relatively low cost are seen to be critical in the battle not only to secure a position in the consumer's mind but also to restrain promotional costs. As a result, the growth of corporate advertising, the combination of the best of advertising and public relations, has been significant.

Finally, marketing communications recognise the development of channel or trade marketing. Many organisations have moved away from the traditional control of a brand manager to a system which focuses upon the needs of distributors and intermediaries in the channel. The organisations in the channel work together to satisfy their individual and collective objectives. The degree of conflict and cooperation in the channel network depends upon a number of factors, but some of the most important factors are the form and quality of the communications between member organisations. This means that marketing communications must address the specific communication needs of members of the distribution network and those other stakeholders who impact on or who influence the performance of the network. Indeed, marketing communications recognise the need to contribute to the communications in the channel network, to support and sustain the web of relationships.

Marketing communications must address the specific communication needs of members of the distribution network and those other stakeholders.

For example, many organisations in the airline industry have shifted their attention to the needs of the travel trade, customers and competitors. United Airlines, British Airways, KLM and Quantas and other airlines have changed their approach, attitude and investment priorities so that channel partnerships and alliances because the environment in which they operated previously has changed radically. Now there is a clear emphasis on working with their partners and their competitors (e.g. British Airways and KLM), and this entails agreement, collaboration and joint promotional activity in order that all participants achieve their objectives.

The marketing communications mix

The marketing communications mix consists of a set of tools which can be used in different combinations and different degrees of intensity in order to communicate with a target audience. This 'bag of tools' is also referred to as the promotional mix and the two terms are used interchangeably in this book. In addition to these tools or methods of communication, there is the media, or the means by which marketing communication messages are conveyed. Tools and media should not be confused as they have different characteristics and seek to achieve different goals.

There are five principal marketing communications tools: these are advertising, sales promotion, public relations, direct marketing and personal selling. However, there have been some major changes in the environment and in the way organisations communicate with their target audiences. New technology has given rise to a raft of different media while people have developed a variety of ways to spend their leisure time. This is referred to as media and audience fragmentation and organisations have developed fresh combinations of the promotional mix in order to reach their audiences effectively. For example, there has been a dramatic rise in the use of direct-response media as direct marketing becomes adopted as part of the marketing plan for many products. The Internet and digital technologies have enabled new interactive forms of communication where the receiver has greater responsibility for their part in the communication process. An increasing number of organisations are using public relations to communicate messages about the organisation (corporate public relations) and also messages about their brands (marketing public relations).

There has been a dramatic rise in the use of direct-response media.

What has happened therefore is that the promotional mix has developed such that the original emphasis on heavyweight mass communication (above-the-line) campaigns has given way to more direct and highly targeted promotional activities using direct marketing and the other tools of the mix. Using the jargon, through-the-line and below-the-line campaigns are used much more these days. Figure 1.2 brings these elements together.

The shift is from an *intervention*-based approach to marketing communications (one based on seeking the attention of a customer who might not necessarily be interested), towards *permission*-based communications (where the focus is upon communications with members of an audience who have already expressed an interest in a particular offering). In other words with permission communications the seedlings for a relationship are established by the audience, not the brand owner. This has a particular impact on direct marketing, on-line communications and to some extent personal selling.

The shift is from an intervention-based approach to marketing communications towards permission-based communications.

Advertising is a non-personal form of mass communication and offers a high degree of control for those responsible for the design and delivery of the advertising message. However, the ability of advertising to persuade the target audience to think or behave in a particular way is suspect. Furthermore, the effect on sales is extremely hard to measure. Advertising also suffers from low credibility in that audiences are less likely to believe messages delivered through advertising than they are messages received through some other tools.

Advertising also suffers from low credibility.

Figure 1.2   Above- and below-the-line communications.

The flexibility of this tool is good because it can be used to communicate with a national audience or a particular specialised segment. Although the costs can be extremely large, a vast number of people can be reached with the message, so the cost per contact can be the lowest of the tools in the mix. Advertising and related media are considered at some depth in Chapters 20–22.

Sales promotion comprises various marketing techniques which are often used tactically to provide added value to an offering, with the aim of accelerating sales and gathering marketing information. Like advertising, sales promotion is a non-personal form of communication but has a greater capability to be targeted at smaller audiences. It is controllable and, although it has to be paid for, the associated costs can be much lower than those of advertising. As a generalisation, credibility is not very high, as the sponsor is, or should be, easily identifiable. However, the ability to add value and to bring forward future sales is as strong as it is important in an economy which focuses upon short-term financial performance. Sales promotion techniques and approaches are the subject of Chapters 22 and 23.

Personal selling is traditionally perceived as an interpersonal communication tool which involves face-to-face activities undertaken by individuals, often representing an organisation, in order to inform, persuade or remind an individual or group to take appropriate action, as required by the sponsor's representative. A salesperson engages in communication on a one-to-one basis where instantaneous feedback is possible. The costs associated with interpersonal communication are normally very large.

The costs associated with interpersonal communication are normally very large.

This tool, the focus of Chapter 29, differs from the previous two in that, while still lacking in relative credibility and control, the degree of control is potentially lower. This is because the salesperson is free at the point of contact to deliver a message other than that intended (Lloyd, 1997). Indeed, many different messages can be delivered by a single salesperson. Some of these messages may enhance the prospect of the salesperson's objectives being reached (making the sale), or they may retard the process and so incur more time and hence costs. Whichever way it is viewed, control is lower than with advertising.

The use of direct marketing by organisations over the past 10 years has been significant as it signals a shift in focus from mass to personalised communications: the use of, in particular, direct mail, telemarketing and the fast developing area of interactive communications, such as the Internet. By removing the face-to-face aspect of personal selling and replacing it with an email communication, a telephone conversation or a direct mail letter, many facets of the traditional salespersons' tasks can be removed, freeing them to concentrate on their key skill areas. Aspects of direct marketing are developed below and in Chapter 28.

Public relations is 'the art and social science of analysing trends, predicting their consequences, counselling organisations' leadership, and implementing planned programmes of action which will serve both the organisation's and the public interest' (Mexican Statement, 1978). This definition suggests that public relations should be a part of the wider perspective of corporate strategy, and this is discussed at length in Chapter 26. The increasing use of public relations, and in particular publicity, is a reflection of the high credibility attached to this form of communications. Publicity involves the dissemination of messages through third-party media, such as magazines, newspapers or news programmes. There is no charge for the media space or time but there are costs incurred in the production of the material. (There is no such thing as a free lunch or a free promotion.) There is a wide range of other tools used by public relations, such as event management, sponsorship and lobbying. It is difficult to control a message once placed in the channels, but the endorsement offered by a third party can be very influential and have a far greater impact on the target audience than any of the other tools in the promotional mix.

This non-personal form of communication offers organisations a different way to communicate, not only with consumers but also with many other stakeholders.

The four elements of the promotional mix discussed so far have a number of strengths and weaknesses. As a response to some of the weaknesses which revolve around costs and effectiveness, direct marketing emerged in the 1990s as a new and effective way of building relationships with customers over the long term.

Direct marketing seeks to target individual customers with the intention of delivering personalised messages and building a relationship with them based upon their responses to the direct communications. In contrast to conventional approaches, direct marketing attempts to build a one-to-one relationship, a partnership with each customer, by communicating with the customers on a direct and personal basis. If an organisation chooses to use direct marketing then it has to incorporate the approach within a marketing plan. This is because distribution is different and changes in the competitive environment may mean that prices need to change. For example, charges for packing and delivery need to be incorporated. The product may also need to be altered or adapted to the market. For example, some electrical products are marketed through different countries on home shopping channels. The electrical requirements of each country or region need to be incorporated within the product specification of each country's offering. In addition to these changes, the promotion component is also different, simply because communication is required directly with each targeted individual. To do this, direct-response media must be used.

In many cases direct-response media are a derivative of advertising, such as direct mail, magazine inserts, and television and print advertisements which use telephone numbers to encourage a direct response. However, direct response can also be incorporated within personal selling through telemarketing and sales promotions with competitions to build market knowledge and develop the database which is the key to the direct marketing approach.

This text regards direct marketing as *the management process associated with the marketing objective of building mutually satisfying customer relationships through a personal and intermediary-free dialogue. Direct-response media are the primary communication tools when direct marketing is an integral part of the marketing plan.* Further discussion of direct marketing and direct-response communications can be found in Chapters 25 and 28.

The Internet is a distribution channel and communication medium that enables consumers and organisations to communicate in radically different ways. It allows for interactivity and is possibly the purest form of marketing communications dialogue. Communication is two-way and very fast, allowing businesses and individuals to find information and enter exchange transactions in such a way that some traditional communication practices and shopping patterns are being reconfigured.

The Internet is a distribution channel and communication medium.

The communication mix is changing: no longer can the traditional grouping of promotional tools be assumed to be the most effective forms of communication. This brief outline of the elements of the promotions mix signals some key characteristics.

Table 1.4   A summary of the key characteristics of the tools of marketing communications

	Advertising	Sales promotion	Public relations	Personal selling	Direct marketing
Communications					
Ability to deliver a personal message	Low	Low	Low	High	High
Ability to reach a large audience	High	Medium	Medium	Low	Medium
Level of interaction	Low	Low	Low	High	High
Credibility given by target audience	Low	Medium	High	Medium	Medium
Costs					
Absolute costs	High	Medium	Low	High	Medium
Cost per contact	Low	Medium	Low	High	High
Wastage	High	Medium	High	Low	Low
Size of investment	High	Medium	Low	High	Medium
Control					
Ability to target particular audiences	Medium	High	Low	Medium	High
Management's ability to adjust the deployment of the tool as circumstances change	Medium	High	Low	Medium	High

These are the extent to which each element is controllable, whether it is paid for by the sponsor and whether communication is by mass medium or undertaken personally. One additional characteristic concerns the receiver's perception of the credibility of the source of the message. If the credibility factor is high then there is a greater likelihood that messages from that source will be accepted by the receivers.

Table 1.4 represents the key characteristics and shows the relative effectiveness of the tools of promotion across a number of different characteristics. The three primary groupings are the ability of each to communicate, the costs involved and the control that each tool can maintain.

Effectiveness of the promotional tools

Each element of the promotions mix has different capacities to communicate and to achieve different objectives. The effectiveness of each tool can be tracked against the purchase decision process. Here consumers can be assumed to move from a state of unawareness through product comprehension to purchase. Advertising is better for creating awareness, and personal selling is more effective at promoting action and purchase behaviour.

Readers are encouraged to see the elements of the mix as a set of complementary ingredients, each drawing on the potential of the others. The tools are, to a limited extent, partially interchangeable and in different circumstances different tools are used to meet different objectives. For example, network marketing organisations such as Avon Cosmetics use personal selling to complete the majority of activities in the purchase decision sequence. The high cost of this approach is counterbalanced by the effectiveness of the communications. However, this aspect of interchangeability only

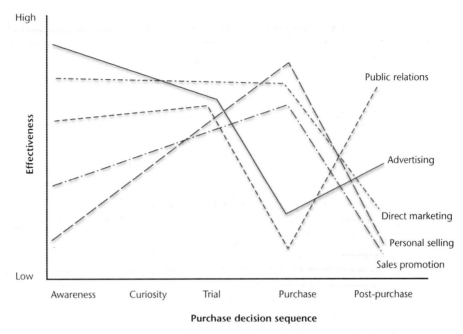

Figure 1.3   The relative effectiveness of the tools of the marketing communications mix.

serves to complicate matters. If management's task was simply to identify problems and then select the correct precision tool to solve the problem, then the issue of the selection of the 'best' promotions mix would evaporate (Figure 1.3).

These five elements of the promotional mix are supplemented by one of the most effective forms of marketing communication, *word-of-mouth* recommendation. As we shall see later, word-of-mouth recommendation is one of the most powerful marketing communication tools and, if an organisation can develop a programme to harness and accelerate the use of personal recommendation effectively, the more likely it will be that the marketing programme will be successful.

One of the most effective forms of marketing communication is word-of-mouth recommendation.

Selection criteria

The key criteria governing an organisation's selection and use of each tool are as follows:

1. The degree of control required over the delivery of the message.
2. The financial resources available to pay a third party to transmit messages.
3. The level of credibility that each tool bestows on the organisation.
4. The size and geographic dispersion of the target audiences.

Control

Control over the message is necessary to ensure that the intended message is transmitted to and received by the target audience. Furthermore, this message must be capable of being understood in order that the receiver can act appropriately. Message control is complicated by interference or negative 'noise' which can corrupt and distort messages. For example, an airline's advertising may be discredited by a major news story about safety checks or even an accident.

Advertising and sales promotion allow for a high level of control over the message, from design to transmission. Interestingly, they afford only partial control or influence over the feedback associated with the original message.

Financial resources

Control is also a function of financial power. In other words, if an organisation is prepared to pay a third party to transmit the message, then long-term control will rest with the sponsor for as long as the financial leverage continues. However, short-term message corruption can exist if management control over the process is less than vigilant. For example, if the design of the message differs from that originally agreed, then partial control has already been lost. This can happen when the working relationship between an advertising agency and the client is less than efficient and the process for signing off work in progress fails to prevent the design and release of inappropriate creative work.

Advertising and sales promotion are tools which allow for a high level of control by the sponsor, whereas public relations, and publicity in particular, is weak in this aspect because the voluntary services of a third party are normally required for the message to be transmitted.

Advertising and sales promotion are tools which allow for a high level of control by the sponsor.

There is a great variety of media available to advertisers. Each media type (for example, television, radio, newspapers, magazines, posters and the Internet) carries a particular cost, and the financial resources of the organisation may not be available to use particular types of media, even if such use would be appropriate on other grounds.

Credibility

Public relations scores heavily on credibility factors. This is because receivers perceive the third party as unbiased and to be endorsing the offering. They view the third party's comments as objective and trustworthy in the context of the media in which the comments appear.

At a broad level, advertising, sales promotion and, to a slightly lesser extent, personal selling are tools that can lack credibility, as perceived by the target audience. Because of this, organisations often use celebrities and 'experts' to endorse their offerings. The credibility of the spokesperson is intended to distract the receiver from the sponsor's prime objective, which is to sell the offering. Credibility, as we shall later, is an important aspect of the communication process and of marketing communications.

Credibility, as we shall later, is an important aspect of the communication process and of marketing communications.

Size and geographic dispersion

The final characteristic concerns the size and geographic dispersion of the target audience. A consumer audience, often national, can only be reached effectively if tools of mass communication are used, such as advertising and sales promotion. Similarly, various specialist businesses require personal attention to explain, design, demonstrate, install and service complex equipment. In these circumstances personal selling, one-to-one contact, is of greater significance. The tools of marketing communications can enable an organisation to speak to vast national and international audiences through advertising and satellite technology, or to single persons or small groups through personal selling and the assistance of word-of-mouth recommendation.

Management of the promotional tools

Traditionally, each of the promotional tools has been regarded as the domain of particular groups within organisations:

1. Personal selling is the domain of the sales director, and traditionally uses an internally based and controlled sales force.
2. Public relations is the domain of the chairperson and is often administered by a specialist PR agency.
3. Advertising and sales promotion are the domain of the marketing manager or brand manager. Responsibility for the design and transmission of messages for mass communications is often devolved to an external advertising agency.

Many organisations have evolved without marketing being recognised as a key function, let alone as a core philosophy. There are a number of reasons why this might be so. First, the organisation may have developed with a public relations orientation in an environment without competition, where the main purpose of the organisation was to disperse resources according to the needs of their clients. The most obvious examples are to be drawn from the public sector: local authorities and the NHS in particular. A second reason would be because a selling perspective ('our job is to sell it') dominated. There would invariably be no marketing director on the board, just a sales director representing the needs of the market.

It is not surprising that these various organisational approaches have led to the transmission of a large number of different messages. Each function operates with good intent, but stakeholders receive a range of diverse and often conflicting messages.

Context and marketing communications

Organisations can be seen as open social systems (Katz and Kahn, 1978) in which all of the components of the unit or system are interactive and interdependent (Goldhaber, 1986). Modify one part of a system and adjustments are made by all the other components to accommodate the change. This effect can be seen at the micro and macro levels. At the macro level the interdependence of organisations has been noted by a number of researchers. Stern and El-Ansary (1995) depict distribution channels as 'a network of systems', and so recognise organisations as interdependent units. At the micro level, the individual parts of an organisation accommodate each other as the organisation adjusts to its changing environment. By assembling the decisions associated

Modify one part of a system and adjustments are made by all the other components to accommodate the change.

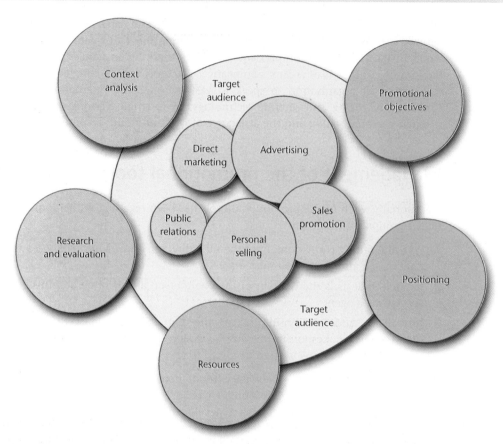

Figure 1.4   The system of marketing communications.

with the development and delivery of a marketing communications strategy (Figure 1.4), it becomes possible to see the complexity and sensitivity of each of the decision components.

The marketing communications undertaken by organisations within these systems can be regarded as a series of communication episodes. These episodes constitute a dialogue and can be seen to have a certain continuity. The amount of time between episodes may vary from the very small, such as those associated with many major FMCG brand campaigns, which run and run, or very large, such as those associated with some business-to-business campaigns or one-off events associated with a single task, such as government drink-driving campaigns held annually each Christmas period.

These episodes occur within situations where specific factors can be identified and where the circumstances are characteristically individual. Indeed, it is unlikely that any two episodes will occur with exactly the same circumstances. The use of marketing communications as a means of influencing others is therefore determined by the specific circumstances or the context in which the episode is to occur. Marketing communications become part of the context and influences and are influenced by the particular circumstances.

It is important therefore, when considering the elements and factors that contribute to marketing communications, to account for the context in which the communications will contribute. For example, falling sales often provoke a response by management to increase or change the advertising. The perception of the brand by the target audience might be inaccurate or not what was intended, or a new product might be launched into a competitive market where particular positions have been adopted by competitors. These contexts contain a set of specific circumstances in which a marketing communication episode might (will) occur. It should be borne in mind that the list of possible contexts is endless and that the task facing marketing communications managers is to identify the key aspects of any situation and deliver promotional messages that complement the context. This enables audiences to interpret messages correctly and maintain a dialogue.

Contexts contain a set of specific circumstances in which a marketing communication episode might (will) occur.

The main tasks facing the management team responsible for marketing communications are to decide the following:

1. Who should receive the messages.
2. What the messages should say.
3. What image of the organisation/brand receivers are to form and retain.
4. How much is to be spent establishing this new image.
5. How the messages are to be delivered. *(media)*
6. What actions the receivers should take.
7. How to control the whole process once implemented.
8. Determining what was achieved. *(measurement)*

These tasks are undertaken within a context within which there may be many episodes or only a few. Note that more than one message is often transmitted and that there is more than one target audience. This is important, as recognition of the need to communicate with multiple audiences and their different information requirements, often simultaneously, lies at the heart of marketing communications. The aim is to generate and transmit messages which present the organisation and its offerings to their various target audiences, encouraging them to enter into a dialogue and relationship. These messages must be presented consistently and they must address the points stated above. It is the skill and responsibility of the marketing communications manager to blend the communication tools and create a mix that satisfies these elements.

Consequently, contexts are not independent or isolated sets of easily identifiable circumstances, but are interrelated and overlapping circumstances in which it is rare for any one organisation to have total knowledge of any single context. Management make judgements based upon their experience, marketing research and limited knowledge of any one identifiable part context, and it might be said that each time a marketing communications programme is rolled out management takes an educated leap into the unknown.

Communication differences

Having identified the need to communicate with a number of different audiences, it seems appropriate to conclude this opening chapter by examining the differences between communications used by and targeted at organisations (commonly referred to as business-to-business) and those aimed at consumer markets. Some writers (Brougaletta, 1985; Gilliland and Johnston, 1997) have documented a variety of differences between consumer and business-to-business markets. The following is intended to set out some of the more salient differences (see also Table 1.5):

1. *Message reception*

   The contextual conditions in which messages are received and ascribed meanings are very different. In the organisational setting the context is much more formal, and as the funding for the purchase is to derived from company sources (as opposed to personal sources for consumer market purchases) there may be a lower orientation to the price as a significant variable in the purchase decision. The purchase is intended to be used by others for company usage, whereas products bought in a consumer context are normally intended for personal consumption.

2. *Number of decision-makers*

   In consumer markets a single person very often makes the decision. In organisational markets decisions are made by many people within the buying centre. This means that the interactions of the individuals needs to be considered. In addition, a variety of different individuals need to be reached and influenced and this may involve the use of different media and message strategies.

Table 1.5 Differences between consumer and business-to-business marketing communications

	Consumer-orientated markets	Business-to-business markets
Message reception	Informal	Formal
Number of decision-makers	Single or few	Many
Balance of the promotional mix	Advertising and sales promotions dominate	Personal selling dominates
Specificity and integration	Broad use of promotional mix with a move towards integrated mixes	Specific use of below-the-line tools but with a high level of integration
Message content	Greater use of emotions and imagery	Greater use of rational, logic- and information-based messages although there is evidence of a move towards the use of imagery
Length of decision time	Normally short	Longer and more involved
Negative communications	Limited to people close to the purchaser/user	Potentially an array of people in the organisation and beyond
Target marketing and research	Great use of sophisticated targeting and communication approaches	Limited but increasing use of targeting and segmentation approaches
Budget allocation	Majority of budget allocated to brand management	Majority of budget allocated to sales management
Evaluation and measurement	Great variety of techniques and approaches used	Limited number of techniques and approaches

3. *The balance of the communications mix*

   The role of advertising and sales promotions in business-to-business communications is primarily to support the personal selling effort. This contrasts with the mix which predominates in consumer markets. Personal selling has a relatively minor role and is only significant at the point of purchase in some product categories where involvement is high (cars, white goods and financial services), reflecting high levels of perceived risk. However, the increasing use of direct marketing in consumer markets suggests that personal communications are becoming more prevalent and in some increasingly similar to the overall direction of business-to-business communications.

4. *The constituents of the marketing communications mix*

   Business-to-business markets have traditionally been quite specific in terms of the promotional tools and media used to target audiences. While the use of advertising literature is very important, there has been a tendency to use a greater proportion of below-the-line activities. This compares with consumer markets, where a greater proportion of funds have been allocated to above-the-line activities. It is interesting that the communications in the consumer market are moving towards a more integrated format, more similar in form to the business-to-business model than was previously considered appropriate.

5. *Message content*

   Generally, there is high involvement in many business-to-business purchase decisions, so communications tend to be much more rational and information based than in consumer markets. However, there are signs that businesses are making increased use of imagery and emotions in the messages (see Chapter 21).

6. *Length of purchase decision time*

   The length of time taken to reach a decision is much greater in the organisation market. This means that the intensity of any media plan can be dissipated more easily in the organisational market.

7. *Negative communications*

   The number of people affected by a dissatisfied consumer, and hence negative marketing communication messages, is limited. The implications of a poor purchase decision in an organisational environment may be far reaching, including those associated with the use of the product, the career of participants close to the locus of the decision and, depending upon the size and spread, perhaps the whole organisation.

8. *Target marketing and research*

   The use of target marketing processes in the consumer market has been more advanced and sophisticated than in the organisational market. This impacts on the quality of the marketing communications used to reach the target audience. However, there is much evidence that the business-to-business markets are using advanced techniques such as the use of psychographics, the Wilson learning 'social style' model and the 'cube' model (Eisenhart, 1988), which use lifestyle and values as a means of segmentation and the formulation of effective messages.

9. *Budget allocation*

   The sales department receives the bulk of the marketing budget in the organisation market and little is spent on research in comparison with the consumer market.

10. *Measurement and evaluation*

The consumer market employs a variety of techniques to evaluate the effectiveness of communications. In the organisation market, sales volume, value, number of enquiries and market share are the predominant measures of effectiveness.

There can be no doubt that there are a number of major differences between consumer and organisational communications. These reflect the nature of the environments, the tasks involved and the overall need of the recipients for particular types of information. Information need, therefore, can be seen as a primary reason for the differences in the way promotional mixes are configured. Advertising in organisational markets has to provide a greater level of information and is geared to generating leads which can be followed up with personal selling, which is traditionally the primary tool in the promotional mix. In consumer markets, advertising plays the primary role with support from the other tools of the promotional mix. Interestingly, new media appears to be reconfiguring the marketing communications mix and perhaps reducing the gulf and distinction between the mix used in business-to-business and consumer markets. Throughout this book, reference will be made to the characteristics, concepts and processes associated with marketing communications and each of these two main sectors.

There are a number of major differences between consumer and organisational communications.

Summary

The concept of exchange transactions is seen by many commentators as underpinning the marketing concept. Of the different types of exchange, market and relational are the two that can be observed most often in industrial societies.

Marketing communications have a number of roles to play in the context of both these types of exchange, but, as will be seen later in this text, there is a strong movement away from the reliance on market exchanges to the longer-term perspective that relational exchanges enjoy and to the development of partnerships. This approach is referred to as 'relationship marketing', and it is here that changes in the use and deployment of marketing communications can be best observed.

There are five traditional elements to the promotional mix: advertising, sales promotion, public relations, direct marketing and personal selling. Each has strengths and weaknesses, and these tools are now beginning to be used in different ways to develop relationships with customers, whether they be consumers or organisational buyers. An example of these changes is the use of the Internet, a communication medium, which has grown rapidly since the mid-1990s and is threatening to reconfigure the way traditional promotional tools are used.

Marketing communications have an important role to play in communicating and promoting the products and services not only to consumers but also to the business-to-business sector and other organisations who represent other stakeholders. The development of partnerships between brands and consumers and between organisations within distribution channels or networks is an important perspective of marketing communications. Communications in this context will be an important part of this text.

Finally, marketing communications can be seen as a series of episodes that occur within a particular set of circumstances or contexts. Marketing managers need to be able to identify principal characteristics of the context they are faced with and contribute to the context with a suitable promotional programme.

Review questions

1. Briefly compare and contrast the different types of exchange transaction.
2. How does communication assist the exchange process?
3. Name the five main elements of the marketing communications mix.
4. Write a brief description of each element of the marketing communications mix.
5. How do each of the elements compare across the following criteria: control, communication effectiveness and cost?
6. How does direct marketing differ from the other elements of the mix?
7. Identify five different advertisements that you think are using direct-response media. How effective do you think they might be?
8. Explain contexts and episodes. Describe the main tasks facing the management team responsible for marketing communications.
9. What is systems theory and how might it apply to marketing communications?
10. Explain how marketing communications supports the marketing and business strategies of the organisation.

MINI CASE

This mini case was written by Lynn Sudbury, Senior Lecturer in Marketing at Liverpool John Moores University.

Marketing to grey consumers isn't black and white

They may be over 50, but many don't feel old. They are increasing in number, and now represent about one-third of the population in Britain, while the number of 16–34 year olds is declining. They hold an estimated 80% of the UK's private wealth and are increasingly willing to spend it. They are on the whole active and healthy. They are the grey market, otherwise known as Woopies (well-off older people), Jollies (jet-setting oldies with lots of loot) and Grampies (growing retired active monied people in an excellent state). The grey market accounts for over half of all UK expenditure on leisure goods and cars and 48% and 43% of home furnishings and electrical goods respectively.

Of course, not all greys are active, healthy and wealthy. There is a great deal of difference between those who are in poor health and live solely on state benefits, those who enjoy good pensions and an active (and perhaps early) retirement, and those who are in the pre-retirement stage of their careers. Likewise, many older consumers are now enjoying the freedom of the empty nest, while others are still depended upon by their older offspring for financial assistance. The majority of greys, however, are relatively free from mortgages and are financially stable.

The financial services and holiday industries have been quick to recognise the importance of this market. SAGA dominates the market for overseas holidays for older consumers, while many other tour operators offer specific packages, such as Thompson's 'Young at Heart' and Airtours 'Golden Years'. Greys are becoming increasingly adventurous in their choice of destination, and long haul breaks are being referred to as 'SKI' (spending kid's inheritance) holidays.

The financial services and holiday sectors are, on the whole, the exception. The majority of marketers of mainstream products, while not denying its importance, have been reluctant to openly target this market. For example, a recent study of 75 advertisements found in magazines aimed at greys revealed that all advertisements for home furnishing products that used older models were for stair-lifts, bath-lifts or orthopaedic beds, depicting how disability and infirmity can be overcome. Given that members of the grey market include Kevin Keegan, Billy Connolly and David Bowie, it is unlikely that such offerings will appeal.

There are several possible reasons for marketer's reluctance to focus on greys. First, there is a belief that the economic future of a brand depends on brand loyalties established early in life. In comparison, an outmoded stereotype persists, depicting all older people as socially isolated, ill and resistant to change. However, evidence suggests that older people are just as likely to switch brands as younger people. Second, many of those who work in marketing and advertising are themselves young, and therefore have difficulty empathising with greys or perceiving grey marketing as glamorous or exciting. Such a view has led to poorly thought-out positioning strategies, for example Empathy shampoo, positioned as beneficial for 'old hair'. Finally, many marketers believe that openly targeting older consumers will alienate younger audiences. This belief has yet to be proved, while it has been suggested that an older spokesperson can lend credibility to a product. On the other hand, marketers obsessed with youth do run the risk of alienating a potentially lucrative market: a recent study conducted by the Millennium Research Bureau found that, of the 750,000 grey con-sumers surveyed, 86.5% thought that TV advertising failed to portray their age group well.

The marketer who wants to successfully target this increasingly important market needs to consider a host of factors. All too often, greys are not considered in market research. Marketers should also remember that well-designed and ergonomically sound products and packaging not only will appeal to those who experience age-related physical problems, but will be easier for everyone to use. Sales promotion techniques such as bonus packs may have less appeal for those who live alone. Those who fear alienating younger consumers through using older models in their advertising have several options. One strategy could be to use younger models in advertisements placed in younger media, and older models in media targeted at older readers and viewers. Alternatively, advertisements featuring people of different ages can bridge the generation gap, while there is no law that states a model must be used in advertising, and creative ideas that focus on product and service benefits can appeal to different ages. For example, a recent Horlicks advertisement depicts a sound-asleep polar bear with the headline 'No kids, no tax forms, no pension shortfall. No wonder he can sleep on an iceberg'. Whatever strategy the marketer uses, it must be remembered that the stereotypical granny image is likely to turn greys off.

Mini-case questions

1. Outline possible approaches to segmenting the grey market. How might this affect the communications used to reach these different groups?
2. Discuss the reasons why many organisations have been reluctant to target greys. How can these barriers be overcome?
3. Outline the possible age-related physical problems that some grey consumers may experience. How can packaging be improved to help older consumers to overcome such difficulties?
4. Identify three different advertisements that you think target the grey market. How effective do you feel these are? How could they be improved?

References

Andersson, P. (1992) Analysing distribution channel dynamics. *European Journal of Marketing*, **26**(2), pp. 47–68.

Bagozzi, R. (1978) Marketing as exchange: a theory of transactions in the market place. *American Behavioural Science*, **21**(4), pp. 257–61.

Bowersox, D. and Morash, E. (1989) The integration of marketing flows in channels of distribution. *European Journal of Marketing*, **23**, p. 2.

Brougaletta, Y. (1985) What business-to-business advertisers can learn from consumer advertisers. *Journal of Advertising Research*, **25**(3), pp. 8–9.

Delozier, M. (1976) *The Marketing Communication Process*. London: McGraw-Hill.

Dwyer, R., Schurr, P. and Oh, S. (1987) Developing buyer–seller relationships. *Journal of Marketing*, **51** (April), pp. 11–27.

Eisenhart, T. (1988) How to really excite your prospects. *Business Marketing* (July), pp. 44–55.

Gilliland, D.I. and Johnston, W.J. (1997) Toward a model of business-to-business marketing communications effects. *Industrial Marketing Management*, **26**, pp. 15–29.

Goldhaber, G.M. (1986) *Organisational Communication*. Dubuque, IA: W.C. Brown.

Houston, F. and Gassenheimer, J. (1987) Marketing and exchange. *Journal of Marketing*, **51** (October), pp. 3–18.

Katz, D. and Kahn, R.L. (1978) *The Social Psychology of Organisations*, 2nd edn. New York: John Wiley.

Kotler, P. (2000) *Marketing Management: The Millennium Edition*. Englewood Cliffs, NJ: Prentice Hall.

Lloyd, J. (1997) Cut your rep free. *Pharmaceutical Marketing* (September), pp. 30–2.

Mason, T. (2000) Cadbury builds café presence, *Marketing*, 2 November, p. 27

Mauss, M. (1974) *The Gift: Forms and Functions of Exchange in Archaic Societies*. London: Routledge & Kegan Paul.

McCarthy, E.J. (1960) *Basic Marketing: A Managerial Approach*. Homewood, IL: Richard D. Irwin.

Mexican Statement (1978) *The Place of Public Relations in Management Education*. Public Relations Education Trust, June.

Mohr, J. and Nevin, J. (1990) Communication strategies in marketing channels. *Journal of Marketing* (October), pp. 36–51.

Pandya, A. and Dholkia, N. (1992) An institutional theory of exchange in marketing. *European Journal of Marketing*, **26**(12), pp. 19–41.

Stern, L. and El-Ansary, A. (1995) *Marketing Channels*, 5th edn. Englewood Cliffs, NJ: Prentice Hall.

Waller, R. (1996) BBC Radio 4 *Today* programme, 29 July.

chapter

2

Communication theory

Only by sharing meaning with members of the target audience and reducing levels of ambiguity can it be hoped to create a dialogue through which marketing goals can be accomplished. To share meaning successfully may require the support of significant others: those who may be expert, knowledgeable or have access to appropriate media channels.

AIMS AND OBJECTIVES

The aims of this chapter are to introduce communication theory and to set it in the context of marketing communications.

The objectives of this chapter are:

1. To understand the basic model of the communication process.
2. To appreciate how the components of the model contribute to successful communications.
3. To provide an analysis of the linkages between components.
4. To examine the impact of personal influences on the communication process.
5. To introduce more recent explanations of communication theory, including networks.
6. To explain how communication theory underpins our understanding of marketing communications.

An introduction to the communication process

It was established in the previous chapter that marketing communications is partly an attempt by an organisation/brand to create and sustain a dialogue with its various constituencies. Communication itself is the process by which individuals share meaning.

Therefore, for a dialogue to occur, each participant needs to understand the meaning of the other's communication. For this overall process to work, information needs to be transmitted (Dibb *et al.*, 1991) by all participants. It is important, therefore, that those involved with marketing communications understand the complexity of the transmission process. Through knowledge and understanding of the communications process, they are more likely to achieve their objective of sharing meaning with each member of their target audiences and so have an opportunity to enter into a dialogue.

For a dialogue to occur, each participant needs to understand the meaning of the other's communication.

In the previous chapter the point was established that there is a variety of reasons why organisations need to communicate with various groups. Of these, one of the more prominent is the need to influence or persuade.

As an initial observation, persuasive communications can be seen in three different contexts. First, persuasion can be viewed in the form of the negotiations that occur between individuals. Here persuasion is based upon a variety of overt and subtle rewards and punishments.

Second, persuasion can be seen in the form of propaganda. Organisations seek to influence their target audiences through the use of symbols, training and cultural indoctrination. The third and final context is that of a speaker addressing a large group. Influence in this context is achieved through the structure of the material presented, the manner in which the presentation is delivered and the form of evidence used to influence the group.

These three perspectives focus upon persuasion, but there is a strong need for organisations also to inform and remind. Furthermore, these approaches are too specific for general marketing purposes and fail to provide assistance to those who wish to plan and manage particular communications.

Linear model of communication

Wilbur Schramm (1955) developed what is now accepted as the basic model of mass communications (Figure 2.1). The components of the linear model of communication are:

1. Source: the individual or organisation sending the message.
2. Encoding: transferring the intended message into a symbolic style that can be transmitted.
3. Signal: the transmission of the message using particular media.
4. Decoding: understanding the symbolic style of the message in order to understand the message.
5. Receiver: the individual or organisation receiving the message.
6. Feedback: the receiver's communication back to the source on receipt of the message.
7. Noise: distortion of the communication process, making it difficult for the receiver to interpret the message as intended by the source.

This is a linear model which emphasises the 'transmission of information, ideas, attitudes, or emotion from one person or group to another (or others), primarily through

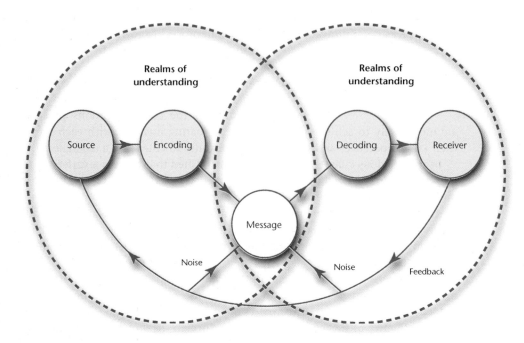

Figure 2.1   A linear model of communication. Based on Schramm (1955) and Shannon and Weaver (1962).

symbols' (Theodorson and Theodorson, 1969). The model and its components are straightforward, but it is the quality of the linkages between the various elements in the process that determine whether the communication will be successful.

Source/encoding

The source, an individual or organisation, identifies a need to transmit a message and then selects a combination of appropriate words, pictures, symbols and music to represent the message to be transmitted. This is called encoding. The purpose is to create a message that is capable of being understood by the receiver.

There are a number of reasons why the source/encoding link might break down. For example, the source may fail to diagnose a particular situation accurately. By not fully understanding a stakeholder's problem or level of knowledge, inappropriate information may be included in the message, which, when transmitted, may lead to misunderstanding and misinterpretation by the receiver. By failing to appreciate the level of education of the target receiver, a message might be encoded in words and symbols that are beyond the comprehension of the receiver.

There are a number of reasons why the source/encoding link might break down.

Some organisations spend a great deal of time and expense on marketing research, trying to develop their understanding of their target audience. This is a point that we shall return to later. The source of a message is an important factor in the communication process. A receiver who perceives a source lacking conviction, authority, trust or expertise is likely to discount any message received from that source, until such time that credibility is established.

Most organisations spend a great deal of time and expense recruiting sales representatives. The risk involved in selecting the wrong people can be extremely large. Many high-tech organisations require their new sales staff to spend over a year receiving both product and sales training before allowing them to meet customers. From a customer's perspective, salespersons who display strong product knowledge skills and who are also

A receiver who perceives a source lacking conviction, authority, trust or expertise is likely to discount any message received.

able to empathise with the individual members of the decision-making unit are more likely to be perceived as credible. Therefore, the organisation that prepares its sales staff and presents them as knowledgeable and trustworthy is more likely to be successful in the communication process than those that do not take the same level of care.

The source is a part of the communication process, not just the generator of detached messages. Patzer (1983) determined that the physical attractiveness of the communicator, particularly if it is the source, contributes significantly to the effectiveness of persuasive communications.

This observation can be related to the use, by organisations, of spokespersons and celebrities to endorse products. Spokespersons can be better facilitators of the communication process if they are able to convey conviction, if they are easily associated with the object of the message, if they have credible expertise and if they are attractive to the receiver, in the wider sense of the word.

This legitimate authority is developed in many television advertisements by the use of the 'white coat', or product-specific clothing, as a symbol of expertise. By dressing the spokesperson in a white coat, he or she is perceived immediately as a credible source of information ('they know what they are talking about'), and so is much more likely to be believed.

Signal

Once encoded, the message must be put into a form that is capable of transmission. It may be oral or written, verbal or non-verbal, in a symbolic form or in a sign. Whatever the format chosen, the source must be sure that what is being put into the message is what is wanted to be decoded by the receiver. The importance of this aspect of the communication process will be developed later when different message strategies are examined in Chapter 21.

The channel is the means by which the message is transmitted from the source to the receiver. These channels may be personal or non-personal. The former involves face-to-face contact and word-of-mouth communications, which can be extremely influential. Non-personal channels are characterised by mass media advertising, which can reach large audiences.

Information received directly from personal influence channels is generally more persuasive than information received through mass media.

Information received directly from personal influence channels is generally more persuasive than information received through mass media. This may be a statement of the obvious, but the reasons for this need to be understood. First, the individual approach permits greater flexibility in the delivery of the message. The timing and power with which a message is delivered can be adjusted to suit the immediate 'selling' environment. Second, a message can be adapted to meet the needs of the customer as the sales call progresses. This flexibility is not possible with mass media messages, as these have to be designed and produced well in advance of transmission and often without direct customer input.

Decoding/receiver

Decoding is the process of transforming and interpreting a message into thought. This process is influenced by the receiver's realm of understanding, which encompasses the experiences, perceptions, attitudes and values of both the source and the receiver. The more the receiver understands about the source and the greater his or her experience in decoding the source's messages, the more able the receiver will be to decode the message successfully.

Feedback/response

The set of reactions a receiver has after seeing, hearing or reading the message is known as the response. These reactions may vary from the extreme of dialing an enquiry telephone number, returning a coupon or even buying the product, to storing information in long-term memory for future use. Feedback is that part of the response that is sent back to the sender, and it is essential for successful communication. The need to understand not just whether the message has been received but also which message has been received is vital. For example, the receiver may have decoded the message incorrectly and a completely different set of responses have been elicited. If a suitable feedback system is not in place then the source will be unaware that the communication has been unsuccessful and is liable to continue wasting resources. This represents inefficient and ineffective marketing communications.

The evaluation of feedback is, of course, vital if sound communications are to be developed. Only through evaluation can the success of any communication be judged. Feedback through personal selling can be instantaneous, through overt means such as questioning, raising objections or signing an order form. Other means, such as the use of gestures and body language, are less overt, and the decoding of the feedback needs to be accurate if an appropriate response is to be given. For the advertiser, the process is much more vague and prone to misinterpretation and error.

Feedback through mass media channels is generally much more difficult to obtain, mainly because of the inherent time delay involved in the feedback process. There are some exceptions, namely the overnight ratings provided by the Broadcasters' Audience Research Board to the television contractors, but as a rule feedback is normally delayed and not as fast. Some commentators argue that the only meaningful indicator of communication success is sales. However, there are many other influences that affect the level of sales, such as price, the effect of previous communications, the recommendations of opinion leaders or friends, poor competitor actions or any number of government or regulatory developments. Except in circumstances such as direct marketing, where immediate and direct feedback can be determined, organisations should use other methods to gauge the success of their communications activities, for example, the level and quality of customer inquiries, the number and frequency of store visits, the degree of attitude change and the ability to recognise or recall an advertisement. All of these represent feedback, but, as a rough distinction, the evaluation of feedback for mass communications is much more difficult to judge than the evaluation of interpersonal communications.

The evaluation of feedback for mass communications is much more difficult to judge than the evaluation of interpersonal communications.

Noise

A complicating factor which may influence the quality of the reception and the feed-back is noise. Noise, according to Mallen (1977), is 'the omission and distortion of information', and there will always be some noise present in all communications. Management's role is to ensure that levels of noise are kept to a minimum, wherever it is able to exert influence.

Noise occurs when a receiver is prevented from receiving the message. This may be because of either cognitive or physical factors. For example, a cognitive factor may be that the encoding of the message was inappropriate, so making it difficult for the receiver to decode the message. In this circumstance it is said that the realms of under-standing of the source and the receiver were not matched. Another reason why noise may enter the system is that the receiver may have been physically prevented from decoding the message accurately because the receiver was distracted. Examples of dis-traction are that the telephone rang, or someone in the room asked a question or coughed. A further reason could be that competing messages screened out the targeted message.

Some sales promotion practitioners are using the word 'noise' to refer to the ambi-ence and publicity surrounding a particular sales promotion event. In other words, the word is being used as a positive, advantageous element in the communication process. This approach is not adopted in this text.

Realms of understanding

The concept of the 'realm of understanding' was introduced earlier. It is an important element in the communication process because it recognises that successful commu-nications are more likely to be achieved if the source and the receiver understand each other. This under-standing concerns attitudes, perceptions, behaviour and experience: the values of both parties to the com-munication process. Therefore, effective communi-cation is more likely when there is some common ground, a realm of understanding between the source and receiver.

Effective communication is more likely when there is some common ground, a realm of understanding between the source and receiver.

Some organisations, especially those in the private sector, spend a huge amount of money researching their target markets and testing their advertisements to ensure that their messages can be decoded and understood by the target audience. The more organisations understand their receivers, the more confident they become in con-structing and transmitting messages to them. Repetition and learning, as we shall see later, are important elements in marketing communications. Learning is a function of knowledge and, the more we know, the more likely we are to understand.

Kelman's model of source characteristics

Kelman (1961) developed a simple scheme for examining the characteristics of a source. Figure 2.2 indicates that these are source credibility, source attractiveness and the degree of compliance required by the source. Each characteristic involves a differ-ent process by which the source influences attitudinal or behavioural change in the receiver.

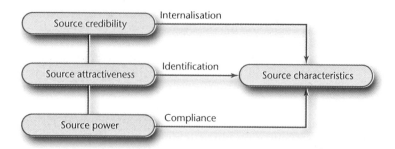

Figure 2.2   Kelman's model of source characteristics. From Kelman (1961); used with kind permission.

Source credibility refers to the extent that receivers perceive the source, or a partici-

> *Source credibility refers to the extent that receivers perceive the source as able and willing to give an objective opinion and as having sufficient relevant expertise.*

pant in the communication process, as able and willing to give an objective opinion and as having sufficient relevant expertise. As explained earlier, a high level of perceived expertise in a source is often more persuasive than if the expertise is perceived as low.

Source credibility – Max Factor

Max Factor claim that their products are so good that they are used by the experts in their industry: 'Make-up for Make-up Artists'. Trustworthiness is important, as the impact of the source will be reduced if receivers perceive the source to be biased.

Max Factor have a problem as it is clear to consumers that the make-up artist used in each advertisement may not necessarily be completely objective in their view because they will have been paid to take part in the advertisement. What we do as viewers is trade off the validity of the claim against the perceived trustworthiness of the individual. The result is that the claim has reduced impact but probably enough, if repeated enough times, for us to accept that the products are very good. If one is already *a Max Factor* customer, then product experience will contribute to a support argument (see Chapter 21) and advertising messages are used to reinforce previous brand choice decisions.

A high level of source credibility is not always an asset, nor is a low-credibility source always a liability. Eagly and Chaiken (1975) found high- and low-credibility sources to be of equal effectiveness when the source is arguing for a position opposing their own best interest. The use of a high-credibility source is of less importance when the receivers have a neutral position. Recent advertisements in the United Kingdom (e.g. Lombard North, Parcelforce) suggest that source credibility and attractiveness need not necessarily be high in order to be effective.

While a great deal of empirical work indicates that the credibility of a message source correlates strongly with a message's ability to induce attitude change, there are factors that can moderate this change (Newell and Shemwell, 1995). Factors such as involvement, product type, message type, experience and expectations are some of the more notable influences.

Source attractiveness develops when a source is perceived as attractive, and persuasion, according to Kelman, occurs through a process known as identification. This is apparent when the receiver is motivated to seek some type of relationship with the source and so adopts a similar position. The receiver may only maintain the attitude or behaviour as long as it is supported by the source or as long as the source remains attractive.

Identification is apparent when the receiver is motivated to seek some type of relationship with the source and so adopts a similar position.

Organisations often select sales staff whose characteristics have a strong correlation with their customers or who have similar backgrounds to those of the target audience. This is thought to be an appropriate way to help build a bond or area of common interest between the two parties. This bond of similarity can also be established through what is referred to as 'slice of life' advertising. This is a technique where the target audience is exposed to a series of messages which represent an everyday occurrence or problem. The receiver is encouraged to believe 'I can see myself in that situation'. Credibility is established by inviting receivers to identify themselves with the situation and by showing how the promoted product can resolve their problem. Food and drink manufacturers often present their products as an integral part of family life (Persil, Oxo and Sunny Delight). By depicting them as part of everyday events and building associations between the event, the brand and the people, the target audience can identify easily and naturally with the overall scene and the associated brand values that complement it.

Source power is said to be present when the source of a message is able to reward or punish. When the receiver perceives source power, the influence process occurs through compliance. In an attempt to be rewarded and to avoid punishment, the receiver complies with the request of the source.

Source power is said to be present when the source of a message is able to reward or punish.

Such power is difficult to apply in advertising, but is more easily identifiable in personal selling, where sales staff, through use of a lavish expense account, for example, may exert power over a buyer. Alternatively, if the seller's organisation is perceived as dominating a market, buyers may comply with the requests of the source to ensure continuity of supply. Dennis, which makes fire engines, develops source credibility through a variety of activities. Trade advertising, testing, prominent name display on each tender, frequent exposure on news programmes at the scene of accidents and disasters and use within high-profile television dramas all help to reduce risk through familiarity and association, build source expertise through the bravery of the those involved and develop trust through continued presence and the reliability of the equipment. See Plate 2.1.

The effect of personal influences on the communications process

One-step flow of communication

The traditional model of communication having been looked at, attention must now be given to the effect that personal influences may have on the process. The traditional view of communication holds that the process consists essentially of one step. Information is directed and shot at prospective audiences, rather like a bullet is

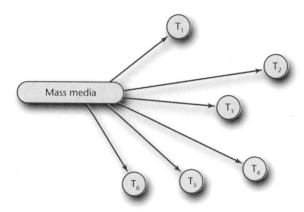

Figure 2.3 One-step model of communication. T = member of the target audience.

propelled from a gun. The decision of each member of the audience to act on the message or not is the result of a passive role or participation in the process (Figure 2.3).

Organisations can communicate with different target audiences simply by varying the message and the type and frequency of channels used. The one-step model has been criticised for its oversimplification, and it certainly ignores the effect of personal influences on the communication process.

Two-step flow of communication

This model depicts information flowing via media channels to particular types of people (opinion leaders and opinion formers; see later) to whom other members of the audience refer for information and guidance. Through interpersonal networks, opinion leaders not only reach members of the target audience who may not have been exposed to the message, but may reinforce the impact of the message for those members that did receive the message (Figure 2.4). For example, editors of travel sections in the Sunday press and television presenters of travel programmes fulfil the role of opinion former and can influence the decision of prospective travellers. It can be seen that targets 5 and 6 were not exposed to the original message, so the opinion leader

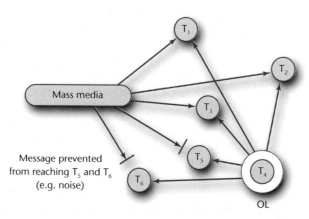

Figure 2.4 Two-step model of communication. OL = opinion leader.

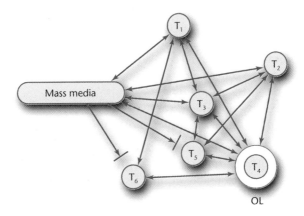

Figure 2.5   Multi-step model of communication.

(OL; T_4) acts as an original information source for them and as a reinforcer for targets 1, 2 and 3.

The implication of the two-step model is that the mass media do not have a direct and all-powerful effect over their audiences. If the primary function of the mass media is to provide information, then personal influences are necessary to be persuasive and to exert direct influence on members of the target audience.

Multi-step flow of communications

This model proposes that the process involves interaction among all parties to the communication process; see Figure 2.5. This interpretation closely resembles the network of participants that are often involved in the communication process.

Word-of-mouth communications

The multi-step model suggests that opinion leaders/formers and members of the target audience all influence each other. The communication process is two way, and interaction by word-of-mouth communications assists and enriches the communication process.

We can see, therefore, the importance of personal influences upon the communication process. Customers use word-of-mouth recommendations to provide information and to support and reinforce their purchasing decisions. At the heart of this approach is the source credibility that is assigned to people whose opinions are sought after and used in the purchase decision process. In comparison to advertising messages, word of mouth communications are more robust (Berkman and Gilson, 1986).

Customers use word-of-mouth recommendations to provide information and to support and reinforce their purchasing decisions.

People like to talk about their product experiences, for a variety of reasons that are explored in the next section. However, by talking with a neighbour or colleague about the good experiences associated with a new car, for example, the first-hand 'this has actually happened to someone I know' effect will be instrumental in the same views

being passed on to other colleagues, irrespective of their validity or overall representation of similar cars. eViral marketing (see Chapter 25) is an electronic version of the
spoken endorsement of a product or service where messages, screen savers and other
information are targeted at key individuals who then voluntarily pass the message to
friends and colleagues and in doing so bestow, endorse and provide the message with
much valued credibility.

But why do people want to discuss products or advertising messages? Dichter
(1966) determined that such motivation fell into four categories:

1. *Product involvement*
   People, he found, have a high propensity to discuss matters that are either dis-
   tinctly pleasurable or unpleasurable. Such discussion serves to provide an opportunity for the experience to be relived, whether it be the 'looking for' or the 'use'
   experience, or both.

2. *Self-involvement*
   Discussion offers a means for ownership to be established and signals aspects of
   prestige and levels of status to the receiver. More importantly, perhaps, dissonance
   can be reduced as the purchaser seeks reassurance about the decision.

3. *Other involvement*
   Products can assist motivations to help others and to express feelings of love,
   friendship and caring. These feelings can be released through a sense of sharing the
   variety of benefits that products can bestow.

4. *Message involvement*
   The final motivation to discuss products is derived, according to Dichter, from the
   messages that surround the product itself, in particular the advertising messages
   and, in the business-to-business market, seminars, exhibitions and the trade press,
   which provide the means to provoke conversation and so stimulate word-of-mouth
   recommendation.

It is interesting to note that Dichter's various forms of involvement, in particular the
'self' and 'other' categories, bear a strong similarity to the market exchanges and reciprocal exchanges explored in Chapter 1. However, word-of-mouth communications are
often undertaken by those who identify very closely with a brand, to the extent that
they might be termed brand advocates. Advocacy can
be demonstrated not only through word-of-mouth
communications but also through behaviour, for
example, by wearing branded clothing or using tools
and equipment. Watts (2000) reports the claim made
by the group marketing director of Dyson that 70% of
sales are generated through recommendation by family
and friends, to the extent that some people would ring up others and offer to lend out
their machine. The issue of advocacy is explored further in Chapter 23 in the section
on loyalty and retention schemes.

*Advocacy can be demonstrated not only
through word-of-mouth communications but
also through behaviour, for example, by
wearing branded clothing or using tools and
equipment.*

These motivations to discuss products and their associative experiences vary
between individuals and with the intensity of the motivation at any one particular
moment. There are two main persons involved in this process of word-of-mouth communications: a sender and receiver. Research indicates that the receiver's evaluation of
a message is far from stable over time and accuracy of recall decays (expectedly)
through time. What this means for marketing communications is that those people

who have a positive product experience, especially in the service sector, should be encouraged to talk as soon as possible after the event (Christiansen and Tax, 2000).

For organisations it is important to target messages at those individuals who are predisposed to such discussion, as this may well propel word-of-mouth recommendations and the success of the communications campaign . The target, therefore, is not necessarily the target market, but those in the target market who are most likely to volunteer their positive opinions about the offering or those who, potentially, have some influence over members. There are three types of such volunteers: opinion leaders, formers and followers.

Opinion leaders

Katz and Lazerfeld (1955) first identified individuals who were predisposed to receiving information and then reprocessing it to influence others. Their studies of American voting and purchase behaviour led to their conclusion that those individuals who could exert such influence were more persuasive than information received directly from the mass media. These opinion leaders, according to Rogers (1962), tend 'to be of the same social class as non-leaders, but may enjoy a higher social status within the group'. Williams (1990) uses the work of Reynolds and Darden (1971) to suggest that they are more gregarious and more self-confident than non-leaders. In addition, they have a greater exposure to relevant mass media (print) and as a result have more knowledge/familiarity and involvement with the product class, are more innovative and more confident of their role as influencer (leader) and appear to be less dogmatic than non-leaders (Chan and Misra, 1990).

Using ordinary people to express positive comments about a product to each other is a very well-used advertising technique.

Opinion leadership can be simulated in advertising by the use of product testimonials. Using ordinary people to express positive comments about a product to each other is a very well-used advertising technique.

Viral campaign – Burn

Reaching the youth market is notoriously difficult and traditional approaches to achieving credibility do not always work. The launch of Coca-Cola's energy drink Burn was characterised by the free distribution of the drink to those opinion formers regarded as 'cool' by the target audience, namely DJs and bar staff at clubs and bars.

The importance of opinion leaders in the design and implementation of communication plans should not be underestimated. Midgley and Dowling (1993) refer to *innovator communicators*: those who are receptive to new ideas and who make innovation-based purchase decisions without reference to or from other people. However, while the importance of these individuals is not doubted, a major difficulty exists in trying to identify just who these opinion leaders and innovator communicators are. While they sometimes display some distinctive characteristics, such as reading specialist media vehicles, often being first to return coupons, enjoying attending exhibitions or just involving themselves with new, innovative techniques or products, they are by their very nature invisible outside their work, family and social groups.

Opinion formers

Opinion formers are individuals who are able to exert personal influence because of their authority, education or status associated with the object of the communication process. Like opinion leaders, they are looked to by others to provide information and advice, but this is because of the formal expertise that opinion formers are adjudged to have. For example, community pharmacists are often consulted about symptoms and medicines, and film critics carry such conviction in their reviews that they can make or break a new production.

Opinion formers are individuals who are able to exert personal influence because of their authority, education or status associated with the object of the communication process.

The BBC radio programme *The Archers*, an everyday story of country folk, has been used to deliver messages about farming issues. The actors in the programme are opinion formers and they direct messages to farmers about farming techniques and methods. The educational use was very important after the Second World War.

Popular television programmes, such as *Eastenders*, *Brookside* and *Coronation Street*, all of which attract huge audiences, have been used as vehicles to bring to attention and open up debates about many controversial social issues, such as contraception, abortion, drug use and abuse, and serious illness and mental health concerns.

Broadcast opinion formers – *The Archers*

The radio soap opera about rural life, centred around a fictional village called Ambridge, has been the source of information about country matters for a long time. Not only does the programme refer to real current affairs, it also mentions organisations where the script demands authenticity. For example, when one of the characters became commercially involved in a riding stable, she decided to get the appropriate qualification from the British Horse Society (BHS).

This mention of BHS provided source credibility for the story and a product placement opportunity for BHS. The programme also fulfilled the role of opinion former as it served to direct those who needed a riding instructor's qualification to a credible organisation.

The influence of opinion formers can be great. For example, the editor of a journal or newspaper may be a recognised source of expertise, and any offering referred to by the editor in the media vehicle is endowed with great credibility. In this sense the editor acts as a gatekeeper, and it is the task of the marketing communicator to ensure that all relevant opinion formers are identified and sent appropriate messages.

The credibility of opinion formers is vital for communication effectiveness.

However, the credibility of opinion formers is vital for communication effectiveness. If there is a suspicion or doubt about the impartiality of the opinion former, then the objectivity of their views and comments are likely to be perceived as tainted and not believed so that damage may be caused to the reputation of the brand and those involved.

Credibility in doubt – wine tasters

The views of an independent third party can be very beneficial as witnessed by Chittenden (2000) who reported that when a Liubimetz merlot was mentioned on the BBC's *Food and Drink* programme, sales of the wine soared by 888%.

So, it was not surprising that an allegation by a member of the Circle of Wine Tasters that some members were not sufficiently independent to give unbiased views of wines caused much resentment. It was suggested that some members were tied into supermarket contracts or television programmes such that there was a conflict of interest and that the advice and recommendations they gave consumers were inevitably biased.

Source: Maurice Chittenden, *The Sunday Times*, London, 26 November 2000.

Many organisations constantly lobby key members of parliament in an effort to persuade them to pursue 'favourable' policies. Opinion formers are relatively easy to identify, as they need to be seen shaping the opinion of others, usually opinion followers.

Opinion followers

The vast majority of consumers can be said to be opinion followers. The messages they receive via the mass media are tempered by the opinions of the two groups of personal influencers just discussed. Some people actively seek information from those they believe are well informed, while others prefer to use the mass media for information and guidance (Robinson, 1976). However, this should not detract from the point that, although followers, they still process information independently and use a variety of inputs when sifting information and responding to marketing stimuli.

Ethical drug manufacturers normally launch new drugs by enlisting the support of particular doctors who have specialised in the therapy area and who are recognised by other doctors as experts. These opinion leaders are invited to lead symposia and associated events to build credibility and activity around the new product. At the same time, public relations agencies prepare press releases with the aim that the information will be used by the mass media (opinion formers) for editorial purposes and create exposure for the product across the target audience, which, depending upon the product and/or the media vehicle, may be GPs, hospital doctors, patients or the general public. All these people, whether they be opinion leaders or formers, are active influencers or talkers (Kingdom, 1970).

Process of adoption

An interesting extension to the concept of opinion followers and the discussion on word-of-mouth communications is the process by which individuals become committed to the use of a new product. Rogers (1983) has identified this as the process of

Prior conditions

1. Previous practice
2. Felt needs/problems
3. Innovativeness
4. Norms of the social systems

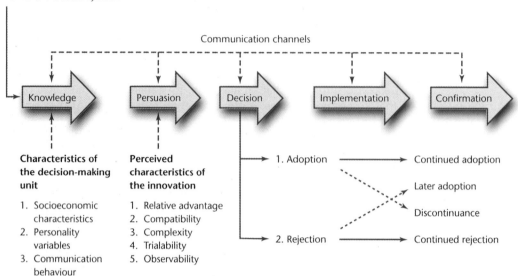

Figure 2.6   Stages in the innovation decision process of adoption. Reprinted from Rogers (1983) with the permission of the Free Press. Copyright 1962, 1971, 1983 by the Free Press.

adoption and the stages of his innovation decision process are represented in Figure 2.6. These stages in the adoption process are sequential and are characterised by the different factors that are involved at each stage (e.g. the media used by each individual).

1. *Knowledge*

   The innovation becomes known to consumers, but they have little information and no well-founded attitudes. Information must be provided through mass media to institutions and people that active seekers of information are likely to contact. Information for passive seekers should be supplied through the media and channels that this group habitually uses to look for other kinds of information (Windahl *et al.*, 1992).

   Jack cleans his teeth regularly, but he is beginning to notice a sensitivity to both hot and cold drinks. He becomes aware of an advertisement for Special Paste on television.

2. *Persuasion*

   The consumer becomes aware that the innovation may be of use in solving known and potential problems. Information from those who have experience of the product becomes very important.

   Jack notices that the makers of Special Paste claim that their brand reduces the amount of sensitive reaction to hot and cold drinks. Special Paste has also been recommended to him by someone he overheard in the pub last week. Modelling behaviour predominates.

3. *Decision*

An attitude may develop and may be either favourable or unfavourable, but as a result a decision is reached whether to trial the offering or not. Communications need to assist this part of the process by continual prompting.

Jack is prepared to believe (or not to believe) the messages and the claims made on behalf of Special Paste. He thinks that Special Paste is potentially a very good brand (or not). He intends trying Special Paste because he was given a free sample (or because it was on a special price deal).

4. *Implementation*

For the adoption to proceed in the absence of a sales promotion, buyers must know where to get it and how to use it. The product is then tested in a limited way. Communications must provide this information in order that the trial experience be developed.

Jack buys 'Special Paste' and tests it.

5. *Confirmation*

The innovation is accepted or rejected on the basis of the experience during trial. Planned communications play an important role in maintaining the new behaviour by dispelling negative thoughts and positively reaffirming the original 'correct' decision. McGuire, as reported in Windahl *et al.* (1992), refers to this as post-behavioural consolidation.

It works, Jack's teeth are not as sensitive to hot and cold drinks as they were before he started using 'Special Paste'. He reads an article that reports that large numbers of people are using these types of products satisfactorily. Jack resolves to buy 'Special Paste' next time.

This process can be terminated at any stage and, of course, a number of competing brands may vie for consumers' attention simultaneously, so adding to the complexity and levels of noise in the process. Generally, mass communications are seen to be more effective in the earlier phases of the adoption process for products that buyers are actively interested in, and more interpersonal forms are more appropriate at the later stages, especially trial and adoption. This model assumes that the stages occur in a predictable sequence, but this clearly does not happen in all purchase activity, as some information that is to be used later in the trial stage may be omitted, which often happens when loyalty to a brand is high or where the buyer has experience in the marketplace.

Process of diffusion

The process of adoption in aggregate form, over time, is diffusion. According to Rogers, diffusion is the process by which an innovation is communicated through certain channels over a period of time among the members of a social system. This is a group process and Rogers again identified five categories of adopters. Figure 2.7 shows how diffusion may be fast or slow and that there is no set speed at which the process occurs. The five categories are as follows:

The process of adoption in aggregate form, over time, is diffusion.

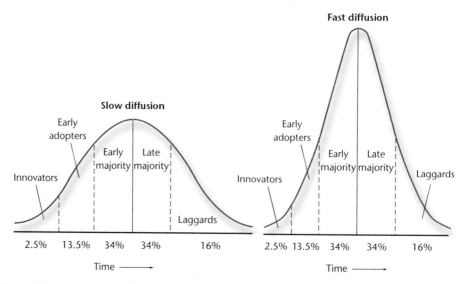

Figure 2.7 Fast and slow diffusion of an innovation. From Hawkins *et al.* (1989); used with kind permission.

1. *Innovators*: these groups like new ideas and have a large disposable income. This means they are more likely to take risks associated with new products.

2. *Early adopters*: research has established that this group contains a large proportion of opinion leaders and they are therefore important in speeding the diffusion process. Early adopters tend to be younger than any other group and above average in education. Other than innovators, this group takes more publications and consults more salespeople than all others. This group is important to the marketing communications process because they can determine the speed at which diffusion occurs.

3. *Early majority*: usually, opinion followers are a little above average in age, education, social status and income. They rely on informal sources of information and take fewer publications than the previous two groups.

4. *Late majority*: this group of people is sceptical of new ideas and only adopts new products because of social or economic factors. They take few publications and are below average in education, social status and income.

5. *Laggards*: a group of people who are suspicious of all new ideas and set in their opinions. Lowest of all the groups in terms of income, social status and education, this group takes a long time to adopt an innovation.

This framework suggests that, at the innovation stage, messages should be targeted at relatively young people in the target group, with a high level of income, education and social status. This will speed word-of-mouth recommendation and the diffusion process. Mahajan *et al.* (1990) observe that the personal influence of word-of-mouth communications does not work in isolation from the other communication tools. Early adopters are more likely to adopt an innovation in response to 'external influences' and only through time will the effect of 'internal influences' become significant. In other words, mass media communications need time to work before word-of-mouth communications can begin to build effectiveness.

A major difficulty associated with the use of this framework, however, is the inability to define which stage of the diffusion process is operating at any time. Furthermore, Gatignon and Robertson (1985) suggest that there are three elements to the diffusion process which need to be taken into account, particularly for the fast-moving consumer goods sector:

1. The rate of diffusion or speed at which sales occur.
2. The pattern of diffusion or shape of the curve.
3. The potential penetration level or size of the market.

Care should be taken to ensure that all three of these elements are considered when attempting to understand the diffusion process. It can be concluded that if a promotional campaign is targeted at innovators and the early majority and is geared to stimulating word-of-mouth communications, then the diffusion process is more likely to be successful than if these elements are ignored.

Interactional approaches to communications

The models and frameworks of the communication process discussed to date can be interpreted as an abstraction. The one-step model is linear and unidirectional, and it suggests that the receiver plays a passive role in the process. The two-step and multi-step models attempt to account for the interactive nature of communication and they proffer a mutually participative role for all parties to the communication process. These models emphasise individual behaviour and exclude the social behaviour implicit in the process. Goffman (1969) advocates an 'interactional' approach which focuses on the roles adopted by the players in the communication process. Through mutual understanding of each other's behaviour, the rules of the communication process are established. McEwan (1992) suggests that this permits formal and informal communication procedures to be established, and that mutual understanding (Rogers and Kincaid, 1981) and increased levels of trust can be developed by the participants.

This is an interesting perspective, as strands of the importance of source credibility can be identified in this approach. Evidence of Goffman's approach can be seen in personal selling. Sellers and buyers, meeting for the first time, often enter negotiations at a formal level, each adopting a justifiable, self-protective position. As negotiations proceed, so the two parties adjust their roles, and, as the likelihood of a mutual exchange increases, so the formal roles give way to a more informal ones.

Relational or contextual approaches to communications

The previous model accounts for social behaviour but does not account for the context within which the behaviour occurs. Communication events always occur within a context (Littlejohn, 1992) or particular set of circumstances, which not only influence the form of the communication but also the nature and the way the communication is received, interpreted and acted upon. There are a huge number of variables that can influence the context, including the disposition of the people involved, the physical environment, the nature of the issue, the history and associated culture, the goals of the participants and the expected repercussions of the dialogue itself.

Littlejohn identifies four main contextual levels. These are interpersonal, group, organisational and mass communication. These levels form part of a hierarchy whereby higher levels incorporate the lower levels but 'add something new of their own'.

There are four main contextual levels: interpersonal, group, organisational and mass communication.

The relational approach means that communication events are linked together in an organised manner, one where the events are 'punctuated' by interventions from one or more of the participants. These interventions occur whenever the participants attempt cooperation or if conflict arises.

Soldow and Thomas (1984), referring to a sales negotiation, state that a relationship develops through the form of negotiations rather than the content. An agreement is necessary about who is to control the relationship or whether there will be equality. Rothschild (1987) reports that 'sparring will continue' until agreement is reached or the negotiations are terminated. In other words, without mutual agreement over the roles of the participants, the true purpose of the interaction, to achieve an exchange, cannot be resolved.

An interesting aspect of relational communication theory is social penetration (Taylor and Altman, 1987). Through the disclosure of increasing amounts of information about themselves, partners in a relationship (personal or organisational) develop levels of intimacy which serve to build interpersonal (interorganisational?) relationships. The relationship moves forward as partners reveal successive layers of information about each other and, as a greater amount or breadth of information is shared, confidence grows. These levels can be seen to consist of orientation, exploratory affective exchange, affective exchange and stable exchange; see Table 2.1. These layers are not uncovered in a logical, orderly sequence. It is likely that partners will return to previous levels, test the outcomes and rewards and reconsider their positions as the relationships unfolds through time. This suggests that social penetration theory may lie at the foundation of the development of trust, commitment and relational exchanges between organisations.

Relationships need not be just dyadic, as the interactional approach suggests, but could be triadic or even encompass a much wider network or array of participants. Through this perspective a 'communication network' can be observed, through which information can flow. Participants engage in communication based upon their perception of the environment in which the communication occurs and the way in which each participant relates to each other.

Rogers (1986) identifies a communication network as 'consisting of interconnected

Table 2.1   Layers of social penetration

Orientation	The disclosure of public information only.
Exploratory affective exchange	Expansion and development of public information.
Affective exchange	Disclosure, based upon anticipated relationship rewards, of deeper feelings, values and beliefs.
Stable exchange	High level of intimacy where partners are able to predict each other's reactions with a good level of accuracy.

Source: Adapted from Taylor and Altman (1987).

individuals who are linked by patterned communication flows'. This is important, as it views communication as transcending organisational boundaries. In other words, it is not only individuals within an organisation that develop patterned communication flows but also individuals across different organisations. These individuals participate with one another (possibly through exchanges) and use communication networks to achieve their agenda items.

The extent to which individuals are linked to the network is referred to as connectedness. The more a network is connected, the greater the likelihood that a message will be disseminated, as there are few isolated individuals. Similarly, the level of integration in a network refers to the degree to which members of the network are linked to one another. The greater the integration, the more potential channels there are for a message to be routed through.

The more a network is connected, the greater the likelihood that a message will be disseminated, as there are few isolated individuals.

Systems theory, as discussed in the previous chapter, recognises that organisations are made of interacting units. The relational approach to communications is similar to systems theory. The various 'criss-crossing' flows of information between reciprocating units allow individuals and groups to modify the actions of others in the 'net', and this permits the establishment of a pattern of communication (Tichy, 1979).

Network approaches to communications

The regular use of these patterned flows leads to the development of communication networks, which have been categorised as prescribed and emergent (Weick, 1987). Prescribed networks are formalised patterns of communication, very often established by senior management within an organisation or by organisational representatives when interorganisational communications are considered. It follows that emergent networks are informal and emerge as a response to the social and task-orientated needs of the participants.

Undoubtedly some of these more recent approaches have made significant contributions to our understanding of communication. They need to be developed further, and for a fuller account of these approaches to communication readers are referred to McEwan (1992). These later approaches, like their predecessors, have been developed as a result of our understanding of individual behaviour, often within an organisational context.

Summary

An appreciation of the way in which communication works is important to understanding and developing planned communications. The classic approach to communication views the process as linear, similar to the actions of a hypodermic syringe injecting its audience with information. Here the sender, message, channel, receiver approach is prevalent. Subsequent models have attempted to reflect the two-way perspective and to account for the interpersonal components of communications, which in themselves stress mutuality and shared perceptions (Windahl *et al.*, 1992).

The linear approach is not rejected, as there are circumstances where a one-way transmission of information is required, such as a flood warning by the National Rivers

Authority or the announcement that a product specification has been altered to meet new legislative requirements. However, in the context of developing relational exchanges (Chapter 1), the network approach to communications is both justified and compatible. Individuals are seen to engage in patterned flows of communication which partly reflect the diversity of their interests.

This text recognises the importance of the linear and interactional approaches to communication, but uses the concept of communication networks, a contextual perspective, to explore marketing communications.

Review questions

1. Name the elements of the linear model of communication and briefly describe the role of each element.

2. What is source credibility and what are the two main components?

3. How does Kelman assist our understanding of the source of a message?

4. Select four television and four print advertisements and identify how the advertisers attempt to establish credibility. Do they succeed?

5. Discuss the differences between one-step, two-step and multi-step communications.

6. How do opinion leaders differ from opinion formers and opinion followers?

7. Why is word-of-mouth communication so important to marketing communications?

8. Draw a graph to show the difference between fast and slow diffusion.

9. What is the relational approach to communications? How might social penetration theory assist our understanding of this interpretation of how communication works?

10. Identify two forms of communication networks.

MINI CASE

This mini case was written by Jill Brown, Senior Lecturer in Marketing at the University of Portsmouth Business School. The author would like to acknowledge the contribution of Tim Miller at HSBC.

Using opinion formers at HSBC

A bar of soap was included in the invitations to the press event when HSBC launched its new TV banking service via Open in 1999. Former *EastEnders* star Martine McCutcheon demonstrated that the innovative new service, accessed via digital satellite TV, was simple enough to be used by anyone and Martyn Lewis hosted the event, providing the required 'weight' and credibility. It was vitally important that key opinion formers attended and were persuaded that HSBC's new interactive TV service was the most exciting and user-friendly development in banking for many years.

Originally owned by a consortium consisting of Matsushita, BT, BSkyB and HSBC, Open was launched to offer greater choice to consumers who wanted to be able to access interactive services from the comfort of their own home, using their TV. Although PC home ownership continues to grow, virtually every household in the UK already has a television. The government's decision to 'switch off' analogue TV some time between 2006 and 2010 means that soon everyone will be watching digital TV. Already, over 5.3 million (early 2001 figure)

Sky Digital households have access to Open.

Matsushita provided the TV technology, BT the telecommunications expertise, BSkyB the broadcast experience and analogue customer base and HSBC developed the transaction management and payment systems.

Open provides shopping, banking, games, email and local information services and whilst the early users tended to reflect the younger, male profile of the typical Web surfer the demographics are now changing and becoming more mainstream.

HSBC developed two main services:

Banking services for its customers (balance checking on current, savings and credit card accounts, transfers, bill payments, standing order and direct debit checking, lists of recent transactions, etc.).

Financial services for non-customers and customers (travel and health insurance, car financing scheme, information on likely repayments on loans, etc.).

HSBC used a carefully crafted and integrated campaign involving outdoor media, direct mail, print advertising, in-branch and on-screen promotions and internal communications. There were live TV banking displays in selected branches and advertising on the HSBC Web site. The image of a red sofa figured strongly throughout and the strapline 'Take remote control of your money' evolved into 'Sit down and take remote control'.

The press launch positioned the launch of HSBC's interactive TV banking services as a historic milestone in the development of television. A series of video clips illustrated key moments in the history of TV – from early footage from the black-and-white era through to the advent of colour, the launch of digital TV and finally the launch of interactive TV services. After Martine's 'live' demo and the video presentation, HSBC's Chief Executive, Bill Dalton took questions from the floor. A lunch followed with plenty of opportunities for questions and discussion. Press packs were also issued, containing press releases, questions and answers, and factsheets about the HSBC service and about Open.

Heavy use was made of public relations to communicate with key opinion formers and unusually for HSBC, which normally conducts all of its PR activity in-house, a PR agency was employed to strengthen the PR effort, demonstrating the weight attached to this particular communications tool for this campaign.

Journalists at the launch were given the opportunity of one-to-one press briefings and senior managers have subsequently given a large number of follow-up interviews. This has ensured sustained press coverage, continuing long after the launch event. Media sections targeted included consumer (e.g. *Best, Woman, FHM*), personal finance (e.g. *Personal Finance, Moneywise*), specialist (e.g. *Parenting, Disability Times*), technology (e.g. *Revolution, Computer Weekly*), on-line media (e.g. FT Your money, UK-invest, thisismoney.com), national personal finance sections (e.g. *Sun Money, Financial Mail on Sunday, Cash*) broadcast media (e.g. BBC2's *Working Lunch*, Radio 4's *Moneybox*), TV listings media (e.g. Sky's customer magazine, *Time Out*) and regional publications (on-screen promotions gave the opportunity to publicise 'local' winners).

A number of accolades have been received by HSBC for the campaign, including winning 'the most innovative marketing campaign' at the Financial Innovation Awards and a World Gold Medal at the International Film and Video Awards (held at the New York Festival) for work on the on-screen video featured within the service.

By March 2001 130,000 people had registered to use HSBC's Open Banking service and 250,000 brochure requests had been received – the role of opinion formers in establishing the credibility and user-friendliness of this new brand cannot be underestimated.

Mini-case questions

1. How do you account for the extensive communications with opinion formers in this case?
2. What factors led to the success of this public relations campaign?
3. How might word-of-mouth communications be used to develop awareness and understanding of the new product?
4. Using the processes of adoption and diffusion, explain how services such as TV banking might develop.

References

Berkman, H. and Gilson, C. (1986) *Consumer Behaviour: Concepts and Strategies*. Boston, MA: Vent.

Chan, K.K. and Misra, S. (1990) Characteristics of the Opinion Leader: a new dimension. *Journal of Advertising*, **19**(3), pp. 53–60.

Chittenden, M. (2000) Store links 'taint' wine critics taste. *Sunday Times*, 26 November, p. 3.

Christiansen, T. and Tax, S.S. (2000) Measuring word of mouth : the questions of who and when. *Journal of Marketing Communications*, **6**, pp. 185–99.

Dibb, S., Simkin, L., Pride, W. and Ferrel, O. (1991) *Marketing: Concepts and Strategies*. New York: Houghton Mifflin.

Dichter, E. (1966) How word-of-mouth advertising works. *Harvard Business Review*, **44** (November/December), pp. 147–66.

Eagly, A. and Chaiken, S. (1975) An attribution analysis of the effect of characteristics on opinion change. *Journal of Personality and Social Psychology*, **32**, pp. 136–44.

Gatignon, H. and Robertson, T. (1985) A propositional inventory for new diffusion research. *Journal of Consumer Research*, **11**, pp. 849–67.

Goffman, E. (1969) *Strategic Interaction*. New York: Doubleday.

Hawkins, D.I., Best, R.J. and Coney, K.A. (1989) *Consumer Behaviour: Implications for Marketing Strategy*. Homewood, IL: Richard D. Irwin.

Katz, E. and Lazarfeld, P.F. (1955) *Personal Influence*. Glencoe, IL: Free Press.

Kelman, H. (1961) Processes of opinion change. *Public Opinion Quarterly*, **25** (Spring), pp. 57–78.

Kingdom, J.W. (1970) Opinion leaders in the electorate. *Public Opinion Quarterly*, **34**, pp. 256–61.

Littlejohn, S.W. (1992) *Theories of Human Communication*, 4th edn. Belmont, CA: Wadsworth.

Mahajan, V., Muller, E. and Bass, F.M. (1990) New product diffusion models in marketing. *Journal of Marketing*, **54** (January), pp. 1–26.

Mallen, B. (1977) *Principles of Marketing Channel Management*. Lexington, MA: Lexington Books.

McEwan, T. (1992) Communication in organisations. In *Hospitality Management* (ed. L. Mullins). London: Pitman.

Midgley, D. and Dowling, G. (1993) Longitudinal study of product form innovation: the interaction between predispositions and social messages. *Journal of Consumer Research*, **19** (March), pp. 611–25.

Newell, S.J. and Shemwell, D.J. (1995) The CEO endorser and message source credibility: an empirical investigation of antecedents and consequences. *Journal of Marketing Communications*, **1**, pp. 13–23.

Patzer, G.L. (1983) Source credibility as a function of communicator physical attractiveness. *Journal of Business Research*, **11**, pp. 229–41.

Reynolds, F.D. and Darden, W.R. (1971) Mutually adaptive effects of interpersonal communication. *Journal of Marketing Research*, **8** (November), pp. 449–54.

Robinson, J.P. (1976) Interpersonal influence in election campaigns: two step flow hypothesis. *Public Opinion Quarterly*, **40**, pp. 304–19.

Rogers, E.M. (1962) *Diffusion of Innovations*, 1st edn. New York: Free Press.

Rogers, E.M. (1983) *Diffusion of Innovations*, 3rd edn. New York: Free Press.

Rogers, E.M. (1986) *Communication Technology: The New Media in Society*. New York: Free Press.

Rogers, E.M. and Kincaid, D.L. (1981) *Communication Networks: Toward a Paradigm for Research*. New York: Free Press.

Rothschild, M. (1987) *Marketing Communications*. Lexington, MA: D.C. Heath.

Schramm, W. (1955) How communication works. In *The Process and Effects of Mass Communications* (ed. W. Schramm). Urbana, IL: University of Illinois Press, pp. 3–26.

Shannon, C. and Weaver, W. (1962) *The Mathematical Theory of Communication*. Urbana, IL: University of Illinois Press.

Soldow, G. and Thomas, G. (1984) Relational communication: form versus content in the sale interaction. *Journal of Marketing*, **48** (Winter), pp. 84–93.

Taylor, D. and Altman, I. (1987) Communication in interpersonal relationships: social penetration theory. In *Interpersonal Processes: New Directions in Communication Research* (eds M.E. Roloff and G.R. Miller). Newbury Park, CA: Sage, pp. 257–77.

Theodorson, S.A. and Theodorson, G.R. (1969) *A Modern Dictionary of Sociology*. New York: Cromwell.

Tichy, N. (1979) Social network analysis for organisations. *Academy of Management Review*, **4**, pp. 507–19.

Watts, J. (2000) Dyson abandons strategy of in-house advertising, *Campaign*, 11 August, p. 22

Weick, K. (1987) Prescribed and emergent networks. In *Handbook of Organisational Communication* (ed. F. Jablin). London: Sage.

Williams, K. (1990) *Behavioural Aspects of Marketing*. Oxford: Heinemann.

Windahl, S., Signitzer, B. and Olson, J.T. (1992) *Using Communication Theory*. London: Sage.

part 2

Contexts

Chapters 3–11

The circumstances, conditions and environments in which marketing communications occur

3

Understanding how customers process information

Understanding the way in which customers perceive their world, the way they learn, develop attitudes and respond to marketing communication stimuli is fundamental if effective communications are to be developed.

AIMS AND OBJECTIVES

The aim of this chapter is to provide an introduction to the main elements of buyer information processing, in order that readers develop an appreciation of the complexities associated with understanding and using information provided through marketing communications.

The objectives of this chapter are:

1. To introduce cognitive theory as an important element in the development of planned communications.

2. To examine personality as a main factor in the determination of successful communications.

3. To explore perception in the context of marketing communications.

4. To understand the main differences between conditioning and cognitive learning processes.

5. To appraise the role of attitudes and the different ways in which attitudes are thought to be developed.

6. To appreciate the importance of understanding an individual's intention to act in a particular way and its part in the decision process.

7. To understand how marketing communications can be used to influence these elements of buyer behaviour and in particular to change attitudes.

8. To provide a brief overview of the other environmental influences that affect the manner in which individuals process information.

Introduction

This chapter will explore the elements that influence the information processing behaviour of two different types of buyer: consumers and organisational buyers. It will then establish how the identification of different behaviour patterns can influence marketing communications.

Marketing is about many things, but one of its central themes is the management of behaviour, in particular behaviour prior to, during and after an exchange. Therefore it makes sense to underpin marketing activities with an understanding of buyer behaviour, in order that marketing strategies and communication plans in particular be more effective. It is not the intention to provide a deep or comprehensive analysis of buyer behaviour, since there are many specialist texts that readers can refer to. However, a basic understanding of the context in which buyers process information, the way they behave, their decision-making processes and the ways in which such knowledge can be utilised in promotional plans is important.

There are a number of theoretical approaches that have been developed to assist our understanding of human behaviour, but the majority have their roots in one of three psychological orientations. These three (Freud's psychoanalytical theory, reinforcement theory and cognitive theory) can be seen to have influenced thinking about buyer behaviour over the last 50 years. This book will explore cognitive theory in the context of marketing communications.

Cognitive theory

Mainstream psychology has moved from a behavourist to a cognitive orientation. Similarly, the emphasis in understanding and interpreting consumer behaviour has progressed from a reinforcement to a cognitive approach.

Cognitive theory is based upon an information-processing, problem-solving and reasoning approach to human behaviour. Individuals use information that has been generated by external sources (e.g. advertisements) and internal sources (e.g. memory). This information is given thought, processed, transferred into meanings or patterns and then combined to form judgements about behaviour (based on Rumelhart in Belk, 1975).

Cognitive theory is based upon an information-processing, problem-solving and reasoning approach to human behaviour.

The cognitive orientation considers the consumer to be an adaptive problem solver, one who uses various processes in reasoning, forming concepts and acquiring knowledge. There are several determinants that are important to our understanding of the

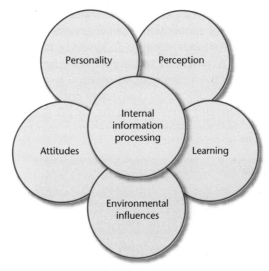

Figure 3.1   Elements of information processing.

cognitive orientation because they contribute to the way in which individuals process information. These are personality, perception, learning, attitudes, certain environmental influences and issues pertinent to an individual's purchase situation (Figure 3.1). Each of these will now be considered.

Personality

Personality is, essentially, concerned with the inner properties of each individual, those characteristics that differentiate each of us. Consideration is given to two main approaches: the Freudian and trait theories of personality.

Freudian theory

Freud believed that the needs which motivate human behaviour are driven by two primary instincts: life and death. The life instincts are considered to be predominantly sexual in nature, whereas the death instincts are believed to be manifested through self-destructive and/or aggressive behaviour.

The personality of the individual is assumed to have developed in an attempt to gratify these needs, and consists of the id, superego and ego; this approach is termed psychoanalytic theory. The id is the repository for all basic drives and motivations. Its function is to seek pleasure through the discharge of tension. The superego acts to restrain the id, to inhibit the impulses of the pleasure-seeking component, partly by acting within the rules of society. These two are obviously in conflict, which the ego attempts to mediate by channelling the drives of the id into behaviour acceptable to the superego.

The application of psychoanalytic theory to buyer behaviour suggests that many of the motives for purchase are driven by deeply rooted sexual drives and/or death instincts.

The application of psychoanalytic theory to buyer behaviour suggests that many of the motives for purchase are driven by deeply rooted sexual drives and/or death instincts. These can only be determined by probing the subconscious, as in work undertaken by motivation researchers, the first of whom were Dichter and Vicary. Motivation research attempts to discover the underlying motivations for consumer behaviour. A variety of techniques have been developed, including in-depth interviews, projective techniques, association tests and focus groups.

Psychoanalytic theory has been criticised as too vague, unresponsive to the environment and too reliant on the early development of the individual. Furthermore, because the samples used are very often small and because of the emphasis on the

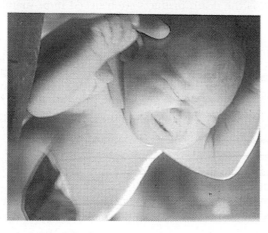

Exhibit 3.1 Audi advertisement using symbols of life. Picture supplied and reproduced with the kind permission of Audi UK.

unconscious, verification and substantiation of the results of experiments are often difficult – and some say impossible.

However, the psychoanalytic approach has been used as the basis for many advertising messages, aimed at deeply rooted feelings, hopes, aspirations and fears. For example, many life assurance companies use fear in their advertising messages to motivate people to invest in life and pension policies. Advertisements for cars often depict symbols: those of life and death in the Audi advertisement in Exhibit 3.1, and that of safety in the Volvo advertisement in Exhibit 3.2. We also know that buyers can be motivated by symbolic as well as functional motives in their purchases. Thus the use of sexual appeals and symbols in advertisements is often undertaken with this information in mind. In addition, many commentators agree that motivation research is the forerunner of the psychographics research often used for market segmentation (see Chapter 5).

Trait theory

In contrast with the largely qualitative approach of the Freudian school is the empirical perspective. Under this approach, personality is measured and quantified. What is being measured are the traits or 'distinguishing, relatively enduring ways in which one individual differs from another' (Guildford, 1959). Personality tests invariably seek to measure individual differences in respect of specific traits. The end result is a label that is applied to the particular traits observed in the individuals being tested. These labels, for example, consider aspects such as the degree of assertiveness, responsiveness to change or the level of sociability an individual might exhibit.

Of specific interest to marketing communicators is the relationship between broad personality traits and general styles of behaviour. Consumer psychologists, working on

Exhibit 3.2
Volvo advertisement using safety as the main motivation. Picture supplied and reproduced with the kind permission of Volvo UK.

behalf of advertising agencies in particular, have spent a great deal of time trying to identify specific traits and then develop consumer profiles which enable a distinct market segment to be determined. The 4Cs was one such programme, developed by Young and Rubicam in the late 1980s. Four distinct types of consumer were identified: aspirers, succeeders, mainstreamers and reformers, each of whom have particular psychographic characteristics.

Mainstreamers are motivated by a basic need for security and belonging. To satisfy that drive, they tend to buy established products and manufacturers' brands, as they perceive purchase risk to be lower. Aspirers seek status and self-esteem and this is directed through identification with materialism. Aspirers are able to express themselves through the possession of goods, which act as symbols of achievement, such as the latest hi-fi or designer clothes. Succeeders are people who are successful but who need to control the events in their lives. Typically they read the *Financial Times* or the *Daily Telegraph* and consume products that have proven quality. Reformers are the antithesis of the aspirers, in that they seek self-fulfilment rather than status. Own brands and natural products are sought by them, as it is the quality of life that is their underlying motivation (*QED*, 1989).

Fiat personality – Spirito di Punto

The brand advertising used to support the launch of Fiat's Punto into the UK car market was influenced partly by a previous pan-European campaign and partly by its positioning and understanding of its target market.

When a new car is launched there is usually a six-month window in which the latest technology remains unique to the car. This credibility window needs to be exploited. However, a bland informationally based ad rarely works in this market so a couple, representative of the target market, were chosen to reflect the Fiat brand personality and values.

The campaign used two ads: the first depicted a male driver making disparaging (tongue-in-cheek) comments about how women might utilise several of the car's attributes. This ran for four or five days with the expectation of building a certain level of indignation, especially among women drivers. Then the second ad was released, which depicted a woman driver making similar derogatory comments about men, in the context of the car's attributes. The aspirational couple were chosen because they embodied the personality of Fiat and associated Italian values. He represented fun and cheekiness and she a Latin, independent feistiness.

The ads were tracked on a standard car industry wide study which measures against awareness (recognition of the ad), branding (understanding of the brand manufacturer name) and overall likeability (did I like it?) indices. It rated so highly that the Spirito di Punto won the best car ad for 1999. See Plates 3.1and 3.2.

Material and photographs kindly supplied by D'arcy

By combining the qualitative approach of the motivational researchers with the quantitative approach of the trait theorists, psychographic variables can be determined. Over the last 20 years this has developed into a popular segmentation technique, called psychographics. This particular technique is discussed in Chapter 5, from both a consumer and an organisational buyer perspective.

Perception

Perception is concerned with how individuals see and make sense of their environment. It is about the selection, organisation and interpretation of stimuli by individuals so that they can understand the world.

Individuals are exposed, each day, to a tremendous number of stimuli. Leslie de Chernatony (1993) suggests that research has shown that on a typical day each consumer is exposed to over 550 advertisements, notwithstanding the thousands of other non-commercial stimuli that we encounter. To cope with this bombardment, our sensory organs select those stimuli to which attention is given. These selected stimuli are organised in order to make them comprehensible and are then given meaning; in other words, there is an interpretation of the stimuli which is influenced by attitudes, values, motives and past experiences as well as the character of the stimuli themselves. Stimuli, therefore, are selected, organised and interpreted.

Perception is concerned with how individuals see and make sense of their environment.

Perceptual selection

The vast number of messages mentioned earlier need to be filtered, as we cannot process them all. The stimuli that are selected result from the interaction of the nature of the stimulus with the expectations and the motives of the individual. Attention is an important factor in determining the outcome of this interaction: 'Attention occurs when the stimulus activates one or more sensory receptor nerves and the resulting sensations go to the brain for processing' (Hawkins *et al.*, 1989).

The nature of the stimuli, or external factors such as the intensity and size, position, contrast, novelty, repetition and movement, are factors that have been developed and refined by marketing communicators to attract attention. Animation is used to attract attention when the product class is perceived as bland and uninteresting, such as margarine or teabags. Unexpected camera angles and the use of music can be strong methods of gaining the attention of the target audience, as used successfully in the Bacardi Breezer and Renault commercials. Sexual attraction can be a powerful means of capturing the attention of audiences and when associated with a brand's values can be a very effective method of getting attention (for example, the Diet Coke advertisement, Plate 3.3).

Sexual attraction can be a powerful means of capturing the attention of audiences.

The expectations, needs and motives of the individual, or internal factors, are equally important. Individuals see what they expect to see, and their expectations are normally based on past experience and preconditioning. From a communications perspective the presentation of stimuli that conflict with the individual's expectations will invariably receive more attention. The attention-getting power of erotic and sexually driven advertising messages (jeans manufacturers often promote their brands, such as Levi 501s and Diesel, using this stimulus) is well known, but, as we shall see later, readers only remember the attention-getting device (e.g. the male or female), not the offering with which an association was intended. Looked at in terms of Schramm's model of communication (Chapter 2), the process of encoding was inaccurate, hence the inappropriate decoding.

Of particular interest is the tendency of individuals to select certain information from the environment. This process is referred to as selective attention. Through attention, individuals avoid contact with information which is felt to be disagreeable in that it opposes strongly held beliefs and attitudes.

Individuals see what they want or need to see. If they are considering the purchase of a new car, there will be heightened awareness of car advertisements and a correspondingly lower level of awareness of unrelated stimuli. Selective attention allows individuals to expose themselves to messages that are comforting and rewarding. For example, reassurance is often required for people who have bought new cars or expensive technical equipment and who have spent a great deal of time debating and considering the purchase and its associated risk. Communications congratulating the new owner on his or her wise decision often accompany post-purchase literature such as warranties and service contracts. If potentially harmful messages do get through this filter system, perceptual defence mechanisms help to screen them out after exposure.

Individuals see what they want or need to see.

Perceptual organisation

For perception to be effective and meaningful, the vast array of selected stimuli needs to be organised. The four main ways in which sensory stimuli can be organised are figure–ground, grouping, closure and contour.

Figure–ground

Each individual's perception of an environment tends to consist of articles on a general background, against which certain objects are illuminated and stand proud. Williams (1981) gives the examples of trees standing out against the sky and words on a page. This has obvious implications for advertisers and the design and form of communications, especially advertisements, to draw attention to important parts of the message, most noticeably the price, logo or company/brand name (see Exhibit 3.3: Renault Mégane Liberté).

Grouping

Objects which are close to one another tend to be grouped together and a pattern develops. Grouping can be used to encourage associations between a product and specific attributes. For example, food products which are positioned for a health market are often displayed with pictures that represent fitness and exercise, the association being that consumption of the food will lead to a lifestyle that incorporates fitness and exercise, as these are important to the target market.

Closure

When information is incomplete individuals make sense of the data by filling in the gaps. This is often used to involve consumers in the message and so enhance selective attention. Advertisements for American Express charge cards or GM credit cards ('if invited to apply'), for example, suggest that ownership denotes membership, which represents exclusiveness and privilege.

Television advertisements that are run for 60 seconds when first launched are often cut to 30 or even 15 seconds later in the burst. The purpose is two-fold: to cut costs and to remind the target audience. This process of reminding is undertaken with the

Exhibit 3.3   A picture using the foreground to highlight the object (car) against a general background. Picture kindly supplied by Renault UK Ltd and Publicis. Photograph by Steve Hoskins.

assistance of the audience, who recognise the commercial and mentally close the message even though the advertiser only presents the first part.

Contour

Contours give objects shape and are normally formed when there is a marked change in colour or brightness. This is an important element in package design and, as the battle for shelf space in retail outlets becomes more intense, so package design has become an increasingly important aspect of attracting attention.

The battles between Sainsbury's and Coca-Cola in the mid 1990s regarding the introduction of an alleged 'copy-cat' (Glancey, 1994) own-label product serves to illustrate this point. This and other own-label products are often packaged in a very similar way to the branded item. This serves to diffuse the impact of the branded item on the shelves and enhances the position and credibility of the own-label item.

Copy-Cat presentations – Puffin and Penguin

United Biscuits took Asda (a multiple retailer) to court when the retailer launched an own-brand chocolate biscuit (Puffin) with very similar packaging to the bar owned by United Biscuits (Penguin). Murphy (1997) reported that the court ruled that the colour, typography and use of the Puffin character were deceptively similar to those of Penguin and Asda were required to change the packaging.

These methods are used by individuals in an attempt to organise stimuli and simplify their meanings. They combine in an attempt to determine a pattern to the stimuli, so that they are perceived as part of a whole or larger unit. This is referred to as gestalt psychology.

Perceptual interpretation

Interpretation is the process by which individuals give meaning to the stimuli once they have been organised. As Cohen and Basu (1987) state, by using existing categories, meanings can be given to stimuli. These categories are determined from the individual's past experiences and they shape what the individual expects to see. These expectations, when combined with the strength and clarity of the stimulus and the motives at the time perception occurs, mould the pattern of the perceived stimuli.

Interpretation is the process by which individuals give meaning to the stimuli once they have been organised.

The degree to which each individual's ascribed meaning, resulting from the interpretation process, is realistic, is dependent upon the levels of distortion that may be present. Distortion may occur because of stereotyping: the predetermined set of images which we use to guide our expectations of events, people and situations. Another distortion factor is the halo effect which occurs when a stimulus with many attributes or dimensions is evaluated on just a single attribute or dimension. Brand extensions and family branding strategies are based on the understanding that if previous experiences with a different offering are satisfactory, then risk is reduced and an individual is more likely to buy a new offering from the same 'family'.

Marketing and perception

Individuals, therefore, select and interpret particular stimuli in the context of the expectations arising from the way they classify the overall situation. The way in which individuals perceive, organise and interpret stimuli is a reflection of their past experiences and the classifications used to understand the different situations each individual frames every day. Individuals seek to frame or provide a context within which their role becomes clearer. Shoppers expect to find products in particular situations, such as rows, shelves or display bins of similar goods. They also develop meanings and associations with some grocery products because of the utility and trust/emotional satisfaction certain pack types evoke. The likelihood that a sale will be made is improved, if the context in which a purchase transaction is undertaken does not contradict a shopper's expectations.

Marketing communications should attempt to present products (objects) in a frame or 'mental presence' (Moran, 1990) that is recognised by a buyer, such as a consumption or purchase situation. A product has a much greater chance of entering an evoked set if the situation in which it is presented is one that is expected and relevant. However, a new pack design can provide differentiation and provoke people into reassessing their expectations of what constitutes appropriate packaging in a product category. See the following Pringles case as an example.

Differentiation through pack design – Pringles

Crisps have traditionally been packaged and presented in sealed foil bags, so, when the cardboard tube format was introduced for the Pringles brand, it represented a radically new package concept. Verebelyi (2000) reports that the challenge to shoppers was whether they would accept the innovative design as an appropriate and suitable way of protecting and storing the savoury product.

Once shoppers proved to themselves that the product was more likely to keep its shape in the tube, then the package (and the brand) was accepted. Indeed, the Pringles tube has provided the brand a powerful means of differentiation and enables it to standout on the shelves. See Exhibit 3.4.

Exhibit 3.4   Pringles – a new packaging concept introduced into an established product category. Picture kindly supplied by Procter and Gamble UK.

Javalgi *et al.* (1992) point out that perception is important to product evaluation and product selection. Consumers try to evaluate a product's attributes by the physical cues of taste, smell, size and shape. Sometimes no difference can be distinguished, so the consumer has to make a judgement on factors other than the physical characteristics of the product. This is the basis of branding activity, where a personality is developed for the product which enables it to be perceived differently from its competitors. The individual may also set up a separate category or evoked set in order to make sense of new stimuli or satisfactory experiences. Consumer perception of salon and shop based haircare products shows important differences and indicates the different roles that marketing communication needs to play: see Figure 3.2. Within each of these sectors many brands are developed which are targeted at different segments based upon demographic, benefit and psychographic factors.

Goodrich (1978) discusses the importance of perception, which can be seen in terms of the choices tourists make when deciding which destination to visit. The decision is influenced by levels of general familiarity, levels of specific knowledge and perception. It follows that the more favourable the perception of a particular destination, the more likely it is to be selected from its competitors.

Finally, individuals carry a set of enduring perceptions or images. These relate to themselves, to products and to organisations. The concept of positioning the product in the mind of the consumer is fundamental to marketing strategy and is a topic that

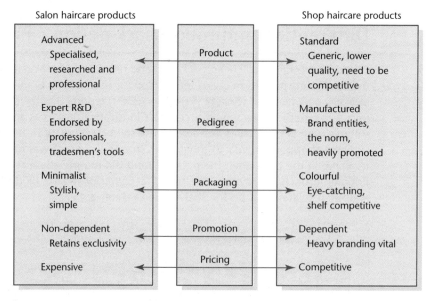

Figure 3.2   Comparison of salon and shop haircare products.

will be examined in greater depth in Chapter 13. The image an individual has of an organisation is becoming recognised as increasingly important, judging by the proportion of communication budgets being given over to public relations activities and corporate advertising in particular.

Organisations develop multiple images to meet the positioning requirements of their end-user markets and stakeholders. They need to monitor and adjust their iden-

Organisations develop multiple images to meet the positioning requirements of their end-user markets and stakeholders.

tities constantly in respect of the perceptions and expectations held by the other organisations in their various networks. For example, the level of channel coordination and control can be a function of the different perceptions of channel members. These concern the perception of the channel depth, processes of control and the roles each member is expected to fulfil. Furthermore, the perception of an organisation's product quality and its associated image (reputation) is becoming increasingly important. Both end-user buyers and channel members are attempting to ensure that the intrinsic and extrinsic cues associated with their products are appropriate signals of product quality (Moran, 1990).

Learning

There are two mainstream approaches to learning: behavioural and cognitive.

Behavioural learning

The behavourist approach to learning views the process as a function of an individual's acquisition of responses. There are three factors important to learning: association, reinforcement and motivation. However, it is the basic concept of the stimulus–response orientation which will be looked at in more detail.

The behavourist approach to learning views the process as a function of an individual's acquisition of responses.

It is accepted that for learning to occur all that is needed is a 'time–space proximity' between a stimulus and a response. Learning takes place through the establishment of a connection between a stimulus and a response. Marketing communications are thought to work by the simple process of people observing messages and being stimulated/motivated to respond by requesting more information or purchasing the advertised product in search of a reward. Behaviour is learned through the conditioning experience of a stimulus and response. There are two forms of conditioning: classical and operant.

Classical conditioning   ~ Pavlov's dogs

Classical conditioning assumes that learning is an associative process that occurs with an existing relationship between a stimulus and a response. By far the best-known example of this type of learning is the experiment undertaken by the Russian psychologist Pavlov. He noticed that dogs began to salivate at the sight of food. He stated that this was not taught, but was a reflex reaction. This relationship exists prior to any experimentation or learning. The food represents an unconditioned stimulus and the response (salivation) from the dogs is an unconditioned response.

Pavlov then paired the ringing of a bell with the presentation of food. Shortly the dogs began to salivate at the ringing of the bell. The bell became the conditioned stimulus and the salivation became the conditioned response (which was the same as the unconditioned response).

From an understanding of this work it can be determined that two factors are important for learning to occur:

1. To build the association between the unconditioned and conditioned stimulus, there must be a relatively short period of time.

2. The conditioning process requires that there be a relatively high frequency/repetition of the association. The more often the unconditioned and conditioned stimuli occur together, the stronger will be the association.

Classical conditioning can be observed operating in each individual's everyday life. An individual who purchases a new product because of a sales promotion may continue to buy the product even when the promotion has terminated. An association has been established between the sales promotion activity (unconditioned stimulus) and the product (conditioned stimulus). If product quality and satisfaction levels allow, long-run behaviour may develop despite the absence of the promotion. In other words, promotion need not act as a key purchase factor in the long run.

Advertisers attempt to associate their products/services with certain perceptions, images and emotions that are known to evoke positive reactions from consumers. Image advertising seeks to develop the associations that individuals have when they think of a brand or an organisation, and hence its reputation. Messages of this type show the object with an unconditioned stimulus that is known to evoke pleasant and favourable feelings. The product becomes a conditioned stimulus eliciting the same favourable response. The advertisements for Bounty Bars use images of desert islands to evoke feelings of enjoyment and pleasure and associations with coconuts.

Classical images – Citroën

Citroën UK and Citroën France have both used Claudia Schiffer in their car advertising. In the UK the international model is only associated with a single product, the Xara in two separate executions. However, research indicates that across all segments she has become the face of Citroën and an association has developed between the two.

CLAUDIA SCHIFFER ON THE SET OF THE LATEST CITROËN XSARA TV COMMERCIAL

CITROËN
PUBLIC AFFAIRS
0870 606 9000
Neg No. 1607

Exhibit 3.5   Classical conditioning – Claudia Schiffer in association with Citroën. Photograph kindly supplied by Citroën UK.

In Exhibit 3.5 Claudia Schiffer is depicted next to the car. The car becomes the conditioned stimulus and the celebrity model acts as an unconditioned stimulus. See the model, think of the Xara or perhaps think of Citroën.

Material and photograph kindly supplied by Citroën UK

Operant conditioning *– Skinner boxes*

In this form of conditioning, sometimes known as instrumental conditioning, learning occurs as a result of an individual operating or acting on some part of the environment. The response of the individual is instrumental in getting a positive reinforcement (reward) or negative reinforcement (punishment). Behaviour that is rewarded or reinforced will be continued, whereas behaviour that is not rewarded will cease.

B.F. Skinner was a pioneer researcher in the field of operant conditioning. His work, with rats who learned to press levers in order to receive food and who later only pressed the lever when a light was on (discriminative stimulus), highlights the essential feature of this form of conditioning: that reinforcement follows a specific response.

Many organisations use reinforcement in their communications by stressing the benefits or rewards that a consumer can anticipate receiving as a result of using a product or brand. For example, Sainsbury's offer 'Reward Points' and Asda offer a reward of money savings which 'makes the difference'. Reinforcement theories emphasise the role of external factors and exclude the individual's ability to process information internally. Learning takes place either through direct reinforcement of a particular response or through an associative conditioning process.

> *Many organisations use reinforcement in their communications by stressing the benefits or rewards that a consumer can anticipate receiving as a result of using a product or brand.*

However, operant conditioning is a mechanistic process which is not realistic, as it serves only to simplify an extremely complex process.

Cognitive learning

This approach to our understanding of learning assumes that individuals attempt to control their immediate environments. They are seen as active participants in that they try to resolve problems by processing information that is pertinent to each situation. Central to this process is memory. Just as money can be invested in short-, medium- and long-term investment accounts, so information is memorised for different periods of time. These memories are sensory, short-term and long-term; see Figure 3.3.

Sensory storage refers to the period in which information is sensed for a split second, and if an impression has been made the information will be transferred to short-term memory where it is rehearsed before transfer to long-term memory. *Short-term*

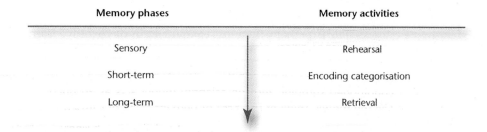

Memory phases	Memory activities
Sensory	Rehearsal
Short-term	Encoding categorisation
Long-term	Retrieval

Figure 3.3 Aspects of internal information processing.

memory lasts no longer than approximately eight seconds and a maximum of four or five items can be stored in short-term memory at any one time. Readers will probably have experienced being introduced to someone at a social event only to forget the name of the guest when they next meet them at the same event. This occurs because the name was not entered into *long-term* memory. Information can be stored for extended periods in long-term memory. This information is not lying dormant, however, it is constantly being reorganised and recategorised as new information is received.

There are four basic functions by which memory operates. These are, first, *rehearsal*, where information is repeated or related to an established category. This is necessary so that the second function, *encoding*, can take place. This involves the selection of an image to represent the perceived object. Once in long-term memory it is *categorised and stored*, the third function.

There are four basic functions by which memory operates.

Retrieval is the final function, a process by which information is recovered from storage.

Cognitive learning is about processing information in order that problems can be resolved. These information-handling processes can range from the simple to the complex. There are three main processes: iconic, modelling and reasoning.

Iconic rote learning involves understanding the association between two or more concepts when there is an absence of a stimulus. Learning occurs at a weak level through repetition of simple messages. Beliefs are formed about the attributes of an offering without any real understanding of the source of the information. Advertisers of certain products (low value, frequently purchased) will try to remind their target audiences repeatedly of the brand name in an attempt to help consumers learn. Through such repetition, an association with the main benefits of the product may be built, if only via the constant reminders by the spokesperson.

Learning through the *modelling* approach involves the observation and imitation of others and the associated outcomes of their behaviour. In essence, a great deal of children's early learning is developed in this way. Likewise, marketing communicators use the promise of rewards to persuade audiences to act in a particular way. By using positive images of probable rewards, buyers are encouraged to believe that they can receive the same outcome if they use the particular product. For example, clothing advertisements often depict the model receiving admiring glances from passers-by. The same admiration is the reward 'promised' to those who wear the same clothing. A similar approach is used by Kellogg's to promote their Special K breakfast cereal. The commercial depicts a (slim) mother and child playing on a beach. The message is that it is important to look after yourself and to raise your family through healthy eating, an outdoor life and exercise.

Learning through the modelling approach involves the observation and imitation of others and the associated outcomes of their behaviour.

Reasoning is perhaps the most complex form of cognitive learning. Through this process, individuals need to restructure and reorganise information held in long-term memory and combine it with fresh inputs in order to generate new outputs. Because of legislation, cigarette advertisers have had to find new ways of reaching their audiences. Benson & Hedges have used innovative complex messages to reach smokers of their Silk Cut brand. The complex messages associated with this brand require much thought and reasoning to deduce the relationship between the image (scissors and silk ribbon) and the brand.

Cognitive processing – Kellogg's All-Bran

Kellogg's All-Bran, a shredded-fibre breakfast cereal, began to lose market share after achieving brand leadership. Research revealed that buyers understood the importance of fibre in their diet but had assumed that fresh fruit, vegetables and wholemeal bread were suitable and easier alternative sources of fibre. Kellogg's used a campaign which compared the fibre content with a variety of commonly assumed rich sources of fibre, such as nine slices of brown bread (see Exhibit 3.6),

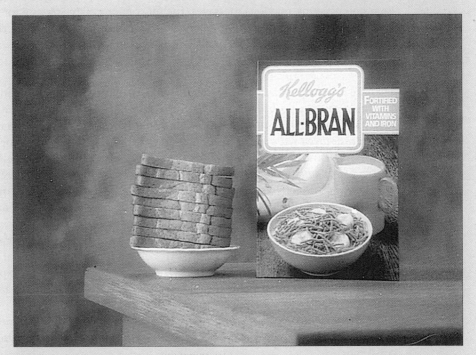

Exhibit 3.6   All-Bran advertisement – an example of the use of reasoning in an advertisement appeal. Picture supplied and used with the kind permission of Kellogg Company of Great Britain Ltd. All rights reserved.

21 new potatoes and eight bananas. The success of this campaign was largely due to both current and lapsed buyers having to re-think their view of All-Bran. They were challenged to reason why they were not using All-Bran when it is the richest source of an ingredient that they value. Buyers were encouraged to make a judgement about their current diet and an alternative that was being presented as patently superior.

Of all the approaches to understanding how we learn, cognitive learning is the most flexible interpretation. The rational, more restricted approach of behavioural learning, where the focus is external to the individual, is without doubt a major contribution to knowledge. However, it fails to accommodate the complex internal thought processes that individuals utilise when presented with various stimuli.

It is useful to appreciate the way in which people are believed to learn and forget as there are several issues which are useful to media planners in particular.

Interference theory

Burke and Srull (1988) suggest that learning and brand recall can be interfered with. This may be caused either by new material affecting previously stored information or by old information being retrieved and interfered with by incoming messages. The first case, where the last message has the strongest recall, is similar to the recency effect discussed in the context of message design (Chapter 21).

In a competitive environment, where there are many messages being transmitted, each one negating previous messages, the most appropriate strategy for an advertiser would be to separate the advertisements from those of its competitors. This reasoning supports much of the positioning work undertaken by brand managers.

Decay

The rate at which individuals forget material assumes a pattern, as shown in Figure 3.4. Many researchers have found that information decays at a negatively decelerating rate. As much as 60% of the initial yield of information from an advertisement has normally decayed within six weeks. This decay, or wear-out, can be likened to the half-life of radioactive material. It is always working, although it cannot be seen, and the impact of the advertising reduces through time. Like McGuire's (1978) retention stage in his hierarchy of effects model (see Chapter 20), the storage of information for future use is important, but with time, how powerful will the information be and what triggers are required to promote recall?

Advertising wear-out is thought to occur because of two factors. First, individuals use selective perception and mentally switch off after a critical number of exposures. Second, the monotony and irritation caused by continued exposure lead to counter-argument to both the message and the advertisement (Petty and Cacioppo, 1979).

Advertisements for John Smith's bitter, Gold Blend and Renault attempt to prevent wear-out by using variations on a central theme to maintain interest and yet provide consistency.

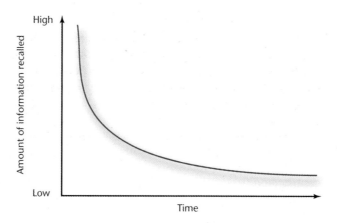

Figure 3.4   A standard decay curve.

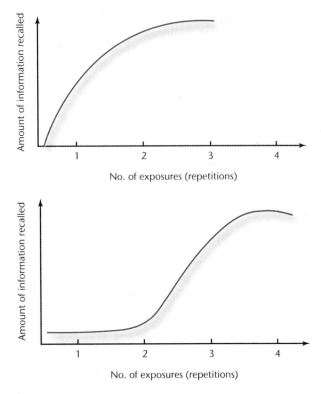

Figure 3.5   Learning curves.

Cognitive response

Learning can be visualised as following either of the curves set out in Figure 3.5. The amount learnt 'wears out' after a certain repetition level has been reached. Grass and Wallace (1969) suggest that this process of wear-out commences once a satiation point has been reached. A number of researchers (Zielske, 1959; Strong, 1977) have found that recall is improved when messages are transmitted on a regular weekly basis, rather than daily, monthly or in a concentrated or dispersed format.

The amount learnt 'wears out' after a certain repetition level has been reached.

An individual's ability to develop and retain awareness or knowledge of a product will, therefore, be partly dependent not only on the quality of the message but also on the number and quality of exposures to a planned message. To assist the media planner there are a number of concepts that need to be appreciated and used within the decisions about what, where and when a message should be transmitted. There are a number of other concepts that are of use to media planners: these are reach and coverage, frequency, gross rating points, effective frequency, efficiency and media source effects.

Attitudes

The perceptual and learning processes may lead to the formation of attitudes. These are predispositions, shaped through experience, to respond in an anticipated way to an object or situation. Attitudes are learned through past experiences and serve as a link between thoughts and behaviour. These experiences may relate to the product itself, to the messages transmitted by the different members of the channel network (normally mass media communications) and to the information supplied by opinion leaders, formers and followers.

Attitudes are learned through past experiences and serve as a link between thoughts and behaviour.

Attitudes tend to be consistent within each individual: they are clustered and very often interrelated. This categorisation leads to the formation of stereotypes, which is extremely useful for the design of messages as stereotyping allows for the transmission of a lot of information in a short time period (30 seconds) without impeding learning or the focal part of the message.

Attitude components

Attitudes are hypothetical constructs, and classical psychological theory considers attitudes to consist of three components:

1. *Cognitive component (learn)*
   This component refers to the level of knowledge and beliefs held by individuals about a product and/or the beliefs about specific attributes of the offering. This represents the learning aspect of attitude formation.

2. *Affective component (feel)*
   By referring to the feelings held about a product – good, bad, pleasant or unpleasant – an evaluation is made of the object. This is the component that is concerned with feelings, sentiments, moods and emotions about an object.

3. *Conative component (do)*
   This is the action component of the attitude construct and refers to the individual's disposition or intention to behave in a certain way. Some researchers go so far as to suggest that this component refers to observable behaviour.

This three-component approach (Figure 3.6) to attitudes is based upon attitudes towards an object, person or organisation. The sequence of attitude formation is learn, feel and do. This approach to attitude formation is limited in that the components are seen to be of equal strength. A single-component model has been developed where the attitude only consists of the individual's overall feeling towards an object. In other words, the affective component is the only significant component.

Figure 3.6   The three-component attitude model.

Multi-attribute attitude models

One of the difficulties with the three- and single-component attitude models is that they fail to explain why an individual has a particular attitude. A different approach views objects as possessing many different attributes, all of which are perceived and believed by individuals with differing strengths and intensity.

Attribute analysis is an important factor in the design and consistency of marketing communication messages. For example, the UK toilet tissue market has been dominated by two main players, Andrex with 24.2% market share and SCA Hygiene's Double-Velvet with 10.4% share (Brabbs, 2000). In 2000 Charmin entered the market.

For many years Andrex has used a puppy to symbolise the softness, strength and length of its product. Table 3.1 indicates how the softness and strength attributes valued by consumers in 1992 have changed so that by 1996 the key attributes had become slightly less significant than they were. However, strong attitudes held by Andrex's loyal customers have enabled market share to rise steadily and market leadership has been maintained. This has been achieved in the light of the increased number of high-quality products (often own label) that are now available, all of which communicate softness and strength as the key attributes; see Plate 3.4.

A different approach views objects as possessing many different attributes.

In 2000 Procter and Gamble introduced Charmin to the UK, from the USA where it has a 30% market share. Apart from a huge £14 million ad spend and strong outdoor, radio, press and direct marketing programme, the launch was notable for the position it took in the market. Andrex positions by features, such as strength, length and softness as symbolised by the puppy. Double-Velvet adopts a similar position but appears to focus on features such as thickness as a surrogate for quality. Charmin's approach has been to highlight a neglected attribute, namely a comfortable cleaning proposition, smooth and strong, even when wet.

Intentions

Of the many advances in this area, those made by Ajzen and Fishbein (1980) have made a significant contribution. They reasoned that the best way of predicting

Table 3.1   Attributes valued by consumers when purchasing toilet tissue

Attributes (%)	1992	1995	Change 1992–95
Softness	66	57	−9
Colour to match decor	47	48	1
Price	45	45	0
Brand loyalty	39	36	−3
Special offers	24	32	8
Strength	42	29	−13
Length of roll	25	24	−1
Own label	6	14	8

Source: Adapted from a Mintel Report (1996).

behaviour was to measure an individual's intention to purchase (the conative component). Underlying intentions are the individual's attitude towards the act of behaviour and the subjective norm. In other words, the context within which a proposed purchase is to occur is seen as important to the attitude that is developed towards the object.

The subjective norm is the relevant feelings others are believed to hold about the proposed purchase, or intention to purchase. Underpinning the subjective norm are the beliefs held about the people who are perceived to 'judge' the actions an individual might take. Would they approve or disapprove, or look favourably or unfavourably upon the intended action?

The subjective norm is the relevant feelings others are believed to hold about the proposed purchase.

Underpinning the attitude towards the intention to act in a particular way are the strengths of the beliefs that a particular action will lead to an outcome. Ajzen and Fishbein argue that it is the individual's attitude to the act of purchasing, not the object of the purchase, that is important. For example, a manager may have a positive attitude towards a particular type of expensive office furniture, but a negative attitude towards the act of securing agreement for him to purchase it.

The theory of reasoned action (Ajzen and Fishbein, 1980; Figure 3.7) shows that intentions are composed of interrelated components: subjective norms, which in turn are composed of beliefs and motivations about relevant others, towards a particular intention, and attitudes, which in turn are made up of beliefs about the probable outcomes that a behaviour will lead to.

This approach recognises the interrelationship of the three components of attitudes and that it is not attitude but the intention to act or behave that precedes

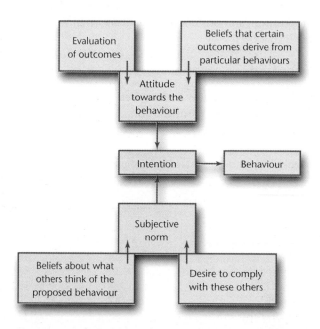

Figure 3.7   Theory of reasoned action model. Based on Ajzen and Fishbein (1980) and adapted from Schiffman and Kanuck (1991). Reproduced with permission of Prentice Hall Inc., Englewood Cliffs, NJ.

observable behaviour that should be the focus of attention. It should be understood that attitudes do not precede behaviour and cannot be used to predict behaviour, despite the attempts of a number of researchers. Attitudes are important, but they are not the sole determinant of behaviour, and intentions may be a better indicator of behaviour.

The objective of marketing communications is often to create a positive attitude towards a product and/or to reinforce or change existing attitudes.

Attitudes impact on consumer decision-making, and the objective of marketing communications is often to create a positive attitude towards a product and/or to reinforce or change existing attitudes. An individual may perceive and develop a belief that British Airways has a friendly and informal in-flight service and that the service provided by Lufthansa is cold and formal. However, both airlines are perceived to hold a number of different attributes, and each individual needs to evaluate these attributes in order that an attitude can be developed. It is necessary, therefore, to measure the strength of the beliefs held about the key attributes of different products. There are two main processes whereby beliefs can be processed and measured: compensatory and non-compensatory models.

Compensatory models

Through this approach, attributes that are perceived to be weak can be offset by attributes that are perceived to be strong. As a result, positive attitudes are determined in the sense that the evaluation of all the attributes is satisfactory. For example, Table 3.2 sets out a possible evaluation of three package holidays. Despite the weakness on hotel cleanliness, the strength of the other attributes in package 2 scores this the highest, so the strongest attitude is formed towards this product. Some individuals make decisions about products on the basis that their attributes must not contain any weaknesses. Therefore package 2 would not be considered, as it fails to reach a minimum level of expected satisfaction on cleanliness, thus, despite its strengths, it is relegated from the decision alternatives.

An understanding of attitude components and the way in which particular attributes can be measured not only enables organisations to determine the attitudes held towards them and their competitors but also empowers them to change the attitudes held by different stakeholders, if it is thought necessary.

Table 3.2   Compensatory and non-compensatory models

Attribute	Weighting	Package 1		Package 2		Package 3	
		Rating	Score	Rating	Score	Rating	Score
Price	5	5	25	6	30	5	25
Hotel cleanliness	3	3	9	2	6	4	12
Travel times	2	7	14	9	18	4	8
Attitude rating			48		54		45
Possible decisions							
Compensatory model		Not considered		*Winner*		Not considered	
Non-compensatory model		*Winner*		Not considered		Considered	

Changing attitudes with marketing communications

Marketing communications is important to either maintain or change attitudes held by stakeholders. It is not the only way as product and service elements, pricing and channel decisions all play an important part in shaping the attitudes held. However, *but* marketing communications have a pivotal role in conveying each of these aspects to the target audience. Branding (Chapter 14) is a means by which attitudes can be established and maintained in a consistent way and it is through the use of the tools of the promotional mix that brands can be sustained. The final point that needs to be made is that there is a common thread between attributes, attitudes and positioning (Chapter 13). Attributes provide a means of differentiation and positions are shaped as a consequence of the attitudes that result from the way people interpret the associated marketing communications.

Environmental influences on the attitudes people hold towards particular products and services are partly a reflection of the way they interpret the marketing communications surrounding them, partly as a result of their direct experience of using them and partly as a result of the informal messages received from family, friends and other highly credible sources of information. These all contribute to the way people position products and services and the way they understand them relative to competing products. Managing attitudes (towards a brand) is therefore very important and marketing communications can play an important part in changing or maintaining attitudes. There are a number of ways in which attitudinal change can be implemented:

1. *Change the physical product or service element*
   At a fundamental level, attitudes might be so ingrained that it is necessary to change the product or service. This may involve a radical redesign or the introduction of a significant new attribute. Only once these changes have been made should marketing communications be used to communicate the new or revised object. When VW bought Skoda they redesigned the total product offering before relaunch.

2. *Change misunderstanding*
   In some circumstances people might misunderstand the benefits of a particularly important attribute and marketing communications are required to correct the beliefs held. This can be achieved through product demonstration of functionally based communications. Packaging and even the name of the product may need to be revised.

3. *Build credibility*
   Attitudes towards a brand might be superficial and lack sufficient conviction to prompt conative behaviour. This can be corrected through the use of an informative strategy, designed to build credibility. Product demonstration and hands-on experience (e.g. through sampling) are effective strategies. Skoda support a rally team to convey durability, speed and performance.

4. *Change performance beliefs*
   Beliefs held about the object and the performance qualities of the object can be adjusted through appropriate marketing communications. For example, by changing the perceptions held about the attributes, it is possible to change the attitudes about the object.

5. *Change attribute priorities*

   By changing the relative importance of the different attributes and ratings it is possible to change attitudes. Therefore, a strategy to emphasise a different attribute can change the attitude not only to a brand but to a product category. By stressing the importance of travel times, it might raise the importance of this attribute in the minds of potential holiday-makers and so give package 2 an advantage over its rivals, using the non-compensatory decision rule. Dyson changed attitudes to carpet cleaning equipment by stressing the efficiency of their new cyclone technology rather than the ease of use, aesthetic design or generic name (Hoover) associations used previously.

6. *Introduce a new attribute*

   Opportunities might exist to introduce a radically different and new (or previously unused) attribute. This provides a means for clear differentiation until competitors imitate and catch up. The solution for package 3 may be to introduce a fourth attribute, one in which the suppliers of package 3 know they have an advantage over the competition. This may be that they have a no-surcharge guarantee and packages 1 and 2 do not. By making prominent the new no-surcharge guarantee in the promotional messages transmitted by package 3, the introduction of a new significant attribute may lead to greater success.

7. *Change perception of competitor products*

   By changing the way competitor products are perceived it is possible to differentiate your own brand. For example, by changing the perception of packages 1 and 2 or changing the association of their packages with the others, package 3 might gain an advantage. This could be achieved by using messages that set the package apart from its rivals, suggesting, for example, that not all package holidays are the same. This is a theme was used by Thomson Holidays, when their copy read, 'We go there, we don't stay there'.

8. *Change or introduce new brand associations*

   By using celebrities or spokespersons with whom the target audience can identify, it might be possible for package 3 to change the way the product is perceived on an emotional basis rather than relying on attributes and a more rational argument.

9. *Use corporate branding*

   By altering the significance of the parent brand relative to the product brand, it is possible to alter beliefs about brands and their overall value. In some situations there is little to differentiate competitive brands and little credible scope to develop attribute-based attitudes. By using the stature of the parent company it is possible to develop a level of credibility and brand values that other brands cannot copy, although they can imitate by using their parent brand. Procter and Gamble have introduced their name to the packs of many of their brands.

10. *Change the number of attributes used*

    Many brands still rely on a single attribute as a means of providing a point of differentiation. This was popularly referred to as a unique selling proposition at a time when attribute- and informationally based communications reflected a *feature*-dominated understanding of branding. Today, two or even three attributes are often combined with strong emotional associations in order to provide a point of differentiation and a set of *benefit*-orientated brand values.

Attitude change – Skoda

Skoda, the eastern European car manufacturer, has long suffered an inferior reputation in western Europe for the poor quality and reliability of its cars. However, Volkswagen bought shares in Skoda in 1991 and set about changing the attitudes of people in the important markets. To do this, it first set about changing the quality of the cars by introducing new design and manufacturing techniques. The first new product was the Felicia, launched in 1994; this was followed by the Octavia in 1996 and then the Fabia in 1999.

The launches of the Felicia and Octavia are interesting because Skoda had virtually 100% unprompted name awareness. The first task was therefore not to build awareness of the name Skoda but to inform the market about changes in the ownership of Skoda. In May 1995 the Felicia was launched with the line, 'We have changed the car, can you change your mind?' Here was a direct challenge to car buyers to revisit their attitude towards the Skoda name.

In October 1995 it launched a campaign based upon the line, 'Who's behind the changes at Skoda?' To support the question, a Volkswagen badge was depicted in the background as a shadow of the Skoda badge. This was an important and risky move as for many VW stands for reliability, the result of a long positioning approach.

In February 1996, advertising was used that showed the Felicia being used by representatives of the Territorial Army, and no immediate reference to Skoda was provided. In January 1997 the line changed to 'Judge for yourself', inviting buyers and the media to test drive and encouraging action (a behavioural and cognitive move) towards changing their attitudes.

The marketing communications used to launch the Fabia in 1999 used the copyline, 'It's a Skoda. Honest' and with tongue-in-cheek humour tried to engage consumers so that they were willing to re-evaluate their perception of Skoda so that they were in line with the current Skoda product, not the pre-Volkswagen model, using press, TV, radio and outdoor work, supported by public relations, product placement, mystery shopping and retraining of retail staff. The new car won numerous awards including 'Car of the Year 2000'.

The results of this latest campaign have been quite amazing: sales up 15%, and 79% of people agreeing that Skodas are better than they used to be (54%) and 33% (20%) of people agreeing that they could imagine themselves driving a Skoda. Above all else, market share rose to 1.3% when the UK car market was experiencing a dramatic fall in volume sales owing to the rip-off Britain crisis.

While attitudes towards Skoda have not been completely changed, this latest campaign theoretically added a million potential customers and has gone a long way to changing brand attitudes. See Plates 3.5 and 3.6.

Material kindly supplied by Skoda UK Ltd

Neither organisations nor consumers exist in a vacuum. They exist in an 'open' system and therefore act upon and are affected by various environmental factors (Figure 3.8). There are a number of externally generated influences that impact upon buyer information processing and decision-making. The main factors are described below.

Figure 3.8   Environmental influences on buyer information processing.

Culture

Culture has been referred to as the unique characteristics that identify the acceptable patterns of behaviour and social relations within a particular society. Culture embodies the norms, beliefs, artifacts and customs that are learned from society and that constitute its values. It is these values that influence consumer behaviour and are of increasing importance to the international advertiser. Indeed, a more detailed consideration of the role of culture on marketing communications can be found in Chapter 16.

Culture is learned and acquired, it is not instinctive. Culture defines acceptable behaviour within a society and so sets the rules for all members who belong to the culture. For marketing communications, culture should be seen as a communication system in its own right. Through verbal and non-verbal actions a society is able to maintain stability, to bind all members with a sense of identity and to provide them with a means of continuity.

Culture is learned and acquired, it is not instinctive.

Subcultures

There are a number of sub-cultures within any given culture. These include age, geography, race, religion and ethnic groupings and they can all influence the way marketing communications are perceived, interpreted and understood.

Social class

Virtually all societies are stratified by class, based upon power, wealth and prestige. Society values individuals and groups on criteria such as education, occupation and level of income. This information is distilled into a social class system, such as upper, middle and lower class, which for a long time has been a main characteristic of UK society.

Marketeers have developed a socioeconomic categorisation which is used as a primary means of segmenting markets. Creative designers have always used symbols to reflect the values, lifestyles, norms and family roles associated with each perceived stratum. Among the many benefits this brings is the ability to transfer a lot of information relatively quickly and so communicate effectively. The process also allows for the continuity of the core values of society.

However, as discussed in Chapter 5, this traditional approach to segmentation is becoming increasingly difficult to utilise as consumers' purchasing habits become more complex and their lifestyles become less rigid and more open. McMurdo (1993) discusses some of the research by the advertising agency J. Walter Thompson. It is now necessary for advertisers to recognise the speed at which consumers can move between purchasing styles, even in the space of a single shopping trip. This is because the requirements of each purchase can be so different that tailor-made segmentation by product is necessary. For example, Dulux recognises that its market for paints consists of 'sloshers' and 'craftsmen'. Paint can be bought for the attic, where it will be 'sloshed', or for the lounge, where it will be applied like a 'craftsman', by the same individual.

Consumers' purchasing habits become more complex and their lifestyles become less rigid and more open.

Groups

Groups are one of the primary factors influencing learning and socialisation. An individual may simultaneously be a member of several groups, each having a different degree of effect. These groups can be categorized as follows:

1. Ascribed groups: one automatically belongs, e.g. family.
2. Primary/secondary groups: where interaction is on a one-to-one basis, e.g. family and friends.
3. Formal/informal groups: where the presence or absence of structure and hierarchy defines the group activity.
4. Aspirational/membership groups: groups to which the individual wishes to belong or does belong.

All these act as reference groups for the individual and influence the individual's behaviour.

Situational influences

The design, encoding and media channels used to transmit communication messages must take into account that buyers are influenced by factors that are unique to each buying situation and are not related specifically to the product or the individual. The situational context impacts on the information-processing capabilities of the buyer. For example, the amount of light in the store or the level of store traffic can influence the amount of time given to decision-making. While this factor will normally have been accounted for in the formulation of the marketing strategy, it must be revisited if the communications are to be effective.

When considering the impact that situational influences might have on information processing, the type of situation needs to be considered. A situational determinant is a factor that is unique to each buying act. These situational influences are connected neither to the purchase object nor to the buyer, and are independent of them. Hansen (1972) identified three types of situation: usage, purchase and communications.

Usage situation

When and where is the offering to be consumed and is consumption to be largely a private act, orientated to the individual (such as chocolate bars) or part of a social activity (such as beer)? For example, some manufacturers of breakfast cereals have been repositioning (Chapter 13) their brands in an attempt to encourage use at other times of the day. Communications need to reflect this strategy and encapsulate the situation in which the desired eating behaviour occurs.

Purchase situation

The act of purchase and the associated environment can influence the behaviour of the target individual. Is shopping a monthly, biannual, weekly or last-minute activity? Mothers shopping with children are more likely to be influenced by product preferences of their children than when shopping without them. This may be due not only to the amount of time available to complete the physical act of shopping but also to the time to process the information. Engel *et al.* (1990) cite information load, format and form as important criteria. Too much information (information overload) can reduce the accuracy of an individual's decision-making, whereas the order in which information is presented both on packages and in terms of store layout can seriously retard the amount of time taken to process information, and this can also influence the motivation of the shopper.

The manner in which information is presented will affect the decision style. For example, the ease of comparing brands, perhaps on an individual attribute basis (e.g. diabetics determining the amount of carbohydrate in competing brands), will influence both perception and purchase behaviour.

The manner in which information is presented will affect the decision style.

What is the environment of the shop like? Are there opportunities to influence the target with in-store promotions and advertising messages? Different individuals prefer different supermarkets and price is not the sole criterion. Store loyalty is a function of a number of issues, among them convenience, layout, product range, car-parking facilities and whether packers are available. Associated with this is the concept of corporate image. Each of the supermarket chains has a particular range of images held by its consumers. Consumer perception of store efficiency and value for money and the totality of corporate communications need to reflect, deflect or reinforce particular images. This element is pursued in greater depth in Chapter 16.

Communications situation

The settings in which marketing communications are received will affect the degree to which the message is understood and acted upon. For example, salespersons cold-calling on organisations (arriving at an organisation and requesting a sales interview without a prior appointment) are not usually received in a positive way. Furthermore, having gained an appointment through a prior arrangement does not mean that the information provided during the visit will be received as intended. The buyer may have been advised of some bad news prior to the meeting and his or her thoughts are not focused on the object of the sales meeting or presentation. Television commercials may be zipped or zapped, clutter may prevent key points of the message getting home or general noise in the form of conversation may also affect the effectiveness of the message. One of the central issues concerning the situation in which communications are received is the need to gain the attention of the receiver.

Having determined that there are particular types of situations where the consumption process occurs, Belk (1975), proposes that there are five main situation variables that should be considered. These are the physical aspects, the social surroundings, the time, the task and the antecedent states.

Physical aspects refer to the store design and layout, the location, the lighting, music, smells and sounds associated with the situation. The *social surroundings* refer to all those involved in the purchase, usage or communications. For example, a child was described in one type of situation as accompanying a mother on the shopping activity, and children have a degree of influence on such an event.

Time was considered in the context of the time available to complete the activity, but it could also be considered in the context of time of day, year or season, or time elapsed since the last purchase. The *task* itself is pertinent. Is the purchase for a third party as a present, or is it for personal consumption? Finally, *antecedent states* are the influences each individual experiences, but state is transitional. For example, states of high elation, despondency, bitterness or pleasure are experienced by all individuals, but they are not enduring characteristics.

The particular impact of various environmental influences can affect the behaviour of buyers during purchase activity, during usage and when information is being processed. Understanding the impact of the physical, time and social influences, together with the nature of the task and antecedent states, provides the marketing communications planner with fresh inputs to the exercise of positioning the product appropriately.

Summary

This chapter has reviewed some of the recent and current thinking about how individuals process information. Cognitive theory provides a valuable insight into the manner in which buyers use externally and internally generated stimuli to solve problems. Personality, perception, learning, attitudes and aspects pertinent to the wider environment and each purchase situation have been considered as major elements of the problem-solving approach adopted by both consumers and organisational buyers.

Marketing communication planners need to be aware of these elements and to understand how they operate in the target audience. Messages can be created to match the cognitive needs of the intended audience and change, for example, perception or attitudes, in such a way that communication with the target audience is likely to be more successful.

Review questions

1. Write a short description of cognitive theory. How does it differ from behaviourism?
2. What are the main elements of information processing?
3. How does Trait theory differ from Freudian theories of personality?
4. Describe a purchase repertoire (or evoked set) and suggest how marketing communications might assist perceptual selection.
5. To what extent are perception and positioning interlinked?
6. Choose three printed advertisements where the user is promised a reward.

7. Attitudes are believed to comprise three elements. Name them.

8. Write a brief explanation of the theory of reasoned action.

9. How might the environment influence marketing communications?

10. Identify the different types of situational influences on the purchase process.

▊ MINI CASE

Changing attitudes at *PerHair*

Market research has shown that pharmaceutically developed shampoos market was at an immature stage of market development. This was characterised by consumers' apparent ignorance about the role and use of these products. They considered that they should only by consumed if and when the need arose; in other words, the market was cause driven. Prescription brands, of which Garanten held a substantial market share, accounted for 90% of the total market. In contrast, manufacturers had not developed the OTC market, where Hyforez held 37% market share and total adspend was just 900,000 euros.

PerHair was launched at the end of 1996 and was targeted AB and C1 men and women aged 25–54. It's positioning was 'the food your hair needs' and 'a successful product now available for you'. Distribution was regulated by legislation, which required that all relevant products be channelled through pharmacies.

In 1996, the goal of all promotional activities was to educate the public regarding the benefits of pharmaceutically developed shampoos containing vitamins, encouraging them to reconsider whether their way of living influenced the quality and quantity of their hair. PerHair marketing communication strategy was tailored for each of the three different target groups: end-users, pharmacists and doctors.

During 1997, the communication with the selected consumer segment included PR activities in order to achieve maximum publicity, TV commercials and inserts in magazines. Additionally, as far as doctors were concerned, a relevant newsletter was created and mailed, sales representatives were hired and a sampling programme was developed to create awareness, encourage trial and through experience develop trust for the new product. Pharmacists were approached, informed and gradually convinced through a launch presentation, constant briefing by the sales force and an attractive sales policy.

In 1997, the total cost of media expenditure in the category reached 2 million euros, an increase of 222% from the previous year. PerHair's SOV was 20% and by the end of 1997, Garanten's market share fell by 11%. The OTC market in the nutrient shampoo category increased its volume of sales by 143%, with PerHair becoming number 2 with 22% market share. Among the consumers, 23% had become to believe that PerHair was a good, benefit giving product, and 11% had either switched from another brand or were convinced to try PerHair.

In 1998, the brand continued to reach all three target groups:

end-users by a TV campaign, inserts in health and lifestyle magazines, outdoor posters and sponsorships of various events;

pharmacists were offered innovative POP material, educational leaflets for customers, window stickers and incentives to recommend the product;

doctors were further informed through PerHair's participation at medical conferences and the periodical edition of a newsletter on hair-health issues.

TV advertising continued to have a strong educational message informing of the benefits of hair products containing vitamins. PerHair also started to build concern about people's hair health. PerHair's message was differentiated from competitive brands, which only really focused on shine and beauty.

During 1998, the market changed dramatically, with Garanten losing 47% of its sales and PerHair doubling its sales. The OTC hair category showed a significant increase reaching 51% of the total market, while sales in the prescription category fell by 50%.

Attitudes were gradually changing towards better hair protection and care. More OTC companies were attracted to the growing market. Five new products were launched and by the end of 1998 it was obvious that competition was increasing and that different OTC brands were starting to defend their market share by increasing marketing expenditure. Total market media expenditure rose by 185%, with PerHair's SOV being 24%, mainly allocated to TV.

Research into pharmacists' attitudes at the end of 1998 showed that 55% of them were already well aware of the brand and had a good perception of it. Of these 15% were persuaded to recommend it to their customers. The brand commanded 10% brand loyalty.

In 1999, there were already 20 OTC brands in the market. Media expenditure remained high. PerHair continued to have a high SOV. The TV ad became more aggressive, stressing the number 1 position of the brand in many countries and the benefits the product gives to the health of hair.

The overall market increased by 14% and at the same time the only prescription brand Garanten fell by another 22%. The OTC category reached 65% of the total market sales. In 1999 the PerHair brand was completed with the introduction of 'PerHair Men', which was developed for the special needs of young men aged 18–30.

In the same year, marketing communication activities were aimed mostly at the end-users, to increase spontaneous brand awareness and brand loyalty. Apart from the TV campaign, many tailored activities were addressed to different target groups, involving inserts in trendy magazines, outdoor work, pharmacy posters and indoor ads in sports centres. In pharmacies and doctors' surgeries educational leaflets were distributed and innovative stands were used. PerHair's leader image was further imprinted through a visual presence at pharmaceutical and medical conferences.

By 2000, the market had been radically transformed. People appreciated and used pharmaceutically developed shampoos containing vitamins as a pre-emptive measure to keep hair healthy. The number of users had dramatically increased and PerHair became market leader with 27% volume share.

Note: The information provided in this mini case is not intended to reflect on any single company or brand. All brands and companies have been disguised and the case does not reflect good or bad management practice.

Mini-case questions

1. Explain how management of the *Perhair* brand demonstrates how consumer attitudes can be effectively changed.
2. To what extent does this mini case demonstrate the role of attributes in the way consumers perceive brands?
3. Prepare brief notes explaining the communication strategies used by *Perhair*.
4. How might the *Perhair* brand be developed in the future?
5. To what extent might the impact of significant others affect the development of the vitamin-enriched shampoo market?

References

Ajzen, I. and Fishbein, M. (1980) *Understanding Attitudes and Predicting Social Behaviour.* Englewood Cliffs, NJ: Prentice Hall.

Belk, R. (1975) Situational variables in consumer behaviour. *Journal of Consumer Research*, **2** (December), pp. 57–64.

Brabbs, C. (2000) Charmin characters take on the Andrex puppy. *Marketing*, 3 February, p. 15.

Burke, R. and Srull, T.K. (1988) Competitive interference and consumer memory for advertising. *Journal of Consumer Research*, **15** (June), pp. 55–68.

Cohen, J. and Basu, K. (1987) Alternative models of categorisation. *Journal of Consumer Research* (March), pp. 455–72.

de Chernatony L. (1993) The seven building blocks of brands. *Management Today* (March), pp. 66–7.

Engel, F., Blackwell, R. and Minniard, P. (1990) *Consumer Behaviour*, 6th edn. New York: Dryden Press.

Glancey, J. (1994) The real thing put to the test. *Independent on Sunday*, 24 April, News Analysis, p. 5.

Goodrich, J.N. (1978) The relationship between preferences for and perceptions of vacation destinations: application of a choice model. *Journal of Travel Research*, **17**(2).

Grass, R.C. and Wallace, H.W. (1969) Satiation effects of TV commercials. *Journal of Advertising Research*, **9**(3), pp. 3–9.

Guildford, J. (1959) *Personality.* New York: McGraw-Hill.

Hansen, F. (1972) *Consumer Choice Behaviour: A Cognitive Theory*. New York: Free Press.

Hawkins, D., Best, R. and Coney, K. (1989) *Consumer Behaviour*. Homewood, IL: Richard D. Irwin.

Javalgi, R., Thomas, E. and Rao, S. (1992) US travellers' perception of selected European destinations. *European Journal of Marketing*, **26**(7), pp. 45–64.

McGuire, W. (1978) An information processing model of advertising effectiveness. In *Behavioural and Management Science in Marketing* (eds H.J. Davis and A.J. Silk). New York: Ronald Press.

McMurdo, M.W. (1993) Chasing butterflies. *Marketing Week*, 21 May, pp. 28–31.

Mintel (1996) Household Paper Products. *Marketing Ingelligence*, January, p. 7.

Moran, W. (1990) Brand preference and the perceptual frame. *Journal of Advertising Research* (October/November), pp. 9–16.

Petty, R.E. and Cacioppo, J.T. (1979) Effects of message repetition and position on cognitive responses, recall and persuasion. *Journal of Personality and Social Psychology*, **37** (January), pp. 97–109.

QED (1989) It's not easy being a dolphin. BBC TV.

Schiffman, L. and Kanuck, L. (1991) Consumer Behavior. Englewood Cliffs, NJ: Prentice Hall.

Strong, E.C. (1977) The spacing and timing of advertising. *Journal of Advertising Research*, **17** (December), pp. 25–31.

Verebelyi, N. (2000) The power of the pack. *Marketing*, 27 April, p. 37.

Williams, K.C. (1981) *Behavioural Aspects of Marketing*. London: Heinemann.

Zielske, H.A. (1959) The remembering and forgetting of advertising. *Journal of Marketing*, **23** (January), pp. 239–43.

4

Customer decision-making

Customers make product purchase related decisions in different ways. Understanding the ways in which buyers make decisions and the factors that impact upon the decision process can affect the effectiveness of marketing communications. In particular, it can influence message structure, content and scheduling.

AIMS AND OBJECTIVES

The aim of this chapter is to consider some of the different processes consumers and organisational buyers use to make purchase decisions.

The objectives of this chapter are:

1. To present a general process for purchase decision-making.
2. To examine the sequence and methods used by consumers to make decisions.
3. To explore the components of perceived risk.
4. To introduce and explain involvement theory and relate it to planned communication activities.
5. To consider the different types of individual who contribute to purchase decisions made by organisations.
6. To understand the stages which organisations use to make purchase decisions.
7. To appreciate the differences in approaches and content of marketing communications between consumer and organisational buying.

Introduction

An understanding of the contextual elements that impact upon individual purchase decision-making and the overall process through which individuals behave and ultimately make decisions is an important first stage in the development of any marketing communications plan. Knowledge of a buyer's decision-making processes is vital if the correct type of information is to be transmitted at the right time and in the right or appropriate manner. There are two broad types of buyer: consumers and organisational buyers. First, consideration will be given to a general decision-making process and then an insight into the characteristics of the decision-making processes for consumers and organisational buyers will be presented. The chapter concludes with a consideration of the differences between the two main approaches.

A general buying decision-making process

Figure 4.1 shows that there are five stages to the general process whereby buyers make purchase decisions and implement them. Marketing communications can impact upon any or all of these stages with varying levels of potential effectiveness.

Problem recognition

Problem recognition occurs when there is a perceived difference between an individual's ideal state and reality. Advertisers often induce 'problem recognition' by suggesting that the current state is not desirable or by demonstrating how consumers can tell whether they have a similar problem (e.g. 'Is your hair dull and lifeless?'). The difficulty in getting buyers to recognise that they have a problem invites the question, do they actually have a problem? If there is no identified need, then it is not marketing but selling that is being practised.

Problem recognition occurs when there is a perceived difference between an individual's ideal state and reality.

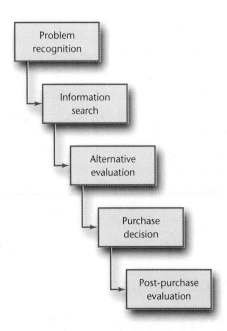

Figure 4.1　Five general stages of a buyer's purchase decision process.

2   Information search

Having identified a problem a prospective buyer will search for information in an attempt to resolve it. There are two main areas of search activity:

1. The internal search involves a memory scan to recall experiences and knowledge, utilising the perceptual processes to see whether there is an 'off-the-shelf' solution.

2. If there is no 'off-the-shelf' solution, the prospective buyer will resort to an external search. This will involve family and friends, reference sources and commercial guides and advertising.

3   Alternative evaluation

Potential solutions need to be evaluated in order that the optimum choice be made. Products considered feasible constitute the *preference set*, and it is from these seven or eight products that a smaller group of products is normally assembled. This is referred to as the *evoked set* (or repertoire) and it is from this that consumers make a choice. Attributes used to determine the sets are referred to as evaluative criteria. Very often these attributes are both objective and subjective in nature.

4   Purchase decision

Having evaluated various solutions, the buyer may develop a predisposition to make a purchase. This will involve matching motives and evaluative criteria with product attributes. This necessitates the use of the processes of learning and attitude formation, discussed in the previous chapter.

5   Post-purchase evaluation

Direct experience of the product is an important part of the decision process. Feedback from use helps learning and attitude development and is the main contributor to long-run behaviour. Communication activity must continue to provide satisfaction and prevent the onset of cognitive dissonance. This is a state where, after the purchase decision has been made, a buyer might feel tension about a past decision either because the product fails to reach expectations or because the consumer becomes aware of a superior alternative.

Much of the advertising undertaken by car manufacturers seeks to prevent the onset of tension and purchase dissatisfaction.

Marketing communications, at this stage, should be aimed at reinforcing past decisions by stressing the positive features of the product or by providing more information to assist its use and application. For example, much of the advertising undertaken by car manufacturers seeks to prevent the onset of tension and purchase dissatisfaction.

Types of consumer decision-making

Buyers do not follow the general decision sequence at all times. The procedure may vary depending upon the time available, levels of perceived risk and the degree of involvement a buyer has with the type of product. Perceived risk and involvement are issues that will be covered later. At this point three types of problem solving behaviour (extended problem solving, limited problem solving and routinised response) will be considered.

1. Extended problem solving (EPS)

Consumers considering the purchase of a car or house undertake a great deal of external search activity and spend a lot of time reaching a solution that satisfies, as closely as possible, the evaluative criteria previously set. This activity is usually associated with products that are unfamiliar, where direct experience and hence knowledge are weak, and where there is considerable financial risk. *eg house, car*

Marketing communications should aim to provide a lot of information to assist the decision process. The provision of information through sales literature, such as brochures and leaflets, web sites for determining product and purchase criteria in product categories where there is little experience, access to salespersons and demonstrations and advertisements are just some of the ways in which information can be provided.

2. Limited problem solving (LPS)

Having experience of a product means that greater use can be made of internal memory-based search routines, and the external search can be limited to obtaining up-to-date information or to ensuring that the finer points of the decision have been investigated.

By differentiating the product, marketing communications provide the buyer with a reason to select that particular product.

Marketing communications should attempt to provide information about any product modification or new attributes and convey messages which highlight those key attributes known to be important to buyers. By differentiating the product, marketing communications provide the buyer with a reason to select that particular product.

3. Routinised response behaviour (RRB)

For a great number of products the decision process will consist only of an internal search. This is primarily because the buyer has made a number of purchases and has accumulated a great deal of experience. Therefore, only an internal search is necessary, so little time or effort will be spent on external search activities. Low-value items which are frequently purchased fall into this category, for example toothpaste, soap, tinned foods and confectionery.

Communicators should focus upon keeping the product within the evoked set or getting it into the set.

Some outlets are perceived as suitable for what are regarded as distress purchases. Alldays and Happy Shopper outlets position themselves as convenience stores for distress purchases (for example, a pint of milk at ten o'clock at night). Many garages have positioned themselves as convenience stores suitable for meeting the needs of RRB purchases. In doing so they are moving themselves away from the perception of being only a distress purchase outlet.

Communicators should focus upon keeping the product within the evoked set or getting it into the set. Learning can be enhanced through repetition of messages, but repetition can also be used to maintain attention and awareness.

Perceived risk

An important factor associated with the purchase decision process is the level of risk perceived by the buyer. This risk concerns the uncertainty of the proposed purchase and the outcomes that will result from a decision to purchase a product.

Risk is perceived because the buyer has little or no experience of the performance of the product or the decision process associated with the purchase. Buyers may lack the ability to make what they see as the right decision and they may be forced to trade the decision to purchase one product in lieu of another because resources, such as time and money, are restricted. Risk is related to not only brand-based decisions but also to product categories, an especially important aspect when launching new technology products, for example. The level of risk an individual experiences varies through time, across products and is often a reflection of an individual's propensity to manage risk. Risk is related to involvement, trust and other buyer behaviour concepts.

Risk is related to not only brand-based decisions but also to product categories.

Settle and Alreck (1989) suggest that there are five main forms of risk that can be identified; the purchase of a hi-fi unit demonstrates each element:

1. Performance risk: will the unit reproduce my music clearly?
2. Financial risk: can I afford that much or should I buy a less expensive version?
3. Physical risk: will the unit damage my other systems or endanger me in any way?
4. Social risk: will my friends and colleagues be impressed?
5. Ego risk: will I feel as good as I want to feel when listening to or talking about my unit?

A sixth element, time, is also considered to be a risk factor (Stone and Gronhaug, 1993). Using the hi-fi example, will purchase of the unit lead to an inefficient use of my time? Or can I afford the time to search for a good hi-fi so that I will not waste my money?

What constitutes risk is a function of the contextual characteristics of each situation, the individuals involved and the product under consideration:

1. Each situation varies according to perceptions of the shopping experience, the time the purchase is to be made in the context of the other activities that need to be completed (last chance to buy a birthday present, only 15 minutes left before meeting my partner), and the image different stores have and the risk that is associated with the products offered by the store.
2. Each individual has a propensity to higher or lower levels of risk. These levels may vary according to their experience of purchasing particular products, demographic factors such as age, level of education and religion, and various personality factors.
3. The product may, if only for price, convey a level of risk to the purchaser. For example, the purchase of a car is not only a large financial commitment for most people, but is also a highly emotive decision that has significant ego and social risks attached to it.

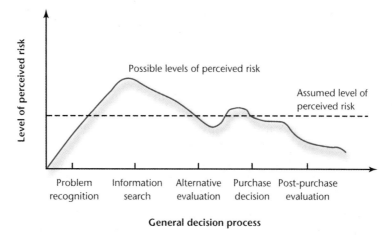

Figure 4.2 Varying levels of perceived risk through the purchase decision process. Adapted from Mitchell and Boustani (1994); used with kind permission.

Perceived risk need not be constant throughout the decision process. Mitchell and Boustani (1994) suggest that the level of perceived risk may vary as depicted in Figure 4.2, although more work is required to determine the validity of their initial findings.

The main question is, how can buyers be helped to alleviate high levels of risk during the pre- and post-purchase stages in the decision process? The main method used by buyers is the acquisition of information. Information through the mass media, through word-of-mouth communications and through personal selling (usually sales representatives) is used to set out the likely outcomes and so reduce the levels of risk. Brand loyalty can also be instrumental in reducing risk when launching new products. The use of guarantees, third-party endorsements, money-back offers (some car manufacturers offer the opportunity to return a car within 30 days or exchange it for a different model) and trial samples (as used by many hair care products) are well-used devices to reduce risk.

Reducing perceived risk – Discover Racing

A campaign devised by the Horserace Betting Levy Board is designed to attract people to horse racing and so increase the amount of betting turnover. Clarke (2001) reports that research found that people were well disposed to horse racing and betting in general but their main obstacle appeared to be a fear that they lacked sufficient knowledge about horse racing, betting and what to do at a race course.

To overcome this inhibitor, the Racing and Betting Marketing Group was constructed which then launched the Discover Racing three-year campaign. This sought to reduce perceived risk by installing a call centre and Web site that provided information and ticketing facilities. Through easy access to information and responding to peoples questions it is hoped to increase the number of visitors to race courses, build interest and enthusiasm before launching jockey fan clubs, merchandise and long-term interest in the sport.

Appreciating the level and types of risk buyers perceive is important for many marketing activities. As Mitchell (1999) points out, new product development, segmentation, targeting, positioning and marketing communications can all be influenced by understanding perceived risk. Services, he points out, have been shown to carry higher levels of risk, mainly because of their characteristics of heterogeneity, perishability, inseparability and intangibility which serve to undermine buyer confidence. For example, Ashford *et al.* (2000) refer to the perceived risk associated with dental care and mention fear and anxiety, the internal environment of the practice, dentists' social and communication skills and patient satisfaction as important elements that may interrelate and influence attitudes and behavioural intentions.

Many direct marketing advertisements in magazines seek to reduce a number of different types of risk. Companies offering wine for direct home delivery, for example, try to reduce performance risk by providing information about each wine being offered. Financial risk is reduced by comparing their 'special' prices with those in the high street, social risk is approached by developing the brand name associations trying to improve credibility and time risk is reduced through the convenience of home delivery.

Involvement theory

A central framework, critical to understanding consumer decision-making behaviour and associated communications, is involvement theory. Purchase decisions made by consumers vary considerably, and one of the factors thought to be key to brand choice decisions is the level of involvement (in terms of importance and relevance) a consumer has with either the product or the purchase process.

The term 'involvement' has become an important concept in the consumer behaviour literature. The concept has its roots in social psychology, but its current form and interpretation by researchers is both interesting and revealing. There is no consensus on a definition of involvement. Kapferer and Laurent (1985) argue that involvement has five different facets. These are interest, risk importance, risk probability, sign value and hedonic value. Their approach tends to be all-consuming, whereas Ratchford (1987), quoting Zaichkowsky (1985) and others, does not perceive involvement as such a broad matter. The majority of researchers do not recognise the importance of hedonic and sign value elements in this context. To some, involvement is about the ego, perceived risk and purchase importance – a cognitive perspective. To those who favour a behavioural perspective, the search for and evaluation of product-orientated information is pertinent (Schiffman and Kanuk, 1991).

To some, involvement is about the ego, perceived risk and purchase importance – a cognitive perspective.

Involvement – characteristics

The various characteristics associated with the involvement concept can be considered in three phases. These are depicted at Figure 4.3. Phase 1 considers the degree of involvement which will vary on a situational basis and will be affected by contextual elements such as the nature of the individual and their experiences, values and expectations. The situation itself concerning the purpose of the purchase (e.g. gift or own

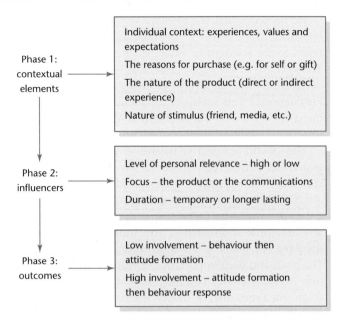

Figure 4.3   Three phases of individual involvement and attitude development.

consumption) will also affect the level of involvement. The product or service will also be a factor taking account of whether the individual has direct or indirect experience of the object. In addition, the nature of the stimulus to purchase will also be an important factor, whether this be an advertisement, friend or general need.

Phase 2 is characterised by three main factors. The intensity of involvement reflects the level or degree of personal relevance and is normally seen as either high or low involvement. The focus of the involvement refers to whether the object or the communications surrounding the product are of primary importance. The third factor concerns the duration of the involvement. Essentially this may be temporary (e.g. if motivated by an advertisement seen for the first time, or buying a gift) or it may be longer lasting or enduring , reflecting some form of loyalty, commitment or interest in the object or product category.

Phase 3 concerns the outcomes or responses individuals give as a consequence of the involvement they experience. The manner and speed at which information is processed (as a result of the level of involvement) leads primarily to either attitudes being formed prior to behaviour (high involvement) or attitudes being formed after product experience or behaviour (low involvement).

The implications for those responsible for marketing communications are many and varied. However, where high involvement is present messages should stress attributes and benefits (functional) so that they feed the more rational, considered information processing style that accompanies this position. Where there is low involvement it is better to use more emotional (expressive) messages simply because individuals do not expend any considered or conscious effort in processing the information.

Following this analysis of the involvement process, it is interesting to consider Laaksonen's (1994) interpretation where he draws upon three perspectives of involvement from the literature. These are the cognitive, predisposition to act and response-based interpretations.

He proposes that the *cognitive view* of involvement regards the perceived personal relevance of an object to an individual as of paramount importance. This approach refers to the strength or extent of the cognitive/attitude structure towards an object. The strength of the psychological linkage between an individual and a stimulus object determines the intensity of involvement. How important is it to purchase PlayStation2? This intensity of attitude is seen to have originated from social judgement theory, where involvement is seen as a variable affected by how others might interpret a purchase; that is, their predisposition to respond to PlayStation2.

The second perspective regards involvement as an individual state or *predisposition to act*. Here, involvement focuses on the mental state of an individual, evoked by a stimulus. It is the degree of perceived importance, the interest or level of emotional attachment, arousal, drive or motivation that defines the intensity of involvement, either present in an individual or present in any given situation. Using the previous analogy, how motivated is the individual to purchase PlayStation 2? Therefore, involvement refers to the motivational state of an individual in a specific situation. The goals and their importance (hierarchy) defined by individuals determine the direction (towards an object/advertisement or perhaps the act of purchasing) and the level (high, medium, low) of involvement. Again, involvement is regarded as a mediating variable in information processing and a predisposition to act.

The third perspective is the *response view*. Here involvement is regarded as a reaction to an external stimulus or stimuli such as marketing communications. These responses are typically characterised by the form of cognitive and behavioural processing (learn–feel–do) directed to accomplishing a task. So the response view of involvement is based on the reaction of an individual to a stimulus, which will affect the learn–feel–do sequence and the depth to which processing occurs. Therefore, the impact of promotional messages for PlayStation2 is likely to be most important in determining the direction and purchase intentions of potential game station purchasers. Here, involvement is considered as a cognitive response to the marketing communication messages (Batra and Ray, 1983). These views do not see involvement as a mediating variable, simply because involvement is regarded as 'an actualised response in itself' (Laaksonen, 1994).

Of these three, no one view can be determined as a correct interpretation. In a way all are wrong and all are right simultaneously. There is agreement among many researchers that involvement should be seen in the context of three main states. These are high, low and zero involvement. The last of these is self-explanatory and requires no additional comment. The other two states are portrayed as two discrete ends of a continuum. Consumers are thought to move along this continuum, from high to low, as purchase experience increases, perceived risk is reduced and levels of overall knowledge improves.

The approach taken here is that involvement is about the degree of personal relevance and risk perceived by members of the target market in a particular purchase situation (Rossiter *et al.*, 1991). This implies that the level of involvement may vary through time as each member of the target market becomes more (or less) familiar with the purchase and associated communications. At the point of decision-making, involvement is either high or low, not some point on a sliding scale or a point on a continuum between two extremes. Involvement is a cognitively bound concept, the strength and depth of which varies among and between individuals.

Involvement is about the degree of personal relevance and risk perceived by members of the target market in a particular purchase situation.

High involvement occurs when a consumer perceives an expected purchase which is not only of high personal relevance but also represents a high level of perceived risk. Cars, washing machines, houses and insurance polices are seen as 'big ticket' items, infrequent purchases that promote a great deal of involvement. The risk described is financial, but, as we saw earlier, risk can take other forms. Therefore, the choice of perfume, suit, dress or jewelry may also represent high involvement, with social risk dominating the purchase decision. The consumer, therefore, devotes a great deal of time to researching the intended purchase and collecting as much information as possible in order to reduce, as far as possible, levels of perceived risk.

A *low-involvement* state of mind regarding a purchase suggests little threat or risk to the consumer. Low-priced items such as washing powder, baked beans and breakfast cereals are bought frequently, and past experience of the product class and the brand cues the consumer into a purchase that requires little information or support. Items such as alcoholic and soft drinks, cigarettes and chocolate are also normally seen as low involvement, but they induce a strong sense of ego risk associated with the self-gratification that is attached to the consumption of these products.

Hedonic consumption

There is a range of products and services that can evoke high levels of involvement based upon the emotional impact that consumption provides the buyer. This is referred to as hedonic consumption, and Hirschmann and Holbrook (1982) describe this approach as 'those facets of consumer behaviour that relate to the multi sensory, fantasy and emotive aspects of one's experience with products'. With its roots partly in the motivation research and partly in the cognitive processing schools, this interpretation of consumer behaviour seeks to explain how and why buyers experience emotional responses to the act of purchase and consumption of particular products. *Historical imagery* occurs when, for example, the colour of a dress, the scent of a perfume or aftershave, or the aroma of a restaurant or food can trigger an individual's memory to replay an event. In contrast, *fantasy imagery* occurs when a buyer constructs an event, drawing together various colours, sounds and shapes to compose a mental experience of an event that has not occurred previously. Consumers imagine a reality in which they derive sensory pleasure. Some smokers imagine themselves as 'Marlboro Men': not just masculine, but as idealised cowboys (Hirschmann and Holbrook, 1982).

The advertising of fragrances and luxury brands is often based on images which encourage individuals to project themselves into a desirable or pleasurable environment or situation, for example, those which foster romantic associations. The Ralph Lauren *Romance* ad is an excellent example of a romantic/fantasy message. To some extent this is a sophisticated example of features and benefits. The left-hand page (features) shows what the brand is, how it is presented (the packaging) and prominently displays the brand name around the neck of the bottle. The right-hand page shows the benefits of usage, namely the depiction of a romantic embrace, presumably fuelled by *Romance* and one which users perceive as desirable. See Exhibit 4.1. Readers should also observe the thematic consistency of the brand name through the visual associations that the ad seeks to make.

There are a number of problems with the hedonic approach, namely measurement

Exhibit 4. 1 *Romance* by Ralph Lauren. An example of romantic fantasy used for fragrance advertising. Picture reproduced with the kind permission of Ralph Lauren and Neville McCarthy Associates.

factors of reliability and validity, but, nevertheless, appreciating the hedonic needs of the target audience can be an important contribution to the creation of promotional messages.

Consumer decision-making processes

From this understanding of general decision-making processes, perceived risk and involvement theory, it is possible to identify two main approaches to consumer decision-making.

High-involvement decision-making

If an individual is highly involved with the initial purchase of a product, EPS is the appropriate decision sequence, as information is processed in a rational, logical order.

The essential element in this sequence is that a great deal of information is sought initially and an attitude is developed before a commitment or intention to trial is determined.

Individuals who are highly involved in a purchase are thought to move through the process shown in Figure 4.4. When high-involvement decision-making is present, individuals perceive a high level of risk and are concerned about the intended purchase. The essential element in this sequence is that a great deal of information is sought initially and an attitude is developed before a commitment or intention to trial is determined.

Information search is an important part of the high-involvement decision-making process. Because individuals are highly motivated, information is actively sought, processed and evaluated. Many media sources are explored, including the mass media, word-of-mouth communications and point-of-sale communications. As individuals require a lot of information, print media are more appropriate as a large volume of detailed information can be transmitted and this allows the receiver to digest the

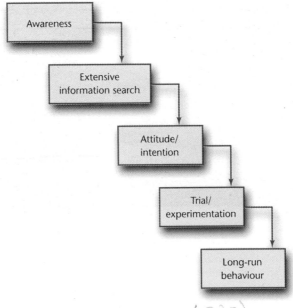

Figure 4.4   High-involvement decision-making process.   *(EPS)*

information at a speed which they can control. Exhibit 4.2 depicts an advertisement for a car. Note the amount of information presented and the balance between the copy and the visual elements of the message.

Evaluation of the information and of the alternatives that have been derived from the information search needs to be undertaken. By comparing and implicitly scoring the different attributes of each alternative, a belief about the overall competitiveness of each alternative can be established. In Chapter 3 a compensatory model was examined. In this approach, individuals do not reject products because an attribute scores low; rather, a weakness is offset or compensated for by the strength and high scores accredited to other attributes. An individual's attitude to a purchase is the sum of the scores given to the range of evaluative criteria used in the decision-making process. As we saw in Chapter 3, Fishbein states that an attitude towards the act of purchasing and the subjective norm (the perceived attitude of others to the act being considered) combine to form an *intention* to act in a particular way. This part of the process is facilitated by the use of credible sources of information. Therefore, personal selling is important to bring individuals closer to the product, in order that it may be demonstrated and allow intense learning to occur.

Trial behaviour will follow if the perceived quality of the product is satisfactory and sufficient triggers, from internal searches, stimulate experimentation. Likewise, long-run behaviour, the goal of all marketing activities, will be determined if the guarantees and product quality combine to meet the expectations of the individual, generated by the information search.

Low-involvement decision-making

If an individual has little involvement with an initial purchase of a product, LPS is the appropriate decision process. Information is processed cognitively but in a passive,

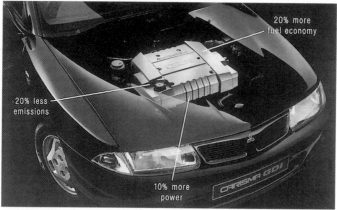

INSIDE THE NEW Carisma is Mitsubishi's revolutionary 1.8 L Gasoline Direct Injection engine. It's been specially designed to be more economical, up to 20% improvement over conventional petrol engines. It releases fewer emissions, including a reduction of carbon dioxide by 20%. Performance is increased too, with a 10% improvement in power output and torque over normal fuel injected petrol engines of the same size. Of course the Carisma GDI® still has all the other important features such as twin airbags, side impact door beams, engine immobiliser and multi-link suspension with passive rear wheel steering. And everything is covered by Mitsubishi's unbeatable 3 year unlimited mileage warranty package. We haven't just re-designed the engine, we've re-invented it.

Prices start from £14,515 on the road.

For more information, simply

Freecall **0800 123 363**.

MITSUBISHI MOTORS
RE-INVENTING THE WHEEL

The Colt Car Company Ltd., Watermoor, Circencester, Glos GL7 1LF. www.mitsubishi-cars.co.uk

GDI is a registered trademark of Mitsubishi Motors Corporation. Price includes delivery, number plate and 12 months road fund licence.

You wait years for an improvement to the petrol engine, then three come along all at once.

Exhibit 4.2 A print advertisement for a product that often evokes high involvement. Picture reproduced with the kind permission of Mitsubishi.

involuntary way. Information is processed using right-brain thinking so information is stored as it is received, in sections, and this means that information is stored as a brand association (Heath, 2000). An advertisement for Andrex toilet tissue featuring the puppy is stored as the 'Andrex Puppy' without any overt thinking or reasoning.

Information is processed cognitively but in a passive, involuntary way.

Because of the low personal relevance and perceived risk associated with this type of processing, message repetition is necessary to define brands and create meaningful brand associations. Individuals who have a low involvement with a purchase decision choose not to search for information and are thought to move through the process shown in Figure 4.5.

Communications can assist the development of awareness in the low-involvement decision-making process. However, as individuals assume a passive problem-solving role, messages need to be shorter than in the high-involvement process and should contain less information. Broadcast media are preferred as they complement the passive learning posture adopted by the individual. Repetition is important because the receiver has little or no motivation to retain information, and his or her perceptual selection processes filter out unimportant information. Learning develops through

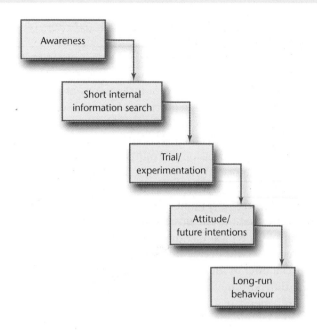

Figure 4.5   Low-involvement decision-making process.

exposure to repeated messages, but attitudes do not develop at this part of the process (Harris, 1987).

Where low involvement is present, each individual relies upon internal, rather than external, search mechanisms, often prompted by point-of-purchase displays. Using non-compensatory decision rules (Chapter 3), where product weaknesses are not offset by strengths, individuals make decisions, often at the point of purchase, to try established or new brands.

Price can be a very important factor by which individuals can discriminate between low-involvement purchase decisions. In high-involvement decisions there is a wide variety of attributes which individuals can use to discriminate between purchase decisions. In low-involvement purchases, price, packaging and point-of-purchase displays, and promotions work together to cue and stimulate an individual into trying a product.

Long-run behaviour is a function of promotional messages, product quality and the degree of loyalty that can be sustained towards the brand.

As a direct result of trying a product (or experimenting) and hence product experience, an attitude develops. By judging the quality of the experience, an attitude is formed which acts as the basis for future decisions. Long-run behaviour is a function of promotional messages, product quality and the degree of loyalty that can be sustained towards the brand.

Subsequent purchase activity

The initial purchase decision process frames all subsequent decisions in the product category. If a high-involvement decision process ends satisfactorily, then levels of brand loyalty are normally high, which means that subsequent decisions can be processed much more quickly. Routinised response behaviour occurs safely, as any risk associated with a purchase can be dispelled through the security associated with a brand. Brand loyalty is the normal outcome of a successful high-involvement decision-making process.

If the high-involvement process ends in partial satisfaction, then, depending upon the nature and extent of the outstanding risk, the next decision may also be EPS. For example, if the purchase of a first savings or investment product results in total dissatisfaction, any second purchase of a similar or financially related product will require a review of the critical attributes to provide up-to-date product and provider information, but not necessarily to inform about what a savings/investment policy is.

If the initial decision was motivated by a low level of involvement and the outcome was satisfactory, then subsequent decisions will be based upon a state of brand ambivalence. This means that individuals relegate these decisions to a habitual process but will consider a number of different brands, and will switch to one of them if they perceive that the circumstances in which the decision is being made are changing. For example, a typical habitual decision concerns the purchase of tinned tomatoes. Most consumers will decide upon their usual brand until they notice a price promotion, special offer or incentive to purchase a different brand. A switch may also be actuated by different merchandising and positioning within the store, different personal requirements (e.g. dietary changes) and levels of brand awareness.

Repeat purchase decisions are often unstable on the grounds that buyers are content to switch between products in their evoked set unless there is a high level of brand loyalty. Manufacturers of products that are associated with low-involvement decision-making are required to engage in promotional activities that keep the awareness of the brand at the top of each individual's mind-set.

Repeat purchase decisions are often unstable on the grounds that buyers are content to switch between products in their evoked set unless there is a high level of brand loyalty.

Otherwise there is a danger that a competitor may change the circumstances in which an individual makes a decision and trigger a motivation to try its offering.

Impact on Communications

Involvement is a theory central to our understanding of the way in which information is processed and the way in which consumers make decisions about product purchases. It was established that there are two main types of involvement: high and low. This concept of involvement leads to two orderings of the hierarchy of effects. In decisions where there is high involvement, attitude precedes trial behaviour. In low-involvement cases this position is reversed. In the former a positive and specific position is assumed by the consumer, whereas in the latter attitudes to the product (not the product class) develop after product use.

As discussed earlier, where there is high involvement, consumers seek out information because they are concerned about the decision processes and outcomes. Because they have these concerns, consumers develop an attitude prior to behaviour. Products that evoke high-involvement decision processes tend to be high cost, to be bought relatively infrequently, to be complex, to elicit feelings of risk and to be visible to others.

Where there is low involvement, consumers are content to select any one of a number of acceptable products and often rely on those that are in the individual's evoked set. Low involvement is thought to be a comfortable state, because there are too many other decisions in life to have to make decisions about each one of them, so an opportunity not to have to seek information and make other decisions is welcome.

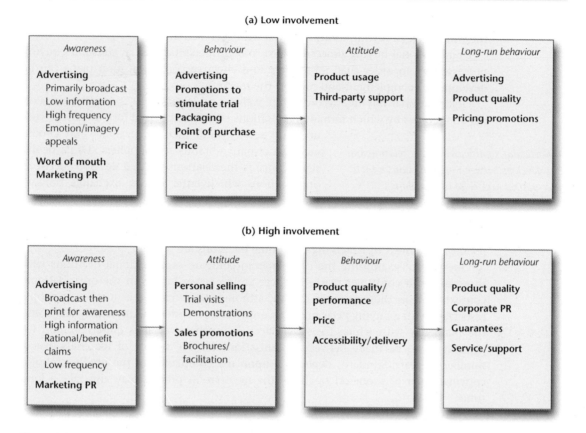

Figure 4.6 Promotional strategies for different levels of involvement.

This suggests that high and low positions are not static or permanent. Involvement is said by some (Vaughn, 1980; Ratchford, 1987) to be a continuum where consumers can move from a high- to a low-involvement position, as their experience of a product increases and their perceived risk is reduced. Figure 4.6 indicates the advertising and promotion strategies best suited for each level within both involvement spectra.

Involvement impacts therefore on what is said, how it is said and when it is said.

Involvement impacts therefore on what is said, how it is said and when it is said. Readers are advised that other material relating to involvement and the strategic implications for marketing communications can be found in Chapters 12 and 20.

Organisational buying decision processes

Organisations have so far been viewed in the context of sellers, but in order to function they need to buy materials, parts, general supplies and services from a range of other organisations. Some texts refer to this as industrial marketing or, in the more current terminology, business-to-business marketing, reflecting the growth and importance of the public sector and the increasing use of the services sector within mature economies. However, the term 'organisational marketing' is used here to reflect the wide range of organisations involved with such activities.

Organisational buying processes need to be understood, just as consumer buying processes do, in order that appropriate and effective communication plans can be developed to complement and support the marketing mix.

Organisational buying, according to Webster and Wind (1972), is 'the decision making process by which formal organisations establish the need for purchased products and services and identify, evaluate and choose among alternative brands and suppliers'. Of particular significance is the relationship that develops between organisations which enter market exchange transactions. As mentioned previously, the various networks that organisations belong to will influence the purchase decisions that other organisations in the network make. However, before exploring these issues, it is necessary to review the context in which organisational decisions are made.

Of particular significance is the relationship that develops between organisations which enter market exchange transactions.

One way of examining the context is to compare organisational decisions with those made in consumer markets. There are far fewer buyers in the organisational context than in the consumer market, although there can be a number of people associated with a buying decision in an organisation. Orders are invariably larger and the frequency with which they are placed is much lower. It is quite common for agreements to be made between organisations for the supply of materials over a number of years. Similarly, depending upon the complexity of the product (photocopying paper or a one-off satellite), the negotiation process may also take a long time.

Many of the characteristics associated with consumer decision-making processes can be observed in the organisational context. However, organisational buyers make decisions which ultimately contribute to the achievement of corporate objectives. To make the necessary decisions, a high volume of pertinent information is often required. This information needs to be relatively detailed and is normally presented in a rational and logical style. The needs of the buyers are many and complex, and some may be personal. Goals, such as promotion and career advancement within the organisation, coupled with ego and employee satisfaction combine to make organisational buying an important task, one that requires professional training and the development of expertise if the role is to be performed optimally.

Buyclasses comprise three types: new task, modified rebuy and straight rebuy.

Buyclasses

Organisational buyers make decisions that vary with each buying situation and buyclass. Buyclasses, according to Robinson *et al.* (1967), comprise three types: new task, modified rebuy and straight rebuy (Table 4.1):

1. *New buy*

   As the name implies, the organisation is faced with a first-time buying situation. Risk is inevitably large at this point, and partly as a consequence there are a large number of decision participants. Each participant requires a lot of information and a relatively long period of time is required for the information to be assimilated and a decision to be made.

Table 4.1   Main characteristics of the buyclasses

Buyclass	Degree of familiarity with the problem	Information requirements	Alternative solutions
New buy	The problem is fresh to the decision-makers	A great deal of information is required	Alternative solutions are unknown, all are considered new
Modified rebuy	The requirement is not new but is different from previous situations	More information is required but past experience is of use	Buying decision needs new solutions
Rebuy	The problem is identical to previous experiences	Little or no information is required	Alternative solutions not sought or required

2. *Modified rebuy*

Having purchased a product, the organisation may request through its buyer that certain modifications be made to future purchases, for example, adjustments to the specification of the product, further negotiation on price levels or perhaps the arrangement for alternative delivery patterns. Fewer people are involved in the decision process than in the new task situation.

3. *Straight rebuy*

In this situation, the purchasing department reorders on a routine basis, very often working from an approved list of suppliers. No other people are involved with the exercise until different suppliers attempt to change the environment in which the decision is made. For example, they may interrupt the procedure with a potentially better offer.

These phases bear a strong resemblance to the extended, limited and routinised response identified earlier with respect to the consumer market.

Buying centres

Reference has been made on a number of occasions to organisational buyers, as if these people are the only representatives of an organisation to be involved with the purchase decision process. This is not the case, as very often a large number of people are involved in the purchase decision. This group is referred to as either the decision-making unit (DMU) or the buying centre.

Buying centres vary in size and composition in accordance with the nature of each individual task.

Buying centres vary in size and composition in accordance with the nature of each individual task. Webster and Wind (1972) identified a number of people who make up the buying centre.

Users are people who not only initiate the purchase process but will use the product, once it has been acquired, and evaluate its performance. *Influencers* very often help set the technical specifications for the proposed purchase and assist the evaluation of alternative offerings by potential suppliers. *Deciders* are those who make purchasing decisions. In repeat buying activities the buyer may well also be the decider. However, it is normal practice to require that expenditure decisions involving sums over a certain financial limit be authorised by other, often senior, managers. *Buyers* (purchasing managers) select suppliers and manage the process whereby the required products are procured. As identified previously, buyers may not decide which product is to be purchased but they influence the framework within which the decision is made. *Gatekeepers* have the potential to control the type and flow of information to the organisation and the members of the buying centre. These gatekeepers may be technical personnel, secretaries or telephone switchboard operators.

The size and form of the buying centre is not static. It can vary according to the complexity of the product being considered and the degree of risk each decision is per-

The size and form of the buying centre is not static.

ceived to carry for the organisation. Different roles are required and adopted as the nature of the buying task changes with each new purchase situation (Bonoma, 1982). It is vital for seller organisations to identify members of the buying centre and to target and refine their messages to meet the needs of each member of the centre.

The task of the marketing communications manager and the corresponding sales team is to decide which key participants have to be reached, with which type of message, with what frequency and to what depth should contact be made. Just like individual consumers, each member of the buying centre is an active problem solver and processes information so that personal and organisational goals are achieved.

Influences on the buying centre

Three major influences on organisational buyer behaviour can be identified as stakeholders, the organisational environment and those aspects which the individual brings to the situation (Table 4.2).

Stakeholders develop relationships between the focus organisation and other stakeholders in the network. The nature of the exchange relationship and the style of communications will influence buying decisions. If the relationship between organisations is trusting, mutually supportive and based upon a longer-term perspective (a relational structure) then the behaviour of the buying centre may be seen to be cooperative and

Table 4.2   Major influences on organisational buying behaviour

Stakeholder influences	Organisational influences	Individual influences
Economic conditions	Corporate strategy	Personality
Legislation	Organisational culture and values	Age
Competitor strategies	Resources and costs	Status
Industry regulations	Purchasing policies and procedures	Reward structure and systems
Technological developments	Interpersonal relationships	
Social and cultural values		
Interorganisation relationships		

Source: Based on Webster and Wind (1972).

constructive. If the relationship is formal, regular, unsupportive and based upon short-term convenience (a market structure-based relationship) then the purchase behaviour may be observed as courteous yet distant.

Without doubt the major determinant of the organisational environment is the cost associated with switching from one supplier to another (Bowersox and Cooper, 1992). When an organisation chooses to enter into a buying relationship with another organisation, an investment is made in time, people, assets and systems. Should the relationship with the new supplier fail to work satisfactorily, then a cost is incurred in switching to another supplier. It is these switching costs that heavily influence buying decisions. The higher the potential switching costs, the greater the loss in flexibility and the greater the need to make the relationship appropriate at the outset.

Behaviour within the buying centre is also largely determined by the interpersonal relationships of the members of the centre.

Behaviour within the buying centre is also largely determined by the interpersonal relationships of the members of the centre. Participation in the buying centre has been shown to be highly influenced by individuals' perceptions of the personal consequences of their contribution to each of the stages in the process. The more that individuals think they will be blamed for a bad decision or praised for a good decision, the greater their participation, influence and visible DMU-related activity (McQuiston and Dickson, 1991). The nature and dispersal of power within the unit can influence the decisions that are made. Power is increasingly viewed from the perspective of an individual's ability to control the flow of information and the deployment of resources (Spekman and Gronhaug, 1986). This approach reflects a network approach to, in this case, intraorganisational communications.

From a communications perspective there is strong evidence that the provision/collection of information is a major contributor to risk reduction (Mitchell, 1995). Figure 4.7 sets out some of the more common approaches used by organisations to reduce risk.

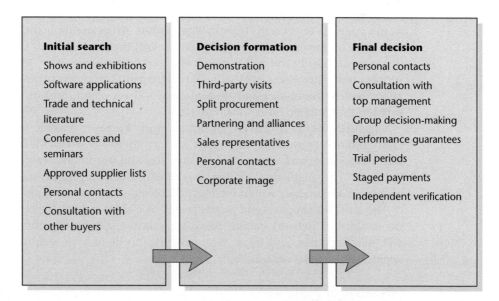

Figure 4.7   Risk reduction approaches for organisational purchase decisions

Buyphases

The organisational buying decision process consists of several stages or buyphases (Robinson *et al.*, 1967). The following sequence of six phases or events is particular to the new task buyclass. Many of these buyphases are ignored or compressed when either of the other two buyclasses are encountered.

Need/problem recognition

Products or services are purchased because of two main events (Cravens and Woodruff, 1986). Difficulties may be encountered first as a result of a need to solve problems, such as a stock-out or new government regulations, and, secondly, as a response to opportunities to improve performance or enter new markets. Essentially, the need/recognition phase is the identification of a gap. This is the gap between the benefits an organisation has now and the benefits it would like to have. For example, when a photocopier breaks down or fails to meet the needs of the organisation, the communication benefits it offers are missed by the users. This gap can be bridged by using a different machine on a temporary basis or by buying a new machine that provides the range of benefits required.

Product specification

As a result of identifying a problem and the size of the gap, influencers and users can determine the desired characteristics of the product needed to resolve the problem. This may take the form of a general description or may require a much more detailed analysis and the creation of a specification for a particular product. What sort of photocopier is required? What is it expected to achieve? How many documents should it copy per minute? Is a collator or tray required? This is an important part of the process, because if it is executed properly it will narrow the supplier search and save on the costs associated with evaluation prior to a final decision.

Supplier and product search

At this stage the buyer actively seeks organisations who can supply the necessary product. There are two main issues at this point. Will the product reach the required performance standards and will it match the specification? Secondly, will the potential supplier meet the other organisational requirements? In most circumstances organisations review the market and their internal sources of information and arrive at a decision that is based on rational criteria.

Organisations, as we have seen before, work wherever possible to reduce uncertainty and risk. By working with others who are known, of whom the organisation has direct experience and who can be trusted, risk and uncertainty can be reduced substantially. This highlights another reason why many organisations seek relational exchanges and operate within established networks and seek to support each other.

The quest for suppliers and products may be a short task for the buyer; however, if the established network cannot provide a solution, the buying organisation has to seek new suppliers, and hence new networks, to be able to identify and short-list appropriate supplier organisations.

Evaluation of proposals

Depending upon the complexity and value of the potential order(s), the proposal is a vital part of the communication plan and should be prepared professionally. The proposals of the short-listed organisations are reviewed in the context of two main criteria: the product specification and the evaluation of the supplying organisation. If the organisation is already a part of the network, little search and review time need be allocated. If the proposed supplier is new to the organisation, a review may be necessary to establish whether it will be appropriate (in terms of price, delivery and service) and whether there is the potential for a long-term relationship or whether this is a single purchase that is unlikely to be repeated.

Once again, therefore, is the relationship going to be a market exchange or a relational exchange? The actions of both organisations, and of some of the other organisations in the network to the new entrant, are going to be critical in determining the form and nature of future relationships.

Supplier selection

The buying centre will undertake a supplier analysis and use a variety of criteria depending upon the particular type of item sought. This selection process takes place in the light of the comments made in the previous section. A further useful perspective is to view supplier organisations as a continuum, from reliance on a single source to the use of a wide variety of suppliers of the same product.

Jackson (1985) proposed that organisations might buy a product from a range of different suppliers, in other words a range of multiple sources are maintained (a practice of many government departments). She labelled this approach 'always a share', as several suppliers are given the opportunity to share the business available to the buying centre. The major disadvantage is that this approach fails to drive cost as low as possible, as the discounts derived from volume sales are not achieved. The advantage to the buying centre is that a relatively small investment is required and little risk is entailed in following such a strategy.

At the other end of the continuum are organisations that only use a single-source supplier. All purchases are made from the single source until circumstances change to such a degree that the buyer's needs are no longer being satisfied. Jackson referred to these organisations as 'lost for good', because once a relationship with a new organisation has been developed, they are lost for good to the original supplier. An increasing number of organisations are choosing to enter alliances with a limited number or even single-source suppliers. The objective is to build a long-term relationship, work together to build quality and help each other achieve their goals. Outsourcing manufacturing activities for non-core activities has increased, and this has moved the focus of communications from an internal to an external perspective.

The objective is to build a long-term relationship, work together to build quality and help each other achieve their goals.

Evaluation

The order is written against the selected supplier and immediately the supplier is monitored and performance is evaluated against such diverse criteria as responsiveness to enquiries and modifications to the specification and timing of delivery. When the product is delivered it may reach the stated specification but fail to satisfy the original need. This is a case where the specification needs to be rewritten before any future orders are placed.

Organisational buying has shifted from a one-to-one dyadic encounter, salesperson to buyer, to a position where a buying team meets a selling team. The skills associated with this process are different and are becoming much more sophisticated, and the demands on both buyers and sellers are more pronounced. The processes of buying and selling are complex and interactive.

Developments in the environment can impact on a consumer or organisation buyer and change both the way decisions are made and their nature. For example, the decision to purchase new plant and machinery requires consideration of the future cash flows generated by the capital item. Many people will be involved in the decision, and the time necessary for consultation may mean that other parts of the decision-making process are completed simultaneously.

There are a number of other issues concerned with the manner in which the members of a buying centre interact and make choices. An interesting new approach to strategic management considers the subjective, cognitive thoughts of the strategist to be more important than has been considered previously. Porter (1980), Ansoff and McDonnell (1990) and others, in what is referred to as the design school of thought, assume that strategic decisions result from rational, logical analysis and interpretation of the environment.

An alternative view is that as environments are too complex and dynamic for objective analysis to be any practical use (Simon, 1976); then strategy or choices are fashioned from individuals' interpretations of their environment. Projections of historical data in uncertain highly unpredictable environments mean that strategists, or members of the buying centre in this case, will rely more on knowledge and experience as the main platform for decision-making and selection among options (Rutter, 1994).

Unifying models of buyer decision-making

The models of decision-making presented here and in the literature are important because they focus attention on key issues and bring out the priorities. They help the development of marketing communications by segregating audiences according to their situational needs. However, two points of contention concern the implied rationality of decision-making, particularly in organisational contexts and the assumption that consumer decision-making is different to organisational decision-making.

For example, there is immediate similarity between the EPS, LPS and RRB consumer-related purchase states and the new task, modified rebuy and rebuy states associated with organisational buying. Risk and involvement are relevant to both categories and, although the antecedents may vary, the marketing communications used to alleviate or reduce these conditions are essentially the same, just deployed in different ways. Wilson (2000) explores the issues related to rationality and implied differences. For example, consumers make product-related purchase decisions based on a wide array of inputs from other people and not just those in the immediate family environment. This is akin to group buying dynamics associated with the DMU. He argues that the rationality normally associated with organisational decision-making is misplaced, suggesting that in some circumstances the protracted nature of decision-making is more a reflection of organisational culture and the need to follow bureaucratic procedures and to show due diligence. In addition, issues concerning established behaviour patterns, difficulties and reluctance to break with established (purchasing) practices, intra- and interorganisational politics and relationships, and the costs associated with supplier switching all contribute to a more interpretive

Consumers make product-related purchase decisions based on a wide array of inputs from other people and not just those in the immediate family environment.

understanding of organisational decision-making. Further support for this view is given by Mason and Gray (1999), who refer to the characteristics of decision-making in the air business passenger travel market and note some strong similarities between the two main groups.

Many of the characteristics of both consumer and organisational decision-making show greater similarities than normally assumed.

What needs to be considered is that many of the characteristics of both consumer and organisational decision-making show greater similarities than normally assumed (or taught). The implication for marketing communications is that a richer deeper understanding of these processes and characteristics may encourage the development of more effective communications.

Summary

The processes which buyers use to make purchase decisions differ according to a variety of factors. These vary with the nature of the purchase situation; that is, whether the purchase is orientated to consumer or organisational buying and the depth of experience held by the buyer. Other factors concerned are the levels of perceived risk, involvement, knowledge and the number of others who are contributing to the final outcome.

Some of the decision processes that have been presented in this chapter appear to be linear and based upon logic and reason. This is not the case, as decisions are often the result of experience, knowledge and an interpretive view of the environment. Therefore, the decision processes used by buyers are not always sequential, nor do they reflect a rational approach to resolving problems and needs.

Marketing communications need to be based on an understanding of the decision processes used by buyers in the targeted market. This means that the content and style of messages and the form of delivery by the tools of the promotional mix (Chapters 20–31) can be dovetailed closely to the needs of the receivers. This also demonstrates how the realm of understanding is an important issue in effective communications.

Review questions

1. Describe the general decision-making process.
2. What are EPS, LPS and RRB?
3. Select a product and a service which you have used recently and relate the six elements of perceived risk to both of them. How do the elements of risk differ?
4. Explain the three broad interpretations of involvement. How does involvement differ from perceived risk?
5. Describe the high- and low-involvement decision-making processes.
6. Highlight the differences between consumer and organisational buying.
7. What are buyclasses and buying centres?
8. How might a salesperson successfully utilise knowledge about the buying centre?
9. Explain the components of the various buyphases.

10. What are the main communication differences between consumer-orientated and business-to-business orientated marketing communications?

MINI CASE

This mini case was written by Ruth Ashford, Senior Lecturer in Public Relations and Marketing Communications at The Manchester Metropolitan Business School.

Motorola

V3688 Cellular phone: 'SMALL is big' – the South Asian PR campaign

Introduction

Motorola sought to reinforce its technology leadership through the launch of its V3688. Qualitative research on this product was conducted in key markets in the South Asian region and findings engaged to develop a communications plan to overcome consumers' negative perceptions of the phone. This case identifies the successful launch of the Motorola V3688 phone in nine South Asian countries.

Motorola's V3688 cellular phones

The Motorola V3688 phone was almost 50% smaller than many of its competitors' offerings. The V3688 pushed the technology envelope one step further, establishing leadership in size, weight and features. The shape of this phone was dramatised with a unique streamlined design and the world's smallest, lightest dual-band cellular phone at the time of launch. The company believed that its features surpassed expectation of what one cellular phone could embody.

Consumer research

Motorola conducted focus groups in Asian regions and found that they needed to address consumers' concerns about their perceptions of poor product performance due to the V3688's small size and light weight. Indeed, this research confirmed that customers perceived the product as toy-like and potentially fragile. Males in Australia perceived it to be small and feminine. Some consumers thought that competitors' products (i.e. Nokia's and Ericsson's) were 'cooler' than Motorola's. Indeed, this research highlighted that there were complex levels of risk perceptions related to performance, physical, social and ego issues. Thus, Motorola had to devise a communications plan to help to alleviate these levels of risk during the consumer decision-making process. Motorola realised that the communications campaign would need to address the problem of the V3688 product being perceived as toy-like, potentially fragile and unfashionable.

Communications campaign

The communication objectives were as follows:

To dramatise the launch of the innovative Motorola V3688 in South Asia.

To clearly differentiate the V3688 in the market place and communicate the 'WOW' factor.

To re-establish and reinforce Motorola's leadership in the market.

Strategic decisions and message

The positioning strategy was to reposition Motorola as the brand of choice for cellular phones and reinforce innovation and technology through the product offerings. The campaign aimed to differentiate the V3688 as the phone that would surpass expectations of what one cellular phone could embody at that time.

One of the key requirements was to develop the brand further and to reduce consumers' perceptions of risk. Therefore, the corporate brand was developed as:

ingenious 5 WOW (in form and function);

inspiring = anything is possible;

always ahead = innovative and style you want to use *now*;

part of you – like your watch or wallet.

The campaign was anchored by a core concept: 'SMALL is Big'. Aimed at the upwardly mobile, style-conscious consumer, this communicated the point of product differentiation (small in size, big on features), with a cool, memorable and humorous tagline. This was used to create hype and reinforced the style factor of the product, as well as the brand, in an effort to reduce consumers' perception of risk.

PR campaign execution

The PR agency Burson-Marsteller devised a campaign for the client – Motorola – with the core concept which could travel across all markets and audiences in the Asian regions. The 'SMALL is big' concept was successful because it was product focused and directly communicated a tangible benefit, with the main point of differentiation in the message.

In Singapore, a high-impact media launch event was staged. Held in a very fashionable venue, a stylish interactive art mystery drama was presented. The Motorola V3688 was central to solving the plot. At this event, journalists experienced first-hand the benefits and features of the product as they were required to use the phone to enable them to obtain 'clues' to solve the mystery. The 'SMALL is big' concept was also dramatised through exaggeration of the magnitude and size of all elements which were present at the event, such as big drinks and big hors d'oeuvres.

Pre-written feature stories were place in key lifestyle media. The titles included 'Motorola sizes up what's BIG today' and 'SMALL things in store'. In particular, a readers' write-in promotion hosted by Motorola with a leading female magazine attracted over 600 consumers to write in with their 'favourite small things in life'. In the business media, release titles included 'The big news from Motorola comes in a small package' and 'Size doesn't matter if you mean serious business'.

Evaluation of success

Motorola reached launch sales objectives for South Asia and in the media and it experienced the first stages of a perceptual shift relating to the brand. Research illustrated that the brand was now seen as a style and technology innovator. The key phone attributes appeared in 85% of all press coverage and 90% of the stories included all key messages.

Clearly this PR campaign indicates that the management of clear and credible brand messages are very important to change consumer's perceptions of risk and thus a successful outcome was achieved.

This case has been adapted from the IPRA Gold Awards submissions with the kind permission of IPRA, Belina Tan from Burson-Marsteller (SEA) Ltd and Jeanette Tan from Motorola Electronics Pte. Ltd.

Mini-case questions

1. Explain the further elements of perceived risk which may have been identified in Motorola's consumer research and explain how perceived risk differs from involvement.
2. Considering the key issues which Motorola was facing, what other possible positioning opportunities could have been considered?
3. Explain the possible problems which marketing communicators could face when working with external agencies on such campaigns.

References

Ansoff, H.I. and McDonnell, E.J. (1990) *Implanting Strategic Management*, 2nd edn. Hemel Hempstead: Prentice Hall.

Ashford, R., Cuthbert, P. and Shani, N. (2000) Perceived risk and consumer decision making related to health services: a comparative study. *International Journal of Nonprofit and Voluntary Sector Marketing,* 5(1), pp. 58–72.

Batra, R. and Ray, M.L. (1983) Operationalizing involvement as depth and quality of response. In *Advances in Consumer Research* (eds R.P. Bagozzi and A.M. Tybout), Vol. **10**, pp. 309–13. Ann Arbor, MI: Association for Consumer Research.

Bonoma, T.V. (1982) Major sales: who really does the buying? *Harvard Business Review* (May/June), p. 113.

Bowersox, D. and Cooper, M. (1992) *Strategic Marketing Channel Management.* New York: McGraw-Hill.

Clarke, A. (2001) Racing to broaden its appeal. *Promotions and Incentives* (January, pp. 26–28.

Cravens, D. and Woodruff, R. (1986) *Marketing.* Reading, MA: Addison-Wesley.

Harris, G. (1987) The implications of low involvement theory for advertising effectiveness. *International Journal of Advertising,* **6**, pp. 207–21.

Heath, R. (2000) Low-involvement processing, *Admap* (March), pp. 14–16.

Hirschmann, E.C. and Holbrook, M.B. (1982) Hedonic consumption: emerging concepts, methods and propositions. *Journal of Marketing,* **46** (Summer), pp. 92–101.

Jackson, B. (1985) Build customer relationships that last. *Harvard Business Review,* **63**(6), pp. 120–8.

Kapferer, J.N. and Laurent, G. (1985) Consumer involvement profiles: a new practical approach to consumer involvement. *Journal of Advertising Research,* **25** (6), pp. 48–56.

Laaksonen, P. (1994) *Consumer Involvement: Concepts and Research.* London: Routledge.

Mason, K.J. and Gray, R. (1999) Stakeholders in a hybrid market: the example of air business passenger travel. *European Journal of Marketing,* 33(9/10), pp. 844–58.

McQuiston, D.H. and Dickson, P.R. (1991) The effect of perceived personal consequences on participation and influence in organisational buying. *Journal of Business,* **23**, pp. 159–77.

Mitchell, V.-M. (1995) Organisational risk perception and reduction: a literature review. *British Journal of Management,* **6**, pp. 115–33.

Mitchell, V.-M., (1999) Consumer perceived risk: conceptualisations and models. *European Journal of Marketing ,* **33**(1/2), pp. 163–95.

Mitchell, V-W. and Boustani, P. (1994) A preliminary investigation into pre and post-purchase risk perception and reduction. *European Journal of Marketing,* **28**(1), pp. 56–71.

Porter, M.E. (1980) *Competitive Strategy: Techniques for Analysing Industries and Competitors.* New York: Free Press.

Ratchford, B.T. (1987) New insights about the FCB grid. *Journal of Advertising Research* (August/September), pp. 24–38.

Robinson, P.J., Faris, C.W. and Wind, Y. (1967) *Industrial Buying and Creative Marketing.* Boston, MA: Allyn & Bacon.

Rossiter, J.R., Percy, L. and Donovan, R.J. (1991) A better advertising planning grid. *Journal of Advertising Research* (October/November), pp. 11–21.

Rutter, K.A. (1994) Strategy formulation in turbulent times: the need for counselling methods. Unpublished working paper, University of Portsmouth.

Schiffman, L. and Kanuk, L. (1991) *Consumer Behavior.* Englewood Cliffs, NJ: Prentice Hall.

Settle, R.B. and Alreck, P. (1989) Reducing buyers' sense of risk. *Marketing Communications* (January), pp. 34–40.

Simon, H.A. (1976) *Administrative Behaviour: A Study of Decision Making Processes in Administrative Organisations.* New York: Free Press.

Spekman, R.E. and Gronhaug, K. (1986) Conceptual and methodological issues in buying centre research. *European Journal of Marketing,* **20**(7), pp. 50–63.

Stone, R.N. and Gronhaug, K. (1993) Perceived risk: further considerations for the marketing discipline. *European Journal of Marketing*, **27**(3), pp. 39–50.

Vaughn, R. (1980) How advertising works: a planning model. *Journal of Advertising Research* (October), pp. 27–33.

Webster, F.E. and Wind, Y. (1972) *Organizational Buying Behaviour*. Englewood Cliffs, NJ: Prentice Hall.

Wilson, D.F. (2000) Why divide consumer and organisational buyer behaviour? *European Journal of Marketing*, **34**(7), pp. 780–96.

Zaichkowsky, J. (1985) Measuring the involvement constraint. *Journal of Consumer Research*, **12**, pp. 341–52.

Purpose and audiences

In order to deliver and maintain effective marketing communications it is important to communicate within the context of the organisation's corporate goals, its marketing intentions and the communication needs and segment characteristics of the relevant target audience.

AIMS AND OBJECTIVES

The aim of this chapter is to examine marketing communications in the light of an organisation's corporate goals and marketing plans.

The objectives of this chapter are:

1. To appreciate the essence of corporate strategy and how the mission provides a context for the marketing (corporate) communications activities.

2. To understand the role of marketing communications in the context of corporate and business-level strategies.

3. To introduce the pivotal role marketing strategy has in the development of marketing communications.

4. To appreciate how segmentation and target marketing assist the development of marketing communications.

5. To provide an example of psychographic segmentation.

6. To appraise the product life cycle and consider its contribution to marketing communications .

7. To introduce the notion of brand equity as a tool for developing marketing communications.

Introduction

The business arena in which an organisation's corporate and product-based communications are to be deployed forms an important contextual element. The achievement of integrated marketing communications (see Chapter 19) requires that all communications be internally compatible with the mission and values of the organisation. These overarching goals are normally embedded within a corporate philosophy that in turn is a reflection of the dominant culture. This philosophy provides a context within which marketing communications are required to operate and convey the strategic intent of the organisation. In themselves the communications provide a further context for the delivery of the strategies, in particular a context whereby organisational members and non-members decode, interpret and respond to the organisation's messages.

Marketing communications is an important activity that must complement the corporate objectives and provide a context through which the philosophy and culture of the organisation are perpetuated. Therefore, marketing communications and the corporate intent are firmly intertwined. Figure 5.1 sets out the interrelationship between these two components.

Marketing communications and the corporate intent are firmly intertwined.

The organisation's mission

The direction and strategy of the organisation are often embedded within its mission and the vision that critical members have of the organisation. An organisation's mission and stated philosophy can form an important dimension which not only shapes relationships with customers, shareholders, suppliers, employees and the general public but also serves to influence the organisation's marketing (and communications) activities that follow.

A mission consists of four interrelated elements: purpose, strategy, behaviour standards and values.

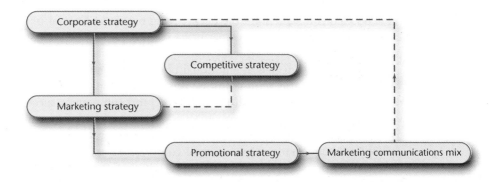

Figure 5.1   The relationship of marketing communications to corporate strategy.

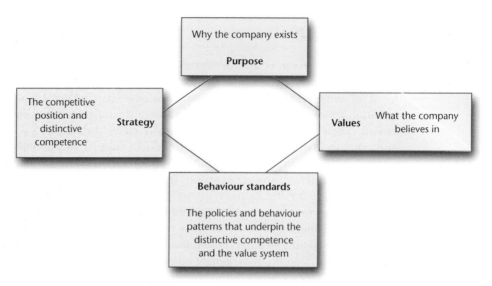

Figure 5.2 The Ashridge mission model. Reprinted from Campbell and Yeung (1991), with permission from Elsevier Science.

According to Campbell and Yeung (1991), a mission consists of four interrelated elements: purpose, strategy, behaviour standards and values (Figure 5.2).

Purpose refers to the question about what the organisation seeks to achieve. Three types were identified: those who are in business just to satisfy shareholders (e.g. Hanson), those who seek to satisfy a range of stakeholders (GlaxoSmithKline) and those that seek to achieve or contribute toward a form of organisational self-actualisation, one where the organisation sets out to accomplish a long-term aim which contributes positively to the needs of society (The Body Shop).

Strategy sets out the way in which the purpose is to be fulfilled. It determines the way the business will compete and the position and advantages it will strive to achieve.

Standards of behaviour are guidelines for the people who are required to action the strategy and to assist them to decide what to do. The authors consider the need for a 'moral rationale to run alongside the commercial rationale'. This is the way people in this organisation are expected to behave.

The final element concerns the *values* of the organisation and is an extension of the previous element. Values are the deeper-lying beliefs and moral underpinnings that are an important part of an organisation's culture. Here there is a concern for what is morally right and what is ethically the correct behaviour.

The impact and degree of emotional bond that organisational members develop with the mission and philosophy of the organisation are important because this degree of bonding is reflected in the energy and subsequent success of the organisation in achieving its aims and objectives. The communications must reflect these four elements by conveying conviction, consistency and a sense of total integration and coordination. In reality, of course, many mission statements are either ill-conceived or badly written with the result that the statement adds very little. Research into US mission statements by Leuthesser and Kohli (1997), suggest that the messages tend to be grouped into benefits, values, identity and focus. See Table 5.1.

Table 5.1   Classification of messages conveyed through mission statements

Message	Explanation
Benefits	For customers = claims of superior value. For employees = claims of superior safety, security and friendliness. For shareholders = claims concerning superior growth, dividends and security.
Value	Refer to the organisation's value system and its norms. For example, values concerning the importance of long-term relationships with customers and suppliers.
Identity	How the organisation wants to be perceived by all its stakeholders.
Focus	Refers to the scope of the activities undertaken by the organisation and often sets out the boundaries.

Source: Adapted from Leuthesser and Kohli (1997). Reprinted with kind permission of *Business Horizons* (3), Copyright (1997) by the Board of Trustees at Indiana University, Kelley School of Business.

Marketing strategy

The marketing plan is a subset of the marketing strategy, which in turn is a part of the business plan and strategy. Marketing communications seeks to deliver the essence of the corporate goals, the direction and intention of the business plan and the conviction and detail of the marketing plan, to its target markets. In other words, marketing communications should provide a means by which the organisation communicates its offering to meet the buyer's needs. It does this in the context of the organisation's overall mission and corporate culture:

Marketing communications should provide a means by which the organisation communicates its offering to meet the buyer's needs.

- It clarifies the role of communications in the context of particular corporate, business and marketing strategies and plans.

- It prevents duplication and confusion among those involved in the development and execution of a communication strategy.

- It anchors a communication strategy in the sense that communications are given a base, a purpose and a means of evaluating the success of the campaign.

- It provides direction to all personnel associated with the development and implementation of communication strategy.

- It focuses attention on the appropriate target audiences.

The first important point is that, by clearly segregating marketing strategy from communications strategy, the role of communications within marketing is highlighted. The role of the latter is to support and communicate the marketing strategy; that is, *not* to duplicate or formulate another approach to the market. The second point is that communications strategy should establish the most appropriate way of communicating the marketing intentions of an organisation to its various target markets and stakeholder audiences.

Marketing strategy acts as the cornerstone of the development of planned marketing communications. It sets the direction and manner in which the marketing objectives are to be achieved and guides the work of those responsible for marketing communications, those other stakeholders working inside the organisation (e.g. employees) and all stakeholders who are external to the organisation (e.g. advertising agencies).

Refocusing the brand – Crown Paints

In the early 1980s Dulux and Crown Paints held virtually equal shares of the domestic gloss and emulsion markets. By 1988 Crown had just 50% of Dulux's share and by 1997 it held just 33%.

Apart from the arrival of several own brands, the main reason for this decline was Crown's failure to concentrate on the mass market. Its competitive response to Dulux was to move into niche markets and create a range of sub-brands. One of the problems with this approach was that the advertising was fragmented, inconsistent and so thinly spread as to confuse and devalue the brand in the eyes of consumers.

The solution lay first in revising the marketing strategy. This entailed the removal of many of the sub-brands and a refocusing on the core colour range. Advertising was required to bring more emotional values to the brand and general new levels of brand awareness. The strategy required the brand to be repositioned in such a way that it was clearly differentiated from conventional paint communications. To support the advertising, the repositioning exercise needed to be taken into the store. Innovative new packaging and redesigned point-of-purchase materials helped consumers reappraise the brand and restore Crown's market position. See Plate 5.1.

Information kindly supplied by Rozina Ali, Akzo Nobel

Marketing strategy is the process whereby target markets are identified and selected. Marketing plans are developed for each selected market segment in order that the needs of buyers in each target group may be satisfied. Each marketing plan consists of the main elements of the marketing mix (see Chapter 1). Each element of this mix has the capacity to communicate in its own right (see Chapter 29 for more details). This management process is systematic and is driven by the need for an organisation to meet and exceed its corporate and marketing objectives. According to Dibb *et al.* (1991), 'A marketing strategy articulates a plan for the best use of the organisation's resources and tactics to meet its objectives'.

Many organisations are placing increasing importance on loyalty and relationship marketing as a vital part of their marketing strategies. The implementation of this strategy requires the use of marketing communications to deliver the key messages and to maintain the dialogue that is crucial to the success of the strategy.

Redirecting the overall strategy – Boots

Boots had failed to adapt to changing market conditions and at the turn of the century its position as one of the UK's premier retail institutions was, like Marks and Spencer, under real threat. Change was necessary if the company was to survive.

The change strategy that was implemented was essentially a massive corporate repositioning exercise to turn Boots into an upmarket supplier of health and beauty products and services (Rushe and Hamilton, 2001).

Apart from restructuring the company to provide a more integrated and complementary portfolio and adjusting the quality of management, the repositioning involved the establishment of two new types of store. One is convenience stores with numerous tills for shoppers in a hurry and the other is for more upmarket health and beauty services. These include opticians, chiropodists, herbalists and dentists. Some stores might even have a gym so that a whole range of health services might be provided.

The communication strategies pursued by the Boots organisation need to reflect this repositioning and communicate information to clarify what the new stores are and convey a fresh set of brand values and associations. The business context for Boots is changing: a new vision, new brands, new values and a new set of associations that need to be established in a tightening market place where the financial community is looking for reasons to increase the value of the Boots share price.

The importance of using the marketing strategy as the base for the communications strategy and for not duplicating it must not be overlooked. This chapter will look first at the process of target market selection and review the elements of the mix in the context of communications.

Target marketing: segmentation

Segmentation is an established and acknowledged technique for dividing a mass market into identifiable subunits, in order that the individual needs of buyers and potential buyers can be more easily satisfied.

The broad process of segmenting a market is set out in Figure 5.3. Essentially, market segmentation seeks to establish particular groups or clusters of buyers. As indicated above, target marketing is the process whereby specific segments are selected and marketing plans are then developed to satisfy the needs of the potential buyers in the chosen segments. The development, or rather identification, of segments can be perceived as opportunities, and, as Beane and Ennis (1987) suggest, 'A company with limited resources needs to pick only the best opportunities to pursue'.

The importance of using the marketing strategy as the base for the communications strategy and for not duplicating it must not be overlooked.

This process of segmentation is necessary because a single product is unlikely to meet the needs of all customers in a mass market. If it were, then a single type of toothpaste, chocolate bar or car would meet all of our needs. This is not so, and there are a host of products and brands seeking to satisfy particular buyer needs. For example, ask yourself the question, 'Why do I use toothpaste?' The answer, most probably, is one of the following:

1. You want dental hygiene.

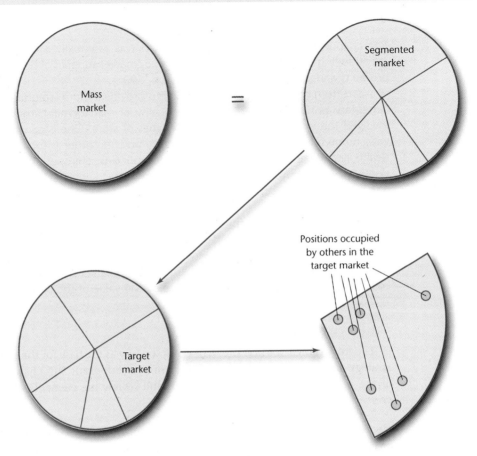

Figure 5.3   The process of target marketing.

2. You like fresh breath and you don't want to offend others.

3. You want white, shining teeth.

4. You like the fresh oral sensation.

5. Other products (e.g. water, soap) do not taste very good.

Whatever the reason, it is unlikely that given a choice we would all choose the same product. In what is now regarded as a classic study, Russell Haley (1968) undertook some pioneering research in this field and from it he established four distinct types of customer. Even after 30 years have elapsed this typology remains a potent practical example of market segmentation: those who bought toothpaste for white teeth (sociables), those who wished to prevent decay (worriers), those who liked the taste and refreshment properties (sensors) and finally those who bought on a price basis (independents). Each of these groups has particular demographic, behaviouristic and psychographic characteristics which can be seen in Table 5.2.

It is not surprising that a range of toothpaste products has been developed that attempts to satisfy the needs of different buyers, for example, Macleans for fresh breath, Crest for dental hygiene, Sensodyne for those sensitive to hot and cold drinks and numerous others promoted on special offers for those independent buyers looking for a low price. There are others who are not very interested in the product and

Table 5.2   Benefit segments for the toothpaste market

Segment name	The sensory segment	The sociables	The worriers	The independents
Principal benefit sought	Flavour, product appearance	Brightness of teeth	Decay prevention	Price
Demographic strengths	Children	Teens, young people	Large families	Men
Special behavioural characteristics	Users of spearmint-flavoured toothpaste	Smokers	Heavy users	Heavy users
Brands disproportionately favoured	Colgate, Stripe	Macleans, Plus White, Ultra Brite	Crest, Sensodyne	Brands on sale
Personality characteristics	High self-involvement	High sociability	High hypochondriasis	High autonomy
Lifestyle characteristics	Hedonistic	Active	Conservative	Value oriented

Source: Haley (1968); used with kind permission.

have continued using a brand that others in their current or past households are comfortable with.

Buyers, therefore, can be clustered or grouped into segments. By definition, each segment has its own specific characteristics and this isolation of buyers with similar lifestyles, needs and outlook permits a greater understanding and appreciation of each cluster. Such an approach is possible with all stakeholders, although very often organisations identify buyers but fail to recognise the different needs of their other stakeholders.

The more we know and understand about all of an organisation's stakeholders and are able to develop a common realm of understanding, the more effective will be the communications.

The more we know and understand about all of an organisation's stakeholders and are able to develop a common realm of understanding, the more effective will be the communications with each target audience. Recognising the existence of different stakeholders, and the increasing impact some stakeholders have upon each other, means that a greater number and variety of messages have to be transmitted.

Market segmentation, therefore, is the division of a mass market into distinct groups which have common characteristics, needs and similar responses to marketing actions. How then can a market be subdivided? Some of the more common methods are as follows.

Bases for segmentation

Demographic

This is the most basic and most often used method of segmenting a market. The underlying principle is that the age, sex, occupation, level of education, religion, social class and income characteristics determine, to a large extent, a potential buyer's ability to enter into an exchange relationship or transaction. Cosmetics are largely targeted at women and toys at appropriate age groupings. Lego has developed a range of products for targeting at children at different stages in their development: Duplo for the under 4-year-olds, Lego System for the 4–8-year-olds and Lego Technic for 8–13-year-old children. All the sets are integrated with one another and continuity is maintained. Interestingly, Lego found that 5-year-old girls tended not to use the product as much as boys. The reason was found to be that girls played in a way that required their imagination to be stimulated differently from boys. Lego developed products such as Paradisa and Scala to meets these needs.

The advertising industry, according to Oliver (1994), was one of the first to build data on socioeconomic grade, an attempt to combine class, type of employment and income (Table 5.3). This has persisted and, despite its shortcomings, is used a great deal by a large number of marketers. The market research industry uses this approach frequently to classify markets. While this high level of credibility might promote further use, the approach can be misleading and prone to generalisations. People are, increasingly, capable of moving between groups, and the disposable income of a member of one group may well be more than that of a group above. That is, a C2 plumber may have a greater income than a C1 office administrator. The argument for their retention as valid tools of segmentation is based on the stability of the identifiable purchase patterns, the reliability of income and occupation relationships and the distinct attitude patterns that exist. For example, the ABC1 groups have a future perspective, while the C2DE groups tend to have a perspective based on present circumstances.

Geographic

This type of segmentation is based upon the premise that the needs of potential customers in one geographic area are different from those in another area. For example, it is often said that Scottish beer drinkers prefer heavy bitters, Northerners in England prefer mild, drinkers in the West prefer cider, and in the South lager is the preferred drink. This demarcation may also reflect the way in which promotional messages are received.

Perception of advertising messages is heavily influenced by the culture of particular member countries.

In Europe, perception of advertising messages is heavily influenced by the culture of particular member countries, and broad patterns of perception can be seen in Latin-based countries, as distinct from their northerly partners. In the USA it has been found

Table 5.3 Socioeconomic groups in the United Kingdom (NRS)

Social grade	Social status	Occupation
A	Upper middle class	Higher managerial, administrative or professional
B	Middle class	Intermediate managerial, administrative or professional
C1	Lower middle class	Supervisory or clerical, and junior managerial, administrative or professional
C2	Skilled working class	Skilled manual workers
D	Working class	Semi- or unskilled manual workers
E	Those at the lowest levels or subsistence	State pensioners or widows (no other earner), casual or lowest grade workers

Note: The social grade of an individual is normally based on the occupation of the head of household.

that the perception of advertisements varies from the north-east to the west. The use of print advertisements is dependent very often on geographic areas rather than, say, the level of education attained by the target group. However, this method of segmentation is only useful at the broadest level. The examples given above are only broad generalisations and any marketing strategy founded on such a basis is unlikely to be very successful.

Geodemographic

This type of segmentation has grown out of the need to combine the best of the two previous bases. The most well-known form of geodemographics is called Acorn (a classification of residential neighbourhoods). This tool and others, such as Mosaic and Pinpoint, assume that there is a relationship between the type of housing people live in and their purchase behaviour. At the root of this approach is the ability to use post-codes to send similar messages to similar groups of households, on the basis that where we live determines how we live.

Geodemographics have been significant in the development of direct mail activities which allow for the accurate delivery of personal messages. Indeed, direct mail has offered advertisers and clients the opportunity to send targeted messages to the extent that it is becoming increasingly possible to achieve the ultimate form of segmentation: customisation. Acorn requires the development of customer profiles, and attached to these profiles are media consumption habits, which are an important adjunct to this form of segmentation.

Psychoanalytic

Psychographics involves the subdivision of a market on the basis of personality or lifestyle (Table 5.4). This is determined by an analysis of the activities, interests and opinions (AIO) of the consumer. Lifestyles or patterns of behaviour are a synthesis of the motivations, personality and core values held by individuals. These AIO patterns are reflected in the buying behaviour and decision-making processes of individuals. By identifying and clustering common lifestyles, a correlation with a consumer's product and/or media usage patterns becomes possible. Teanby (1999) reports that the data generated through the AC Nielsen Homescan consumer panel (weekly analysis of the purchases made by 10,500 UK households) are used

Psychographics involves the subdivision of a market on the basis of personality or lifestyle.

Table 5.4   Elements of lifestyle

Activities	Interests	Opinions	Demographics
Work	Family	Themselves	Age
Hobbies	Home	Social issues	Education
Social events	Job	Politics	Income
Vacation	Community	Business	Occupation
Entertainment	Recreation	Economics	Family size
Club membership	Fashion	Education	Dwelling
Community	Food	Products	Geography
Shopping	Media	Future	City size
Sports	Achievements	Culture	Stage in life cycle

Source: Plummer (1974); used with kind permission.

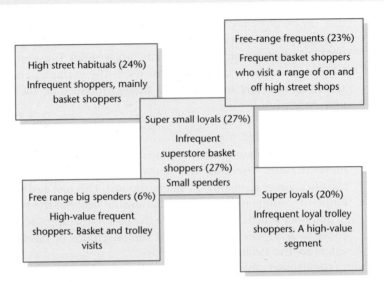

Figure 5.4 Shoppergraphics (UK households), a five-part typology. From Teanby (1999); used with kind permission.

to identify five different types of shopper, from which typologies have been determined. These 'shoppergraphics' can be used not only to determine better marketing strategies but to also communicate with each group more effectively. See Figure 5.4.

The values and lifestyle programme (Vals) developed by SRI International in 1978 classified consumers according to their values and lifestyles. Both Vals 1 and the updated Vals 2 (1989) have been used successfully in the USA. The Values Company is marketing and extending a typology for use in the UK and European markets using Maslow's hierarchy of needs. Three primary motivations (sustenance, inner and outer directed) are used to cluster groups of individuals who share common characteristics. These groupings result in seven segments, each with its own distinctive attitudes, behaviours and decision-making styles. See the social value groups section for more information about each of the social value groups.

Behaviouristic

In this form of segmentation the market is differentiated on the basis of the use of the offering by individuals, the benefits they derive from use, the levels of loyalty buyers display and the stage which buyers have reached in the decision-making process.

Usage

Pareto's rule states that 80% of purchases are made by just 20% of consumers. The development of customer profiles for these groups is a priority task. The main clusters should focus attention upon heavy, medium, light and non-users. In the air travel industry, business customers can be clustered according to the number of times they use particular routes or airlines. There are many outcomes to this type of segmentation, including frequent-flier programmes and the special facilities designed for these business customers.

The main clusters should focus attention upon heavy, medium, light and non-users.

Table 5.5   Five elements of lifestage

Young single	Bank accounts, credit cards, unsecured loans, fashion chain store cards, 'booze and sex' singles holidays
First-time house buyers	Mortgages, insurance, unsecured loans, department store cards
Families with children	Family holidays, life and health assurance, pensions
Empty nesters	Cars, cruise and investment schemes
Pensioners	Financial schemes, holidays for the elderly

Source: Goften (1999); used with kind permission.

Usage of soft drinks can be determined in terms of purchase patterns (two bottles per week), usage situations (parties, picnics or as an alcohol substitute) or purchase location (supermarket, convenience store or wine merchant).

Lifestage

Associated with usage is the concept of lifestage. For a long time marketing activities have been based on the principle that people have varying amounts of disposable income and different needs, at different stages in their lives. Their priorities for spending change at different trigger points and these points or lifestages do not occur at the same date. See Table 5.5.

Not only is the recognition of these lifestages important for reaching new groups as people move through stages but also it is a vitally important aspect of communication strategy in terms of message and media planning. Used alone lifestage information is insufficient and needs to be supplemented with other data drawn from appropriate databases; see the Tesco example below.

Lifestage mailings – Tesco

Tesco distributes a quarterly magazine to nine million loyalty Clubcard holders. However, they do not receive the same version as they are segmented according to lifestage and the recipes and offers are varied accordingly. Information such as the degree of affluence, frequency of shop visits, where you live and which brands are purchased can help build a multidimensional picture. The layered approach helps build a richness of information that enables the development of customer profiles, which can further improve the quality of the communications used to reach them (Goften, 1999).

Social value groups

The social value groups used by The Values Company are based on the premise that people have a set of values, beliefs and motivations that are relatively consistent through time. It has been shown that there is a strong correlation between people's values and their purchase behaviour. This is because individuals' values provide one of the primary ways of scanning their environment and of interpreting and understanding the variety of cues presented to them.

While individual experiences may shape interpretation and understanding, people who hold similar values tend to behave in a cohesive way. It is this cohesion that provides the depth and richness of this approach to segmentation. While the typologies that have emerged from various longitudinal studies in the UK (and the USA) are of direct benefit to strategic management and for identifying key changes in society and future market opportunities, the key benefits for marketing communications are for brand (re)positioning (Chapter 13), message strategy (Chapter 21), media planning (Chapter 22) and corporate identity issues (Chapter 16).

To appreciate the nature and scope of the social value groups (Figure 5.5) it is necessary to understand the broad motivational groups and subgroups into which the population has been classified.

Inner-directed people are orientated towards personal growth and individual freedom, and are concerned about people. They tend to prefer niche, high-quality markets, and their drive for individualism may lead them to a small, round-the-corner restaurant rather than the expensive, well-known and status-orientated restaurant where 'anybody who is anybody' must be seen.

Outer-directed people have a more competitive outlook on life than the inner-directed group. They are continually seeking to improve their position and moving forward their careers and their social lives. They have a more materialistic approach and use products to signal their position.

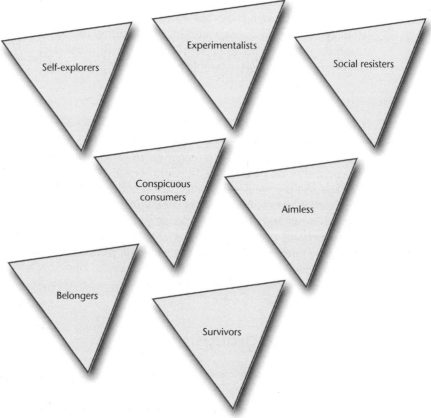

Figure 5.5   Social value groups.

Sustenance-driven people are concerned about the maintenance of the status quo. Consequently, safety, security and comfort are prime issues. Purchase behaviour is characterised by caution, low risk and tradition.

Readers will be able to see the similarity of these main groups to those of Maslow's hierarchy of needs (see Mullins, 1999).

The following material attempts to present a snapshot of the seven value groups into which the population has been classified. Further information can be provided by The Values Company Ltd.

Self-explorers (11% of the population)

These people cannot tolerate restriction unless it is self-imposed. They are independent and modern in outlook, economically comfortable and psychologically complex. They are driven by their needs for self-expression and personal satisfaction. They tend to be tolerant, confident, intelligent, imaginative and responsive.

Products promoted for their newness are unlikely to be received very well by this group. Promotional messages based on time saving or an environmental basis have a greater chance of success. People in this group have a low television diet but consume a lot of information in a variety of publications, which include *Marie Claire*, *Elle*, *Q* and newspapers such as the *Mail on Sunday* and *The Guardian*. 'Horizon', classical British costume dramas, and 'Have I Got News for You?' are the more likely television programmes watched by this group.

Core values are inner directed.

Experimentalists (5% of the population)

These people are characterised by their need for new ideas and experiences. Predominantly men in their late 20s and early 30s, experimentalists are energetic, confident, gregarious and intelligent. This group wants to find exciting approaches to life. Work is important for personal growth, but security within work is not required.

Because experimentalists enjoy an above-average level of risk-taking, new products are very attractive to them. To some extent these people are impulsive in their desire to experiment with innovations. However, they are just as likely to become bored and will drop products just as quickly. They are crucial to the development of markets, not to those that are mature or established. For example, they helped create the Häagen-Dazs market share, but cannot be relied on to be users in five years' time.

Packaging and the presentation of promotional messages are important attributes looked for by this group. Their media consumption is heavy and reveals widespread tastes. Newspapers such as the *Sun* and the *Sunday Mirror* feature a great deal. *Empire*, *Perfect Home* and various special-interest magazines are also popular. Because they are out a great deal their television consumption is light, but they prefer programmes such as *Ali G*, *Big Breakfast* and *Top of the Pops*.

Core values are combined inner and outer directed.

Conspicuous consumers (18% of the population)

This is a significant group who are marked by their strong concern for appearances, where value is expressed in the eyes of others. It is the image of themselves that is important. Energy is directed to generating a romantic notion of their own personal status through material possessions.

Conspicuous consumers use a variety of cues in order that others can develop an image of them with respect to status, personality and acceptability. Therefore, they use products that others use in order to gain respect and recognition of personal worth. Importance is attached to the opinion of others, and in advertising messages the use of the 'expert' can be useful because these people like to be able to be in the know. Work serves as an instrument in order that limited status needs are fulfilled, but is really only a means by which their standard of living can be improved.

By emphasising status, personality and lifestyle, messages aimed at this group are more likely to be received well. As decision-making is often difficult for these people, strong brand and corporate-based communications can provide reassurance and the confidence to buy. Advertisements such as those for American Express and Rolex, which feature well-known style-orientated celebrities, are powerful and effective in communicating with this group.

Living, House Beautiful and *Company* are popular magazines because they help to romanticise their lives. Mass soaps such as *Neighbours* and *EastEnders* are very popular, as are other mainstream programmes such as *They Think its All Over* and *The Clothes Show*.

Core values are outer directed.

Belongers (20% of the population)

This group is strongly orientated towards the family, country and establishment, and has a great deal of trust in large established organisations. The belonger prefers the family environment partly because of the comfort of rigid routines and the reassurance that stability brings. They are Mr and Mrs (not Ms) Average.

Work is important to members of this group, but they know their rights and place in society and do not seek to disturb the balance, as they see it. For example, it is unlikely that belongers would complain about any goods or services, and research suggests that they are more satisfied than any other group with newspapers, banks, TV and health issues.

Belongers buy large safe brands which are recommended with a parental appeal or by a figure of authority (e.g. tyres or home burglar alarms endorsed by the police force). They will also drop a brand if it lets them down or fails to get family acceptance. Belongers feel that they must do well for their children, so the parental appeal and approval is of particular significance to them. The *Mail on Sunday, Sun* and the *Express* are the papers most likely to be read by this group. Their television consumption is slightly above average and is geared towards the 'proper' channels, i.e. BBC and ITV, but not Channel 4 or any of the cable or satellite offerings. Nice safe programmes appear to be the most popular, e.g. *Antiques Roadshow, Only Fools and Horses* and *BBC News*. Advertisements for the Churchill Insurance (British Bulldog logo) Halifax (safe, secure houses) and Abbey National are well received by this group.

Core values are sustenance to outer driven.

Survivors (23% of the population)

These people have a strong inclination to accept the direction given by the establishment and institutions. They see the establishment as threatening and impenetrable, hence a set of values emerge that classify groups as 'Them and Us'. The establishment provides security and protection, and in return survivors offer to surrender their personal goals and ambitions (if they ever had any). The catchphrase 'the way things have always been done' serves to encapsulate their orientation towards the 'Them and Us' position.

Survivors have a low expectation of what life will bring to them. Work, for example, is seen as necessary to make a living, but any mention of issues such as self-development and self-fulfilment can only provoke strong negative feelings. It is quite usual to find survivors remaining with organisations who are trying to become structurally flatter and slimmer. Apparently, voluntary retirement programmes tend to attract the inner- and outer-directed groups. It is unfortunate that survivors remain, because these new organisations require creativity and new approaches to work, and survivors are the least equipped to manage it.

Ownership of household items is below average and brand choices are not required as selection is invariably made on price. Therefore, survivors find little pleasure at work or through their own personal resources and turn to escapism for diversion in their lives. Papers such as the *Sun*, *Mirror* and *News of the World* are the most popular, and survivors tend to be the heaviest users of television as they search for ways to be taken out of themselves. *The Bill*, *Blind Date*, *Crimewatch UK* and *Gladiators* are preferred programmes, all of which reflect, slightly, the 'Them and Us' disposition.

Core values are sustenance driven.

Social resisters (12% of the population)

This group of people believe that by maintaining the *status quo* change can be resisted for as long as possible. The need for control is vital and is achieved through stereotypical roles and acceptance of authority, so that ethical and moral codes of behaviour can be sustained.

Social resisters are driven by their sense of moral duty, which is often focused on the family. Careers or jobs are instrumental in supporting the family; there is no need for there to be any enjoyment or self-expression in work.

Reassurance and reduction of risk are achieved through the purchase of established, reliable brands. Consequently, their level of brand loyalty is high and hence difficult to change. Promotional messages should convey approval and family advantage. Social resisters approve of products that are perceived to be tried and trusted and which express values of concern and care. Television programmes such as *Songs of Praise*, *Survival* and *Holby City* are preferred as are newspapers such as the *Sunday Express* and the *Sun*.

Core values are sustenance driven.

Aimless (6% of the population)

Without a goal or any orientation within society, the aimless resent the authorities, who are unable to provide employment for them. Unlike survivors, the aimless believe that hard work or education will not produce the rewards of work. Their world is orientated to the present, as they have no vision of the future or of the needs of others.

Work, if they have it, is perceived as a means of survival. It has no intrinsic value and they accept meaningless work much more readily than those in other groups. Their levels of self-esteem are low, they have virtually no desire for excitement and have lower levels of fear (compared with survivors) in their lives. This is because of their resigned attitude towards authority and society.

Their purchase behaviour is driven by price and their need for consumer durables is severely capped by their limited disposable income. The aimless are 70% more likely to read the *Sun* and the *News of the World* than any other group and are unlikely to read any magazines. Their average television consumption is not reflected in any dominant style, yet *Police Camera Action*, *Stars in their Eyes* and *Airline* draw a high proportion of the aimless.

Core values are sustenance driven.

To illustrate how this form of segmentation can be used, Menumaster, a range of frozen ready-to-eat meals, used packaging with heavy red triangles and a 'bird of freedom' to symbolise the free time that these instantaneous meals provided users. Advertising messages focused upon familiarity and traditional family scenes. Sales for some of the products in the range lagged behind others. Analysis showed that the traditional recipe products, such as cottage pie and steak and kidney pie, were successful (survivors and belongers), but meals with slightly more esoteric recipes, such as lasagne and fish mornay, were failing to establish themselves.

A decision was made to split the brand into two brands: Menumaster and Healthy Options. The traditional recipe meals would continue to be presented to the survivors and belongers in the current way, under the Menumaster brand. The new recipes would be targeted at younger people and would be clearly differentiated though Healthy Options. This was accomplished by using lighter colours on the packaging and depicting couples leading a modern lifestyle, in other words, appealing to the needs of different groups (experimentalists and self-explorers), by showing the up-to-date roles of younger, busy, often career-orientated people. The decision was successful, as these products gained market share quickly. The Menumaster brand had been re-presented to the market based upon an understanding of the values and lifestyles of the target groups. By careful coordination of the packaging and advertising images, a consistency was developed that members of the target market were able to appreciate and identify.

What is clear from the work that has been undertaken to understand psychographics is that the previous reliance on generally bland demographic data is receding. More incisive information based on the lifestyles and attitudes of people is revealing groups that are of greater potential to marketers and communications strategists. (Used with the kind permission of The Values Company.)

Benefit

Benefit segmentation refers to consumers who purchase products and services in order to satisfy specific needs and wants. The grouping of consumers on the basis of attributes sought is a widely used form of segmentation. For example, camera buyers may be seeking good quality pictures, durability, ease of use, low price or a prestigious name, to name just a few benefits.

Following the Lego System example used previously, it is interesting to note that the Lego concept is built on two main benefits that children derive from using this type of product. The first main benefit is the building of the models, and the second is the play component once models are completed. These brand values can be articulated as stimulating imagination, creativity and learning. Normally, the building element is of equal importance to the play component in most children's desire to use the product. However, research undertaken by Lego has discovered that certain types of children derive greater enjoyment from the play component. Consequently, a new

Table 5.6   Kitchen stoves – customer profiles

Group	Characteristics
Entertainers	These people like to cook at home and entertain at the same time. The kitchen will probably have a table in it.
Ostentatious non-cooks	Cooking for this group is not a pleasure, reflected in the purchase of ready-cooked prepared meals. The kitchen, however, must reflect their sense of style and design.
Traditional grandmas	This group consists of people who like to prepare family-type meals and whose cooker is changed quite infrequently. The 'eye-level' grill is a firm favourite.
Liberated home-lovers	Kitchens are an important family area to this group. They believe strongly in self-sufficiency and natural products, and like lots of space in which to prepare casseroles and healthy food.
Apathetic non-cooks	Harassed mothers preparing convenience meals for demanding children.

Source: Adapted from J. Lawless (1998) *The Sunday Times*, London, 5 April.

product was launched called Belville. The models are relatively quick and easy to construct and the environments created (pony club, restaurants, etc.) seek to maximise the play component.

Further examples of this form of segmentation can be seen in the toothpaste market, which was examined earlier, and the kitchen stove market and the different attitudes people have towards their kitchens and the impact this has on the types of cooker they might buy. See Table 5.6

Loyalty

Most markets consist of four levels of loyalty: hard core, soft core, shifting loyals and switchers. An organisation is capable of learning a great deal from analysing loyalty patterns, especially those of the hard-core loyals.

Most markets consist of four levels of loyalty: hard core, soft core, shifting loyals and switchers.

The level of loyalty shoppers have for their preferred supermarket is an important aspect of the marketing programmes developed by the major supermarkets, such as Sainsbury's, Safeway and Tesco. Increasing attention is being given to the shifting loyals in an attempt to expand the local base that each supermarket commands.

Buyer readiness stage

This refers to the stage individuals have reached as they prepare to purchase a product. It could be that they are unaware of a product's existence, that they are informed but have not formed an opinion or that they have decided they are convinced of the benefits that will come with purchase and intend buying. The numbers within each stage have an important bearing upon the communication plan.

This correlates with the process of adoption (Chapter 2) that individuals differ in the speed at which they are prepared to try new products. Marketing communications need to be targeted at those individuals who are more ready to commit themselves. NatWest Bank, working in association with Avon, an insurance company, has been offering term life assurance to clients of the bank. By gradually increasing the total value of the cover for a small percentage increment in the premiums, Avon has identified customers who are prepared to make further investments. Such an approach allows it to determine the readiness of each customer to the acceptance of each new offer.

A combination of approaches is required in order that a significant and insightful consumer profile can be developed.

What should be clear from this very brief overview is that no single segmentation tool will suffice. A combination of approaches is required in order that a significant and insightful consumer profile can be developed. Without this understanding, appropriate media and message development work cannot be effective, as will be seen later.

Targeting

The next task is to decide which, if any, of the segments discovered should be the focus of the marketing programme. Kotler (1997) advises that, unless the following criteria are met, it is probably unwise to continue with the segmentation plan:

- All segments should be *measurable* – is the segment easy to identify and measure?
- All segments should be *substantial* – is the segment sufficiently large to provide a stream of profits?
- All segments should be *accessible* – can the buyers be reached with promotional programmes?

To this list can be added the following:

- All segments should be *differentiable* – is each segment clearly different from other segments so that different marketing mixes are necessary?
- All segments should be *actionable* – has the organisation the capability to reach the segment?

Decisions need to be made about whether a single product is to be offered to a range of segments, whether a range of products should be offered to multiple segments or a single segment or whether one product should be offered to a single segment. Whatever the decision, always a reflection of the resources available to an organisation, a marketing mix is developed to meet the needs of the segment to be entered and be within the resource capability of the organisation.

The segmentation exercise will have been undertaken previously as part of the development of the marketing strategy. The marketing communications strategist will not necessarily need to repeat the exercise. However, work is often necessary to provide current information about such factors as perception, attitudes, volumes, intentions and usage, among others. It is the accessibility question that is paramount: how can the defined group be reached with suitable communications? What is the media consumption pattern of the target audience?

Positioning

Positioning is the natural outcome of the target marketing process and is the subject of Chapter 13. Positioning is the communications element of the segmentation process in that the marketing mix needs to be communicated to the target market buyers. This communication should be executed in such a way that the product occupies a particular position in the mind of each buyer, relative to the offerings of competitive products. As Dibb and Simkin (1991) state, 'the paying public do not always perceive a product or brand in the same way the manufacturer would like' (or believes they do). Successful positioning can only be achieved by adopting a customer perspective and by understanding how customers perceive products in the class and how they attach importance to particular attributes.

Positioning is the communications element of the segmentation process.

Marketing communications and segmentation

Segmentation is an important ingredient in an organisation's marketing strategy and must be fully understood by all those responsible, in whatever way, for the development of a viable promotional strategy. The process of segmentation need not be repeated by the communications team, but certain aspects of the buyer's profile need to be developed and explored in greater depth. The segmentation base must be understood if coherence, uniformity of approach and subsequent communications are to be accomplished and be successful.

Rothschild's (1987) approach to the use of segmentation in the context of marketing communications is useful because he groups the various bases for segmenting markets into the following:

1. *Enduring variables*

   These variables do not change across product classes; they stay relatively constant and they live with the individual. They include demographics, geographics and psychographic variables.

2. *Dynamic variables*

   These variables, by way of contrast, change through different product classes, and therefore an individual's relationship with a product is unique. The main segmentation tools are usage, time of adoption, loyalty level and benefit sought.

It is very important, as Rothschild says, to be able to describe the consumer/stakeholder on a number of dimensions for the precise purpose of developing effective and efficient communication plans. Broadly speaking, enduring variables are used for the design of media plans (Chapter 22). These are the different media each individual prefers to read or view on a regular basis. Dynamic variables are used in message design (Chapter 21) and positioning (Chapter 13). This refers to what is said, the advertising copy and symbolism, or the sales representative's prepared introduction and product description, for example.

The development of a positioning statement is the outcome of the review of the segmentation process and it is of vital importance if the communications strategy is to be successful.

A further aspect of the message strategy is how it is said, the colours and fonts used, and the tone and style of the communication. The development of a positioning statement is the outcome of the review of the segmentation process and it is of vital importance if the communications strategy is to be successful.

Product life cycle

The product life cycle (PLC) is a concept that has been used exhaustively to explain and predict sales patterns of products through time. Underpinning the concept is the

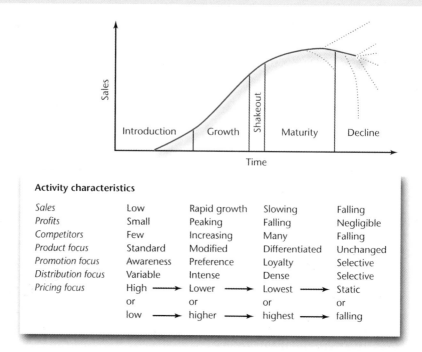

Figure 5.6 Traditional activities associated with the PLC.

belief that products move through a sequential logical pattern similar to the path that life forms follow: from birth through growth to maturity, before decline and inevitable death occur. At each stage of the cycle, a set of strategies or activities can be identified that are thought to be appropriate to the development of a product. One such assembly of activities is reproduced in Figure 5.6.

Since Levitt (1965) attempted to make the PLC concept much more manageable, the popularity of the concept has been maintained. Various strategies have been devised for each stage in the PLC, very often just to legitimise the concept and continue its use as a simple, easily understood predictive tool.

However, as Lambkin and Day (1989) comment, few management concepts have been so widely accepted or thoroughly criticised as the PLC. Meenaghan and O'Sullivan (1986) have empirically tested the sales curve and highlighted the divergence in thinking about the PLC. The concept may have had value when market conditions were stable and relatively predictable, but current markets are hostile, complex and turbulent (Wood, 1990), to the extent that the PLC is rendered inflexible and generally irrelevant. The PLC has been exaggerated in terms of its usefulness and its use as a strategic tool. It is not an accurate reflection of the pattern of a product's life.

As a generalisation, however, it can be observed that sales increase in the initial phases of a product's life before levelling as market stagnation occurs (Tellis and Crawford, 1981). It is the mature phase that provokes most discussion, as different organisations pursue different brand strategies, there are changes in technology and buyers' preferences change. The levels of resources that have been made available to support the product vary and the marketing strategies and competitive environments in which products are expected to perform differ widely. As Lambkin and Day point out, the life-cycle frameworks fail to mention the total uncertainty about the emerging markets into which new products are launched. Furthermore, there is no account of the manner in which organisations deploy their skills and resources.

Phases of development

There is increasing acceptance that the PLC is now seen as a sterile predictive tool in marketing strategy. The concept is misleading and can lead to prescriptive approaches to strategy formulation. If it has any use, it is as an educational tool and as a means of identifying periods of past development. By conceptualising zones or phases of development, overall approaches to the development of communication strategies can be identified that aid understanding, discussion and planning (Table 5.7).

By conceptualising zones or phases of development, overall approaches to the development of communication strategies can be identified that aid understanding, discussion and planning.

Marketing communicators need to be aware of the *phase* which the product or brand has reached within the development of the relevant product class. When sales growth slows (overall market sales slow) the effectiveness of competitive strategies becomes vitally important in shaping the sales curve in the mature phase. Strategies resulting from this knowledge should be created carefully in response to the anticipated market conditions. No set formula exists, and it is dangerous to be strategically prescriptive.

The marketing communicator needs to understand the phase in which a brand is situated. Having achieved that through the use of historical data and environmental scanning techniques, a general appreciation of the characteristics associated with marketing communications activities in the phase is of general assistance. The information may be useful to guide broad approaches to communications (awareness or persuasion), and to coordinate and focus thinking about the formulation and timing of competitive communications.

The information may be useful to guide broad approaches to communications.

The successful development of any new offering must be accompanied by an announcement to the target market of the product's existence. Consequently, in the

Table 5.7   Communication activities for product development phases

Introductory phase	Development phase	Established phase
Consumer		
Awareness	Differentiation	Sustain loyalty
• Advertising	• Advertising	• Sales promotion
• Public relations		• Advertising
		• Marketing public relations
		• Direct-response media
Channels		
Awareness	Conviction and preference	Sustain brand exposure
• Sales promotion	• Personal selling	• Sales promotion
• Personal selling	• Direct-response media	• Personal selling
• Public relations	• Joint advertising	• Merchandising
		• Corporate public relations
		• Direct-response media

introductory phase, building awareness in both the consumer markets and the different channels is of paramount importance to establish the product's presence and to build distribution, respectively.

However, the nature of the brand's entering market needs to be observed perhaps with even more attention than in the past. *Brand challengers* or *entrepreneurial revolutionaries* (Cooper and Simmons, 1997) are brands that take a radical new approach to the needs of the market and break away from the frame in which brands in the sector are normally perceived. These brands have a strategy which seeks to reorientate the market to a new way of competing. Cooper and Simmons quote brands such as Virgin, Microsoft, Sony and PlayStation, to which can be added Direct Line and Toys R Us. These brands undermine those in the mature zone and jeopardise their brand values.

As development occurs and volume of sales increases, so does the number of organisations supplying the market. They have been attracted by the potential profitability, and this means that the emphasis of the communications strategy moves to the creation of differentiated awareness. In the introductory phase, demand was generated for the product concept; in the development phase, the increased number of suppliers forces demand generation to be driven by the need to create brand awareness. As this phase evolves, so the level of competitive activity intensifies, witnessed by indicators such as the level of advertising expenditure, the nature of the messages transmitted and the increasing number of players in the market.

When sales in the product class appear to level off, it could be interpreted as the onset of the established phase. The need to remain competitive remains vitally important, because sales growth in the market has possibly ceased, the market has become stagnant, and growth within individual brands will usually only be achieved by converting non-loyals and switchers into brand loyals. Where limited problem-solving (Chapter 4) has created low levels of loyalty and high levels of brand switching, more funds should be moved into sales promotion at the expense of advertising. If extended problem-solving has created high levels of brand loyalty, a higher level of advertising than sales promotion is required.

The termination of a product can be deliberate, the result of market forces or the development of new technology. Communication strategy will be influenced by marketing strategy. If the policy is to extinguish the product and divest of all stocks, then it is probable that there will be a dramatic withdrawal of nearly all forms of promotion. Some promotional activity will continue with the trade in an effort simply to keep open the flow and availability of products. This serves two factors: first, to reduce stocks to a minimum and so reduce the level of working capital tied up in stocks, and, secondly, it allows brand management to continue influencing the form of relationships with the members of the channel network. By seeking to support and assist channel members to attain their objectives, continuous and supportive communications will provide for future transactions.

If the policy is to allow the product to provide positive cash flows for a further period, until market forces take hold, it is probable that promotional investments will be required, albeit at lower levels than before.

Summary

The corporate strategy is a foundation upon which business and functional strategies are developed. Marketing strategy is very closely allied to business strategy, and mar keting communications, a subactivity of marketing, is responsible for communicating the organisation's offering and corporate intentions to its various stakeholders, not just its customers.

To do this requires an appreciation of the needs of the buyers, non-buyers, intermediaries and other stakeholders (see Chapter 10) so that the organisation can shape its offering.

The marketing mix is an organisation's response to the identified needs of target customers. Marketing communications seek to convey the essence of the tangible and intangible elements of the offering represented in the mix. Many organisations will not have developed their marketing strategy into a form that can be formally articulated. This poses a dilemma in as much that communication planners might be drawn into developing a marketing strategy in its absence. This should be resisted, as it is not the responsibility of the marketing communications strategy to undertake this type of work.

The marketing strategy provides the communications planner with a view of the target market and a profile of the target customer, often based upon a combination of segmentation variables. Depending upon the object of the communications, whether a brand or an organisation, research can unveil the manner in which communications should be encoded and the media that need to be used to deliver the messages to the target audience. Above all else, the marketing strategy and the specification of target audiences are paramount for the development of effective marketing communications. The target audience provides a context within which marketing communications attempts to convey meaningful messages and sustain a viable dialogue with selected stakeholders.

Review questions

1. What is the difference between corporate and business level strategy?

2. Describe the elements of the Ashridge mission model.

3. Define marketing strategy and discuss its relevance to marketing communications.

4. Why is segmentation important?

5. How might you segment the markets for calculators, air travel, pencils, hand soaps and breakfast cereals?

6. What are enduring and dynamic segmentation variables?

7. Using the segments determined in answer to Question 5, suggest how the dynamic variables have influenced the marketing communications of organisations in these markets.

8. Comment on the utility of the product life cycle concept.

9. Identify the principal promotional activities associated with the product lifecycle.

10. List the seven social value groups and identify their prime core values.

This mini case was written by Martin Evans of the Cardiff Business School.

Big B

Segmentation and customer databases

The Big B supermarket chain has introduced a card-based loyalty scheme. Customers complete an application form giving the name, address and birth dates of all household members. The supermarket's EPOS system records customers' transactions and these are also recorded against their name as they have their card swiped. Customers are given points against their purchases and these can be redeemed as money off future purchases.

Overlays of the basic profile data and transactional data are provided by use of geodemographic systems such as Acorn and Mosaic. Lifestyle data are also purchased. This provides personalised data concerning what specific individuals claim they purchase.

These data sources are 'fused' and then 'mined'. The mining is based on two approaches. First a structured model is used to segment customers. This looks like a family tree with family life stage at the top, with each stage further subdivided according to whether the customer buys only vegetarian foods, foods for diabetes, alcohol and so on.

The second approach refers to the digging around in databases in a relatively unstructured way with the aim of discovering links between customer behaviour and almost any variable that might potentially be useful. For example, consumers' individual biorhythms and star signs are examined as potential predictors of purchasing patterns. Also, transactional and profile data are mined with respect to meteorological databases to predict, perhaps months ahead, what demand there might be for ice cream or soup.

Transactional data are at the heart of Big B's databases, then, overlaid with a variety of profile data. The supermarket refers to the amal-gam of the fusion of profile and transaction data as *biographics*. Database linking, providing the company with credit history, actual purchasing behaviour, media response and the recency, frequency, and monetary (RFM) value of purchases can potentially describe its customers' lives in their 'consumer' role.

So far 100,000 different segments have been identified and there are the same number of different versions of the Big B customer magazine that are mailed, each with a (slightly) different set of incentives. The aim is to personalise these offers as far as possible. However, there are four major groupings, based on RFM analysis. Each customer's transactions are analysed to calculate their average order value, how frequently they buy and how recently they made their last purchase. On this basis, the 'best' customers get a gold card and are sent the best offers. Silver and bronze customers spend less and are therefore not targeted so fully. Those not spending much on a regular basis are not targeted at all. Big B has been advised that according to the 80:20 rule, prospects further up the league table should be treated differently.

Big B is experimenting with an approach that allows customers to insert their loyalty cards in a reader, on entry to the store, which will print a shopping list of their usual items plus offers on what the database analysis produces as being incentives. They will be directed to shelves along which these individual specific offers can be found.

Big B is keen to retain customers because it recognises that retention costs are significantly lower than acquisition costs and, if 'retained' customers can be moved into a meaningful 'relationship' based on mutual trust, mutual benefit, mutual respect, mutual commitment, the 'lifetime values' of these customers can be extremely lucrative.

There is also an acquisition strategy at Big B.

Local catchment areas can be analysed according to the geodemographic characteristics of its best customers in order to select names and addresses of current non-customers who possess similar profiles. The company also uses this approach to analyse potential locations to site new branches.

Big B has created strategic alliances with their fast-moving consumer goods suppliers based on sharing aggregated (not personalised) data in order to exploit the resulting synergy – akin to the concept of 'category management'.

The supermarket has now moved into financial services and offers a banking service and insurance policies. The company recognises the importance of stringent assessment of risk for its insurance policies and is considering using genetic data for this purpose.

Mini-case questions

1. It is clear, then, that large quantities of personalised data are available to marketers through their loyalty schemes. In order to access and harness customer information for more accurate targeting of relevant 'offers', customer details must be available and this is the trade-off . What are the implications of this for (a) marketers and (b) customers? To what extent is Big B Big Brother?

2. Loyalty isn't just 'repeat purchasing', it is also concerned with favourable attitudes toward the company. Therefore even the most sophisticated demographic and behavioural data doesn't inform about how consumers feel about the supermarket. They might be frequenting the store because of convenience or 'deal loyalty' rather than real loyalty. What is your considered reaction to this?

3. In terms of developing a relationship strategy, is the concept of a supermarket loyalty scheme an oxymoron? Why or why not?

4. In terms of segmentation and targeting, what are the implications of the 80:20 concept for both marketers and customers?

References

Beane, T.P. and Ennis, D.M. (1987) Market segmentation: a review. *European Journal of Marketing*, **2**, p. 5.

Campbell, A. and Yeung, S. (1991) Creating a sense of mission. *Long Range Planning*, 24 August, pp. 5–20.

Cooper, A. and Simmons, P. (1997) Brand equity lifestage: an entrepreneurial revolution. TBWA Simmons Palmer, unpublished working paper.

Dibb, S. and Simkin, L. (1991) Targeting, segments and positioning. *International Journal of Retail and Distribution Management*, **19**(3), pp. 4–10.

Dibb, S., Simkin, L., Pride, W.M. and Ferrel, O.C. (1991) *Marketing: Concepts and Strategies*. New York: Houghton Mifflin.

Goften, K. (1999) Age-old way to define marekts. *Marketing*, 15 July, pp. 31–2.

Haley, R.I. (1968) Benefit segmentation: a decision orientated research tool. *Journal of Marketing*, **32** (July), p. 33.

Kotler, P. (1997) *Marketing Management: Analysis, Planning Implementation and Control*, 9th edn. Englewood Cliffs, NJ: Prentice Hall.

Lambkin, M. and Day, G.S. (1989) Evolutionary processes in competitive markets: beyond the product life cycle. *Journal of Marketing*, **53** (July), pp. 4–20.

Lawless, J. (1998) Cooker buyers have wide range of tastes. *Sunday Times*, Business Section, 5 April, p. 9.

Levitt, T. (1965) Exploit the product life cycle. *Harvard Business Review* (November/December), pp. 81–94.

Leuthesser, L. and Kohli, C. (1997) Corporate identity: the role of mission statements. *Business Horizons*, **40**(3) (May–June), pp. 59–67.

Meenaghan, T. and O'Sullivan, J. (1986) The shape and length of the product lifecycle. *Irish Marketing Review*, **1**, pp. 83–102.

Mullins, L.J. (1999) *Management and Organisational Behaviour*, 5th edn. London: Pitman.

Oliver, G. (1994) *Marketing Today*, 4th edn. Hemel Hempstead: Prentice Hall.

Plummer, J. (1974) The concept and application of lifestyle segmentation. *Journal of Marketing*, **38**(1) (January), pp. 33–7.

Rothschild, M. (1987) *Marketing Communications*. Lexington, MA: D.C. Heath.

Rushe, D. and Hamilton, K. (2001) Muddy boots. *Sunday Times*, Business Focus, 18 February, p. 5.

Teanby, D. (1999) Changing times in retail. *Admap*, May, pp. 21–24

Tellis, G.J. and Crawford, C.M. (1981) An evolutionary approach to product growth theory. *Journal of Marketing* (Fall), pp. 125–32.

Wood, L. (1990) The end of the product life cycle? *Journal of Marketing Management*, 6(2), pp. 145–55.

6

Ethics in marketing communications

Richard Christy

Ethical considerations – questions of right and wrong – are an inseparable part of real-life marketing communications. Any part of an organisation's marketing communications can send messages about its ethical stance, either intentionally or otherwise. Organisations need to cultivate an active awareness of the ethical consequences of their marketing communications.

AIMS AND OBJECTIVES

The aim of this chapter is to introduce the ideas of business ethics and to review how they are relevant to marketing communications.

The objectives of this chapter are:

1. To review briefly the main ideas in ethics and the way they are applied to business in general.

2. To discuss the differing viewpoints of the ethics of marketing communications as a whole.

3. To understand how ethical considerations affect specific issues in marketing communications, such as truth-telling, respect for personal privacy, the treatment of vulnerable groups and questions of taste and decency.

4. To introduce frameworks and models that can help managers to think through these issues in planning their marketing communications.

Introduction

In this book, the word 'good' is probably used dozens of times, often in the sense of 'likely to contribute to effective marketing communications', or similar. 'Good', however, can also have a moral, or ethical (the two words are used interchangeably here), connotation, which may be quite distinct: something that is functionally effective may or may not be ethically acceptable. This chapter looks at how ethical questions of good and bad or right and wrong might be applied to marketing communications.

Familiar concerns

How do these questions make themselves felt in real life? Everyone will have their own list, but common concerns include:

- misleading or false advertising;
- shocking, tasteless or indecent material in marketing communications;
- high-pressure sales techniques, particularly when applied to vulnerable groups;
- telesales calls that seem to intrude on personal privacy;
- PR communications that seem to distract and obfuscate, rather than inform;
- the payment of bribes to win business.

Why is it worth paying attention to these matters? For many, the main reason for wanting to understand how ethics may bear upon marketing communications will be a natural desire to know how good things can be promoted and bad things avoided. For others, interest in these questions will result from a realisation that if a company conducts its marketing communications (or any other aspect of its business) in a way that others find unethical, then it may have negative consequences that can outweigh any functional benefits. Finally, many may believe that there is no necessary contradiction between being effective in business and behaving ethically, and perhaps even that true long-term effectiveness in business is more likely to be achieved by companies who set and stick to high ethical standards.

There has been a growing emphasis on business ethics in recent years.

Importance of judgement and experience

There has been a growing emphasis on business ethics in recent years, partly as a consequence of an increased public interest in how businesses behave (i.e. not just in the products and services they produce) and a more sceptical and less respectful attitude to the place of business and business people in society. This growing awareness has also been fuelled by a far wider availability of information about corporate actions: it is much more difficult to keep things permanently secret in the Internet age. Business ethics as a subject addresses itself to the complete range of activities of an organisation, part of which is to do with the ethical implications of the way an organisation approaches its marketing communications. As we shall see, many of the issues that arise are not simple 'black-and-white' questions, but more complex situations in which judgement and experience have to be applied to arrive at an ethically acceptable solution.

More complex situations in which judgement and experience have to be applied to arrive at an ethically acceptable solution.

For example, most people would presumably object to a sales presentation whose content was designed to mislead consumers about a product or make deliberately false claims about its benefits, but few would go as far as to require every marketing communication to provide full 'warts and all' detail about the advantages and possible disadvantages of buying and using the product. Finding the balance between these two extremes is not wholly an ethical question – practical and legal issues, for example, are also likely to intrude – but one in which an understanding of ethics as applied to the conduct of business can be very valuable.

This chapter provides a brief introduction to some of the main ideas in ethics and to the way in which ethical thinking can be applied to business. For all that common sense plays a major role in the resolution of many real-life ethical questions, these issues can be highly complex, with solutions sometimes depending strongly on the approach adopted to analysis. Understanding moral concepts may help a decision-maker to analyse the ethical ramifications of a situation in order to make a better ethical choice. Sometimes, in real-life business situations, resolving to do the right thing can be easier than determining what the right thing actually *is*.

Sometimes, in real-life business situations, resolving to do the right thing can be easier than determining what the right thing actually is.

Ideas in business ethics

Ethics is the study of morality: those practices and activities that are importantly right and wrong (De George, 1999); business ethics considers the application of ethical principles to the conduct of business. This distinction may seem obvious, but it makes an important point: just as medical ethics considers the application of ethics to medicine, business ethics is about the way general ethical principles should be applied to business. In particular, business is not 'exempt' from the moral considerations that apply to human affairs in general, nor should a separate set of moral standards be developed for the set of human activities that fall under the heading of business (or marketing communications in particular).

Business ethics considers the application of ethical principles to the conduct of business.

Questions of right and wrong have occupied thinkers and writers over many millennia, and it is impossible to provide anything but a superficial overview in the space available here. Those who wish to follow up in more detail some of the theoretical ideas mentioned here should consult a specialist business ethics text: De George's (1999) book, for example, is one of many in the field that provide a clear and accessible account of the application of ethical principles to business.

Two major schools of thought can be distinguished in ethics.

Duties and consequences

Two major schools of thought can be distinguished in ethics, which broadly lie on either side of the means/ends debate:

- The first is concerned with *duties*, and argues that some actions are always bad and others always good.
- The second approach focuses on *consequences*, holding that whether an act is good

or bad depends on what happens as a result of taking that action, no matter what the action is. Utilitarianism is a well-known form of this approach, seeking to identify actions that (very broadly) can be expected to result in the greatest good of the greatest number.

Problems of the main approaches

To make this distinction is to oversimplify a very complex and long-running debate and also to overlook the many sophisticated variants and hybrid theories that have been developed. In the course of this debate, the problems inherent in either approach have been well rehearsed – an approach to ethics based on duty alone is likely to be inflexible and difficult to put into practice in a complex real world. By contrast, the alternative approach of considering only outcomes seems unsatisfactory to many. Crude utilitarianism, for example, is (by definition) 'unprincipled' and insufficiently concerned with the idea of justice. Also, in practical terms, it can also be very difficult to arrive at a satisfactory assessment of 'the greatest good', however that is defined.

Neither approach on its own seems to offer a practical and foolproof guide to ethical business decision-making. As has been suggested above, a simple and apparently unarguable duty-based rule like 'Always tell the truth in marketing communications' may cause problems as soon as we start to plan an advertising campaign. Is it our duty to provide a detailed and reasoned discussion of all of the reasons for and against buying the product, whatever the medium we are using? Must we refrain from using ironic statements that are plainly designed to entertain, rather than inform? For example, Heineken's famous '. . . refreshes the parts that other beers cannot reach' campaign would have to be excluded by this rule. The simple rule is unworkable: it must either be made platitudinously general (e.g. 'Do no intentional harm') or it must be expanded to a long list of qualifications, definitions and exceptions.

A simple and apparently unarguable duty-based rule like 'Always tell the truth in marketing communications' may cause problems as soon as we start to plan an advertising campaign.

Basing the ethical evaluation of our actions only on the expected consequences brings a separate set of problems. If, for example, a company designs an advertising campaign that most people will find mildly amusing but which a small religious minority will (quite foreseeably) find highly offensive, then the publication of research data showing a weighted average calculation of approval for the adverts will be unlikely to reassure most people's intuitive concerns about the campaign. In practical terms, it can also be extraordinarily difficult to forecast all of the consequences of a proposed action, however concerned one may be to achieve a balanced assessment.

It can also be extraordinarily difficult to forecast all of the consequences of a proposed action.

Other approaches to business ethics

These practical difficulties in applying simple rules or methods to complex real-life situations have caused many writers in business ethics to leave the theoretical ends/means argument to one side and to propose alternative bases for judging the ethical implications of proposed business actions. Jackson (1996), for example, explains how a focus on moral virtues in business life can provide a much more practical basis for assessing good conduct in business. The concept of virtues seeks to express those qualities and dispositions in a person that will help to ensure a good life, often seeking a 'mean' between two undesirable poles. Courage, for example, can be defined as a virtue that lies between the extremes of cowardice on the one hand and foolhardiness on the other. One of the strengths of this approach is the way in which it helps to temper the absolutism to which a duty-based approach to ethics is prone as well as the unprincipled expedience of crude utilitarianism. Finding the 'mean', however, is far from straightforward. Murphy (1999) argues that a virtues approach is appropriate and useful in analysing the ethics of organisations, as well as individuals and discusses five virtues that are particularly relevant to the ethical conduct of international marketing: integrity, fairness, trust, respect and empathy.

A different alternative is proposed by Sternberg (1994), in which the assessment of business ethics is based upon a definition of the *purpose* of the company (for this reason, her approach to business ethics is described as teleological):

> To be an ethical business, an organisation must be a business and must conduct its activities ethically. An organisation is a business if its objective is maximising long-term owner value; a business acts ethically, if its actions are compatible with that aim and with distributive justice and ordinary decency
>
> (Sternberg, 1994, p. 93)

In this definition, 'distributive justice' refers to the principle by which rewards are allocated in proportion to the contribution made to organisational ends, while the constraint of 'ordinary decency' obliges a firm to refrain from coercion, lying, cheating and so on, whether or not they appear at the time to further the business purpose. These two restrictions acknowledge the vital importance of confidence and trust in the business world.

In adopting this approach, a manager would be mainly concerned with the consequences of a proposed action, but would concentrate on those consequences that are directly or indirectly relevant to the firm's long-term interests, rather than seeking to judge what is in the general interest. On first reading, this may seem to some be nothing more than a formal statement of the 'Greed is good' values which are sometimes associated with the aggressive 'Anglo-Saxon' model of capitalism of the 1980s. The teleological approach, however, is importantly different from the excesses of that era:

A manager would be mainly concerned with the consequences of a proposed action, but would concentrate on those consequences that are directly or indirectly relevant to the firm's long-term interests.

- The concept of 'long-term owner value' is not the same thing as that of short-term rewards: the pursuit of long-term value may require very different actions from a policy designed to maximise, say, the next dividend payment.

- The requirement to behave with 'common decency' firmly excludes actions on the part of the firm such as lying, cheating, stealing and coercion, no matter how expedient or financially attractive they may seem in the short term: these things are always unethical.

- An intelligently self-interested firm will generally not wish to pursue activities that give it a bad reputation among customers, suppliers, potential recruits and so on, because to do so would be to fail to maximise long-term owner value. This is not to say that individual employees may have no other reasons for this restraint, but rather to suggest that the teleological principle will often provide sufficient reason to behave ethically in business.

This teleological principle, and the primacy it accords to the interests of the shareholders, has been criticised as incomplete by some (see, for example, Sorrell and Hendry, 1994) and many argue for a much more extensive view of corporate social responsibility. However, thinking broadly and clearly about the long-term interests of a business can in many cases help to identify the ethical way forward, as will be argued in this chapter.

An intelligently self-interested firm will generally not wish to pursue activities that give it a bad reputation among customers, suppliers, potential recruits and so on, because to do so would be to fail to maximise long-term owner value.

Stakeholder theories

Although it is framed in terms that may seem to be disconcertingly stark – even provocative – this teleological principle may help to illuminate the difference between the ideas of 'stakeholder' theory and the seemingly narrower concerns of agency theory. One example of this theory is provided by Milton Friedman's (1970) suggestion that the social responsibility of business is to use its resources to engage in activities designed to increase its profits, within the 'rules' of free competition and without deception or fraud. This type of approach views directors and managers as agents of the owners, with a prime duty to maximise their wealth. By contrast, some forms of stakeholder theory define a far wider set of external interests, to which the firm is in some way 'accountable' (see Chapter 10 for a fuller discussion of the implications of stakeholder theory).

Some forms of stakeholder theory define a far wider set of external interests, to which the firm is in some way 'accountable'.

Whatever view is taken of a firm's relationship with and duties towards its various stakeholders, the mere acknowledgement of complexity and plurality does not of itself help managers to know what to *do* about this plurality in practice. Managers seeking to 'balance' stakeholder interests will quickly encounter the very practical problem of how that 'balance' should be defined. Consider, for example, opportunities for a firm to contribute to or become involved with charitable causes. The available range of local, national and global causes will in total outweigh any conceivable budget. What is needed is both an ethical basis for deciding whether to lend support at all and, if so, which causes to support. Asking the question 'Which actions best support the long-term goals of this firm?' in an intelligent and enlightened way may well help to illuminate the complex ethical issues facing firms today. The word 'enlightened' is used here to describe an outlook that deliberately considers the long term as well as the short term, that thinks more broadly than the immediate transactions carried out by the firm and is active and searching, rather than passive.

Managers seeking to 'balance' stakeholder interests will quickly encounter the very practical problem of how that 'balance' should be defined.

The teleological principle requires that stakeholder interests be acknowledged and taken into account, because not to do so would be a violation of the principle. Importantly, it also provides guidance on *how* those interests are to be taken into account (i.e. by assessing their impact on the long-term interests of the owners of the firm). As Sternberg (1994, p. 50) points out, however, 'taking something into account' is not the same being accountable to it.

The scope of ethical issues in marketing communications

Before looking at the application of these ideas to marketing communications, one or two things need to be clarified. The first of these is the importance of distinguishing between:

■ those critiques of marketing communications that are based upon a belief that the activity as a whole is undesirable;

■ criticisms of some aspects of marketing communications in practice that are based on an acceptance that the activity is in principle justifiable.

The next section provides a brief review of some of the first type of critique, not least because these arguments are frequently encountered in public debate; in effect, they are part of the world in which marketing takes place. The rest of the chapter, however, concerns itself with the second category of criticisms – ethical issues that are raised by the practice of marketing communications, with a clear implication that advertising, selling, PR and so on are things that can be done ethically or unethically, depending upon the choices that are made.

It is also important to clarify that the discussion here concentrates on marketing communications in particular, rather than marketing in general, meaning that many issues relating to marketing as a whole have been excluded. It is certainly unethical to advertise a product that is known to be so badly designed or manufactured as to be dangerous, for example, but the ethical issue in this case has more to do with the practice of product management than advertising. Those interested in ethical issues affecting marketing in general should consult a specialised text such as Schlegelmilch (1999), or the review of the literature presented in Tsalikis and Fritzsche (1989).

The final clarification is to point out that the main ethical questions in marketing communications are considered one by one in this chapter, rather than looking at the individual elements of the promotional mix in turn. Questions of truth-telling, decency, privacy and so on have some bearing on every part of the promotional mix, although the context of each medium may affect the way in which ethical considerations have to be applied.

Marketing communications: a diabolical liberty?

In the 1968 comedy film *Bedazzled*, Peter Cook plays a jaded, weary devil, who complains that since introducing the seven deadly sins, he has done very little except invent advertising. The line is just a joke, of course, but does rely upon one familiar view of advertising: that it is inherently bad, manipulative or corrupting. Nor is this disapproval confined to advertising: the image of the smooth, fast-talking 'snake oil' salesman is an enduring one, with many modern counterparts. Similarly, the public relations industry has suffered from some extremely *poor* PR in recent years: the term 'PR' sometimes seems to be used in a way that is almost synonymous with half-truths, insincerity and manipulation. In contemporary

One familiar view of advertising: it is inherently bad, manipulative or corrupting.

politics, the term 'spin' is generally pejorative, suggesting a growing impatience with slick presentation at the expense of candour and truth.

If these views – in effect, that marketing communication is inherently undesirable and unworthy – are taken seriously, then the ethical response must presumably be to indulge in these activities as little as possible, if at all. Happily, however, this is not the only view that can be taken: an alternative view regards marketing communication as playing a key role in the market economy, assisting the process through which consumer needs are identified and satisfied. From this perspective, the ethics of advertising, PR and so on depend upon how they are carried out: in themselves, these activities are ethically neutral. Most of this chapter takes the latter perspective, but it is certainly worth briefly highlighting the more fundamental critiques of advertising.

The ethics of advertising, PR and so on depend upon how they are carried out: in themselves, these activities are ethically neutral.

Advertising as mass manipulation?

Vance Packard's famous book about mass communications *The Hidden Persuaders* (Packard, 1960) had a major impact. His concern was what he saw as the manipulative widespread use of psychological techniques in advertising, PR, politics and so on:

> *many of us are being influenced and manipulated – far more than we realise – in the patterns of our everyday lives. Large-scale efforts are being made, often with impressive success, to channel our unthinking habits, our purchasing decisions, and our thought processes by the use of insights gained from psychiatry and the social sciences. Typically these efforts take place beneath our level of awareness, so that the appeals which move us are often, in a sense, 'hidden'.*
>
> (Packard, 1960, p. 11)

Today's hard-pressed advertisers, trying to engage the attention of a sophisticated, knowing and demanding public, might be forgiven for wryly wishing that anything like that level of influence could be achieved. However, Packard's book provided a powerful expression of a point of view that is often found in press and academic commentaries on advertising, sometimes linked to more fundamental political critiques of the capitalistic society in which advertising takes place. Forty years later, a similar concern is evident in Klein's (2000) account of the anti-capitalist protests that have taken place in several cities internationally. One of the strands of this diverse movement has been concern about the dominance of global brands in everyday life.

Pollay's (1986) review of social science commentaries on advertising drew together a wide range of material into a general framework. This synthesis suggested that advertising was seen – by social scientists – as a powerful and intrusive means of communication and persuasion, whose (unintended) effects could be to reinforce materialism, cynicism, irrationality, selfishness and a number of other undesirable outcomes. Holbrook's (1987) reply to this paper challenged some of its implicit assumptions (e.g. that advertising is monolithic, somehow acting in concert; that it appeals to a mass audience; that it manipulates social values; that it relies mainly upon emotional impact)

A powerful and intrusive means of communication and persuasion, whose (unintended) effects could be to reinforce materialism, cynicism, irrationality, selfishness and a number of other undesirable outcomes.

and suggested that the 'conventional wisdom or prevailing opinion' represented in the Pollay model was unfairly destructive of a much more diverse reality.

This discussion of ethics in marketing communications takes for granted a number of much broader issues to do with the ethical acceptability of marketing as an activity and of the capitalist system which engendered it.

Space does not permit anything like an adequate discussion of these serious and important arguments. The important point to be taken forward is that this discussion of ethics in marketing communications takes for granted a number of much broader issues to do with the ethical acceptability of marketing as an activity and of the capitalist system which engendered it. As Robin and Reidenbach (1993) point out:

> The degree to which the basic marketing functions are seen to be ethical or unethical must ... be measured within our understanding of their history, the times in which they are applied, the context in which they are applied, the expectations of society, the requirements of capitalism and our best understanding of human behaviour.

> (Robin and Reidenbach, 1993, p. 104)

Similarly, Thompson (1995) recommends a 'contextualist' model of marketing ethics, in which ethical dilemmas are to be recognised and addressed through the interplay of social values, cultural meanings, stakeholder interests and values and the organisational contexts within which individual marketing agents operate. At a practical level, Vallance (1995) observes that it is usually more valuable in business to ask a specific question like 'Is it ethical for us to run this advert now?' than to wonder more generally 'Is advertising ethical?'

Truth-telling

The general ethical requirement to tell the truth is one that bears upon every type of marketing communication. Reflecting the widespread public distaste for lying and deceit, there are plenty of legal and other regulatory deterrents to this type of unethical conduct in advertising, selling, public relations and so on. Clearly, no responsible business will wish to be found on the wrong side of these requirements, but there remains plenty of scope for judgement in respect of which aspects of the truth are to be presented in marketing communications and how they are to be put across.

The general ethical requirement to tell the truth is one that bears upon every type of marketing communication.

As discussed at the beginning of this chapter, we expect a salesperson not to lie to us, but few would require from a salesperson a full and balanced account of the advantages and disadvantages of our entering into the proposed transaction. There are perhaps two reasons why: mainly, it is unreasonable to expect the salesperson or advertiser to have enough information about us to be able to carry this out; also, however, there is a general acceptance that the principle of *caveat emptor* ('let the buyer beware') should play some sort of moderating role.

A general acceptance that the principle of caveat emptor *('let the buyer beware') should play some sort of moderating role.*

As Sternberg (1994) observes, the aim of a salesperson is to sell the company's products, not to provide consumer guidance. Both buyer and seller have their own interests and it is normally up to either party to look after these interests during the purchase process. Thus there is no ethical requirement that customers should ensure that the transaction is profitable for the seller, nor – in every case – that the seller must go to great lengths to ensure that the buyer is making a wise and prudent purchase (although many sellers will choose to provide some advice of this nature, in order to appeal more effectively to customers). Much depends on the context of the sales dialogue: the nature of the product or service, the awareness and expectations of the customer and so on (see also Smith's (1995) 'Consumer sovereignty' test discussed below). It is also usually important for the seller to make it plain in some way that selling is actually taking place: the Market Research Society, for example, defines the unacceptable practice of 'sugging' – selling under guise (of conducting research). The distinction between selling and giving independent advice is also embodied in the regulations relating to the marketing of financial services in the UK.

Misrepresentation and 'puffery'

Some way short of the extreme of deceit or lying, but nonetheless the wrong side (for most people) of the ethical divide, is the problem of deliberate or reckless misrepresentation in selling. Chonko (1995) defines misrepresentation as occurring when salespeople make incorrect statements or false promises about a product or service. The dividing line is not always absolutely clear: a salesperson can be generally expected to show enthusiasm for the product, which may result in some

A sales negotiation can be seen as a performance in which both buyer and seller may make some claims that do not represent their actual or final position.

degree of exaggeration. Up to a point, of course, a sales negotiation can be seen as a performance in which both buyer and seller may make some claims that do not represent their actual or final position. Most, however, would accept this as perfectly normal, perhaps even seeing it as an effective way of identifying and delineating the area within which both buyer and seller are prepared to participate.

Misrepresentation in advertising is likely to be condemned by codes of practice, if not by actual statute. The American Marketing Association's code of ethics, for example, is clear that it is the responsibility of members to avoid false and misleading advertising and sales promotions that use deception or manipulation (American Marketing Association, n.d.).

Much advertising, however, contains some degree of what might be called 'embellishment' or 'puffery'.

Much advertising, however, contains some degree of what might be called 'embellishment' or 'puffery' – the enthusiastic use of language and images to convey the most optimistic view of the product or service being portrayed. Those who find embellishment to be a natural, obvious and harmless aspect of advertising language will have some difficulty in providing a firm dividing line between harmless embellishment and deception. Chonko (1995) points out that the American Federal Trade Commission regards puffery as acceptable because such statements are not likely to be relied upon by consumers in making their choice. However, this approach seems itself to place great reliance upon being able to identify those parts of a marketing communication that *are* likely to be relied upon. Similar issues are raised by the visual images created for advertising, which naturally seek to show the product as appealingly as possible. Images of sports cars parked outside large country houses are unlikely to delude any potential buyers as to the lifestyle benefits of the model. Nor can there be any serious concern about using mashed potato to represent easily melted ice cream in an advertising photo session. However, for some products aimed at some audiences

– and children's toys are often mentioned in this context – exaggerated images may have a greater potential to delude. These questions are complex in detail: the extent

The extent to which consumers should be held responsible for critically evaluating the commercial messages is not a simple issue.

to which consumers should be held responsible for critically evaluating the commercial messages is not a simple issue, since so much depends upon the circumstances of an individual case. For Attas (1999), for example, it is preferable to think about the effects of deceptive advertising in terms of the effect on society as a whole (i.e. as if deception at a particular level were commonplace), rather than seeking to make firm statements about the possible effects on an individual.

The importance of context: selling complex products

The importance of context in judging ethical behaviour can be seen in the debate in the UK over the problems arising from the selling of private pensions during the 1980s. In many cases, customers were persuaded by salespeople to switch out of existing pension schemes into new schemes whose subsequent performance left them worse off. In these cases, the complex nature of the services, together with the unfamiliarity of many of the customers with the various types of product and how to choose between them, led them to place an unusually

This should have placed a greater than normal ethical duty on the salesperson to ensure that the customers were properly informed of the consequences and implications.

great reliance on the advice provided by the salesperson. Put another way, the extent to which the buyer was foreseeably *able* to 'beware' in these cases was very limited, which in turn should have placed a greater than normal ethical duty on the salesperson to ensure that the customers were properly informed of the consequences and implications of the switch. The fact that these ethical standards were clearly not met in a large

number of cases has caused a great deal of loss, anxiety and inconvenience for the customers who lost out, but also a great deal of difficulty, expense and embarrassment for the pensions industry as a whole. The issue rumbled on for years, with the UK government adopting a policy of publicly 'naming and shaming' formerly well-respected financial services companies who were failing to meet regulatory targets for compensating these customers.

Writing about ethical issues in insurance selling in general, Diacon and Ennew (1996) point out that marketing transactions in financial services have greater than

Marketing transactions in financial services have greater than normal potential for ethical complications.

normal potential for ethical complications. The unavoidable complexity of many financial services products is heightened by the fact that the evaluation may depend upon individual calculations carried out for the customer by the salesperson; also, risk for the

customer may be significant, in that the actual benefits received will often depend upon the performance of the economy over a long period. The authors highlight a number of other ethical issues relevant to insurance selling, including:

■ the issue of 'fitness for purpose' in both the design of the products and the way in which they are matched to customer needs;

■ the transparency of the price for these products, such that any commissions payable to the intermediary organisation or individual salesperson are clearly visible;

- the need for truth in promotion, not only in terms of strict factual correctness, but also in terms of what the consumer might be expected to understand from a phrase;

- the effect of the sales targeting and reward systems of the selling organisation on the behaviour of salespeople, particularly in view of the important advisory component of this type of selling.

In their survey of the industry, the authors found some awareness of these ethical issues and also evidence of initial moves to address the main cause of problems: the potentially dangerous combination of commission-based selling and imperfect information on the part of customers.

In the teleological approach to business ethics described above, businesses are encouraged to act in ways that can be expected to maximise the long-term wealth of owners. The serious problems arising from personal pension selling during the 1980s provide an example of how important it is for businesses to maintain an active awareness of the likely effects of their actions. A decade and a half later, it is all too clear that a failure to address problems that should have been quite foreseeable has caused misery and distress for many customers and – tellingly – major disadvantage for the industry as a whole. It is difficult to escape the conclusion that a more enlightened assessment of the long-term interests of the business on the part of financial service providers would have helped to avert many of the problems, to the great benefit of all involved. This is easy to conclude with hindsight: the effective ethical businesses are those that manage to cultivate this type of foresight.

The relational context and expectations

The importance of the buyer/seller context in which the statement is made is also reflected in Gundlach and Murphy's (1993) paper on the ethics of relational marketing exchanges. In these relational exchanges, the value of the arrangement for both sides depends critically upon the mutual maintenance of trust, equity, responsibility and commitment (i.e. as opposed to the more contractual regulation of shorter term transactional relationships). Clearly, the expectations as regards the content and openness of marketing communications in the former would be different from the latter. A customer might, for example, feel upset if a car salesperson with whom he had dealt for many years failed to tell him that the model he was buying was about to be superseded, because that would seem to be inconsistent with the trust built up over the years. The same customer might not be at all upset to find the same thing happen with a personal computer bought from a discount store in London, not only because computers are known to date more quickly than models of cars, but also because there was no long-term relationship to be brought into question.

In these relational exchanges, the value of the arrangement for both sides depends critically upon the mutual maintenance of trust, equity, responsibility and commitment.

Truth-telling and PR

The practice of PR is also likely to raise many truth-telling issues. The purpose of PR is to create and manage relationships between the firm and its various publics and there must always be a temptation in so doing to place undue emphasis on the positive aspects of the firm's actions. The question of what is 'due' emphasis is no easier in this area of marketing communications than in selling or advertising: a firm must strike an ethical balance, based upon its understanding of its impact on others and its own long-term interests and reputation. Firms that make a habit of using PR techniques to mislead stakeholder groups are in effect consuming in the short term the trust upon which their long-term profitable existence may depend.

PR campaigns have been recommended as more effective than overt advertising for firms seeking to restore their corporate reputation after times of difficulty. As Curtis (1999) reported, Shell seemed to be taking a risk in running a high-profile advertising campaign to announce its adoption of a 'triple bottom line' (reporting on environmental and social performance as well as financial). Some commentators in the article felt that a PR-driven approach would be more effective, leading to the much more credible third-party endorsement, rather than self-funded proclamations that may attract cynicism and further attacks.

Botan (1997) distinguishes between the 'monologic' and 'dialogic' approaches to PR, suggesting that dialogue is a more ethical basis for planning PR campaigns, particularly in an information society. More pragmatically,

PR firms above all must rely upon a basic level of public trust in their activities if they are to do any good for their clients.

Barton (1994) warns that, following the major business scandals of the 1980s, courts may increasingly hold PR firms liable for making false or misleading statements on behalf of their clients, placing a prudential burden of proof and research on the PR firms themselves. Onerous though such burdens may turn out to be, they appear to be little different from that which an enlightened view of long-term self-interest on the part of PR firms might indicate – PR firms above all must rely upon a basic level of public trust in their activities if they are to do any good for their clients at all.

Vulnerable groups

The question of truth-telling leads directly to the special requirements for the treatment of vulnerable groups in marketing communication campaigns. Many countries, for example, have much stricter controls on the content and timing of advertising to children than on advertising in general, based upon an enhanced concern for the potential of advertisements and other promotional material to delude and disturb these audiences.

These special regulations, however, should not distract attention from the general ethical requirement to design marketing communications that show an enlightened understanding of and concern for the needs of the recipient of the communication. The often-discussed tragic problems resulting from the sale of baby milk products in some developing countries had much to do with marketing and other communications from the seller that simply did not take adequate account of the reality of life in developing countries. As De George (1999, p. 264) observes:

> In an attempt to increase sales, Nestlé, as well as other producers of infant formula [milk], extended the sale of their product to many countries in Africa. They followed some of the same marketing techniques that they had followed with success and without customer complaint elsewhere.
>
> One standard technique was advertising on billboards and magazines. A second was the distribution of free samples in hospitals to new mothers as well as to doctors. In themselves, these practices were neither illegal nor unethical. Yet

their use led to charges of following unethical practices and to a seven-year world-wide boycott of all Nestlé products.

Firms that cultivate an enlightened awareness of their impact on their surroundings will have a greater chance of perceiving and anticipating these issues before they become problems.

In retrospect, it is easy to point out that the company should have paid greater attention to the likelihood in this environment of the product being made up with water from a contaminated source or of the product being over-diluted by users who were unfamiliar with it. Again, firms that cultivate an enlightened awareness of their impact on their surroundings will have a greater chance of perceiving and anticipating these issues before they become problems.

Vulnerable groups – children or parents?

Parents can experience real stress at Christmas time in trying to track down this year's 'must-have' toy for their children. TV advertisements and sophisticated merchandising fuel this demand, reinforced by peer pressure at school, and child-oriented marketing is becoming increasingly evident on the Internet. In some parts of Europe, TV advertising aimed at children is prohibited and some voluntary restraints have been introduced in the UK. Some have expressed concern about the way advertisements for fashionable toys and clothing can reinforce social exclusion by making children without these expensive products feel abnormal. Others, however, are wary of extending existing limitations on advertising, emphasising the need for parents to manage the expectations of their children and sometimes to refuse demands.

Adapted from Daniel Lee, *The Guardian*, 20 December 2000

Privacy and respect for persons

One aspect of the duty-based view of ethics referred to at the beginning of this chapter is the importance of treating others as ends in themselves, rather than merely as means: in other words, not merely using others, but treating them with the respect they deserve as fellow human beings. This ethical requirement finds a number of potential applications in the world of marketing communications, for example:

- avoiding the annoyance and harassment that can result from the inappropriate application of high-pressure sales techniques;
- respecting the wish that some may have at some times to be private, not to be approached with sales calls and – for some – not to be sent unsolicited direct mail communications;
- refraining from causing unwarranted distress or shock by ensuring that the content of any marketing communication remains within generally accepted boundaries of taste and decency'.

The first of these issues is perhaps easiest to deal with here: harassment is something that can be subjectively defined (i.e. by the recipient of the unwelcome attention) and no ethical business will wish to cross that line. The reason for this is both to do with the standards of common decency that an ethical firm will wish to maintain and also the view that harassing customers is unlikely to be consistent with the long-term interests of the business. The fact that sales harassment does take place does not undermine the principle, but rather suggests that some businesses have a flawed view of their long-term interest, or, in the most opportunistic cases, that they are making no plans to have a long-term future. As in some of the other cases discussed above, the need for regulation is primarily to support and reinforce the action that an ethical company would be likely to choose anyway.

Responding to individual preferences for privacy

The issue of privacy is a little more complex, especially if it is treated as a question of 'rights'. It is not very easy to define a separate and defensible right to privacy in respect of direct marketing approaches. Privacy is essentially a subjective concept, to do with not being perceived or disturbed at a particular time or while engaged in a particular activity. To express this as a right seems to involve a corresponding obligation on others to sense in some way that a person is in a private state and then not to perceive or disturb that person, which sounds impractical in many circumstances. In the context of a capitalist society, it is also difficult to think about general prohibitions on the making of commercial approaches.

Privacy is essentially a subjective concept.

This is not at all to argue that concerns about privacy in respect of direct marketing have no basis, but rather to suggest that they can be more productively addressed by regarding them as a reasonable request (rather than the assertion of a right) and then considering how an ethical firm ought to respond (Christy and Mitchell, 1999). Privacy-related concerns in this area seem to fall into two main categories: unwelcome sales approaches (e.g. teleselling calls in the evening) and a more general concern about the implications of large amounts of personal data being collected, stored and processed for sale to those involved in direct marketing.

In the first case, the ethical response is the same as for sales harassment: ethical firms will refrain as far as possible from making unwelcome approaches, for reasons of enlightened self-interest. They will, for example, support and encourage the development of general schemes through which individuals can signify their general wish not to be contacted. They will also seek out and use mailing lists that are a very close match with their target segments, which will both make the mailing more effective and also reduce the chance of the mailing piece being seen as 'junk'. They will also provide a clear means for those who do not wish to be contacted to indicate their wish.

An ethical company can also respond to the second and more general concern about privacy, both by offering clear opportunities to individuals to have their details excluded from files and also by ensuring as far as possible that information about individuals used in direct marketing has been ethically collected, processed and stored (e.g. such that it is still up to date, thus minimising the risk of, say, causing distress by inadvertently mailing to deceased people). Sometimes, even these efforts may not be enough to avoid causing offence inadvertently, and an ethical firm will ensure that it has in place clear and effective systems to receive and respond to the complaint.

Taste and decency

The question of taste and decency in the content of marketing communications is also one which may have an ethical aspect. This is not only to do with the use of 'pin-up' images in corporate calendars and trade advertising; separate, but related concerns may apply to the use by a charity of particularly distressing images in order to raise funds or even the apparently innocent use of stereotypical images in advertising.

Images of women and men in advertising

The first point to be made is that public standards of what is acceptable in this area do clearly change over time. The portrayal of women in early TV advertisements, for example, now often seems so obviously inappropriate as to be hilarious: no advertiser adopting a similar tone today could expect to communicate effectively (except perhaps as a spoof). The extent to which contemporary images of women and men in advertising may also be creating stereotypes is beyond the scope of this chapter, but it should be clear that an advertisement that annoys or alienates its target audience is unlikely to be effective. Effective (and ethical) advertisers will wish to treat their prospective audiences with respect, if only because in a competitive market they cannot afford to behave otherwise. David Ogilvy's (1963, p. 96) often-quoted remark that:

Public standards of what is acceptable in this area do clearly change over time.

> the consumer isn't a moron; she is your wife

provided a much-needed reminder to fellow advertisers of the need to avoid insulting the intelligence of their audiences. The fact that this (no doubt entirely well-intentioned) advice would probably be expressed differently today also underlines the point that standards and expectations do change over time. Ethical advertisers will seek to understand their target audiences well enough to be able to communicate effectively, without giving inadvertent offence. Building up this level of understanding is also very important in a cross-cultural context, where the risk of giving offence inadvertently is much higher. The point is obviously true for international or global marketing, but many domestic markets are also increasingly multicultural in nature.

Ethical advertisers will seek to understand their target audiences well enough to be able to communicate effectively, without giving inadvertent offence.

The interplay of public taste and choices made by advertisers

The annual reports of the Advertising Standards Authority (ASA) provide a crude barometer of public attitudes towards advertising images.

For example, in its commentary on complaints received in 1996, the ASA pointed out that complaints had fallen by 12% from the record 1995 level of 12,804. Complaints about the portrayal of women, however, doubled during that

Plate 1.1 Magnum. The Magnum brand has achieved market leadership through strong consistent branding and positioning. See Chapter 1, page 2. Picture reproduced with the kind permission of Bird's Eye Walls.

Plate 1.2 Dyson. The manufacturer of this revolutionary new domestic appliance uses marketing communications to differentiate, remind, inform and persuade audiences. See Chapter 1, page 8. Picture reproduced with the kind permission of Dyson.

Plate 2.1 Dennis Fire Engines. The characteristics of the source of any marketing communication message are vitally important. The manufacturer of Dennis Fire Engines uses source credibility as an integral part of its promotional activities. See Chapter 2, page 37. Picture reproduced with the kind permission of Dennis Fire Engines.

Plates 3.1 and 3.2 Spirito di Punto. Fiat brand values and aspects of Italian personality were projected through a series of ads designed to portray aspects of the target market male and female values. See Chapter 3, page 62. Pictures reproduced with the kind permission of Fiat.

Plate 3.3 'Diet Coke'. Coca-Cola uses sexual overtones to gain the attention of the target market. See Chapter 3, page 63. Diet Coke is a registered trade mark of the Coca-Cola Company. This image has been reproduced with kind permission of the Coca-Cola Company.

Plate 3.4 Andrex puppy. The use of product attributes in marketing communications is long established. Here the Andrex puppy is used to symbolise (through time) the length and strength of the brand. See Chapter 3, page 77. Picture reproduced with the kind permission of Kimberley-Clark Ltd.

If we've changed the company so much, why didn't we change the name?

Why should we? We have a long history of making motor
cars and we're not about to toss it all away.

What's more, we're proud of our achievements. Year in,
year out, our cars win world championship rallies. Last year we
even won the World F2 Championship. And in Europe's leading customer satisfaction survey, Skoda trounced
the likes of BMW, Rover and Ford.

That's not to say, however, that there weren't some things we
couldn't improve. Since the Volkswagen Group became involved
with us, we've reviewed everything we do, and the way that we do it.

Our quality control and safety programmes mean that the new Skoda meets all the latest European standards.
The result is the new Felicia. A brand new Skoda, made in a brand
new way. We may not have changed the name, but we have changed the
company. And we have changed the car.
Which leaves us with one question to ask you. Are you open enough
to change your mind?

We've changed the car. Can you change your mind?

FOR A FULL INFORMATION PACK AND WHERE TO FIND YOUR NEAREST SKODA DEALER CALL 0345-745 745

Plate 3.5 Skoda. Attitude Change. A major part of many marketing communication campaigns (and advertising in particular) is to either maintain or change the attitudes held by the target market towards the brand or product category. The picture shows Skoda using the VW silhouette to help change attitudes through the suggestion of reliability and trust of VW towards Skoda cars in the UK shortly after the company was bought by its German parent. See Chapter 3, page 82. Picture reproduced with the kind permission of Skoda UK Ltd.

Plate 3.6 Skoda. This more recent campaign used humour to change perceptions and attitudes towards the Skoda brand and raised market share to an all time high. See Chapter 3, page 82. Picture reproduced with the kind permission of Skoda UK Ltd.

Plate 5.1 Crown Paints. Advertising was required to bring more emotional values to the brand and generate new levels of brand awareness. See Chapter 5, page 122, and Chapter 12, page 288. Picture reproduced with the kind permission of Akzo Nobel.

Plate 7.1
B&Q. The use of staff in television commercials provides authenticity and a sense of shared ownership with regard to the B&Q brand promise. See Chapter 7, page 178. Picture reproduced with the kind permission of B&Q.

Plate 7.2
B&Q. As part of the process of involving staff, the daily exercise work-out seeks to bond staff as well as provide for improved health and fitness. See Chapter 7, page 178. Picture reproduced with the kind permission of B&Q.

National Health Servings.

Today, nutrition, diet and the health of the nation are top of the agenda. And not a moment too soon as far as Kellogg's is concerned. Of course, there's a limit to what a Kellogg's breakfast can do. But it can make a real contribution. And we've always done everything in our power to make that contribution as big as possible.

For instance, we were the first cereal manufacturer in the UK to fortify our products with vitamins back in 1960. And we followed not long after with extra iron.

Then in 1987, before the virtues of folic acid were widely acknowledged, we started adding that as well.

What's more, at a time when half of us are officially overweight, we have now taken steps to ensure that every breakfast cereal we make will always be at least 90% fat-free. For further information and advice please phone Kellogg's 0800 626 066.

Kellogg's

Serving The Nation's Health

Plate 9.1 Kellogg's. The need to recognise and reflect social values is an important dimension when building an understanding of the target market and developing a brand's position. This picture reflects part of a campaign by Kellogg's to 'Serve the Nation's Health'. The campaign was built on four pillars: weight control, disease prevention, mental and physical stimulation and winter protection. See Chapter 9, page 221. Picture reproduced with the kind permission of the Kellogg Company of Great Britain.

Plate 12.1 Crown Paints. A business-to-consumer pull strategy designed to reposition the brand. See Chapter 12, page 288 and Chapter 5, page 122. Picture reproduced with the kind permission of Akzo Nobel.

Plate 12.2 'Tim Nice but Dim'. Having identified a need to show consumers how to use beef and lamb for midweek meals, the Harry Enfield character 'Tim Nice but Dim' was used as part of a pull-based strategy to gain the attention of, and then inform, consumers in an amusing manner. See Chapter 12, page 296. Picture and material reproduced with the kind permission of the Meat and Livestock Commission.

period, causing the ASA to recommend that 'Advertisers need to be more sensitive to public opinion when portraying women, especially when such images appear on posters'. However, just a few years later, an advertisement for the Yves Saint Laurent perfume 'Opium' featuring the model Sophie Dahl naked and in a reclining position was ordered to be withdrawn by the ASA after it had attracted more complaints than any other single advertisement in the preceding five years. The advertisement had appeared for some months in magazines, but it was its appearance as a poster that sparked the surge of complaints.

ASA Web site (http://www.asa.org.uk/), accessed 27 February 2001;
The Herald, 19 December 2000

Images designed to shock

The question of the use of shocking images in marketing communications is one in which an organisation would do well to consider its own long-term interest as broadly as possible. In the short term, a shocking image may be effective, but used to excess the tactic will be counter-productive for a growing number of recipients of the message. The controversy resulting from Oliviero Toscani's famous poster campaigns for Benetton certainly succeeded in gaining publicity for the knitwear company. As the images used in successive waves of the campaign became more and more uncomfortable, however, newspapers sometimes refused to carry the advertisements. Eventually in 2000, a campaign featuring prisoners on America's death row caused such an outcry in that country that a key deal between Benetton and Sears was jeopardised. Toscani and Benetton parted company shortly afterwards, as was related in an episode of the BBC series *Blood on the Carpet* (http://www.bbc.co.uk/, accessed 29 February 2001).

The same concerns may apply to a charity: those appealing for funds to help alleviate distressing problems around the world may be tempted to make use of shocking real-life images of the situations that they encounter. Being aware of the ever-present risk of 'compassion fatigue' on the part of donors, as well as the possibility of causing unwarranted distress to some recipients of the message, most charity fund-raising communications remain within limits of taste and decency for what are likely to be purely prudential reasons.

Hospitality, incentives, inducements, and bribery and extortion

The ethical questions surrounding the payment of bribes in business feature prominently in most textbooks on business ethics. These difficult issues need to be mentioned here both because they are important and because they may well involve sales staff. Bribes are unofficial – and usually illegal – payments to individuals 'to procure services or gain influence' (*Collins Concise English Dictionary*). These payments may be to secure orders, for example, or to expedite deliveries.

Distinguishing between bribery and extortion

It is useful to draw a distinction between extortion and bribery: the former is demanded by the would-be receiver, while the latter is offered by the individual or organisation wishing to buy the influence. In a situation in which informal payments of this nature are thought to be commonplace, a company's decision to go along with extortion is ethically different from a decision to offer a bribe. But in either case, the familiar distinction between short-term and long-term benefits is important.

Finding the balance – the Vegetarian Society

A recent example of shocking images illustrates the tension between the desire to make a point powerfully and the need to avoid undue offence. The UK-based Vegetarian Society ran a brief press advertising campaign in 1997 which drew attention to recently published research findings of possible links between diets that are high in red meat and an increased risk of some types of cancer: readers were recommended to reduce or eliminate meat consumption and to eat more vegetables and fruit.

Expressed in this way, the proposition seems to be a reasonable and unsurprising communication from an organisation with the aims of the Vegetarian Society. The campaign, however, attracted an adverse adjudication from the Advertising Standards Authority in December 1997, for reasons that were mainly to do with *how* the point was made, rather than the underlying proposition. The advertisements were deliberately hard-hitting in style, showing photographs of cancer operation scars and including headlines such as 'It's much easier to cut out meat'. Objectors – who included bodies such as the Meat and Livestock Commission and the National Farmers Union – claimed that the advertisements had in a number of ways exaggerated the research findings and government recommendations alluded to in the text and that the advertisements were shocking to those directly or indirectly affected by cancer and unduly distressing.

Most of these complaints – including that of undue distress – were upheld by the ASA. The adjudication was followed by a defiant response from the Vegetarian Society, maintaining that the evidence upon which the advertisements were based was robust and pointing out that the Society had received around 2,500 telephone calls responding positively to the advertisement. Two years later, Barnardos, the children's charity ran a press advertisement featuring a baby sitting alone in a filthy flat and holding a syringe. The advert was headed 'John Donaldson, Age 23' and the copy explained how the work of the charity sought to prevent child abuse victims from the bleak future that could await them. Protestors objected that the advertisement was shocking and offensive, but the ASA did not uphold the complaints, noting that the advertiser had behaved responsibly in researching the advert among its target audience in order to ensure that the message was understood and was unlikely to cause offence.

The purpose of these examples is not to comment on the decisions made, but rather to illustrate the complex issues that have to be weighed in these situations in marketing communications. The Vegetarian Society, Barnardos and other cause-promoting organisations are not businesses in the normal sense, but they do need to make similarly broad and balanced judgements in deciding how to communicate their ideas.

ASA Web site (http://www.asa.org.uk/), accessed 29 February 2001; Vegetarian Society press release of 9 December 1997

Difficult choices

The ethical company will need to take account of the effects on its image and wider relationships of taking part in bribery or extortion: these illegal practices have harmful effects on local economies and are likely to be regarded negatively by most stakeholders. The normal conduct of business relies heavily upon trust and the rule of law, both of which are undeniably jeopardised by corruption.

Even where these practices are in fact commonplace, the position of a company that makes informal payments while at the same time actively pressuring the government to take action against corruption is likely to be seen as different from one that pays bribes on the basis of short-term expediency. Sometimes, companies may consider some sort of arm's-length arrangement, in which local agents are required to 'look after' any needs of this sort, with payments eventually appearing under headings such as 'consultancy fees'. Although expectations and practices may well vary from one industry to another, an ethical analysis of these arm's-length arrangements cannot fail to take account of the fact that corrupt payments are being made, however well they are hidden in the short term.

These illegal practices have harmful effects on local economies and are likely to be regarded negatively by most stakeholders.

For Sternberg (1994), offering a bribe is an attempt to cheat and a violation of ordinary decency, while taking a bribe is a violation of distributive justice: decisions are made because of the bribe, rather than the relevant merits of the business offering. These are difficult questions in practice, which may involve hard choices, including the choice of whether to take part in markets in which corruption is endemic. Dunfee *et al.* (1999) examine the question of bribery in some detail from a social contract theory point of view (based upon a multilayered analysis of what affected parties and society might agree to), arguing that acceptability can only be judged by such a broad analysis.

Corporate hospitality: what are the limits?

Far less serious than actual bribery, but arguably on the same continuum, is the question of the scale of entertainment and hospitality that should be provided by the selling organisation to the buying organisation. It is entirely natural for a company to seek to build up closer relationships with its major customers, and corporate hospitality would normally be seen as an entirely legitimate part of this process. Even in this area, however, sales staff may be conscious of 'grey areas', in which the lavishness of the hospitality or gift-giving may seem to be out of proportion to the purpose of building a business relationship. Many companies recognise this potential hazard by providing guidelines to staff on what is to be regarded as acceptable in accepting and offering corporate hospitality. Those guidelines will naturally take account of normal practice within the industry and may well differ from one industry to another and – within any given industry – from one period to another.

Hospitality expenditure, like any other business expense, needs to be assessed in terms of its intended purpose and in the context of the long-term aims of the business.

Again, however, the appropriate judgement about corporate entertainment is likely to be the one that maximises the company's long-term interests, within the limits of common decency and distributive justice. Hospitality expenditure, like any other business expense, needs to be assessed in terms of its intended purpose and in the context of the long-term aims of the business. At one extreme, to ban all corporate entertainment would damage a firm's commercial relationships and hence its interests in most situations; at the other end of the scale, however, a different type of damage to the firm's long-term interests would be caused by practising over-lavish hospitality.

Ethical influence of supervisory and reward systems in sales management

The previous section mentioned the beneficial role that company codes can play in promoting and facilitating ethical decision-making on the part of sales and other staff. It is also worth highlighting that the management framework itself can also exert a powerful positive or negative influence on the ethical decision-making environment. Sales recruitment, training and briefing systems, for example, can be designed to encourage ethical behaviours on the part of sales staff, but equally may (e.g. through neglect) provide an uncertain context for individual employees, in which inexperienced or opportunistic staff may start to take decisions that are against the long-term interest of the company.

Fostering ethical behaviour by the sales force

The same is true, of course, of the approach taken to sales motivation and reward: a sales targeting and reward system that has been designed without due consideration of the long-term reputation of the company may have the effect of encouraging and rewarding some highly damaging behaviours on the part of staff, especially in the run-up to year-end with everyone under pressure to meet targets. Ethical companies design sales motivation and reward systems that encourage sales behaviour that maximises the long-term company interest. In an empirical study in this area, Hunt and Vasquez-Parraga (1993) found that sales managers did consider both the behaviours of sales staff and the consequences of those behaviours: unethical behaviour was likely to be more severely disciplined, for example, if the consequences were negative for the organisation. The authors suggest that:

Ethical companies design sales motivation and reward systems that encourage sales behaviour that maximises the long-term company interest.

> A culture emphasizing ethical values may be best developed and maintained by having sales people and their supervisors internalising a set of [duty-based] norms proscribing a set of behaviours that are inappropriate, 'just not done', and prescribing a set of behaviours that are appropriate, 'this is the way we do things'. In both cases, sales people and their supervisors should know that when ethical issues are involved, rewards (or punishments) flow from following (or violating) the [duty-based] norms, not from organisationally desirable or undesirable outcomes.
>
> (Hunt and Vasquez-Parraya, 1993, p. 87)

This suggestion, with its emphasis on duties for salespeople, rather than consequences, may at first sight seem to be at odds with the Sternberg's (1994) general recommendation that a business should take that course of action that is consistent with maximising long-term owner value within the constraints of common decency and distributive justice. There is, however, no necessary contradiction: the recommended sales management framework may well be the best way for the firm to maximise long-term owner value, reflecting, for example, the difficulty that individual salespeople may have in judging the long-term interests of the firm reliably. It will also be very helpful to create a culture in which individual salespeople feel able to report unexpected difficulties that they encounter in applying the ethical code of practice as they understand it, either because the code seems inappropriate or because a new type of problem has arisen. In this way, a company can help to ensure that its good intentions concerning ethical behaviour are realised in practice.

Ethical decision-making models in marketing

A number of contributions to the literature have proposed models to facilitate ethical decision-making in business in general and in marketing in particular. In looking at these models, we necessarily stray beyond the specific topic of this chapter: the models offer approaches to decision-making that are certainly applicable to marketing communications, but can also be applied more widely in business affairs.

At a general business level, for example, Sternberg (1994) proposes a four-stage process for identifying and resolving ethical issues in business:

- clarify the question (e.g. look carefully for unintentional vagueness or false assumptions);
- determine the relevance for *this* business (i.e. is this actually a problematic issue relevant to this particular business?);
- identify the circumstantial constraints (which may include legal and regulatory issues, but also contractual, cultural, economic, physical and technical considerations);
- assess the available options (i.e. against the tests of maximising long-term owner value and respecting distributive justice and common decency).

Chonko (1995) characterises the ethical decision-making process in marketing as comprising:

- the ethical situation itself (e.g. the opportunity, or scope for action, the ethical decision history and the moral intensity of the situation);
- characteristics of the decision-maker (for example, knowledge, experience, achievement motivation, need for affiliation);
- significant influences (e.g. the organisation, the law, economics, technology);
- the decision itself;
- the outcomes of the decision (e.g. in terms of performance, rewards, satisfaction, feedback).

From a different point of view, Smith (1995) suggests that marketing ethics can be seen as depending upon the prevailing outlook, ranging along a continuum from *caveat emptor* ('let the buyer beware') at one end, moving through intermediate points of industry standards, ethics codes and consumer sovereignty to the position of *caveat venditor* ('let the seller beware'). In his view, ethics in marketing has for some time been

Ethics in marketing has for some time been moving away from the simple caveat emptor *position towards the position of consumer sovereignty.*

moving away from the simple *caveat emptor* position towards the position of consumer sovereignty. He proposes a consumer sovereignty test for companies to apply:

- *Consumer capability:* is the target market vulnerable in ways that limit consumer decision-making?
- *Information:* are consumer expectations at purchase likely to be realised? Do consumers have sufficient information to judge?
- *Choice:* can consumers go elsewhere? Would they incur substantial costs or inconvenience in transferring their loyalty?

The answers to these test questions in any situation will help the firm to realise what actions it needs to take in order to behave ethically.

Laczniak and Murphy (1991, p. 264) also list some rules of thumb for marketers facing what appears to be an ethical dilemma:

- The golden rule – act in a way that you would expect others to act towards you.
- The *professional ethic* – take only actions which would be viewed as proper by an objective panel of your professional colleagues.
- Kant's *categorical imperative* – act in a way such that the action taken under the circumstances could be a universal law of behaviour for everyone facing those same circumstances.
- The *TV test* – a manager should always ask, would I feel comfortable explaining this action on TV to the general public?
- The outcomes of the decision (e.g. in terms of performance, rewards, satisfaction, feedback).

Laczniak and Murphy also propose a set of questions for marketers to help to analyse an issue in ethical terms. The questions cover issues of law, moral obligations, consequences and intent. As they point out, exploring the sometimes conflicting answers to these questions is likely to enhance the moral reasoning capabilities of managers, which – in parallel with company and other codes of ethics – is likely to result in better ethical decisions.

In these decision models, the literature provides a checklist of questions or characteristics which aim to help a firm think its way through ethical issues. As should be clear, the answers to the questions are very much up to the judgement made by the managers involved in the process.

Why strive to be ethical in marketing?

In closing this chapter, it is perhaps worth highlighting some of the research that has been conducted into the ethical behaviour of real-life marketing people. As Goolsby and Hunt (1992) point out, marketing as a function is often linked in the public mind with ethical abuse, mainly because of the way marketing operates at the boundary between the firm and its customers. In their study, however, the authors found that marketing people (and especially marketing women) compared favourably with those from other functions in terms of cognitive moral development (broadly, an individual's capacity for independent moral reasoning).

Marketing people compared favourably with those from other functions in terms of cognitive moral development.

Singhapakdi *et al.* (1995) concluded from a survey of US marketing professionals that marketers seem to believe that ethics and social responsibility are important components of organisational effectiveness. The survey also partly indicated that ethical corporate values seem to sensitise marketers to the need to include ethics and social responsibility in marketing decisions. This view is supported by Creyer and Ross (1997), who found that many consumers do take a company's ethics into account in making purchase decisions and that they may pay a higher price to a firm whose behaviour they approve of. Clear, readily accessible and credible information about corporate behaviour is an essential element in this relationship.

These findings would seem to indicate that there may be a positive reception within the marketing profession for Thompson's (1995, p. 188) suggestion:

> For marketers, adopting a more caring orientation offers an opportunity to become ethical innovators within their organisation. In most firms, those in marketing positions are closest to consumers, in terms of direct interaction and knowledge of their lifestyles. One role for marketers would be to regard themselves as more explicit advocates of consumer interests – both immediate and long term.

This general proposal about the role of marketing in general has special relevance for the activities of marketing communications.

Summary

This chapter has provided a brief introduction to the main ideas in business ethics and looked at some of the implications of these ideas for the practice of marketing communications. Just as there are no special ethical rules for business in general, ethics in marketing communications is a matter of applying normal ethical principles to the practice of marketing communications. Some of the difficulties in business of deciding between general ethical systems based upon duties and those based upon consequences may be avoided by taking a teleological or purpose-based approach, seeking to identify actions which will have the effect of maximising the long-term interest of the firm and its owners, remaining always within the important constraints of common decency and distributive justice. Done properly, this approach obliges managers to take an intelligent and enlightened view of the likely consequences of their actions on others.

It is sometimes argued that practices such as advertising are inherently undesirable: powerful means of manipulation, with destructive consequences. This chapter, however, has taken the view that ethics in marketing communications need to be considered in the context of a market economy, meaning that advertising, selling and so on are activities that are in themselves ethically neutral, but can be carried out in ethical or unethical ways. Applying the teleological approach helps to resolve many problems in marketing communications, including those to do with truth-telling, behaviour towards vulnerable groups, privacy and respect for persons, taste and decency, inducements and approaches to sales supervision and reward.

Marketing communications managers, with their special responsibility for the dialogue between the firm and the outside world, have every reason to take business ethics seriously (and generally seem, in fact, to do so) and may well have the opportunity to play an influential role in this respect within the firm as a whole.

Review questions

1. What are the practical problems of adopting a simple duties-based or consequences-based approach to ethics in marketing communications?

2. Explain why a practical approach to ethical business has to be based upon a clear idea of the purpose of a business.

3. What are the limitations, if any, of the principle *caveat emptor* (let the buyer beware) as a guide to ethics in personal selling?

4. What guiding principles can help a company to decide about the proposed use of a shocking image in its advertising?

5. Why is it both difficult and important for a company to take account of individual privacy in designing and implementing its marketing communications?

6. What ethical lessons for marketing communications managers in financial services companies should be learned from the private pensions scandal in the UK in the 1980s?

7. What is the difference between lying, misrepresentation and puffery in advertising? What tests should an advertiser apply to avoid misrepresentation?

8. What evidence would help to differentiate between legitimate corporate hospitality and unethical inducements, such as bribery?

9. Describe, with examples, the way in which Smith's consumer sovereignty test can help a company to design ethical marketing communications.

10. Explain Sternberg's four-stage process for identifying and resolving ethical issues in business.

MINI CASE

Pure and Simple Fashions

It was late in the evening and marketing director Jane Carson was reflecting on how quickly difficult situations seemed to develop in the business environment of the new century. It was only last month that she had organised a very successful launch of the new season's designs, coupled with a launch of her company's new interactive Web site, which would allow customers to order on line. Recent events, however, had demonstrated that modern communications media could just as effectively carry bad news.

Pure and Simple Fashions (PSF) was a familiar retail brand on the high street, providing mid-priced fashions aimed at younger women. From its launch 10 years earlier, its competitive positioning had also been pure and simple, as reflected in its advertising line: 'Fashion that doesn't cost the earth'. Pure and Simple clothes were made from natural fibres, grown organically and processed in ways that supported the environmental notion of 'sustainability': working with natural resources without reducing the future availability of those resources. This idea – coupled with some inspired and widely praised innovative designs – had connected very effectively with PSF's target segment and the organisation had built up a loyal following over the years. Indeed, PSF's positioning seemed to appeal just as strongly to the new generation of young women customers as to the organisation's original clients, many of whom had stayed with PSF. PSF had grown steadily, with retail outlets in most UK cities and large towns, and an enviable profit growth record, based upon its well-established positioning. This business development had been supported by extensive and very popular press and poster advertising, based upon appealing natural images from ecosystems around the world. Two years ago, PSF had initiated an expansion into continental Europe, based upon franchised outlets in a growing number of major cities. This had now been complemented by the introduction of an interactive Web site, whose design had been nominated for a national award for ease of access and use. Customers could view the ranges in three dimensions, match colours and order clothes manufactured to exactly their own sizes. The new distribution channel was underpinned by extensive customer relationship management software, which PSF hoped would enable it to build a closer relationship with its individual customers, as well as providing the basis for increasing growth into international markets.

The current crisis for PSF had its roots in a TV documentary programme broadcast two weeks before. The documentary had set out to investigate what some saw as the negative effects of increasing globalisation. The agenda was a familiar one, focusing on the enormous economic power wielded by very large multinational corporations in smaller developing countries. Part of the programme had focused on working conditions in factories in developing countries, showing the manufacture of branded clothing and other products for world markets. Pure and Simple was one of many well-known brands mentioned in this part of the programme, in a sequence that also contrasted bright and appealing advertising images from Europe with distressing views of unpleasant and oppressive working environments and interviews with employees about their experiences. No specific allegations about PSF or any other brand were made in the programme, although allusions were made to earlier, well-documented allegations about the use of child labour by some manufacturers. Street interviews with shoppers

in London were used to suggest a disparity between the promoted image of branded goods and the reality of life for those who made them.

In the days following the broadcast of the programme, newspapers and magazines took up the themes of the programme, resulting in a flood of letters from readers: it was clear that the programme had – at least at an emotional level – been very effective. Soon, PSF branch managers began to report increasing numbers of hostile questions from customers about the company's sourcing policy; the levels of telephone and email enquiries into PSF's headquarters confirmed this development. The problem had escalated to a new level with the threat from a previously little-known anti-capitalist lobbying group to 'jam' the communications of number of brand-owning organisations, including PSF, by flooding their Web sites with vast amounts of communications traffic. The experiences of other organisations in the recent past had shown that threats of this nature needed to be taken seriously: the effect for PSF at the beginning of the present season could be disastrous, particularly given the strength and clear focus of its present environmentalist positioning.

Although Pure and Simple had never made any public statement about its policy concerning the manufacture of its products, Jane Carson knew that PSF had always insisted that working conditions in its suppliers were in line with – and in many cases significantly better than – local 'best practice', although of course actual wage rates were low by European standards. Objectively, PSF could argue strongly that its suppliers maintained high standards and that its participation in developing countries was of clear benefit to those economies. However, the present public debate was not being conducted objectively and Jane wondered how to regain the initiative. What seemed to be happening was that those customers who had been attracted to Pure and Simple because of its environmental commitment were those who were expressing the greatest concern about the issues raised by the TV programme.

For some time, it had been possible to see the growing links between previously disparate specialist lobbying organisations, together with the increasing interest on the part of affluent and well-educated customers in the values embodied in the brands they chose. Had Pure and Simple sat on its environmental laurels in recent years and been caught napping by these new developments? Or was it PSF's very strong public image and accessibility that rendered it vulnerable to these protests, whatever the reality of its case? The textbook injunction to 'balance stakeholder interests' seemed to be particularly problematic this evening, as Jane worked on her company's response.

Note: this case is wholly imaginary; no reference is intended to actual organisations or people.

Mini-case questions

1. What ethical issues for Pure and Simple Fashions arise in this case?

2. How would an evaluation of these ethical issues based on broad stakeholder theory differ from one based on Sternberg's teleological perspective?

3. Outline a possible marketing communications strategy for PSF that will allow it to respond to its current difficulties and continue its successful and profitable growth as a fashion retailer.

4. What lessons might PSF learn concerning the management of its relationship with its various stakeholders?

References

American Marketing Association (n.d.) Code of ethics, http://www.ama.org/ (accessed 1 March 2001).

Attas, D. (1999) What's wrong with deceptive advertising?, *Journal of Business Ethics*, **21**, pp. 49–59.

Barton, L. (1994) A quagmire of ethics, profit and the public trust: the crisis in public relations services. *Journal of Professional Services Marketing*, **11**(1), pp. 87–99.

Botan, C. (1997) Ethics in strategic communication campaigns: the case for a new approach to public relations. *Journal of Business Communication*, **34**(2), pp. 188–202.

Chonko, L.B. (1995) *Ethical Decisions in Marketing*. Thousand Oaks, CA: Sage.

Christy, R and Mitchell, S.M. (1999), Direct marketing and privacy. *Journal of Targeting, Measurement and Analysis for Marketing*, **8**(1), pp. 8–20.

Creyer, E.H. and Ross, W.T. (1997) The influence of firm behaviour on purchase intention: do consumers really care about business ethics? *Journal of Consumer Marketing*, **14**(6), pp. 421–33.

Curtis, J. (1999) Is TV too much for Shell's ethical rebuild? *Marketing*, 7 October 1999, p. 21.

De George, R.T. (1999) *Business Ethics*, 5th edn. Englewood Cliffs, NJ: Prentice Hall.

Diacon, S.R. and Ennew, C.T. (1996) Ethical issues in insurance marketing in the UK. *European Journal of Marketing*, **30**(5), pp. 67–80.

Dunfee, T.W., Smith, N.C .and Ross, W.T. (1999) Social contracts and marketing ethics. *Journal of Marketing*, **63**(3), pp. 14–32.

Friedman, M. (1970) The social responsibility of business is to increase its profits. *New York Times Magazine*, 13 September, pp. 32 *et seq.*

Goolsby, J.R. and Hunt, S.D. (1992) Cognitive moral development and marketing. *Journal of Marketing*, **56** (January), pp. 55–68.

Gundlach, G.T. and Murphy, P.E. (1993) Ethical and legal foundations of relational marketing exchanges. *Journal of Marketing*, **57** (October), pp. 35–46.

Holbrook, M.B. (1987) Mirror, mirror, on the wall, what's unfair in the reflections on advertising? *Journal of Marketing*, **51** (July), pp. 95–103.

Hunt, S.D. and Vasquez-Parraga, A.Z. (1993) Organisational consequences, marketing ethics and salesforce supervision. *Journal of Marketing Research* (February), pp. 78–90.

Jackson, J.C. (1996) *An Introduction to Business Ethics*. Oxford: Blackwell.

Klein, N. (2000) *No Logo*. London: Flamingo

Laczniak, G.R. and Murphy, P.E. (1991) Fostering ethical marketing decisions. *Journal of Business Ethics*, **10**, pp. 259–71.

Murphy, P.E. (1999) Character and virtue ethics in international marketing: an agenda for managers, researchers and educators. *Journal of Business Ethics*, **18**, pp. 107–24.

Ogilvy, D. (1963) *Confessions of an Advertising Man*. London: Longman.

Packard, V. (1960) *The Hidden Persuaders*. Harmondsworth: Penguin.

Pollay, R.W. (1986) The distorted mirror: reflections on the unintended consequences of advertising. *Journal of Marketing*, **50** (April), pp. 18–36.

Robin, D.P. and Reidenbach, R.E. (1993) Searching for a place to stand: toward a workable ethical philosophy for marketing. *Journal of Public Policy and Marketing*, **12**(1), pp. 97–105.

Schlegelmilch, B. (1998) *Marketing Ethics: An International Perspective*. London: International Thomson Business Press.

Singhapakdi, A., Kraff, K.L., Vitell, S.J. and Rallapalli, K.C. (1995) The perceived importance of ethics and social responsibility on organisational effectiveness: a survey of marketing. *Journal of the Academy of Marketing Science*, **23**(1), pp. 49–56.

Smith, N.C. (1995) Marketing strategies for the ethics era. *Sloan Management Review* (Summer), pp. 85–97.

Sorell, T. and Hendry, J. (1994) *Business Ethics*. Oxford: Butterworth Heinemann.

Sternberg, E. (1994) *Just Business*. London: Warner.

Thompson, C.J. (1995) A contextualist proposal for the conceptualization and study of marketing ethics. *Journal of Public Policy and Marketing*, **14**(2), pp. 177–91.

Tzalikis, J. and Fritzsche, D.J. (1989) Business ethics: a literature review with a focus on marketing ethics. *Journal of Business Ethics*, **8**, pp. 695–743.

Vallance, E.M. (1995) *Business Ethics at Work*. Cambridge: Cambridge University Press.

chapter 7

Internal marketing communications

The concept of 'internal marketing' recognises the importance of organisational members (principally employees) as important markets in their own right. These markets can be regarded as segments (and can be segmented), each of which has particular needs and wants that require satisfaction in order that an organisation's overall goals be accomplished. Internal (marketing) communications serve to not only convey managerial intentions and members' feelings but in many circumstances represent an integral aspect of communications with external stakeholder groups.

AIMS AND OBJECTIVES

The aim of this chapter is to examine the context of internal marketing and how such issues might impact on an organisation's overall marketing communications.

The objectives of this chapter are:

1. To introduce the notion of internal marketing.

2. To understand the significance of organisational issues when developing marketing communication strategies.

3. To introduce the notion of organisational identity and the impact that employees can bring to the way that organisations are perceived by members and non-members.

4. To examine the impact of corporate culture on planned communications.

5. To provide an insight into the notion of strategic credibility and stakeholder perception of the focus organisation.

6. To appreciate the interaction and importance of corporate strategy to planned communications.

7. To examine how communication audits can assist the development of effective marketing communications.

Introduction

It was established earlier that marketing communications are concerned with the way in which various stakeholders interact with each other and with the focus organisation. Traditionally, external stakeholders (customers, intermediaries and financiers) are the prime focus of marketing communications. However, recognition of the importance of internal stakeholders as a group who should receive marketing attention has increased, and the concept of *internal marketing* emerged in the 1980s. This developed with greater impetus in the 1990s and is likely to be a major area of attention for both academics and practitioners in the first decade of the third millennium.

Berry (1980) is widely credited as the first to recognise the term 'internal marketing', in a paper that sought to delineate between product- and service-based marketing activities. The notion that the delivery of a service-based offering is bound to the quality of the personnel delivering it has formed the foundation of a number of research activities and journal papers.

The popular view is that employees constitute an internal market in which paid labour is exchanged for designated outputs. An extension to this is that employees are a discrete group of customers with whom management interact (Piercy and Morgan, 1991), in order that relational exchanges can be maintained (developed) with external stakeholders. Therefore, as a legitimate type of customer they should be subject to similar marketing practices.

Both employees and managers impose their own constraints upon the range and nature of the activities the organisation pursues, including its promotional activities. Employees, for

Both employees and managers impose their own constraints upon the range and nature of the activities the organisation pursues, including its promotional activities.

example, are important to external stakeholders not only because of the tangible aspects of service and production that they provide but also because of the intangible aspects, such as attitude and the way in which the service is provided: 'how much do they really care?' Images are often based more on the intangible than the tangible aspects of employee communications.

Management, on the other hand, is responsible for the allocation of resources and the process and procedures used to create added value. Its actions effectively constrain the activities of the organisation and shape the nature and form of the communications the organisation adopts, either consciously or unconsciously. It is important, therefore, to understand how organisations can influence and impact upon the communication process.

Each organisation is a major influence upon its own marketing communications. Indeed, the perception of others is influenced by the character and personality of the organisation.

Member/non-member boundaries

The demarcation of internal and external stakeholders is not as clear as many writers suppose. The boundaries which exist between members and non-members of an organisation are becoming increasingly less clear as a new more flexible workforce emerges. For example, part-time workers, consultants and temporary workforces spread themselves across organisational borders (Hatch and Schultz, 1997) and in many instances assume multiple roles of employee, consumer (product) and financial stakeholder (e.g. Halifax or Northern Rock employees, who may be borrowers or savers and now also shareholders).

The boundaries which exist between members and non-members of an organisation are becoming increasingly less clear as a new more flexible workforce emerges.

According to Morgan (1997), many organisations have a problem as they do not recognise that they are themselves part of their environment. The context in which they see themselves and other organisations is too sharp. They see themselves as discrete entities faced with the problem of surviving against the vagaries of the outside world, which is often constructed as a domain of threat and opportunity. He refers to these as *egocentric* organisations. They are characterised by a fixed notion of who they are or what they can be and are determined to impose or sustain that identity at all times. This leads to an overplay of their own importance and an underplay of the significance of the wider system of relationships of which they are a part. In attempting to sustain unrealistic identities they produce identities that end up destroying important elements of the context of which they are part. The example provided by Morgan is of typewriter manufacturers who failed to see technological developments leading to electronic typewriters and then word processors.

It would appear that by redrawing or even collapsing boundaries with customers, competitors and suppliers, organisations are better able to create new identities and use internal marketing communications to better effect.

Purpose of internal marketing

Research by Foreman and Money (1995) indicates that managers see the main components of internal marketing as falling into three broad areas, namely development, reward and vision for employees. These will inevitably vary in intensity on a situational basis.

Managers see the main components of internal marketing as falling into three broad areas, namely development, reward and vision for employees.

All of these three components have communication as a common linkage. Employees and management (members) need to communicate with one another and with a variety of non-members, and do so through an assortment of methods. Communication with members, wherever they are located geographically, needs to be undertaken for a number of reasons. These include the DRIP factors (Chapter 1), but these communications also serve the additional purposes of providing transaction efficiencies and affiliation needs; see Table 7.1.

The values transmitted to customers, suppliers and distributors through external communications need to be reinforced by the values expressed by employees, especially those who interact with these external groups. Internal marketing communications are necessary in order that internal members are motivated and involved with the brand such that they are able to present a consistent and uniform message to non-members. This is an aspect of integrated marketing

This process whereby employees are encouraged to communicate with non-members so that organisations ensure that what is promised is realised by customers is referred to as 'living the brand'.

Table 7.1   The roles of internal marketing communications

DRIP factors	To provide information
	To be persuasive
	To reassure/remind
	To differentiate employees/groups
Transactional	To coordinate actions
	To promote the efficient use of resources
	To direct developments
Affiliation	To provide identification
	To motivate personnel
	To promote and coordinate activities with non-members

communications and involves product and organisation centered messages. If there is a set of shared values then internal communications are said to blend and balance the external communications. This process whereby employees are encouraged to communicate with non-members so that organisations ensure that what is promised is realised by customers is referred to as 'living the brand'.

'Living the Brand' – British Airways

Back in the 1980s British Airways introduced a training programme which all staff attended. This was referred to as 'Putting People First' and a part of each weekly session was attended by a senior director, very often the CEO (now Lord Marshall ,the chairman), to reflect the importance and significance of the training and to be customer orientated. This scheme has been reintroduced as 'Putting People First – Again', partly in an effort to remind staff what the brand represents and to involve them in its development. Goften (2000) reports that the programme is about the past, the present and the future, that is pride in the past, passion for the present and faith in the future. In doing so staff are developed and encouraged to live the brand and, in a service-based business, the quality of the customer service encounter can seriously enhance or damage brand reputation.

In a large number of both b2b and b2c organisations, new products and services are often developed through the use of project teams. According to Lievens and Moenart (2000), project communication is characterised by both flows of communication among project members (intra-project communication) and flows across boundaries with external members (extra-project communication). Boundary spanners act as mediators facilitating communications flows internally (for resources) and externally to customers, suppliers, competitors and technologies. Project teams perceive differing levels of uncertainty associated with their task and these are related to external (user needs, technologies and the competition) and internal (human and financial resources) factors.

Uncertainty about the resources needs to be reduced in order to reduce uncertainty associated with external stakeholders, improve communication effectiveness and achieve project tasks. As we will see later, the integration of internal and external communications is a key factor in the development of integrated marketing communications. Project teams have an important role to play in enhancing corporate reputation, particularly in the b2b sector.

The integration of internal and external communications is a key factor in the development of integrated marketing communications.

Organisational identity

Organisational identity is concerned with what individual members think and feel about the organisation to which they belong. When their perception of the organisation's characteristics accords with their own self-concept then the strength of organisational identity will be strong (Dutton *et al.*, 1994). Organisational identity also refers to the degree to which feelings and thoughts about the distinctive characteristics are shared among the members (Dutton and Dukerich, 1991). There are therefore, both individual and collective aspects to organisational identity.

Albert and Whetten (1985) stated that organisations must make three main decisions: who they are, what business they are in and what they want to be. In order that these decisions be made they claim that consideration must be given to what is central, what is distinctive and what is enduring about the character of the organisation.

Non-members of an organisation also develop feelings and thoughts about what are the central, enduring and distinctive characteristics of an organisation. It is highly probable that there will be variances between the perceptions and beliefs of members and non-members, and this may be a cause of confusion, misunderstanding or even conflict.

Non-members of an organisation also develop feelings and thoughts about what are the central, enduring and distinctive characteristics.

This discrepancy between what Goodman and Pennings (1977) termed private and public identities can impair the 'health' of the organisation. The 'unhealthier' or greater the discrepancy, the more will be the difficulty in generating the resources required to guarantee corporate survival. In other words, the closer the member/non-member identification, the better placed the organisation will be to achieve its objectives.

Organisational identity is deemed to be important at a collective level, when an organisation is formed or when there is a major change to the continuity of the goals of the organisation or when the means of accomplishment are hindered or broken; see Table 7.2.

According to Dutton and Penner (1993), what an individual sees as important, distinctive and unique about an organisation will affect the individual's assessment of the importance of an issue facing the organisation and also the degree to which it is of personal importance.

For members, organisational identity may be conceptualised as their perception of their organisation's central and distinctive attributes, including its positional status and relevant compositional group. Consequently, external events that refute or call into question these defining characteristics may threaten the perception that organisational members have of their organisational identity (Dutton and Dukerich, 1991).

External events that refute or call into question these defining characteristics may threaten the perception that organisational members have of their organisational identity.

Table 7.2 When organisational identity is important

During the formation of the organisation
At the loss of an identity-sustaining element
On the accomplishment of an organisation's *raison d'être*
Through extremely rapid growth
If there is a change in the collective status
Retrenchment

Source: Albert and Whetten (1985).

Research by Elsbach and Kramer (1996) found that members of a high-ranking organisation (MBA schools) perceived a threat because the ranking devalued their central and cherished identity dimensions and so refuted their prior claims of positional status.

Members used selective categorisations to re-emphasise positive perceptions of their organisational identities for both themselves and their non-member audiences by highlighting identity dimensions or alternative groups with which they should be compared and which were not previously identified, the intention being to deflect attention.

Dutton and Dukerich state that there is a significant interdependence between individuals' social identities and their perceptions of their organisational identities. So, as they care about how their organisations are described and how they are compared with other organisations, so they experience cognitive distress (identity dissonance) when they think that their organisation's identity is being threatened by what they perceive as inaccurate descriptions or misleading (unfair) comparisons with other organisations.

In response to this distress members restore positive self-perceptions by highlighting their organisation's membership in alternative comparison groups.

It is normal to assume that identity is relatively static. However, just as organisations can experience strategic drift when the corporate strategy and performance move further away, each period, from the intended or expected pattern, so organisations can suffer from identity drift away from the expected life cycle. Kimberley (1980) argues that this can occur for three main reasons: environmental complexity, identity divestiture and organisational success.

Care must be given to understanding and managing the organisational identity.

This indicates that care must be given to understanding and managing the organisational identity to ensure that any discrepancy between members' and non-members' perceptions of what is central, enduring and distinctive is minimised and to be aware of identity dissonance should the organisation be threatened and the values upheld by its members challenged.

Organisational culture

According to Beyer (1981), organisational identity is a subset of the collective beliefs that constitute an organisation's culture. Indeed, internal marketing is shaped by the prevailing culture, as it is the culture that provides the context within which internal marketing practices are to be accomplished.

Corporate culture, defined by Schein (1985), is 'the deeper level of basic assumptions and beliefs that are shared by members of an organisation, that operate unconsciously and define in a basic taken for granted fashion an organisation's view of its self and its environment'. A more common view of organisational culture is 'the way we do things around here'. It is the result of a number of factors, ranging through the type and form of business the organisation is in, its customers and other stakeholders, its geographical position, and its size, age and facilities. These represent the more tangible aspects of corporate culture. There are a host of intangible elements as well. These include the assumptions, values and beliefs that are held and shared by members of the organisation. These factors combine to create a unique environment, one where norms or guides to expected behaviour influence all members, whatever their role or position.

Shared values – B&Q

B&Q is a do-it-yourself retailer employing over 22,000 people spread across 286 sites. This means that communicating a consistent message to these employees is a complex yet important task, if there is to be brand consistency.

B&Q utilises a number of different internal communications tools to undertake this task, including email, team briefs and energise sessions (early morning team work-out sessions). The company has a distinct and visible personality in that it requires employees to act as brand ambassadors. There are five main values that act as the central pillar of the organisation. These are:

a down to earth approach;

respect for people;

being customer driven;

being positive;

striving to do better.

In part fulfilment of these values B&Q staff feature in the retailer's advertising. These show staff offering advice on tools and materials, ideas for gardening and indoor projects plus information about prices. This reflects the importance of integration because (real) staff are shown endorsing their brand and in essence challenging all customers to ask any employee about a range of matters. To make this loop work, staff need to know about the product range and how products might apply to different customers. If the message transmitted by employees (the promise) is not realised and experienced by customers, then there will be disappointment, falling expectations and a failing corporate image.

B&Q recognises that its staff are a major part of the organisation's success. It also recognises that the continuing commitment of its staff is essential, and effective internal communications are an important component in the process to gain this commitment.

See Plates 7.1 and 7.2.

Material kindly provided by B&Q

Levels of organisational culture

Corporate culture, according to Schein, consists of a number of levels. The first of these, according to Thompson (1990), is the most visible level. This includes physical aspects of the organisation, such as the way in which the telephone is answered, the look and style of the reception area, and the general care afforded to visitors. Other manifestations of these visible aspects are the advertisements, logos, letterheads and other written communications that an organisation generates.

The second level consists of the values held by key personnel. For example, should particular sales teams who regularly better their targets have their targets increased or should certain members of the sales team be redeployed to less successful teams or new markets? If the decision is made to increase the target, and the outcome is successful, then the decision is more likely to be repeated when the same conditions arise again.

The third level in Schein's approach is achieved when the decision to increase the target becomes an automatic response to particular conditions. A belief is formed and becomes an assumption about behaviour in the organisation. This automatic approach can lead to complementary behaviour by members of the sales team. The placing of orders can become manipulated, to the extent that orders placed in month 6 may be 'delayed' or stuck in the top drawer of the sales representative's desk, until some point in month 7, when it is appropriate to release them.

This behaviour leads to relative stability for all concerned.

The belief that the targets will be increased can lead to a behaviour that is referred to as 'the way we do things around here'. This behaviour leads to relative stability for all concerned and need not be disturbed unless a change is introduced, whose source is elsewhere in the system; that is, outside the team.

Culture and communication

Corporate culture is not a static phenomenon; the stronger the culture, the more likely it is to be transmitted from one generation of organisational members to another, and it is also probable that the culture will be more difficult to change if it is firmly embedded in the organisation. Most writers acknowledge that effective cultural change is difficult and a long-term task. Achieving a cultural fit is necessary if an organisation wishes to embrace a strategy that is incompatible with the current mind set of the organisation. Hunger and Wheelan (1993), for example, state that, to bring about cultural change, good communication, throughout the organisation, is a prerequisite for success. Mitchell (1998) considers the strong corporate culture that exists at Procter and Gamble. Depending upon one's perspective, this rigid formal hierarchical culture may be considered an advantage or a disadvantage. On the plus side it allows for strong identity, consistency and people development opportunities, as the company has a 'promote from within' policy. On the downside, the strength and penetration of the culture and need to toe the party line can restrict innovation, entrepreneurship and the use of initiative. This strength of culture and the cautious approach to risk taking may be responsible for the consistent emphasis on product attributes, performance and pack shots in its advertising and communications, unlike its close rival Unilever which makes greater use of emotions in its advertising. Procter and Gamble appear to recognise this as a limitation and have recently embarked upon a change of emphasis and have incorporated a more emotional approach in its communications. Changing the culture will be a challenge, but to be successful senior management will, among other things, need to be 'obsessive' about communicating the following to all members of the organisation (Gordon, 1985):

Corporate culture is not a static phenomenon; the stronger the culture, the more likely it is to be transmitted from one generation of organisational members to another.

1. the current performance and position of the organisation in comparison with its competition and the outlook for the future;

2. the vision of what the organisation was to become and how it would achieve it;

3. the progress the organisation had made in achieving those elements identified previously as important.

The focus of this communication is internal, usually through training and development programmes. However, if the concept of the superorganisation is accepted (Chapter 10), then this level of communication activity should also occur in the channel networks, especially when the network is destabilised owing to environmental turbulence. Certain complex offerings, such as information technology-based products, require channel members to provide high levels of training and support. It is also important to communicate the objectives of the network and to share responsibility for the performance of the channel as a whole. This is partly achieved by members fulfilling their roles as successful dealers, retailers or manufacturers, but there is still a strong requirement for the channel leader to set out what is required from each member of its different networks and to report on what has been achieved to date.

This is partly achieved by members fulfilling their roles as successful dealers, retailers or manufacturers.

Management of the communication finances, through time, will show the degree to which an organisation values such investments. Brands need time, the long term, to build and develop strength. Cutting back on investment in communications, especially advertising, in times of recession and difficulty, reveals management to view such activities as an expense, a cost against short-run needs. Furthermore, the expectation of channel members may be that a certain volume of marketing communications is necessary not only to sustain particular levels of business but also because competitors are providing established levels of communication activity. What is important is that the communications manager understands the culture of the organisation and the primary networks, values, styles, motivations and norms so that the communications work with rather than against the corporate will.

Brands need time, the long term, to build and develop strength.

Corporate strategy and communication

The relationship between corporate strategy and communications is important. Traditionally, these communications are perceived as those that make the network between an organisation's employees and its managers. This internal perspective of communications is important, particularly when organisations are in transition. This is only one part of the communication process. Employees are just one of the many stakeholders each organisation must seek to satisfy. Communications regarding strategic issues should also be targeted at members of the support and performance networks in order to gain their goodwill, involvement and understanding.

Advertising and the impact on employees

Gilly and Wolfinbarger (1998) concluded that an organisation's advertising can have both a positive and a negative effect on the employees of an organisation. Such advertising can serve to clarify roles, make promises that can be realistically delivered and demonstrates that the organisation values its employees. These positive outcomes can be seen in terms of improved morale and commitment.

Conversely, negative effects ensue when the advertising promises are unrealistic and cannot be delivered, messages are not true or the roles portrayed are far from flat-tering. For example, Boots used a campaign to inform consumers about its 'mix-and-match' offer. The ads depicted a member of staff explaining the deal to a confused colleague, who then apologises announcing that it is her first day. Staff, according to Witt (2001), complained that they were made to look stupid and incompetent. The outcome is low morale, distrust and unfavourable attitudes that can be perceived by non-members. It seems important therefore to generate advertising messages that are perceived by employees to be transparently achievable and consistent and this may involve the participation of a few staff in the development of advertising strategy.

Advertising can serve to clarify roles, make promises that can be realistically delivered and demonstrates that the organisation values its employees.

Gilly and Wolfinbarger developed a framework which presents the impact of advertising on employees (Figure 7.1).

This model shows that employees use three main criteria when evaluating the advertising used by their employers, namely accuracy of the message, value congruence and effectiveness. In order to reduce any gap that might emerge as a result of an advertising campaign (and consequent deterioration in morale and commitment), the increased vertical and horizontal communications are deemed necessary. This might require staff

Employees use three main criteria when evaluating the advertising used by their employers, namely accuracy of the message, value congruence and effectiveness.

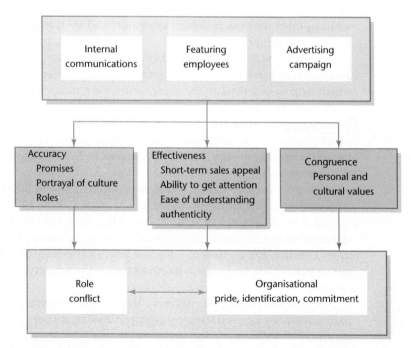

Figure 7.1   The impact of advertising on employees. Adapted from Gilly and Wolfinbarger (1998); used with kind permission.

to be involved in both advertising development and in some cases actual participation in the advertisement, the pretesting of ideas and the dissemination of the advertising and the supporting rationale.

All stakeholders need to know what the objectives of the focus organisation are, particularly the mission and overriding vision the organisation has, as this will impact on the other organisations in the performance network. For example, if Heinz or Pedigree Petfoods were to announce that, in the future, all their products were to be presented in containers that are capable of being recycled, then current suppliers might need to reformulate their offerings and any future suppliers would be aware of the constraint this might place on them. The information is provided in order that others may work with them and continue supplying offerings to end users with a minimum of interruption.

Barich and Kotler (1991) suggest that the concept of positioning (the process whereby offerings are perceived by consumers relative to the competition) applies at the brand and corporate level. If an organisation is pursuing a generic strategy of differentiation, then the positioning statements of the organisation need to reflect this. The image that stakeholders have of an organisation and its offerings affects their disposition towards the organisation, their intentions to undertake market transactions and the nature of the relationships between members.

Good external communications are important because, among other benefits, they can provide a source of competitive advantage. Perrier has built its share of the mineral water market on the volume and style of its planned communications. It has dominated communications in the market and has effectively set a mobility barrier which demands that any major challenger must be prepared to replicate the size of Perrier's investment in communications. The quality of the Perrier communications has also led distributors and other network members to support and want to be involved with the organisation, as evidenced by the swift recovery in market share after all world stocks had to be withdrawn because a small number of bottles had been identified as 'contaminated'. Morden (1993) refers to these positive external perceptions as intangible benefits which help to differentiate the organisation from its competitors.

Good external communications are important because, among other benefits, they can provide a source of competitive advantage.

All marketing strategies, such as those to harvest, build, hold and divest, require different communication strategies and messages. Similarly, market penetration, product development, market development and product penetration strategies all require varying forms of support which must be reflected in the communications undertaken by the organisation.

Marketing research may indicate that different stakeholders do not perceive the corporate and marketing strategies of an organisation in the same way as that intended by management. Some stakeholders may perceive the performance of an organisation inaccurately. This means that the organisation is failing to communicate in an effective and consistent way, and any such mismatch will, inevitably, lead to message confusion and relative disadvantage in the markets in which the organisation operates.

The communication of strategic intent and corporate performance must be harmonised. By understating or even misleading different stakeholders, performance may be influenced, and if claims are made for an organisation which suggest a level of performance or intent beyond reality, then credibility may be severely jeopardised.

Strategic credibility

A relatively new development concerning the role of corporate strategy and corporate communications is the concept of strategic credibility. According to Higgins and Bannister (1992), strategic credibility refers to 'how favourably key stakeholders view the company's overall corporate strategy and its strategic planning processes'.

If stakeholders perceive the focus organisation as strategically capable, it is suggested that it will accrue a number of benefits. The benefits vary from industry to industry and according to each situation, but it appears from the early research that those organisations experiencing transition and who are not regulated in any way have potentially the most to gain from open corporate communication with their stakeholders. The benefits from this open attitude include improved stock market valuations and price/earnings multiples, better employee motivation and closer relationships with all members of the performance and support networks, particularly those within the financial community.

Strategic credibility refers to 'how favourably key stakeholders view the company's overall corporate strategy and its strategic planning processes'.

There are four main determinants of strategic credibility:

1. an organisation's strategic capability;
2. past performance;
3. communication of corporate strategy to key stakeholders;
4. the credibility of the chief executive officer (CEO).

Strategic capability

Capability is a prerequisite for credibility. The perception that stakeholders have of the strategic processes within an organisation will influence their belief that the focus organisation can or cannot achieve its objectives. This is important in networks which are characterised by close working arrangements and high levels of interdependence. Should one organisation indicate that it lacks the necessary capability to perform strategically, then other members of the network are likely to be affected. The sharing of a strategic vision, one that may be common to all members of the stakeholder network, is a positive indicator of the existence of the acceptance that the focus organisation is strategically capable.

Past performance

The maintenance of a sustained strategic capability profile is partly dependent upon corporate performance. Poor performance does not sustain confidence, but even the existence of a strong performance is only worthwhile if it is communicated properly. The communication should inform the target audiences that the performance was planned and that there was sound reasoning and management judgement behind the performance.

Communication should inform the target audiences that the performance was planned and that there was sound reasoning and management judgement behind the performance.

Corporate communications

Organisations should inform members of the network of their strategic intentions as well as their past performance. This requires the accurate targeting and timing of the messages at a pace suitable and appropriate to the target's requirements. Higgins and Bannister refer to financial analysts, in particular, as stakeholders in need of good information. They argue that trying to evaluate the performance of a diversified organisation operating in a number of different markets, of which many of the analysts lack knowledge and expertise, is frustrating and difficult. Good information delivered through appropriate media and at particular times can be of benefit in the development of the realm of understanding between parties.

By keeping financial analysts aware of the strategic developments and the strategic thinking of the focus organisation and the industries in which it operates, the value of the organisation is more likely to reflect corporate performance. ICI experienced a major undervaluation in the 1980s because the financial markets and other key network members were not kept informed of the new strategies and thinking behind the corporate revival in the period 1982–86.

The credibility of the CEO

The fourth element proposed by Higgins and Bannister concerns the ability of the CEO to communicate effectively with a variety of audiences. By projecting strong, balanced and positive communications, it is thought that a visible CEO can improve the overall reputation of the organisation. Coupled with the improvement will be a perception of the strategic capability of the organisation. The CEO therefore can be regarded as a major determinant of the organisation's perceived strategic credibility.

Haji-Ioannou, Anita Rodderick, Terence Conran, Alan Sugar, James Dyson, Bernard Mathews and Richard Branson are some of the major CEOs to promote themselves on behalf of their organisations but there are many others who have tried and failed. However, research by Newell and Shemwell (1995) suggests that care should be taken when using CEOs as an endorser. They argue that the impact of source credibility may be reduced because of beliefs about product attributes, and this in turn may impact on behavioural intentions. Therefore, CEOs might be best used as endorsers when informationally, rather than emotionally or transformationally, based messages predominate.

For example, Richard Branson has been used as CEO endorser of the Virgin group. As chairman he has been a focal point in the promotion of Virgin financial products (mainly informational messages), but has not played such a central role in the persuasive communications concerning the airline Virgin Atlantic, where emotionally based messages have been used to influence brand choice decisions. In this instance a celebrity spokesperson (actress Marianne Faithful) was used to endorse the airline. See plate 21.2.

Strategic credibility is an interesting concept which can be used to develop an understanding of the perception held by key support network members of an organisation's strategic management processes.

Communication audit

Research, as we have seen, is an important element in the design of communication plans. Associated with this should be an evaluation of the most recent attempts at

CEO endorsers – Vision Express

Vision Express decided to use its chairman, Daniel Abittan to endorse the brand in its television commercials. Utilising his charisma and French accent to deliver messages about tangible product attributes (multiflex) and intangible attribures (good looks and sexiness) a high level of perceived credibility was achieved among member and non-member audiences. See Exhibit 7.1.

Exhibit 7.1   CEO endorser – Daniel Abittan. Picture reproduced with the kind permission of Vision Express and Webber Shandwick.

communicating with target audiences. The accumulation of this type of short-run information is useful because it builds into a database that can be used to identify key factors over the long run. Regression analysis can be used eventually to identify key variables in the marketing communications and marketing plans.

The communication strategies of competitors should also be measured and evaluated. Organisations and offerings do not exist in isolation from each other and competitor activities; messages, styles and levels of spend should also be taken into account. If a strategy of differentiation is being pursued, it would appear pointless and wasteful to position an offering in the same way as a main competitor.

The communication strategies of competitors should also be measured and evaluated.

The process by which an organisation communicates with its target audiences is, as we have seen, extremely important. To assist the process of evaluating the effectiveness of past communication strategies, strategic credibility and the corporate image held by different members of all networks, a communication audit should be undertaken. Financial audits examine the processes by which organisations organise and systematically manage their financial affairs. Some of the underlying agenda items may be to prevent fraud and malpractice, but the positive aspects of the financial audit are to understand what is happening, to develop new ways of performing certain tasks and to promote efficiency and effectiveness. The same principle holds for the communication audit. How is the organisation communicating and are there better ways of achieving the communication objectives?

A communication audit is a process which can assist the communications planner in assessing whether or not an organisation is communicating with its consumers and other stakeholders in an effective and meaningful way. A further important goal of such an exercise is to determine whether the communications perceived and understood by the target audiences are the messages that were intended in the first place. Are the messages being decoded in the manner in which they were designed when they were encoded? This exercise helps organisations to develop their realm of understanding with their respective network members and includes all internal and external communications, whether overt or covert.

Procedures associated with a communication audit

All forms of printed and visual communications (brochures, leaflets, annual reports, letterheads, advertisements, etc.) need to be collected and assembled in a particular location. Examples of main competitors' materials should also be brought together, as this will provide benchmarks for market evaluation. Once collated, the task is to identify consistent themes and the logic of the organisation's communications.

Ind (1992) suggests that one way of accomplishing this is to develop a communications matrix (Figure 7.2). Information needs to be grouped by type of offering (ver-

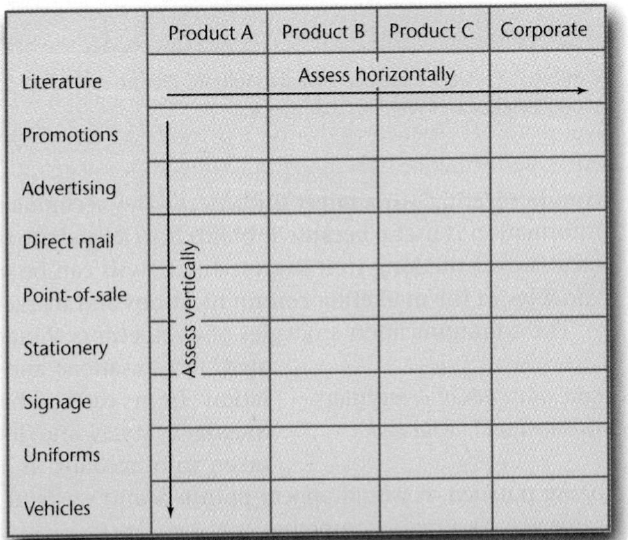

Figure 7.2 A communications audit matrix. From Ind (1992); used with kind permission.

tically) and then by each type of medium (horizontally). The vertical grouping helps determine the variety of messages that customers receive if they are exposed to all the communications relating to a single offering. Are the messages consistent? Are the messages logically related, is the related logic one that is intended and what is the total impact of these communications? The horizontal grouping helps determine message consistency across a number of different offerings, perhaps from different divisions. If a single dealer or end-user receives the communications relating to a product line or even a particular product mix, is the perception likely to be confusing?

Internal communications should be included in the audit. An analysis of official publications, such as in-house magazines, is obvious, but materials posted on notice-boards and the way in which the telephone is answered affect the perception that stakeholders have of the organisation.

The audit needs to incorporate research into the attitudes of employees to the organisation and the perceptions held by various stakeholders. This will involve both qualitative and quantitative research. The objective is to determine whether the image of the organisation reflects reality. If corporate performance exceeds the overall image, then corporate communications are not working effectively. If the image is superior to performance, then the operations of the organisation need to be improved.

In the mid-1980s, ICI's corporate performance was more advanced than its image. The organisation's communications were not working effectively. Research eventually revealed the gulf between performance and image, but had a communications audit been used on a regular basis, in conjunction with an image tracking system, then the amount of damage or loss of goodwill might have been considerably reduced.

Organisations need to understand how they are perceived by their stakeholders. A communications audit focuses attention on the totality of messages transmitted and provides a framework for corporate identity programmes.

Organisations need to understand how they are perceived by their stakeholders.

 ## Functional capability

The final elements to be reviewed as part of the internal marketing context are those that relate to the individual functional areas within an organisation. A firm's overall core competence may be the result of a number of competencies held at functional level. Internal marketing can be regarded as a key to providing strong external marketing performance (Greene *et al.*, 1994). This is achieved by releasing high levels of internal service provision within the functional areas. As Varey (1995) confirms, 'Internal service quality is necessary for superior external service quality'.

Financial capability

Before any communications plan can be devised in any detail, it is necessary to have a broad understanding of the financial capability of the organisation; in other words, how much money is available for communications? This is important, as it impacts upon the objectives that are to be set later and the choice of media necessary to carry the organisation's messages. For example, it is pointless asking dealers to undertake training programmes with end-users if the manufacturer does not have the sales representatives and training staff to instruct the dealers in the first place. Most medium-sized tour operators do not have the capital to fund television-based campaigns, even though some of the major national tour operators regularly use television.

Manufacturing capability

One of the main aims of the communication plan is to stimulate and maintain demand. If the production resources are limited, the capacity needs to be aligned with the potential demand of a region or local area rather than nationally. Equally, the communication programme should be geared to the same area. All demand must be satisfied and likewise much of the communication programme will be ineffective in the short term if full production capacity has been reached.

Marketing capability

Discussion so far has assumed that the available corporate and marketing expertise is of sufficient calibre not only to formulate but also to implement a marketing strategy and its associated communication requirements. This raises questions about the customer orientation of the organisation, its attitude towards marketing planning and its general disposition towards the provision of a sustained level of customer service and satisfaction. Research shows that only a minority of organisations use a formal marketing planning process (Greenley, 1985).

In a study by Doyle (1987) it was found that only 50% of UK organisations claimed to have a marketing philosophy, one where the satisfaction of customer needs predominated over either a sales-orientated or a production-orientated philosophy. There may be a variety of reasons for this, and Boydell (1977), among others, claims that the culture of the organisation may trap or constrict the organisation and reduce the effectiveness of marketing planning. This lack of belief in marketing planning is a reflection of the values and beliefs of the organisation. Leppard and McDonald (1991) conclude their study by stating that if the values of the organisation are generally consistent with the underlying values of a complete marketing planning process, then it is probable that the planning process will be adopted. The necessary values, according to Doyle, are partly driven by the CEO and his or her beliefs in marketing.

Many CEOs had a poor understanding of what marketing is: to a number of them marketing is about selling and promotion. Such a shallow perspective is unlikely to lead to an organisational culture which will support a marketing orientation. The study concluded by reference to the fact that less than half of the organisations in the study had a marketing director supporting the CEO, but 89% had a financial director.

It seems reasonable to extend these conclusions by surmising that the same values and beliefs are necessary for the successful adoption of a planned approach to marketing communications, if only because it is a subsystem of marketing planning.

Summary

Intraorganisational issues need to be appreciated when building a communications plan. One of the key factors to be considered is the corporate strategy, including the degree to which it is understood by stakeholders and the credibility that management has to manage strategic processes.

A major influence on the communication style is the prevailing culture. Culture is a reflection of the personality of the organisation, which in turn affects the corporate identity or the way in which an organisation presents itself to its stakeholders. This presentation of visual cues can be managed deliberately or left unattended. Either way, stakeholders develop a picture of the organisation which enables them to position it among others. This corporate image may well be an accurate interpretation of the real organisation. However, it may be inaccurate, in which case marketing communications need to address the problem and narrow the gap between reality and image.

Review questions

1. Write a short definition of internal marketing and explain how marketing communications needs to assume both internal and external perspectives.

2. What is the role of internal marketing communications?

3. Write short notes explaining why organisational boundaries appear to be less clear than was once thought.

4. What is organisational identity and what do Albert and Whetton (1985) consider to be the three important aspects of identity?

5. Write a brief paper explaining why an understanding of corporate culture is important for successful marketing communications.

6. Why should marketing communications accommodate corporate strategy?

7. What are the elements of strategic credibility?

8. Select three different CEOs from a variety of organisations and evaluate their strategic credibility. What is the justification for selecting these individuals?

9. Prepare a communications matrix for an organisation (or brand/product) with which you are familiar.

10. Why might the functional capabilities of an organisation impact upon an organisation's marketing communications?

MINI CASE

This mini case was written by Stuart Roper, Senior Lecturer in Marketing at Manchester Metropolitan University. Material supplied by MANSELL plc and used with its kind permission.

Building a brand

MANSELL plc

MANSELL plc is a business-to-business construction firm that operates within the property refurbishment, repair and maintenance market, as well as the commercial new build market. Founded in 1908 in the south-east of England,

MANSELL has grown into one of the top 10 construction firms in the UK by a combination of engendering repeat business from a loyal customer base together with the strategic acquisition of businesses that add strength to MANSELL's portfolio.

MANSELL is keen to build its brand

nationally and to this end companies such as HALL & TAWSE and STM acquired by MANSELL have been rebranded under the MANSELL name. The company now has 3,000 staff working from 40 offices dispersed throughout the British Isles. Internal marketing and research are being used to help bring the newly acquired staff into the MANSELL family and to ensure that all stakeholders have a consistent view of the organisation. The company is aware of the significance of branding itself under a single corporate identity. The construction industry has traditionally been regionally rather than nationally oriented with subsequent regional loyalties. MANSELL, however, now has many national and international clients and such clients are happier dealing with one single entity rather than a cluster of regional firms.

The company has grown quickly and MANSELL is aware that in order to present a coherent brand to its customers, it must first ensure that its staff embrace the brand values. Many staff work in the field rather than in an office-bound environment and therefore a concise, relevant communications/corporate identity strategy is necessary. A valuable part of this is the publication *MANSELL News*. Published twice a year, this professionally produced magazine is circulated to the home address of all 3,000 staff as well as 15,000 customer contacts. MANSELL wants staff to feel a part of the company rather than just their region and *MANSELL News* helps give a flavour of the all the market sectors it is engaged in. The company wishes to be seen as a 'property service provider' rather than as a builder so it is important that employees are aware of the wide range of activities that the business is becoming involved in.

In support of *MANSELL News*, the company intranet provides details of all contracts awarded to the company each month. The intranet is a valuable resource that is used by all field staff as it details health and safety information – a daily necessity on construction sites. Internal marketing messages are targeted to staff via the intranet together with a bulletin board on the company-wide email system.

New employees are inducted into the company and provided with a manual, which helps give them an overview of MANSELL, its history and what it stands for.

Because of its rapid growth by acquisition, MANSELL has had to work hard to build a consistent corporate identity. Management was aware that the new brand could only be sold to customers via employees. A corporate identity manual was produced and issued to all regions outlining how all materials should be displayed. These include the colour schemes, fonts, sizes and type of material to be used on signage (both in house and on site), vehicles, brochures and numerous items of stationary. This has considerably reduced the number of styles that were previously being used, a problem that the introduction of personal computers had made worse owing to the individual interpretation they allow.

Regular team briefings take place regionally where messages from head office are disseminated. These are supplemented by a national conference each spring where external speakers and clients present to staff from throughout the group. MANSELL has been keen not to offend regional operators that it has acquired. It still allows local management autonomy, for example, to organise its own training, and the changeover to the MANSELL brand was not imposed but rather agreed with local management who were then given parameters to work within, together with a framework and left to implement the changes. The company has managed the harmonisation of identity in England without losing any business.

The dedication to internal communication reflects MANSELL's approach to external partnering and supply-chain management. The company recently won *Building Magazine*'s Construction Best Practice award. This award was used to reassure newly acquired staff of the strength of the MANSELL brand, and all staff received a letter and gift from the chief executive thanking them for their contribution.

The company is serious about its brand and has commissioned research to investigate its 'brand personality' both internally and externally. Both staff and clients rated the organisation highly on sincerity and competence. The harmonisation of internal and external feelings towards the company is a key component of brand building. On a limited budget and in an industry not famous for its marketing expertise, MANSELL is building a solid national brand based upon coordinated internal marketing.

Mini-case questions

1. Appraise the role of the newsletter as a form of internal communications. How might MANSELL plc have better used this method of communication?

2. To what extent might the member/non-member demarcation be applied to this scenario?

3. How else might the intranet be used to develop employee motivation and identification with the organisation?

4. List three ways in which the role of internal marketing communication can be identified at MANSELL plc.

5. Evaluate the extent to which MANSELL plc has used internal marketing communications to develop the corporate brand.

References

Albert, S. and Whetten, D.A. (1985) Organisational identity. In *Research in Organisational Behavior* (eds L.L. Cummings and B.M. Staw). Greenwich, CT: Jai Press.

Barich, H. and Kotler, P. (1991) A framework for marketing image management. *Sloan Management Review*, **94** (Winter), pp. 94–104.

Berry, L.L. (1980) Services marketing is different. *Business* (May/June), pp. 24–9.

Beyer, J.M. (1981) Ideologies, values and decision making in organisations. In *Handbook of Organisational Design* (eds P. Nystrom and W. Swarbruck). London: Oxford University Press.

Boydell, T. (1977) BACIE Conference, London, July.

Doyle, P. (1987) Marketing and the British chief executive. *Journal of Marketing Management*, 3(2), pp. 121–32.

Dutton, J.E. and Dukerich, J.M. (1991) Keeping an eye on the mirror: image and identity in organisational adaptation. *Academy of Management Review*, **34**, pp. 517–54.

Dutton, J.E. and Penner, W.J. (1993) The importance of organisational identity for strategic agenda building. In *Strategic Thinking: Leadership and the Management of Change* (eds J. Hendry, G. Johnson and J. Newton). Chichester: Wiley.

Dutton, J.E., Dukerich, J.M. and Harquail, C.V. (1994) Organisational images and member identification. *Administrative Science Quarterly*, **39**, pp. 239–63.

Elsbach, K.D. and Kramer, R.M. (1996) Members' responses to organisational identity threats: encountering and countering the *Business Week* rankings. *Administrative Science Quarterly*, **41**, pp. 442–76.

Foreman, S.K. and Money, A.H. (1995) Internal marketing: concepts, measurements and application. *Journal of Marketing Management*, **11**, pp. 755–68.

Gilly, M.C. and Wolfinbarger, M. (1998) Advertising's internal audience. *Journal of Marketing*, **62** (January), pp. 69–88.

Goften, K. (2000) Putting staff first in brand evolution. *Marketing*, 3 February, pp. 29–30.

Goodman, P.S. and Pennings, J.M. (1977) *New Perspectives on Organisational Effectiveness*. San Francisco, CA: Jossey-Bass.

Gordon, G. (1985) The relationship of corporate culture to industry sector and corporate performance. In *Gaining Control of the Corporate Culture* (eds R.H. Kilman, M.J. Saxton, R. Serpa, and associates). San Francisco, CA: Jossey-Bass.

Greene, W.E., Walls, G.D. and Schrest, L.J. (1994) Internal marketing – the key to external marketing success. *Journal of Services Marketing*, **8**(4), pp. 5–13.

Greenley, C.E. (1985) Marketing plan utilisation. *Quarterly Review of Marketing*, **4** (Summer), pp. 12–19.

Hatch, M.J. and Schultz, M. (1997) Relations between organisational culture, identity and image. *European Journal of Marketing*, **31**(5/6), pp. 356–65.

Higgins, R.B. and Bannister, B.D. (1992) How corporate communication of strategy affects share price, *Long Range Planning*, **25**(3), pp. 27–35.

Hunger, J.D. and Wheelan, T. (1993) *Strategic Management*, 4th edn. Reading, MA: Addison-Wesley.

Ind, N. (1992) *The Corporate Image: Strategies for Effective Identity Programme*, rev. edn. London: Kogan Page.

Kimberley, J. (1980) Initiation, innovation and institutionalisation in the creation process. In *The Organisational Lifecycle* (eds. J. Kimberley and R. Miles). San Francisco, CA: Jossey-Bass.

Leppard, J.W. and McDonald, H.B. (1991) Marketing planning and corporate culture: a conceptual framework which examines management attitudes in the context of marketing planning. *Journal of Marketing Management*, **7**, pp. 213–35.

Lievens, A. and Moenart, R.K. (2000) Communication flows during financial service innovation. *European Journal of Marketing*, **34**(9/10), pp. 1078–110.

Mitchell, A. (1998) P&G's new horizons. *Campaign*, 20 March, pp. 34–5.

Morden, T. (1993) *Business Strategy and Planning*. London: McGraw-Hill.

Morgan, G. (1997) *Images of Organisation*, 2nd edn. New York: Sage.

Newell, S.J. and Shemwell D.J. (1995) The CEO endorser and message source credibility: an empirical investigation of antecedents and consequences. *Journal of Marketing Communications*, **1**, pp. 13–23.

Piercy, N. and Morgan, R. (1991) Internal marketing – the missing half of the marketing programme. *Long Range Planning*, 24 (April), pp. 82–93.

Schein, E.H. (1985) *Organisational Culture and Leadership*. San Francisco, CA: Jossey-Bass.

Thompson, J.L. (1990) *Strategic Management: Awareness and Change*. London: Chapman & Hall.

Varey, R.J. (1995) Internal marketing: a review and some interdisciplinary research challenges. *International Journal of Service Industry Management*, **6**(1), pp. 40–63.

Witt, J. (2001) Are your staff and ads in tune? *Marketing*, 18 January, p. 21.

8

Financial resources

Organisations need to ensure that they achieve the greatest possible efficiency with each unit of resource (£s, $s, Gldrs, euros, SKrs) they allocate to promotional activities. They cannot afford to be profligate with scarce resources and managers are accountable to the owners of the organisation for the decisions they make, including those associated with the costs of their marketing communications.

AIMS AND OBJECTIVES

The aim of this chapter is to examine the financial context within which organisations undertake promotional campaigns.

The objectives of this chapter are:

1. To determine current trends in advertising and promotional expenditure.
2. To discuss the role of the promotional budget.
3. To clarify the benefits of using promotional budgets.
4. To examine various budgeting techniques, both practical and theoretical.
5. To provide an appreciation of the advertising-to-sales (A/S) ratio.
6. To set out the principles where share of voice (SOV) can be used as a strategically competitive tool.
7. To consider some of the issues associated with brand valuation.

Introduction

The rate at which promotional expenditures, and in particular those associated with advertising, have outstripped the retail price index has been both alarming and

Table 8.1   Top UK advertisers January–December 1999

Organisation	£m total (1999)
Procter and Gamble	165.5
Central Office of Information	92.2
Renault UK	84.9
BT	84.6
Vauxhall Motors	84.1
L'Oréal	67.1
Mars Confectionery	63.7
Ford Motor Company	57.4
Kellogg	53.1
Van den Bergh Foods	52.7
Other 90 organisations	981.0
Total	**3,189.3**

Source: ACNeilsen MMS. Used with kind permission.

troublesome. This disproportionate increase in the costs of advertising has served to make it increasingly less attractive to clients and has spurred the development of other forms of promotion, most notably direct marketing.

Some advertising agencies have argued that this disproportionately high increase is necessary because of the increasing number of new products and the length of time it takes to build a brand. Levels of advertising spend have continued to grow. In 1999 both cinema (46%) and outdoor media have grown considerably as clients continued to build their brands. Procter and Gamble spent £165 million in the UK across 160 products, with Sunny Delight spend at £8.3 million. Kellogg's and Coca Cola cut back by 30% and 20% respectively (Bainbridge, 2000), but the remaining amounts are still huge (Table 8.1).

Large investment and commitment are required over a period of years if long-term, high-yield performance is to be achieved. Many

Large investment and commitment are required over a period of years if long-term, high-yield performance is to be achieved.

accountants, on the other hand, view advertising from a different perspective. Their attitude has, for a long time, been to consider advertising as an expense, to be set against the profits of the organisation. Many of them see planned marketing communications as a variable, one that can be discarded in times of recession.

These two broad views of advertising and of all promotional activities, one as an investment to be shown on the balance sheet and the other as a cost to be revealed in the profit and loss account, run consistently through discussions of how much should be allocated to the promotional spend. For management, the four elements of the promotional mix are often divided into two groups. The first contains advertising, sales promotion and public relations, while the second group contains the financial aspects that relate to personal selling.

This division reflects not only a functional approach to marketing but also the way in which, historically, the selling and marketing departments have developed. This is often observed in older, more established, organisations which find innovation and change more difficult to come to terms with. Accountability and responsibility for promotional expenditure in the first group often fall to the brand or product manager. The second group is managed by a sales manager, often at national level, reporting to a sales director.

The promotional costs that need to be budgeted include the following. First, there is the air time on broadcast media or space in print media that has to be bought to carry the message to the target audience. Then there are the production costs associated with generating the message and the staff costs of all those who contribute to the design and administration of the campaign. There are agency and professional fees, marketing research and contributions to general overheads and to expenses such as cars, entertainment costs and telephones that can be directly related to particular profit centres. In addition to all these are any direct marketing costs, for which some organisations have still to find a suitable method of cost allocation. In some cases a particular department has been created to manage all direct marketing activities, and in these cases the costs can be easily apportioned.

The budget for the sales force is not one that can be switched on and off like an electric light. Advertising budgets can be massaged and campaigns pulled at the last minute, but communication through personal selling requires the establishment of a relatively high level of fixed costs. In addition to these expenses are the opportunity costs associated with the long time taken to recruit, train and release suitably trained sales personnel into the competitive environment. For example, this process can take over 15 months in some industries, especially in the fast-changing, demanding and complex information technology markets.

Strategic investment to achieve the right sales force, in terms of its size, training and maintenance, is paramount. It should be remembered, however, that managing a sales force can be rather like turning an ocean liner: any move or change in direction has to be anticipated and actioned long before the desired outcome can be accomplished. Funds need to be allocated strategically, but for most organisations a fast return on an investment should not be expected.

This chapter will concentrate on the techniques associated with determining the correct allocation of funds to the first group of promotional tools and, in particular, emphasis will be placed upon the advertising appropriation. Attention will then be given to the other measures used to determine the correct level of investment in sales promotion, public relations and the field sales force. Finally, the question of brand valuation and its place on the balance sheet is considered.

Trends in promotional expenditure

It was stated earlier that advertising expenditure in the United Kingdom has risen faster than consumer expenditure. While this is true, the rapid increases in advertising spend in the 1980s slowed at the beginning of the 1990s, then speeded up again as the economy recovered only to waver again in 2001 after a buoyant previous year.

This noticeable cutback in advertising expenditure when trading conditions tightens reflects the short-term orientation that some organisations have towards brand development or advertising. What is also of interest is the way in which the promotional mix has been changing over the past 10–15 years. For a long time the spend on media advertising dominated the promotional budget of consumer products and services. Now, it is sales promotion that often has the strongest influence together with sponsorship and direct marketing activities. The reasons for this shift, first reported by Abraham and Lodish (1990), are indicative of the increasing attention and accountability that management is attaching to the promotional spend. Increasingly,

Management is attaching increasing attention and accountability to the promotional spend.

marketing managers are being asked to justify the amounts they spend on their entire budgets, including advertising and sales promotion. Senior managers want to know the return they are getting for their promotional investments, in order that they meet their objectives and that scarce resources can be used more effectively in the future.

In recent years some organisations have deliberately reallocated their budgets in order to make more funds available for price cutting and discounting. Supermarket chain Safeway chopped its £14 million annual above-the-line spend so that it could focus on local sales promotion activities. The French car manufacturer Citröen cut its £31 million budget in late 1999 to help fund discounting in an increasingly price-sensitive market.

These two organisations were experiencing trading difficulties and it is not uncommon to find companies in these circumstances slashing their ad spend, if only on a

In recent years some organisations have deliberately reallocated their budgets in order to make more funds available for price cutting and discounting.

temporary basis. Marks & Spencer and Sainsbury's are also experiencing difficulties but have either increased or maintained their above-the-line spend. According to Hall (1999), Procter and Gamble set *'strict guidelines about how much can be spent below-the-line if a brands equity is to be maintained'*. Research by Profit Impact on

Market Strategy (PIMS) (Tylee, 1999; Tomkins, 1999) found that companies that maintain or even increase their adspend during a recession are likely to grow three times faster than those companies that cut the adspend when the economy turns round. The Renault Clio and the Nescafé Gold Blend brands were cited as examples of advertisers that had increased their adspends during the last downturn and succeeded in increasing their profitability and market performance.

A report undertaken for the Advertising Association however, found that the majority of brand leaders who use advertising as a substantial proportion of the promotional mix continue to dominate their markets, just as they did 30 years ago. In doing so, the report concludes, they have thwarted the challenge of own brands. In other words, advertising can protect brands, as long as the adspend is large.

The role of the promotional budget

The role of the promotional budget is the same whether the organisation is a multinational, trading from numerous international locations, or a small manufacturing unit on an industrial estate outside a semi-rural community. Both organisations want to ensure that they achieve the greatest efficiency with each pound they allocate to promotional activities. Neither can afford to be profligate with scarce resources, and each is accountable to the owners of the organisation for the decisions it makes.

There are two broad decisions that need to be addressed. The first concerns how much of the organisation's available financial resources (or relevant part) should be allocated to promotion over the next period. The second concerns how much of the total amount should be allocated to each of the individual tools of the promotional mix.

Benefits of budgeting

The benefits of engaging in budgeting activities are many and varied, but in the context of marketing communication planning they can be considered as follows:

1. The process serves to focus people's attention on the costs and benefits of undertaking the planned communication activities.

2. The act of quantifying the means by which the marketing plan will be communicated to target audiences instills a management discipline necessary to ensure that the objectives of the plan are capable of being achieved. Achievement must be at a level which is acceptable and which will not overstretch or embarrass the organisation.

3. The process facilitates cross-function coordination and forces managers to ensure that the planned communications are integrated and mutually supportive.

4. The process provides a means by which campaigns can be monitored and management control asserted. This is particularly important in environments that are subject to sudden change or competitive hostility.

5. At the end of the campaign, a financial review enables management to learn from the experiences of the promotional activity in order that future communications can be made more efficient and the return on the investment improved.

The process of planning the communications budget is an important one. Certain elements of the process will have been determined during the setting of the promotion objectives. Managers will check the financial feasibility of a project prior to committing larger resources. Managers will also discuss the financial implications of the communication strategy (that is, the push/pull dimension) and those managers responsible for each of the individual promotional tools will have estimated the costs that their contribution to the strategy will involve. Senior management will have some general ideas about the level of the overall appropriation, which will inevitably be based partly upon precedent, market and competitive conditions and partly as a response to the pressures of different stakeholders, among them key members of the performance network. Decisions now have to be made about the viability of the total plan, whether the appropriation is too large or too small and how the funds are to be allocated across the promotional tools.

The process of planning the communications budget is an important one.

Communication budgets are not formulated at a particular moment in a sequence of management activities. The financial resources of an organisation should be constantly referred to, if only to monitor current campaigns. Therefore, budgeting and the availability of financial resources are matters that managers should be constantly aware of and be able to tap into at all stages in the development and implementation of planned communications.

Difficulties associated with budgeting for communications spend

There are a number of problems associated with the establishment of a marketing communications budget. Of them all, the following appear to be the most problematic.

First, it is difficult to quantify the precise amount that is necessary to complete all the required tasks. Second, communication budgets do not fit neatly with standard accounting practices. The concept of brand value is accepted increasingly as a balance sheet item, but the concept of investment in communication to create value has only recently begun to be accepted, e.g. by Jaguar and Nestlé. Third, the diversity of the promotional tools and the means by which their success can be measured renders like-for-like comparisons null and void. Finally, the budget-setting process is not as clear-cut as it might at first appear.

It is difficult to quantify the precise amount that is necessary to complete all the required tasks.

There are four main stakeholder groups that contribute to the decision. These are the focus organisation, any communication agencies, the media whose resources will be used to carry the designated messages and the target audience. It is the ability of these four main stakeholders to interact, to communicate effectively with each other and to collaborate in a way that will impact most upon the communications budget. However, determining the 'appropriate appropriation' is a frustrating exercise for the marketing communications manager. The allocation of scarce resources across a promotional budget presents financial and political difficulties, especially where the returns are difficult to identify. The development and significance of technology within marketing can lead to disputes concerning ownership and control of resources. For example, in many companies management and responsibility for the Web site rests with the IT department, which understandably take a technological view of issues. Those in marketing, however, see the use of the Web site from a marketing perspective and need a budget to management it. Tension between the two can result in different types of Web site design, and effectiveness and this leads to different levels of customer support.

Tension between the two can result in different types of Web site design.

Smallbone (1972) suggested a long time ago that the allocation of funds for promotion is one of the primary problems facing marketers, if not one of the major strategic problems. Audience and media fragmentation, changed management expectations and a more global orientation have helped ensure that budgeting remains problematic.

Models of appropriation

At a broad level there are a number of models proposed by different authors concerning the appropriation of the promotional mix. In particular, Abratt and van der Westhuizen (1985) refer, among others, to Smallbone's (1972) and Gaedeke and Tootelian's (1983) models of promotional appropriation. Abratt and van der Westhuizen have determined, among other things, that personal selling dominated the promotion mix of all their respondents in a particular study of business-to-business markets and that the models themselves were too simplistic to be of any direct benefit.

These broad approaches to budget allocation are not therefore appropriate, and it is necessary to investigate the value of using particular techniques. It is useful to set out the theoretical approach associated with the determination of communication and, in particular, advertising budgets.

Techniques and approaches

Theoretical approaches: marginal analysis and response curves

This method is normally depicted as a tool for understanding advertising expenditures, but, as Burnett (1993) points out, it has been used for all elements of the promotional mix, including personal selling, so it is included here for understanding the overall promotional allocation.

Marginal analysis enables managers to determine how many extra sales are produced from an extra unit of promotional spend. A point will be reached when an extra pound spent on promotion will generate an equal amount (a single pound's worth) of revenue. At this point marginal revenue is equal to marginal costs, the point of maximum promotional expenditure has been reached and maximum profit is generated.

Another way of looking at this approach is to track the path of sales and promotional expenditure. Even with zero promotional effort some sales will still be generated. In other words, sales are not totally dependent upon formal promotional activity, a point we shall return to later. When there is a small amount of promotion effort, the impact is minimal, as the majority of potential customers are either unaware of the messages or they do not think the messages are sufficiently credible for them to change their current behaviour. After a certain point, however, successive increments in promotional expenditure will produce more than proportionate increments in sales. The sales curve in Figure 8.1 can now be seen to rise steeply and the organisation moves into a position where it can begin to take advantage of the economies of scale in promotion. Eventually the sales curve starts to flatten out as diminishing returns to promotion begin to set in. This is because the majority of the potential target market have become aware of the offering and have decided whether or not to become customers.

This model suffers from a number of disadvantages (Table 8.2). First, it assumes that communications can be varied smoothly and continuously. This is not the case. Second, it assumes that communications are the only influence upon sales. As discussed previously, sales are influenced by a variety of factors, of which planned

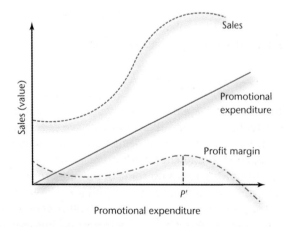

Figure 8.1   Marginal analysis for promotional expenditures. P′ is the point of maximum profit, the optimal level of promotional expenditure.

Table 8.2   Difficulties with the marginal analysis as a way of setting promotional budgets

Assumes promotional activities can be varied in a smooth and uniform manner.

Requires perfect data which in reality are very difficult to obtain.

Assumes only promotional activities impact upon sales.

Does not consider all the costs associated with promotional activities.

No account is made of the actions of direct and indirect competitors.

Adstock effects are ignored.

All messages are regarded as having equal impact. No consideration is given to the quality of messages as perceived by the target audience.

communications is but one. Controllable and uncontrollable elements in the environment influence sales. Next, no account is taken of the other costs associated indirectly with the presentation of the offering, such as those allied to distribution. Each promotional thrust will often be matched, or even bettered, by the competition. Furthermore, the actions of rivals may even affect the sales performance of all products in the same category.

It is fair to say, therefore, that the marginal approach fails to account for competitor reactions. The model assumes that sales are the result of current promotional campaigns. No attempt is made to account for the effects of previous campaigns and that adstock may well be a prime reason for a sale occurring. The time parameters used to compute the marginal analysis could be totally inaccurate.

The marginal approach fails to account for competitor reactions.

One of the most important shortcomings of the theory is its failure to account for the qualitative effects of the messages that are transmitted. It is assumed that all messages are of a particular standard and that relative quality is unimportant. Clearly this cannot be the case.

The marginal approach is suspect in that it operates outside the real world, and it requires data and skill in its implementation that are difficult and expensive to acquire. Theoretically, this approach is sound but the practical problems of obtaining the necessary information and the absence of qualitative inputs render the technique difficult for most organisations to implement.

Practical approaches

If the marginal approach is not practical then a consideration of the alternative approaches is necessary. Practitioners have developed a range of other methods which tend to reflect simplicity of deduction and operation but raise doubts over their overall contribution and effectiveness.

The following represent some of the more common approaches. It should be noted, at this point, that none of the techniques should be seen in isolation. Organisations should use a variety of approaches and so reduce any dependence, and hence risk, on any one method. The main methods are arbitrary, inertia, media multiplier, percentage of sales, affordable, and objective and task.

The main methods are arbitrary, inertia, media multiplier, percentage of sales, affordable, and objective and task.

Arbitrary

Sometimes referred to as 'chairperson's rules', this is the simplest and least appropriate of all the techniques available. Under chairperson's rules, what the boss says or guesses at is what is implemented. The fact that the boss may not have a clue what the optimal figure should be is totally irrelevant. Very often the budget is decided on the hoof, and as each demand for communication resources arrives so decisions are made in isolation from any overall strategy.

Apart from the merit of flexibility, this method has numerous deficiencies. It fails to consider customer needs, the demands of the environment or marketing strategy, and there is an absence of any critical analysis. Regretfully this approach is used often by many small organisations.

Inertia

An alternative to guesswork is the 'let's keep it the same' approach. Here all elements of the environment and the costs associated with the tasks facing the organisation are ignored.

Media multiplier

One step more advanced is the method that recognises that media rate card costs may have increased. So, in order to maintain the same impact, the media multiplier rule requires last year's spend to be increased by the rate at which media costs have increased.

Percentage of sales

One of the more common and thoughtful approaches is to set the budget at a level equal to some predetermined percentage of past or expected sales. Invariably, organisations select a percentage that is traditional to the organisation, such as 'we always aim to spend 5.0% of our sales on advertising'. The rationale put forward is that it is the norm for the sector to spend about 4.5–5.5% or that 5.0% is acceptable to the needs of the most powerful stakeholders or is set in recognition of overall corporate responsibilities. For example, a local authority will be mindful of the needs of its council tax payers, whose finances contribute to the funding and maintenance of local tourism activities, for example, a museum or park facilities.

There are a number of flaws with this technique. It is focused upon the sales base on which the budget rests. Planned communications, and advertising in particular, are intended to create demand, not to be the result of past sales. If the demand generators of the promotional mix are to be based on last period's performance, then it is likely that the next period's results will be similar, all things being equal. This must be the logical implication when the percentage is based on past performance.

Another way of looking at this method is to base the spend on a percentage of the next period's sales. This overcomes some of the problems, but still constrains the scope and the realistic expectations of a budget. No consideration is given to the sales potential that may exist, so this technique may actually limit performance.

Affordable

This approach is still regarded by many organisations as sophisticated and relatively free of risk. It requires each unit of output to be allocated a proportion of all the input costs and all the costs associated with the value-adding activities in production and manufacturing, together with all the other costs in distributing the output. After making an allowance for profit, what is left is to be spent on advertising and communication. In other words, what is left is what we can afford to spend.

The affordable technique is not in the least analytical, nor does it have any market or task orientation. It is a technique which is used by organisations of differing sizes (Hooley and Lynch, 1985), that are product rather than customer orientated. Their view of advertising is that it is a cost and that the quality of their product will ensure that it will sell itself. Organisations using this technique will be prone to missing opportunities that require advertising investment. This is because a ceiling on advertising expenditure is set and borrowings are avoided. As sales fluctuate in variable markets, the vagueness of this approach is unlikely to lead to an optimal budget.

Objective and task

The methods presented so far seek to determine an overall budget and leave the actual allocation to products and regions to some arbitrary method. This is unlikely to be a realistic, fair or optimal use of a critical resource.

The objective and task approach is different from the others in that it attempts to determine the resources required to achieve each promotion objective. It then aggregates these separate costs into an overall budget. For example, the costs associated with achieving a certain level of awareness can be determined from various media owners who are seeking to sell time and space in their media vehicles. The costs of sales promotions and sales literature can be determined and the production costs of these activities and those of direct marketing (e.g. telemarketing) and PR events and sponsorships can be brought together. The total of all these costs represents the level of investment necessary to accomplish the promotion objectives that had been established earlier in the marketing communications plan.

The objective and task approach is different from the others in that it attempts to determine the resources required to achieve each promotion objective.

The attractions of this technique are that it focuses management attention upon the goals that are to be accomplished and that the monitoring and feedback systems that have to be put in place allow for the development of knowledge and expertise. On the downside, the objective and task approach does not generate realistic budgets, in the sense that the required level of resources may not be available and the opportunity costs of the resources are not usually determined. More importantly, it is difficult to determine the best way to accomplish a task and to know exactly what costs will be necessary to complete a particular activity. Very often the actual costs are not known until the task has been completed, which rather reduces the impact of the budget-setting process. What is also missing is a strategic focus. The objective and task method deals very well with individual campaigns, but is not capable of providing the overall strategic focus of the organisation's annual (period) spend. The case of Procter and Gamble illustrates this point.

The use of this approach leads to the determination of a sum of money. This sum is to be invested, in this case, in promoting the offerings of the organisation, but it could equally be a new machine or a building. To help discover whether such a sum should be invested and whether it is in the best interests of the organisation, a 'payout plan' can be undertaken:

1. *Payout plans*

These are used to determine the investment value of the advertising plan. This process involves determining the future revenues and costs to be incurred over a two- or three-year period. The essential question answered by such an exercise is 'how long will it take to recover the expenditure?'

2. *Sensitivity analysis*
Many organisations use this adjusting approach to peg back the advertising expenditure because the payout plan revealed costs as too large or sales developing too slowly. Adjustments are made to the objectives or to the strategies, with the aim of reducing the payback period.

Competitive parity

In certain markets, such as the relatively stable fast-moving consumer goods (FMCG) market, many organisations use promotional appropriation as a competitive tool. The underlying assumption is that advertising is the only direct variable that influences sales. The argument is based on the point that while there are many factors that impact on sales, these factors are all self-cancelling. Each factor impacts upon all the players in the market. The only effective factor is the amount that is spent on planned communications. As a result, some organisations deliberately spend the same amount on advertising as their competitors spend: competitive parity.

Some organisations deliberately spend the same amount on advertising as their competitors spend: competitive parity.

Competitive parity has a major benefit for the participants. As each organisation knows what the others are spending and while there is no attempt to destabilise the market through excessive or minimal promotional spend, the market avoids self-generated turbulence and hostile competitive activity.

There are, however, a number of disadvantages with this simple technique. The first is that, while information is available, there is a problem of comparing like with like. For example, a carpet manufacturer selling a greater proportion of output into the trade will require different levels and styles of advertising and promotion from another manufacturer selling predominantly to the retail market. Furthermore, the first organisation may be diversified, perhaps importing floor tiles. The second may be operating in a totally unrelated market. Such activities make comparisons difficult to establish, and financial decisions based on such analyses are highly dubious.

The competitive parity approach fails to consider the qualitative aspects of the advertising undertaken by the different players. Each attempts to differentiate itself, and very often the promotional messages are one of the more important means of successfully positioning an organisation. It would not be surprising, therefore, to note that there is probably a great range in the quality of the planned communications. Associated with this is the notion that, when attempting to adopt different positions, the tasks and costs will be different and so seeking relative competitive parity may be an inefficient use of resources. The final point concerns the data used in such a strategy. The data are historical and based on strategies relevant at the time. Competitors may well have embarked upon a new strategy since the data were released. This means that parity would not only be inappropriate for all the reasons previously listed, but also because the strategies are incompatible.

Advertising-to-sales ratio

An interesting extension of the competitive parity principle is the notion of advertising-to-sales (A/S) ratios. Instead of simply seeking to spend a relatively similar amount on promotion as one's main competitors, this approach attempts to account for the market shares held by the different players and to adjust promotional spend accordingly.

If it is accepted that there is a direct relationship between the volume of advertising (referred to as weight) and sales, then it is not unreasonable to conclude that if an organisation spends more on advertising then it will see a proportionate improvement in sales. The underlying principle of the A/S ratio is that, in each industry, it is possible to determine the average advertising spend of all the players and compare it with the value of the market. Therefore, it is possible for each organisation to determine its own A/S ratio and compare it with the industry average. Those organisations with an A/S ratio below the average may conclude either that they have advertising economies of scale working in their favour or that their advertising is working much harder, pound for pound, than some of their competitors. Organisations can also use A/S ratios as a means of controlling expenditure across multiple product areas. Budgets can be set based upon the industry benchmark, and variances quickly spotted and further information requested to determine shifts in competitor spend levels or reasons leading to any atypical performance.

It is possible to determine the average advertising spend of all the players and compare it with the value of the market.

Each business sector has its own characteristics, which in turn influence the size of the advertising expenditure. In 1998 the A/S ratio for female fragrances was 8.1%, confectionery 1.9%, indigestion remedies 21%, cameras 5.9%, ice-cream 2.4%, cereals 8% and shampoo 18% (Advertising Association). It can be seen that the size of the A/S ratio can vary widely. It appears to be higher (that is, a greater proportion of revenue is used to invest in advertising) when the following are present:

1. The offering is standardised, not customised.
2. There are many end-users.
3. The financial risk for the end-user customer is small.
4. The marketing channels are short.
5. A premium price is charged.
6. There is a high gross margin.
7. The industry is characterised by surplus capacity.
8. Competition is characterised by a high number of new product launches.

A/S ratios provide a useful benchmark for organisations when they are trying to determine the adspend level. These ratios do not set out what the promotional budget should be, but they do provide a valuable indicator around which broad commercial decisions can be developed.

Share of voice

Brand strategy in the FMCG market has traditionally been based upon an approach which uses mass media advertising to drive brand awareness, which in turn allows premium pricing to fund the advertising investment (cost). The alternative approach has been to use price-based promotions to drive market share. The latter approach has often been regarded as a short-term approach which is incapable of sustaining a brand over the longer term.

The concept underlying the A/S ratio can be seen in the context of rival supporters chanting at a football match. If they chant at the same time, at the same decibel rating, then it is difficult to distinguish the two sets of supporters, particularly if they are chanting the same song. Should one set of supporters shout at a lower decibel rating, then the collective voice of the other supporters would be the one that the rest of the crowd, and perhaps any television audience, actually hears and distinguishes.

This principle applies to the concept of share of voice (SOV). Within any market the total of all advertising expenditure (adspend), that is all the advertising by all of the players, can be analysed in the context of the proportions each player has made to the total. Should one advertiser spend more than any other then it will be its messages that are received and stand a better chance of being heard and acted upon. In other words, its SOV is the greater. This implies, of course, that the quality of the message transmitted is not important and that it is the sheer relative weight of adspend that is the critical factor.

Within any market the total of all advertising expenditure (adspend), that is all the advertising by all of the players, can be analysed in the context of the proportions each player has made to the total.

This concept can be taken further and combined with another, share of market (SOM). When a brand's market share is equal to its share of advertising spend, equilibrium is said to have been reached (SOV = SOM).

Strategic implications of the SOV concept

These concepts of SOV and SOM frame an interesting perspective of competitive strategy based upon the relative weight of advertising expenditure. Schroer (1990) reports that, following extensive research on the US packaged goods market (FMCG), it is noticeable that organisations can use advertising spend to maintain equilibrium and to create disequilibrium in a market. The former is established by major brand players maintaining their market shares with little annual change to their advertising budgets. Unless a competitor is prepared to inject a considerable increase in advertising spend and so create disequilibrium, the relatively stable high spend deters new entrants and preserves the *status quo*. Schroer claims that if the two market leaders maintain SOV within 10% of each other then competitive equilibrium will exist. This situation is depicted in Figure 8.2. If a market challenger launches an aggressive assault upon the leader by raising advertising spend to a point where SOV is 20–30% higher than the current leader, market share will shift in favour of the challenger.

In Figure 8.2, brands 1, 3, 4 and 6 have an SOM that is greater than their SOV. This suggests that their advertising is working well for them and that the larger organisations have some economies of scale in their advertising. Brands 2 and 5, however, have an SOM that is less than their SOV. This is because brand 2 is challenging for the larger market (with brand 1) and is likely to be less profitable than brand 1 because of the increased costs. Brand 5 is competing in a niche market, and, as a new brand, may be spending heavily (relative to its market share) to gain acceptance in the new market environment.

This perspective brings implications for advertising spend at a strategic level. This shown in the matrix, Figure 8.3, which shows that advertising spend should be varied

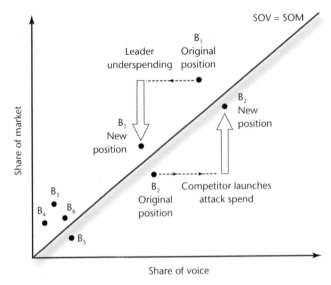

Figure 8.2   Strategy to gain market share by an increase in adspend. From Schroer (1990); used with kind permission.

according to the spend of the company's competitors in different markets. The implications are that advertising budget decisions should be geared to the level of adspend undertaken by competitors in particular markets at particular times. Decisions to attack or to defend are also set out. For example, promotional investments should be placed in markets where competitors are underspending. Furthermore, if information is available about competitors' costs, then decisions to launch and sustain an advertising spend attack can be made in the knowledge that a prolonged period of premium spending can be carried through with or without a counter-attack.

Advertising budget decisions should be geared to the level of adspend undertaken by competitors in particular markets at particular times.

This traditional perspective of static markets being led by the top two brands using heavy above-the-line strategies and the rest basing their competitive thrusts on price-based promotions has been challenged by Buck (1995) by reference to a study of Superpanel data by Hamilton. It was found that the brand leaders in many FMCG markets spent nearly 50% more than the industry average on advertising, while the number 2 brand spent about 8% less than the industry average. In addition, the gap with the other

		Share of market	
		High	**Low**
Competitor's share of voice	**High**	Defend position by increased adspend	Find niche position, decrease adspend and deploy other tools
	Low	Stabilise position by moderating adspend and use other tools	Attack competitors and use large adspend

Figure 8.3   Strategies for advertising spend. Reprinted by permission of Harvard Business School Press, from Ad spending: growing market share, *Harvard Business Review* (January/February), by J. Schroer, Boston, MA 1990, pp. 44–8, copyright © 1990 by Harvard Business School Publishing Corporation, all rights reserved. One-time permission to reproduce granted by Harvard Business School Publishing 2001.

actors was not as significant as Schroer reported. This is, of course, a comparison of European and US markets, and there is no reason why they should be identical or at least very similar. However, the data are interesting in that the challenge of brand 2, postulated by Schroer, is virtually impossible in many of the UK, if not also in European, markets.

The concepts of SOV and SOM have also been used by Jones (1990) to develop a new method of budget setting. He suggests that those brands that have an SOV greater than their SOM are 'investment brands', and those that have a SOV less than or equal to their SOM are 'profit-taking brands'.

There are three points to notice. First, the high advertising spend of new brands is an established strategy and represents a trade-off between the need for profit and the need to become established through advertising spend.

The high advertising spend of new brands is an established strategy and represents a trade-off between the need for profit and the need to become established through advertising spend.

The result, invariably, is that smaller brands have lower profitability because they have to invest a disproportionate amount in advertising. Second, large brands are often 'milked' to produce increased earnings, especially in environments which emphasise short-termism. The third point is that advertising economies of scale allow large brands to develop with an SOV consistently below SOM.

Using data collected from an extensive survey of 1,096 brands across 23 different countries, Jones 'calculated the difference between share of voice and share of market and averaged these differences within each family of brands'. By representing the data diagrammatically (Figure 8.4), Jones shows how it becomes a relatively simple task to work out the spend required to achieve a particular share of market. The first task is to plot the expected (desired) market share from the horizontal axis; then move vertically to the intersect with the curve and read off the SOV figure from the vertical axis.

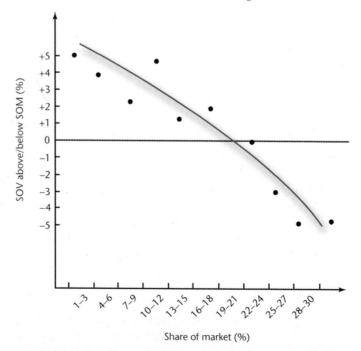

Figure 8.4   Curve comparing SOV with SOM. Reprinted by permission of Harvard Business School Press, from Ad spending: maintaining market share, *Harvard Business Review* (January/February), by J.P. Jones, Boston, MA 1990, pp. 38–42, copyright © 1990 by Harvard Business School Publishing Corporation, all rights reserved. One-time permission to reproduce granted by Harvard Business School Publishing 2001.

Appropriation brand types

From this approach it is possible to determine three main types of brands, based upon the amount of advertising expenditure. In each market there are brands which are promoted without the support of any advertising. These small niche players can be regarded as zero-based brands.

Where brands are supported by token advertising, which represents a small SOV, the brand is probably being milked and the resources are being channelled into developing other brands. New launches are typified by the heavy advertising investment necessary to get them off the ground. Here the SOV will be larger than the SOM and these can be referred to as investment brands.

In situations where the SOM is very large and the SOV much smaller, these profit-taking brands are running a risk of losing market share if a competitor spots the opportunity to invest a large sum in a prolonged attack. Finally, there is a group of brands which maintain stability by respecting each other's positions and by not initiating warfare. These brands can be referred to as equilibrium brands.

1. Investment brands – SOV > SOM; heavy advertising to drive growth.
2. Milking brands – SOV < SOM; low-level advertising to take profits out of the brand.
3. Equilibrium brands – SOM = SOV; steady-level advertising to maintain position and avoid confrontation.

Assessing brands in the context of the advertising resources they attract is a slightly different way of reflecting their power and importance to their owners. If the SOV approach is limited by its applicability to stable, mature market conditions then at least it enables the promotional spend to be seen and used as a competitive weapon.

Profit Impact on Market Strategy (PIMS)

One of the problems with the SOV approach is that it fails to take into account how much of a finite budget should be allocated to the other elements of the promotional mix. Considering the relative amounts that are spent on advertising and sales promotions, let alone direct marketing, it is important to try to understand and determine how much of the budget should be spent on the other tools. In many markets a more useful strategic approach is to determine the relative spend of above- to below-the-line promotional activities. As noted earlier, Procter and Gamble actually set limits on what proportion of a brand can be spent below-the-line.

An alternative approach is the impact of marketing communications on profitability. One of the more notable commercial research organisations is PIMS. PIMS is a major database of the performance of 3,500 business units and includes profiles of over 200 variables measured over a rolling four-year period. The database records data of business performance enabling managers to understand and develop strategies based upon empirical results of businesses in particular sectors. One of the major findings is that total advertising spend is not correlated with profitability. What has emerged is that profitability is related to an opti-

Total advertising spend is not correlated with profitability.

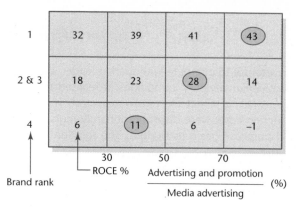

Figure 8.5   Brand leaders to concentrate on media advertising. From PIMS (2000).

mum promotional mix which is dependent upon a number of key factors: again, an argument for integrated marketing communications.

The questions that brand managers need to answer are 'should promotional investment be used to build brand image or should the goal be to drive sales off the shelf?' and 'where is the balance?'

According to PIMS, brand leaders spend 70% plus above-the-line and make 43% return on capital employed (ROCE). As if to make the point, Mistry (2001) reports that market leader snack food manufacturer Walkers spends approximately 33% of its overall marketing budget below-the-line. Brands ranked 2 or 3 should invest a smaller amount above the line but above 50% whereas brands ranked 4 or lower should only really use below-the-line investments if they are to be less than moderately successful. See Figure 8.5.

The evidence from the database reveals many statistical relationships, too many to present here. Some of the other pointers are that brands should use advertising in declining markets and use sales promotions in expanding or rapid growth markets. One other outcome appears to be that above-the-line advertising should be used when there are many distributors and where there is little innovation or sister brands.

There is some debate about the applicability and real usefulness of the PIMS data and PIMS themselves point out the limitations of their work. However, the database serves to counter the arguments of the SOV school of thought that media advertising alone is the only significant variable that determines performance. One measures market share, and the other uses market share to determine ROCE.

Which methods are most used?

From this review and commentary it is necessary to draw out the degree to which these particular tools are used in practice. Mitchell's (1993) study to determine the methods and criteria used by companies to determine their advertising budgets found that 40% of respondents claimed to use the objective and task approach, 27% used percentage of future sales (8% used past sales) and 19% used a variety of company-specific methods that do not fit neatly with any one item from the list presented above.

Lateral Thinking – Golden Wonder

In an attempt to compete with market leader, Walkers Crisps, Golden Wonder used expensive film-style TV campaigns. It realised that this approach was not working and was failing to get the return expected. The main reason for this was that the production costs were disproportionately high to the media time Golden Wonder could purchase given its budget. The solution was to use 20-second animated TV ads and in doing so Golden Wonder reduced its overall TV spend by 60%, improved awareness and sold more product.

Although the figures resulting from the study can only be used to indicate trends of overall preferences, another other set of important factors also emerged from this study. These are the range of organisational influences that impact on individual organisations. Over half the respondents reported that the method used to set these budgets actually varied, internally, across product categories. Different methods were used for new and established products.

The criteria used by organisations to set their communication budgets are many and varied. Mitchell (1993) suggested that the criteria used could be grouped as *controllables* (41%), such as financial, product, production and goals, *uncontrollables* (41%), such as sales, competition, market, media and distribution and *signals* (18%), such as national activities, experience, effectiveness of expenditures and awareness. He reported that the processes used to determine the budgets were found as either essentially centralised or top down (52%), decentralised or bottom up (13.5%) or bargaining (top down and bottom-up) (21%).

The main factors associated with the determination of marketing communications (advertising) budgets are:

1. Organisational strategy and direction, values and cultural perspective.
2. The relative amount of financial resources that are available.
3. Competitive activities and market conditions.
4. The overall level of economic confidence felt by buyers and sellers.
5. The level of product/brand development and the marketing objectives.

Over time a number of models and methods have been developed to manage these criteria to enable an appropriation to be determined.

Budgeting for the other elements of the promotional mix

The methods presented so far have concentrated on the FMCG sector. The assumption has been that only one product has been considered. In reality, a range of products will need promotional finances and the allocation decision needs to reflect the needs of an organisation's portfolio of brands. Broadbent (1989) suggests that this situation and others (e.g. direct marketing, corporate advertising) require particular combinations of the approaches presented so far. The recommendation again is that no single method will help organisations to determine the optimal investment sum.

Sales promotion activities can be more easily costed, than advertising, in advance of a campaign. Judgements can be made about the expected outcomes, based upon experience, competitive conditions and the use of predictive software tools. The important variable with sales promotion concerns the redemption rate. How many of the extra pack, price deals and samples will customers demand? How much extra of a brand needs to be sold if all the costs associated with a campaign are to be covered? The production and fulfilment costs can also be determined, so in general terms a return can be calculated in advance of a sales promotion event. However, there are a large number of sales promotion activities and these will often overlap. From a management perspective the brand management system is better, since a single person is responsible for the budget, one who is able to take a wider view of the range of activities. While the objective and task approach appears to be more easily applied to this element of the mix, other methods, such as competitive parity and fixed ratios, are often used.

> Sales promotion *activities can be more easily costed, than advertising, in advance of a campaign.*

The costs of *public relations* activities can also be predicted with a reasonable degree of accuracy. The staffing and/or agency costs are relatively fixed and, as there are no media costs involved, the only other major factor is the associated production costs. These are the costs of the materials used to provide third parties with the opportunity to 'speak' on the organisation's behalf. As with sales promotion, if a number of public relations events have been calculated as a necessary part of the overall promotional activities of the organisation, then the costs of the different tasks need to be anticipated and aggregated and a judgement made about the impact the events will make. The relative costs of achieving a similar level of impact through advertising or other elements of the mix can often be made, and a decision taken based upon relative values.

It has already been stated that the costs associated with the *sales force* are the highest of all the elements of the mix. This would indicate that the greatest degree of care needs to taken when formulating the size and deployment of the sales force. The different approaches to the determination of the sales force are covered in Chapter 29. The costs associated with each activity of personal selling and the support facilities (e.g. car, expenses, training) can be calculated easily, but what is more difficult to predict is the return on the investment.

These approaches to calculating the amount that should be invested in promotional activities vary in their degree of sophistication and usefulness. Of all these methods, none is the ideal answer to the question of how much should be allocated to marketing communications or, more specifically, the advertising spend. Some of the methods are too simplistic, while others are too specific to particular market conditions. For example, formulating strategy to gain market share through increasing SOV seems to ignore the dynamic nature of the markets and the fact that organisations need to satisfy a range of stakeholders and not concentrate solely on winning the greatest market share.

The reader may well have reached the conclusion that the most appropriate way forward for management is to consider several approaches in order to gather a ball-park figure. Such a composite approach negates some of the main drawbacks associated with particular methods. It also helps to build a picture of what is really necessary if the organisation is to communicate effectively and efficiently.

Of all the methods and different approaches, the one constant factor that applies to them all concerns the objectives that have been set for the campaign. Each element of the promotional mix has particular tasks to accomplish and it is these objectives that drive the costs of the promotional investment. If the ultimate estimate of the promotional spend is too high, then the objectives need to be revised, not the methods used.

Brand valuation

The importance of brands cannot be understated. Indeed, many organisations have attempted (and succeeded) in valuing the worth of their brands and have had them listed as an asset on their balance sheets. While this has stimulated the accountancy profession into some debate, the concept of a brand's worth to an organisation cannot really be refuted. Among other things, companies buy the potential income streams that brands offer, not just the physical assets of plant, capital and machinery.

Butterfield (1999) argues that marketers will be required to account for their activities in terms of the contribution they make to the financial performance of an organisation. This will mean that markets and customers will be viewed as assets, which in turn will become subject to development, cultivation and leverage. Marketers will also be required to use different measures of performance. Market share, margin and revenues will give way to terms such as net present value of future cash flows, or just shareholder value. It will not be just a question of how much your ad-spend is, but how much you spend relative to your main competitors market share.

It will not be just a question of how much your ad spend is, but how much you spend relative to your main competitors market share.

At the end of the promotional process, one of the benefits that management hope will emerge is an overall increase in the valuation of the brand. This net value arises as a result of the investment (for example, promotional expenditures) generating a return to reward those who risked the capital invested in the brand. Some believe that this value arises from these activities and that the brand itself is worth £x; this should therefore be regarded as an asset and be placed on the balance sheet.

Why then are brands valued? Birkin (1995) suggests that the reasons are quite varied, including the need to assist in merger and acquisition activities, to establish royalty rates for brand licensing, to support financing decisions (e.g. bank loans), to allocate marketing resources among brands and to formulate brand measurement systems. Perhaps the most important of these is that, through understanding the value of a brand, all those involved with the delivery of the brand are aware of the risks a brand strategy might bear and the returns most likely to be achieved on any further investment in the brand.

All this begs the questions: when does a brand add value to the organisation's overall net worth and when should it be axed? Many of the sub-brands and line extensions developed in the 1980s have become subject to investigation in the 1990s. Clarity of communication has been difficult to achieve as markets have become increasingly competitive and it is difficult to make any form of meaningful differentiation or position by which users should continue to purchase. Nestlé axed its Chambourcy yoghurt brand in 1995 and replaced it

Clarity of communication has been difficult to achieve as markets have become increasingly competitive and it is difficult to make any form of meaningful differentiation or position by which users should continue to purchase.

with a Nestlé-branded offering. Birds Eye phased out eight sub-brands in 1996. Part of the reasoning was to focus brand-related resources across the 'mother' brand (Birds Eye) rather than have resources spread thinly across, for example, four sub-brands in the ready meals category alone (Curtis, 1996). The equity that each of these brands held (that is, their overall value) had diminished to the point that management decided that the opportunity costs of maintaining the brand in the current context could and should not be sustained. Brand equity is discussed more fully in Chapter 14.

Summary

The task of assigning financial resources to an organisation's marketing communications is difficult and imprecise, and as yet there is no method that can be used on a prescriptive basis. Theoretically, the task can be understood and resources allocated easily. Unfortunately, the quality and availability of information required to use marginal analysis are poor and practitioners have to rely on other methods. These other methods range from the simplistic ('this is what I think we should spend') to the more complex analysis associated with the spend incurred by competitors and the relationship of share of voice with market share that some believe is operable in certain market conditions, or purchase database information such as PIMS.

The decision to invest in marketing communications is a difficult one. This is because the direct outcomes are intangible and often distant, as the advertising effects are digested by potential buyers until such time as they are prepared and ready to purchase.

The methods presented in this chapter represent some of the more commonly used techniques. No one method is sufficient, and two or three approaches to the investment decision are required if management are to decide with any accuracy or confidence. Some commentators (Jones, 1990; Buzzell *et al.*, 1990) suggest that the actual amounts invested by some organisations are larger than is necessary. The consequence is that there is wastage and inefficiency, which contributes to a dilution of the profits that brands generate. Management have to make a trade-off between investing and growing the brand to secure a position compared with relaxing the promotional investment and harvesting some profit, perhaps as a reward for the previous investment activity.

Review questions

1. How might organisations benefit from adopting an appropriation-setting process?
2. What problems might be encountered when setting them?
3. Write a brief paper outlining the essence of marginal analysis. What are the main drawbacks associated with this approach?
4. Why is the objective and task method gaining popularity?
5. What is a payout plan?
6. Discuss the view that if the A/S ratio only measures average levels of spend across an industry then its relevance may be lost as individual organisations have to adjust levels of promotional spend to match particular niche market conditions.

7. How might the notion of SOV assist the appropriation-setting process?

8. What are 'profit-taking' and 'investment' brands?

9. Determining the level of spend for sales promotion is potentially difficult. Why?

10. What are the main reasons justifying the valuation of brands?

MINI CASE

Xioniene

Analgesics are made of three main types of formulation: aspirin, paracetamol and ibuprofen, and each of the leading suppliers has a brand in each of these sectors. Paracetamol is the leading formulation as it does not have the side effects of aspirin, and ibuprofen has been gaining share because it is perceived as fast acting, strong and because it can command a premium price. A fourth type of formulation has recently been developed which uses a combination of the other types of formulation. By adding codeine to the formulation, a much more powerful analgesic can be offered. See Table 8.3.

Distribution

Analgesics are available as an OTC ('over-the-counter') product and can be sold either through pharmacies or through retail outlets such as CTNs and grocery multiples. 'P' line products may be sold only through pharmacies employing a resident pharmacist. Retail outlets without an in-store pharmacy can only sell general sales list (GSL) analgesics. Government controls on analgesic classification and pack sizes

Table 8.3   Sales of OTC analgesics by product type

(£m RSP)	1999 (£m RSP)	2000
Paracetamol	55.2	62.1
Aspirin	49.5	51.3
Ibuprofen	14.1	17.5
Combinations	15.2	23.1
Total	134.00	154.00

RSP, retail selling price.

Table 8.4   Sales of analgesics by type of outlet

(£m rsp)	1999 (£m rsp)	2000
Boots	36	39
Other chemists	54	58
Grocery multiples	36	46
Other drugstores and CTNs	8	9
Total	134.00	154.00

RSP, retail selling price.

determine which types of analgesics retailers are allowed to sell (Table 8.4).

Research shows that there is a trend towards the use of stronger and more ailment-specific analgesics. These products permit premium prices to be charged, as a result of which a greater proportion of sales are being channelled through pharmacies.

Industry structure

Four major companies dominate the industry: Clearmill Laboratories, Healthline, Brookes and Infol International.

Clearmill brands enjoy good distribution in both the pharmacy and retail sectors. Direx accounts for the majority of Clearmill's sales with an estimated 16% total market share in 1997, a loss of 14.6% on its 1999 performance.

Of the three main brands offered by Healthline, the market shares for Nured (3% MS) and Zendol (5% MS) remained constant over the past two years. The main new brand from Healthline in recent years has been Fennadiene with a 9.5% market share in 2000, which represents a dramatic increase of 39.7% on its 1999 share. This particular brand is of specific interest to Infol International as it is a combination analgesic, which incorporates codeine and paracetamol and has been responsible for much of Healthline's recent growth.

The principal business of Brookes is the supply of own-label and branded products to the extent that they are the largest UK supplier of analgesics. Brookes developed Alophine as its own brand with a premium price, when ibuprofen was deregulated in 1993. In 2000 it increased its market share to 12.1% from 8.45% in 1999. This spectacular achievement was thought to have been the result of two actions. First, a major TV advertising campaign was launched in which the message was conveyed in an interesting, innovative and entertaining way. Second, there was a great deal of favourable press coverage as a result of the high ratings Alophine achieved in independent tests.

Infol holds 11.0% MS with its ClearHead brand (5.3% MS) and the recently launched Xioniene (5.7% MS). ClearHead is an aspirin-based product and has been losing market share in each of the past four years. Like Fennadiene, Xioniene is a 'P' line product and requires the support of the retail pharmacist if an offering is to be successful.

Other players, including own brands, make up 55.9% of the analgesics market.

The market is growing by value and to a limited extent by volume. Real growth is expected to continue at 4.5% per annum, although faster rates are expected in the combination formulations. It is a very competitive market with product development concentrating on attributes of strength and taste. Further competition has arisen from substitutes such as natural remedies and alternative medicines. These are seen as a potential key influence on attitudes towards the use of analgesics.

Consumers

Market research has shown that women are twice as likely to be users of analgesics as men and that the use of leading brands is closely linked to income. The higher the income, the greater the usage of branded products. Many

men avoid using analgesics as they are seen as either 'unnecessary' or simply because the current brands are perceived as ineffective.

The success of ibuprofen-based products such as Alophine was based on the trend towards more effective and 'stronger' analgesics. Use of analgesics is highest amongst those suffering most stress, for example, those with children and among women under 45.

However, following health scares in the 1970s and 1980s concerning each base formulation, some consumers in the 1990s are aware of the health risks associated with analgesics. There appears to be no correlation between age and non-usage of analgesics associated with health concerns. There is, however, a higher awareness of health issues in the upper socioeconomic group and, as a consequence, they read the pack details. It is this group who are most likely to take analgesics.

Infol International

Infol International developed Xioniene so that it would combine the better qualities of paracetamol and ibuprofen with codeine. Others had attempted such a combination but failed because of the side-effects generated by certain active ingredients, thought necessary to stabilise the codeine. Infol had developed a technique that brought about stabilisation, without the inclusion of the other active ingredients. The launch was very successful with a high number of recommendations by pharmacists. A 9% market share was expected this year.

The management team of Infol International was preparing to meet in order to discuss the marketing plans for Infol's range of analgesics. The objective was to obtain 16% market share by the end of next year. This growth was to be achieved through a range of new products, to be launched over a three-year period, the first of which was Xioniene last year. The next to be launched, this year, was XLT, a replacement for ClearHead and paracetamol based.

Vivian Shepherd, brand manager for Xioniene, was considering the promotional mix and the appropriation. Media expenditure in the market, she noted, had fallen over the last two years but television is still the prime medium for brand leaders. Industry spend on press and magazine advertising was increasing and she considered diverting a proportion of next year's spend on Xioniene into print. She knew that promotional expenditure by Healthline, especially on Fennadiene, was set to increase again next year and she was anxious to persuade her group brands manager that Infol should increase the Xioniene spend. She was also aware that others in the team favoured a 50% increase on last year's Xioniene spend, based largely on their experience. Others thought that there was a need to spread the budget more equally over both the current brands and others thought that funds should be redirected to making a greater number of

Table 8.6 Media spend on major analgesic brands

(£m)	1999 (£m)	2000
Direx	1.1	1.5
Alophine	1.6	2.1
Zendol	0.6	0.7
Fennadiene	1.8	2.0
Xioniene	N/A	1.4
ClearHead	0.7	0.4

personal visits to the community pharmacists in order that they recommend Xioniene rather than depend upon brand strength and consumer recall. Preparing her arguments she obtained details on media expenditure on the market, (Table 8.5) and the media spend by brand (Table 8.6).

Table 8.5 Main media expenditures on OTC analgesics

	£m
1994	13.3
1995	11.2
1996	11.6
1997	12.1
1999	12.7
2000	14.5

Mini-case questions

1. Evaluate the different methods which Shepherd could use to determine the promotional budget for Xioniene.
2. What amount would you recommend should be spent on above-the-line promotion, for Xioniene, based on the limited information that is available in the mini case?
3. How might the promotional mix for Xioniene differ from that for XLT?
4. How might SOV calculations help Shepherd?

References

Abraham, M. and Lodish, L.M. (1990) Getting the most out of advertising and sales promotion. *Harvard Business Review* (May/June), pp. 50–60.

Abratt, R. and van der Westhuizen, B. (1985) A new promotion mix appropriation model. *International Journal of Advertising*, **4**, pp. 209–21.

Bainbridge, J. (2000) Top 1000 advertisers. *Marketing*, 2 March, p. 26

Birkin, M. (1995) Why brands are valued. *Admap* (March), pp. 18–19.

Broadbent, S. (1989) *The Advertising Budget*. Henley-on-Thames: NTC Publications.

Buck, S. (1995) The decline and fall of the premium brand. *Admap* (March), pp. 14–17.

Burnett, J. (1993) *Promotion Management*. New York: Houghton Mifflin.

Butterfield, L. (1999) *Excellence in Advertising: The IPA Guide to Best Practice*. Oxford: Butterworth Hienemann.

Buzzell, R.D., Quelch, J.A. and Salmon, W.J. (1990) The costly bargain of sales promotion. *Harvard Business Review* (March/April), pp. 141–9.

Curtis, J. (1996) Till death do us part. *Marketing*, 25 July, pp. 20–1

Gaedeke, R.M. and Tootelian, D.H. (1983) *Marketing: Principles and Application*. St Paul, MN: West.

Hall, E. (1999) When advertising becomes an expensive luxury. *Campaign*, 10 December, p. 18.

Hooley, G.J. and Lynch, J.E. (1985) How UK advertisers set budgets. *International Journal of Advertising*, **3**, pp. 223–31.

Jones, J.P. (1990) Ad spending: maintaining market share. *Harvard Business Review*, (January/February), pp. 38–42.

Mistry, B. (2001) Walkers revives Tazo route. *Promotions and Incentives*. (March), pp. 26–8.

Mitchell, L.A. (1993) An examination of methods of setting advertising budgets: practice and literature. *European Journal of Advertising*, **27**(5), pp. 5–21.

PIMS (2000) www.PIMS-Europe.com.

Schroer, J. (1990) Ad spending: growing market share. *Harvard Business Review* (January/ February), pp. 44–8.

Smallbone, D.W. (1972) *The Practice of Marketing*. London: Staple Press.

Tomkins, R. (1999) If the return is right, keep spending. *Financial Times*, 19 March, p. 8.

Tylee, J. (1999) Survey warns against adspend cuts. *Campaign,* 12 March, p. 10.

chapter 9

Environmental influences on marketing communications

The environment provides a setting within which largely uncontrollable elements have the potential to shape and reshape the nature and form of the marketing communications used by participant organisations. The task is to use the environment to shape messages and images rather than ignore or fight these forces which have the potential to cause major damage to a company's marketing communications and reputation.

AIMS AND OBJECTIVES

The aims of this chapter are to introduce some of the wider environmental factors associated with marketing communications.

The objectives of this chapter are:

1. To appreciate the complexity of the environmental context and its impact on marketing communications.
2. To understand the principal forces that operate within the context of the environment.
3. To discern the impact of societal forces on marketing communications.
4. To appreciate how technological advances have affected planned communications.
5. To provide an insight into how economic conditions affect such programmes.
6. To explore the way in which legislative changes can shape the content of promotional messages.
7. To establish the role of communications in the context of corporate responsibility.

Introduction

It has been established that organisations are open systems and that they seek to satisfy their objectives through networks of other organisations. They are, therefore, subject to the influences of these other organisations and the network as a whole. At the same time, however, the focus organisation seeks to influence different parts of the network, and much of that activity is undertaken through its promotional programme. The quality of interaction that an organisation enjoys with its environments will be a significant contribution to the success of the organisation in its attempt to meet its objectives. Planned marketing communications influence the quality of the relationships held and consequently the outcomes of the partnerships, in the form of relational exchanges.

The wider environment cannot be ignored and is a factor in the development of planned communications. Most of the elements discussed so far are, to a large extent, capable of being controlled by the organisation. The context within which buyers and organisations function means that changes in buyer preferences and buying patterns can be determined through marketing research and programmes can be adjusted to meet changed conditions. Competitors may change the way in which they present their offerings and in doing so seek to reposition not only themselves but also some of the other players in the market.

The wider environment cannot be ignored and is a factor in the development of planned communications.

There are opportunities to overcome these difficulties through such tools as advertising (to transmit messages to mass audiences), direct marketing (to focus messages on individual customers) and sales promotions (to stimulate purchase activity). However, there is a range of other forces which constitute a context which organisations are unable to influence to any significant degree; that is, they are largely uncontrollable, at least in the short run.

The context of these forces may be beyond the influence of an organisation and, rather than attempt to influence the source of these forces, the only feasible course of action is to adapt to the expected or prevailing environmental conditions. The pharmaceutical industry is now required by the European Union to list on the packaging, or on leaflets provided with drugs, many of the ingredients contained in each product. When this is considered in the light of the vast number of compounds that are used in each formulation and the requirement to provide suitable usage instructions and all necessary warnings concerning any possible side effects, it becomes apparent that the design of the label and hence promotional message associated with over-the-counter (OTC) and pharmacy only (P line) offerings become exceedingly complex.

The main characteristics of this contextual element are that these forces are largely uncontrollable.

The purpose of this chapter is therefore to consider the wider external environment as a context within which organisations seek to deploy planned (and unplanned) marketing communication messages. The main characteristics of this contextual element are that these forces are largely uncontrollable and that the communications activities have to be designed and implemented in a way that accommodates the key constraining and restraining forces.

The environmental context

Potentially, there are an extremely large number of elements in the environment that indirectly or directly affect the communications of an organisation. The skill of the marketing communications manager is to sense those elements that may be unobtrusive now but which may gather strength and have a stronger impact on the organisation or its offerings at some point in the future. Having sensed new environmental developments and determined that their impact cannot be ignored, the next step is to adjust the way in which messages are encoded, delivered or decoded so that the impact is diffused and, where possible, used to the advantage of the organisation. The environmental context can be regarded as consisting of a number of sub-contexts within which driving and restraining forces seek to influence the established norms. The main forces are political, economic, societal, technological (PEST), plus seasonal impacts and those concerning corporate responsibility (Figure 9.1).

Adjust the way in which messages are encoded, delivered or decoded so that the impact is diffused and, where possible, used to the advantage of the organisation.

Before considering each of these forces it is important to remember the reason for considering these environmental elements. Organisations need to be aware of environmental developments because some of them, not all, have the potential to increase or decrease the effectiveness of their communications. If the communications are not effective, the implication is that the communications are not efficient and the organisation is wasting resources. The other critical aspect is that the roots of a crisis may be embedded in an environmental force which, if not observed or attended to, might lead to serious consquences and damage a brand's reputation (see Chapters 16 and 26). Changes in consumers' fashion preferences and the entry of new brands (e.g. Matalan) went unnoticed by Marks and Spencer for many years, or least they were not attended to. As a result, the largest UK clothing retailer has suffered declining market share and profitability and been forced to adopt crisis communications. Management have reconsidered its brand proposition and introduced radically different forms of communication, including television advertising in an attempt to communicate a new set of brand values.

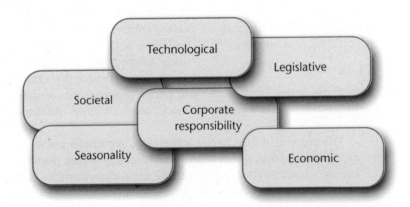

Figure 9.1 Elements of the environmental context.

Societal forces

One of the most significant of the environmental forces acting in the societal subcontext concerns changes in the demographic balance. The number of people in each of the age bands (e.g. 18–24 year olds) is changing. This demographic shift in population bands means that by 2010 there will be more than three times the number of people over 60 years old than there were in the 1960s. The growth in the number of older people brings implications for the production capacity of the economy and the opening of new markets. Already the 'grey market' (over-50-year-olds) is well established. In 1991 24% of the UK population was over 55 years old, and the size of this band is expected to increase significantly. This new segment requires different products and services from all others, as they possess different readership habits and viewing patterns. This will mean a change not only in the nature and form of products which are of value to them but also in the way products and services are presented to them.

This new segment requires different products and services from all others, as they possess different readership habits and viewing patterns.

Another force is that the number of single-parent families has grown and the size and shape of the family unit are shifting as divorce rates remain high and the number of births outside the traditional family unit increases. Apart from addressing the impact that these new units have on levels of disposable income, marketing communications need to be sensitive to the fact that the 2+2 family unit is no longer dominant. For example, family scenes such as those that used to be depicted in advertisements for Allied Dunbar and Oxo, have now been replaced with scenes that are more reflective of contemporary life. Sales promotions that offer bonus packs or family tubs offer no value to these emerging units. Sensitivity to and awareness of these issues are more important if a message is to have credibility with the target audience.

Changing social values – Kellogg's

Kellogg's had traditionally positioned itself around family values, quality and choice. In the UK it was found to be the most trusted brand, but it was facing declining market share (Datamonitor), stagnant market conditions and increasing attack from own-label products. Kellogg's needed to reconsider its approach.

In January 1998 the company announced a new positioning approach following extensive consumer research. It found from a series of focus groups that consumers believed that stress and weight control, together with family health, constituted the primary issues facing people. As a result of this, Kellogg's launched a radically different campaign that focused on raising awareness of the importance of diet in leading a healthy lifestyle. Its positioning is now about 'Serving the Nation's Health'.

Kellogg's claims that 'Serving the Nation's Health' was a return to the corporate philosophy established by its founder, who claimed that Kellogg's 'makes quality products for a healthier world'. See Plate 9.1

Adapted from Rogers (1998)

Further to this point and at a more subtle level, the changing nature of society brings difficulties and opportunities for advertisers. How should messages be presented to target audiences? For example, the role of women in society has changed considerably over the past decade. The traditional role of mother and housewife has changed, and there are a growing number of households where domestic chores are shared more equally (Bartos, 1983). The pattern of women's lives has changed considerably over the last 20 years. Many more are now pursuing educational qualifications before commencing careers. Increasing numbers of those who previously were unable to study are returning to education later in life. The roles women now assume at work have also changed, as a greater number now hold middle and senior management positions. Promotional messages have tried to reflect this change (e.g. Actimel by Danone) , and some advertisers have moved away from narrow stereotyping. Messages showing women as supercharged, multi-skilled heroines who manage homes, partners, families, business and local community activities emerged in the 1980s as a reaction to these changes in society. However, these have now given way in the light of reality and the guilt that some women experienced in trying to live up to these implausible expectations.

Changes in the environment are not always negative and uncontrollable as they can be used and incorporated within a campaign to good advantage. By seizing the initiative it is possible to associate topicality and flexibility with a brand. For example, American Express used Lennox Lewis (heir apparent world heavyweight boxing champion) when he failed to win the champion's crown at the first attempt. The fight was declared a draw yet it was widely assumed that he had won by a substantial margin. 'Being Robbed in America' was a humorous response, one that fitted the brand and helped to develop appropriate brand associations and values. See Exhibit 9.1.

Changes in the environment are not always negative and uncontrollable as they can be used and incorporated within a campaign to good advantage.

When the perfume Charlie was first launched in the United Kingdom in the mid-1970s, it was the first to position itself as a fragrance for the independent woman. One of the main ways of appealing to this emerging segment was to dress the strident actress in trousers, something that had not occurred previously. This approach was soon copied by others, of course, including Chanel, who disguised their actress in a male suit and placed her unnoticed in a gentlemen's club in an attempt to position on equality and assertiveness. Chanel in 2001 still use a (younger looking) striding women in a trouser suit to represent the brand.

The attitudes held by society have changed faster than demographics. Increasingly, towards the end of the 1980s, environmentalists became a force which businesses and consumers finally came to understand and appreciate. Organisations began to incorporate environmental issues in their communications and purchasing activities. The ecological perspective has become more important as psychographic segments become more significant, witnessed by the sales growth of organic products, Iceland positioning themselves against GM products and the growth and sustainability of The Body Shop, the most successful 'green retailer' (Dibb and Simpkin, 1991). The force with which ecological issues impact upon consumers and organisations can only intensify. Organisations should determine whether ecological matters present any opportunities in the form of untapped market segments, new promotional messages to reposition organisations and their brands, or new media vehicles to carry messages to this audience.

The attitudes held by society have changed faster than demographics.

HANDY

IF YOU GET
ROBBED
IN AMERICA.

American Express® has travel offices

in all corners of the globe.

So should you have the misfortune

to be relieved of your moneybelt

we can provide emergency cash,

and replace your card, usually within

24 hours. Now who would you rather

have in your corner?

do more.

Exhibit 9.1
Complementary brand values: American Express and Lennox Lewis. Picture kindly used with the permission of American Express Europe Ltd.

A further consideration is the way in which consumers use brands to reflect lifestyle and personality factors. In the 1980s, research indicated that brands were bought partly to reflect status and achievement, but consumers in the 1990s were more sceptical about brand claims and were considered to be more thoughtful about their purchases. Consumers in the new century continue to be more caring and considerate,

London Zoo

Towards the end of the 20th century, many zoos, including London Zoo, experienced a marked decline in the number of visitors. One of the reasons for this is that the public's attitude to zoos has changed (for a variety of reasons) and they do not want animals taken out of their natural environment and caged in pens that are inappropriate. London Zoo, like many others, has tried to reposition itself as an organisation charged with the protection of endangered species, mainly through the development of breeding programmes. These actions represent a contextual adjustment. London Zoo adapted itself to the environment within which it functioned and determined a more appropriate context for its continued existence, a context that would be more acceptable to its wide array of stakeholders, most notably the paying public.

although it will be interesting to observe how this changes as the retail landscape alters with technological developments (e.g. interactive home shopping). This is, of course, a reflection of the economic conditions, but it means that the messages transmitted to target audiences need to be decoded in such a way that quality and benefits are easily understood (McMurdo, 1993). Luxury advertising is also changing as tastes change. Rawsthorn (1993) observed that advertisements in glossy upmarket magazines, such as *Tatler*, *Vanity Fair* and *Vogue*, could be seen to 'dwell on exclusivity and craftsmanship and the long history of their companies, rather than the materialistic imagery of the 1980s'. The context portrayed by these messages is consistent and often aspirational, motivating members of the target audience to change aspects of their lifestyle.

Consumers use brands to reflect lifestyle and personality factors.

A further issue concerns marketing communication messages that attempt to break established conventions. In order to gain attention in cluttered markets and to be contemporary, some advertisements infringe upon societal norms and are rejected (Gossard lingerie rejected for sexual overtones, Ford Fiesta advertisements that depicted speed as the primary attribute), while others infringe yet are accepted (Tango, Wonderbra), and in so doing alter the context for future communications and expectations for advertisers, consumers and agencies either at large or within the product sector and market. The dynamism of the advertising business itself provides a mechanism by which society acts as an important context for marketing communications.

A further issue concerns marketing communication messages that attempt to break established conventions.

Tango demonstrated its responsibility and speed of reaction to the environment when it changed its advertising following the report of an accident. The 'You've been Tango'd' campaign involved one character slapping another around the cheeks with both hands, and this soon led to a play ground craze. However, the agency (HHCL) received a call one day from a doctor who reported that a child had suffered a perforated eardrum as a result of being 'Tango'd'. The ad was pulled immediately and replaced with a 'kiss' (Howell, 2000).

Society provides both legislative and voluntary regulatory frameworks through which marketing communications messages are designed, vetted and delivered. In a

Society, therefore, is a framework or context within which marketing communication messages have value.

way this is a form of censorship, society's self-imposed mechanism for maintaining the contextual norms for the marketing communications we experience. Society, therefore, is a framework or context within which marketing communication messages have value, are valued and which legitimise the current culture and the marketing communications that contribute to it.

Technological forces

The pace at which technology has advanced over the past decade has had a tremendous impact upon advertisers, media owners, marketing research, advertising and newly born new media agencies. The principal effect has been to fragment the audience in such a way that targets can be more easily defined and reached with pinpoint accuracy. Some of the secondary effects of fragmentation are that organisations now employ different promotional mixes to reach these diverse groups. A greater emphasis has been placed on sales promotion at the expense of mass advertising. Direct marketing has attained a greater level of acceptability and more organisations are using multiple sales channels rather than only relying on the field sales force. One of the reasons for the rapid development of direct marketing has been technological advance, bringing the ability for organisations to harness computing facilities at speeds and costs that are increasing and falling respectively. For example, the surge in telemarketing activities and segmentation approaches through database management typify the advances made and society's attitudes towards to direct response television (DRTV) and personalised, unsolicited mail have changed.

New technology has enabled supermarkets to scan purchases at the checkout and record the data so that in-store promotion campaigns can be run more effectively. Single-source data, that is the electronic measurement of television exposure and purchase behaviour (Assael and Poltrack, 1991), have facilitated testing the effectiveness of advertisements under semi-controlled conditions, where all the data emanate from the same household.

The explosion of video recorders and the steady growth of satellite and cable networks have reduced, and will continue to do so, the power of the central broadcast networks. This means that advertisers have more opportunities to reach particular targets and viewers are able to select a greater range of programmes. Zipping and zapping between channels enables viewers to avoid television commercials, so lowering the perceived effectiveness of the medium.

Advertisers have more opportunities to reach particular targets and viewers are able to select a greater range of programmes.

The recently launched TiVo system enables consumers to record programmes yet blank out advertisements. This represents a further impetus away from above-the-line communications. Home shopping channels are expanding and while the penetration of interactive (digital) television is limited it will grow quickly. Experiments with interactive television advertising (e.g. Dove), built on the ideas associated with permission marketing, will inevitably expand as cable and satellite penetration increases.

New on-line and interactive communications have begun to change the way in which shopping, entertainment, banking and education, for example, are undertaken and delivered to a wide variety of audiences.

Technological breakthroughs have occurred in the print industry. Colour printing for newspapers, at an economical rate, is now a commercially attractive strategy for some advertisers. Magazine publishers have developed new techniques to attract advertisers. Scent strips, for example, allow perfume houses to invite readers to try a new fragrance without them having to visit a store. Personalised magazines can now be assembled in response to reader enquiries about particular products and product categories. The advent and development of commercial radio has provided new opportunities to reach buyers, typified by the success of Classic FM and Virgin 1215.

Advertisers need to be aware of the changes that are occurring in the technological environment and be prepared to review them as they may provide better opportunities to reach their target audiences.

Economic forces

The condition of the national economy is beyond the control of any single organisation. The effects can be seen in tangible elements, such as the level of disposable income, and intangible elements, such as the confidence that organisations and consumers have to invest. The balance between an individual's propensities to save and to spend can have an immediate impact upon the way in which promotional messages are designed, delivered and received. For example, it is not uncommon for advertisers to promote economy packs and price deals during times of recession and to cut back on media expenditure. Many consumers become cautious about non-necessary expenditures and less receptive to messages inducing them to enter exchange transactions, unless there is an incentive or some form of added value associated with the purchase. When the economy is strong or gathering strength, so the desire to save gradually gives way to a greater propensity to spend. Consumers become more receptive to a variety of messages, and the content of advertising messages in particular becomes more expansive. Message appeals become more emotional and tend to replace the rational, price-orientated messages that dominate during a recession.

When the economy is strong or gathering strength, so the desire to save gradually gives way to a greater propensity to spend.

The 1980s was a period of self-orientated affluence, the 1990s saw a more value-orientated perspective and in the early years of the new century a period characterised by uncertainty. These changes impact upon attitudes, buying patterns and the structure of organisations as they adapt to the radically different environments and the new strategies that they seek to sustain competitiveness and viability. For example, many food manufacturers are having to adapt their products in the wake of the growing assertiveness of retailers and the success of their own brands. Marketing communications have changed, witnessed by the way in which the promotional mix is deployed and by the shift in budget away from mass advertising to sales promotions and direct marketing.

Seasonal forces

Many products have purchase cycles that are short and regular. Promotional messages can be spread across the year, according to the objectives of each campaign. Some products, however, are consumed on a seasonal basis, which impacts upon promotional strategy and media scheduling in particular. These seasonal factors may occur because of climatic and natural elements, whereas others may result from past practices or cultural norms. For example, the most important purchase period in the toy market is the period leading to Christmas; this represents a cultural determinant. However, the main sales of ice-cream occur in the summer months, and gardening products sell best in the spring and early summer. These result from climatic conditions and will vary from country to country. These seasonal forces are usually uncontrollable (they cannot normally be changed), so organisations must adapt their promotional activities to meet the environmental conditions.

Some products, however, are consumed on a seasonal basis, which impacts upon promotional strategy and media scheduling in particular.

The market for new cars in the UK used to surge at the new registration letter date, 1 August. During this period, over 25% of each year's new car sales occurred. However, unlike the weather and climatic issues, the new car purchase and registration issue was originally induced as a societal requisite and as such was capable of change. A number of stakeholders were adversely affected by this system and a move was made to change it so that there are two points within each year when new registrations can be made. This development serves to reduce the congestion and excessive activity at car dealerships in August, but also impacts on the marketing communication schedules of car manufacturers. The nature of the competitive communication activity alters and budgets are reorganised to reflect the new market requirements. In addition to this, the activities of agencies and those involved in media planning in particular have altered, and advertising creatives need to find new ways of reminding people about their clients' products, as well as differentiating them, on perhaps a greater number of occasions each year.

Legislative forces

Some of the most important stakeholders that all organisations have are their national governments and other associated (often higher-level) affiliations. In the UK the latter would be represented by the European Union, in South-East Asia by SEATO and in the USA by NAFTA. The potential force that these parties have through legislation and regulation is enormous and it is this overall context of guidelines and boundaries of behaviour that sets limits on the behaviour of organisations and the marketing communication dialogue they seek to generate and maintain.

The end of commission payments – The Prudential

Financial services company, The Prudential announced in February 1998 that it was to abolish the payment of commission as a means of rewarding its sales force.

Merrell (1998) suggests that this decision can be traced back to the introduction of a legal requirement that the amount of commission earned had to be declared to consumers. Because these sums are normally taken out of the fund at the beginning of a policy term, it cut the value of the fund to be invested, and customers were unhappy at the amounts of commission declared. In addition, the drive to earn commission in the absence of adequate salaries has been regarded as a prime cause of the pension misselling that occurred in the late 1980s and early 1990s. Not only has The Prudential been admonished by the regulatory authorities and had to set aside £450 million for compensation, but it has also had its reputation severely challenged.

The changes have led to a new sales force structure with retail-style distribution based around telephone account management and a culture that encourages the development of customer relationships. As Sir Peter Davis, the then group chief executive, said, 'we want to change the sales force from hunters to farmers'.

The processes by which new laws are developed provide opportunities for industry to put forward its views. These are normally heard formally through committee procedures and informally through lobbying practices. In this sense, legislation can be influenced and is to some extent controllable. However, the vast majority of legislation is in place and has to be complied with. The legislation regarding the promotion of products and services within a product class must always be considered as a part of the planning process. Legislation changes frequently and it is important that advertisers are up to date and aware of current legislative requirements. These requirements include not only advertising but also packaging, sales promotions, logo and brand name issues.

European Union initiatives

For products targeted at children, advertising which is aimed at children under 10 is not allowed in Sweden. In Greece, TV toy advertising between 7:00 a.m. and 10:00 p.m. is banned; some countries require ads for sweets to carry a toothbrush symbol and others have rules intended to curb advertisers from encouraging children to exercise 'pester power'.

Alcohol, tobacco, pharmaceuticals and financial services are also subject to similarly diverse regulations and rules about how much of the human body can be revealed, whether prices can be discounted for special offers, and the use of free gifts in sales promotions.

Sponsorship in The Netherlands was seen as having particularly restrictive curbs on event sponsorship, while the UK and Denmark were seen to impose strict rules on broadcasting of free gifts in sales promotions (adapted from Summers, 1996).

The EU is seeking to harmonise the way in which member countries use marketing communications. Variations in the standards, guidelines and regulations governing aspects of promotion are seen by some as inappropriate and it is thought that consumers should receive greater levels of protection for unscrupulous operators.

The legislative framework is supplemented by the activities of the institute or trade association to which an advertiser might belong and the voluntary codes of practice that the Independent Television Commission (ITC) and the Committee of Advertising Practice (CAP) enforce as custodians of the British Code of Advertising Practice.

Adherence to these guidelines is normally enforced through the threat of blacklisting and ejection from the relevant professional body. The need for members to remain within these groups can be strong. This is because membership is often regarded as a sign of credibility, which in turn is a factor that can determine whether they will continue to attract business.

Force for corporate responsibility

A fast-growing and important area of interest is the level of responsibility organisations are prepared to accept for their role in the systems in which they operate. The breadth of vision that organisations have with regard to their system responsibilities has expanded considerably over the past decade. Some would argue that there are three main driving forces behind this new vision. The first an increased awareness and understanding of how production and consumption of resources impact upon the environment and how an organisation contributes to the cycle. The second is the recognition and acceptance that organisations need to cooperate and collaborate with other organisations, principally in their performance networks, if they are to have any strategic advantage. The third reason lies with the increasing impact consumers are having in terms of their rights and understanding of business and communication issues and their associated willingness to make known their views.

Some would argue that there are three main driving forces behind this new vision.

One of the responses to this new vision was the proliferation of total quality management programmes. These were introduced in the 1990s by organisations to improve efficiency, reduce costs and increase levels of customer satisfaction. Some organisations will only collaborate with others if it can be shown that they have an acceptable standard of quality procedures, namely a kite mark or British Standard. What has happened is that quality standards have become 'standardised' and are no longer a means by which differentiation can be sustained.

Another outcome of the new vision has been the awareness and interest associated with the development of business ethics and codes of conduct. Business ethics are essentially concerned with the morality associated with the decisions that an organisation and its members make and how these decisions, both right and wrong and good and bad, affect society or particular stakeholder groups. This has been discussed at length in Chapter 6.

Issues concerning, for example, cash for passports, vehicle defects and delayed recall by car manaufacturers, misselling or pensions and bank and computer fraud all make headline news. But there are a vast number of other matters, concerning golden handshakes, insider dealing, making promises about delivery in the full knowledge that it will not be met, whistle blowing and salespersons using pressurised or misleading methods of selling, that occur frequently and which receive little public attention. One exception to this last point concerns the problems resulting from the misselling of pensions by a number of organisations in the financial services sector in the 1990s.

Much of the work of marketing communications, and public relations in particular, is to present the organisation as a morally correct and socially responsible organisation.

Indeed, much of the work of marketing communications, and public relations in particular, is to present the organisation as a morally correct and socially responsible organisation. This is achieved by informing stakeholders of its various public good works, such as charitable donations and sponsorships, and its position on particular social issues. All of these activities or cues provide visibility so that others perceive it as an acceptable network member, one from whom they can comfortably buy goods or with whom they can sustain a viable business relationship.

Some target audiences are aware of organisations who practise good or bad business ethics, or at least, in their perception, are distinguished one way or another. Managers should not underestimate the potential for resistance or opposition by their customers, through, for example, refusing to buy their products or use their services (Thompson, 1990). Readers are advised to refer to Chapter 6 for a deeper consideration of these and other related issues.

Summary

Organisations operate in environmental contexts that are largely controllable. Indeed, it is management's responsibility to ensure that the organisation influences its environments in order that the organisation can achieve its objectives. There are, however, areas where management has little, if any, influence. Management's task is to be aware of the nature, speed and direction of the changes that are occurring in these uncontrollable areas and to shape corporate, unit and functional strategies accordingly.

This wider environmental context is maintained by a number of forces. These forces are derived from a number of principal sources, however, many changes stem from government initiatives. Societal and cultural developments, economic conditions, technological surges and legislative frameworks continually shape the nature of the context within which organisations operate. In turn, the marketing communications undertaken by organisations need to accommodate and reflect these changes, not only in terms of the content but also the direction and speed with which they are transmitted. When developing marketing communication strategies and preparing plans a PEST analysis can be very useful. However, a common mistake is to make a linkage between a PEST factor and a brand or organisation, but failure to translate that into an impact on a brand/organisation's communications.

Review questions

1. Identify the main forces that maintain the environmental context and which affect organisations.

2. What is the prime characteristic common to all of these forces?

3. Using an organisation with which you are familiar, identify the various forces acting upon it. How strong is each force and is the strength likely to change?

4. Suggest ways in which attitudes towards each of the following might have changed over the past 30 or 40 years: cars, aftershave, margarine, package holidays, pollution and waste disposal, shopping and criminals.

5. How have technological forces impacted upon the promotional activities of grocery retailers?

6. Write a brief report outlining some of the legislative forces that can affect particular organisations. How can marketing communications be used in this context?

7. Discuss the view that buyers are not interested in marketing communications that present an organisation and/or its products honestly and truthfully.

8. Identify three seasonal forces that are driven by natural forces and three that are driven by artificial or cultural criteria.

9. Select a brand of your choice and determine how environmental forces might affect its marketing communications.

10. Identify two organisations that, in your opinion, manage these uncontrollable forces well. Justify your decisions.

MINI CASE

This case was written by Yasmin Sekhon, Lecturer in Marketing at the Southampton Business School.

Petrol crisis

Crippling the country

September 2000 saw the UK come to a near standstill. As social pressure gained force, economic issues were argued and political bickering began, the country was put on red alert.

Fuel protests began, as consumers and freight hauliers in particular made accusations that oil companies and petrol retailers were not passing recent cuts in the price of crude oil on to the consumer fast enough and that the rate of fuel tax was far higher than in other European countries. Irate farmers and truckers brought Britain to a virtual standstill by preventing tankers from delivering fuel to petrol stations. The social outcry affected the economy and the country in general. Not only did petrol stations close and people were unable to get to work, supermarket chains reported bulk buying by consumers and certain stores ran low on bread and other essentials.

The emergency services considered using their own supplies of fuel to ensure that services were not disrupted. Public transport saw a significant increase in the number of passengers as people gave up on their cars. British industry was worried that much-needed manufacturing components would not arrive in time.

Technologically, the fuel crisis meant certain supermarkets had to temporarily suspend their Internet shopping services, as fulfilment companies could not get fuel to make deliveries, thus impacting on the promotional activities of grocery retailers and others.

Politically, the Labour government was under immense pressure. Not wishing to be seen to give in to bullying but needing to resolve the crisis quickly, it had to communicate firmness and authority, yet be seen to be sympathetic and understanding. This had political repercussions, with the Conservatives moving ahead of Labour in the opinion polls for the first time in eight years. However, the Prime Minister stated: 'we could not possibly start introducing emergency budgets, cutting and raising tax on the basis of highly volatile moves in the world oil market'.

The media and marketing world took advantage of this situation, as British newspapers damned the government, backed consumers and published numerous editorials, calling on the government to cut fuel prices and accusing it of ignoring long standing public opposition. WHSmith began mass advertising campaigns, playing on the fuel crisis by stating in its print advertising campaign: 'sorry no unleaded pencils'.

This crisis also meant that many planned

marketing communications campaigns were largely ignored, as consumers were far more concerned with the developments of the fuel crisis. It also meant that reactionary campaigns, as illustrated by WHSmith, were quick to make the most of the situation in hand.

After the protest had died down, the country began to get back on its feet and consumers were given a 1p decrease per litre. However, it is feared that in the near future this chaos will once again affect the environment as a whole. Although the affect of these actions on the British market will almost certainly be reduced because the government and oil firms will be prepared to respond immediately and because many consumers will not want such disruption of that scale again.

The issue still remains that the environment does not only affect industry, but in this instance also the marketing communications environment as a whole. Consumers reverted to panic buying, long-planned media campaigns were largely ignored and reactionary campaigns became popular. Also, from a perceptual point of view, petrol retailers were regarded by many as greedy, taking advantage of consumers. In addition, the government had to begin a public relations campaign to restore consumer confidence and generate goodwill.

This crisis reflects the impact of largely uncontrollable environmental events and the severity of the repercussions.

Mini-case questions

1. Identify the main PEST factors that affected Britain as a whole within the fuel crisis.
2. Identify the impact of each of these PEST factors on the marketing communications of oil companies, independent petrol retailers, the government and grocery retailers.
3. Assume the role of a marketing communications manager for a major petrol retailer and prepare a marketing communications campaign to restore consumer confidence and change the perception of you to a friendly and caring retailer.

References

Assael, H. and Poltrack, D.F. (1991) Using single source data to select TV programmes based on purchasing behaviour. *Journal of Advertising Research* (August/September), pp. 9–17.

Bartos, R. (1983) Women in advertising. *International Journal of Advertising*, **2**, pp. 33–45.

Dibb, S. and Simpkin, L. (1991) Targeting, segments and positioning. *International Journal of Retail and Distribution Management*, **19**(3), pp. 4–10.

Howell, R. (2000) 100 Best Ads, Channel 4.

McMurdo, M.W. (1993) Chasing butterflies. *Marketing Week*, 21 May, pp. 28–31.

Merrell, C. (1998) Pru has a new sales policy. *The Times*, 28 February, p. 64

Rawsthorn, A. (1993) A little luxury goes a longer way. *Financial Times*, 18 November, p. 12.

Rogers, D. (1998) Why Kellogg has crossed the thin line. *Marketing*, 5 March, pp. 12–13.

Thompson, J.L. (1990) *Strategic Management: Awareness and Change.* London: Chapman & Hall.

10

Stakeholders, supply chains and interorganisational relationships

It is necessary to consider the whole system of relationships between organisations because the relationship between any two is contingent upon the direct and indirect relationships of all the actors (Andersson, 1992). A network of relationships therefore provides the context within which exchange and associated marketing communication behaviour occur.

AIMS AND OBJECTIVES

The aims of this chapter are to introduce the concepts of networks and stakeholders with a view to understanding business-to-business relationships of which marketing channel relationships and associated supply chain networks are important elements.

The objectives of this chapter are:

1. To introduce fundamental issues concerning network analysis.

2. To develop a methodology for stakeholder analysis and network mapping.

3. To show how organisations combine to form partnerships with particular stakeholders, coordinating their efforts to provide buyer satisfaction.

4. To establish marketing communications as a vital management process between stakeholders in a network of organisations.

5. To introduce two main common distribution networks, the conventional and vertical marketing systems.

6. To examine some of the behavioural issues involved with the management of channel networks, including conflict and leadership.

7. To explain how planned communications, in both network and intra-organisational contexts, can be improved by focused responsibilities and integration of communications activities.

Introduction

Distribution is a vital part of the marketing mix and accounts for a large percentage of the cost of a product. Its importance, however, is often overlooked by managers and students of marketing, and marketing communications in particular.

The distribution of products concerns two main elements. The first is the management of the tangible or physical aspects of moving a product from the producer to the end-user. This must be undertaken in such a way that the customer can freely access an offering and that the final act of the buying process is as easy as possible. The second element is the management of the intangible aspects or issues of ownership, control and flows of communication between parties responsible for making the offering accessible to the customer. The focus of this chapter will be on the second of these elements, commonly referred to as channel management or, as it is increasingly referred to, supply chain management.

Channel management: the intangible aspects or issues of ownership, control and flows of communication between parties.

Products flow through a variety of organisations, who coordinate their activities to make the offering readily available to the end-user. Coordination is necessary to convert raw materials into a set of benefits that can be transferred and be of value to the end-user. These benefits are normally bundled together and represented in the form of a product or service. The various organisations who elect to coordinate their activities each perform different roles in a chain of activity. Some perform the role of manufacturer, some act as agents and others may be distributors, dealers, value-added resellers, wholesalers or retailers. Whatever their role, it is normally specific and geared to refining and moving the offering closer to the end user.

Distribution channels – Snapple

Quaker Oats bought the Snapple drink in 1994 for $1.7 billion, when the drink's turnover had reached $674 million, having risen three-fold in as many years. Quaker saw synergies with its existing drink Gatorade and the logic of the acquisition looked sound (Miles, 2000).

By 1997 Quaker had sold the drink to Triarc Companies of New York for just $300 million, a drop of $1.4 billion, or a loss of $1.3 million per day. The reasons for this disaster were thought to be a failure to understand the previous distribution channels and the lack of synergy in logistics and the associated brand values.

Adapted from *Marketing Business*, the magazine for The Chartered Institute of Marketing, Issue 91. Used with kind permission

Each organisation is a customer to the previous organisation in an industry's value chain. Some organisations work closely together, coordinating and integrating their activities, while others combine on a temporary basis. In both cases, however, these organisations can be observed to be operating as members of a partnership (of differing strength and dimensions) with the express intention of achieving their objectives with their partner's assistance and cooperation. So, in addition to the end-user, a further set of customers (partners) can be determined: all those who make up the channel of distribution.

Each organisation is a customer to the previous organisation in an industry's value chain.

It was seen in Chapter 2 that effective communications are developed by building a positive realm of understanding with all those who impact upon the organisation and with whom communication is necessary and important: the target audiences. It is important, therefore, to identify who these other organisations (the target audiences) are, what their needs are and how important they are to the focus organisation and its products. Further questions include what the aims and objectives of these other organisations are and what the nature of the relationships between them is. Having undertaken this analysis it is then possible to develop complementary messages, to coordinate their transmission and to monitor and assess their effectiveness.

To help accomplish this, organisations must not only understand which other organisations interact with them but also determine the nature and the form of the relationships between organisations both inside and outside of the distribution channel. For example, organisations operating within the 'fast-moving consumer goods' or the 'over-the-counter' markets will invariably be able to identify two particular clusters: first, all those that contribute to the value-adding activities and directly affect the performance of the focus organisation, such as dealers, distributors, wholesalers and retailers, and second, all those that affect the performance in an indirect way, such as banks, market research agencies, recruitment organisations and local authorities.

Organisations must determine the nature and form of relationships between organisations inside and outside the distribution channel.

The stakeholder concept

All organisations develop a series of relationships with a wide variety of other organisations, groups and indeed consumers who buy their products. These relationships and individual partnerships vary considerably in their intensity, duration and function. Nevertheless, these partnerships are entered into on the grounds that each organisation anticipates benefit from mutual cooperation.

The concept of different groups influencing an organisation and in turn being influenced is an important element in the development of integrated marketing communications. The concept enables an organisation to identify all those other organisations and individuals who can be or are influenced by the strategies and policies of the focus organisation. Understanding who the stakeholders are also helps to determine where power is held, and this will in turn influence strategy at a number of levels within the focus organisation. According to Freeman (1984), stake-

The concept of different groups influencing an organisation and in turn being influenced is an important element in the development of integrated marketing communications.

holders are 'any group or individual who can affect or is affected by the achievement of an organisation's purpose'. These stakeholders may be internal to the organisation, such as employees or managerial coalitions, or external to the organisation in the form of suppliers, buyers, local authorities, shareholders, competitors, agencies or the government.

The essential purpose of stakeholder analysis is to determine which organisations

The essential purpose of stakeholder analysis is to determine which organisations influence the focus organisation and what their aims, objectives and motivations are.

influence the focus organisation and what their aims, objectives and motivations are. This enables the development of a more effective strategy, one that considers the power and interests of those who have a stake in the focus organisation. Freeman suggested that the stake held by any organisation could be based upon one of three forms. The first is a stake based upon the equity held in the organisation, the second is a stake based upon an economic perspective, reflecting a market exchange-based relationship, and the third is a stake based upon the influence of organisations which affect the focus organisation but 'not in marketplace terms'.

The horizontal dimension reflects the type of power that stakeholders can have over the focus organisation. Again, Freeman highlights three elements. The first is the formal power to control the actions of the organisation. The second is economic power to influence the organisation through the markets in which they operate, and the final element is political power generated by the stakeholders' ability to influence an organisation through legislation and regulation. He constructed a matrix, Figure 10.1, which represents the dominant influence of each stakeholder. This acknowledges that stakeholders could be placed in a number of different cells, but as Stahl and Grigsby (1992) point out, by showing their dominant role the focus organisation is in a better position to gauge the influence of each stakeholder group.

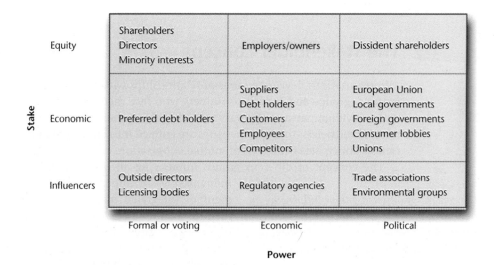

		Formal or voting	Economic	Political
	Equity	Shareholders Directors Minority interests	Employers/owners	Dissident shareholders
Stake	Economic	Preferred debt holders	Suppliers Debt holders Customers Employees Competitors	European Union Local governments Foreign governments Consumer lobbies Unions
	Influencers	Outside directors Licensing bodies	Regulatory agencies	Trade associations Environmental groups

Power

Figure 10.1 Participant stakeholders: the grid location denotes the primary but not necessarily sole orientation of the stakeholder. From Freeman (1984); used with kind permission.

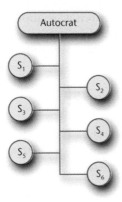

Figure 10.2   The autocrat model of stakeholder management.

Stakeholder models

Following Freeman's work various authors have attempted to interpret or develop our understanding of the stakeholder concept (e.g. Carroll, 1993; Johnson and Scholes, 2000; Donaldson and Preston, 1995; Mason and Gray, 1999). However, following the work of Rowe *et al.* (1994), there are two main models which underpin the way organisations cope with the diversity of interests of a variety of stakeholders. The first of these is the autocratic model shown in Figure 10.2, which clearly suggests that the power and the right to lead a channel are placed in a single organisation.

The second model, Figure 10.3, is the integrator model. This interpretation suggests that the power and right to govern the organisation or channel are vested among many stakeholders and subgroups. The organisation, as a networker or channel leader (see later), attempts to balance the conflicting aims and objectives and hence 'weave' a path through the conflicting influences on the organisation. The integrator model

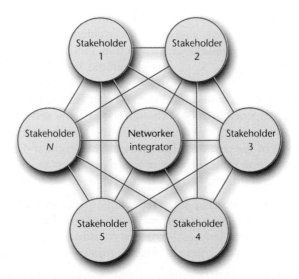

Figure 10.3   The integrator model of stakeholder management.

clearly shows the two-way relationship between the organisation and each of the stakeholders. It also illuminates the direct and indirect interaction among the different stakeholders and the power positions relative to the focus organisation.

Stakeholder analysis

The first step in stakeholder analysis is to list all stakeholders and then position them on a map. Those organisations with a primary relationship are then linked together so that 'patterns of interdependence emerge' (Rowe *et al.*, 1994). Figure 10.4 is a stakeholder map for WorkSpace, an office furniture manufacturer. Here it can be seen not only that WorkSpace interacts with primary and secondary stakeholders but that there is also interaction between the different stakeholders. This application of systems theory is important, as it highlights the point that stakeholders who may be far removed or distant from an original change to the system may well be affected to a greater degree than a number of other stakeholders who are closer to the point of change. This aspect of change within a system is referred to as 'structural change' and can affect stakeholders regardless of their distance from the focus organisation or the point within the system where change was initiated.

It is also important to recognise that coalitions and individuals can belong to more than one stakeholder group.

It is also important to recognise that coalitions and individuals can belong to more than one stakeholder group. For example, lorry drivers/transport owners and the UK government may be in conflict over the latter's position of fuel tax. However, the two parties may also be locked together in opposition to a European Union ruling that the maximum weight of lorries be increased to allow larger European juggernauts wider access to the UK road network, even though UK hauliers are discriminated in other ways when travelling across the Continent.

Stakeholder groups can also emerge as a result of a specific event. This is of particular relevance to organisations planning for disaster and crisis situations. Relatives of patients who have been afflicted or harmed as a result of using particular drugs or who have been involved in an accident, such as an aircraft disaster, often form action groups when lobbying for compensation. For example, friends and relatives of the victims of the two boats, the *Marchioness* and the *Bowbelle*, which were involved in a collision on the River Thames in 1989, have acted together to have the case reopened in 2000, although the case was settled legitimately early in the 1990s.

The current position an organisation holds within the stakeholder map is partly a result of the past decisions of the organisation and its other stakeholders.

The current position an organisation holds within the stakeholder map is partly a result of the past decisions of the organisation and its other stakeholders, and is also a reflection of the balance of forces acting on an organisation: those that drive it forward and those that try to restrain it. As Rowe *et al.* (1994) suggest:

> the present status of the organisation, is at best, a temporary balance of opposing forces. Some of these forces provide resources and support to the organisation, while some serve as barriers or constraints. The forces are generated by stakeholders in the course of pursuing their own interests, goals, and objectives.

Having mapped the different stakeholders and made judgements about the inter-relationships between different stakeholders, the next task is to make assumptions

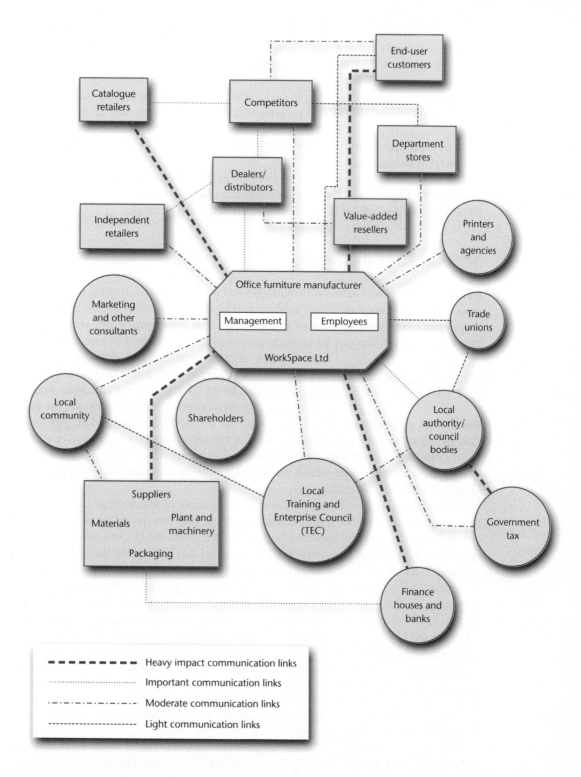

Figure 10.4   A stakeholder map for WorkSpace.

about the effects a proposed strategy might have on them. For example, a marketing strategy to terminate a particular product line and substitute it with one that is targeted at a different target market, one that will require different types of distribution, may well arouse opposition from particular members of the channel network. These assumptions then need to be listed as supporting or resisting the strategy and then be evaluated by the use of two simple rules. The first rule determines the importance of the assumption and the second its reliability. While the numerical analysis may be prone to subjectivity and bias, the exercise is useful because, as Greenley (1989) says, 'it helps focus attention upon those influences or forces that are likely to be extremely beneficial or detrimental'.

The outcome of this process is an evaluation of the likelihood of the success of a proposed strategy. Should the support be greater than the resistance, management has a better basis upon which to proceed with the proposed strategy.

Stakeholder networks

Stakeholders represent actors within marketing channel analysis. Indeed, the degree of congruence between stakeholder analysis and channel analysis is strong. Stakeholder maps reflect the complex web of relationships that all organisations weave. These maps also suggest that the focus organisation operates within a dynamic system of interacting organisations. As mentioned earlier, the map indicates the primary relationships and patterns of interdependence. These patterns and webs suggest the existence of a number of networks within each stakeholder map. Owing to the relative power positions of stakeholders, particular stakeholder networks focus upon functional activities and so have priority over others, or are perceived as more important than certain other networks. This suggests that certain organisations and individuals within each network may have a disproportionate level of power and influence.

Stakeholder maps reflect the complex web of relationships that all organisations weave.

The marketing channel is a vitally important network of organisations, and in order to distinguish between the traditional linear and vertical interpretation of distribution channels, which emphasises a bipolar and dyadic relationship (Andersson, 1992), a perspective of *a network of organisations, collaborating and working together in partnership, to provide end-user satisfaction,* is introduced as a more useful, realistic but conceptually more challenging approach. These networks not only constitute those organisations that make up the marketing channel but also seek to integrate all those other organisations that assist the channel members to achieve their objectives of satisfying customer needs. Therefore a stakeholder network can be identified, which in turn can be subdivided into two major sub-networks: the performance and support networks.

The performance network consists of organisations which are directly involved with the value-adding processes in the production and distribution of the product or service. Examples would be producers, manufacturers, suppliers, distributors (such as wholesalers and retailers) and also competitors. The performance network for WorkSpace is shown in Figure 10.5.

The support network consists of those organisations or groups that influence, indirectly, the value-adding processes.

The support network consists of those organisations or groups that influence, indirectly, the value-adding processes. For some organisations these may be financial institutions, local and national government

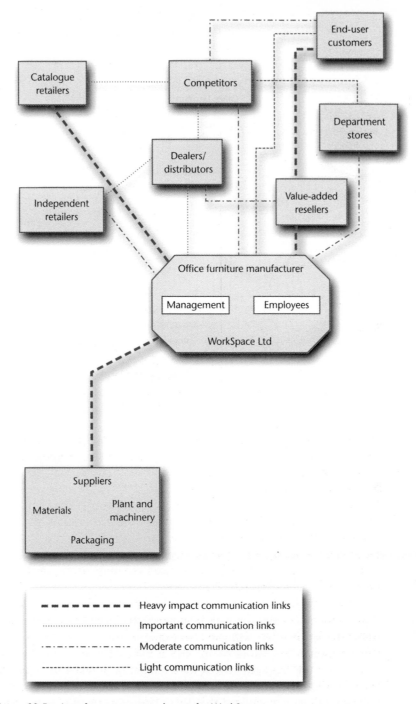

Figure 10.5   A performance network map for WorkSpace.

and legislature, consultancies and support agencies, training and professional bodies, and pressure groups, such as consumer interest organisations. All of these organis-ations may influence the value-adding processes in an indirect way and on an irregu-lar basis, and are characterised by their irregular, infrequent and low level of

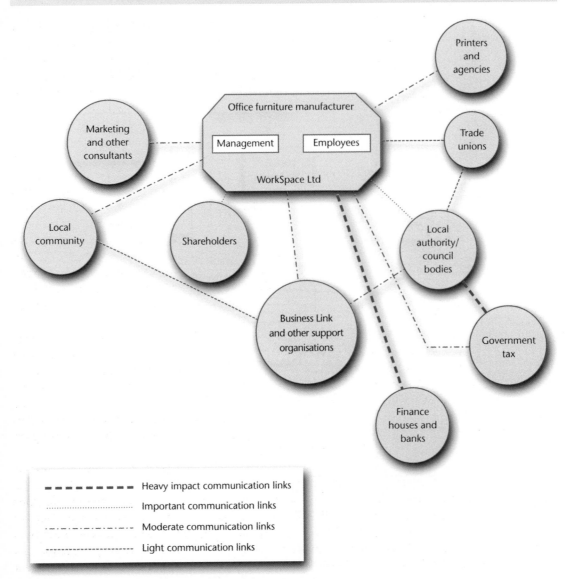

Figure 10.6   A support network map for WorkSpace.

interaction in comparison with members of the performance network. Membership of the different networks will vary. For example, the government is a key stakeholder in the performance network of an NHS hospital. However, the same government is a member of the support network for a retailer or provider of wholesale services in the food or clothing markets. The support network for WorkSpace is shown in Figure 10.6.

It should be remembered that these two subnetworks are not mutually exclusive. Indeed, they are interdependent and interactive. However, for ease of analysis it is often appropriate to distinguish between the two. The identification of these networks is an important foundation for the development of marketing communications. As seen in Chapter 2, when examining communication theory, relational communication networks take into account the context in which the communication takes place, and in particular the roles participant organisations play in the network.

The context for the performance network is the interdependence between organisations in the value-adding processes, each with the common aim of satisfying buyer needs. The context for the support network is a market exchange relationship between each actor and the focus organisation, and the absence of any mutual interdependence. For example, a bank may provide loan facilities to the focus organisation, but the arrangement is relatively short term. The loan is only normally 'discussed' by both parties at the initiation and at periodic reviews and, while important, is not necessarily vital to the long-term process of adding value or to the performance of the organisation or the other organisations involved in the value chain.

Stakeholder analysis is an important concept for developing knowledge and understanding about the other organisations in the environment. From the stakeholder map it is possible to distinguish or at least derive particular networks of organisations. The performance and support networks help identify groups of organisations which have different needs and relationships, which in turn will affect the marketing communications undertaken by the focus organisation, in particular those organisations in the performance network with whom tight couplings or partnerships are formed.

Stakeholder analysis is an important concept for developing knowledge and understanding about the other organisations in the environment.

Stakeholder analysis is seen, increasingly, as a significant part of corporate strategy (analysis, formulation, implementation and evaluation). However, its use as a tool within marketing communications has generally been overlooked, but is of importance. Of particular interest are the mapping and assumption rating exercises. Mapping is important in its own right to identify stakeholders and their interrelationships. The assumption rating exercise is important not only to evaluate the support for a particular strategy but also to evaluate the general support stakeholders have for each other and in particular for the focus organisation.

The strength of the current (or expected) relationships between key stakeholders and the degree of fit with corporate and competitive strategies will impact on the form, nature, strength and desired effectiveness of the marketing communications between members (Chapter 15). For example, if a pharmaceutical manufacturer experiences difficulties convincing hospital doctors that a new drug is as effective as claimed, particularly in comparison with a competitive offering, the preparation of a stakeholder map may well reveal that a number of different stakeholders interact with the hospital doctors to a greater or lesser extent. The share price may also be wavering in expectation of the success or failure of the new drug, so the financial community will be seen to have a stake and may be in need of reassurance. This information should be known prior to the launch, but what may not be known is that the strength of the relationships between certain stakeholders may have waxed or waned.

Recently, hospital pharmacists have been urged by another stakeholder, the government, to prescribe generic instead of branded drugs and, being budget driven, have started to exert some control over the prescribing habits of hospital doctors. As a form of resistance to the management drive, the new drug is being recommended by the doctors but is being rejected by the pharmacists, who incidentally have increased powers over the hospital drugs budget. The creation of business managers, another recent development in the NHS, has established a new stakeholder, once again with budget-holding responsibilities and a vested interest in the drugs bill. Add to this the drug wholesalers, with their objectives of moving high-margin offerings such as branded drugs, and the communications tasks appear increasingly complex.

By preparing performance and support network maps, a visual interpretation of the communication tasks begins to emerge.

By preparing performance and support network maps, a visual interpretation of the communication tasks begins to emerge. Communications have to be targeted at the following:

1. The pharmacists, to persuade them of the efficacy and value of using the drug.
2. The doctors, to remind them that the drug represents better value effectiveness than all other offerings.
3. The financial community, to ensure continuing confidence in the manufacturer and all the manufacturer's related activities.
4. The business managers, to keep the drug at the top of their awareness, or in their evoked set.
5. The wholesalers, to keep them informed of developments, to involve them in the management of the network and to maintain their distribution facilities and stock levels.
6. The sales representatives of the manufacturer, to support and provide continuous relevant information in order that they maintain credibility with the pharmacists whom they are trying to influence.
7. The staff of the manufacturer, to maintain morale and motivation.

Marketing channels and networks

The structural pattern that any channel assumes is a result of the relationships between the individual organisations that compose the channel. The channel is dynamic, so the structure should be flexible in order that it can respond to the changing environment. Two main channel patterns can be identified: conventional channels and vertical marketing channels. Both are representations of the performance network described earlier.

Two main channel patterns can be identified: conventional channels and vertical marketing channels.

Conventional marketing channels

Traditionally, organisations group together because independently their objectives cannot be achieved. By working together each member can concentrate upon those activities that it does best. This may be retailing or manufacturing, but, whatever it is, the objectives of each organisation are best served by allowing others to perform alternative, specialist functions for them. Through this approach, organisations form temporary, often loosely aligned, partnerships with a range of organisations and retain their independence and autonomy. Bipolar relationships typify these structures, as decisions are often self-orientated and reflect the needs of just the two members (Figure 10.7).

As a consequence of this self-interest, the level of control that any member has over the other members of the channel is minimal, except where access to an important raw material or product can be affected. This framework allows offerings to move

Figure 10.7   A conventional marketing channel.

through the entire system or through parts of it. There is no single controlling organisation and the framework is viewed as a set of independent organisations working in free association with one another. There is, as Oliver (1990) puts it, 'no controlled coverage of the market'. Attempts to secure coverage usually result in a loss of control in the marketing channel. Furthermore, the level of loyalty is low, which is indicative of the instability that exists in these configurations (as organisations are able to enter and exit with relative freedom) and the lack of impact on the remaining actors in the overall system.

Communication within these channels is often framed within the needs of any two partners, and a wider systems perspective is absent. As a result, communications tend to be *ad hoc,* reactionary, unidirectional (in the sense that messages are not reciprocated) and do not occur on a very frequent basis.

Vertical marketing systems

Vertical marketing systems (VMSs) attempt to trade off coverage against the lack of control – more control means less coverage. They have developed since the mid-1970s and consist of vertically aligned and coordinated marketing partners. They function as a system, centrally driven by a controlling organisation, designed to achieve economies of scale and to maximise market impact in a collaborative partnership attempting to satisfy customer needs. The tighter cooperation and interdependence of member partners is formally recognised and a planned approach ensures that a greater degree of stability is achieved. The entry and exit of partners to the system is controlled to meet the needs of the channel and not any one member. The coupling between members is tight and the level of connectedness is similarly strong.

Vertical marketing systems (VMSs) attempt to trade off coverage against the lack of control – more control means less coverage.

There are three types of VMS: administered, contractual and corporate.

Administered VMSs

The administered system is similar to that of the standard channel in that the participants work together, tied by the attraction of potential rewards. 'The point at which the conventional channel stops and the administered one begins must be made on the basis of judgements about the degree of effective interorganisational management taking place in the channel' (Rosenbloom, 1983).

Organisations work together to fulfil strategies developed by a limited number of channel partners. These strategies are then administered through informal 'voluntary' collaborative agreements by all interested parties. It is important to recognise that members retain their own authority and that each member's commitment to the system is largely determined by self-interest, but a system-wide perspective and a view of the longer term helps bind members together.

Contractual VMSs

Developing out of administered VMSs are contractual partnerships which consist, essentially, of a written agreement between a dominant member and the other members of the channel. These contracts set out members' rights and obligations. There are three kinds of contractual arrangement.

1. *Wholesaler-sponsored chains*
   These consist of organisations which agree to work together to obtain discounts and other advantages in purchasing, distribution and promotion, e.g. Mace.

2. *Retailer-sponsored chains*
   These are similar to the wholesaler chains and, for the individual organisation, represent a trade-off between independence and performance potential. The sponsored chain approach allows small and medium-sized organisations to compete against the purchasing power of many retail and wholesale multiples. Spar and VG are examples of retailer cooperatives.

3. *Franchise*
   There are three forms of franchise:
   (a) manufacturer-driven retailer systems, e.g. Ford;
   (b) manufacturer-driven wholesaler systems, e.g. Coca-Cola;
   (c) service-driven retailer systems, e.g. McDonald's.

   Franchise arrangements have grown in popularity over the last 20 years. Under these arrangements the right to market a particular offering is agreed between two parties (a bipolar arrangement).

   There are two main approaches to franchising. The first is a *product franchise*, where the channel's dominant organisation authorises particular organisations to distribute their offering. In other words, organisations are selected into a channel and each is permitted to use the trade name and promotional materials (which are deemed to be of value to the customer) of the dominant organisation. Various German kitchen appliance and furniture manufacturers use this form of authorisation to allow particular UK retailers (independent kitchen design and fit organisations) to distribute their offerings. The second form of franchise can be referred to as a *business franchise*. Under this format not only is the product permitted to be used by the franchisee but the whole trading approach

Product franchise: *organisations are selected into a channel and each is permitted to use the trade name and promotional materials.*

Business franchise: *the whole trading approach must be utilised.*

must be utilised. McDonald's restaurants are an example of the latter, with franchisees having to adopt the entire established trading style.

What is of importance to those responsible for marketing communications is that the relationships between the franchisor and franchisee can determine the style, breadth and form of the communications between partners. For example, under the product franchise arrangement, the relationship is such that, once each new franchise operation is established, contact between the two parties is limited to periodic performance review, a relationship often characterised by non-involvement and a market-structured orientation.

Under the business franchisee arrangement, a closer relationship, formed partly to protect the brand and the associated investment, means that the communications can be more relational and hence supportive, rather than market structured. As McGrath and Hardy (1986) point out, those organisations that seek to develop understanding through substantial communications programmes will improve relationships and reduce the level of channel conflict. It will be shown later (Chapter 15) that the form of the relationship is an important factor in the communications strategy adopted by organisations. Whether the franchise arrangements are product or business formats is not necessarily important in itself, but the outcomes of the arrangements are important for subsequent analysis and strategy formulation.

Corporate VMSs

A corporate vertical marketing system is a discrete grouping of organisations that are owned, and hence controlled, by one dominant member. This form provides for the greatest control in comparison with the other two systems. Laura Ashley not only designs and makes products but distributes them through its own retail outlets. Thomson, the tour operator, owns Lunn Poly travel agencies and Britannia Airways and in turn controls not only the distribution of its own offerings (and is not dependent upon other travel agencies) but also the carrier with whom clients travel. Another tour operator, Airtours, purchased and merged competitor travel agencies Hogg Robinson and Pickfords and relaunched them as Going Places. Of the many benefits that this format provides, control over the information flow is an important one. Information can be dispersed to selected areas of the organisation at a time that meets management's requirements.

Corporate systems are achieved through vertical integration. Organisations can choose to integrate upstream to control their sources of supply (their inputs), or they can move downstream and seek to control the distribution of their offerings. Complete control is virtually impossible and the scale economies and cost savings that

Corporate systems are achieved through vertical integration.

are important attractions of vertical integration can often only be achieved through large investment. Indeed some writers feel that contractual systems can provide many of the benefits that corporate systems provide and that there must be sound reasons to enter into a corporate system (Buzzell, 1983). The inherent lack of flexibility associated with corporate systems has been a prime reason for organisations to move away from such rigidity.

Channel design

The design of a marketing channel can only be predetermined if the focus organisation is considering the development of a VMS; otherwise, the decision is normally based upon whether to enter a particular system or how to adjust a system in which they are currently operating. These decisions need to be made on the basis of the answers to the following two questions:

1. How many sales outlets are required to provide optimal service for current and future customers?

2. How should the outlets participate in order for customer satisfaction to be achieved?

These questions are answered by the level of market coverage offered to the customer segment. There are three choices available: intensive, selective and exclusive.

1. *Intensive distribution*

   This is normally applicable to items that are low priced and frequently purchased, where customer involvement is low and perceived risk minimal. Chewing gum, newspapers and soft drinks are good examples. By offering the product through a large number of outlets, so the wide availability promotes the opportunity for high-volume sales.

2. *Selective distribution*

   By placing the offering in a limited number of outlets a more favourable image can be generated and the producer can determine which intermediaries would be best suited to meet the needs of the channel. Customers are more involved with the purchase, and the level of perceived risk is correspondingly higher. As a result, buyers are prepared to seek out appropriate outlets, and those that best match the overall requirements of the customer will be successful. Televisions, hi-fi equipment and clothing are suitable examples of this form of distribution.

   These questions are answered by the level of market coverage offered to the customer segment. There are three choices available: intensive, selective and exclusive.

   As the costs of each channel are evaluated by a greater number of organisations, so it is likely that they will determine that the commonly accepted guide that 80% of sales are often driven by just 20% of outlets will apply. It is therefore highly probable that in the future selective distribution will be used by an increasing number of organisations.

3. *Exclusive distribution*

   Some customers may perceive a product to be of such high prestige or to be positioned so far away from the competition so that just a single outlet in a particular trading area would be sufficient to meet the needs of the channel. For example, BMW cars are normally only available from a single outlet in any one area. If the offering requires complex servicing arrangements or tight control then the exclusive form of distribution may be best, as it fosters closer relationships.

Coughlan et al (2001) warn against the temptation of moving to an intensive distribution strategy in the expectation that sales volume will improve. For example, if Jaeger, manufacturers of high-quality clothing, now distributed through selective distribution outlets, decided to use multiples, discount stores and variety stores, any short-term sales improvement would rapidly fall away for the following reasons:

1. New outlets would use Jaeger products as loss leaders to attract customers. Prices generally would fall and the smaller margins might not be attractive to the original outlets.

2. Service and customer care would vary from store to store and generally deteriorate.

3. Promotion would have to be increased and more stock held by Jaeger rather than channel members. Increased costs and smaller margins would lead eventually to an unattractive business characterised by poor profitability and conditions in which no participant can win.

The selection criteria for entry to a performance network are a function of the following factors, as identified by Cravens and Woodruff (1986):

1. anticipated revenue flows and costs;

2. legal considerations;

3. level of channel control required;

4. channel availability.

To this list should be added the expected levels of cooperation and goodwill which will frame the relationship between members. Indeed, a further question should be asked of the focus organisation itself. If accepted into an established channel will it be able to fulfil the role expected of it and what will be the form of the relationship with the other members? Will it fit in?

Expected levels of cooperation and goodwill will frame the relationship between members.

 ## Coordination, conflict and power

As noted previously, if a marketing channel is to function effectively, cooperation between members is paramount. To work effectively and efficiently the interdependence, specialisation and expertise of individual organisations should be encouraged (Rosenbloom, 1983). However, interdependence is rarely distributed in a uniform and equitable way. This inequality is a major source of power for members of the channel configuration. This disproportionate distribution means that no single organisation can have absolute power (Stern and Gorman, 1969). For example, by owning and controlling resources that are valued by another organisation, channel power can be established. Relationships between members can be seen to be a reflection of the balance of power that exists between them.

Interdependence is rarely distributed in a uniform and equitable way.

Emerson (1962) referred to power as a function of dependence. The more dependent X is on Y, so the greater power Y has over X. As all members of the channel network are interdependent then all members have a degree of power. It is therefore imperative that the power held by constituent members is utilised to further the development of the superorganisation and the achievement of its objectives and goals. If used otherwise, power may lead to negative consequences for the member and in turn for the channel network.

It is therefore imperative that the power held by constituent members is utilised to further the development of the superorganisation and the achievement of its objectives and goals.

Social exchange theory is used by Stern and El-Ansary (1992) to look at the issue of dependence: 'This theory rests on two major constructs: comparison level (CL) and comparison level of alternatives (CLalt)'. The former concerns the expected performance levels of channel members based on experience. The latter is based on the expected performance of the best alternative organisation to a current channel member. As this is true for all channel members, there is a certain level of dependence upon each other. This means that each channel member can affect, by its own actions, the performance of others. It is this ability to influence the performance of others that is seen by advocates of social exchange theory as a source of power.

Sources of power

French and Raven (1959), in a classic study, determined five bases for power: rewards, coercion, expertise, legitimate and reference bases. *Rewards* are one of the more common, where, for example, a manufacturer might grant a wholesaler particular discounts dependent upon the volume of products bought during an agreed period. *Coercion* is the other side of the 'reward-based' coin, where negative measures may be brought in to sanction a channel member. If a wholesaler becomes dissatisfied with the payment cycle adopted by a retailer, deliveries may be slowed down or the discount structure revised. Power based upon *expertise*, perceived by other channel members, makes them dependent upon the flow of information from the source. Interestingly, the expert power exercised by leading pharmaceutical manufacturers is derived from the dependence of the pharmacies and general practitioners (GPs) on them and not so much on the dependence of the wholesalers. *Legitimate* power, whereby the authority to manage the channel is recognised rather like a manager recognises the authority of an executive director, is uncommon in conventional channels. Only in contractual and corporate vertical marketing systems (for example, franchisors) can legitimate power be exercised. Finally, *reference* power works on the basis of association and identification – 'being in the same boat' as Rosenbloom (1983) refers to it. If members of a network are able to share and empathise with the problems of their 'network partners', then a channel-wide solution to a common problem may well result in increased understanding, collaboration and trust.

Only in contractual and corporate vertical marketing systems (for example, franchisors) can legitimate power be exercised.

By recognising and understanding the bases of power, the levels of cooperation and the form of the relationships between members, the nature of communication, its pattern, its frequency and its style can be adjusted to complement the prevailing conditions. Furthermore, such an understanding can be useful to help shape the power relationships of the future and to enhance the corporate/marketing strategy. Once the current and expected power bases are determined, marketing communications can assist the shaping process. Of the power propositions provided by French and Raven, reward and coercion seem more apt for use within channels, where market exchange-based transactions predominate. Legitimate and expert power might be better applied in channels with a high level of relational exchanges.

Channel conflict

Conflict within and between all channels is endemic. Indeed, Hunt and Nevin (1974) found conflict to be widely prevalent in channel relationships. Conflict represents a breakdown or deterioration in the levels of cooperation between partners (Shipley and Egan, 1992). Cooperation is important because members of any channel are, to varying degrees, interdependent; hence their membership in the first place.

The reasons for conflict need to be clearly appreciated, as identification of the appropriate cause can lead to communication strategies that remedy, or at least seek to repair, any damage. Some of the more common reasons for channel conflict, suggested by Stern and Gorman (1969), are failure to enact a given or agreed role, issues arising among the participant organisations, selective perception and inadequate communications. For example, because channel members undertake particular *roles*, any failure to fulfil the expected role may be a cause of conflict. An *issue* may arise within the channel that causes conflict. For example, a wholesaler and a manufacturer may disagree about margins, training, marketing policies or, more commonly, territorial issues. McGrath and Hardy (1986) see conflict emanating from manufacturers' policies, such as sales order policies. The tighter and more constricting they are, the greater the likelihood that conflict will erupt than if the policies are flexible and can be adjusted to meet the needs of both parties.

Channel conflict – Mercedes

News of the decision to terminate the contracts of a large majority of its UK franchised dealerships was not received enthusiastically by those faced with losing their businesses. The remaining dealerships are to be renamed Mercedes-Benz and the owners will not be able to use their individual names (Barrett and Storey, 2001). The net result is that the network of Mercedes retail outlets is to be changed from a franchise to a directly owned group (from contract VMS to corporate VMS).

Mercedes wants to create more brand contact for its customers and plans to build 'World of Mercedes' experience centres, many on sites as large as 20 acres. By having more control over the brand, it believes increased brand loyalty can be achieved. The reaction of the dealers has been to form a 'dealer council', appoint legal representatives to challenge the legality of the decision and a public relations consultancy to manage a media campaign.

Through the process of selective perception any number of members may react to the same stimulus in completely different and conflicting ways. The objectives of each of the channel members are different, however well bonded they are to the objectives of the distribution system. It is also likely that each member perceives different ways of achieving the overall goals, all of which are recipes for conflict. The final reason is perhaps one of the most important, and central to the issue of this particular key factor. *Communication* is a coordinating mechanism for all members of the system. Its absence or failure will inevitably lead to uncoordinated behaviour and actions that are not in the best interests of the channel system. The channel can become destabilised through poor or inadequate communication, as the processes of selective perception can distort encoded messages and lead to conflict and disunity. The decision by Heinz back in 1994 to cut out all brand television advertising and move to direct marketing seriously destabilised the partnerships between multiple grocers and manufacturers of branded products (plus the advertising agencies and television contractors). Manufacturers needed to respond to the growth of supermarket own-label lookalike products, so that they could protect their brand-loyal customers. Heinz also wanted to control the discounting policy regarding its products, rather than leave it to the discretion of the supermarkets (Snoddy, 1994).

Conflict emerged in a previously stable system, as certain members saw their cor-

Through the process of selective perception any number of members may react to the same stimulus in completely different and conflicting ways.

porate and marketing objective capable of being achieved through new channels which required new members and new roles. The response of the supermarkets was to threaten not to redeem any Heinz coupons that had been sent to customers via direct mail. This is against the food manufacturers' rules about misredemption, but the disequilibrium was easy to observe. The performance network broke down as a result of a shift in the perceptions of members of the best way to achieve their own objectives.

The response of the supermarkets was to threaten not to redeem any Heinz coupons that had been sent to customers via direct mail.

Management of channel communications

Communications between members of marketing channels, and VMSs in particular, are normally the responsibility of a particular member in the channel system. This member assumes this dominant role by virtue of the dependence of the other actors (members). This dependence provides for the exercise of power, as set out earlier. The organisations that are perceived to be powerful in the context of the distribution channel are said to be channel leaders or channel captains.

The organisations that are perceived to be powerful in the context of the distribution channel are said to be channel leaders or channel captains.

Channel leadership carries a responsibility to coordinate the activities of the other members. Therefore, all communications should be designed to assist the network as a whole and not just those of the leader. As Frazier and Sheth (1985) suggest, the objective of channel leadership is to contribute to the improved performance of the channel network. If the channel performance improves, then the channel leader is likely to benefit and its role as leader will be confirmed for a further period.

The communications that the channel leader masterminds consist of two main strands. The first is the operational data flow, enhancing the performance of the network at an operational level. The advances in information technology (IT) have been crucial to the distribution of data between organisations. Indeed, IT now provides an opportunity for organisations to develop competitive advantage. For example, the installation of computerised reservation systems in travel agencies by tour operators not only helps to provide for a high level of customer satisfaction through real-time processing but also signals the existence of a considerable mobility barrier. Those travel agents who wish to exit the network and those tour operators wishing to enter a more compelling relationship with certain travel agents must now account for all the costs of changing systems, including the hardware, software, training and support associated with information technology.

The second strand is marketing communications. This concerns the deployment of the range of tools in the promotional mix, established earlier. These flows of largely persuasive information are designed to influence organisations and individuals to take a particular course of action. Information is distributed in order to influence the decisions that members make about the marketing mix they each adopt.

Particular organisations can be seen to adopt the role of channel leader and to become responsible for the discharge and regulation of the information in the network or superorganisation.

Management of organisational communications

As a broad generalisation, formal communication with all other organisations and individuals, that is all stakeholders, has been the responsibility of two individual managers, each within different departments and reporting to different senior executives:

1. The first of these is the brand manager, who traditionally has been responsible for the communications and, in particular, the promotion of the brand. Recently, a number of organisations have been appointing trade or channel managers, reflecting the increasing recognition of the significance and power associated with certain channel intermediaries, such as the multiple retailers. These channel managers have many responsibilities, including the establishment of suitable relationships with all organisations in the performance network.

2. The second is the public relations manager, whose department has historically been responsible for communications with other non-trade organisations and the establishment of goodwill with organisations in the wider environment.

By spreading responsibility for an organisation's communications across two separate departments, each trying to accomplish different, often conflicting, objectives, organisations can only suboptimise and fail to communicate effectively. Different and uncoordinated messages, conveyed at different times, lead to confusion and misunderstanding by stakeholders. At worst, there may be a change to a more negative perception and a fall in confidence and goodwill towards the organisation, which, unless corrected, can in the long term affect not only consumer perception and sales but also the share price and value of the organisation.

Different and uncoordinated messages, conveyed at different times, lead to confusion and misunderstanding by stakeholders.

Other problems brought about by this divided approach to the management of organisational communications are changes to employees' motivation and the shared values held by the organisation. Changes in attitude and the image held of the organisation by all stakeholders, and failure to communicate corporate strategy and marketing plans to particular organisations, are illustrative of further problems, as are the missed opportunities to develop strategic alliances and to satisfy changing customer needs.

Many researchers (Mallen, 1969; Rosenbloom, 1978) have concluded that channel conflict is reduced, but never eliminated, by building cooperation among members of the channel. To help build cooperation it is essential that there is consensus about the overall objectives and sound communication. To assist the development of a cooperative network of relationships, the generation of integrated marketing communications by all members, particularly channel leaders, is fundamental. One of the first steps is to appoint a communications coordinator. This person should be responsible for the development and implementation of a communications strategy that controls all the message outputs of the organisation and assists the organisation through the complex web of channels to which all organisations belong.

Networks

The ideas expressed so far in this chapter are well founded, accepted and researched but use, as their focus, the dyadic relationship between organisations based upon the functionality whereby each organisation is able to achieve their own goals. This perspective while still current in many respects has been challenged and some now consider a supply chain perspective as more valid, one where interorganisational functionality across the whole network of interacting organisations is more prevalent.

Business-to-business relationships are characterised by organisations that choose to coordinate their activities in such a way that their individual goals are achieved, but not necessarily at the expense of other organisations with whom they interact. Relational exchanges are sought with a variety of organisations and McLoughlin and Horan (2000) identify five main exchange elements:

Financial and economic exchange

Technological exchange

Knowledge exchange

Legal exchange

Information exchange

These exchanges are both formal and informal and occur in different degrees between two or more organisations through time.

In marketing channels, organisations manage a trade-off between the desire to remain independent (autonomous) and the need to be interdependent (cooperative). Much of the literature and the discussion so far depicts these channels as a vertical alignment of organisations, one which is linear and essentially bipolar. That is, the interorganisational relationships are regarded as one to one or dyadic in nature, as if to exclude the impact and influence that other organisations bring to the relationship. One of the difficulties of this approach is that organisations are regarded out of the true context in which they operate. It is necessary to consider the whole system of relationships because the relationship of any two actors (organisations) is contingent upon the direct and indirect relationships of all the actors (Andersson, 1992). A network of relationships therefore provides the context within which exchange behaviour occurs.

These exchanges are both formal and informal and occur in different degrees between two or more organisations through time.

A systems view accepts that the actions of an organisation impact, to a greater or lesser degree, upon many other organisations, not just the one to whom action is directed. Indeed, it is the interdependence and web of relationships that organisations develop with one another that characterises the nature and intensity of network behaviour.

A systems view accepts that the actions of an organisation impact, to a greater or lesser degree, upon many other organisations, not just the one to whom action is directed.

Networks hold together partly through 'an elaborate pattern of interdependence and reciprocity' (Achrol, 1997). Indeed, the development of relationship marketing appears to coincide with the emergence of network approaches to interorganisational

Networks and alliances – P&G and Coca-Cola

In February 2001 Procter and Gamble and Coca-Cola announced a joint venture for their snacks and beverages products. The deal is based around the access Coca-Cola will have to Procter and Gamble's formidable product innovation amd management skills while P&G will have access to a huge world wide distribution outlet where Coke 'is just an arm's reach away'.

analysis. This approach is referred to as industrial network analysis, and has evolved from its original focus on dyadic relationships (Araujo and Easton, 1996). Now the position of an organisation in a network is regarded as important. Positions are determined by the functions performed, their importance, the strength of relationships with other organisations and the identity of the organisations with which there are direct and indirect relationships (Mattsson, 1989). Some researchers (e.g. Lancioni, 2000) argue that there has been a transition from thinking of channels of distribution where the focus is upon making each constituent firm more productive and hence more efficient (an intrafunctional view) to one which looks at enhancing the level of efficiency of the entire network by focusing on the need for collaboration and mutual support (an interfunctional view). A more recent step holds that the objectives and strategies of constituent firms become one and the same, such that the network assumes a customer focus so that improvements are achieved by firms acting together (an interorganisational approach). Those supporting this supply chain management perspective maintain that management's role is to ensure that the coalition runs smoothly and that a focus on conflict resolution is paramount (Ballou *et al.*, 1999). This view is not shared (e.g. Achrol, 1997) as, although a customer focus is regarded as important, others regard the current paradigm to be built around cooperating and coordinating networks which are built upon trust and commitment and in which there is a noticeable absence of power, overt conflict and political jousting. However, there is agreement that networks of interacting organisations is a more acceptable interpretation of management practice than the more rigid distribution channels approach so widely accepted in the 1970s and 1980s.

The position an organisation has and the degree to which an organisation is connected or coupled to other organisations partly determines the extent to which organisations are able to mobilise resources and achieve corporate goals. As Achrol states, the strength and duration of a relationship are partly dependent upon 'the network of relationships that collectively define and administer the norms by which dyadic relationships are conducted'. He goes on to quote Macneil (1978) who suggested that the more relational an exchange becomes the more it takes on the properties of 'a minisociety with a vast array of norms beyond those centered on the exchange and its immediate processes'. Network approaches provide a more dynamic interpretation of the relationships that organisations have with one another. Networks provide a context for understanding the actions that actors take and in particular provide a means for understanding or interpreting the communications used to maintain or enhance relationships. This text uses a network approach to understand the context within which organisations interact.

Network approaches provide a more dynamic interpretation of the relationships that organisations have with one another.

The superorganisation concept

Dibb *et al.* (1991) declare, quite rightly, that 'the marketing channel is a social system each with its own conventions and behaviour patterns'. As mentioned above, each member of the network has a role to perform, and with the role are conferred particular responsibilities, rewards and punishments. The roles of each member are understood by all partners in the channel network, therefore, there are certain expectations of each organisation participating in the system. The totality of this interorganisational behaviour is the establishment of what Stern *et al.* (1996) term a 'superorganisation'.

Such a label may be openly rejected by member organisations anxious to preserve their independence and autonomy, but at the end of the day they all need each other, and the more organisations require others in the channel network to perform specific functions, so the efficiency of the channel improves. Just as organisations need good management, so do superorganisations – they require direction and purpose, and they need cooperation, conflict resolution and, perhaps above all else, leadership.

Network cooperation

The term 'superorganisation' is a useful concept in that it binds constituent organisations together as a coordinated unit and provides for a level of self-protection, purpose and direction. This in turn may foster competitive intentions, which may result in a channel network seeing itself in competition with other channel networks or superorganisations. No individual member organisation will take actions which may jeopardise the overall channel performance unless, of course, conflict has not been satisfactorily resolved. The term can also be interpreted as limiting the scope of the member organisations, one which the term 'performance network' overcomes.

Finally, it is worth noting that that there appears to be a move away from a focus on shareholders and financial measures of success. For example, *The Tomorrow's Company Inquiry Report* argues that companies that sustain competitive success in the future will be those that focus on all their stakeholder relationships (Desmond, 2000).

Summary

This chapter has introduced network theory as a means of exploring some of the issues associated with an organisation's interorganisational relationships, in particular those actor organisations involved with what is traditionally viewed as the marketing channel.

Stakeholder theory provides a similar perspective to network analysis, and issues concerning the manner in which stakeholder maps can be drawn to assist marketing communications were presented. Following this, the distribution channels were presented as a network of interacting organisations, some of whom contribute directly to the value-added activities of the focus organisation (referred to as performance networks) and some of whom provide activities and services that support the focus organisation (referred to as support networks) but do not contribute directly to the channel of distribution.

Understanding who the key stakeholders are, and knowing their positions and roles in the various networks, represents an important key factor in the development of planned communications. Communications are regarded as an important element in the smooth working of, and reduction in the level of conflict in, any network. Understanding the quality and form of the current relationships helps to shape future marketing communications with members of the different networks.

Review questions

1. What are the four factors that are considered to determine the position of an organisation in a network?

2. Explain the central characteristics of industrial network analysis.

3. Determine the main stakeholders for an organisation with which you are familiar and rank them in order of importance.

4. Select those that directly influence the value-adding processes performed by the organisation.

5. Prepare a performance network map. Indicate on the map the main flows of marketing communications currently established and the promotional flows that should be in position.

6. Suggest ways in which new flows of promotional information can be established.

7. What are the differences between conventional channel networks and vertical marketing systems?

8. How might marketing communications be influenced by the type of franchise in place?

9. To what extent might the emergence of a powerful organisation reflect levels of interdependence in a network?

10. French and Raven identified several bases for power. What are they?

MINI CASE

This mini case was written by Richard Scullion, Senior Lecturer in Marketing at Bournemouth University.

A day in the life of a political communications director

Early March 1997 and a general election seems likely. Opinion polls all tell the same story; the man (TB) about to walk into the meeting at Millbank Towers is likely to be the next Prime Minister of Great Britain. He had cut short filming his first party political broadcast (PPB) which was to portray him as a 'family man', to ensure he attended this critical meeting, a meeting to consider how best to convince trade union leaders to keep a low profile during the election campaign. His director of communications (DC) has bought a document based on results from recent focus groups showing that Labour's Achilles heel with 'middle England' was the perception that unions would have too much power if Labour were elected. The DC wanted to convince TB that a pre-emptive move was vital; indeed, the party needed to appear tough on the unions at this time. Despite some uncomfortable moments, the meeting went

well, the DC's document was used to good effect and TB managed to tread a fine line between being a friend and a foe. He finished the meeting by emphasising to the union bosses how a businesslike relationship would serve them well if Labour were to win power.

The DC had little time to congratulate TB as he had to attend a breakfast meeting being hosted by the shadow chancellor. Leaders from the financial markets were listening to Labour's vision for 'Enterprise Britain' and the DC wanted to be there for the question/answer session. As it turned out, the questions were not particularly hostile and were dealt with succinctly by the shadow chancellor.

Excellent news soon reached him: the evening news programmes (and the following day's papers) were to be on cue or, as Labour communication managers called it, 'on message'. Headlines of 'Blair to be tough on the

Unions' were to be followed up on the business pages with 'Top financiers like what they hear from Labour'. The DC understandably felt a sense of great satisfaction.

He was interrupted by a phone call informing him of a confidential call that had just taken place between TB and the leader of one of the opposition parties. The call was about forming some kind of pact/alliance. Immediately questions whirled around the DC's head. Doing deals behind closed doors might look sleazy to the electorate who were highly sensitive to this issue at the moment, but then again it could look very statesmanlike. It was obvious to the DC that this was too complex an issue to make quick decisions about. The issue was quickly stored in his mind as he made his way to the party's advertising agency DMBMD for a strategy meeting.

The top man at the agency had just began to present the agency case as he arrived entitled 'THE CASE FOR GOING "SUBTLY" NEGATIVE'. It was a well-rehearsed, strong case summarised by:

1. You don't need to get too dirty as you are so far ahead in the polls – and remember you will have to work alongside the Conservatives in parliament for the next four or five years.

2. Go too negative and the electorate will turn off so none of your other messages will get through. Even worse they may turn against you. (We were reminded of the famous Blair Eyes campaign of 1996 which backfired badly for the sponsors of the ad – the Tories.)

3. But, despite the points above, many people need more than a reason to vote for you, they need a reason not to vote for the opposition. This was particularly true for voters who had got into the habit of voting Conservative over the years.

One of the Labour team put a forceful case for engaging in a much more negative advertising campaign, suggesting Labour support demanded it. The agency team was more cautious. They pointed out the electorate was basi-

cally made up of three groups: us, them and the undecided, and that it was the last group that had to be appealed to because they would determine the election result. A junior member of the agency team suggested a need to segment the electorate more comprehensively, arguing that the electorate's level of involvement and interest in politics should influence the kind of messages to use. The DC was impressed but time was moving on so the meeting finally agreed with an R&R campaign 'Reassure and Remind':

Reassure – people that Labour is a party you can trust to govern responsibly.

Remind – people of the recent weaknesses and failures of the Conservatives whilst in government.

The DC considered the outcome to be straightforward and this would make it easy to sell to TB and other senior politicians.

En route to the Park Lane Hotel he had to sign off final copy for a Labour newsletter. The front-page story was headed 'Tories bring out the big guns': the article reminded members of the Tories' ability to win elections. It went on to highlight the importance for party members to work tirelessly to ensure a victory.

The dining room was full of black suits and posh dresses; the well heeled were paying £500 each to rub shoulders with TB and to be entertained by celebrity endorsers of the party. The DC's only worry tonight was for the event not to be portrayed as a victory party or seen as elitist. He made sure he introduced some of the invited guests to certain journalists. These included a nurse who had recently won an award for bravery: 'Good human interest story there', he said as he made the introductions.

Later he got a call from his counterpart in Washington. Negotiations were continuing to get President Clinton to endorse TB without it appearing like blatant electioneering. The details of what Clinton would say had been agreed, focusing on the personal warmth between the two men, what an intelligent, determined man TB was, etc. The conversation tonight was about the context and timing.

At home he called his office to check the content of the next morning's newspaper headlines: always nice to hear good news before sleep.

Mini-case questions

1. Why might it be important for the DC to draw up a network of his parties' stakeholders?
2. Who do you consider to be the most import-

ant of this network from a marketing communications perspective and why?

3. Do you think it is sufficient for the electorate to be considered as three groups: 'us', 'them' and 'others'? What other ways might you want to segment them for communications purposes?

4. Apply the notion of a 'support' and 'performance' network to the Labour party – what issues does it raise in terms of overlap, timing and co-ordination of messages?

References

Achrol, R.S. (1997) Changes in the theory of interorganisational relations in marketing: toward a network paradigm. *Journal of the Academy of Marketing Science*, 25(1), pp. 56–71.

Andersson, P. (1992) Analysing distribution channel dynamics: loose and tight coupling in distribution networks. *European Journal of Marketing*, 26(2), pp. 47–68.

Araujo, L. and Easton, G. (1996) Networks in socioeconomic systems: a critical review. In *Networks in Marketing* (ed. D. Iacobucci). CA: Sage.

Ballou, R., Gilbert, S. and Mukherjee, A. (1999) New managerial challenges from supply chain opportunities. *Industrial Marketing Management*, 29, pp. 7–18.

Barrett, L. and Storey, J. (2001) Protected identit., *Marketing Week*, 25 (January), pp. 28–31.

Buzzell, R.D. (1983) Is vertical integration profitable? *Harvard Business Review*, 61 (January/February), pp. 96–100.

Carroll, A.B. (1993) *Business and Society: Ethics and Stakeholder Mangement*. Cincinnatti, OH: South-Western.

Coughlan, A.T., Anderson, E. Stern, L. and El-Ansary, A. (2001) *Marketing Channels*, 6th edn. Englewood Cliffs, NJ: Prentice Hall.

Cravens, D.W. and Woodruff, R.B. (1986) *Marketing*. Reading, MA: Addison-Wesley.

Dermody, J. and Scullion, R. (2000) Perceptions of negative political advertising, meaningful or menacing? *International Journal of Advertising*, 19(2).

Desmond, P. (2000) Reputation builds success – tomorrow's annual report. *Corporate Communications: An International Journal*, 5(3), pp. 168–173.

Dibb, S., Simpkin, L., Pride, W.M. and Ferrel, O.C. (1991) *Marketing*. New York: Houghton Mifflin.

Donaldson, T. and Preston, L.E. (1995) The stakeholder theory of the corporation: concept, evidence, implications. *Academy of Management Review*, 20(1) (January), pp. 65–91.

Emerson, R. (1962) Power–dependence relations. *American Sociological Review*, 27 (February), pp. 32–3.

Frazier, G.L. and Sheth, J. (1985) An attitude–behavior framework for distribution channel management. *Journal of Marketing*, 43(3), pp. 38–48.

Freeman, R.E. (1984) *Strategic Management*. Boston, MA: Pitman.

French, J.R. and Raven, B. (1959) The bases of social power. In *Studies in Social Power* (ed. D. Cartwright). Ann Arbor, MI: University of Michigan.

Greenley, G. (1989) *Strategic Management*. Hemel Hempstead: Prentice Hall.

Hunt, S.B. and Nevin, J.R. (1974) Power in channel of distribution: sources and consequences. *Journal of Marketing Research*, 11, 186–93.

Johnson, G. and Scholes, K. (2000) *Exploring Corporate Strategy*, 6th edn. Harlow: Prentice Hall Europe.

Lancioni, R. (2000) New developments in supply chain management, *Industrial Marketing Management*, **29**(1), pp. 1–6.

Macneil, I.R. (1978) Contracts: adjustment of long-term economic relations under classical, neoclassical and relational contract law. *Northwestern University Law Review*, **72** (January–February), pp. 854–905.

Mallen, B.E. (1969) A theory of retailer–supplier conflict. In *Distribution Channels: Behavioural Dimensions* (ed. L.W. Stern). New York: Houghton Mifflin.

Mason, K.J. and Gray, R. (1999) Stakeholders in a hybrid market: the example of air business passenger travel. *European Journal of Marketing*, **33**(9/10), pp. 844–58.

Mattsson, L.-G. (1989) Development of firms in networks: positions and investments. *Advances in International Marketing*, **3**, pp. 121–39.

McGrath, A. and Hardy, K. (1986) A strategic paradigm for predicting manufacturer–reseller conflict. *European Journal of Marketing*, **23**(2).

McLoughlin, D. and Horan, C. (2000) Perspectives from the Markets-as-networks approach. *Industrial Marketing Management*, **29**(4), pp. 285–92.

Miles, L. (2000) Sleeping with the enemy. *Marketing Business* (July–August), pp. 17–19.

Oliver, G. (1990) *Marketing Today*, 3rd edn. Hemel Hempstead: Prentice Hall.

Rosenbloom, B. (1978) Motivating independent distribution channel members. *Industrial Marketing Management*, **7** (November), pp. 275–81.

Rosenbloom, B. (1983) *Marketing Channels: A Management View*. Hinsdale, IL: Dryden Press.

Rowe, A.J., Mason, R.O., Dickel, K.E., Mann, R.B. and Mockler, R.J. (1994) *Strategic Management: A Methodological Approach*, 4th edn. Reading, MA: Addison-Wesley.

Shipley, D. and Egan, C. (1992) Power, conflict and co-operation in brewer–tenant distribution channels. *International Journal of Service Industry Management*, **3**(4), pp. 44–62.

Snoddy, R. (1994) Heinz drops TV adverts in move to direct marketing. *Financial Times*, 3 May, p. 1.

Stahl, M. and Grigsby, D. (1992) *Strategic Management for Decision Making*. Boston, MA: P.W.S. Kent.

Stern, L., El-Ansary, A. (1992) Marketing Channels, 4th edn. Englewood Cliffs, NJ: Prentice Hall.

Stern, L.W. and Gorman, R.H. (1969) *Conflict in Distribution Channels: An Exploration in Distribution Channels: Behavioural Dimensions* (ed. L.E. Stern). Boston, MA: Houghton Mifflin.

Stern, L. El-Ansary, A. and Coughlan, A.T. (1996) Marketing Channels, 5th edn. Englewood Cliffs, NJ: Prentice Hall.

11

The communications industry

The marketing communications industry is evolving rapidly as new technology and increasing competition induces audience and media fragmentation. Clients, media and agencies continually adapt themselves to the changing environment as they attempt to understand the complexity and opportunities that are continually arising around them.

AIMS AND OBJECTIVES

The aims of this chapter are to introduce the communications industry, the various organisations involved and some of the issues affecting the operation of the industry.

The objectives of this chapter are:

1. To provide an introduction to the communications industry.
2. To consider the nature and role of the main types of organisations involved.
3. To explore relationships and methods of remuneration used within the industry.
4. To outline some of the statutory and voluntary controls used to regulate the industry.
5. To introduce some of the wider European and global issues facing the industry.
6. To anticipate some of the future trends which might affect the industry.

Introduction

The marketing communications industry consists of four principal actors. These are the media, the clients, the agencies (the most notable of which are advertising agen-

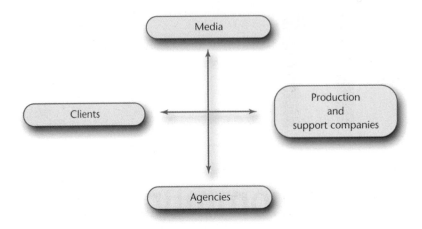

Figure 11.1   The principal organisations in the marketing communications industry.

cies) and finally the thousands of support organisations, such as production companies and fulfilment houses, who enable the whole process to function. It is the operations and relationships between these organisations that not only drive the industry but also form an important context within which marketing communications needs to be understood. Figure 11.1 sets out the main actor organisations in the industry.

The marketing communications industry consists of four principal actors.

The number of relationships that can be developed in this industry, as with others, is enormous. To further complicate matters, the slow yet enduring move towards integrated marketing communications (Chapter 19) requires participants to form new relationships and acquire new skills. The argument that marketing communications activities should be kept in-house is now weak, as manufacturing and service industry providers continue to increase their level of outsourcing activities and de-layer and hollow out their organisations even more finely. There is little or no room to maintain people with skills and expertise that are only drawn upon infrequently and where the notion of critical mass is important for media buying. Most observers would argue that it could not be done as effectively as by agencies and others who are dealing with a number of clients and are, by definition, in constant touch with developments in the industry. In the field of media buying, for example, many would argue that it is unlikely that the necessary expertise could be developed in-house. The increased emphasis on accountability and efficiency means that it is necessary to outsource such activities in order to use expertise, specialised resources and take advantage of collective discounts from media houses. Marketing practitioners, therefore, need to use some of the other organisations in the communications industry. A level of interdependence exists which requires cooperative and collaborative behaviour if the system is to function efficiently.

Many would argue that it is unlikely that the necessary expertise could be developed in-house.

A level of interdependence exists which requires cooperative and collaborative behaviour if the system is to function efficiently.

Growth and development of the marketing communications industry

It is useful to consider the size and value of the industry by considering the sums of money spent by clients on marketing communications. Some of these figures are acknowledged to be estimates, and there is some evidence of 'double counting' (one or more sectors claiming part of the overall spend for itself), so any figures produced cannot be seen as being totally accurate. That said, however, the total spend for advertising, as can be seen from Table 11.1, was £17 billion in 2000.

The total spend for advertising was £17 billion in 2000.

The Institute of Sales Promotion claims that the growth of sales promotion has been 'explosive', but measuring the growth is difficult because there are no rate cards (price lists) and the breadth of activities that are attributable to sales promotion are many and varied. However, the Institute estimates that expenditure on sales promotion has grown from £6.5 billion in 1992 to £9.0 billion in 1996 and perhaps to £13.0 billion in 2000. Although not yet formally exceeding the spend on advertising, this area of activity is fast catching up and, despite published figures, it is widely believed inside the industry that sales promotion has already overtaken advertising in terms of the proportion of client spend.

it is widely believed inside the industry that sales promotion has already overtaken advertising in terms of the proportion of client spend

Estimates vary, mainly because of problems of definition, but of the other areas in the industry sponsorship has grown significantly to £620 million in 2000. Direct marketing had risen spectacularly, with direct mail alone worth £2.0 billion in 2000, and telemarketing worth roughly £800 million in 2000 (McLuhan, 2001).

Other areas of the industry include public relations which has experienced steady development and was worth approximately £1.3 billion in 2000 and exhibitions of which there were 817 in 1999, each over 2,000 sq ft and in total worth approximately £1,300m.

Expenditure patterns do change, albeit at different rates, and, given the domination of advertising and sales promotion, the overall balance is unlikely to change dramatically in the short term. However, it is clearly important for those responsible for the

Table 11.1   Total UK advertising expenditure (including direct mail) £m

	2000 (£m)	1996 (£m)	1995 (£m)	1994 (£m)
Press	7,541	6,400	5,900	5,500
Television	5,393	3,300	3,100	2,900
Direct mail	2,049	1,400	1,100	1,000
Outdoor and transit	823	426	378	350
Radio	595	344	296	243
Cinema	128	73	69	53
Total	17,000	11,994	10,981	10,136

Source: Advertising Statistics Yearbook; used with kind permission.

future and current planning of marketing communications activities to monitor trends, particularly those in the fastest growing sectors of the industry, in order to identify and target creative opportunities.

One area that has experienced significant change has been in media. Industry concentration and the development of global networks has shifted the structure and composition of the industry. Clients have responded by centralising their business into a single media network agency in search of higher discounts and improved efficiency. As a general rule, the stronger the competitive forces, the lower the profitability in the market. An organisation needs to determine a competitive approach that will allow it to influence the industry's competitive rules, protect it from competitive forces as much as possible and give it a strong position from which to compete. The media networks have yet to find a competitive form of differentiation although some are offering additional services as a way of trying to enhance brand identities (Griffiths, 2000). It appears that the power of the media agencies, the low switching costs of buyers and the large threat of substitute products make this a relatively unattractive industry in its current form. Finer segmentation to determine markets that permit higher margins and a move to provide greater differentiation among agencies, together with a policy to reduce the threats from substitute products, perhaps through more visible alliances and partnerships, would enable the industry to recover its position and provide greater stability. It is interesting to note that many leading agencies have moved into strategic consultancy, away from the reliance on mass media, where a substantially higher margin can be generated.

One area that has experienced significant change has been in media.

Many direct marketing companies have evolved out of sales promotion agencies.

Many direct marketing companies have evolved out of sales promotion agencies. According to Goften (2000), both have tried to reposition themselves with the sales promotion houses adopting a wide variety of promotional activities and direct marketing agencies moving their focus of business activity to one that is either orientated towards ecommerce or customer relationship management.

Agency branding

As if to emphasise the above point about differentiation, and despite the move into strategic planning, agency marketing activity is regarded by many as inadequate. Clients, it is reported, have difficulty in distinguishing one brand from another, with the result that agencies appear to have poor brand identities.

One of the reasons for this is poor staff training. Abrahams (1997) reports a study undertaken by Tutt's Consultancy of 40 top advertising agencies. All chairmen responded that their companies had a clearly defined mission and positioning and that it had been communicated clearly to all staff. However, only 20% of staff knew of the mission and positioning intentions (and fewer believed in them).

Brands are developed through consistent communication, delivery and performance. Therefore, agencies need to consider internal marketing communications (Chapter 7) as a means of improving this aspect of their business and thus enhancing their opportunities to deliver a more consistent brand proposition.

Brands are developed through consistent communication, delivery and performance.

Brand philosophies and values are often subsumed when working with a client's culture and values. If an agency developed a strong set of values (by which it was positioned) and took these into a client's working environment there might well be a clash or conflict, which might not be constructive or easy to resolve. So far the policy has been to smother the agency values, but this may need to change in order that agencies can provide points of differentiation for clients to identify and accept.

Selecting an agency

In the areas which have traditionally dominated marketing communications, advertising and sales promotion, there has never been a shortage of advice on how to select an agency. Articles informing readers how to select an agency (Young and Steilen, 1996; Woolgar, 1998; Finch, 2000) appear regularly, and there are a large number of publications and organisations to assist in the process.

According to Barnett and Clarke, 'while choosing an agency is rarely easy, it is often made more difficult than it need be because of the personalities of the people involved and their sometimes contradicting requirements'. The theory behind the process is relatively straightforward. A *search* is undertaken to develop a list of potential candidates. This is accomplished by referring to publications such as *Campaign Portfolio* and the *Advertising Agency Roster*, together with personal recommendations. The latter is perhaps the most potent and influential of these sources. As many as 10 agencies could be included at this stage although six or seven are to be expected.

Next, the client will visit each of the short-listed candidates in what is referred to as a *credentials presentation*. This is a crucial stage in the process, as it is now that the agency is evaluated for its degree of fit with the client's expectations and requirements. Agencies could develop their Web sites to fulfil this role which would save time and costs. The agency's track record, resources, areas of expertise and experience can all be made available on the Internet from which it should be possible to short-list three or possibly four agencies for the next stage in the process: the pitch.

In the PR industry agencies are selected to pitch on the basis of the quality and experience of the agency people, its image and reputation and relationships with existing clients. In addition, Pawinska (2000) reports that the track record of the agency and the extent of its geographical coverage are also regarded as important.

To be able to make a suitable bid the agencies are given a brief and then required to make a formal presentation (the *pitch*) to the client some 6–8 weeks later. This presentation is about how the agency would approach the strategic and creative issues and the account is awarded to whichever produces the most suitable proposal. Suitability is a relative term, and a range of factors need to be considered when selecting an organisation to be responsible for a large part of a brand's visibility. A strategic alliance is being formed and therefore a strong understanding of the strategic objectives of both parties is necessary, as is an appreciation of the structure and culture of the two organisations. The selection process is a bringing together of two organisations whose expectations may be different but whose cooperative behaviour is essential for these expectations to have any chance of materialising. For example, agencies must have access to comprehensive and often commercially confidential data about products and markets if they are to operate efficiently. Otherwise, they cannot provide the service which is expected.

A strategic alliance is being formed and therefore a strong understanding of the strategic objectives of both parties is necessary.

The immediate selection process is finalised when terms and conditions are agreed and the winner is announced to the contestants and made public, often through trade journals such as *Campaign*, *Marketing* and *Marketing Week*.

This formalised process is now being questioned as to its suitability. The arrival of dotcom companies and their need to find communication solutions in one rather than eight weeks has meant that new methods have had to be found. In addition, agencies felt that they were having to invest a great deal into a pitch with little or no reward if the pitch failed. Their response has been to ask for payment to pitch which has not been received well by clients. The tension that arises is that each agency is required to generate creative ideas over which they have little control once a pitch has been lost. The pitching process also fails to give little insight into the probable working relationships and is very often lead by senior managers who will not be involved in the day-to-day operations. One solution adopted by Iceland and Dyson (Jardine, 2000) has been to invite agencies to discuss mini-briefs. These are essentially discussion topics about related issues rather than the traditional challenge about how to improve a brand's performance. By issuing the mini-brief on the day it eliminates weeks of preparation and associated staff costs, and enables the client to see agency teams working together.

This formalised process is now being questioned as to its suitability.

The pitching process also fails to give little insight into the probable working relationships.

Agency types and structures

As with any industry, growth and development spawn new types and structures. Adaptation to the environment is important for survival. The same applies to the marketing communications industry, where, to take the advertising industry as an example, many different organisational configurations have evolved.

The first option for a client is to undertake the communications functions in house. However, this is both costly and inefficient, and most outsource their requirements to agencies.

Full-service agencies

The first and most common type of agency (advertising) is the full-service agency. This type of organisation offers the full range of services that a client requires in order to advertise its products and services. Agencies such as J. Walter Thompson, Saatchi & Saatchi and Leo Burnett offer a full service consisting of strategic planning, research, creative development, production and media planning. Some of these activities may be subcontracted, but overall responsibility rests with the full-service agency.

A derivative of this type of agency is the creative shop.

Further discussion of some of the issues concerning full-service agencies follows later.

Creative shops

A derivative of this type of agency is the creative shop, which forms when creative personnel (teams) leave full service agencies to set up their own business. These

'HotShops' provide specialist services for clients who wish to use particular styles and approaches for their creative work.

Media independents

Similarly, media independents provide specialist media services for planning, buying and monitoring the purchase of a client's media schedule. There are two main forms: media independents, where the organisation is owned and run free of the direction and policy requirements of a full service agency, and media dependents, where the organisation is a subsidiary of a creative or full service organisation. The largest dependent in the UK is Zenith Media, owned originally by Saatchi & Saatchi, and the largest independent is Carat.

A la carte

Partly in response to the changing needs of clients and consumers, many organisations require greater flexibility in the way their advertising is managed. Consequently these clients prefer to use the services of a range of organisations. So, the planning skills of a full service agency, the creative talent of a particular HotShop and the critical mass of a media-buying independent provide an *à la carte* approach. This process needs to be managed by the client, because when the services of other marketing communications providers are included flexibility is increased while coordination and control become more complex and problematic.

New media

New media agencies have developed as a result of the growth of the new media industry which has seen huge growth in the last few years of the last decade and the first few of the new millennium. The growth has come from two main areas. The first concerns the surge of dotcoms that hit the market full of expectation of transforming the way business is conducted and the second concerns established bricks and mortar brands seeking to reach customers by adding to their marketing channels.

New media agencies have developed as a result of the growth of the new media industry which has seen huge growth.

The provision of Internet facilities has been the main area of work, mainly communication and business operation activities. This has been followed by WAP technology activity and interactive television (see Chapter 25). The market appears to have formed into three main parts of a spectrum of activities. At one end are those agencies that are marketing orientated and at the other are technology-based organisations. Murphy (2000) feels that the real growth is likely to develop in the middle with organisations referred to as 'interactive architects' who can offer a blend of skills and consultancy services. Merger and acquisition activity has been intense, mainly a reaction to rapid industry growth which was not capable of being sustained.

The move towards integrated marketing communications (see Chapter 19) was an inevitable development to bring about greater efficiency and harmonisation. Therefore, if established advertising agencies could offer all marketing communications services the client need only deliver a single brief and await results. Accordingly, WPP and Saatchi & Saatchi set about building the largest marketing communications empires in the world. According to Green (1991), Saatchi & Saatchi attempted to become the largest marketing services company in the world. The strategy adopted in the early 1980s was to acquire companies outside its current area of core competence, media advertising. Organisations in direct marketing, market research, sales promotion and public relations were brought under the Saatchi banner.

By offering a range of services under a single roof, rather like a 'supermarket', the one-stop shopping approach made intrinsic sense. Clients could put a package together, rather like eating from a buffet table, and solve a number of their marketing requirements – without the expense and effort of searching through each sector to find a company with which to work.

Green also refers to the WPP experience in the late 1980s. J. Walter Thompson and Ogilvy and Mather were grouped together under the umbrella of WPP and it was felt that synergies were to be achieved by bringing together their various services. Six areas were identified: strategic marketing services, media advertising, public relations, market research, non-media advertising and specialist communications. A one-stop shopping approach was advocated once again.

The recession of the early 1990s brought problems to both of these organisations, as well as others. The growth had been built on acquisition, which was partly funded from debt. This required considerable interest payments, but the recession brought a sharp decline in the revenues of the operating companies, and cash flow problems forced WPP and Saatchi & Saatchi to restructure their debt and their respective organisations. As Phillips (1991) points out, the financial strain and the complex task of managing operations on such a scale began to tell.

However, underpinning the strategy was the mistaken idea that clients actually wanted a one-stop shopping facility. It was unlikely that the best value for money was going to be achieved through this, so it came as no surprise when clients began to question the quality of the services for which they were paying. There was no guarantee that they could obtain from one large organisation the best creative, production, media and marketing solutions to their problems. Many began to shop around and engage specialists in different organisations (*à la carte*) in an attempt to receive not only the best quality of service but also the best value for money. Evidence for this might be seen in the resurgence of the media specialists whose very existence depends on their success in media planning and buying. By 1990 it was estimated that in the UK 30% of market share in media buying was handled by media specialist companies.

Underpinning the strategy was the mistaken idea that clients actually wanted a one-stop shopping facility.

It is no wonder then, that clients, and indeed many media people working in agencies who felt constrained to leave and set up on their own account, felt that full-service agencies were asking too much of their staff, not only in terms of providing a wide range of integrated marketing services generally, but also in giving full attention and bringing sufficient expertise to bear in each of the specific services it has to offer (account management, creative, production, media research etc.).

The debate about whether or not to use a full-service agency becomes even more crucial, perhaps, for those in specialist areas. In business-to-business marketing, for example, Yovovich and Lawler (1991) cite the experiences of a number of companies, some of which have left large agencies for smaller specialist agencies and vice versa. In many ways it comes back to the quality of relationships. They present arguments for the specialist agency based upon the point that, while there may be some convergence of approaches between consumer goods marketing and business-to-business advertising, it can be easier for a business-to-business advertising firm to do consumer advertising than it is to do the reverse.

They report that business-to-business shops survive on their ability to execute some very fundamental techniques for clients, such as direct mail or sales promotion. In contrast, the large, consumer goods-oriented shops, whose traditional skills are market research, planning and media advertising, often lack the core skills, initiative or expertise to deliver business-to-business marketing services.

The same has been said of direct marketing where there appears to be the same sort of disenchantment with the full-service agency. Criticisms include the exclusion of direct marketing experts from presentations to clients, a lack of education among mainstream agency types as to what direct marketing actually does or the complaint that clients don't want to be force fed a direct marketing subsidiary that may be incompetent or inappropriate. The experience of those involved in direct marketing has been further destablised by the the growth in the Interent. Direct mail has gained rather than lost because dotcoms have used direct mail as off-line promotion to drive Web site traffic. Telemarketing has flourished because call centres have repositioned themselves as multimedia contact centres and have extended their range of services.

Criticisms include the exclusion of direct marketing experts from presentations to clients.

There is a spectrum of approaches for clients. They can find an agency which can provide all of the required marketing communication services under one roof, or find a different agency for each of the services, or mix and match. Clearly the first solution can only be used if the budget holder is convinced that the best level of service is being provided in *all* areas, and the second only if there are sufficient gains in efficiency (and savings in expenditure) to warrant the amount of additional time he or she would need to devote to the task of managing marketing communications.

Agency operations

Advertising agencies are generally organised on a functional basis. There have been moves to develop matrix structures utilising a customer orientation, but this is very inefficient and the low margins prohibit such luxuries. There are departments for planning, creative and media functions coordinated on behalf of the client by an account handler or executive.

The account handler fulfils a very important role in that these people are responsible for the flow of communications between the client and the agency. The quality of the communications between the two main parties can be critical to the success of the overall campaign and to the length of the relationship between the two organisations. Acting at the boundary of the agency's operations, the account handler needs to perform several roles, from internal coordinator and negotiator to presenter (of the agency's work), conflict manager and information gatherer. Very often account handlers will experience tension as they seek to achieve their clients' needs while trying to balance the needs of their employer and colleagues. These tensions are similar to those experienced by salespersons and need to be managed in a sensitive manner by management.

Once an account has been signed a client brief is prepared which provides information about the client organisation (Figure 11.2). It sets out the nature of the industry it operates in together with data about trends, market shares, customers, com-

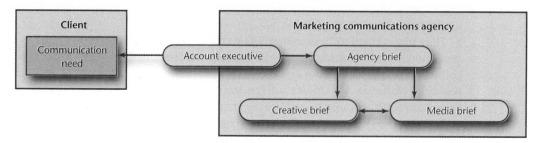

Figure 11.2 The briefing process.

petitors and the problem that the advertising agency is required to address. This is used to inform agency personnel. In particular, the account planner will undertake research to determine market, media and audience characteristics and make proposals to the rest of the account team as to how the client problem is to be resolved.

Much of this information is translated into a creative brief for the development of copy and visuals by the appointed creative team. This is a team of two, a copy writer and an art director, supported by a service team. This team is responsible for translating the proposal into an advertisement. Later, a media brief will also be generated, informing the media planning and buying department of the media required and the type of media vehicles required.

In recent years, partly as as a response to the growth of new media, a raft of small entrepreneurial agencies emerged, to exploit the new opportunities arising from the digital revolution. Although these agencies are often founded by people who have started their careers in larger and highly structured agencies, many of them run their own organisations in a more organic manner.

A raft of small entrepreneurial agencies emerged, to exploit the new opportunities arising from the digital revolution.

While dedicated teams might be the theoretically best way to manage a client's project, reality in many cases is the use of project teams comprising expert individuals working on a number of projects simultaneously. This is not, of course, a new phenomenon but as a result many people are multitasking and they assume many roles with new titles. For example, the title head of content has arisen to reflect the significance of content issues in the new media market. Project managers assume responsibility for the implementation phase and the coordination of all aspects of a client's technological facilities. In addition, there are positions such as head of marketing, mobile (increasing focus on WAP technology), production and technology. The result is flat structures, no hierachies and flexible working practices and similar expectations.

Relationships

If the briefing process provides the mechanism for the agency operations, it is the nature of the relationships between the agency and the client that very often determines the length of the contract and the strength of the solutions advanced for the client.

There are a number of agency/client relationships that have flourished over a very long period of time, and some of these are shown in Table 11.2. There are a huge

Table 11.2   Some of advertising's longest held accounts

Client	Agency	Arrival
SmithKline Beecham	O & M	1896
Lever Bros	APL	1898
Brooke Bond Foods	BMP DDB	1914
Kraft	JWT	1922
Nestlé	JWT	1927
British Aerospace	BMP DDB	1938

Source: *Campaign*, 6 September 1996, p. 34.

number of other accounts who have excellent relationships that have lasted a long time. However, these appear to be in the minority, as many relationships appear to founder as clients abandon agencies and search for better, fresher solutions or because of takeovers and mergers between agencies, which require that they forfeit accounts that cause a conflict of interest.

From a contextual perspective these buyer/seller relationships can be seen to follow a pattern of formation, maintenance and severance, or pre-contract, contracting process and post-contract stages (Davidson and Kapelianis, 1996). Clients and agencies enter into a series of interactions (West and Paliwoda, 1996) or exchanges through which trust and commitment is developed.

Clients and agencies enter into a series of interactions or exchanges through which trust and commitment is developed.

Hakansson (1982) identified different contexts or atmospheres within which a relationship develops. These contexts had several dimensions: closeness/distance, cooperation/conflict, power/dependence, trustworthiness and expectations. Therefore, the client/agency relationship should be seen in the context of the network of organisations and the exchanges or interactions that occur in that network. It is through these interactions that the tasks that need to be accomplished are agreed, resources made available, strategies determined and goals achieved. The quality of the agency/client relationship is a function of trust, which is developed through the exchanges and which fosters confidence. Commitment is derived from a belief that the relationship is worth continuing and that maximum effort is warranted at maintaining the relationship (Morgan and Hunt, 1994). The development of new forms of remuneration (see below) based around payment by results, also signifies a new client focus and a willingness to engage with clinets and to be paid acording to the success and contribution the agancy can provide (Lace and Brocklehurst, 2000).

Poor relationships between agencies and clients are likely to result from a lack of trust and falling commitment. As it appears that communication is a primary element in the formation and substance of relational exchanges, clients might be advised to consider the agencies in their roster as an extended department of the core organisation and use internal marketing communication procedures to assist the development of identity and belonging.

One last point to be made is the increasing age gap between those in the industry, both agency and client, and their audiences. Those that produce marketing communications tend to be under 35 and the average age of those targeted to receive the communications is rising. According to Starkey (1999),

There is an increasing age gap between those in the industry, both agency and client, and their audiences.

Nike talks to agencies about £9 million UK ad task

Nike was reported to have begun talking to UK agencies about the future of its business. This was despite the fact that the account was still placed with TBWA Simons Palmer.

Clare Dobie, the Nike UK Advertisement Manager, confirmed that discussions were taking place with other agencies but stated that there were no plans to resign TBWA Simons Palmer. She said that 'it is a long time since we talked to any agencies and we want to be sure that we are working with the best people'. She went on to say that 'Park Life' (a particular football ad for Nike using football stars such as Eric Cantona, Robbie Fowler, David Seaman and Ian Wright) was, in her opinion, probably the best ever football advertisement.

This faltering commitment suggests an impending divergence of intentions, and a fall in trust between the two parties was expected. Indeed, in November 1997 the account was awarded to a US agency (Wieden & Kennedy) that was about to enter the UK market from its European base in Amsterdam. Nike claimed that the appointment assisted its strategy to develop a coordinated global campaign in order to defend its market leadership position.

Adapted from various sources including Barrett (1997) and Hall (1997)

this may increase the chance of misunderstanding of older consumers and this misunderstanding becomes a self-fulfilling prophecy.

Agency remuneration

One factor that has a significant impact on the quality of the relationship between the parties is the remuneration or reward for the effort (added value) the agency makes in attempting to meet and satisfy the needs of its client. One major cause for concern and complaint among marketing managers is the uncertainty over how much their marketing communications programmes will finally cost and the complexity surrounding the remuneration system itself.

There are three main ways in which agencies are paid. These are *commission, fees* and *payment by results*. A fourth is a mixture or combination of these approaches.

Traditionally, advertising agencies were paid a commission by media owners for selling space in their publications. A figure of 15% emerged as the norm and seemed a fair reward for the efforts of the agency. However, as

There are three main ways in which agencies are paid.

relationships between agencies and clients strengthened, it seemed only reasonable that the clients should feel that agencies should act for them (and in their best interests), and not for the media owners. A number of questions were raised about whether the agency was actually being rewarded for the work it did and whether it was being objective when recommending media expenditure. As media independents emerged, questions started to be asked about why media agencies received 3% and the creative agency received 12%.

Client discontent is not the only reason why agency remuneration by commission has been called into question, and alternatives are being considered. In times of recession marketing budgets are inevitably cut, which means less revenue for agencies. Increasing competition means lower profit margins if an agency is to retain the business, and if costs are increasing at the same time the very survival of the agency is in question. As Snowden stated as long ago as 1993, 'Clients are demanding more for less'. She goes on to say, 'It is clear to me that the agency business needs to address a number of issues; most important amongst them, how agencies get paid. It is the key to the industry's survival.'

During the early 1990s there was a great of discussion and energy directed towards non-commission payment systems. This was a direct result of the recession, in which clients cut budgets and there was a consequent reduction in the quantity of media purchased and hence less revenue for the agencies. Fees became more popular, and some experimented with payment by results. Interestingly, as the recession died and the economy lifted, more revenue resulted in larger commission possibilities, and the death throes of the commission system were quickly replaced by its resuscitation and revival.

It is likely that there will continue to be a move away from a reliance on the payment of commission as the only form of remuneration to the agency.

It is likely that there will continue to be a move away from a reliance on the payment of commission as the only form of remuneration to the agency. Fees have been around for a long time, either in the form of retainers or on a project-by-project basis. Indeed, many agencies charge a fee for services over and above any commission earned from media owners. The big question is about the basis for calculation of fees (and this extends to all areas of marketing communications, not just advertising), and protracted, complicated negotiations can damage client/agency relationships.

For many, payment by results seems a good solution. There are some problems, however, in that the agency does not have total control over its performance and the final decisions about how much is spent and which creative ideas should be used are the client's. The agency has no control over the other marketing activities of the client, which might determine the degree of success of the campaign. Indeed, this raises the very thorny question of what 'success' is and how it might be measured. Despite these considerations, it appears that PBR is starting to become an established form of remuneration with over 30% of agency–client contracts containing an element of PBR. Lace (2000) explains that this is due to the inadequacies of both commission- and fee-based systems in the 'new age of cost cutting and accountability'.

A different way of looking at this is to consider what the client thinks the agency does and from this evaluate the outcomes from the relationship. Jensen (1995) proposes that advertising agencies can be seen as an *ideas business* which seeks to build brands for clients. An alternative view is that agencies are *advertising factories*, where the majority of the work is associated with administration, communication, coordination and general running around to ensure that the advertisement appears on the page or screen as desired.

A different way of looking at this is to consider what the client thinks the agency does and from this evaluate the outcomes from the relationship.

If the 'ideas business' view is accepted then the ideas generated add value for the client, so the use the client makes of the idea should be rewarded by way of a royalty type payment. If the 'factory concept' is adopted, then it is the resources involved in the process that need to be considered and a fee-based system is more appropriate. Both parties will actively seek to reduce costs that do not contribute to the desired outcomes. These are different approaches to remuneration and avoid the volume of media purchased as a critical and controversial area.

Controlling the marketing communications industry

There are two types of control in the marketing communications industry: statutory (the legal framework) and voluntary (or self-regulatory). This is a detailed and complex area of marketing and it is clearly beyond the scope of this chapter to give a comprehensive description of all existing controls (which are being constantly revised, updated and added to). However, what follows is intended to give the reader some idea of the nature of existing controls and reactions to them.

The self-regulatory system of advertising control in the United Kingdom has been in existence for over 40 years. The Advertising Standards Authority (ASA) oversees the non-broadcast system on which broadcast codes are based and ensures that it functions in the public interest. The Committee of Advertising Practice (CAP), the industry arm, operates in parallel to coordinate the activities of the trade and professional organisations that comprise the advertising business. Together, they ensure that the British Code of Advertising Practice functions in the interests of consumers and is observed by those who commission, prepare and publish advertisements. Finally, the Advertising Standards Board of Finance exists independently to raise a levy on advertising expenditure to fund the system.

There are two types of control in the marketing communications industry: statutory and voluntary.

It is to the ASA that the public and the industry complain if they suspect that a non-broadcast advertisement is less than 'Legal, Decent, Honest and Truthful'. In addition to receiving over 10,678 complaints (1997), the Authority conducts a substantial monitoring programme, scrutinising more than 15,000 advertisements. This allows the ASA to anticipate and resolve problems and to spot trends that require intervention before they are revealed by complaints. In addition it is noticeable that the copy advice service offered to advertisers is being used much more than in the past. Perhaps this is a reflection of a more sensitive and protective attitude towards customers and the public and the need to protect brand reputation much more in harsher competitive environments. It is also interesting to note the relatively steady number of complaints received about advertisements and the sudden increase in the number of advertisements withdrawn: see Table 11.3.

All advertisements investigated are adjudicated by the Council of the Authority, which consists of 12 members serving as individuals and appointed by an independent chairman. The Council's rulings are published in a monthly report, which is

Table 11.3   Number of complaints received and advertisements withdrawn

	1995	1996	1997	2000
Number of complaints received	12,804	12,055	10,678	12,262
Number of advertisements withdrawn	515	720	512	1,427

Source: Advertising Standards Association.

widely circulated. In composition, the Council must be dominated by members who have no connection with the advertising business.

Television advertising in the UK, including satellite and cable, is governed by the Independent Television Commission (ITC), which has its own Code of Advertising Standards and Practice. In 2000, the ITC decided that 1,427 advertisements were adjudged to be not in good taste, were indecent or were socially irresponsible. These advertisements were withdrawn.

Advertising on radio is regulated by the Radio Authority (RA) which, likewise, has its own Code. Both bodies are statutorily regulated and both Codes therefore have statutory force (i.e. the force of law). The ITC and the RA, as well as responding to complaints, provide advice on the interpretation of their codes.

The CAP predates the ASA and was the genesis of the self-regulatory system. In the early 1960s it was recognised by those working in the industry that effective controls were needed to set standards for those preparing and publishing advertisements. The ASA administers and the CAP formulates and updates the British Code of Advertising Practice. Any advertisement in press, posters, cinema, direct mail, viewdata, sales promotion or the management of lists and databases is governed by the rules in the Code.

In addition to the British Code of Advertising Practice, many industries have now instituted their own sectoral codes of practice which require observance of the CAP code but also contain more detailed rules on specialised advertisements and trading practices.

Since the Code was first published, there has been a significant enlargement of the amount of legislation designed to protect the consumer. This is true not only domestically but also in relation to directives emanating from the EU, which must be drawn into the UK's existing register of more than 80 statutes, orders and regulations affecting advertising.

The Code, and the self-regulatory framework that exists to administer it, was designed to work within and to complement those legal controls. Its scope, speed and flexibility provide an alternative, and in some instances the only, means of resolving disputes about advertisements. It also stimulates the adoption of high standards of practice in numerous areas, such as taste and decency, that are extremely difficult to judge in law but which fundamentally affect the reputation of the advertising industry.

In addition, the Office of Fair Trading, the Department for the Environment, Food and Rural Affairs, the Department of Trade and Industry, the Home Office, the Securities and Investments Board, the Bank of England and the Department of Health (to name a diverse but not exhaustive selection) have consumer protection legislation which ranges far wider and deeper than could be executed through a judicially non-punitive Code of Practice; in some instances, companies and individuals who break the laws administered by these offices face criminal as well as civil prosecution.

The British Code of Sales Promotion Practice is published by the CAP and conforms to the principles of the International Code of Sales Promotion Practice, published by the International Chamber of Commerce. Implementation of the Code is in the hands of the CAP under the general supervision of the ASA. Day-to-day supervision of the Code, including pre-publication advice for promoters, is in the hands of the Committee's subcommittee on sales promotion, the members of which have wide experience of sales promotion matters. The Code sets out basic principles and gives general guidelines applying to all forms of sales promotion and how these apply in particular cases. The Code also lists the main legislative controls on sales promotions and associated advertising: the fifth edition (Alderson, 1990) identifies 19 Acts, orders and regulations. The Institute of Sales Promotion, itself a member of the CAP, provides a recommended reading list, much of which is concerned with the regulatory framework for sales promotion and which is an invaluable guide for potential promoters. The Direct Selling Association has its own Code of Practice within which all member companies must operate. The Direct Mail Services Standards Board monitors postal advertising and unaddressed leaflet material to ensure compliance with the law and the Code. Public relations has its own Code of Practice and there have even been suggestions (Week, 1990) that sales representatives should have their own codes of ethics.

It seems, therefore, that the consumer is well protected against any attempts to defraud, mislead or even offend. However, it does seem that these codes are constantly being challenged by clients and consumers. This may be a reflection of boundaries being tested in the name of advancement and progress, especially as offending clients are, in many cases, only lightly rebuffed and told not to do it again. But this raises the question of whether there is too much control. Some argue that freedom of expression, freedom of speech and even freedom of choice are under threat. Others point out that even more control is on the way, talking about 'the plethora of legislation on advertising regulations now being considered by the European Commission'. The further question is, of course, does it work? The evidence, from the number of complaints and prosecutions in any one year, is that examples of malpractice are few and far between. There will always be some who are guilty (deliberately or otherwise) of 'circumventing the voluntary codes designed to regulate them' (Hoek *et al.*, 1993) and there will always be contentious issues, such as the promotion of tobacco products, especially to young people, which will, almost inevitably, lead to further controls. What is certain is that those responsible for marketing communications need to keep up to date by seeking best advice on this most important and potentially dangerous area.

Summary

This chapter has attempted to demonstrate the complex nature of the marketing communications industry by considering the size, trends, players, operations and competitive aspects. It should be noted, however, that in the space available this analysis has not attempted to be, and cannot be regarded as, a comprehensive treatment.

The structure that advertising agencies have adopted and the operational aspects may be a little outdated, and the industry might be advised to find new ways of presenting itself to its buyers. Of the many issues facing the industry one of the key ones concerns the relationships between agencies and their clients. The context that the industry presents and which influences the relationships of the main participants, the media, clients and agencies, must not be ignored.

The industry will continue to evolve and further integration between agencies and those that own and manage many of the new marketing communication tools is likely to accelerate.

Review questions

1. How might an organisation determine the sum to be spent on marketing communications and how might that sum be apportioned between the various activities available?

2. Which are the principal types of organisation in the marketing communication industry?

3. Write notes for a presentation explaining the different types of agency available to clients.

4. Outline the arguments for and against using an agency.

5. What factors should be taken into consideration and what procedure might be followed when selecting an agency?

6. What problems might be encountered in agency/client relationships?

7. What are the basic dimensions for the development of good agency/client relationships?

8. Write brief notes about the briefing system.

9. Explain the commission payment system, and outline alternative approaches.

10. How can an organisation best acquaint itself with the relevant controls in a chosen area of marketing communications?

MINI CASE

This mini case was written by Jonathan Lace, Allied Domecq Associate Professor in Advertising at Southampton Business School.

MegaPark in talks with GBH on new pay structure

MegaPark (the client) is an international company with diversified activities. It pays the London agency (GBH) a commission of 10% net with an additional 2.5% on net media spending to an independent media agency for media buying and schedule planning. The advertising investment in the brands handled by GBH for the past ear was £3.5 million, with advertising on TV, and in print and radio.

Given fluctuating budgets in the past year (and perhaps worse to come in an uncertain market), there is little certainty of income to the agency, making it difficult to for them to plan the resource allocation to the account. In addition, the client is keen to allocate a higher proportion of the spending on both new media (mainly Web advertising) and sponsorship in the coming year.

Chris Pearson, the marketing director, has decided to meet with the advertising agency managing director (Sarah Holden) specifically to explore an alternative method of agency remuneration. The following is an excerpt of this discussion.

Client   Sarah, our account has been with you in one guise or another for about five years now. During that time we've not really considered the role that remuneration can play in ensuring success. Clearly the world has moved on considerably and commission is becoming less relevant, especially since media buying and planning are now handled by the media agency.

Agency   We'd be happy to move away from commission. The majority of our clients now pay us by fee anyway. If you wanted to use fees, a good starting point would be to give us a clear indication of what your requirements are over the next year, so that we can determine the likely staff resource we need to service your account, and then to cost these up.

Client   Well, of course I can let you know what we are planning, but the difficulty is, as you know, that plans change. I'd like a fee proposal from you that ensures some flexibility – we don't want to end up paying for resource that we don't use.

Agency   And we don't want to undercost the work we actually do for you. A greater certainty may be better for both of us. One possibility to enable flexibility is to reconcile our actual time put against the account with the budgeted time. We can ask our key people to keep timesheets of hours worked. Thus at the end of the period we can see whether we're on track or not, and adjust payments accordingly. Part of the fee proposal would be for certain agency costs such as key people and overheads which would be guaranteed regardless of fluctuating workloads and budgets – a minimum income guarantee.

Client   One problem with this arrangement that I can see straight away is that every time the account people pick up the phone the clock starts ticking. It may make for worse rather than better communication. Indeed, it goes against our aim of working together better to improve our return on advertisement investment. Of course, if we, the client, continue to use the agency as we have done, and wish to do, there's no limit to how much we could spend under this new arrangement. If we install a minimum, we'd also need to have a maximum limit to agency remuneration.

Agency   Well we need to explore this in greater detail based on an understanding of your needs – the type and level of input that you think you are going to need. Besides fees another possibility is base part of our remuneration on performance – on success of the advertising. For instance, if a campaign achieves or exceeds, say, targeted advertising or brand awareness levels we would receive extra payments.

Client   I'd also be keen to introduce an element of payment by results. Our problem is that we have several brands and campaigns – this could get quite complicated. In addition, I don't see my board to agreeing to additional remuneration unless there is also a penalty for poor performance or base, i.e. certain remuneration has been revised down accordingly.

Perhaps we should consider the contribution that advertising makes to sales?

Agency   Yes that's always a valuable exercise but could be unstable for remuneration purposes. As we don't have anything like that in place the cost might be significant and disproportionate to the benefits for pbr purposes alone.

Client   Hmm that's true. It might be easier to consider just measures of our performance, like market share growth?

Agency   Yes, if you like. If our remuneration was to be linked to your sales or market share performance, we would naturally wish to share in your plans and thinking to assess the viability of your targets. As we would be staking certain income on something over which we would have less control, we would need to assess the risk involved. Furthermore, we would be looking for a potentially higher return for the risk we would be taking. What would happen, say, if one of your factories burnt down?

Client   Clearly there are plenty of issues here – how much to stake, how to set the appropriate measures and how to evaluate the results. The whole thing could get very complicated. Clearly the last thing we want to do is to spend hours discussing what the measures should be for a pbr scheme rather than getting on with the business in hand. What we need is something simple, that's equitable and encourages both of us to work together better.

Agency   Well yes. What is your motivation for wanting to have pbr?

Client   I suppose, in the broadest sense it is about tying our fortunes together – to more fairly reward the agency for the contribution it makes, while at the same time ensuring that we get the best for our investment; in one word – accountability.

Agency   Why don't we think about what type of pbr scheme makes he best sense on this account? Perhaps we could discuss this in a couple of weeks?

This case has been prepared for teaching purposes only. It is not intended to be illustrative of an actual situation, rather to convey some of the issues involved in the negotiation of a mutually satisfactory remuneration agreement. For further information on agency remuneration please consult the publications listed on *www.advertising-research.com*.

Mini-case questions

1. Consider the benefits and drawbacks to both agency and client of switching from a remuneration agreement based on commission on media spending to one based on fees.

2. Consider how an element of payment by results could be structured to suit both client and agency – to achieve a win–win solution.

3. How would your recommendation in question 2 vary for a client in different product sectors (e.g. lager, cars, bank)?

References

Abrahams, B. (1997) Branding the agency. *Marketing*, 26 June, pp. 24–5.

Alderson, M. (1990) *The British Code of Sales Promotion Practice*, 5th edn. CAP.

Barrett, P. (1997) Nike dumps UK shop. *Marketing*, 27 November, p. 15.

Curtis, J. (1999) Why grey is golden. *Marketing*, 15 July, pp. 25–5.

Davidson, S. and Kapelianis, D. (1996) Towards an organisational theory of advertising: agency–client relationships in South Africa. *International Journal of Advertising*, **15**, pp. 48–60.

Finch, M. (2000) How to choose the right marketing agency, *Admap* (October), pp. 46–7.

Goften, K. (2000) Mergers shake up DM and SP groups. Agency 2001 *Marketing Report* 13, 30 November, pp. 15–16.

Green, A. (1991) Death of the full-service ad agency? *Admap* (January), pp. 21–4.

Griffiths, A. (2000) More than a media network. *Campaign Report*, 20 October, pp. 3–4.

Hakansson, H. (1982) *International Marketing and Purchasing of Industrial Goods: An Interaction Approach*. Chichester: John Wiley.

Hall, E. (1997) Nike talks to agencies about £9M UK ad task. *Campaign*, 10 October, p. 2.

Hoek, J., Gendall, P. and Stockdale, M. (1993) Some effects of tobacco sponsorship advertisements on young males. *International Journal of Advertising*, **12**, pp. 25–35.

Jardine, A. (2000) Will workshops replace the pitch? *Marketing*, 13 April, p. 16

Jensen, B. (1995) Using agency remuneration as a strategic tool. *Admap* (January), pp. 20–2.

Lace, J. M. (2000) Payment-by-results. Is there a pot of gold at the end of the rainbow? *International Journal of Advertising*, **19**, pp. 167–83.

Lace, J. M. and Brocklehurst, D. (2000) You both win when you play the same game. *Admap* (October), pp. 40–2.

McLuhan, R. (2001) Technology spurs call centre growth, *Marketing*, 12 April, pp. 33–42.

Morgan, R.M. and Hunt, S.D. (1994) The commitment–trust theory of relationship marketing. *Journal of Marketing*, **58** (July), pp. 20–38.

Murphy, D. (2000) New media's year of good fortunes. *Agency 2001 Marketing Report 13*, 30 November, p. 33.

Pawinska, M. (2000) The passive pitch. PR Week, 12 May, pp. 14–15.

Phillips, W. (1991) From bubble to rubble. *Admap* (April), pp. 14–19.

Snowden, S. (1993) The remuneration squeeze. *Admap* (January), pp. 26–8.

Starkey, R. (1999) cited in Curtis (1999).

Week, W.A. (1990) Corporate codes of ethics and sales force behaviour: a case study. *Journal of Business Ethics*, **11**, pp. 753–60.

West, D.C. and Paliwoda, S.J. (1996) Advertising client–agency relationships. *European Journal of Marketing*, **30**(8), pp. 22–39.

Woolgar, T. (1998) Choosing an agency. *Campaign Report*, 9 October, pp. 6–7.

Young, M. and Steilen, C. (1996) Strategy based advertising agency selection: an alternative to 'spec' presentation. *Business Horizons*, **39** (November/December), pp. 77–80.

Yovovich, B.G. and Lawler, E.O. (1991) Big agency – small agency, *Business Marketing* (May), pp. 13–18.

part 3

Strategies

Chapters 12–19

The direction, purpose and overall orientation of an organisation's communications activities, with regard to both its products/services and the overall organisation

12

Marketing communication strategies and planning

A marketing communication strategy refers to an organisation's preferred orientation and emphasis of its communications with its customers and stakeholders, in the light of its business and marketing strategies. A marketing communications plan is concerned with the development and managerial processes involved in the articulation of an organisation's marketing communication strategy.

AIMS AND OBJECTIVES

The aims of this chapter are to explore the nature of marketing communications strategies, to familiarise readers with the elements and concepts associated with marketing communication planning and to introduce the marketing communications planning framework.

The objectives of this chapter are:

1. To introduce the notion of marketing communication strategy as a separate concept to marketing communications plans.
2. To consider three main marketing communication strategies: pull, push and profile.
3. To examine involvement as a basis for developing promotional strategies.
4. To evaluate the FCB grid as a tool for strategy development.
5. To use the Rossiter–Percy grid as a means of creating strategic direction.
6. To consider the different elements involved in marketing communication plans.
7. To highlight the linkages and interaction between the different elements of the plan.
8. To present a framework for the development of marketing communication plans.

Introduction

It is assumed by many that marketing communication strategy is simply the combination of activities in the communications mix. In other words, strategy is about the degree of direct marketing, personal selling, advertising, sales promotion and public

Key decisions concern the overall direction of the programme and target audiences.

relations that is incorporated within a planned sequence of communication activities. This is important, but it is not the essence of marketing communications strategy. From a strategic perspective, key decisions concern the overall direction of the programme and target audiences, the fit with marketing and corporate strategy, the desired position the brand is to occupy in the market, the resources to be made available, the key message and overall goals.

In order to adopt a customer perspective on which to build marketing communications strategy, rather than adopt a production orientation around the resource base, it is useful to revisit the buying behaviour and characteristics of the different target audiences. Consumer purchase decisions are characterised

It is useful to revisit the buying behaviour and characteristics of the different target audiences.

(very generally and see Chapter 4) by a single-person buying centre whereas organisational buying decisions can involve a large number of different people, fulfilling different roles and all requiring different marketing communication messages. It follows from this that the approach to communicating with these two very different target sectors should be radically different, especially in terms of what, where, when and how a message is communicated. Once promotional objectives have been established, it is necessary to formulate appropriate strategies. Promotional objectives that are focused upon consumer markets require a different strategy from those formulated to satisfy the objectives that are focused on organisational customers. In addition, there are circumstances and reasons to focus communications upon the development of the organisation and a corporate brand. Often, these corporate brands need to work closely with the development of product brands. As a result, it is possible to identify three main marketing communication strategies:

pull strategies to influence end-user customers (consumers and b2b);

push strategies to influence trade channel buyers;

profile strategies to influence a range of stakeholders.

These can be referred to as the 3Ps of promotional strategy. Push and pull relate to the direction of the communication to the marketing channel: pushing communications down through the marketing channel or pulling consumers/buyers into the channel

These can be referred to as the 3Ps of promotional strategy.

via retailers, as a result of receiving the communications. They do not relate to the intensity of communication and only refer to the overall approach. Profile refers to the presentation of the organisation as a whole and therefore the identity is said to be profiled to various other target stakeholder audiences, which may well include consumers, trade buyers and business-to-business customers. Normally, profile strategies do not contain or make reference to specific products or services that the organisation offers. See Table 12.1. This may be blurred where the name of a company is the name of its primary (only) product. For example, messages about Kwik-Fit are very often designed to convey meaning about the quality and prices of its services, however, they often reflect on the organisation itself,

Table 12.1   Marketing communications strategy options

Strategy	Target audience	Communication focus	Communication goal
Pull	Consumers	Product/service	Purchase
	End-user b2b customers	Product/service	Purchase
Push	Channel intermediaries	Product/service	Developing relationships & distribution network
Profile	All relevant stakeholders	The organisation	Building reputation

especially when its advertising shows members of staff in workwear, doing their work. Now that Marks and Spencer have dropped their St Michael brand, messages about the retailer will inevitably be more orientated to the company and the broad range of products rather than any one product brand.

Within each of these overall strategies, individual approaches should then be formulated to reflect the needs of each particular case. So, for example, the launch of a new shampoo product will involve a push strategy to get the product on the shelves of the appropriate retailers. The strategy would be to gain retailer acceptance of the new brand and to position it as a profitable new brand to gain consumer interest. Personal selling supported by trade sales promotions will be the main promotional tools. A pull strategy to develop awareness about the brand will need to be created, accompanied by appropriate public relations work. The next step will be to create particular brand associations and thereby position the brand in the minds of the target audience. Messages may be functional or expressive but they will endeavour to convey a brand promise. This may be accompanied or followed by the use of incentives to encourage consumers to trial the product. To support the brand, care lines, and a Web site will need to be put in place to provide credibility as well as a buyer reference point.

In order that these strategies be implemented, it is normal procedure to develop a marketing communications plan. The degree to which these plans are developed varies across organisations and some rely on their agencies to undertake this work for them. However, there can be major benefits as a result of developing these plans in-house, for example, by involving and discussing issues internally and developing a sense of ownership.

Planning is not the same as strategy, although the two are often used interchangeably. Strategy is about the direction, approach and implementation of an organisation's desired marketing communications (in this case) whereas planning is usually about the formalisation of the strategy and ideas, into a manageable sequence of activities that are linked, coherent and capable of being implemented in the light of the resources that are available. Strategy is about the way an organisation prefers to communicate with its customers and stakeholders. It must do this in the light of its business and marketing strategies to encourage a degree of dialogue with selected stakeholders.

Planning is not the same as strategy, although the two are often used interchangeably.

A marketing communications plan is concerned with the development and managerial processes involved in the articulation of an organisation's marketing communication strategy. This will be considered later in this chapter.

There is little doubt that planning and strategy are interlinked but it is useful to

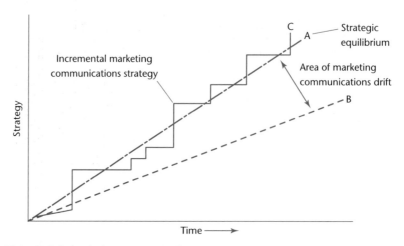

Figure 12.1 Drift in marketing communications strategy.

consider strategy as something that needs to be attended to on a regular basis. With so many variables and an external environment that is subject to tremendous change, promotional strategy can be seen to drift, to move away from its central message. The only way to correct drift is to change the marketing communications strategy by an amount according to the degree to which messages have drifted. This might be best observed in Figure 12.1.

Line B suggests that if current marketing communications remain as they are, then the size of the gap with the central theme of marketing communications will widen and any attempt to get back will be large and expensive.

Line C depicts a brand that has adapted its marketing communications on a more frequent basis (than B) and as a result follows an incremental strategy, one that results in a more consistent message. This concept might be interpreted in terms of positioning and repositioning brands and the changing of agencies in order to revitalise and change the direction of the communications strategy currently being pursued.

A pull strategy

If messages are to be directed at targeted end-user customers, then the intention is invariably to generate increased levels of awareness, change and/or reinforce attitudes, reduce risk, encourage involvement and ultimately provoke a motivation within the target group. This motivation is to stimulate action so that the target audience expect the offering to be available to them when they decide to enquire, experiment or make a repeat purchase. This approach is known as a *pull* strategy and is aimed at encouraging customers to 'pull' products through the channel network. See Figure 12.2. This usually means that consumers go into retail outlets (shops) to enquire about a particular product and/or buy them, or to enter a similar transaction direct with the manufacturer or intermediary through direct mail or the Internet. B2b customers are encouraged to buy from dealers and distributors whilst both groups of consumers and b2b customers have opportunities to buy through direct marketing channels where there is no intermediary.

To accomplish and deliver a pull strategy, the traditional approach has been to deliver

A pull strategy and is aimed at encouraging customers to 'pull' products through the channel network.

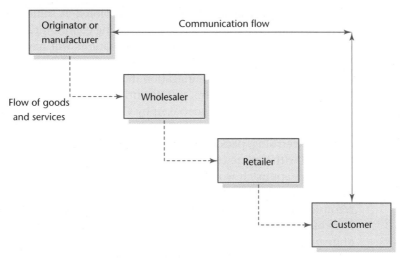

Figure 12.2   Direction of communication in a pull strategy.

mass media advertising supported by below-the-line communications, most notably sales promotions. There has been greater use of direct marketing in non-fast-moving consumer goods sectors and the arrival of the Internet has presented opportunities to reach audiences in new ways and so reduce reliance on the old formulaic approach to pull-based strategies. The decision to use a pull strategy has to be supported by a core message proposition. This will vary according to the context analysis and the needs of the target audience. However, it is probable that the core message will seek to differentiate (position), remind or reassure, inform or persuade the audience to think, feel or behave in a particular way. Agencies and clients have their own approach to this labelling activity. One way might be to term a communication strategy pull/remind or pull/position as this describes the audience and what the strategy seeks to achieve.

The decision to use a pull strategy has to be supported by a core message proposition.

Alternative pull strategies – UK supermarkets

ASDA (Wal-mart) has developed a strong market share in the UK based mainly on price competition or on what is referred to as everyday low pricing (pull/price). Tesco runs everyday low pricing but uses sales promotions as a form of complementary positioning (pull/price/promotions). In their wake, Sainsbury's and Safeway have used differing pull strategies to regain lost share, increase profitability and stave off takeover threats.

Safeway has abandoned all national advertising and its loyalty scheme. In its place is a direct marketing approach based largely on direct mail flyers sent to households on a weekly basis. Some of the money saved by not advertising has been put into selected sales promotions and discounts (pull/direct/promotions).

Although Sainsbury's uses EDLP on 1,000 selected lines, it has adopted a classic branding campaign, based around the celebrity chef Jamie Oliver. Making heavy use of television, the brand is positioned around a quality proposition emphasised by the personality and the associated redesign of major stores (pull/quality/repositioning).

The level and degree of involvement, explored at some depth in Chapter 4, has some implications for pull strategies. Marketing communication messages can be considered to be a stimulus which in some situations will have a strong impact on the level of involvement enjoyed by the target audience. A strategic response to this would be to adapt marketing communication messages so that they are effective at different levels of involvement, a form of differentiation.

For example, research undertaken by Crown Paints found that the brand was perceived to be very male, very traditional and a bit dull and staid. A pull strategy based around advertising, packaging and point-of-purchase materials was used to reposition the brand with a more contemporary identity. See Plate 12.1.

Another approach would be to turn low-involvement decisions into high involvement which through communications, encourage members of the target audience to reconsider their perception of a brand or of the competition. Again, this represents a form of differentiation. A third approach is to segment the market in terms of the level of involvement experienced by each group and according to situational or personality factors, and then shape the marketing communication messages to suit each group.

FCB matrix

Vaughn (1980) developed a matrix utilising involvement and brain specialisation theories. Brain specialisation theory suggests that the left-hand side of the brain is best handling rational, linear and cognitive thinking, whereas the right-hand side is better able to manage spatial, visual and emotional issues (the affective or feeling functions).

Vaughn proposed that by combining involvement with elements of thinking and feeling, four primary advertising planning strategies can be distinguished. These are informative, affective, habitual and self-satisfaction (see Figure 12.3). According to Vaughn, the matrix is intended to be a thought provoker rather than a formula or model from which prescriptive solutions are to be identified. The FCB matrix is a useful guide to help analyse and appreciate consumer/product relationships and to develop appropriate communication strategies. The four quadrants of the grid identify particular types of decision-making and each requires different advertising approaches. Vaughn suggests that different orderings from the learn–feel–do sequence can be observed (see Figure 12.3). By perceiving the different ways in which the process can be ordered, he proposed that the learn–feel–do sequence should be visualised as a continuum, a circular concept. Communication strategy would, therefore, be based on the point of entry that consumers make to the cycle.

The matrix is intended to be a thought provoker rather than a formula or model from which prescriptive solutions are to be identified.

Some offerings, generally regarded as 'habitual', may be moved to another quadrant, such as 'responsive', to develop differentiation and establish a new position for the product in the minds of consumers relative to the competition. This could be achieved by the selection of suitable media vehicles and visual images in the composition of the messages associated with an advertisement. There is little doubt that this model, or interpretation of the advertising process, has made a significant contribution to our understanding of the advertising process and has been used by a large number of advertising agencies (Joyce, 1991).

This model has made a significant contribution to our understanding of the advertising process and has been used by a large number of advertising agencies.

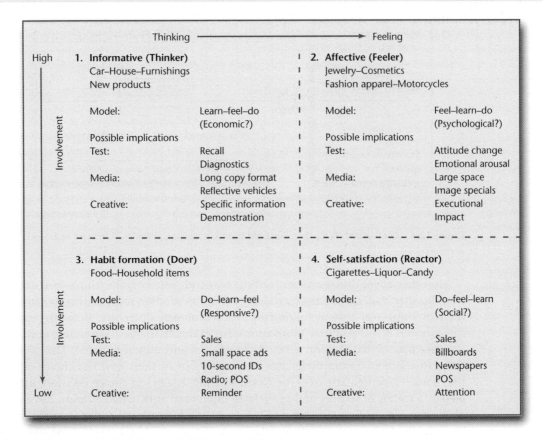

Figure 12.3 FCB grid. From Vaughn (1980); used with kind permission.

The Rossiter–Percy grid

Rossiter *et al.* (1991), however, disagree with some of the underpinnings of the FCB grid and offer a new one in response (revised 1997) (Figure 12.4). They suggest that involvement is not a continuum because it is virtually impossible to decide when a person graduates from high to low involvement. They claim that the FCB grid fails to account for situations where a person moves from high to low involvement and then back to high, perhaps on a temporary basis, when a new variant is introduced to the market. Rossiter *et al.* regard involvement as the level of perceived risk present at the time of purchase. Consequently, it is the degree of familiarity buyers have at the time of purchase that is an important component.

They suggest that involvement is not a continuum.

A further criticism is that the FCB grid is an attitude-only model. Rossiter *et al.* quite rightly identify the need for brand awareness to be built into such grids as a prerequisite for attitude development. However, they cite the need to differentiate different purchase situations. Some brands require awareness recall because the purchase decision is made prior to the act of purchasing. Other brands require awareness recognition at the point of purchase, where the buyer needs to be prompted into brand choice decisions. Each of these situations requires different message strategies, and these are explored in Chapter 21.

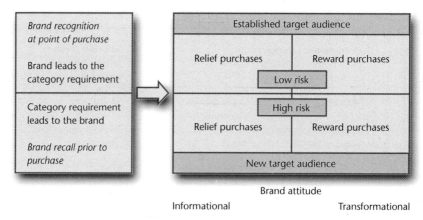

Figure 12.4   The Rossiter–Percy grid. Adapted from Rossiter and Percy (1997); used with kind permission.

The other major difference between the two grids concerns the 'think–feel' dimension. Rossiter *et al.* believe that a wider spectrum of motives must be incorporated, as the FCB 'think–feel' interpretation fails to accommodate differences between product category and brand purchase motivations. For example, the decision to use a product category may be based upon a strictly functional and utilitarian need. The need to travel to another country designates the necessity of air transport. The choice of carrier, however, particularly over the North Atlantic, is a brand choice decision, motivated by a variety of sensory and ego-related inputs and anticipated outputs. Rossiter *et al.* disaggregate motives into what they refer to as informational and transformational motives. By detailing motives into these classifications, a more precise approach to advertising tactics can be developed (Chapter 21). Furthermore, the confusion inherent in the FCB grid, between the think and involvement elements, is overcome.

It should be understood that these 'grids' are purely hypothetical, and there is no proof or evidence to suggest that they are accurate reflections of advertising. It is true that both models have been used as the basis for advertising strategy in many agencies, but that does not mean that they are totally reliable or, more importantly, that they have been tested empirically so that they can be used in total confidence. They are interpretations of commercial and psychological activity and have been instrumental in advancing our level of knowledge. It is in this spirit of development that these models are presented in this text.

These 'grids' are purely hypothetical, and there is no proof or evidence to suggest that they are accurate reflections of advertising.

There are parts in both of these frameworks that have a number of strong elements of truth attached to them. However, for products that are purchased on a regular basis, pull strategies should be geared to defending the rationale that current buyers use to select the brand. Heavy buyers select a particular brand more often than light users do from their repertoire. By providing a variety of consistent stimuli, and by keeping the brand alive, fresh buyers are more likely to prefer and purchase a particular brand than those that allow their brands to lose purchase currency and the triggers necessary to evoke memory impressions. For example, the long-running Renault campaign using the Nicole and Papa characters sought to use fresh ideas based on buyers' transformational motives. Normally car purchase evokes high involvement, but only at the time of purchase. In order to build reputation and positive association with the Renault brand, key messages need to be delivered in the intervening (non-purchase) period. Nicole provided a point of attention, curiosity (see Chapter 20) and consistency, while delivering messages about flair and style to be associated with Renault.

For products purchased on an irregular basis, marketing communications need only touch the target audience on a relatively low number of occasions. Strategies need to be developed that inform and contextualise the purchase rationale for consumers. This means providing lasting impressions that enable consumers to understand the circumstances in which purchase of a particular product/brand should be made once a decision has been made to purchase from the product category.

The priorities are to communicate messages that will encourage consumers to trust and bestow expertise on the product/brand that is offered.

Here the priorities are to communicate messages that will encourage consumers to trust and bestow expertise on the product/brand that is offered.

Changing perceptions and attitudes – Land Rover

Following a brief to sell 300 Land Rovers, research conducted by the direct marketing agency Craik Jones found that the attitudes held by prospective Land Rover buyers were based on serious misconceptions about the brand. Not only did they feel that Land Rovers were essentially a rural vehicle but they also drove like a truck rather than a luxury car.

These attitudes had been developed as a result of information and perceptions of the brand, without ever having driven the car. This is typical of the order in which attitudes are formed when there is high involvement (learn–feel–do). In order to overcome this, a direct marketing strategy was developed by the agency to encourage trial in order that attitudes could be based on direct experience (learn–do–feel). Direct mail was used to stimulate a test drive and this was followed up a week later to thank the drivers and to find out their reactions to the experience of actually driving a Land Rover. Not only were over 700 orders placed as a direct result of this campaign but the reaction and knock-on effect on the dealer network was very positive. Direct marketing had been used as part of a pull strategy to change attitudes and increase sales.

A pull strategy, therefore, refers to messages targeted at particular customer audiences and to the overall task that a campaign might seek to achieve. This might be to differentiate or position a brand (e.g. by reference to specific attributes), remind/reassure, inform (by raising awareness) or persuade (stimulate action). To accomplish this, a functional or expressive branding policy needs to be agreed and understood by all relevant parties (see Chapters 13 and 14).

A push strategy

A second group or type of target audience can be identified, based firstly on their contribution to the marketing channel and secondly because these organisations do not consume the products and services they buy, but add value before selling the product on to others in the supply chain. The previous strategy was targeted at customers who make purchase decisions related largely to their personal (or organisational) consumption of products and services. This second group buys products and services, performs some added-value activity and moves the product through the marketing channel network. This group is a part of the b2b sector, and the characteristics and issues associated with trade channel marketing communications are explored in greater detail in Chapter 15.

The degree of cooperation between organisations will vary and part of the role of marketing communications is to develop and support the relationships that exist.

Trade channel organisations and indeed all b2b organisations are actively involved in the development and maintenance of interorganisational relationships. The degree of cooperation between organisations will vary and part of the role of marketing communications is to develop and support the relationships that exist.

The 'trade' channel has received increased attention in recent years as the strategic value of intermediaries has become more apparent. As the channel networks have developed, so has their complexity, which impacts upon the marketing communications strategies and tools used to help reach marketing goals. The expectations of buyers in these networks have risen in parallel with the significance attached to them by manufacturers. The power of multiple retailers, such as Tesco, Sainsbury's, Safeway and Asda, is such that they are able to dictate terms (including the marketing communications) to many manufacturers of branded goods.

Below-the-line branding – Matika

Black and Decker discovered that they were losing sales in the trade sector because their products were perceived to be more suitable for consumers and the do-it-yourself market. Their response was to develop a separate brand for this particular trade sector. They used a new name 'Matika', identified the product range through the colour yellow and made it available through different trade channels. The promotional materials and support documentation needed a different 'tone of voice' to reflect a more rugged and stronger position. The messages were integrated in order to reinforce the desired positioning.

Defn

A *push* communication strategy involves the presentation of information in order to influence other trade channel organisations and, as a result, encourage them to take stock, to allocate resources (e.g. shelf space) and to help them to become fully aware of the key attributes and benefits associated with each product with a view to adding value prior to further channel transactions. This strategy is designed to encourage resale to other members of the network and contribute to the achievement of their own objectives. This approach is known as a *push* strategy, as it is aimed at pushing the product down through the channel towards the end-users for consumption. See Figure 12.5.

A push communication strategy involves the presentation of information in order to influence other trade channel organisations.

The channel network (Chapter 10) consists of those organisations with whom others must cooperate directly to achieve their own objectives. By accepting that there

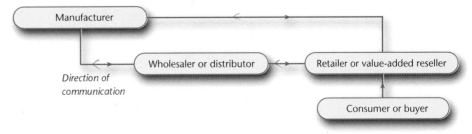

Figure 12.5   Direction of communication in a push strategy.

is interdependence, usually dispersed unequally throughout the network, it is possible to identify organisations that have a stronger/weaker position within a network. Communication must travel not only between the different levels of dependence and role ('up and down' in a channel context) and so represent bidirectional flows but also across similar levels of dependence and role, that is horizontal flows. For example, these may be from retailer to retailer or wholesaler to wholesaler.

B2B   Marketing communications targeted at people involved in organisational buying decisions are characterised by an emphasis on personal selling. Trade advertising, trade sales promotions and public relations all have an important yet secondary role to play. Direct marketing has become increasingly important and the development of the Internet has had a profound impact on b2b communications and interorganisational relationships. However, personal selling has traditionally been the most significant part of the promotional mix where a push strategy has been instigated.

Personal selling has traditionally been the most significant part of the promotional mix where a push strategy has been instigated.

Finally, just as it was suggested that the essence of a pull strategy could be articulated in brief format, a push strategy could be treated in a similar way. The need to consider the core message is paramount as it conveys information about the essence of the strategy. Push/inform, push/position or push/key accounts/discount might be examples of possible terminology. Whether or not this form of expression is used it is important that marketing communication strategy be referred to more than just push; what is to be achieved also needs to be understood.

A profile strategy

The strategies considered so far concern the need for dialogue with customers (pull) and trade channel intermediaries (push). However, there is a whole range of other stakeholders, many of whom need to know about and understand the organisation rather than actually purchase its products and services. See Figure 12.6. This group of stakeholders may include financial analysts, trade unions, government bodies, employees or the local community. It should be easy to understand that these different stakeholder groups can influence the organisation in different ways and, in doing so, need to receive (and respond to) different types of messages. So, the financial analysts need to know about financial and trading performance and expectations, and the local community may be interested in employment and the impact of the organisation on the local environment, whereas the government may be interested in the way

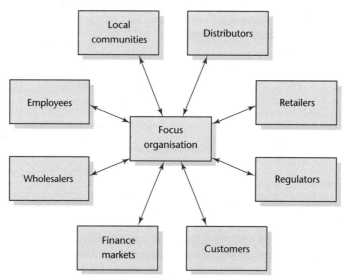

Figure 12.6   Direction of communication in a profile strategy.

the organisation applies health and safety regulations and pays corporation, VAT and other taxes. It should also be remembered that consumers and business-to-business customers may also be more interested in the organisation itself and so help initiate an umbrella branding strategy, which is considered in Chapters 14 and 16.

Traditionally these organisationally orientated activities have been referred to as corporate communications, as they deal more or less exclusively with the corporate entity or organisation. Products, services and other offerings are not normally the focus of these communications. It is the organisation and its role in the context of the particular stakeholders' activities that is important. However, it should be noted that as more corporate brands appear, the distinction between corporate and marketing communications begins to become much less clear. Indeed, when considered in the light of the development and interest in internal marketing (and communications), it may be of greater advantage to consider corporate communications as part of an organisation's overall marketing communications activities.

Communications used to satisfy this array of stakeholder needs and the organisation's corporate promotional goals are developed through what is referred to as a profile strategy, a major element of which is corporate branding, the subject of Chapter 16.

The awareness, perception and attitudes held by stakeholders towards an organisation need to be understood, shaped and acted upon. This can accomplished though continual dialogue, which will lead to the development

The awareness, perception and attitudes held by stakeholders towards an organisation need to be understood, shaped and acted upon.

of trust and commitment and enable relationships to grow. This is necessary in order that stakeholders act favourably towards an organisation and enable strategies to flourish and objectives be achieved.

According to Anderson (2000), merger and acquisition activity in the first six months was up 26% in 2000 (£1.2 trillion). To build corporate brands, organisations must develop modern integrated communication programmes with all of their key stakeholder groups. Audiences demand transparency and accountability and instant on-line access to news, developments, research and networks means that inconsistent

To build corporate brands, organisations must develop modern integrated communication programmes with all of their key stakeholder groups.

or misleading information must be avoided. As if to reinforce this, a survey reported by Gray (2000) found that CEOs rated the reputation of their organisations as more important than that of their products. However, the leading contributor to the strength of the corporate brand is seen to be their products and services, followed by a strong management team, internal communications, PR, social accountability, change management and the personal reputation of the CEO.

Stakeholder analysis is used in the development of strategic plans, so if an organisation wants its communications to support the overall plan, it makes sense to communicate effectively with the appropriate stakeholders. Rowe *et al.* (1994) point out that, because of the mutual interdependence of stakeholders and the focus organisation, 'each stakeholder is in effect an advocate of any strategy that furthers its goals'. It follows, therefore, that it is important to provide all stakeholders with information that enables them to perceive and position the focus organisation so as to generate the desired corporate image. This requires a communication strategy that addresses these particular requirements, even though there may not be any immediately recognisable shift in performance.

However, it would be incorrect to perceive corporate communications as just a means of shaping or influencing the attitudes and behaviour of other stakeholders.

A profile strategy is one which focuses the majority of an organisation's communications upon the development of corporate image and reputation.

Organisations exist within a variety of networks, which provide a context for the roles and actions of member organisations (Chapter 10). Bidirectional communication flows exist and organisations adapt themselves to the actions and behaviour of others in the network. Therefore, corporate communications provides a mechanism by which it can learn about the context(s) in which it exists and is itself shaped and influenced by the other stakeholders with whom it shares communications. Reference is made to the work of Grunig and Hunt (1984), considered in Chapter 15.

A *profile* strategy is one which focuses the majority of an organisation's communications upon the development of corporate image and reputation, whether that be just internally, just externally or both. To accomplish and deliver a profile strategy, public relations, including sponsorship and corporate advertising, becomes the pivotal tool of the promotional mix. Personal selling may remain a vital element delivering both product/service and corporate messages.

Strategic balance

While the pull, push and profile strategies are important, it should be remembered that they are not mutually exclusive. Indeed, in most organisations it is possible to identify an element of each strategy at any one time. In reality, most organisations are structured in such a way that those responsible for communications with each of these three main audiences do so without reference to or coordination with each other. This is an example of how integrated marketing communications, which is examined in Chapter 19, needs to have one senior person responsible for all the organisational communications. Only through a single point of reference is it really possible to develop and communicate a set of brand values that are consistent and credible.

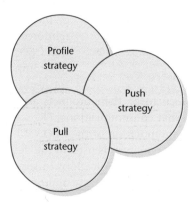

Figure 12.7   Marketing communication strategic eclipse

Recognising these limitations that organisations often place on themselves, the 3Ps should be considered as part of a total communication effort. Figure 12.7 depicts how the emphasis of a total communication strategy can be shift according to the needs of the various target audiences, resources and wider elements such as the environment and the competition. The marketing communications eclipse provides a visual interpretation of the balance between the three strategic dimensions. The more that is revealed of any one single strategy, the greater its role in any campaign. Conversely, the less that is revealed, the smaller the contribution. In any one campaign, one or two of the three strategies might be used in preference to another and will often reflect branding approaches. For example, a brand manager's use of a profile strategy at Procter and Gamble or Mars will be virtually zero and will almost certainly be entirely pull as trade communications are developed in a separate trade channel or category department.

The marketing communications eclipse provides a visual interpretation of the balance between the three strategic dimensions.

The role of each element of the promotional mix is important in promotional strategy. Each tool has different strengths and should be used accordingly. For example, direct marketing and sales promotion are more likely to be effective in persuading consumer audiences, while personal selling is likely to be used in a b2b situation. A profile strategy designed to change perception and understanding of the organisation is more likely to utilise public relations and corporate advertising.

Combining strategies – beef and lamb, nice and simple

Research undertaken by the Meat and Livestock Commission identified that sales of beef and lamb for mid-week meals had been falling because consumers did not know how to prepare meat in a sufficiently quick or easy way. Consumers lacked cooking ideas and inspiration and, although meat was perceived as a traditional source of protein by consumers, other more convenient foods were being used. Therefore, issues concerning customer and business context matters were prevalent.

Convenience is a function of speed, ease and versatility. To increase consumption of meat, therefore, it was necessary to enable consumers to learn how to prepare beef and lamb in a convenient way. This was accomplished by generating a number of meal ideas and then communicating them in an informative yet credible way: a pull strategy.

It was decided that television was necessary to reach the target audience and the Harry Enfield character 'Tim Nice but Dim' would be a suitable opinion former. The reaction 'well if he can cook these dishes then so can I' was seen as an integral part of the way the message needed to be understood (decoded) by the target audience. See Plate 12.2.

The TV campaign ran for five weeks and was supported by a number of integrated promotional activities. All multiple retailers received on-pack stickers featuring a picture of 'Tim', recipe details and a reminder of the necessary ingredients. Other in-store support included shelf barkers and hanging posters.

Free point of purchase material was received by 9,200 independent butchers and the campaign included six sheet posters placed outside Tesco and Sainsbury's stores: a push strategy. Public relations activities included the briefing of consumer journalists prior to the campaign burst, press releases to the regional press and radio interviews with celebrity chef James Martin to give a 'foodie' feel to the campaign.

A sales promotion programme using soundbites from the television commercial was used by some radio stations as part of a 'Listen and Win with Tim' campaign. Listeners had to answer a relevant question with a chance of winning some high-quality cookware. To complete the programme, the www.meatmatters.com site was refreshed and included a Tim microsite focusing solely on the campaign.

The 'Beef & Lamb, Nice & Simple' campaign had its origins in an understanding of the way consumers perceived the preparation of meat-based meals. The solutions sought to reposition beef and lamb as appropriate ingredients for modern weekday meals. This was achieved by educating consumers and helping them to learn how to use the product. They were invited to reason with the new knowledge inputs provided by the stimulus 'Tim' and then make a judgement about whether they could do the same.

By using marketing communications to inform and remind, consumers learnt to reconsider their views of meat-based mid-week meals. By providing easy means to access relevant information, sales of beef and lamb increased, and qualitative research through Millward Brown found a positive shift in the way consumers perceived beef and lamb as a suitable mid-week meal. Members of the trade channel were kept informed and integrated into the campaign. Both pull and push strategies were used and they eclipsed those of a profile campaign for the Meat and Livestock Commission.

Material kindly supplied by Phil Toms, Meat and Livestock Commission

Marketing communication strategy, regardless of the overall focus, is normally composed of a number of different elements. When considering strategy there are a number of key issues that need to be considered. These are shown in Table 12.2.

Strategy needs to be understood in terms of how the communication goals that have been set are to be achieved, and how we are going to accomplish them in terms of complementing the business and marketing strategies, with our current resources and opportunities and at the same time encourage target audiences to respond to our communications.

Table 12.2 Issues to be considered when developing marketing communications

Element	Issue
Target audiences	Which type of audience do we need to reach and why?
Channel strategies	How do we make our products/services available – direct or indirect?
Objectives	What do we need to achieve, what are our goals?
Positioning	How do we want to be perceived and understood?
Branding	How strong and what values and associations do stakeholders make with our brand?
Integration	How consistent are our communications internally and externally?
Competitors	How do our communications compare with those of our key competitors?
Resources	What resources do we have and which do we need to secure?

Answers to these questions are not always easy to find and very often there will be conflicting proposals from different coalitions of internal stakeholders. In other words, there is a political element that needs to be considered and there may also be a strong overriding culture that directs the communication strategy and may hinder innovation or the development of alternative methods of communication. Everyone who is involved with the development of marketing communications campaigns (internally and externally) should agree and prioritise necessary activities. The development of a marketing communications plan facilitates this process and enables the strategy to be articulated in such a way that the goals are achieved in a timely, efficient and effective manner.

A marketing communications plan facilitates this process and enables the strategy to be articulated in such a way that the goals are achieved in a timely, efficient and effective manner.

Developing a marketing communications plan

The marketing communications planning framework (MCPF) aims to bring together the various elements of marketing communications into a logical sequence of activities. The rationale for promotional decisions is built upon information generated at previous levels in the framework. It also provides a checklist of activities that need to be considered.

The MCPF represents a way of understanding the different promotional components, of appreciating the way in which they relate to one another and is a means of writing coherent marketing communications plans.

The MCPF represents a way of understanding the different promotional components, of appreciating the way in which they relate to one another and is a means of writing coherent marketing communications plans for work or for examinations, such as those offered by the Chartered Institute of Marketing in the Integrated Marketing Communications paper.

The second part of this book explores various contexts that influence or shape marketing communications. All marketing managers (and others) need to understand these contextual elements and appreciate how they contribute and influence the development of marketing communication programmes. In addition, there are a number of other elements and activities that need to be built into a programme in order that it can be implemented. These elements concern the goals, the resources, the promotional tools to be used and measures of control and evaluation. Just like the cogs in a clock, these elements need to be linked together, if the plan is to work.

To help students and managers comprehend the linkages between the elements and to understand how these different components complement each other, the rest of this chapter deals with the development of marketing communication plans. To that extent it will be of direct benefit to managers seeking to build plans for the first time or for those familiar with the activity to reconsider current practices. Secondly, the material should also be of direct benefit to students who are required to understand and perhaps prepare such plans as part fulfilment of an assessment or examination in this subject area.

The marketing communications planning framework

It has been established (Chapter 1) that the principal tasks facing marketing communications managers are to decide:

1. Who should receive the messages.
2. What the messages should say.
3. What image of the organisation/brand receivers are expected to retain.
4. How much is to be spent establishing this new established image.
5. How the messages are to be delivered.
6. What actions the receivers should take.
7. How to control the whole process once implemented.
8. What was achieved.

Note that more than one message is transmitted and that there is more than one target audience. This is important, as recognition of the need to communicate with multiple audiences and their different information requirements, often simultaneously, lies at the heart of marketing communications. The aim is to generate and transmit messages which present the organisation and their offerings to their various target audiences, encouraging them to enter into a dialogue. These messages must be presented consistently and they must address the points stated above. It is the skill and responsibility of the marketing communications planner to blend the communication tools and to create a mix that satisfies these elements.

A framework for integrated marketing communications plans

To enable managers and students to bring together the various promotional elements into a cohesive plan, which can be communicated to others, an overall framework is required.

The MCPF (Figure 12.8) seeks to achieve this by bringing together the various elements into a logical sequence of activities where the rationale for promotional decisions is built upon information generated at a previous level in the framework. Another advantage of using the MCPF is that it provides a suitable checklist of activities that need to be considered.

The MCPF represents a sequence of decisions that marketing managers undertake when preparing, implementing and evaluating communication strategies and plans. It does not mean that this sequence reflects reality; indeed many marketing decisions are made outside any recognisable framework. However, as a means of understanding the different components, appreciating the way in which they relate to one another and bringing together various aspects for work or for answering examination questions such as those offered by the Chartered Institute of Marketing in the Integrated Marketing Communications paper, this approach has many advantages and has been used by a number of local, national and international organisations.

The MCPF brings together the various elements into a logical sequence of activities where the rationale for promotional decisions is built upon information generated at a previous level in the framework.

Marketing communications require the satisfaction of promotional objectives through the explicit and deliberate development of communication strategy. The MCPF will be used to show first the key elements, second some of the linkages and third the integrated approach that is required.

The process of marketing communications, however, is not linear, as depicted in this framework, but integrative and interdependent. To that extent, this approach is a

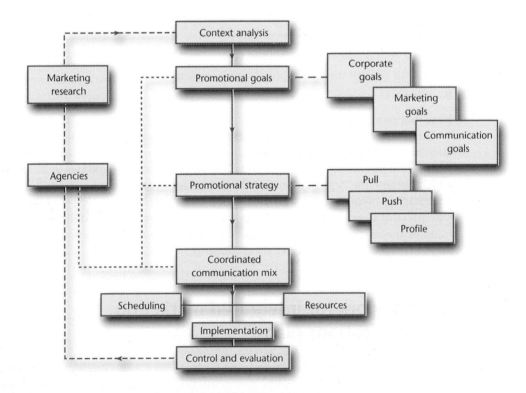

Figure 12.8 The marketing communications planning framework.

The process of marketing communications, however, is not linear, as depicted in this framework, but integrative and interdependent.

recognition of the value of stakeholder theory and of the requirement to build partnerships with buyers and other organisations networked with the organisation.

Other 'decision sequences' have been advanced, in particular one by Rothschild (1987) and another by Engel *et al.* (1994). One of the difficulties associated with their frameworks is that they fail to bring strategy into the development of the promotional mix. Their frameworks rely on the objective and task approach, whereby plans are developed for each of the individual promotional tools, and then aggregated to form strategy.

Another more recent framework is the SOSTAC approach. This is essentially a sound system and moves closer than most of the others to achieving suitable marketing communication plans. However, as the framework is multipurpose and is intended for application to a variety of planning situations, there is a strong danger that the communication focus is lost at the situation analysis phase. This can lead to a reiteration of a SWOT and/or a general marketing plan, with subsequent problems further down the line in terms of the justification and understanding of the communications strategy and promotional mixes that need to be deployed. In addition, the SOSTAC model does not give sufficient emphasis to the need to identify and understand the characteristics of the target audience, which is so important for the development of a coherent marketing communications plan.

The MCPF approach presented here is not intended to solve all the problems associated with such plans, but is robust enough to meet the needs of employers and examiners, and is recommended.

Elements of the plan

Marketing communications plans consist of the elements in the MCPF, as set out in Table 12.3.

Context analysis

The MCPF consists of a number of elements, the first of which is the context analysis (CA). The purpose of compiling a CA is to determine and understand the key market and communication drivers which are likely to influence (or already are influencing) a brand (or organisation) and either help or hinder its progress towards meeting its long-term objectives. This is different from a situation analysis, because the situation

---

Table 12.3   Elements of a marketing communications plan

Context analysis
Promotional objectives
Marketing communications strategy
Promotional mix (methods, tools and media)
Resources (human and financial)
Schedule and Implementation
Evaluation and control

analysis considers a range of wider organisational factors, most of which are normally considered in the development of marketing plans (while the communication focus is lost). Duplication is to be avoided, as it is both inefficient and confusing.

The compilation of a CA is very important, as it presents information and clues about what the promotional plan needs to achieve. Information and market research data about target audiences (their needs, perception, motivation, attitudes and decision-making characteristics), the media and the people they use for information about offerings, the marketing objectives and time-scales, the overall level of financial and other resources that are available, the quality and suitability of agency and other outsourced activities, and the environment in terms of societal, technological, political and economic conditions, both now and at some point in the future, all need to be considered.

At the root of the CA is the marketing plan.

At the root of the CA is the marketing plan. This will already have been prepared and contains important information about the target segment, the business and marketing goals, competitors and the time-scales on which the goals are to be achieved.

The rest of the CA seeks to elaborate and build upon this information so as to provide the detail in order that the plan can be developed and justified.

The CA provides the rationale for the plan. It is from the CA that the marketing objectives (from the marketing plan) and the marketing communications objectives are derived.

The CA provides the rationale for the plan. It is from the CA that the marketing objectives (from the marketing plan) and the marketing communications objectives are derived. The type, form and style of the message are rooted in the characteristics of the target audience, and the media selected to convey messages will be based upon the nature of the tasks, the media habits of the audience and the resources available.

The main components of the context analysis are:

1. *The customer context*
   Segment characteristics
   Levels of awareness, perception and attitudes towards the brand/organisation
   Level of involvement
   Types of perceived risk
   DMU characteristics and issues

2. *The business context*
   Corporate and marketing strategy and plans
   Brand/organisation analysis
   Competitor analysis

3. *The internal context*
   Financial constraints
   Organisation identity
   Culture, values and beliefs
   Marketing expertise
   Agency suitability

4. *The external context*
   Who are the key stakeholders and why are they important?
   What are their communication needs?
   Social, political, economic and technological restraints and opportunities

Promotional objectives

The promotional objectives are drawn from the CA and they should consist of three main elements:

- *Corporate objectives*

  These are derived from the business or marketing plan. They refer to the mission and the business area that the organisation believes it should be in.

- *Marketing objectives*

  These are derived from the marketing plan and are output orientated. Normally these can be considered as sales-related objectives, such as market share, sales revenues, volumes, ROI and profitability indicators.

- *Marketing communication objectives*

  These are derived from an understanding of the current context in which a brand exists and the future context in the form of where the brand is expected to be at some point in the future. These will be presented as awareness levels, perception, comprehension/knowledge, attitudes towards and overall degree of preference for the brand. The choice of communication goal depends upon the tasks that need to be accomplished. In addition, most brands need either to maintain their current brand position or reposition themselves in the light of changing contextual conditions.

These three elements constitute the promotional objectives and they all need to be set out in SMART terminology (see Chapter 13). What also emerges is a refinement to the positioning that managers see as important for success. Obviously, not all plans require express attention to positioning (e.g. government information campaigns) but most commercial and brand-orientated communication programmes need to communicate a clear position in their market. So, at this point the positioning intentions are developed and these will be related to the market, the customers or some other dimension. The justification for this will arise from the CA.

The promotional objectives are drawn from the CA.

Communication strategy

The communication strategy should be customer not method/media orientated. Therefore, the strategy depends upon whether the target audience is a consumer segment, a distributor or dealer network or whether all stakeholders need to be reached. In addition, it is imperative that the strategy be geared to the communication needs of the target audience which is revealed during the customer and business context analyses. This will show what the task is that marketing communications needs to achieve. Having established who the audience is, push-, pull- or profile-dominated strategies can be identified. The next step is to determine the task that needs to be accomplished. This will have been articulated previously in the marketing communications objectives but the approach at this stage is less quantitative and softer. The DRIP roles of marketing communications can be used to suggest the strategy being pursued. For example, if a new brand is being launched, the

The communication strategy should be customer not method/media orientated.

Having established who the audience is, push-, pull- or profile-dominated strategies can be identified.

first task will be to inform and differentiate the brand for members of the trade before using a pull strategy to inform and differentiate the brand for the target end-user customers. An organisation wishing to signal a change of strategy and/or a change of name following a merger or acquisition may choose to use a profile strategy and the primary task will be to inform of the name change. An organisation experiencing declining sales may choose to remind customers of a need or it may choose to improve sales through persuasion.

Promotional methods

Having formulated, stated and justified the required position, the next step is to present the basic form and style of the key message that is to be conveyed. Is there to be a lot of copy or just a little? Is there to be a rational or emotional approach or some weighting between the two? What should be the tone of the visual messages? Is there to be a media blitz (e.g. a Microsoft-type day, as used for the launch of Windows 95, or Cable & Wireless yellow saturation)? It is at this point that those responsible for the development of these plans can be imaginative and try some new ideas. Trying to tie in the message to the strategic orientation is the important part, as the advertising agency will refine and redefine the message and the positioning.

Trying to tie in the message to the strategic orientation is the important part.

From this the promotional mixes need to be considered *for each* of the strategies proposed, that is, a mix for the consumer strategy, a mix for trade strategy and a distinct mix for the communications to reach the wider array of stakeholders.

The choice of promotional methods should clearly state the methods and the media to be used.

The choice of promotional methods should clearly state the methods and the media to be used. A short paragraph justifying the selection is very important, as the use of media in particular is to a large extent dependent upon the nature of the goals, the target audience and the resources. The key is to provide message consistency and a measure of integration.

The schedule

The next step is to schedule the deployment of the methods and the media. This is best achieved by the production of a Gantt chart (see the suggested answer later in the appendices).

Events should be scheduled according to the goals and the strategic thrust. So, if it necessary to communicate with the trade prior to a public launch, those activities tied into the push strategy should be scheduled prior to those calculated to support the pull strategy.

Similarly, if awareness is a goal then, if funds permit, it may be best to use television and posters first before sales promotions (unless sampling is used), direct marketing, point of purchase and personal selling.

Resources

This is a vitally important part of the plan, one that is often avoided or forgotten about. The resources necessary to support the plan need to be determined and these refer not only to the financial issues but to the quality of available marketing expertise and the time that is available to achieved the required outcomes.

Gantt charts and other project planning aids are best used to support this part of the plan. The cost of the media and methods can either be allocated in a right-hand column of the chart, or a new chart can be prepared. Preferably, actual costs should be assigned, although percentages can be allocated if examination time is at a premium. What is of importance is the relative weighting of the costs and that there is a recognition and understanding of the general costs associated with the proposed individual activities.

What is of importance is the relative weighting of the costs and that there is a recognition and understanding of the general costs associated with the proposed individual activities.

It must be understood that a television campaign cannot be run for less than £1.5 million and that the overall cost of the strategy should be in proportion to the size of the client organisation, its (probable) level of profitability and the size and dynamics of the market in which it operates.

Control and evaluation

Unless there is some form of evaluation, there will be no dialogue and no true marketing communications. There are numerous methods to evaluate the individual performance of the tools and the media used, and for examination purposes these should be stated. In addition, and perhaps more meaningfully, the most important measures are the promotional objectives set in the first place. The success of a promotional strategy and the associated plan is the degree to which the objectives set are achieved.

Links and essential points

It was mentioned earlier that there are a number of linkages associated with different parts of the promotional plan. It is important to understand the nature of these links as they represent the interconnections between different parts of the plan and the rationale for undertaking the contextual analysis in particular. The contextual analysis (CA) feeds the items shown in Table 12.4. The promotional objectives derived from the CA feed the items shown in Table 12.5.

Table 12.4 Linkages within the MCPF *(fed by CA)*	
Objectives	From the marketing plan, from the customer, stakeholder network and competitor analysis and from an internal marketing review
Strategic balance between push, pull and profile	From an understanding of the brand, the needs of the target audiences including employees and all other stakeholders and the marketing goals
Brand positioning	From users' and non-users' perceptions, motivations, attitudes and understanding about the brand and its direct and indirect competitors
Message content and style	From an understanding about the level of involvement, perceived risk, DMU analysis, information-processing styles and the positioning intentions
Promotional tools and media	From the target audience analysis of media habits, involvement and preferences, from knowledge about product suitability and media compatibility, from a competitor analysis and from the resource analysis

Table 12.5 The role of promotional objectives

Balance of the promotional strategy
Positioning requirements
Promotional methods in terms of the most appropriate tools and media
Schedule (that is, when particular activities need to be completed)
Evaluation of what was achieved

The promotional strategy is derived from an overall appreciation of the needs of the target audience (and stakeholders) regarding the brand and its competitive position in the market.

To help explain the MCPF and the linkage, a mini-case study follows the Summary and Review Questions. You are required to prepare a marketing communications plan. It is suggested that you prepare one using the material in this chapter as a guide. An answer is provided in Appendix A which you can use to compare with your own response. The prepared answer is not the only possible answer: there are other plans which could be of equal significance and use.

Summary

The development of a marketing communications strategy is important if an organisation is to communicate effectively with its various target audiences. Unlike planning, which is an articulation of strategy, marketing communications needs to be rooted in its target audiences and the task that needs to be completed.

Push, pull and profile strategies can be combined in different ways to meet the needs of different communication tasks. In addition to the broad target, it is important to express strategy in terms of the differentiation (positioning), reminding /reassuring, informing and persuading of audiences.

The marketing communications planning framework offers a sequential format for the development of marketing communication plans. In real life such plans are developed in parallel and involve different individuals and stakeholders in varying degrees. The framework presented here is practical and robust, yet the linear approach should not be accepted without question.

Communication strategy is about the direction and coordination of messages to specific audiences. It is about the delivery of timely, accurate messages that are of significant value for their recipients.

Review questions

1. Write brief notes explaining the role strategy plays in marketing communications.

2. What are the 3Ps of marketing communications strategy? Explain the differences between each of them and use the marketing communications eclipse to support your answer.

3. Compare strategy with planning. In what ways might planning be the same as strategy?

4. Explain the key characteristics associated with a pull strategy.

5. Draw the FCB grid and place on it the following product categories: shampoo, life assurance, sports cars, kitchen towels, box of chocolates.

6. Prepare a report explaining the differences between the Rossiter–Percy and FCB grids.

7. Draw two diagrams depicting the direction of communications in both the push and the pull strategies.

8. Describe what the 'core message' is and provide four examples.

9. Sketch the marketing communications planning framework – from memory.

10. Following on from the previous question, check your version of the MCPF with the original and then prepare some bullet-point notes, highlighting the critical linkages between the main parts of the framework.

MINI CASE

Porridge matters

Alternative Health Foods Ltd (AHF) was formed in the early 1980s when the F-Plan diet was first spawned on a wave of publicity. The high level of interest shown by the public in fibre, oat and natural products (such as All-Bran) spurred Roger Tomkinson to develop his own cereal mixes for his family and then local consumption. Using a high proportion of various natural ingredients, many locally sourced, he developed a small range of cereal mixes.

He was soon encouraged to supply local health food shops with small quantities of three of his cereal mixes. From this point AHF has grown substantially and is now a major supplier of cereals to health food shops, chemists and a number of hotels.

The cereal products are sold under the Rainbow Foods brand and all are made from natural ingredients, with no additives or preservatives. Many of the ingredients are sourced in the UK. The breakfast cereal range consists of four main products: three muesli and one porridge mix. The three muesli are Natural (sweet), Organic (low salt and sugar) and Coated (honey clusters). A range of cereal bars has also been developed successfully under the Snappy brand. All products command a premium price, which is consistent with their position in the health foods sector.

The cereals are packaged in recycled cardboard containers with simple and straightforward labels in toning green, beige and other natural colours.

AHF also supplies a range of own-label products for many of the main supermarket multiples. The ingredients for the own-label products are significantly different from those for the branded market. The own-label muesli mixes need fewer ingredients but have to be either richer or stronger in taste. Prices are much lower on the own-label range, reflected in a 30% margin compared with 65% earned on the branded 'Rainbow Foods' range sold into the chemists and health food shops.

Turnover reached £22 million last year and profitability was a respectable 12%. Market share in the breakfast cereal market had reached 8% and it had been clearly articulated by the directors that this was expected to rise over the next three years (to 12%) as the company prepared to grow organically and through acquisition. Promotional expenditure was approximately 7% of turnover.

Currently the branded products are supplied to approximately 2,300 independent retail outlets throughout the UK. These are a mix of health food shops, independent chemists and hotels. Many of the hotels supplied are located in metropolitan areas, in contrast to the chemists and health food shops, which are often located close together in the same street in suburban areas.

Own-label products are distributed to 18 accounts in the UK. There are some export sales to Europe, looked after by a Swiss agent who has substantial contacts in the French, Swiss and German supermarket businesses.

Consumer research indicated that Rainbow muesli was perceived as a high-quality brand by muesli users. Fifty-two per cent of all muesli users are aware of the Rainbow brand, however, levels of awareness in non-user segments were low. Current consumers are mainly women, in the 40–60 age band, well educated, ABC1, with an active interest in healthy foods. Their slightly conservative approach to life was reflected in their comfortable lifestyle and their dietary need to eat muesli and similar nutritious foods.

The market was changing, however, as an increase in consumption of muesli by younger people, mainly in the 18–35 band, had been detected. Some were interested in the health aspect but others in this emerging segment saw the value for money associated with muesli products. As a number commented at a series of focus groups 'not only was it good for you, but it is quick to prepare, fills you up and can be eaten at any time'. A report in a Sunday paper commented that a number of television advertisements for different snack foods were stressing speed and satisfaction and were obviously targeted at young and busy executives.

Recently, a government report found that the food content in most packaged breakfast cereals was so low as to be of little or no value. Some commentators revived the old joke that the cardboard container was more nutritious than the contents. At around the same time, however, reports from the USA were suggesting that a high intake of oats was an important factor in preventing certain diseases and had been shown to speed recovery from illness and major operations.

After much discussion and consultation, AHF decided that the Rainbow brand should be repositioned to appeal to the emerging younger market. In the short term, however, the brand should not be positioned so as to alienate current customers.

References

Anderson, Q. (2000) Anderson on ... corporate branding. *Campaign*, 8 September, p. 39.

Engel, J.F., Warshaw, M.R. and Kinnear, T.C. (1994) *Promotional Strategy*, 8th edn. Homewood, IL: Richard D. Irwin.

Gray, R. (2000) The chief encounter. *PR Week*, 8 September, pp. 13–16.

Grunig, J. and Hunt, T. (1994) *Managing Public Relations*. New York: Holt, Rineholt & Winston.

Joyce, T. (1991) Models of the advertising process. *Marketing and Research Today* (November), pp. 205–12.

Killgren, L. (1996) The hole story. *Marketing Week*, 11 October, pp. 93–4.

Rossiter, J.R. and Percy, L. (1997) *Advertising, Communications and Promotion Management*, 2nd edn. New York: McGraw-Hill.

Rossiter, J.R., Percy, L. and Donovan, R.J. (1991) A better advertising planning grid. *Journal of Advertising Research* (October/November), pp. 11–21.

Rothschild, M. (1987) *Marketing Communications*. Lexington, MA: DC Heath.

Rowe, A.J., Mason, R.O., Dickel, K.E., Mann, R.B. and Mockler, R.J. (1994) *Strategic Management: A Methodological Approach*, 4th edn. Reading, MA: Addision–Wesley.

Vaughn, R. (1980) How advertising works: a planning model. *Journal of Advertising Research* (October), pp. 27–33.

13

Promotional objectives and positioning

The formal setting of promotional objectives is important because they provide guidance concerning what is to be achieved and when. These objectives form a pivotal role between the business/marketing plans and the marketing communications strategy.

▨ AIMS AND OBJECTIVES

The aims of this chapter are to establish the nature and importance of the role that objectives play in the formulation of promotional strategies and to explore the concept of positioning.

The objectives of this chapter are:

1. To examine the need for organisational objectives.

2. To set out the different types of organisational goals.

3. To specify the relationship between corporate strategy and promotional objectives.

4. To determine the components of promotional objectives.

5. To examine the differences between sales- and communication-based objectives.

6. To evaluate the concept of positioning.

7. To explore the technique of perceptual mapping.

8. To understand and determine various positioning strategies.

▨ Introduction

There are many different opinions about what it is that marketing communications seek to achieve. The conflicting views have led some practitioners and academics to polarise their thoughts about what constitutes an appropriate set of objectives. First, much effort and time has been spent trying to determine what promotion and marketing communication activities are supposed to achieve in the first place. Second, how should the success of a campaign be evaluated? Finally, how is it best to determine the degree of investment that should be made in each of the areas of the promotional mix? The process of resolving these different demands that are placed upon organisations has made the setting of promotional objectives very complex and difficult. It has been termed 'a job of creating order out of chaos' (Kriegel, 1986).

This perceived complexity has led a large number of managers to fail to set promotional objectives. Many of those that do set them do so in such a way that they are

The most common promotional objectives set by managers are sales related.

inappropriate, inadequate or merely restate the marketing objectives. The most common promotional objectives set by managers are sales related. These include increases in market share, return on investment, sales volume increases and improvements in the value of sales made after accounting for the rate of inflation.

Such a general perspective ignores the influence of the other elements of the marketing mix and implicitly places the entire responsibility for sales performance with the promotional mix. This is not an accurate reflection of the way in which businesses and organisations work. In addition, because sales tests are too general, they would be an insufficiently rigorous test of promotional activity and there would be no real evaluation of promotional activities. Sales volumes vary for a wide variety of reasons:

1. Competitors change their prices. *activities*
2. Buyers' needs change.
3. Changes in legislation may favour the strategies of particular organisations.
4. Favourable third-party communications become known to significant buyers.
5. General economic conditions change.
6. Technological advances facilitate improved production processes, economies of scale, experience effects and, for some organisations, the opportunity to reduce costs.
7. The entry and exit of different competitors.

These are a few of the many reasons why sales might increase and conversely why sales might decrease. Therefore, the notion that marketing communications are entirely responsible for the sales of an offering is clearly unacceptable, unrealistic and incorrect.

The role of objectives in corporate strategy

Objectives play an important role in the activities of individuals, social groups and organisations because of the following:

1. They provide direction and an action focus for all those participating in the activity.
2. They provide a means by which the variety of decisions relating to an activity can be made in a consistent way.

3. They determine the time period in which the activity is to be completed.

4. They communicate the values and scope of the activity to all participants.

5. They provide a means by which the success of the activity can be evaluated.

It is generally accepted that the process of developing corporate strategy demands that a series of objectives be set at different levels within an organisation (Thompson, 1990; Greenley, 1989). This hierarchy or objective consists of mission, strategic business unit (SBU) or business objectives and functional objectives, such as production, finance or marketing goals.

The first level in the hierarchy (mission) requires that an overall direction be set for the organisation. If strategic decisions are made to achieve corporate objectives, both objectives and strategy are themselves constrained by an organisation's mission. Mission statements are 'management's vision of what the organisation is trying to do and to become over the long term' (Thompson and Strickland, 1990). A mission statement outlines who the organisation is, what it does and where it is headed. A clearly developed, articulated and communicated mission statement enables an organisation to define whose needs are to be satisfied, what needs require satisfying and which products and technologies will be used to provide the desired levels of satisfaction.

Mission statements are 'management's vision of what the organisation is trying to do and to become over the long term'.

a|ca

Conventionally, setting the mission answers the question 'What business are we in?' (Levitt, 1960). Obvious answers such as 'engineering', 'food processing', 'import and export' or 'retailing' miss the point. These are merely activities. Missions must be linked, explicitly, first and foremost to the needs met, rather than to markets or industries (Rosen, 1995). According to IBM, its original success was tied to its founder's principle of 'offering the best customer service in the world', not to technological innovation.

The mission then, should clearly identify the following:

1. The customers/buyers to be served.

2. The needs to be satisfied.

3. The products and/or technologies by which these will be achieved.

In some organisations these points are explicitly documented in a mission statement. These statements often include references to the organisation's philosophy, culture, commitment to the community and employees, growth, profitability and so on, but these should not blur or distract attention from the organisation's basic mission. The words mission and vision are often used interchangeably, but they have separate meanings. Vision refers to the expected or desired outcome of carrying out the mission over the agreed period of time.

Vision refers to the expected or desired outcome of carrying out the mission over the agreed period of time.

The mission (see Chapter 5) provides a framework for the organisation's objectives, and the objectives that follow should promote and be consistent with the mission.

While the word 'mission' implies a singularity of purpose, organisations have multiple objectives because of the many aspects of the organisation's performance and behaviour that contribute to the mission, and should, therefore, be explicitly identified. However, as

Organisations have multiple objectives because of the many aspects of the organisation's performance and behaviour that contribute to the mission.

Rosen points out, many of these objectives will conflict with each other. In retailing, for example, if an organisation chooses to open larger stores, then total annual profit should rise, but average profit per square metre will probably fall. Short-term profitability can be improved by reducing investment, but this could adversely affect long-term profitability. Organisations therefore have long-term and short-term objectives.

At the SBU level, objectives represent the translation of the mission into a form that can be understood by relevant stakeholders. These objectives are the performance requirements for the organisation or unit and these in turn are broken down into objectives or targets that each functional area must achieve, as their contribution to the unit objectives. Marketing strategies are functional strategies, as are the strategies for the finance, human resource management and production departments. Combine or aggregate them and the SBU's overall target will, in reductionist theory, be achieved.

The various organisational objectives are of little use if they are not communicated to those who need to know what they are. Traditionally, such communication has focused upon employees, but there is increasing recognition that the other members of the stakeholder network need to understand an organisation's purpose and objectives. The marketing objectives developed for the marketing strategy provide important information for the communications strategy. Is the objective to increase market share or to defend or maintain the current situation? Is the product new or established? Is it being modified or slowly withdrawn? The corporate image is shaped partly by the organisation's objectives and the manner in which they are communicated. All these impact upon the objectives of the communications plan.

Promotional objectives consist of three main components.

Promotional objectives consist of three main components. The first component concerns issues relating to the buyers of the product or service offered by the organisation. The second concerns issues relating to sales volume, market share, profitability and revenue. The third stream relates to the image, reputation and preferences that other stakeholders have towards the organisation. Each of these three streams is developed later in this chapter.

The role of promotional objectives and plans

Many organisations, including some advertising agencies, fail to set realistic (if any) promotional objectives. There are several explanations for this behaviour, but one of the common factors is that managers are unable to differentiate between the value of promotion as an expenditure and as an investment. This issue was addressed earlier (Chapter 8), but for now the value of promotional objectives can be seen in terms of the role they play in communications planning, evaluation and brand development.

The setting of promotional objectives is important for three main reasons. The first is that they provide *a means of communication and coordination* between groups (e.g. client and agency) working upon different parts of a campaign. Performance is improved if there is common understanding about the tasks the promotional tools have to accomplish. Secondly, objectives constrain the number of options available to an organisation. As Rothschild (1987) says, 'the key is to eliminate those strategies that have no chance of allowing the firm to meet its objectives'.

Promotional objectives act as a guide for decision-making and provide a focus for decisions that follow in the process of developing promotional plans.

Promotional objectives act as *a guide for decision-making* and provide a focus for decisions that follow in the process of developing promotional plans. The third reason is that objectives provide *a benchmark* so that the relative success or failure of a programme can be determined.

There is no doubt that organisations need to be flexible to be able to anticipate and adjust to changes in their environments. This principle applies to the setting of promotional objectives. To set one all-encompassing objective and expect it to last the year (or whatever period is allocated) is both hopeful and naive; multiple objectives are necessary.

The content of promotional objectives has also been the subject of considerable debate. Two distinct schools of thought emerge: those that advocate sales-related measures as the main factors and those that advocate communication-related measures as the main orientation.

The sales school

As stated earlier, many managers see sales as the only meaningful objective for promotional plans. Their view is that the only reason an organisation spends money on promotion is to sell its product or service. Therefore, the only meaningful measure of the effectiveness of the promotional spend is in the sales results.

These results can be measured in a number of different ways. Sales turnover is the first and most obvious factor particularly in business-to-business markets. In consumer markets and the fast-moving consumer goods sector, market share movement is measured regularly and is used as a more sensitive barometer of performance. Over the longer term, return on investment measures are used to calculate success and failure. In some sectors the number of products sold (or cases), or volume of product shifted, relative to other periods of activity, is a common measure.

Sales result from a variety of influences.

There are a number of difficulties with this view. One of these has been looked at above, that *sales result from a variety of influences*, such as the other marketing mix elements, competitor actions and wider environmental effects, such as the strength of the currency or the level of interest rates.

A second difficulty rests with the concept of *adstock or carryover*. The impact of promotional expenditure may not be immediately apparent, as the receiver may not enter the market until some later date but the effects of the promotional programme may influence the eventual purchase decision. This means that, when measuring the effectiveness of a campaign, sales results will not always reflect its full impact.

Sales objectives *do little to assist the media planner, copywriters and creative team* associated with the development of the communications programme, despite their inclusion in campaign documents such as media briefs.

Sales-orientated objectives are, however, applicable in particular situations. For example, where direct action is required by the receiver in response to exposure to a message, measurement of sales is justifiable. Such an action, a behavioural response, can be solicited in direct-response advertising. This occurs where the sole communication is through a particular medium, such as television or print.

The retail sector can also use sales measures, and it has been suggested that packaged goods organisations, operating in markets which are mature with established pricing and distribution structures, can build a databank from which it is possible to isolate the advertising effect through sales. For example, Sainsbury's was able to monitor the stock movements of particular ingredients used in its 'celebrity recipe' commercials. This enables it to evaluate the success of particular campaigns and particular celebrities. Its current use of celebrity chef Jamie Oliver is so successful that it can stock ingredients in anticipation of particular advertisements being screened. However, despite this cause-and-effect relationship, it can be argued that this may ignore the impact of changes in competitor actions and changes in the overall environment. Furthermore, the effects of the organisation's own corporate advertising, adstock effects and other family brand promotions need to be accounted for if a meaningful sales effect is to be generated.

This may ignore the impact of changes in competitor actions and changes in the overall environment.

The sales school advocates the measure on the grounds of simplicity. Any manager can utilise the tool, and senior management does not wish to be concerned with information which is complex or unfamiliar, especially when working to short lead times and accounting periods. It is a self-consistent theory, but one that may misrepresent consumer behaviour and the purchase process (perhaps unintentionally), and to that extent may result in less than optimal expenditure on marketing communications.

The communications school

There are many situations, however, where the aim of a communications campaign is to enhance the image or reputation of an organisation or product. Sales are not regarded as the only goal. Consequently, promotional efforts are seen as communication tasks, such as the creation of awareness or positive attitudes towards the organisation or product. To facilitate this process, receivers have to be given relevant information before the appropriate decision processes can develop and purchase activities established as a long-run behaviour.

Sales are not regarded as the only goal.

Various models have been developed to assist our understanding about how these promotional tasks are segregated and organised effectively. AIDA and other hierarchy of effects models are considered in Chapter 20 at some length and need not be repeated here. However, one particular model was developed deliberately to introduce clear objectives into the advertising development process: Dagmar.

Dagmar

Russell Colley (1961) developed a model for setting advertising objectives and measuring the results. This model was entitled 'Defining Advertising Goals for Measured Advertising Results – Dagmar'. Colley's rationale for what is effectively a means of setting communications-orientated objectives was that advertising's job, purely and simply, is to communicate to a defined audience information and a frame of mind that stimulates action. Advertising succeeds or fails depending on how well it communicates the desired information and attitudes to the right people at the right time and at the right cost.

Advertising succeeds or fails depending on how well it communicates the desired information and attitudes to the right people at the right time and at the right cost.

Colley proposed that the communications task be based on a hierarchical model of the communications process: awareness – comprehension – conviction – action.

Awareness

Awareness of the existence of a product or an organisation is necessary before purchase behaviour can be expected. Once awareness has been created in the target audience, it should not be neglected. If there is neglect, the audience may become distracted by competing messages and the level of awareness of the focus product or organisation may decline. Awareness, therefore, needs to be created, developed, refined or sustained, according to the characteristics of the market and the particular situation facing an organisation at any one point in time (Figure 13.1).

In situations where the buyer experiences high involvement and is fully aware of a product's existence, attention and awareness levels need only be sustained, and efforts need to be applied to other communication tasks, which may be best left to the other elements of the communications mix. For example, sales promotion and personal selling are more effective at informing, persuading and provoking purchase of a new car once advertising has created the necessary levels of awareness.

Where low levels of awareness are found, getting attention needs to be a prime objective so that awareness can be developed in the target audience.

Where low levels of awareness are found, getting attention needs to be a prime objective so that awareness can be developed in the target audience.

Where low involvement exists, the decision-making process is relatively straightforward. With levels of risk minimised, buyers with sufficient levels of awareness may be prompted into purchase with little assistance of the other elements of the mix. Recognition and recall of brand names and corporate images are felt by some (Rossiter and Percy, 1987) to be sufficient triggers to stimulate a behavioural response. The requirement in this situation would be to refine and strengthen the level of awareness in order that it provokes interest and stimulates a higher level of involvement during recall or recognition.

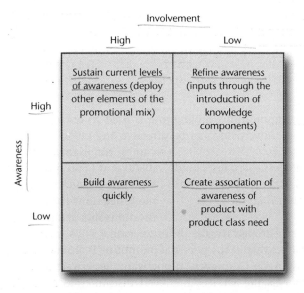

Figure 13.1   Awareness grid.

Where low levels of awareness are matched by low involvement, the prime objective has to be to create awareness of the focus product in association with the product class.

It is not surprising that organisations use awareness campaigns and invest a large amount of their resources in establishing their brand or corporate name. Many brands seek to establish 'top of mind awareness' as one of their primary objectives for their advertising spend.

Comprehension

Awareness on its own is, invariably, not enough to stimulate purchase activity. Knowledge about the product (or what the organisation does) is necessary, and this can be achieved by providing specific information about key brand attributes. These attributes and their associated benefits may be key to the buyers in the target audience or may be key because the product has been adapted or modified in some way. This means that the audience needs to be educated about the change and shown how their use of the product may be affected. For example, in attempting to persuade people to try a different brand of mineral water, it may be necessary to compare the product with other mineral water products and provide an additional usage benefit, such as environmental claims.

Awareness on its own is, invariably, not enough to stimulate purchase activity.

Conviction

Having established that a product has particular attributes which lead to benefits perceived by the target audience as important, it is then necessary to establish a sense of conviction. By creating interest and preference, buyers are moved to a position where they are convinced that one particular product in the class should be tried at the next opportunity. To do this, the audience's beliefs about the product need to be moulded, and this can be accomplished by using messages that demonstrate a product's superiority over its main rival or by emphasising the rewards conferred as a result of using the product, for example, the reward of social acceptance associated with many fragrance, fashion clothing and accessory advertisements, and the reward of self-gratification associated with many confectionery messages (Cadbury's Flake).

High-involvement decisions are best supported with personal selling and sales promotion activities, in an attempt to gain conviction. Low-involvement decisions rely on the strength of advertising messages, packaging and sales promotion to secure conviction.

Action

A communications programme is used to encourage buyers to engage in purchase activity. Advertising can be directive and guide buyers into certain behavioural outcomes, for example, to the use of toll-free numbers (0800 and 0500 in the UK), direct mail activities and reply cards and coupons. However, for high-involvement decisions the most effective tool in the communications mix at this stage in the hierarchy is personal selling. Through the use of interpersonal skills, buyers are more likely to want to buy a product than if the personal prompting is absent. The use of direct marketing activities by Avon Cosmetics, Tupperware, Betterware and suppliers of life assurance and double-glazing services has been instrumental in the sales growth experienced by organisations in these markets. Colley's dissatisfaction with the way in which adver-

Through the use of interpersonal skills, buyers are more likely to want to buy a product than if the personal prompting is absent.

tising agencies operated led him to specify the components of a good advertising objective: 'A specific communications task to be accomplished among a defined audience to a given degree in a given period of time'. An analysis of this statement shows that it is made up of four distinct elements:

1. A need to specify the communications task.
2. A need to define the audience.
3. A need to state the required degree of change.
4. A need to establish the time period in which the activity is to occur.

Colley's statement is very clear – it is measurable and of assistance to copywriters. Indeed, Dagmar revolutionised the approach taken by advertisers to the setting of objectives. It helped to move attention from the sales effect to the communication effect school and has led to improved planning processes, as a result partly of a better understanding of advertising and promotional goals.

Many of the difficulties associated with sequential models (Chapter 20) are also applicable to Dagmar. In addition to problems of hierarchical progression, measurement and costs are issues concerning the sales orientation, restrictions upon creativity and short-term accountability.

Sales orientation

This criticism is levelled by those who see sales as the only valid measure of effectiveness. The sole purpose of communication activities, and advertising in particular, is to generate sales. So, as the completion of communications tasks may not result in purchases, the only measure that need be undertaken is that of sales. This point has been discussed earlier and need not be reproduced here.

Restrictions upon creativity

Dagmar is criticised on the grounds that creative flair can be lost as attention passes from looking for the big idea to concentration upon the numbers game, of focusing on measures of recall, attitude change and awareness. It is agreed that the creative personnel are held to be more accountable under Dagmar and this may well inhibit some of their work. Perhaps the benefits of providing direction and purpose offset the negative aspects of a slight loss in creativity.

Short-term accountability

To the above should be added the time period during which management and associated agencies are required to account for their performance. With accounting periods being reduced to as little as 12 weeks, the communications approach is impractical for two reasons. The first is that the period is not long enough for all of the communication tasks to be progressed or completed. Sales measures present a much more readily digestible benchmark of performance.

The second concerns the unit of performance itself. With the drive to be efficient and to be able to account for every communication pound spent, managers themselves need to use measures that they can understand and which they can interpret from published data. Sales data and communications spend data are consistent measures and make no further demands on managers. Managers do not have enough time to spend analysing levels of comprehension or preference and to convert them into formats that are going to be of direct benefit to them and their organisations. Having said that, those organisations that are prepared to invest in a more advanced management information system will enable a more sophisticated view to be taken.

The communication school approach is not accepted by some, who argue that it is too difficult and impractical to translate a sales objective into a series of specific communications objectives. Furthermore, what actually constitutes adequate levels of awareness and comprehension and how can it be determined which stage the majority of the target audience has reached at any one point in time? Details of measurement, therefore, throw a veil over the simplicity and precision of the approach taken by the communication orientation school.

Some argue that it is too difficult and impractical to translate a sales objective into a series of specific communications objectives.

From a practical perspective, it should be appreciated that most successful marketing organisations do not see the sales and communications schools as mutually exclusive. They incorporate both views and weight them according to the needs of the current task, their overall experience, the culture and style of the organisation and the agencies with whom they operate.

Derivation of promotional objectives

It has been established that specific promotional objectives need to be set up if a suitable foundation is to be laid for the many communication decisions that follow. Promotional objectives are derived from understanding the overall context in which the communications will operate. Comprehending the contexts of the buyer and the organisation allows the objectives of the planned communications to be identified: the *what* that is to be achieved. For example, objectives concerning the perception that different target customers have of a brand, the perception that members of a performance network have of the organisation's offerings, the reactions of key stakeholders to previous communications and the requirements of the current marketing plan all impact upon the objectives of the communication plan. Therefore, promotional objectives evolve principally from a systematic audit and analysis of the key communication contexts, and specifically from the marketing plan and stakeholder analysis.

Promotional objectives evolve principally from a systematic audit and analysis of the key communication contexts, and specifically from the marketing plan and stakeholder analysis.

It was established earlier that there are three main streams of objectives. These are set out in Figure 13.2. The first concerns issues relating to the buyers of the product or service offered by the organisation. The second concerns issues relating to market share/sales volume, profitability and revenue. The third stream relates to the image, reputation and preferences that other stakeholders have towards the organisation.

All these objectives are derived from an analysis of the current situation. The marketing communication brief which flows from this analysis should specify the sales-related objectives to be achieved, as these can be determined from the marketing plan. Sales-related objectives might concern issues such as market share and sales volume.

Customer-related objectives concern issues such as awareness, perception, attitude, feelings and intentions towards a brand or product. The exact issue to be addressed in the plan is calculated by analysing the contextual information driven by the audit.

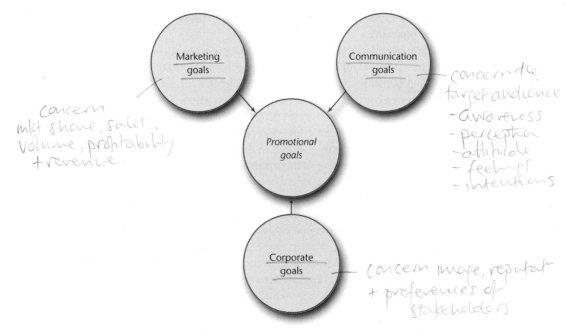

[handwritten annotation left: Concern mkt share, sales volume, profitability + revenue.]

[handwritten annotation right: concern the target audience
- awareness
- perception
- attitude
- feelings
- intentions]

[handwritten annotation lower right: concern image, reputation + preferences of stakeholders]

Figure 13.2   Three principal topics for promotional objective setting.

Issues related to the perception of the organisation are often left unattended or, worse, ignored. Research may indicate that the perception of particular stakeholders, in either the performance or the support network, does not complement the current level of corporate performance or may be misplaced or confused. Objectives will need to be established to correct or reinforce the perception held of the organisation. The degree of urgency may be directly related to the level of confusion or misunderstanding or be related to competitive or strategic actions initiated by competitors and other members of the network. Corporate strategy may have changed and, as identified earlier, any new strategy will need to be communicated to all stakeholders.

The need for realism when setting promotional objectives

Hierarchy of effects models which specify stages of development were first proposed as far back as 1898 by E. St Elmo Lewis (Barry and Howard, 1990) and similar views were expressed by Colley (Dagmar) in 1961. Yet despite the passage of time since their publication, a large number of organisations still either fail to set any promotional objectives or confuse objectives with strategy.

A large number of organisations still either fail to set any promotional objectives or confuse objectives with strategy.

Organisations seeking to coordinate their communications need to recognise the necessity of setting multiple objectives at different times in the campaign period and of being prepared to adjust them in the light of environmental changes. These changes may be due to ever-decreasing product life cycles or technological developments that may give a competitor comparative advantage, and perhaps legislative developments (or the timing of management's interpretation and implementation of certain legislation) may bring about a need to reconfigure the promotional mix.

Management's failure to set objectives is often the result of a lack of awareness of the current position, or a lack of understanding of how and why appropriate objectives need to be established. With increasingly competitive and turbulent environments, a greater number of organisations are turning their attention to ways in which they can communicate more effectively with their stakeholders. Furthermore, as more executives undertake management education programmes, so a higher level of skill is being transferred to organisations, and this in turn will bring a higher incidence of better practice.

The overall objective of any promotional programme is to increase the level of sales. While it seems unreasonable to expect the promotional mix to bear total responsibility for this, it is also unreasonable and impractical to expect the communications approach to bear total responsibility. It is imperative that organisations are willing and prepared to set promotional objectives which utilise basic communications tasks, such as awareness and intentions, and that they utilise sales benchmarks as means of determining what has been achieved and how. Promotional objectives are a derivative of both marketing and corporate strategies. Just as revenue and income targets are part of marketing strategy, so they should form part of the promotional objectives. They cannot be separated and they cannot be neglected.

Figure 13.2 shows the different types of objectives that can be set for a promotional strategy. The choice depends on the situation facing each manager and, in particular, whether the product or organisation is new. Establishing and maintaining levels of awareness is, however, paramount to any communications programme, and must be considered one of the primary communication objectives.

Promotional objectives need to be set which reflect the communication and sales tasks that the product or organisation needs to accomplish. It should be appreciated that promotional objectives are vitally important, as they provide the basis for a string of decisions that are to be taken at subsequent stages in the development of the communication plan.

Promotional objectives need to be set which reflect the communication and sales tasks that the product or organisation needs to accomplish.

Management's next task is to make decisions regarding which of these different promotional objectives will receive attention first. In order that decisions can be made regarding promotional strategy, the communications mix and the level of resources allocated to each promotional tool, it is necessary to rank and weight the objectives at this stage in the management process. The criteria used to weight the different objectives will inevitably be subjective. This is because they reflect each manager's perception, experience and interpretation of his or her environment. However, it is also his or her skill and judgement that are the important elements, and as long as the criteria are used and applied in a consistent manner the outcome of the communication plan is more likely to be successful.

SMART objectives

To assist managers in their need to develop suitable objectives, a set of guidelines has been developed, commonly referred to as SMART objectives. This acronym stands for specific, measurable, achievable, relevant, targeted and timed.

The process of making objectives SMART requires management to consider exactly what is to be achieved, when, where, and with which audience. This clarifies thinking, sorts out the logic of the proposed activities and provides a clear measure for evaluation at the end of the campaign:

- *Specific*

  What is the actual variable that is to be influenced in the campaign? Is it awareness, perception, attitudes or some other element that is to be influenced? Whatever the variable, it must be clearly defined and must enable precise outcomes to be determined.

- *Measurable*

  Set a measure of activity against which performance can be assessed. For example, this may be a percentage level of desired prompted awareness in the target audience.

- *Achievable*

  Objectives need to be attainable, otherwise those responsible for their achievement will lack motivation and a desire to succeed.

- *Realistic*

  The actions must be founded in reality and be relevant to the brand and the context in which they are set.

- *Targeted and timed*

  Which target audience is the campaign targeted at, how precisely is the audience defined and over what period are the results to be generated?

For example, Argos might have set the following marketing communication objective when launching its credit/loyalty card into the UK market. This goal is realistic, bearing in mind the marketing pedigree and resources available to Argos and its parent company, Great Universal Stores.

> *The marketing communications objective for the period October to March 2000 (timed) is to create 85% (measurable and achievable) prompted awareness (specific) of current female customers, in the 24 to 45 year old age group and earning £15,000 plus (targeted).*

Having determined what levels of awareness, comprehension or preference are necessary or how attitudes need to be developed, the establishment or positioning of these objectives as a task for the organisation to accomplish should be seen as a primary communication objective. The attitude held or what individuals in the target market perceive, comprehend or prefer is a focus for campaign activity and subsequent evaluation.

Positioning: an introduction

The final act in the target marketing process of segmentation and targeting is positioning. Following on from the identification of potential markets, determining the size and potential of market segments and selecting specific target markets, positioning is the process whereby information about the organisation or product is communicated in such a way that the object is perceived by the consumer/stakeholder to be differentiated from the competition, to occupy a particular space in the market. According to Kotler (1997), 'Positioning is the act of designing the company's offering and image so that they occupy a meaningful and distinct competitive position in the target customers' minds'.

This is an important aspect of the positioning concept. Positioning is not about the product but what the buyer thinks about the product or organisation. It is not the

Positioning is not about the product but what the buyer thinks about the product or organisation.

physical nature of the product that is important for positioning, but how the product is perceived that matters. This is why part of the context analysis (Chapter 12), requires a consideration of perception and attitudes and the way stakeholders see and regard brands and organisations. Of course, this may not be the same as the way brand managers intend their brands to be seen or how they believe the brand is perceived.

Attitude research and positioning – Pernod

Following a television-based campaign to position the Pernod brand for the 18–24 year old market, attitude research revealed that the brand would be better suited to an older demographic group. McCawley (2001) reports that a campaign in 2001 was designed to reposition the brand so that it appealed to professionals in their late 20s to mid-30s and complemented their attitude set.

In the consumer market, established brands from washing powders (Ariel, Daz, Persil) and hair shampoos (such as Wash & Go, Timotei), to cars (for example, Peugeot, Saab, Nissan) and grocery multiples (Sainsbury's, Tesco) each carry communications that enable receivers to position them in their respective markets.

The positioning concept is not the sole preserve of branded or consumer-orientated offerings or indeed those of the business-to-business market. Organisations are also positioned relative to one another, mainly as a consequence of their corporate identities, whether they are deliberately managed or not. The position an organisation takes

Organisations are also positioned relative to one another, mainly as a consequence of their corporate identities.

in the mind of consumers may be the only means of differentiating one product from another. King (1991) argues that, given the advancement in technology and the high level of physical and functional similarity of products in the same class, consumers' choices will be more focused on their assessment of the company they are dealing with. Therefore, it is important to position organisations as brands in the minds of actual and potential customers.

One of the crucial differences between the product and the corporate brand is that the corporate brand needs to be communicated to a large array of stakeholders, whereas the product-based brand requires a focus on a smaller range of stakeholders, in particular, the consumers and buyers in the performance network.

Whatever the position chosen, either deliberately or accidentally, it is the means by which customers understand the brand's market position, and it often provides signals to determine a brand's main competitors, or (as is often the case) customers fail to understand the brand or are confused about what the brand stands for.

The development of the positioning concept

This perspective was originally proposed by Ries and Trout (1972). They claimed that it is not what you do to a product that matters; it is what you do to the mind of the prospect that is important. They set out three stages of development: the product era, the image era and the positioning era.

The product era occurred in the late 1950s and early 1960s and existed when each product was promoted in an environment where there was little competition. Each product was accepted as an innovation and was readily accepted and adopted as a natural development. In the pharmaceutical market, drugs such as Navidex, Valium and Lasix became established partly because of the lack of competition and partly because of the ability of the product to fulfil its claims. This was a period when the features and benefits of products were used in communications; the unique selling proposition was of paramount importance.

The image era that followed was spawned by companies with established images, which introduced new me-too products against the original brands. It was the strength of the perceived company image that underpinned the communications surrounding these new brands that was so important to their success. Products such as Amoxil, Tagamet and Tenormin were launched on an image platform.

The positioning era has developed mainly because of the increasingly competitive market conditions, where there is now little compositional, material or even structural difference between products within each class. Consequently, most products are now perceived relative to each other. In most markets the level and intensity of 'noise' drives organisations to establish themselves and their offerings in particular parts of the overall market. It is now the ability of an offering to command the attention of buyers and to communicate information about how an offering is differentiated from the other competitive offerings that helps to signal the relative position the offering occupies in the market.

The positioning concept

All products and all organisations have a position. The position held by each stakeholder can be managed or it can be allowed to drift. An increasing number of organisations are trying to manage the positions occupied by their brands and are using positioning strategies to move to new positions in buyers' minds and so generate an advantage over their competitors. This is particularly important in markets that are very competitive and where mobility barriers (ease of entry and exit to a market, e.g. plant and production costs) are relatively low.

All products and all organisations have a position.

Positioning is about visibility and recognition of what a product/service represents for a buyer. In markets where the intensity of rivalry and competition are increasing and buyers have greater choice, identification and understanding of a product's intrinsic values become critical. Network members have limited capacities, whether this be the level or range of stock they can carry or the amount of available shelf space that can be allocated. An offering with a clear identity and orientation to a particular target segment's needs will not only be stocked and purchased but can warrant a larger margin through increased added value.

Positioning, therefore, is the natural conclusion to the sequence of activities that constitute a core part of the marketing strategy. Market segmentation and target marketing are prerequisites to successful positioning. From the research data and the marketing strategy, it is necessary to formulate a positioning statement that is in tune with the promotional objectives.

One of the roles of marketing communications is to convey information so that the target audience can understand what a brand stands for and differentiate it from other competitor brands. Clear, consistent positioning is an important aspect of integrated marketing communication. So the way in which a brand is presented to its audience determines the way it is going to be perceived. Therefore, accepting that there are extraneous reasons why a brand's perception might not be the same as that intended, it seems important that managers approach the task of positioning task in an attentive and considered manner.

Generally there are two main ways in which a brand can be positioned, these are functional and expressive (or symbolic). Functionally positioned brands stress the features and benefits, and expressive brands emphasise the ego, social and hedonic satisfactions that a brand can bring. Both approaches make a promise, a promise to deliver a whiter, cleaner and brighter soap powder (functional) or clothes that we are confident to hang on the washing line (for all to see), dress our children in and send to school and not feel guilty, or dress ourselves and complete a major business deal (symbolic).

There are two main ways in which a brand can be positioned, these are functional and expressive.

Functional brand positioning – adhesives

Marketing communications in the consumer and trade adhesives market places heavy reliance on demonstrating the performance of the individual brands. Solvite, for example, presents a man glued to a board and suspended in dangerous situations (above sharks, towed into the sky and at a theme park on a 'vertical drop' ride). Another brand, 'No More Nails', uses a similar functional approach. One execution shows a man sitting on a chair that has been glued half-way up a wall inside a house.

Adhesives provoke low-involvement decision-making and there is generally little consumer interest in the properties of each brand. The essential information that consumers require is that the brand has strong performance characteristics. This sets up umbrella brand credibility so that sub-brands for different types of glue are perceived to have the same properties as the umbrella brand and that will do the 'job'. Advertising needs to have dramatic qualities in order to attract attention and to build up a store of images that enable people to recall a brand of adhesives that actually do stick.

Expressive brand positioning – ice-cream

The UK super-premium ice-cream sector was first developed by Haagen Dazs which presented the product as a luxury, fashion-orientated food for adults. The advertising showed partially dressed young adult couples enjoying each other's company and using the ice-cream product as an integral part of their sensual pleasure. The focus was on the couple and their pleasure, with Haagen Dazs as a means by which that pleasure could be fulfilled. Although quality was a central issue, the focus was not on the product, its ingredients or the packaging.

When Ben and Jerry's ice-cream was presented in the UK market it was deliberately positioned so that it did not try to emulate the position adopted by Haagen Dazs. So, rather than stress the values of individuality, quality and sensual pleasure, Ben and Jerry's signalled off-beat humour, variety and social/environmental responsibility. When it was launched, advertising through posters, buses, cinema and even 280,000 postcards in bars and nightclubs in London and the south-east was used to feature humorous cartoon parodies of classic/cult films such as *Jaws*, *King Kong* and *Close Encounters* (Anon, 2000) They sponsored wacky world championships such as gurning, conkers, bog snorkelling and nettle eating. In addition, however, communications surrounding the brand emphasised the importance of being environmentally aware and even developed a brand (Rain Forest Crunch) which used nuts from the Brazilian rain forests to call attention to the need to preserve the rain forests by harvesting them and providing the local inhabitants with an income and incentive to harvest and protect, rather than to destroy their environment.

Both of the leading brands in the super-premium segment use symbolic brand positioning: Haagen Dazs uses sensual pleasure as its main platform and Ben and Jerry's depict themselves as wacky and non-conformist, yet socially aware.

Developing and managing a position

To develop a position, managers should be guided by the following process:

1. Which positions are held by which competitors? This will almost certainly require consumer research to determine attitudes and perceptions and possibly the key attributes that consumers perceive as important. Use perceptual mapping.

2. From the above, will it be possible to determine which position, if any, is already held by the focus brand?

3. From the information gathered so far, will it be possible to determine a positioning strategy, that is, what is the desired position for the brand?

4. Is the strategy feasible in view of the competitors and any budgetary constraints? A long-term perspective is required, as the selected position has to be sustained.

5. Implement a programme to establish the desired position.

6. Monitor the perception held by consumers of the brand, and of their changing tastes and requirements, on a regular basis.

Perceptual mapping

In order to determine how the various offerings are perceived in a market, the key attributes that stakeholders use to perceive products in the market need to be established. A great deal of this work will have been completed as part of the research and review process prior to developing a communications plan. The next task is to determine perceptions and preferences in respect of the key attributes as perceived by buyers.

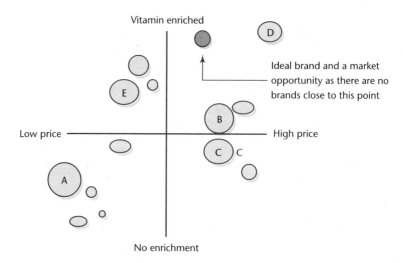

Figure 13.3   A perceptual map for a shampoo market.

The objective of the exercise is to produce a perceptual map (brand and multidimensional maps) where the dimensions used on the two axes are the key attributes, as seen by buyers. This map represents a geometric comparison of how competing products are perceived (Sinclair and Stalling, 1990). Figure 13.3 shows that the key dimensions for consumers in the shampoo market could be price and enrichment. Each product is positioned on the map according to the perception that buyers have of the strength of each attribute of each product. By plotting the perceived positions of each brand on the map, an overall perspective of the market can be developed.

The closer products are clustered together, the greater the competition. The further apart the positions, the greater the opportunity to enter the market, as competition is less intense. From the map, it can be seen that brand A dominates the bottom left-hand sector where a low price and little enrichment have attracted a number of buyers and competitive brands. Brands B and C are in direct competition, positioned closely together on a fairly high price yet medium level of enrichment.

Each product is positioned on the map according to the perception that buyers have of the strength of each attribute of each product.

Brand D is isolated and may need to be repositioned as it may start losing share to a competitor, especially if the ideal position is occupied by B or any of the brands clustered around brand E.

Substitute products are often uncovered by their closeness to each other (Day *et al.*, 1979). It is also possible to ask buyers and other stakeholders what an ideal brand would consist of. This perfect brand can then be positioned on the map, and the closer an offering is to the ideal point, the greater its market share should be, as it is preferred more than its rivals. These maps are known as preference maps.

By superimposing the position of an ideal brand on the map, it is possible to extend the usefulness of the tool. Perceptions of what constitutes the right amount of each key attribute can assist management in the positioning exercise. Marketing communications can, therefore, be designed to convey the required information about each attribute and so adjust buyers' perceptions so that they are closer to the ideal position, or to the position on the map that management wants the brand to occupy. For example, brand C may wish to reposition by changing the perception that users have of the quality of the shampoo. Following any necessary adjustments to the product, marketing communications would emphasise the enrichment atribute and hope to move it away from any association with brand B.

Neal (1980) offered the following reasons why perceptual mapping is such a powerful tool for examining the position of products:

1. It develops understanding of how the relative strengths and weaknesses of different products are perceived by buyers.

2. It builds knowledge about the similarities and dissimilarities between competing products.

3. It assists the process of repositioning existing products and the positioning of new products.

4. The technique helps to track the perception that buyers have of a particular product, and assists the measurement of the effectiveness of communication programmes and marketing actions, intended to change buyers' perceptions.

Perceptual mapping is an important tool in the development and tracking of promotional strategy. It enables brand managers to identify gaps and opportunities in the market and allows organisations to monitor the effects of past marketing communications. For example, in the early 1980s, none of the available brands in the newly emerging lager market was seen as refreshing. All brands were perceived as virtually the same. Heineken saw the opportunity and seized the position for refreshment, and has been able to occupy and sustain the position since then.

Positioning strategies

The development of positions which buyers can relate to and understand is an important and vital part of the marketing communications plan. In essence, the position adopted is a statement about what the brand is, what it stands for and the values and beliefs that customers (hopefully) will come to associate with the particular brand. The visual images or the position statement represented in the strapline may be a significant trigger which buyers use to recall images and associations of the brand.

The visual images or the position statement represented in the strapline may be a significant trigger which buyers use to recall images and associations of the brand.

There are a number of overall approaches to developing a position. These can be based on factors such as the market, the customer or redefining the appeal of the brand itself; see Table 13.1.

To implement these three broad approaches, various strategies have been developed. The list that follows is not intended to be comprehensive or to convey the opinion that these strategies are discrete. They are presented here as means of conveying the strategic style, but in reality a number of hybrid strategies are often used.

Product features

This is one of the easier concepts and one that is more commonly adopted. The brand is set apart from the competition on the basis of the attributes, features or benefits that the brand has relative to the competition. For example, Volvos are safe; Weetabix contains

Table 13.1   Positioning approaches

Approach	Type of application
Market related	*First into a market* Heineken was first to take the refreshment position *Redefine the market* AA repositioned itself as the fourth emergency service Miller Lite said the *lite* meant not heavy, not low alcohol
Customer related	*A unique buying reason* Fairy Liquid cleans 50% more dishes, so lasts longer and provides greater value *Particular type of buyer* Tia Maria became a girl's magic password rather than just a drink to be consumed on special occasions
Appeal related	*Distinct personality* Pepperami became a crazy/mad 'bit of an animal' *Decision criteria* Virgin Upper Class was presented as a sensible rational business decision, not a whim or a risk *Imaginative or interesting* Castrol made oil into liquid engineering Lil-lets are discreet, just like the advertising

all the vitamins needed each day; and the Royal Bank of Scotland promotes its credit card by extolling the benefits of its interest rate compared with those of its competitors.

Price/quality

This strategy is more effectively managed than others because price itself can be a strong communicator of quality. A high price denotes high quality, just as a low price can deceive buyers into thinking a product to be of low quality and poor value. Retail outlets such as Harrods and Aspreys use high prices to signal high quality and exclusivity. At the other end of the retail spectrum, Littlewood's, BHS and Woolworth's position themselves to attract those with less disposable income and to whom convenience is of greater importance. The price/quality appeal is best observed in Sainsbury's, 'where good food costs less' and with the alcoholic lager Stella Artois, which is positioned as 'refreshingly expensive'.

The price/quality appeal is best observed in Sainsbury's, 'where good food costs less' and with the alcoholic lager Stella Artois, which is positioned as 'refreshingly expensive'.

Use

By informing markets of when or how a product can be used, a position can be created in the minds of the buyers. For example, Kellogg's, the breakfast cereal manufacturer, has repositioned itself as a snack food provider. Its marketing strategy of moving into new markets was founded on its overdependence on breakfast consumption. By becoming associated with snacks, not only is usage increased, but the

Repositioning – Harveys Bristol Cream

Harveys Bristol Cream sherry was for a long time the undisputed UK market leader, but the brand began to experience difficulties at a time when sherry consumption world-wide had fallen by 45% since the late 1970s. This was due primarily to increased competition, new lifestyles and the development of own brands. Indeed, own label claimed 40% market share, and the emergence of a new prime competitor, Croft Original, threatened Harveys' position.

A series of research exercises was undertaken. First, psychological tests indicated that the emotional sensory profile of the brand itself was inhibiting. The taste was not quite right and the packaging evoked negative imagery and product expectations. Consumers 'taste with their eyes', so what they see frames their perception and provides a context within which they experience a brand. Therefore, research suggested a change in the physical product and a change in the packaging.

The challenge was to expand the context for the brand, and this required finding a new position that provoked positive brand associations.

The next stage in the research found that people's perception of sherry as a category of drink inhibited use. What emerged were new ways of drinking sherry – with ice, long or with mixers – and this allowed new usage occasions to be identified. Sherry could now be drunk on occasions when it was socially acceptable to drink, not just at weddings and functions, but at pubs, relaxing at home and generally anywhere where drinking was expected/accepted.

From the data and information collected through focus groups and tastings, a communication hierarchy was developed (Figure 13.4). The left-hand side of the pyramid indicated the current brand image and the right-hand side suggested the new context for the brand. To utilise the brand heritage, an idea emerged to use blue glass for the packaging. This type of glass originated in Bristol and was used to make high-quality products. A smaller version of the current label was transferred and after further extensive research, mainly with brand switchers and the not-so-loyals, a relaunch was confirmed. Saatchi & Saatchi were given a brief and an advertising campaign broke for the Christmas market in 1994 (see Plate 13.1).

Awareness indices have all improved; the bottle is accepted in preference to the original and sales have increased substantially, by 46% at one point. In addition, other objectives have been achieved: margins have improved against Croft and its brand leadership position has been enhanced.

Adapted from Hodder *et al.* (1996)

opportunity to develop new products becomes feasible. The launch of Pop Tarts is a testimony to this strategy. Milky Way, 'the sweet you can eat between meals', informs just when it is permissible to eat chocolate and After Eight chocolate mints clearly indicate when they should be eaten. The hair shampoo Wash & Go positions the brand as a quick and easy to use (convenience) product, for those whose lifestyles are full and demanding.

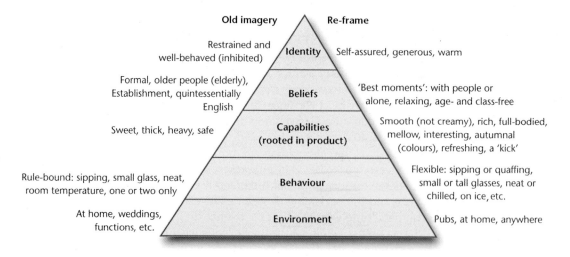

Figure 13.4   Communication hierarchy for Harveys Bristol Cream. From Hodder *et al.* (1996); used with kind permission.

Product class dissociation

Some markets are essentially uninteresting, and most other positions have been adopted by competitors. A strategy used by margarine manufacturers is to disassociate themselves from other margarines and associate themselves with what was commonly regarded as a superior product, butter. The Alliance and Leicester Building Society used to proclaim that 'not all building societies are the same'. The suggestion was that they were different from the rest and hence offered better services and customer care. The moisturising bar Dove is positioned as ' not a soap'.

User

A sensible extension of the target marketing process is to position openly so that the target user can be clearly identified. Flora margarine was for men, and then it became 'for all the family'. American Express uses several leading business celebrities, including Sir Terence Conran and Anita Roddick, to suggest that users can have a lifestyle profile that complements those who use and endorse the Amex card. Some hotels position themselves as places for weekend breaks, as leisure centres or as conference centres. Le Creuset has recently repositioned itself to appeal to a younger customer segment (see Exhibit 13.1).

Le Creuset has recently repositioned itself to appeal to a younger customer segment.

Competitor

For a long time, positioning oneself against a main competitor was regarded as dangerous and was avoided. Avis, however, performed very successfully 'trying even harder' against Hertz, the industry number one. Saab contested the 'safest car' position with Volvo and Qualcast took on its new rival, the hover mower, by informing everyone that 'it is a lot less bovver than a hover', because its product collected the grass

Exhibit 13.1   Le Creuset repositioned for a younger market. Picture reproduced with the kind permission of Le Creuset.

cuttings and produced the manicured lawn finish that roller-less mowers cannot reproduce.

Benefit

Positions can also be established by proclaiming the benefits that usage confers on those that consume. Sensodyne toothpaste appeals to all those who suffer from sensitive teeth, and a vast number of pain relief formulations claim to smooth away headaches or relieve aching limbs, sore throats or some offending part of the anatomy. Daewoo entered the UK offering car buyers convenience by removing dealerships and the inherent difficulties associated with buying and maintaining cars.

Heritage or cultural symbol

An appeal to cultural heritage and tradition, symbolised by age, particular heraldic devices or visual cues, has been used by many organisations to convey quality, experience and knowledge. Kronenbourg 1664, 'Established since 1803', and the use of coats of arms by many universities to represent depth of experience and a sense of permanence are just some of the historical themes used to position organisations.

Whatever the position adopted by a brand or organisation, both the marketing and promotional mixes must endorse and support the position so that there is consistency throughout all communications. For example, if a high-quality position is taken, such as that of the Ritz Carlton Hotel Group, then the product quality must be relatively high compared with competitors, the price must be correspondingly excessive and distribution synonymous with quality and exclusivity. Sales promotion activity will be minimal so as not to convey a touch of inexpensiveness, and advertising messages should be visually affluent and rich in tone and copy, with public relations and personal selling approaches transmitting high-quality, complementary cues.

The dimensions used to position brands must be relevant and important to the target audience and in the image cues used must be believable and consistently credible.

The dimensions used to position brands must be relevant and important to the target audience and in the image cues used must be believable and consistently credible. Positioning strategies should be developed over the long term if they are to prove effective, although minor adaptions to the position can be carried out in order to reflect changing environmental conditions.

Repositioning

Technology is developing quickly, consumer tastes evolve and new offerings and substitute products enter the market. This dynamic perspective of markets means that the relative positions occupied by offerings in the minds of consumers will be challenged and shifted on a frequent basis. If the position adopted by an offering is strong, if it was the first to claim the position and the position is being continually reinforced with clear simple messages, then there may be little need to alter the position originally adopted.

However, there are occasions when offerings need to be repositioned in the minds of consumers/stakeholders. This may be due to market opportunities and development, mergers and acquisitions or changing buyer preferences, which may be manifested in declining sales. Research may reveal that the current position is either inappropriate or superseded by a competitor, or that attitudes have changed or preferences surpassed; whatever the reason, repositioning is required if past success is to be maintained. However, repositioning is difficult to accomplish, often because of the entrenched perceptions and attitudes held by buyers towards brands.

Repositioning – Shell

In 1999 Shell announced its intention to reposition itself as a new open and socially accountable company. The new position that Shell wanted to own was as an energy company that was committed to sustainable development. One of the ads depicted staff talking about how their work and role within Shell helps to protect the environment. Interactive media, including its Web site, are also used to provoke discussion and debate about environmental issues and stimulate feedback so that the company can continually measure stakeholder feelings and adapt its position accordingly. This represents the two-way symmetric model of public relations (Grunig and Hunt, 1984; see Chapter 26).

Exhibit 13.2   The AA: the fourth emergency service. Picture and material kindly supplied by the Automobile Association.

P&O's positioning with the advent of Le Shuttle and the Channel tunnel was to 'cruise across the channel' and to present the channel crossing cleverly as an integral part of the holiday/travel experience. Another demonstration of the name change position could be observed when Marriott took over Holiday Inn in the United Kingdom. The name Marriott is perceived as a much stronger name than that of Holiday Inn. However, in order to sustain the strength of the name, yet retain the previous Holiday Inn clients who wanted a decent business class hotel but who could not afford the new rates and opulence of Marriott, a new product was created and positioned for this segment, called Courtyard by Marriott.

The need to reposition a brand may be stimulated because of the actions of a major competitor. The United Kingdom's car recovery and driver support service market is dominated by two mainstream organisations, the AA and the RAC. In the early 1990s the AA tried to reposition itself away from the RAC as the market became increasingly cluttered, more competitive and depressed as consumer spending became constricted with the recession. The RAC then positioned itself as the 'knights of the road', with all the heroic rescue overtones that a knight confers, while the AA, having tried to be seen as a 'a very, very nice man', portrayed itself as highly professional and demanding high standards, since a vehicle breakdown was regarded as an emergency similar in scale to that requiring the assistance of the fire, police or ambulance services. AA's new position, 'to our members we are the fourth emergency service', is an attempt to be pre-eminent and gain 'top of mind' awareness by conveying a rational benefit approach against the more emotive imagery suggested by the 'knight' (see Exhibit 13.2).

The need to reposition a brand may be stimulated because of the actions of a major competitor.

Summary

The use of objectives in the management process is clearly vital if the organisation's desired outcomes are to be achieved. Each of the objectives, at corporate, unit and functional levels, contributes to the formulation of the promotional objectives. They are all interlinked, interdependent, multiple and often conflicting.

The major task for the promotional objectives is twofold: first, to contribute to the overall direction of the organisation by fulfilling the communication requirements of the marketing mix; second, to communicate the corporate thrust to various stakeholders so that they understand the focus organisation and can respond to its intentions.

Promotional objectives are derived from an initial review of the current situation and the marketing plan requirements. They are not a replication of the marketing objectives but a distillation of the research activities that have been undertaken subsequently. Such objectives consist of two main elements: sales orientated and communication orientated. A balance between the two will be determined by the situation facing the organisation, but may be a mixture of product and corporate tasks. These objectives, once quantified, need to be ranked and weighted in order that other components of the plan can be developed.

Part of the information generated at the research stage informs how buyers and stakeholders position the offering relative to the other players in the target market and how the product itself is perceived (see the Harveys Bristol Cream example). This aspect of the management process is very important, as the communications undertaken by the organisation help to shape the context that individuals have of the offering (or the organisation). The way in which an organisation decides to position itself and/or its offerings determines the form, intensity and nature of the messages transmitted through the promotional mix.

Review questions

1. Why do organisations use objectives as part of their planning processes?

2. What should a mission statement clearly identify?

3. Suggest three reasons why the setting of promotional objectives is important.

4. Write a brief report arguing the case both for and against the use of an increase in sales as the major objective of all promotional activities.

5. Repeat the exercise as for the previous question but this time focus upon communication-based objectives.

6. How and from where are promotional objectives derived?

7. Why is positioning an important part of marketing communications?

8. What is perceptual mapping?

9. Select four print advertisements for the same product class and comment on the positions they have adopted.

10. What are the main positioning strategies?

MINI CASE

This mini case was written by Debbie Clewes, Senior Lecturer in Marketing, Nottingham Trent University.

Carling Lager

Brand planning

The lager brand director at Bass Brewers was reading the 1999/00 brand plan overview for Carling. He was considering what details to include in the brand plan to support this initial overview.

Brand plan overview

- *Vision*
  To be Britain's best-loved beer – one of life's essential ingredients, part of the British social fabric and a brand consumers are proud to be seen drinking.

- *Objectives*
  To maintain the market leadership position in the British lager category with 24% market share in the on-trade (pubs and clubs) and 14% market share in the off-trade (off-licences, supermarkets).

- *Target consumers*
  Primary: younger male mindset – sharp, quick witted and cosmopolitan. They drink in bars as well as boozers, with a repertoire that runs from Guinness to Stella, Bud to Caffrey's. The heart of Carling is rooted in the needs of everyday pint drinking – stimulating, laughter fuelled, mickey taking.
  Secondary: 30–40 year old mindset, male (plus female purchasers in off-trade), mainstream lager drinkers.

- *Strategy (top level)*
  Achieve the highest brand image scores of any mainstream beer to:
  Generate trial by new drinkers
  Generate re-appraisal by, and affinity with, occasional drinkers
  Drive bonding with existing devotees.

- *Key areas and action plan*
  Be seen everywhere
  Drive on-trade distribution
  Dominate display
  Overinvest in South-East
  Support major below-the-line activity above the line.

- *Be front of mind*
  National TV
  Innovative PR
  Constantly surprise
  Integrate relationship marketing into a cohesive affinity programme.

- *Widen brand relevance and appeal*
  New brand design
  Revised stock keeping unit range
  Develop brand communication beyond football.

- *Celebrate contemporary Britishness*
  Reflect British attitude in all communications
  Fully exploit Carling Premiership
  Develop new platforms to reinforce British credentials.

- *Key issues*
  Consumer
  Relatively low spontaneous awareness
  Outperformed by some competitors on key brand image measures
  Lack of affinity in South-East
  Relatively low household penetration
  Over-reliance on football to communicate brand values.

- *Market/competitors*
  Relatively low off-trade presence
  Relatively low on-trade distribution
  Continued move to lower margin channels (such as social clubs)
  Off-trade price convergence between Carling and Premium lagers.

■ *Trade*

Bass take home (off-trade)

Lack of insight to support strategy

Inability to compete in stubby format

Maintaining volume growth without devaluing the category

Bass Leisure Retail (BLR) on-trade outlets

Gaining BLR buy-in to major brand initiatives

Brand visibility within branded concepts

BLR premiumisation policy

Heavy competitor investment.

Independent on-trade

The cost of securing new business

Throughput in 'quality' new distribution tends to be below traditional outlets

Ensuring coverage by World of Carling kiosks

Defending/gaining solus supply without restricting consumer choice.

National account sales

Few 'big-win' accounts will be available in 99/00

Reliance on Bass national sales to deliver growth

Takeover implications of high volume accounts (e.g. Greenalls)

Increasing distribution in existing estates.

Mini-case questions

1. Having read the overview, key questions in the Brand Director's mind are as follows. How should the brand be positioned?
   - ■ consumer insight;
   - ■ consumer profile;
   - ■ rational brand values;
   - ■ emotional brand values;
   - ■ brand essence and strapline;
   - ■ brand personality, tone of voice;
   - ■ the positioning strategies mentioned earlier in the preceding chapter.

2. Where do we currently fall short of the desired position?

   What do we need to change?

   What communications plan will we need this year?

   How can this be integrated with the price, pack and place tactics?

   What consumer research do we need to support the plan?

References

Anon (2000) Cream of the crop. *Marketing Business* (July–August), p. 16.

Barry, T. and Howard, D.J. (1990) A review and critique of the hierarchy of effects in advertising. *International Journal of Advertising*, 9, pp. 121–35.

Colley, R. (1961) *Defining Advertising Goals for Measured Advertising Results*. New York: Association of National Advertisers.

Day, G., Shocker, A.D. and Srivastava, R.K. (1979) Customer orientated approaches to identifying product markets. *Journal of Marketing*, 43(4), pp. 8–19.

Greenley, G. (1989) *Strategic Management*. Hemel Hempstead: Prentice Hall.

Grunig, J. and Hunt, T. (1984) *Managing Public Relations*. New York: Holt, Rinehart & Winston.

Hodder, R., Gordon, W. and Swan, N. (1996) From four weddings and a funeral to blue velvet? *Admap* (March), pp. 38–44.

King, S. (1991) Brand building in the 1990s. *Journal of Marketing Management*, 7, pp. 3–13.

Kotler, P. (1997) *Marketing Management – Analysis, Planning, Implementation and Control*. Englewood Cliffs, NJ: Prentice Hall.

Kriegel, R.A. (1986) How to choose the right communications objectives. *Business Marketing* (April), pp. 94–106.

Levitt, T. (1960) Marketing myopia. *Harvard Business Review* (July/August), pp. 45–56.

McCawley, I. (2001) Pernod to rebrand in pursuit of older people. *Marketing Week*, 25 January, p. 8.

Neal, W.D. (1980) Strategic product positioning: a step by step guide. *Business (USA)* (May/June), pp. 34–40.

Ries, A. and Trout, J. (1972) The positioning era cometh. *Advertising Age*, 24 April, pp. 35–8.

Rosen, R. (1995) *Strategic Management: An Introduction*. London: Pitman.

Rossiter, J.R. and Percy, L. (1987) *Advertising and Promotion Management*, Lexington, MA: McGraw-Hill.

Rothschild, M. (1987) *Marketing Communications*. Lexington, MA: D.C. Heath.

Sinclair, S.A. and Stalling, E.C. (1990) Perceptual mapping: a tool for industrial marketing: a case study. *Journal of Business and Industrial Marketing*, **5**(1), pp. 55–65.

Thompson, J.L. (1990) *Strategic Management: Awareness and Change*. London: Chapman & Hall.

Thompson, A. and Strickland, A.J. III (1990) *Strategic Management*. Homewood, IL: BPI Irwin.

14

Branding and the role of marketing communications

The images and associations that customers make with brands and the brand identities that managers seek to create need to be closely related if long-run brand purchasing behaviour is to be achieved. Marketing communications can play an important and integral part in the development of positive brand associations that have meaning and purpose for buyers.

AIMS AND OBJECTIVES

The aims of this chapter are to explore the nature and characteristics of branding and to identify the way in which marketing communications can be used to develop and maintain brands that are of significance to their respective target audiences.

The objectives of this chapter are:

1. To introduce and explore the nature of branding.
2. To examine the common characteristics of brands.
3. To determine the benefits to both buyers and owners of brands.
4. To identify the different types of brands and the relationships they can have with the parent organisation.
5. To appreciate the strategic importance of brands.
6. To understand the contribution and the way in which marketing communications can be used to build and support brands.
7. To appraise the nature and significance of brand equity.

Introduction to branding

A successful brand is one which creates and sustains a strong, positive and lasting impression in the mind of a buyer. The elements that make up this impression are numerous and research by Chernatony and Dall'omo Riley (1998a) suggests that there is little close agreement on the definition of a brand. They identified 12 types of definition: among them is the visual approach adopted by Assael (1990), that a brand is the name, symbol, packaging and service reputation. The differentiation approach is

A successful brand is one which creates and sustains a strong, positive and lasting impression in the mind of a buyer.

typified by Kotler (2000) who argues that a brand is a name, term, sign, symbol or design or a combination of them intended to identify the goods, or services of one seller or group of sellers, and to differentiate them from those of competitors. What these researchers identified was that brands are a product of the work of managers who attempt to augment their products with values and associations that are recognised by and are meaningful to their customers. In other words, brands are constructs of the identity that managers wish to portray and images are construed by customers (and other stakeholders) of the identities they perceive.

In addition to this, it is important to recognise that both managers and customers are involved in branding as a method by which all parties are able to differentiate among similar offerings and associate certain attributes or feelings and emotions with a particular brand.

Quality and satisfaction through time can lead buyers to learn to trust a brand, which may lead to a priority position in the evoked set and repeat purchasing activity. The acceptance of buyers as active problem solvers means that branding can be seen as a way that buyers can reduce the amount of decision-making time and associated perceived risk. This is because brand names provide information about content, taste, durability, quality, price and performance, without requiring the buyer to undertake time-consuming comparison tests with similar offerings or other risk-reduction approaches to purchase decisions. In some categories brands can be developed through the use of messages that are entirely emotional or image based. Many of the 'products' in fast-moving consumer goods (FMCG) sectors base their communications on imagery, assuming low involvement and the use of peripheral cues. Other sectors, such as cars or pharmaceuticals, require rational information-based messages supported by image-based messages (Boehringer, 1996). In other words, a blend of messages may well be required to achieve the objectives and goals of the campaign.

Brand perceptions – Birds Eye Walls

Ice-cream accounts for 11% of Unilever's £4 billion turnover and is one of seven global product categories that have been marked out for growth.

Carte d'Or is an established European brand but needed further work in the UK to improve market share. Newland (2000) reports that this was achieved by repositioning the brand as fun and mainstream rather than luxurious and expensive, to encourage ice-cream eaters to consume Carte d'Or in social situations. £2.8 million was allocated to the three-month UK campaign.

Branding is a task that requires a significant contribution from marketing communications and is a long-term exercise. Organisations that cut their brand advertising in times of recession reduce the significance and power of their brands. The Association of Media Independents claims, not surprisingly, that the weaker brands are those that reduce or cut their advertising when trading conditions deteriorate.

Branding is a task that requires a significant contribution from marketing communications and is a long-term exercise.

Some organisations are moving the balance of their promotional mixes away from above-the-line work (advertising) towards tools below-the-line. For example, mobile phone companies have used advertising to develop brand awareness and positioning and then have used sales promotion and direct marketing activities to provide a greater focus on loyalty and reward programmes. These companies operate in a market where customer retention is a problem. Customer loss (or churn rate) exceeds 30% and there is a strong need to develop marketing and communications strategies that reduce this figure and provide for higher customer satisfaction levels, and from that improved profitability.

Brand characteristics

Brands consist of two main types of attributes: intrinsic and extrinsic. Intrinsic attributes refer to the functional characteristics of the product such as its shape, performance and physical capacity. If any of these intrinsic attributes were changed, it would directly alter the product. Extrinsic attributes refer to those elements that are not intrinsic and if changed do not alter the material functioning and performance of the product itself: devices such as the brand name, marketing communications, packaging, price and mechanisms that enable consumers to form associations that give meaning to the brand. Buyers often use the extrinsic attributes to help them distinguish one brand from another because in certain categories it is difficult for them to make decisions based on the intrinsic attributes alone.

Brands consist of two main types of attributes: intrinsic and extrinsic.

Luxury brands

Luxury brands such as Rolex, Cartier and Donna Karan have been developed mainly by advertising which is focused not on the intrinsic but the extrinsic attributes. The strategy has been to develop brand name associations which appeal to the aspirational needs and social psychological motivations of their target audiences.

Curtis (2000) says that, in order to grow, these brands face a common problem as they need to reach new target markets. The problem they all face is that lowering the price in order to attract these audiences threatens to impact the perception of the main brand by undermining its values and reputation, the one point of differentiation that has made these brands successful. The route forward is to introduce sub-brands which cannot be seen to be part of the main brand. So, Klein Cosmetics splits its business into two, Classic Brands and the CK Franchise line which includes CkOne and CkB fragrances. Tudor is a sub-brand of Rolex and Donna Karan uses Signature and DKNY as associate labels.

Biel (1997) refers to brands being composed of a number of elements. The first refers to the functional abilities a brand claims and can deliver. The particular attributes that distinguish a brand are referred to as brand skills. He quotes the cold remedy, Contact, whose brand skill is to relieve cold symptoms for 12 hours.

The second element is the personality of a brand and its fundamental traits concerning lifestyle and perceived values, such as being bland, adventurous, exciting, boring or caring. The idea of brand personification is not new, but it is an important part of understanding how a brand might be imagined as a person and how the brand is different from other brands (people). Exhibit 14.1 depicts the world-famous golfer Severiano Ballesteros endorsing the Hugo Boss brand. In doing so, there is a measure of association between the Hugo Boss brand (and its values) and the personality of the Spanish golfing maestro.

The third branding element is about building a relationship with individual buyers. People are said to interact with brands. A two-way relationship can be realistically developed when it is recognised that the brand must interact with the consumer just as much as the consumer must interact with the brand. Blackston (1993) argues that successful branding depends on consumers' perceptions of the attitudes held by the brand towards them as individuals. He illustrates the point with research into the credit card market, where different cards share the same demographic profile of users and the same conventional brand images. Some cards provide recognition or visibility of status, which by association are bestowed upon the owner in the form of power and authority. In this sense the card enhances the user. This contrasts with other cards, where the user may feel intimidated and excluded from the card because as a person the attitudes of the card are perceived to be remote, aloof, condescending and hard to approach.

The third branding element is about building a relationship with individual buyers.

Exhibit 14.1   Hugo Boss endorsed by Severiano Ballesteros. Picture reproduced with the kind permission of Hugo Boss Gmbh.

BOSS
HUGO BOSS

GOLF

For example, respondents felt the cards were saying, 'if you don't like the conditions, go and get a different card' and 'I'm so well known and established that I can do as I want'. The implications for brand development and associated message strategies become clearer.

In line with this thinking, Biel cites Fournier (1995), who considers brand/consumer relationships in terms of levels of intimacy, partner quality, attachment, interdependence, commitment and love.

A more recent approach to brand development work involves creating a brand experience. The Tango roadshows, which enable Tango drinkers to bungee jump, trampoline and do other out of the norm activities, are really seeking to provide extra brand-related experiences. Retail environments based entirely around a brand have been developed, for example, Levi shops. The Virgin brand can be drunk as a cola or vodka, invested as a PEP, transported by flight or rail, viewed at a cinema, listened to or simply used to get married (adapted from Croft, 1996).

A more recent approach to brand development work involves creating a brand experience.

Therefore, Biel sees brands as being made up of three elements: brand personality, brand skills and brand relationships. These combine to form what he regards as 'brand magic' and which underpins added value.

All brands consist of a mixture of intrinsic and extrinsic attributes and management's task is to decide on the balance between them. Indeed, this decision lies at the heart of branding in the sense that it is the strategy and positioning that lead to strong brands. Twivy (2000) suggests that there are two main types of brands, passionate and pseudo.

Passionate brands are those that have a strong positioning and are recognisable, have a core ideology, a DNA that reproduces itself in every aspect of the brand's behaviour and a set of values that engages an entire community of stakeholders. He cites Orange, Sony, Nike, Virgin and Channel 4. Also quoted is a recent new brand, the low-cost airline Go. Corporate design (Wolff Olins) through the use of smart Stansted airport and the use on board of Costa Coffee are all aspects which reflect attention to passionate brand detail.

Passionate brands are those that have a strong positioning and are recognisable.

Pseudo brands on the other hand lack core values and have experienced positioning drift. They might once have had such values but these have since been lost, forgotten or just abused or copied by competitors. Pseudo brands rely on USPs, redesigned logos and advertising and PR campaigns, line extensions to disguise an essential lack of depth. M&S, it says, once had a passion for textiles where there was an attention to simplicity yet really well-made clothes.

Pseudo brands, on the other hand, lack core values and have experienced positioning drift.

Benefits of branding

As a brand becomes established with a buyer, so the psychological benefits of ownership are preferred to competing offerings, and a form of relationship emerges. Brands are said to develop personalities and encapsulate the core values of a product. They are a strong means by which a product can be identified, understood and appreciated. Marketing communications play an important role in communicating the essence of the personality of the brand and in providing the continuity for any relationship, a necessity for a brand to be built through time. This can be achieved through the development of emotional links and through support for any product symbolism that might be present.

Just as brands can provide benefits for buyers, so important direct benefits for manufacturers or resellers also exist. Brands provide a means by which a manufacturer can augment its product in such a way that buyers can differentiate the product, recognise it quickly and make purchase decisions that exclude competitive products in the consideration set. Premium pricing is permissible, as perceived risk is reduced and high quality is conveyed through trust and experience formed through an association with the brand. This in turn allows for loyalty to be developed, which in turn allows for cross-product promotions and brand extensions. Integrated marketing communications becomes more feasible as buyers perceive thematic ideas and messages, which in turn can reinforce positioning and values associated with the brand. For a summary of the benefits of branding, see Table 14.1.

Brand fingerprinting

All branding activities need to extend across all key consumer contact points, a policy that needs to be pursued when developing integrated marketing communications (Chapter 19). One of the main tasks is to remind the market continually of the brand's presence, position and quality. When developing a marketing communications plan, it is vitally important to consider the information arising from a brand audit and then develop a

One of the main tasks is to remind the market continually of the brand's presence, position and quality.

Table 14.1   Benefits of branding

Customer benefits	Supplier benefits
■ Assists the identification of preferred products	■ Permits premium pricing
■ Can reduce levels of perceived risk and so improve the quality of the shopping experience	■ Helps differentiate the product from competitors
■ Easier to gauge the level of product quality	■ Enhances cross-product promotion and brand
■ Can reduce the time spent making product-based decisions and in turn reduce the time spent shopping	■ Encourages customer loyalty/retention and repeat-purchase buyer behaviour
■ Can provide psychological reassurance or reward	■ Assists the development and use of integrated marketing communications
■ Provides cues about the nature of the source of the product and any associated values	■ Contributes to corporate identity programmes
	■ Provides for some legal protection
	■ Provides for greater thematic consistency and uniform messages and communications

brand fingerprint, as Vyse (1999) refers to it. The management and development of a brand require resources and processes to ensure that the brand associations that buyers make are as intended and that the gap between managers' and buyers' expectations is tolerable. With the completion of a brand audit comes an understanding of consumers, but understanding consumers is worthless unless the information is in a form that can be read and understood by everyone involved in the brand development process.

Brands suffer midlife crises, they lose friends and need to be vigorously rejuvenated, often through exceptional creativity (Tango, Harveys Bristol Cream). Vyse comments that brands need to be up-to-date and speak the current language. Gap has a look and feel that travels across its store design, its through-the-line communications, and on packaging which expresses the visual, tactile, emotional and functional values of the clothes. Brand fingerprinting is about developing a single document that can be used by everyone involved with the brand development process. The benefits are:

Brands need to be up to date and speak the current language.

- It allows for continuity when brand managers move on in their careers.
- When the retail environment changes in a radical manner (e.g. eCommerce).
- It focuses on the consumer and so helps maintain the relationship.
- It fosters good team practice.

A brand fingerprint consists primarily of a document that summarises the essential character of the brand. According to Vyse, this comprises the following elements:

Target: a description of the person for whom the brand is always the first choice by defining their attitudes and values.

Insight: a description defining the elements about the consumer and his or her needs upon which the brand is founded.

Competition: a picture of the market and alternative choices as seen by the consumer and the relative values the brand offers in the market.

Benefits: the various functional and emotive benefits that motivate purchase.

Proposition: the single most compelling and competitive statement the target consumer would make for buying the brand.

Values: what the brand stands for and believes in.

Reasons to believe: the proof we offer to substantiate positioning.

Essence: the distillation of the brand's generic code into one clear thought.

Properties: the tangible things of which the merest glimpse, sound, taste, smell or touch would evoke the brand.

For a brand to grow and be sustained, the functional aspects of the product must be capable of meeting the expectations of the buyer. If the quality of the physical and functional aspects of the product is below acceptable standards, marketing communications activities alone cannot create and sustain a brand. When Jaguar cars were first exported to the USA, the car was soon rejected by the market because the first buyers of Jaguars (innovators in the process of adoption) experienced a variety of problems. These included overheating, because thermostats failed to work, and gearboxes and clutches that needed replacing too soon. This led to a poor image of Jaguar, which meant that market penetration would be slow, at least until the product defects were corrected. A quality initiative at the production plant resulted in a car that performed at exceptionally high levels on all functions. Promotional work then built upon the new credibility, so that Jaguar became one of the most sought-after prestige cars in the USA.

Types and forms of branding

There are many forms of branding but primarily there are manufacturer, distributor, price and generic brands.

Manufacturers' brands help to identify the producer of a brand at the point of purchase. For example, Cadbury's chocolate, Ford cars and Coca-Cola are all strong manufacturers' brands. This type of brand usually requires the assistance of channel intermediaries for wide distribution, and the promotional drive stems from the manufacturer in an attempt to persuade end-users to adopt the brand, which in turn stimulates channel members to stock and distribute the brand.

Distributor (or own-label) brands do not associate the manufacturer with the offering in any way. The distributor brand is owned by a channel member, typically a wholesaler, such as Nurdin & Peacock, or a retailer, such as Tesco, Boots and Woolworth's. This brand strategy offers many advantages to both the manufacturer, who can use excess capacity, and retailers, who can earn a higher margin than they can with manufacturers' branded goods and at the same time develop organisational (e.g. store) images. Channel members have the additional cost of promotional initiatives, necessary in the absence of a manufacturer's support. Some manufacturers refuse to make distributor products, and in the mid-1990s there was increased attention paid to this area, as some of the multiple grocers launched products that were alleged to be too similar to main manufacturer brands. Using a similar name and packaging the product in the same style has led to conflict in the channel network.

There has been considerable debate about the shift in volumes between manufacturers and distributor brands. A study by Nielsen reported by Sargent (1995) attempted to isolate the key factors that contribute to longer-term brand development. The study, which focused on 45 major UK-based FMCG markets, found a decline in the volume of manufacturer brands sales and an increase in the volume of distributor sales over the three-year period of the study. TV advertising was isolated as one of the key elements in the development of the brands that had grown (at the expense of price-based sales promotions). The study also confirmed the general view that new product development and being first into a market were of major significance when seeking brand growth over the longer term.

Consumers value or expect a certain level of brand choice in stores.

The growth of distributor brands at the expense of manufacturer brands need not be expected to continue unchecked. Consumers value or expect a certain level of brand choice in stores, and as some store traffic and spend per visit rates have declined, some grocery multiples have taken steps to stem the volume of their distributor brand provision and increased the volume of manufacturer brands on their shelves.

Price brands are produced by manufacturers in an attempt to compete with private brands. Tesco has used this approach to respond to the arrival of a number of low-cost retailers such as Kwik Save and Aldi. The product is low priced and is further characterised by an absence of any promotional support. The effect on the other brands in the manufacturer's portfolio may be to stimulate promotional support to prevent the less loyal buyers from trading over to the low-priced offering.

The final type is the *generic brand*. This is sold devoid of any promotional materials and the packaging only displays information required by law. Manufacturers are even less inclined to produce these 'white carton' products than price brands. They are often sold at prices 40% below the price of normal brands. They consume very few promotional resources, for obvious reasons, but their popularity, after a burst in the 1970s, has waned considerably, particularly in the supermarket sector where they gained their greatest success. However, generics are significant in some markets. The pharmaceutical industry has experienced a growth in the use of generic products, spurred by the NHS reforms of the government (Blackett, 1992).

Brands and their parent organisations

Branding decisions are partly a reflection of an organisation's view of the relationship of its products to each other and to the corporate body and the organisation's strategy (Gray and Smeltzer, 1985). The approach each organisation adopts shapes the marketing communications. These authors recognise five different relationships: single form, brand form, balanced form, variety form and corporate form.

Single-form organisations offer a single product so that the images of the organisation and the product tend to be the same. Kwik-Fit, Pirelli, Coca-Cola and Gillette provide products and services that are keyed into a single strategic business area (SBA).

Single-form organisations offer a single product so that the images of the organisation and the product tend to be the same.

Problems may be expected if they diversify into different areas of activity or if they deviate from their current strategies. For example, Levi failed in its attempt to move into quality men's clothing because the target market associated Levi and the Levi brand with the production of jeans. Had the brand not been so closely associated with the single-product focus, there would have been a greater chance of success in its attempt to broaden the range. However, JCB has extended its brand into fashion, DIY and toys based around the core strength of the brand, namely yellow, durability and functionality (Irvin, 2000). See the JCB example later in this chapter.

The *brand form* reflects a decision not to relate the brands to the parent organisation. This *multi-brand* approach has been followed by manufacturers Procter and Gamble and Lever Bros for many years. Only recently has Lever started to put its name on the packaging of each of its household brands. This form requires promotional expenditure to support the individual brands, but, should a particular brand be damaged, the other brands in the portfolio and the corporate name are protected.

In the *balanced form*, divisions within an organisation convey individual identities, but each one is related to the corporate body. A good example of this approach is Ford UK. Each car in each of its product lines is prefixed by Ford. The Ford Fiesta 1.3L, Ford Escort 1.4GL and Ford Transit all convey the balance between the corporate name and the individual brands.

The *variety form* is identified by organisations who stress either the brand or the organisation, depending upon particular circumstances. Gray and Smeltzer (1985) offer the example of the German organisation Bosch Gmbh. This organisation identifies its spark plugs and power tools under the Bosch name, but elects to use the name Blaupunkt for its radios.

The final approach is referred to as the *corporate form*. Although the organisation may operate in a number of different SBAs, this approach requires all communications to be targeted at reinforcing the corporate image. IBM, Mars, Hewlett-Packard and Black & Decker are examples of this form.

Corporate identity, which will be looked at in detail later (Chapter 16), is also a form of branding. Woolworth's, Tesco and Boots are examples of the growth of retail or distributor brands. All are recognised and perceived by consumers to have particular advantages and disadvantages. All have taken a long time to develop. All have invested heavily in various forms of promotion to build their brands.

There are new types of brand emerging such as dotcom brands. These virtual entities, many spawned with vigour and drive in 1999, need to establish their credentials in order not only to satisfy customers but also to attract investment funding on a medium term basis. Many of the early entrant dotcom companies attempted to provide ecommerce facilities for particular target audiences without necessarily thinking through the whole marketing strategy. Those organisations developing their marketing channels need to balance the trust established in their bricks and mortar brand and develop new images with their clicks only brands. There is no one successful formula and some organisations have developed completely new brands to compete in the new media environment, such as the financial services brand *If* from Halifax and *Egg* from Prudential.

There are new types of brand emerging such as dotcom brands.

There are other brands which seek to provide customers with a level of trust such that the brand is strong enough to carry customers into a variety of unrelated markets. The Virgin brand has demonstrated its ability to attract customers, even though it was understood that Virgin had no prior experience of the particular market at the time it entered (for example, air travel, financial services and cosmetics). What appears to be emerging is that the Virgin brand is associated with success and is seen as one that challenges the established norms by which each market operates. By promising and delivering tangible benefits for customers, Virgin has become a people's brand that seeks out opportunities and rewrites the way markets operate.

There are other brands which seek to provide customers with a level of trust such that the brand is strong enough to carry customers into a variety of unrelated markets.

When BMW and Daihatsu announced their separate intentions to enter the financial services sector, the corporate strategy was based upon a redefinition of their business interests and extending their brands into areas where they would be salient and strong. BMW is a trusted car brand and by moving into financial services it is in a better position to compete with (un)likely competitors such as Virgin, Marks & Spencer, Tesco and Sainsbury's. Essentially the car brand is repositioned as a service brand. With the enhanced mobility, BMW can move into new market sectors that before the redefinition would have been unavailable to it, and it might have been vulnerable to attack in its car market from new service-based brands.

Strategic role of branding

From a strategic perspective, brands play an important role. They can be used as a means of defending market share or group brands, protecting established positions, they can be used to attack competitor brands and provide a means of deterring market entry by others, in other words, act as a market entry barrier or aid customer reten-

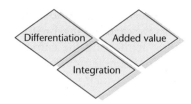

Figure 14.1 The strategic dimensions of branding.

There are three broad aspects of branding which enable these strategic roles to be accomplished, namely differentiation, added value and integration.

tion, as mentioned earlier. However, there are three broad aspects of branding which enable these strategic roles to be accomplished, namely differentiation, added value and integration. See Figure 14.1.

Differentiation

Brands provide the means by which a product can be seen to be different from a competitor's product. Branding is a method of separation and positioning so that customers can recognise and understand what a brand stands for, relative to other brands. However, not all brands choose to be different as there is some strategic advantage for smaller new-entry brands to associate themselves closely with the market leader. This is witnessed by the disagreements between distributors and manufacturers over the packaging, names and type faces used for some products (e.g. Coca-Cola and Sainsbury's Cola, Puffin and Penguin bars).

Added value

The second key aspect is that of added value. Brands enable customers to derive extra benefits as one brand can provide different advantages to another. These advantages might be in the form of rational attribute-based advantages (e.g. whiter, stronger or longer) or they may be more emotionally based advantages derived through the augmented aspects of the products (e.g. the way you feel about a brand).

This issue is evidenced by the vigour with which Levi's resisted the distribution of their jeans through price-orientated distributors such as Asda. One of the arguments proposed by Levi's was that the inherent brand value was effectively removed through this form of distribution.

Integration

For a brand to be maintained and to work, it is important that the communications used to develop and maintain the brand are consistent and meaningful. Part of the essence of integrated marketing communications is that all the tools used to support a brand and the messages that are used to convey brand values must be consistent, uniform and reinforcing. Therefore, successful branding is partly the result of effective integrated marketing communications.

Successful branding is partly the result of effective integrated marketing communications.

Developing the Levi's example a stage further, we know that marketing channels should reflect the desired positioning, in order to develop IMC. If Asda continued to sell Levi products, market forces would ultimately determine whether the positioning determined by Levi's was valued by customers. It is probable that, because of the strength of the resistance, Levi's feared that they would lose their core target market and hence their brand position.

The role of marketing communications in branding

Marketing communications play a vital role in the development of brands and are the means by which products become brands, that is how customers can see how a product is different and understand what a brand stands for and what its values are.

Marketing communications play a vital role in the development of brands.

The way in which marketing communications are used to build brands is determined strategically by the role that the brand is expected to play in achieving an organisation's goals. Chernatony and Dall'Olmo Riley (1998b) argue that there are several roles that marketing communications can play in relation to brand development. For example, they suggest the role during brand extensions is to show buyers how the benefits from the established brand have been transferred or extended to the new brand. It may be that some of the problems currently experienced by Lego are due to a brand extension strategy that has not been suitably supported by marketing communications or the poor financial situation may be due to a move away from core brand values (Benady, 2001). Another role might be to clarify each individual's role within the organisation. Developing Ehrenberg's ideas it might be argued that the role of brand-based marketing communications is to remind buyers and reinforce their perceptions in order to defend market share.

Whatever the role, one major determinant that applies to all organisations is the size of the financial resources that are made available. Should the budget be high, advertising will be the main way in which brand name associations are shaped. The brand name itself will not need to be related to the function or use experience of the brand as the advertising will be used to create and maintain brand associations.

When few financial resources are available, a below-the-line approach is necessary. In particular, the brand name will need to be closely related to the function and use experience of the product, while packaging will also play a significant role in building brand associations.

Brand building through advertising

When advertising is used to enable consumers to make brand associations, two main approaches can be used, the rational and the emotional.

When a rational approach is used, the functional aspects of a brand are emphasised and the benefit to the consumer is stressed. Very often product performance is the focus of the message and a key attribute is identified and used to position the brand.

When a rational approach is used, the functional aspects of a brand are emphasised.

Typically, unique selling propositions (USPs) are used to draw attention to a single functional advantage that a brand claims to have and which consumers find attractive. Many brands try to present two or even three brand features as the USP has lost ground. The rational approach is sometimes referred to as an informative approach (and complements functional positioning; see Chapter 13). For example, when Britvic launched Juice Up into the chilled fruit juice sector to compete with Sunny Delight, it used the higher fruit juice and lower sugar attributes as the main focus of the communication strategy.

When an emotional approach is used, advertising should provide positive psychosocial associations such that consumers develop positive feelings and values with a brand. Product characteristics and their performance remain dormant while the goal is to create positive attitudes to the advertising which in turn are used to make associations with the brand. In other words, the role of likeability, discussed later in Chapter 20, becomes paramount when using an emotional (or lifestyle) basis for advertising. Therefore, these types of advertisements should be relevant and meaningful, credible and be of significant value to the consumer. In essence, therefore, emotional (or transformational) advertising is about people enjoying the advertisement (and complements expressive positioning; see Chapter 13).

When an emotional approach is used, advertising should provide positive psychosocial associations.

Brand building through below-the-line techniques

When the marketing communications budget is limited or where the target audience cannot be reached reasonably or effectively through advertising, then it is necessary to use below-the-line techniques to develop brands. Although sales promotion is traditionally perceived as a tool that erodes rather than helps build a brand as it has a price rather than value orientation, it can be used strategically. In recent years new technology has enabled innovative sales promotion techniques to be used as a competitive weapon and to help build brand presence.

Strategy, technology and sales promotion – Doritos

Doritos is regarded as an irreverent and independent brand in comparison with its sister brand Walkers crisps, which is positioned much more as a homely brand. Clarke (2000) reports a sales promotion undertaken for Doritos, which involved over 15 million gamecards inserted into 50 million promotional packs of Doritos. The gamecards invited consumers to kiss the lips (on the card), which through a heatseal mechanism revealed whether they had won a prize. The top prize was £10,000 and the chance to kiss a top British film star. The film theme builds on the brand's deliberate association with films and movie events and in that sense provides a form of integration and has strategic consistency.

Direct marketing and public relations are important methods used to build brand values especially when consumers experience high involvement. However, experience suggests that the sole use of direct marketing in FMCG markets has been less than satisfactory from those that have experimented (e.g. Heinz in the mid-1990s). The Internet offers opportunities to build new dotcom brands and the financial services sector has tried to harness this method as part of a multichannel distribution policy. What appear to be overridingly important for the development of brands operating with limited resources are the brand name and the merchandising activities, of which packaging, labelling and POP are crucial. In

The development of loyalty schemes and carelines for FMCG, durable and service-based brands is a testimony to the importance of developing and maintaining positive brand associations.

addition, as differentiation between brands becomes more difficult in terms of content and distinct symbolism, the nature of the service encounter is now recognised to have considerable impact on brand association. The development of loyalty schemes and carelines for FMCG, durable and service-based brands is a testimony to the importance of developing and maintaining positive brand associations.

When advertising is the main source of brand development consumers develop associations about the content and positioning of the brand through advertising messages. As a substitute for advertising, it is the merchandising, packaging and the brand name itself that need to convey the required symbolism in such a way that the content and positioning are understood by the target audience. Indeed, the brand name needs to be closely aligned with the brand's primary function, more so than when advertising is able to convey the product's purpose and role. See Exhibit 14.2 and the mini case at the end of this chapter.

Exhibit 14.2   Bioform® – A new brand launch using a below-the-line strategy. Picture reproduced with the kind permission of Charnos and Lewis Moberly.

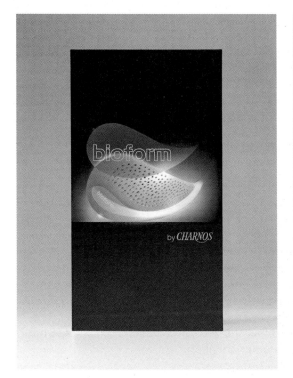

Table 14.2   Devices used to develop brand associations

Mechanism	Explanation
Co-branding	Refers to two or more brands that consumers can clearly identify – Microsoft and NSPCC
Geographical identifiers	Attempt to provide source credibility – country of origin labels, brand names (e.g. British Airways), pictures of country origins (e.g. Cobra beer from India has a map of India on the label) and use of national symbols (e.g. flags)
Ingredient brands	Brands that are only available within other brands – Lycra, Intel and Dolby
Support services	Attempt to provide relationship strength and continuity of contact – loyalty cards (e.g. Tesco, ClubCard, Air Miles), brand-based carelines, technical help and assistance facilities (AOL)
Award symbols	Additional qualifying marks granted by independent organisations – ISO, etc.

Source: Adapted from Riezbos (2002).

The below-the-line route needs to achieve a transfer of image. Apart from the clarity of the brand name (which needs to describe the product functions) and the shape, nature and information provided through the packaging and associated labelling, there are additional mechanisms through which brand associations can be developed. There are five such devices: co-branding, geographical identifiers, the use of ingredient brands, support services and award symbols. See Table 14.2.

There are many occasions where advertising funds are not available to develop brand associations and where the brand name and merchandising needs to be the predominant force in enabling buyers to develop managed and positive brand associations. An increasing number of organisations in the b2b sector are using branding approaches and recognise the benefits of co-branding in particular. Charities and organisations in the not-for-profit sector are increasingly using commercial organisations to co-brand. The former receive commercial expertise and funding while the latter gain in terms of association with good deeds, giving (rather than taking) and being seen to care.

Brands, finance and associations – the cola market

Coca-Cola had UK sales of £620 million in 1999 and Virgin Cola just £29 million. The difference is immense and is reflected in the resources that each company can bring to support the brand and reinforce and develop brand images. While Coke spends approximately £27 million per year above the line, Virgin spends £5 million and places great reliance on innovation and loyalty schemes. One such promotion, called I-can, required ring-pulls to be redeemed for money off Virgin products. Virgin Coke has not made the market penetration that was expected and, according to Witt (2000), it could be argued that this is because the brand name has not be augmented enough to inspire consumer attention.

Marketing communications are the means by which products become brands. Buyers make associations immediately they become aware of a brand name. It is the brand manager's task to ensure that the associations made are appropriate and provide a means of differentiation. By communicating the key strengths and

Marketing communications are the means by which products become brands.

differences of a brand, by explaining how a brand brings value to a customer and by reinforcing and providing consistency in the messages transmitted, a level of integration can be brought to a brand or rather the way it is perceived by the target market.

Finally in this section the importance of branding as a part of integrated marketing communications should not be forgotten and to do this internal brand education is crucial. The way a brand relates internally to departments and individuals and the way the brand is articulated by senior management is an important part of brand education. Brands are not just external elements; they should be a part of the way in which an organisation operates, part of its cultural configuration.

Business-to-business branding

The branding concept has been used by a number of manufacturers (Intel, Teflon, Nutrasweet) to achieve two particular goals. Rich (1996) reports that the first goal is to develop an identity which final end-users perceive as valuable. For example, Intel has developed its microprocessors such that PCs with the Intel brand are seen to be of high quality and credibility. This provides the PC manufacturer with an added competitive advantage.

The second goal is to establish a stronger relationship with the manufacturer. Nutrasweet works with food manufacturers advising on recipes simply because the final product is the context within which Nutrasweet will be evaluated by end-users.

A b2b brand is often tied closely to the company itself as opposed to b2c brands which often take preference to the manufacturer or company name. For example, a

A b2b brand is often tied closely to the company itself.

Rolls Royce power turbine is branded Rolls Royce because the perception of tradition, high quality, performance and global reach that are associated with the Rolls Royce name.

The marketing communications should be developed so that they incorporate and perpetuate the personality of the brand. So, all the Rolls Royce advertising materials should be in corporate colours and contain the logo. All copy should be in the house style and reinforce brand perceptions.

The use of event sponsorship, whereby an organisation provides financial support for a conference or exhibition, has become increasingly popular (Miller, 1997). Mainly because of the costs involved, event organisers have sought sponsorship aid. For sponsors, events provide a means of promoting visibility within a narrowly focused target market. In addition,

Manufacturers will use joint promotional activities as a means of forging close relationships with retailers and as a means of strengthening exit barriers (routes away from relationships).

they provide a means of highlighting their own particular contribution within the conference or their exhibition stand.

The use of joint promotional activities between manufacturers and resellers will continue to be an important form of communication behaviour. The desire to build networks which provide cooperative strength and protection for participants will continue.

Business-to-business branding – JCB

JCB is Europe's leading manufacturer of construction equipment and has developed a unique promotional style based upon demonstrating the features and versatility of its products, in an entertaining way. The JCB *Dancing Diggers* consist of a series of trick routines that the company's demonstration team performs. The *Dancing Diggers* perform at exhibitions and draw huge crowds as the giant earth-moving equipment shows off its capabilities. This activity feeds advertising, sales literature and, of course, public relations work, providing a strong means of arresting attention and building tremendous levels of credibility. See Plate 14.1.

One little touch of personal selling and publicity skill can be observed in the development and launch of a machine called the 3D. The owner, Joe Bamford, designed the cab so that the operator could make a cup of tea. He promised to personally deliver the first 100 orders with a free kettle, which he did for each purchaser.

Manufacturers will use joint promotional activities as a means of forging close relationships with retailers and as a means of strengthening exit barriers (routes away from relationships).

Brand equity

If the PLC fails to deliver appropriate data to assist marketing management and the developmental phase approach is a little too broad, a more precise tool is required to assist the development of marketing communications.

Arising from the increasing recognition of the value that brands bring to organisations, is a relatively new concept referred to as brand equity. According to Ehrenberg (1993), brand equity is just a reflection of a brand's market share. However, this is a view that excludes the composition of brands and the values that consumers place in them. There is a behavioural element and an attitudinal element (Richards, 1997).

Brand equity is a measure of a number of different components, including the beliefs, images and core associations consumers have about particular brands.

Brand equity is a measure of a number of different components, including the beliefs, images and core associations consumers have about particular brands. For example, these may be *vibrant, green, upstart, vigorous, approachable* or *caring*. These will vary between groups and represent fresh segmentation and targeting opportunities. A further component is the degree of loyalty or retention the brand is able to sustain. Measures of market penetration, involvement, attitudes and purchase intervals (frequency) are typical. In addition to these, Cooper and Simmons offer brand future as a third dimension. This is a reflection of a brand's ability to grow and remain unhindered by environmental challenges such as changing retail patterns, alterations in consumer buying methods and developments in technological and regulative fields.

Attempts to measure brand equity have to date been varied and without a high level of consensus, although the spirit and ideals behind the concept are virtually the same. Table 14.3 sets out some of the approaches adopted.

Table 14.3   Five approaches to measuring brand equity

Source	Factors measured
David Aaker	Awareness, brand associations, perceived quality and market leadership, loyalty, market performance measures
Brand dynamics (Millward Brown)	Presence, relevance to consumer needs, product performance, competitive advantage, bonding
Equitrend (Total Research)	Salience, perceived quality, user satisfaction
3-D3 (TBWA Simmons Palmer)	Brand quality, quantity and future measured against a variety of stakeholders
Brand asset valuator (Young & Rubicam)	Strength (differentiation and relevance), stature (esteem and knowledge)

Source: Adapted from Cooper and Simmons (1997) and Haigh (1997).

As a means of synthesising these approaches the following are considered the principal dimensions through which brand equity should be measured:

■ *Brand dominance*: a measure of its market strength and performance.

■ *Brand associations*: measure of the beliefs held by buyers about what the brand represents and stands for.

■ *Brand prospects*: a measure of its capacity to grow and extend into new areas.

A brand with a strong equity is more likely to be able to preserve its customer franchise and so fend off competitor attacks.

Brand equity is considered important because of the increasing interest in trying to measure the return on promotional investments and so value brands for balance sheet purposes. A brand with a strong equity is more likely to be able to preserve its customer franchise and so fend off competitor attacks.

Summary

Branding provides customers with a quick and easy way of understanding what a product is, what value it represents and can represent a measure of psychosocial reassurance. Branding provides manufacturers and distributors with a means of differentiating their products in order to gain competitive advantage in such a way that customers perceive added value. This allows for premium pricing and the improved margin can be used to invest in new opportunities for commercial initiatives through, for example, innovation or improved levels of customer service.

Marketing communications has an important role to play in brand development and maintenance. In many circumstances advertising is used to develop strong brands. To help customers make associations with brands either a rational, information-based approach might be adopted or alternatively a more emotional relationship might be forged, one based more on imagery and feelings.

In a large number of cases the opportunity to use advertising is restricted and many smaller and b2b organisations need to rely on a below-the-line approach. In these circumstances, the brand name is important as it needs to symbolise or convey meaning about the functionality of the brand. In addition, merchandising, packaging and other POP elements will be prominent in brand development.

There are many other factors that can influence the development of brands. Co-branding, geographic signals and award symbols can impact on brand associations so that ultimately risk is reduced, trust is enhanced and there is sufficient confidence to purchase the brand on a regular basis.

Branding is a key strategic communication issue and not only affects FMCG products but is increasingly used by b2b organisations as a means of differentiation.

Review questions

1. Write brief notes explaining what branding is.

2. How do brands assist customers and brand owners?

3. Summarise Biel's concept of 'brand magic'.

4. Select five consumer brands and evaluate their characteristics.

5. Find two examples for each of the different forms of branding.

6. Identify the three elements that determine the strategic aspect of branding.

7. Explain advertising's role in the development of brands.

8. Find three non-FMCG brands and evaluate how their brand strength has been developed without the aid of advertising. How might you improve the strength of these brands?

9. Explain how business-to-business markets might benefit from adopting a branding approach.

10. Discuss two approaches to brand equity.

MINI CASE

This case was written by Janet Hull, Managing Partner, Lewis Moberley.

Bioform®

The UK branded lingerie market is characterised by slow growth, over-supply and fierce competition. Since 1994 lingerie growth has crept ahead of womenswear by a small margin, only to slip back in 1999, in large part caused by poor sales performance at Marks & Spencer, the single biggest retail outlet for lingerie sales, representing over one-third of the total market.

Bras continue to represent the most important sector within the lingerie market, in value terms. This is largely due to branded manufac-turer activity designed to stimulate consumer demand. Branded manufacturers have focused on promoting different bra-wearing occasions and the consequent requirement for a repertoire of bra purchases. Wonderbra and Gossard Ultra Bra, in particular, have triggered the market and stimulated new competition.

Charnos, however, had played no part in this upsurge and was in decline. Its promotional budget had dwindled to nothing and there had been little innovation in its product range. It had lost saliency with consumers and was disadvantaged with the trade because of unfavourable price comparisons. Indeed, one of its major customers (Debenhams) had decided to delist it and others were likely to follow suit, unless corrective action were taken.

The situation facing Charnos was particularly serious as its business was increasingly reliant on lingerie. Its core business, hosiery, was suffering volume losses in line with the market as consumer wardrobe habits changed and trousers became everyday wear. As it entered its 1998/99 financial year, Charnos was aware that, in order to reverse the decline in its business, major product development or diversification would be necessary.

To assist the decision-making process, research was used which showed that *bust sizes were increasing*, that *the majority of women were wearing the wrong size of bra* and that there was considerable *consumer dissatisfaction with bra products on the market*. Bigger-busted ladies felt as though they were being treated like second-class citizens by both retailers and manufacturers. They were made to feel like problem people, rather than valued customers. Larger bra sizes tended to be relegated in store to the section furthest from the main display, alongside maternity bras. Some women, therefore, had both a physical and emotional need associated with the bras currently available. Charnos saw an opportunity with this new market segment.

However, in order to satisfy this market need, it had to first find a new bra design and this was achieved when Charnos was approached by production company, TV6, to get involved in a high-profile Channel 4 TV series, in which product designers Seymour Powell were challenging design conventions across a number of different product sectors. Charnos had everything to gain and nothing to lose so it agreed to participate.

Charnos challenged Seymour Powell to re-think bra design to bring improved shape and support, particularly to bigger bust sizes. Their response was the invention of a prototype three-dimensional undercup support component to replace the traditional bra underwire. The essence of the component is a two-shot moulding process where the inner core armature replicates the underwire but is infused in a softer moulded polymer that holds and shapes the bust. It does not contort or distort the bust but simply shapes and supports it in the most flattering, comfortable way.

After numerous rounds of prototypes and consumer testing, a new product was developed which reached the performance targets set, in terms of shape, support and comfort. Discussion then began about how it should be positioned and branded. There were two main views about how this should be achieved:

1. as a new Charnos brand;
2. as a new ingredient brand.

The new technological breakthrough had the power to revolutionise perceptions of the Charnos lingerie brand. It also had potential to live outside of the Charnos brand, as a stand-alone brand. Analogies were drawn between the new three-dimensional product component and 'Intel inside' in the computer context. Potentially this new product, appropriately positioned and branded, could sit alongside other manufacturer brands as a 'magic ingredient'. By not restricting it to Charnos, there was potential to license the new technology to other branded lingerie, sportswear and fashion manufacturers and thereby enjoy a new, additional income stream. In the optimistic words of the brand chairman 'one day, all bras will be made this way'.

Thoughts then turned to naming the new product. The brand needed to:

> sound technical;
>
> suggest 'better' shape;
>
> be perceived as 'natural'.

In consumer tests the word 'bio' was found to have natural connotations, and 'form' was perceived as meaning well-formed or of good shape. The name 'Bioform' was generated and, when compared with recent sub-brand introductions, such as Wonderbra or Ultra Bra, it was felt to be tonally different and sound more genuine, carrying less hype and more authenticity.

The qualitative research also confirmed that consumer targeting was needed and condition-based rather than age-based. Bigger-busted women occurred in the population across all ages. However, for the purposes of promotion, it was agreed to depict a 25–34 year old who could be assumed to have had a first child, as this was felt to be aspirational to all age groups, younger and old.

Lewis Moberly recommended a brand identity for Bioform® which combined a logotype and a symbolic shape. Importantly, both were capable of being trade-mark registered, served to create a brand mark which could exist outside of the launch packaging and were capable of coexisting alongside other brand names.

A revolutionary new pack form and structure to reflect the brand's product credentials was developed. Because it was important for consumers to handle the bra in order to check the material and structure, it was an important design objective to make the pack easy to open. Another priority was to make it easy for consumers to check the colour of the bra. This was made possible by keeping the sides of the box transparent, while fully coating the front and back panels.

Innovative new pack graphics which defied market convention were also developed so that the Bioform® component became the hero of the pack and appeared centre stage, in computer-generated graphic form, on the front face. External bra features and size and wash details were relegated to top and back of pack.

Bioform® proved a difficult concept to advertise. Early advertising development had followed the conventions of other bra and hosiery advertising, and focused on sex or science, and 'bombed' in consumer research. The route finally decided upon reflected the approach taken by the design consultancy in relation to the packaging. This was based around the adage, 'the medium is the message'. The agency worked with Adshel to take advantage of new three-dimensional photographic and reproductive techniques, to create the first ever three-dimensional poster visible to the human eye.

The headline endorsed the brand positioning – the revolutionary bra that shapes you in 3D. The strapline, Try it, wear it, love it – a phrase now identified more than any with the whole marketing operation – is used in all point of purchase and marketing support. This also became an important selling message on the Bioform® Web site – Bioform.co.uk

In parallel with the advertising, Charnos produced in-store posters, shelf-cards and leaflets announcing the arrival of Bioform®. It also supplied, on demand, freestanding display units, which combined box shelving and hanging space, to present the total concept in the most effective way.

Mini-case questions

1. To what extent has Charnos used a rational or emotional approach to branding?
2. Write brief notes about the degree to which an above- or below-the-line strategy has been followed to develop the Charnos Bioform® brand.
3. To what extent does the brand name agree with the theory that it should represent the functionality of the brand itself?
4. Explain what an ingredient brand is and then evaluate the probability that Bioform® might become an ingredient brand.
5. Identify the brand form adopted by Charnos.

References

Assael, H. (1990) *Marketing: Principles and Strategy*. Orlando, FL: Dryden Press.
Benady, D. (2001) A brick too far. *Marketing Week*, 15 March 2001, pp. 26–9.
Biel, A. (1997) Discovering brand magic: the hardness of the softer side of branding. *International Journal of Advertising*, **16**, pp. 199–210.

Blackett, T. (1992) Branding and the rise of the generic drug. *Marketing Intelligence and Planning*, **10**(9), pp. 21–4.

Blackston, M. (1993) A brand with an attitude: a suitable case for treatment. *Journal of Market Research Society*, **34**(3), pp. 231–41.

Boehringer, C. (1996) How can you build a better brand? *Pharmaceutical Marketing* (July), pp. 35–6.

Chernatony de, L. and Dall'omo Riley, F. (1998a) Defining a brand: beyond the literature with experts' interpretations. *Journal of Marketing Management*, **14**, pp. 417–43.

Chernatony de, L. and Dall'omo Riley, F. (1998b) Expert practitioners' views on roles of brands: implications for marketing communications. *Journal of Marketing Communications*, **4**, pp. 87–100.

Clarke, A. (2000) Doritos' SWALK attack. *Promotions and Incentives* (June), pp. 24–6.

Cooper, A. and Simmons, P. (1997) Brand equity lifestage: an entrepreneurial revolution. TBWA Simmons Palmer, unpublished working paper.

Croft, M. (1996) Stretched marks. *Marketing Week*, 8 March, pp. 47–8.

Curtis, J. (2000) Not taking luxury for granted. *Marketing*, 24 August, pp. 26–7.

Ehrenberg, A.S.C. (1993) If you are so strong why aren't you bigger? *Admap* (October), pp. 13–14.

Fournier, S. (1995) A consumer–brand relationship perspective on brand equity. Presentation to Marketing Science Conference on Brand Equity and the Marketing Mix, Tucson, Arizona, pp. 2–3 March.

Gray, E.R. and Smeltzer, L.R. (1985) SMR Forum: corporate image – an integral part of strategy. *Sloan Management Review* (Summer), pp. 73–8.

Haigh, D. (1997) Brand valuation: the best thing to ever happen to market research. *Admap* (June), pp. 32–5.

Irvin, C. (2000) From crib to consumer. *Marketing Business* (March), pp. 18–20.

Kotler, P. (2000) *Marketing Management: The Millennium Edition*, Upper Saddle River, NJ: Prentice Hall.

Miller, R. (1997) Make an event of it. *Marketing*, 5 June, p. 28.

Newland, F. (2000) Walls embraces Unilever's new creative approach, *Campaign*, 19 May, p. 26.

Rich, M. (1996) Stamp of approval. *Financial Times*, 29 February, p. 9.

Richards, T. (1997) Measuring the true value of brands. *Admap* (March), pp. 32–6.

Riezbos, R. (2002) *Brand Management*. Harlow: Pearson Education.

Sargent, J. (1995) Building brands in the UK. *Admap* (January), pp. 45–7.

Twivy, P. (2000) Passionate brands will win the race. *Marketing*, 9 March, p. 19.

Vyse, K. (1999) Fingerprint clues identify the brand. *Marketing*, 30 September, p. 38.

Witt, J. (2000) Preparing Virgin Cola for the fight of its life. *Marketing*, 2 November, p. 23.

15

Business-to-business marketing communications

Organisations have many reasons to enter into exchange relationships with one another, rather than with consumers. This is referred to as the business-to-business sector and marketing communications need to reflect the characteristics of the buyer behaviour inherent in these relationships. Effective communications are important for helping to build long-term relationships, closer levels of collaboration and cooperative behaviours and help secure some advantage in the market system.

AIMS AND OBJECTIVES

The aims of this chapter are to introduce and explore business-to-business (b2b) marketing communications and to consider the factors that influence and shape relationships between organisations.

The objectives of this chapter are:

1. To establish the primary characteristics of the b2b sector.

2. To develop an understanding of the particular types of risk associated with organisational decision-making.

3. To introduce a model of b2b marketing communications.

4. To examine trust and commitment as major components of interorganisational communications.

5. To appraise the role and structural determinants of marketing communications within marketing channels.

6. To explore the notions of collaborative and autonomous communication strategies.

7. To consider the notion of communication quality.

8. To examine issues concerning eCommerce and b2b relationships.

9. To introduce key account management as an important strategic approach to communications with intermediaries.

Introduction

The characteristics of the business-to-business (b2b) market are very different to those of the consumer market (b2c). The larger size of markets, the lower number of customers, the high average spend per customer, the wider geographic spread and the relatively complex nature of buyer behaviour are significant differences. Of all of these factors, it is the buyer behaviour element that is the primary distinguishing element and the one that impacts most on marketing communications. It should not be surprising therefore that the marketing communications in these two major sectors are very different.

Of all of these factors, it is the buyer behaviour element that is the primary distinguishing element and the one that impacts most on marketing communications.

The commercial b2b sector is made up of four main subsectors, all of which share common buyer behaviour characteristics and communication needs, i.e. goods/services for:

1. Own consumption – vending machines, office furniture, stationery.

2. Incorporation and assembly – materials and supplies necessary for the production of your products and services. The identity of the materials can be lost within the larger product. These organisations are sometimes referred to as original equipment manufacturers (OEMs).

3. Resale to another organisation – acting as a member of a marketing channel, perhaps taking ownership and possession, adding value before passing the products on to another organisation that will add value to it in some way.

4. Retail – the most common example where goods and services are sold to end-user consumers.

In all of the situations organisations are involved in the buying of products, and only in the last situation are consumers at all involved. Therefore, the nature and form of the cooperation and the interorganisational relationships that develop from the exchanges influence the nature of the marketing communication activities used. The degree of cooperation between organisations will vary and part of the role of marketing communications is to develop and support the relationships that exist between partner organisations.

The degree of cooperation between organisations will vary and part of the role of marketing communications is to develop and support the relationships that exist between partner organisations.

In this sector organisations buy products and services and they use processes and procedures that can involve a large number of people. Fuller details about these characteristics can be found in Chapter 4. What is central, however, is the decision-making unit and the complexities associated with the variety of people and processes involved in making organisational purchase decisions and the implications for sup-

Table 15.1   Seven types of organisational decision-making risk

Risk type	Explanation
Technical risk	Will the parts, equipment or product/service perform as expected?
Financial risk	Does this represent value for money, could we have bought cheaper?
Delivery risk	Will delivery be on time, complete and in good order? Will our production schedule be disrupted?
Service risk	Will the equipment be supported properly and within agreed time parameters?
Personal risk	Am I comfortable dealing with this organisation, are my own social and ego needs threatened?
Relationship risk	To what extent is the long-term relationship with this organisation likely to be jeopardised by this decision?
Professional risk	How will this decision affect my professional standing in the eyes of others and how might my career and personal development be impacted?

pliers in terms of the length of time, and nature of the communication mix and messages necessary to reduce the levels of risk inherent in these situations. Mitchell (1999) refers to Haakansson and Wootz (1979), who identified need, transaction and market uncertainties, and Valla (1982) who suggested that there are five categories of risk which must be addressed by buyers and suppliers. From these it is possible to identify seven types of risk that are relevant to organisational buyers. These are shown at Table 15.1.

Valla (1982) suggested that there are five categories of risk which must be addressed by buyers and suppliers.

Personal selling is very important in b2b markets, often because of the need to help build relationships with members of buying centres and the need to demonstrate and explain technicalities associated with the products and services being marketed. In support of the personal selling effort (and exhibitions), trade promotions, trade advertising, direct marketing and public relations all play important roles. See Exhibit 15.1 for an example of B2B advertising. Increasingly, the Internet provides not only new direct routes to customers and intermediaries but also a vibrant new communications medium.

Networks and interorganisational relationships

The strategic value of marketing channels, partnerships and alliances and business networks has become increasingly more significance in recent years. As channel networks have developed, so has their complexity, which impacts upon the marketing communications strategies and tools used to help reach these customers, partners and fellow intermediaries. The expectations of buyers in these networks have risen in parallel with the significance attached to them by manufacturers. The power of multiple retailers, such as Curry's, Comet, Boots and Superdrug, is such that they are able to dictate terms (including the marketing communications) to many manufacturers of branded goods. For example,

As channel networks have developed, so has their complexity, which impacts upon the marketing communications strategies and tools used to help reach these customers, partners and fellow intermediaries.

It's a Chargecard.

Cut admin time and petty cash time and reduce the number of cheques issued.

It's an Information Card.

Track and control expenses with detailed monthly statements and management information.

It's a Travel Card.

Full travel booking service including free travel insurance when you use your card.

It's a Negotiation Card.

Allowing you to negotiate discounts on travel and entertainment.

It's a Security Card.

You decide each card's limit. You're also protected with free Cardholder Misuse Insurance too.

(Sorry, we forgot about the birthday card.)

For further information on our Corporate Card call 0845 721 2111 and quote 1015 or visit our website.
Company Barclaycard P.O. Box 3000 Teesdale Business Park Stockton-on-Tees TS17 6YG
www.company.barclaycard.co.uk

Exhibit 15.1
Company Barclaycard. An example of B2B advertising. Advertisement reproduced with the kind permission of Barclaycard.

many consumer-related sales promotion events are prompted by retailers in response to claims for shelf space and in-store visibility.

The basic structure of any network consists of a focal organisation which is tied with a number of other functionally specialised organisations. The network uses relational exchanges to regularise and sustain cooperative activities. This is a general view and it is recognised that there is a variety of network forms, some of which were explored previously (Chapter 10). However, to repeat an important point, it is necessary to distinguish the type of networks an organisation belongs to from traditional perspectives, if only because it is now generally accepted that all organisations are networks in their own right and that there is a variety of internal and external networks to which all organisations belong.

Network organisations can be distinguished from traditional organisational forms because the exchanges are based upon membership.

Therefore, network organisations can be distinguished from traditional organisational forms because the exchanges are based upon membership, which encourages mutually determined relational transactions. This long-term perspective reflects the density, closeness and shared values that such networks seek to perpetuate.

B2B communications – Sharwood's Asian foods

Sharwood's network of independent retailers is vitally important to provide shelf space and visibility for its brand of sauces. However, it found that the sale of its Chinese sauces through the independent retailer network was low compared with those of Indian sauces. To help rectify the imbalance, it used a direct marketing campaign to coincide with the Chinese New Year.

Incentivised mailpacks were sent to selected independent retail outlets, inviting them to purchase cases of Oriental products and in return receive money-off coupons. The campaign also sought to educate retailers so that they provided their customers with a breadth of suitable products. After a two-week interval, telemarketing was used to identify those retailers who had either purchased or wanted to order over the phone. Darby (1997) reports that a 34% take-up resulted from this approach and Sharwood's market share rose to 26% over the new year period.

Many commentators have observed that organisations are forging relationships with other organisations that are based around a network in order to achieve new, fresh advantages. These advantages may be driven by competitive goals, but the behaviour exhibited is increasingly cooperative. These networks vary in the strength of their ties (degrees of interconnectedness), but success can be seen to be a function of the partnerships that are developed in these networks. A key question has to be, what determines a successful partnership and how is success characterised and replicated? An underlying principle of relational exchanges is the pivotal role of trust and commitment (Morgan and Hunt, 1994) (see Figure 15.1).

Commitment to a partnership, that is the relationship with other network members, is key because of the 'enduring desire to maintain a valued relationship' (Moorman *et al.*, 1992). Of comparable importance is the degree to which partners are confident that each will act in the best interests of the relationship. *Trust*, therefore, is also regarded as a key aspect of relational exchanges and is a composite of the level of reliability and integrity that exists between partners.

Commitment to a partnership is key because of the 'enduring desire to maintain a valued relationship'.

According to Mohr and Spekman (1994), partnership success is based upon three key parameters. These are the attributes the partnership exhibits, the communication behaviour and the techniques used to resolve conflict (see Figure 15.2). Their view is that partnership success is dependent upon a wider array of factors than just commit-

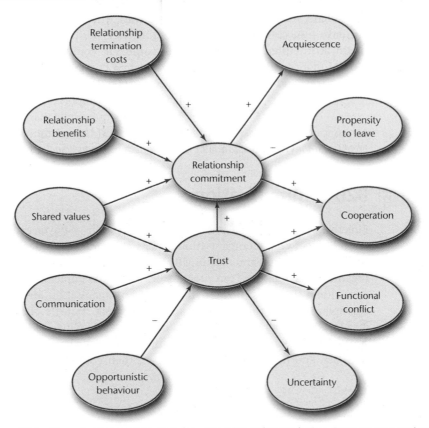

Figure 15.1   The role of commitment and trust in relationship marketing. From Morgan and Hunt (1994); reprinted with permission from *Journal of Marketing*, published by the American Marketing Association.

Figure 15.2   Characteristics of partnership success. From Mohr and Spekman (1994); used with kind permission.

Communication problems are associated with a lack of partnership success *and communication* might be interpreted as an overt manifestation of more subtle phenomenon, such as trust and commitment.

ment and trust. These are recognised as important, but in addition they posit communication- and conflict-related issues. It could be argued that Mohr and Spekman define commitment and trust in a relatively narrow way, such that the other factors need to be made explicit. What is important, however, is that these authors state unequivocally that *communication problems are associated with a lack of partnership success* and that communication *might be interpreted as an overt manifestation of more subtle phenomena, such as trust and commitment.*

B2B communications

Effective communication is key to the satisfaction of buyer expectations and is the main link between an organisation and its environment. Indeed, the systems used to transfer information and meaning from people and machines, in both inter- and intra-organisational contexts, can progress or hinder the implementation of corporate and operational strategies. If the dynamics of an organisation are to be understood, for example, in order that effective and appropriate strategic change processes can be developed, then all its communication systems and networks need to be appreciated.

What are their communication requirements in the light of the objectives that have been set, and more importantly what are their communication expectations? Once

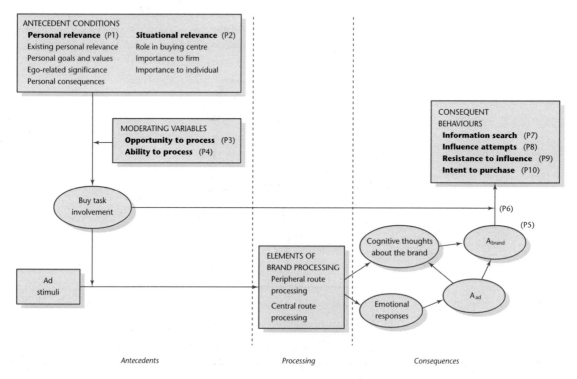

Figure 15.3   Model of business-to-business marketing communications. From Gilliland and Johnston (1997); used with kind permission.

these have been considered, it is possible to consider the communication strategies that may be best suited to achieving these goals and then determine the means by which strategies will be implemented.

Gilliland and Johnston (1997) published a model of b2b marketing communication effects, which has been reproduced as Figure 15.3. In this model the buy task involvement (BTI) represents the degree to which individual members of the DMU feel personal relevance (involvement) with each purchase decision. They identify four main elements that can impact on an individual's level of personal involvement, as set out in Table 15.2.

The model then follows a similar path to the elaboration likelihood model (ELM), which is explained in a consumer market context in Chapter 20. Essentially those involved with the purchase decision will process information via the central route, and will be more attentive to well-argued messages and look for rational logical information in order to support their decision. Those less involved will use the peripheral route and not pay attention to the arguments or information provided. So for this group it will be the design and layout of the advertisement or the attractiveness of the expert sources used that will determine whether there is a change in attitude. Attitude change through the central route tends to be longer lasting than attitude change through peripheral cues.

The buy task involvement (BTI) represents the degree to which individual members of the DMU feel personal relevance (involvement) with each purchase decision.

The authors of this model also recognise that there are political dynamics associated with the roles each member of the DMU adopts. Indeed, there will be a degree of intergroup persuasion according to the degree of affiliation or identification with the products and brands being considered. The more positive the association and the higher the BTI, the more likely an individual will be to engage in behaviour that will seek more information and attempt to influence others.

There are political dynamics associated with the roles each member of the DMU adopts.

Table 15.2   The antecedents associated with BTI

Relevance factor	Explanation
Personal	Refers to personal goals, any ego-related significance and the perceived personal consequences of the purchase decision. The higher the personal relevance, the higher the BTI.
Situational	Refers to the importance of the decision to the individual and to the firm. The higher the situational relevance, the higher the BTI.
Opportunity to process	Refers to the level of distractions and noise that might impede exposure or prevent comprehension of a marketing message. The higher the number of opportunities to process information, the higher the BTI.
Ability to process	Refers to the knowledge an individual has about the product under consideration as the more the individual knows, the greater his/her ability to process information about it. The greater the ability to process information, the higher the BTI.

Source: Adapted from Gilliland and Johnston, (1997); used with kind permission.

The significance of this model is that it brings to attention the importance of emotion and feeling in b2b advertising messages. For a long time the focus of this work has been on producing information advertisements that present product-related information. This will be an effective appeal to those who have a higher BTI. However, there are many others involved with purchase decisions who have a low BTI but who may have a significant input to the decision process. There are also implications for the media schedule with more reason to use television and consumer print media in particular.

Interorganisational communication

The important role that communication plays in determining the effectiveness of any group or network of organisations is widely recognised (Grabner and Rosenberg, 1969; Stern and El-Ansary, 1992). According to Mohr and Nevin (1990), communication is 'the glue that holds together a marketing channel'. It is recognised that, from a managerial perspective, communication is important because many of the causes of tension and conflict in interorganisational relationships stem from inadequate or poor communication. Communication within networks serves not only to provide persuasive information and foster participative decision-making but also to provide for coordination, the exercise of power and the encouragement of loyalty and commitment, so as to reduce the likelihood of tension and conflict.

Communication within networks serves not only to provide persuasive information and foster participative decision-making but also to provide for coordination, the exercise of power and the encouragement of loyalty and commitment.

The channel network (Chapter 10) consists of those organisations with whom others must cooperate directly to achieve their own objectives. By accepting that there is interdependence, usually dispersed unequally throughout the network, it is possible to identify organisations who have a stronger/weaker position within a network. Communication must travel not only between the different levels of dependence and

Changing marketing channels – UK car market

In 1999 new car registrations in the UK fell by nearly 25%. At the same time, the Competition Commission inquiry into UK car pricing was widely predicted to bring about a major reduction in car prices. An interim report from the Commission stated that the current system of 'selective and exclusive distribution' was driving prices higher than perhaps they need be. Consumer dissatisfaction with the process of buying cars from dealerships also fuelled the move to bring about change in the sector's marketing channels.

Moves towards dealerships that are not tied to a particular manufacturer, plus increased Internet opportunities, would help induce competition and reduce prices (Murphy, 1999). Some possible outcomes of this move would be to encourage dealerships to project a stronger brand identity with their target consumers and also encourage the development of a multichannel approach to the market, using direct marketing strategies, ecommerce facilities as well as corporate branding cues to enable differentiation and the creation of brand value.

role ('up and down' in a channel context) and so represent bidirectional flows, but also across similar levels of dependence and role, that is, horizontal flows. For example, these may be from retailer to retailer or wholesaler to wholesaler.

There are some specialised messages that need to be distributed across a variety of networks, for example, messages proclaiming technological advances, business acquisitions and contracts won. It is also apparent that communication flows do not change radically over the short term. On the contrary, they become established and regularised through use. This allows for the emergence of specialised communication networks (Chapter 2). Furthermore, it is common for networks to be composed of subnetworks, overlaying each other. The complexity of an organisation's networks is such that unravelling each one would be dysfunctional.

What is necessary is the establishment of those elements that contribute to the general communications in a b2b situation, and a marketing channel environment in particular. The development of a planned, channel-orientated communications strategy, a push strategy, should be based on identifiable elements that contribute to and reinforce the partnerships in the network. A number of these can be identified, namely a consideration of the movement of flows of information and in particular the timing and permanence of the flows (Stern and El-Ansary, 1992). It should also take into account the various facets of communication and the particular channel structures through which communications are intended to move (Mohr and Nevin, 1990). These will now be considered in turn.

Timing of the flows

Message flows can be either simultaneous or serial. Where *simultaneous* flows occur, messages are distributed to all members so that the information is received at approximately the same time. Business seminars and dealer meetings, together with direct mail promotional activities and the use of integrated IT systems between levels (overnight ordering procedures), are examples of this type of flow. *Serial* flows involve the transmission of messages so that they are received by a preselected number of network members who then transmit the message to others at lower levels within the network. Serial flows may lead to problems concerning the management of the network, such as those concerning stock levels and production.

Message flows can be either simultaneous or serial.

Permanence of the flows

The degree of permanence that a message has is determined by the technology used in the communication process. Essentially, the more a message can be recalled without physical distortion of the content, the more permanent the flow. This would indicate that the use of machines to record the message content would have an advantage over person-to-person messages transmitted at a sales meeting. Permanence can be improved by recording the meeting with a tape recorder or by putting the conversation on paper and using handouts and sales literature.

Mohr and Nevin (1990) suggest that the performance outcomes of a channel network are a result of the interaction of the communication strategy used within a network and the structure of the channel within which the communications flow. Figure 15.4 depicts the relationships between strategies and structure. Therefore, by examin-

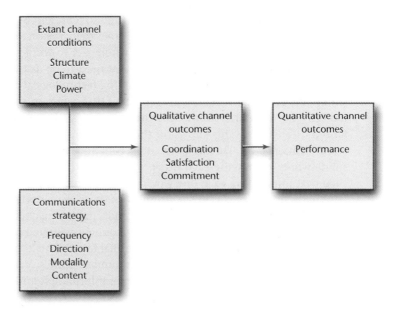

Figure 15.4   A model of communication for marketing channels. From Mohr and Nevin (1990); used with kind permission.

ing the constituent elements and moulding the variables to meet the channel conditions, it may be possible to enhance the performance/success of the network.

Communication facets

Communication strategy results from a combination of four facets of communication. These facets are the frequency, direction, modality and content of communications:

1. *Frequency*

   The amount of contact between members of the performance network needs to be assessed. Too much information (too frequent, aggregate volume or pure repetition) can overload members and have a dysfunctional effect. Too little information can undermine the opportunities for favourable performance outcomes by failing to provide necessary operational information, motivation and support. As a consequence, it is important to identify the current volume of information being provided and for management to make a judgement about the desired levels of communication.

2. *Direction*

   This refers to the horizontal and vertical movement of communication within a network. Each network consists of members who are dependent upon others, but the level of dependence will vary: hence, the dispersion of power is unequal.

   Communications can be unidirectional in that they flow in one direction only. This may be from a source of power to subordinate members (for example, from a major food retailer such as Sainsbury's or Tesco to small food manufacturers). Communications can also be bidirectional, that is, to and from powerful organisations. The relative power positions of manufacturer/producer and reseller need to be established and understood prior to the creation of any communication plan.

3. *Modality*

Modality refers to the method used to transmit information. Mohr and Nevin agree that there is a wide variety of interpretations of the methods used to convey information. They use modality in the sense that communications can be either formal and regulated, such as meetings and written reports, or informal and spontaneous, such as corridor conversations and word-of-mouth communications, often carried out away from an organisation's formal structures and environment.

4. *Content*

This refers to what is said. Frazier and Summers (1984) distinguish between direct and indirect influence strategies. Direct strategies are designed to change behaviour by specific request (recommendations, promises and appeals to legal obligations). Indirect strategies attempt to change a receiver's beliefs and attitudes about the desirability of the intended behaviour. This may take the form of an information exchange, where the source uses discussions about general business issues to influence the attitudes of the receiver.

Channel structures

Communication facets can be seen in the light of three particular channel conditions: structure, climate and power:

1. *Channel structure*

Channel structure, according to Stern and El-Ansary (1988), can be distinguished by the nature of the exchange relationship. These are relational and market structure relationships. Relational exchanges have a long-term perspective and high interdependence and involve joint decision-making. Market exchanges are by contrast *ad hoc* and hence have a short-term orientation where interdependence is low (Chapter 1).

2. *Channel climate*

Anderson *et al.* (1987) used measures of trust and goal compatibility in defining organisational climate. This in turn can be interpreted as the degree of mutual supportiveness that exists between channel members.

3. *Power*

Dwyer and Walker (1981) showed that power conditions within a channel can be symmetrical (with power balanced between members) or asymmetrical (with a power imbalance).

Table 15.3 shows the relationships between communication facets and channel conditions. This is the combination of elements identified above.

Two specific forms of communication strategy can be identified. The first is a combination referred to as a 'collaborative communication strategy' and includes higher-frequency, more bidirectional flows, informal modes and indirect content. This combination is likely to occur in channel conditions of relational structures, supportive climates or symmetrical power. The second combination is referred to as an 'autonomous communication strategy' and includes lower-frequency, more unidirectional communication, formal modes and direct content. This combination is likely to occur in channel conditions of market structures, unsupportive climates and asymmetrical power.

Communication strategy should, therefore, be built upon the characteristics of the situation facing each organisation in any particular network. Not all networks share the

Table 15.3 The relationships between channel conditions and the facets of communication

Channel conditions	Communication facets			
	Frequency	Direction	Content	Modality
Structure				
Relational	Higher	More bidirectional	More indirect	More informal
Market	Lower	More unidirectional	More direct	More formal
Climate				
Supportive	Higher	More bidirectional	More indirect	More informal
Unsupportive	Lower	More unidirectional	More direct	More informal
Power				
Symmetrical	Higher	More bidirectional	More indirect	More informal
Asymmetrical	Lower	More unidirectional	More indirect	More informal

Source: Mohr and Nevin (1990); used with kind permission.

same conditions, nor do they all possess the same degree of closeness or relational expectations. By considering the nature of the channel conditions and then developing communication strategies that complement them, the performance of the focus organisation and other members can be considerably improved, and conflict and tension substantially reduced. Where channel conditions match communication strategy, the outcomes of the performance network are said, by Mohr and Nevin (1990), to be enhanced. Likewise, when the communication strategy fails to match the channel conditions, the outcomes are not likely to be enhanced (Figure 15.5).

Communication strategy should, therefore, be built upon the characteristics of the situation facing each organisation in any particular network.

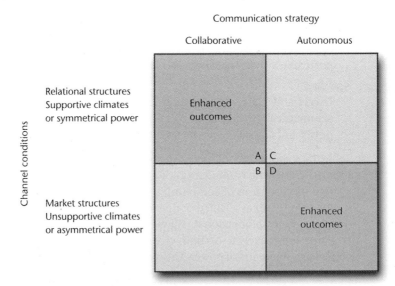

Figure 15.5 Proposed relationships between communication strategies and channel conditions. The shaded areas represent enhanced outcome levels, or where communication strategies fit channel conditions. The unshaded areas represent non-enhanced outcome levels, or where communication strategies do not fit channel conditions. From Mohr and Nevin (1990); used with kind permission.

Communication quality

Recently, an interesting new perspective on marketing channel communications has emerged, namely issues concerning the quality of the communications and the success that might be attributed to the communication behaviours of the partners in any loose or tight networks.

Mohr and Sohi (1995) considered whether communication quality might be a function of the propensity to share information. The inclination among members to share information could be assumed to be positive in networks where members show high levels of trust and commitment. Frequency of communication flows, the level of bidirectional communications in a network and the level of communication formality are assumed to be the main elements of the propensity to share information.

Another aspect considered by the researchers was the degree to which information might be withheld or distorted (deviance). Information deviance might be high when there is an absence of rules (norms) determining what information needs to communicated. Informality may lead to vagueness or inattentiveness and higher levels of deviance.

Also considered was the degree to which information might be withheld or distorted (deviance).

The research sought to determine whether any (or all) of the three factors indicated that there was a linkage between the variables and the quality of information perceived by channel members. The results indicated that in the sample sector (computer dealers) the only significant variable was the frequency of information. The higher the frequency of communications received by channel members, the higher the perception of the quality of the communications. Issues concerning information overload and irritance are discounted.

Satisfaction levels appear to be correlated with higher levels of bidirectional communications. So, frequency impacts on perceived quality (and hence satisfaction) and the degree of bidirectional communications is significant in determining levels of satisfaction with the communications in a channel (network) environment.

eCommerce

Following on from the discussion about the propensity to share information is the rise of eCommerce and the opportunities to share information electronically. The development of Extranets, in particular, enables organisations to share information for mutual benefit and to develop a form of competitive advantage through collaboration. Extranets allow organisations to work together in privacy and to deliver more efficient transactions. One of the difficulties experienced by Extranet users is that all participants must use a common software system and those not hosting the system are invariably required to change their business operations behind their IT interface. New technology is changing that as eCollaboration was launched in 2000. This business model uses software that enables two different operating systems to talk to each other and to share information. All that is required is a portal through which all parties must pass.

The development of Extranets, in particular, enables organisations to share information for mutual benefit and to develop a form of competitive advantage through collaboration.

eCollaboration – Kellogg

Kellogg installed the eCollaboration software in conjunction with a number of UK supermarkets. The fuel blockades in September 1999 led shoppers to panic buying and purchase habits and patterns were soon lost. Normally, Kellogg's would adjust its production schedules according to retailers reports of expected demand, usually with a three-day lag. However, the information would lack precision, would take considerable to time to be disaggregated from the system and the amalgamation of the data from each of the supermarkets had to be completed manually.

During the panic-buying phase, Hewson (2000) reports that consumer demand reverted to staple products (cornflakes rather than cinnamon muesli) but the new system allowed Kellogg to track the emerging demand patterns quickly, to consolidate information from each of the supermarkets, and then adjust production on a daily basis. As a result of this ability to closely monitor purchasing trends, Kellogg's was able to maintain supplies, not lose sales for its business partners or itself, and, of course, strengthen its relationships with the supermarkets.

Source: David Hewson, *The Sunday Times*, London, 26 November 2000.

A b2b communication strategy will often consist of a series of activities designed to ultimately influence the audience and persuade a percentage of them to take a particular action, very often to purchase the product/service itself. For example, a five-stage strategy to launch a new Web site for the purchase of office services might be to:

1. Build brand name awareness among the target audience. This would involve both off-line and on-line communications. The goal would be to drive site traffic and to encourage site visitors.

2. Drive site registration and generate reasons for visitors to return to the site.

3. Convert registrations into purchasers and the use of on-line and off-line sales promotions might be effective.

4. Ensure that a certain percentage of purchasers are retained and are encouraged to return to the site. Not necessarily loyalty but a retention facility based upon a points collection scheme could be useful.

5. Build into the communication strategy a means of personalising communications such that each buyer would receive special offers and notices of products and services that reflect their purchase patterns to date.

To support this strategy, a creative proposition will need to be developed so that there is a central theme around which all communications are linked. This might be related to particular attributes such as product features, for example, a colour, size or speed of service. The benefits of the attributes might also be used, for example, no production downtime or improved staff efficiency might be valid claims. In contrast, an emotional feeling might be generated through the use of a tag line, gimmick, slogan, music or perhaps a mood. In other words, some form of branding needs to be used to differentiate the Web site and create longer-lasting memories which can

To support this strategy, a creative proposition will need to be developed so that there is a central theme around which all communications are linked.

be easily recalled through the mention of the brand name or perhaps an attribute or central theme.

The promotional mix and b2b

As stated earlier, the use of the tools of the promotional mix is very different to that in consumer markets. The prime tool is personal selling supported by both above- and below-the-line activities. The Internet and related digital technologies have had a very significant role in changing the way business is conducted and the speed at which transactions can be undertaken and costs reduced. The WWW is of course both a new distribution channel and communication medium. As a form of communication it is impersonal and more disposed to information search and retrieval than to information that is heavily branded and has emotional overtones. The nature of communications in b2b is that they are very personal, often require face-to-face interaction and the interactive nature lends itself to tailored messages and rapid feedback.

The rest of this chapter will be spent reviewing each of the tools of the mix and role they play within a b2b context. For a fuller exposition of these tools, readers are advised to refer to Part 4 of this text, commencing at Chapter 20.

Advertising and b2b

Perhaps the most important role of advertising in this context is to inform and remind.

Apart from increasing use of on-line advertising, the most important form is print advertising in trade journals and newspapers. Perhaps the most important role of advertising in this context is to inform and remind, whereas differentiation and persuasion are delivered through other tools of the promotional mix, namely sales promotion and personal selling.

B2B advertising – Reebok

Reebok uses advertising in trade magazines to inform its dealers and trade customers of special events, product launches and news relating to the brand. Plate 15.1 depicts an award-winning ad which was targeted at its dealers informing them of the launch of the new Liverpool FC kit. Using scouse humour, Reebok drew attention to the brand and informed dealers of the kit's availability.

Material kindly provided by Reebok International

Direct marketing and b2b

Telemarketing has played an important role in recent years as a support mechanism to the sales force. It is used to facilitate customer enquiries, to establish leads, make appointments and in certain circumstances provide a direct sales channel. One of the more common uses is as a sales order processing system to collect routine low-value orders. This frees up the sales force to concentrate on other more profitable activities.

Direct mail has been an important part of the communications mix in b2b markets

for some time. Direct mail can be used to support personal selling by building awareness, enhancing image, establishing credibility and taking orders, and it can provide
levels of customer management. The significance of this part of the communications
is not in doubt, even though some of it is being surpassed by the use of the Internet
and eCommerce practices.

Therefore, it would appear sensible to be able to measure direct mail activities and
in the b2b sector this is usually accomplished through measurement of response rates.

There are a number of stages through which a receiver of direct mail moves. These are the opening, scanning, (re)reading and response behaviours.

However, this is not entirely satisfactory (Vöegle, 1992)
because there are a number of stages through which a
receiver of direct mail moves. These are the opening,
scanning, (re)reading and response behaviours. Vriens
et al. (1995) suggest that there are three main parts to
the process. The first is the opening behaviour which is
influenced by the attractiveness of the envelope and situational factors. Reading
behaviour is influenced by the opening behaviour, the reader's situational characteristics and the attractiveness of the mailing and its contents. The final behaviour concerns the response generated which is affected by the attractiveness of the offer, by the
reading behaviour that preceded the response and the characteristics of the individual
reader and their situation.

Wulf *et al.* (2000) used this framework to find ways in which response rates to direct
mail could be increased. They found that the attractiveness of the envelope did impact
on opening behaviour but so did the envelope size, material, colour and even type of
postage. Surprisingly the volume of direct mail each manager received had no impact
on opening behaviour. With regard to reading behaviour, it was the attitudes of the
reader that were found to be significant, not the situational factors. Finally, response
behaviour appeared to be determined more by the reading behaviours of the individual rather than any other factor.

Sales promotions and b2b

The use of sales- or rather trade-based promotions is very often unnoticed by consumers. However, trade promotions and interorganisa-

Price-based promotions and delayed discounts are used to encourage organisations to place business.

tional incentives are common and generally effective.
Manufacturers will use competitions and sweepstakes
to incentivise the sales forces of its distributors, to
motivate technical and customer support staff in retail
organisations and as an inducement to encourage other businesses to place orders and
business with them.

Price-based promotions and delayed discounts are used to encourage organisations
to place business. Another popular approach is to discount technical support and
bundle up a range of support facilities. Whatever the package, the purpose remains the
same, to add value in order to advance (or gain) a purchase commitment.

Public relations and b2b

The effectiveness of public relations in a b2b context should not be underestimated.
The range of public relations tools and techniques enable credibility to be developed
in an environment where advertising is relatively ineffective, personal selling critical
to the development of relationships and sales promotion limited to short-term sales

Public relations provide credibility and richness to an organisation's communications.

shifts. Direct marketing and particularly interactively based communications are increasingly important in this sector but public relations provide credibility and richness to an organisation's communications.

Personal selling and b2b

Personal selling is the most important tool of the marketing communication mix in b2b markets. Readers are referred to the substantial space that has been allocated to this topic in Chapter 29. However, one area that has developed in recent years owing to the use of direct marketing and interactive technology is key account management (KAM).

It has long been recognised that particular customer accounts represent an important, often large, proportion of turnover. Such accounts have been referred to variously as national accounts, house accounts, major accounts and key accounts. Millman and Wilson (1995) argue that the first three are orientated towards sales, tend to the short term and are often only driven by sales management needs.

Key accounts may be of different sizes in comparison with the focus organisation, but what delineates them from other types of 'account' is that they are strategically important. Key accounts are customers who, in a business-to-business network, are willing to enter into relational exchanges and who are of strategic importance to the focus organisation.

Key accounts are customers who, in a business-to-business network, are willing to enter into relational exchanges and who are of strategic importance to the focus organisation.

There are two primary aspects of this definition. The first is that relational exchanges are a necessary component and the relationship is perceived by both parties as long term. The second aspect refers to the strategic issue. The key account is strategically important because the account might offer opportunities for entry to new markets; it might represent access to other key organisations; or resources or it might provide symbolic value in terms of influence, power and stature.

Points of contact

The importance of the long-term relationship as a prime part of key account identification raises questions about how these relationships are developed, what resources are required to manage and sustain them and what the long-term success and effectiveness of identifying these accounts is.

The main point of contact is through the sales force, as personal selling is the principle conduit for communication. The assignment of sales executives to these important accounts is common in smaller organisations. Those organisations that have the resources are able to incorporate the services of senior executives. They assume this role and with it they bring the flexibility and responsive service that are required as the account grows in stature. They can make decisions about stock, price, distribution and levels of customisation.

These accounts may be major or national accounts, as very often their strategic significance is not recognised. There is a tendency for these accounts to receive a disproportionate level of attention, as the executives responsible for these major customers lose sight of their own organisation's marketing strategy.

A further way of managing these accounts is to create a key account division. The main advantage of this approach is that it offers close integration of production, finance, marketing and sales. The main disadvantage is that resources are duplicated and the organisation can become very inefficient. It is also a high-risk strategy as the entire division is dependent upon a few customers.

Key account management (KAM)

A number of researchers have attempted to gain a greater understanding of KAM by considering the development cycles that relationships move through. Millman and Wilson (1995) offer the work of Ford (1980), Dwyer *et al.* (1987) and Wotruba (1991) as examples of such development cycles (Table 15.4).

Millman and Wilson have attempted to build upon the work of the others (included in Table 15.4) and have formulated a model which incorporates their own research as well as that established in the literature. McDonald (2000) has since elaborated on their framework, providing further insight and explanation.

The cycle develops with the exploratory KAM level where the main task is to identify those accounts that have key account potential.

The cycle develops with the *exploratory KAM* level where the main task is to identify those accounts that have key account potential and those that do not in order that resources can be allocated efficiently. Buying organisations are considering each other: the buyer in terms of the supplier's offer in terms of its ability to match their own requirements and the seller in terms of the buyer providing sufficient volumes, value and financial suitablity.

The next level is *basic KAM*, where both organisations enter into a transactional period, essentially trialling each other as potential long-term partners. Some relationships may stabilise at this level while others may develop as a result of the seller seeking and gaining tentative agreement with prospective accounts about whether they would become 'preferred accounts'.

At the cooperative KAM *level more people from both organisations are involved in communications.*

At the *cooperative KAM* level more people from both organisations are involved in communications. At the basic KAM level both parties understand each other and the selling company has established its credentials with the buying organisation, through experience. At this next level opportunities to add value to the relationship, perhaps by spreading the

Table 15.4 Comparison of relational models

Ford (1980), Dwyer *et al.* (1987)	Wotruba (1991)	Millman and Wilson (1995)	McDonald. (2000)
Pre-relationship awareness	Provider	Pre-KAM	Exploratory
Early stage exploration	Persuader	Early KAM	Basic
Development stage expansion	Prospector	Mid-KAM	Cooperative
Long-term stage commitment	Problem solver	Partnership KAM	Interdependent
Final stage institutionalisation	Procreator	Synergistic KAM	Integrated
		Uncoupling KAM	Disintegrated

Source: Updated from Millman and Wilson (1995); used with kind permission.

range of products and services transacted, are considered. As a result, more people are involved in the relationship.

At the *interdependent KAM* level of their relationship both organisations are able to recognise the importance of the other to its operations with the supplier either first choice or only supplier. Retraction from the relationship is now problematic as 'inertia and strategic suitability', as McDonald phrases it, holds the partners together.

Integrated KAM is achieved when the two organis-

Integrated KAM is achieved when the two organisations view the relationship as consisting of one entity where they create synergistic value in the marketplace.

ations view the relationship as consisting of one entity where they create synergistic value in the marketplace. Joint problem-solving and the sharing of sensitive information are strong characteristics of the relationship and withdrawal by either party can be traumatic at a personal level for the participants involved, let alone at the organisational level.

The final level is *disintegrating KAM*. This can occur at any time for a variety of reasons, ranging from company takeover to the introduction of new technology. The relationship may return to another lower level and new terms of business are established. The termination or readjustment of the relationship need not be seen as a negative factor as both parties may decide that the relationship holds no further value.

McDonald develops Millman and Wilson's model by moving away from a purely sequential framework. He suggests that organisations may stabilise or enter the model at any level, indeed he states that organisations might readjust to a lower level. The time between phases will vary according to the nature and circumstances of the parties involved. The labels provided by McDonald reflect the relationship status of both parties rather than of the selling company (e.g. prospective) or buying company (e.g. preferred supplier). Whilst the Millman and Wilson and the McDonald interpretations of the KAM relationship cycle provide insight, they are both primarily dyadic perspectives. What also needs to be considered is the influence of significant others, in particular, those other network member organisations that provide context and interaction in particualr networks and influence the actions of organisations and key individuals who are strategic decision makers.

Summary

The b2b market is characterised by the decision-making processes that organisational buyers use. As these can be very different from those used by consumers, it is not surprising that the marketing communications will also vary in many ways. The b2b market consists of four main types of interorganisational relationships, reflecting the role the product/service plays in the business activity of the organisation (e.g. for resale, as OEM).

Seven different types of risk were identified with organisational decision-making. Consequently, the marketing communications used to reach different organisations, predominantly personal selling, need to be adaptive to reduce different typres of risk.

The model of b2b marketing communications suggests that the level of involvement experienced by the main participants in the buying process will affect the level and type of communications used. However, while the simplicity and logical reasoning associated with the model are intuitively appealing, the authors of the model accept that the political ambience in which these decisions are made does in fact 'muddy' the view and reflect the complexity of network relationships.

In order that the promotional objectives relating to members of the marketing channel network can be accomplished, it is necessary to establish and implement a communication strategy that is particular to this type of target audience. This form of marketing communication strategy is referred to as a *push* strategy. Communication strategy in the marketing channel needs to reflect the relationships that exist between members and match prevailing conditions. Commitment and trust are important variables in determining the nature of the relational exchanges that develop in networks, but in addition communications are vitally important to help build long-term relationships.

There are costs associated with communication in these networks. These costs may be direct, in the form of dealer conferences and house magazines. Costs may also be indirect in nature. For example, the views of particular retailers or manufacturers' representatives may go unheard or unreported. These views might be critical to the development of particular markets and hence be of strategic importance.

An examination of the communication networks, perhaps through a channel-wide communication audit, will reveal the need to develop communication networks appropriate to the needs of each organisation and the network as a whole.

The strategic importance of key accounts has gained increased attention in recent years. One of the prime dimensions of key accounts is the long-term relationship that can develop. McDonald has developed Millman and Wilson's interpretation of the different phases that can be associated with key account relationships. Marketing communications, principally through personal selling, is an important tool in fostering, nurturing and sustaining strategically important accounts.

Review questions

1. Who are the principal target audiences for push-orientated communications and how do these communications differ from pull-based communication strategies?

2. Discuss the role that trust and commitment might play in marketing communications with intermediaries.

3. What are the three parameters upon which partnership success is thought to be built?

4. Prepare notes for a short article to be included in a marketing magazine, about the importance of communications within marketing channels.

5. Describe the main elements of promotional informational flows in performance networks.

6. How can communication facets and channel structures be effectively combined?

7. What are the differences between collaborative and autonomous communication strategies?

8. Outline the concept of communication quality and identify the main dimension upon which quality is perceived to be based.

9. Identify the main difference between house or major accounts and key accounts.

10. Explain the concept of key account relationship cycles using the McDonald framework.

MINI CASE

Glymo

Glymo is a long established medium-sized engineering company, which distributes its range of electrically powered garden equipment products through a variety of retail outlets. One of its main products is lawnmowers, which traditionally have been distributed through ironmongers and garden centres and more recently through discount stores, hypermarkets and DIY superstores. For a long time Glymo's marketing channels and management of its distribution was particularly successful and was regarded as a major competitive strength. This success was attributed to the high reputation which had been established within the trade; the product, service, ordering, delivery and above all the company were all perceived to be trustworthy and very reliable. The mainstay of its communications with these outlets was the sales force.

The established market segment that Glymo reached through garden centres consisted of men, over 45 years old, who agreed that 'they took gardening seriously' and 'gardening is my main hobby'. This segment valued solid designs, reliability and preferred to buy from garden centres where there was experienced advice and support. Information compiled from guarantee registration cards indicated that customers had much larger gardens than average and that two-thirds were in the South and West of England.

Sales growth was aided by the introduction of new models, often prompted by sales force suggestions, customers and growing competition. One of these new products (Whirlybird) had been developed following the recognition of a new customer segment, the convenience gardener. This group wanted a lawnmower that would be simple to use, sufficiently light weight so that men and women could use it, and be easy to store. The rotary hover mower with grass collection facilities appeared to satisfy the needs of the convenience gardener. In contrast to traditional buyers, this segment preferred to use DIY superstores to obtain their lawnmowers and related garden equipment. Whirlybird sales soon took off and now contributed to 65% of turnover.

Originally marketing communications had been geared to servicing the garden centres and ironmongers with sales literature, leads and joint promotions with key accounts. Salesmen provided a point of personal contact; they were trained engineers and could provide technical support that was valued by their retail customers. The operation was very successful, profitable and the envy of many of its traditional competitors. However, as the emphasis switched to DIY superstores so the support shifted as well. Now the emphasis was on EDI and stock control with marketing communications orientated to the provision of leaflets and in-store merchandising. Gone was the need for personal support and advice; a salesman's job was now orientated to maintaining relationships with the major buyers of each of the major groups who owned the DIY superstores.

Although sales of Whirlybird related products were strong, Glymo realised that it was losing market share in the traditional market sector. Garden centre business was not central to Glymo and many of the personal friendships and relationships with the garden centres had withered as a result. Sales had slowed partly because Glymo could not support each garden centre in the way it used to. Sales force costs were very high and the reduced size of the sales force meant that they had to be concentrated on the most profitable parts of Glymo's business, the DIY superstores. Gone then were the technical support, the advice for garden centre sales staff and customers from the traditional gardeners segment.

It was not surprising that garden centre owners perceived Glymo as distant and uncaring about their type of business. Glymo had tried to use advertising and direct mail to reach traditional gardeners and build the brand.

However, when these potential customers arrived at garden centres to see the products and test them, they were faced with little Glymo stock, sales staff with little up-to-date knowledge and large ranges of competitor machines.

Glymo began to feel that it would be unable to retrieve its market position. It perceived garden centres as geographically isolated units, too costly to support but potentially profitable if only the company could find the right marketing mix. Glymo was increasingly concerned about the high levels of dealer dissatisfaction, many of whom had switched their business to Glymo's major competitor and other niche manufacturers. Glymo wanted to re-establish its market leadership but knew that to do this it had to re-establish relationships with each garden centre and associated networks. To be competitive it was necessary to provide high levels of support and advice, process sales orders quickly, provide fast customer service an attend to gardeners' needs for advice, not only on machinery but other aspects of lawn and garden care as well. Support through the sales force was not an option.

Mini-case questions

1. To what extent can we apply the collaborative and autonomous communications strategies to this situation?
2. What technological solution would you propose and how would you justify it?
3. What might be the benefits for the traditional gardeners and garden centres from this new approach?
4. Using some of the academic material, discuss the way in which Glymo's relationships with its retailers has evolved.
5. Comment on the degree to which the Gilliland and Johnston model of b2b marketing communications might apply.

References

Anderson, E., Lodish, L. and Weitz, B. (1987) Resource allocation behaviour in conventional channels. *Journal of Marketing Research* (February), pp. 85–97.

Darby, I. (1997) Korma chameleon. *Marketing Direct* (May), pp. 29–30.

Dwyer, R. and Walker, O.C. (1981) Bargaining in an asymmetrical power structure. *Journal of Marketing*, **45** (Winter), pp. 104–15.

Dwyer, F.R., Shurr, P.H. and Oh, S. (1987) Developing buyer–seller relationships. *Journal of Marketing*, **51**(2), pp. 11–28.

Ford, I.D. (1980) The development of buyer–seller relationships in industrial markets. *European Journal of Marketing*, **14**(5/6), pp. 339–53.

Frazier, G.L. and Summers, J.O. (1984) Interfirm influence strategies and their application within distribution channels. *Journal of Marketing*, **48** (Summer), pp. 43–55.

Gilliland, D.I. and Johnston, W.J. (1997) Towards a model of marketing communications effects. *Industrial Marketing Management*, **26**, pp. 15–29.

Grabner, J.R. and Rosenberg, L.J. (1969) Communication in distribution channel systems. In *Behavioural Dimensions in Distribution Channels: A Systems Approach* (ed. L. Stern). Boston, MA: Houghton Mifflin.

Haakansson, H. and Wootz, B. (1979) A framework of industrial buying and selling. *Industrial Marketing Management*, **8**, pp. 28–39.

Hewson, D. (2000) Keeping control of panic buying. *Sunday Times eBusiness Report*, 26 November, p. 5.

McDonald, M. (2000) Key account management – a domain review. *Marketing Review*, **1**, pp. 15–34.

Millman, T. and Wilson, K. (1995) From key account selling to key account management. *Journal of Marketing Practice: Applied Marketing Science*, **1**(1), pp. 9–21.

Mitchell, V.-M., (1999) Consumer perceived risk: conceptualisations and models. *European Journal of Marketing,* **33**(1–2), pp. 163–95.

Mohr, J. and Nevin, J.R. (1990) Communication strategies in marketing channels. *Journal of Marketing* (October), pp. 36–51.

Mohr, J. and Sohi, R.S. (1995) Communication flows in distribution channels: impact on assessments of communication quality and satisfaction. *Journal of Retailing,* **71**(4), pp. 393–416.

Mohr, J. and Spekman, R. (1994) Characteristics of partnership success: partnership attributes, communication behaviour and conflict resolution techniques. *Strategic Management Journal,* **15**, pp. 135–52.

Moorman, C., Zaltman, G. and Despande, R. (1992) Relationships between providers and users of marketing research: the dynamics of trust within and between organisations. *Journal of Marketing Research,* **29** (August), pp. 314–29.

Morgan, R.M. and Hunt, S.D. (1994) The commitment–trust theory of relationship marketing. *Journal of Marketing,* **58** (July), pp. 20–38.

Murphy, C. (1999) How long can car makers hold out? *Marketing,* 28 October, p. 15.

Stern, L. and El-Ansary, A.I. (1988) *Marketing Channels.* Englewood Cliffs, NJ: Prentice Hall.

Stern, L. and El-Ansary, A.I. (1992) *Marketing Channels,* 4th edn. Englewood Cliffs, NJ: Prentice Hall.

Valla, J.-P. (1982) The concept of risk in industrial buying behaviour. Workshop on Organisational Buying Behaviour, European Institute for Advanced Studies in Management, Brussels, December, pp. 9–10.

Vöegle, S. (1992) *Handbook of Direct Mail. The Dialogue Method of Direct Written Sales Communication.* New York: Prentice Hall.

Vriens, M., van der Scheer, Hiek, R., Hoekstra, J.C. and Bult, J. (1995) Conjoint experiments for direct mail response optimisations. *Graduate School/Research Institute Systems, Organisations and Management, Research Report,* 95 B11.

Wotruba, T.R. (1991) The evolution of personal selling. *Journal of Personal Selling and Sales Management,* **11**(3), pp. 1–12.

Wulf, K.D., Hoekstra, J.C and Commandeur, H.R. (2000) The opening and reading behaviour of business-to-business direct mail, *Industrial Marketing Management,* **29**(2) (March), pp. 133–45.

16

Corporate identity and reputation

The awareness, perception and attitudes held by an organisation's various stakeholders will vary in intensity and need to be understood and acted upon. This can be accomplished though a strategy that develops the profile of an organisation, one that seeks continual dialogue and which leads to the development of trust based relationships. This is necessary in order that stakeholders think and act favourably towards an organisation and enable the organisation to develop strategies that are compatible with the environment and its own objectives.

AIMS AND OBJECTIVES

The aim of this chapter is to consider those communications that are designed to encourage a dialogue with stakeholders, with a view to influencing the image and reputation of the organisation.

The objectives of this chapter are:

1. To introduce the notion of corporate communications and profile strategies.
2. To appraise the term 'corporate image' and the associated concepts corporate personality, identity and reputation.
3. To explore methods of evaluating corporate image.
4. To introduce a framework incorporating corporate identity with the process of strategic management.
5. To suggest ways in which transactional analysis can assist the understanding of corporate communications.
6. To consider specialised networks as a means of communicating with members of different networks.

Introduction

An organisation's corporate communications are bound by its identity. Identity is like a badge: organisations can choose what the badge looks like, select its colours, shape and message, but once visible to the outside world, the badge becomes a representation of the organisation. People form an image of the organisation based on those bits that are visible, namely the badge, regardless of whether it is still correct or distorted. More importantly, it is people who wear badges, and it is the associations that people make between the badge and behaviour and actions of those who wear the badge that shape the impressions we have of organisations. This is commonly referred to as corporate image.

Organisations are said to have a personality, a persona that reflects the inner spirit and heart of the organisation. From this cultural core, identities (badges) are hewn and presented to the outside world. The management of the corporate identity is vital if the image held of the organisation by all stakeholders is to be consistent and accurately represent the personality of the organisation (Dowling, 1993).

From this cultural core, identities (badges) are hewn and presented to the outside world.

Gorb (1992) refers to a continuum of differentiation where at one end there is a total loss of personality and the other end a schizoid position is achieved. The trick is to change with the environment and maintain a differentiated position by providing continuity to the way the identity is represented and, of course, perceived. He quotes Shell, whose logo, established over a century ago, appears to have been preserved unchanged. In reality it has undergone many changes and what we see today is nothing like that of the original. This has occurred through careful continuity of the idea of the sea shell and adaptation of it to the various contexts through time.

The phrase corporate identity is gradually being replaced by corporate branding. Balmer (1998) suggests that corporate identity was the accepted terminology in the 1980s, that this gave way to corporate branding in the 1990s and, although it can be argued that there are some intrinsic differences in this terminology, the two are used interchangeably in this chapter. Perhaps the first decade of the 21st century will be orientated to corporate reputation.

The phrase corporate identity is gradually being replaced by corporate branding.

Identity crisis – the Halifax

In the summer of 1997 the Halifax converted from being the world's largest building society into a bank. The transition received a high level of media interest, mainly because of the volume and value of shares that were distributed to eligible members of the former building society.

The change in designation and status was enormous for the organisation to manage. From being a dominant player, indeed market leader, it became a smaller player in a different market, which it knew less about and in which it was far less influential.

Some months after conversion, a customer inquired whether the Halifax offered a safe deposit service, as available in the majority of other banks. The customer was informed that the Halifax did not offer such a service. 'Why not?' was the retort, reports Wright (1997).

The member of staff then investigated the matter internally with the customer relations department and relayed the answer to the customer. 'Having referred your query to head office, I have been advised that Halifax plc is not a bank.'

The question therefore is, if Halifax plc is not a building society and is not a bank, what is it?

The identity crisis experienced by the few staff involved in this example may be atypical or may be replicated across the organisation. What is clear is that the personality of the organisation and the identity it wished to project are not complementary, and further self-analysis and clearer internal communication are required in order that its external communications do not lead to confusion and misunderstanding.

(Adapted from Wright, 1997)

Corporate communications

Corporate communications are simply a part of the process that translates corporate identity into corporate image (Ind, 1992). Increasingly organisations are taking an active interest in corporate branding (Cowlett, 2000) mainly because of the benefits that can be achieved across the organisation. By attempting to control the messages that it transmits, an organisation can inform and motivate stakeholders of what it is, what it does and how it does it in a credible and consistent way. Traditionally the bulk of this communication work has been the responsibility of public relations.

Corporate communications are simply a part of the process that translates corporate identity into corporate image.

Corporate identity programmes require good management of change. Employees are probably the most important stakeholders in the sense that they are not only an audience but also an important group of communicators to external stakeholder groups. Most programmes requiring change should attempt to adapt employee perceptions first and then their attitudes and behaviour.

The gap between organisational image and identity uncovered during research determines the nature of the communications task. A communications strategy is required to address all matters of structure and internal communications and the conflicting needs of different stakeholders so as to produce a set of consistent messages, all within the context of a coherent corporate identity programme. The British Broadcasting Corporation changed its identity partly as a means of enabling it to compete more effectively in an environment that was changing quickly. With the advent of digital television, the emerging international competitive arena and the impending launch a range of new services it was important that the BBC logo became distinctive and reflected the BBC core values of quality, fairness, accuracy and artistic fairness. The

The gap between organisational image and identity uncovered during research determines the nature of the communications task.

previous identity was expensive (four colour), not suitable for the increasing volumes and range of applications, had become increasingly fragmented and reproduced in an inconsistent manner. In addition, it did not work on digital formats and was technically difficult to integrate with other graphics. The new identity signalled changes about the BBC and the culture, attitudes and behaviour of the people who work there. However, at the time of writing the BBC is proposing to change the visual identity (the balloon) again, in an attempt to maintain the currency of its brand.

Analysis of the perceptions and attitudes of stakeholders towards the organisation will have revealed the size of the gap between actual and desired perception. The extent of this gap will have been determined and objectives set to close the gap. This corporate perception gap may be large or small, depending upon who the stakeholder is. Organisations have multiple images and must develop strategies that attempt to stabilise, and if possible equalize, the images held.

Using a four-cell matrix (Figure 16.1), where the vertical axis scales the size of the perceived gap and the horizontal axis the number of stakeholders who share the same perception, a series of strategies can be identified. Should a large number of stakeholders be perceived to hold an image of an organisation that is a long way from reality, then a correction strategy is required to communicate the desired position and performance of the focus organisation. Most common of these is the gap between perceived corporate performance and the real performance of the organisation when put in the context of the actual trading conditions.

If a small number of stakeholders perceive a large gap, then a targeted adjustment strategy would be required, aimed at particular stakeholder groups and taking care to protect the correct image held by the majority of stakeholders. For example, some students perceive some financial institutions (e.g. banks) as not particularly attractive for career progression or compatible with their own desired lifestyles. A targeted adjustment strategy would be necessary by the banks to alter this perception in order that they attract the necessary number of high-calibre graduates.

Should research uncover a small number of stakeholders holding a relatively small

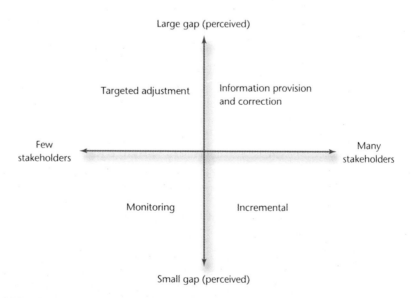

Figure 16.1   Corporate perception gap.

disparity between reality and image, a monitoring strategy would be appropriate and resources would be better deployed elsewhere. The best position would be if the majority of stakeholders perceived a small difference, in which case a maintenance strategy would be advisable and the good corporate communications continued. The natural extension of this approach is to use it as a base tool in the determination of the communication budget. Funds could be allocated according to the size of the perceived perception gap.

If the image they hold is incorrect and the organisation's performance is good, then it is poor communications that are to blame.

The reasons for the gap do not necessarily rest solely with stakeholders. If the image they hold is incorrect and the organisation's performance is good, then it is poor communications that are to blame, which are the fault of the organisation. If the image is correct and accurately reflects performance, then management must take the credit or the criticism for their performance as managers (Bernstein, 1984).

Management of the corporate identity

The first level denoted by Schein (1985) in his hierarchy of corporate culture concerns what are referred to as 'visible artefacts'. These are the more immediately observable aspects of the culture, such as the letterheads, logos and signage. This general view of corporate image is misplaced, and many graphic designers must accept partial responsibility for the popular misconception that the logo is the corporate image. This view is incorrect, as it fails to account for what the logo, other visible cues provided by organisations and the behaviour actually stand for, and from where they have been derived.

The image that stakeholders have of organisations is important for many reasons. They main ones are listed in Table 16.1, where it can be observed that the dimensions of corporate image are quite diverse.

The relational dimension refers to the exchange of attitudes and perceptions with stakeholders of the organisation itself. As will be seen later, organisations consider who they are and what they would like to be and then project identity cues to those stakeholders who it is believed need to be informed. A more advanced understanding then allows for the adaptation of the organisation based upon the feedback or the dialogue thus created.

Management also benefit from corporate identity programmes as they encourage them to reflect upon the organisation's sense of purpose and then provide a decision framework for the decisions that they and others, perhaps functional managers, follow.

Table 16.1   Dimensions of corporate image

Relational dimension
   Government, local community, employees, network members
Management dimension
   Corporate goals, decision-making, knowledge, understanding
Product dimension
   Product endorsement and support, promotional distinctiveness, competitive advantages

The final dimension refers to the advantages that a strong positive identity can give products and services. It is possible to develop more effective and efficient promotional programmes by focusing on the organisation's distinctiveness and then allow for the ripple to wash over the variety of offerings. Banks have traditionally used this approach, and car manufacturers have also partially attempted this strategy. Although the car marque is a very important decision determinant (e.g. Rover, Honda, BMW, VW, Nissan), it is common for particular models within the marque (brand) to be featured heavily.

The principal reason for managing the corporate identity is to make clear to all stakeholders what the values and beliefs of the organisation are and how it is striving

The principal reason for managing the corporate identity is to make clear to all stakeholders what the values and beliefs of the organisation are and how it is striving to achieve its objective.

to achieve its objectives. There are a number of secondary benefits, but these distil down to creating a supportive environment for the offerings, employees and external stakeholders associated with the focus organisation.

Abratt and Shee (1989) attempt to disentangle the confusion surrounding identity and image. They identify three main elements that are central to the development of corporate image (Figure 16.2). These are corporate personality, identity and image. Individuals and organisations project their personalities through their identity. The audience's perception of the identity is the image they have of the object, in this case, the corporate body.

Corporate personality

The first of these elements requires the recognition and acceptance that organisations have personalities, or at least significant characteristics. As Bernstein (1984) states, just as individuals have personalities, so do organisations. Corporate personalities are derived partly from the cultural characteristics of the organisation: the core values and beliefs which in turn are part of a corporate philosophy. Essential to corporate personality is the strategy process adopted by the organisation. The degree to which the strategic process is either formalised and planned or informal and emergent, and whether strategy is well communicated, plays a major role in shaping the personality of the organisation.

For example, management now recognises the powerful influence that an organisation's corporate objectives have in informing and guiding the operations of each of the functional departments. The formulation of the mission statement requires management and employees to understand what the organisation seeks to achieve. To understand what the organisation wants to achieve means understanding what the organisation values and believes in, and this in turn involves and reflects the involvement of all members of the organisation, either deliberately or involuntarily. Indeed, the stated philosophy and values that are articulated through the mission statement (and other devices) are important in establishing the preferred relationship it has with its various constituencies (Leuthesser and Kohli, 1997).

Figure 16.2   Elements of corporate identity. From Abratt and Shee (1989); used with kind permission.

The corporate personality can be considered to be composed of two main facets: the culture and overall strategic purpose (Markwick and Fill, 1997). Organisational culture is a composite of the various sectional interests and drives held by various key members. The blend of product offering, facilities, values and beliefs, staff, structure, skills and systems leads to the formation of particular characteristics or traits. Traits are rarely uniform in their dispersal throughout an organisation, so the way in which these interests are bound together impacts upon the form of the primary culture.

The corporate personality can be considered to be composed of two main facets: the culture and overall strategic purpose.

The strategic processes adopted by organisations are relatively constant because the roots of a process are embedded within the spectrum of organisational activities. Changing the strategic process is very different from changing the content of a strategy.

There was a great deal of merger activity in the late 1990s but management appears to be guilty of not paying enough attention to a vision of what the new culture will be like and how it will be expressed through the identity. The merger between Mannesmann which is over 100 years old and Vodafone, a mere 18 years old, was made on the basis of share value and global expansion, not cultural fit. The evidence suggests that it is the financial business model that dominates and not the brand model. Mergers do not result in amalgamated cultures, as experience shows that one will be pre-eminent, usually as a result of one or two key individuals reaching top positions. People also leave because they do not like the new way of doing things.

Merger cultures – DaimlerChrysler

These two car companies merged in 1998 in a deal worth £28 million, a bringing together of equals designed to combine the best of German depth and American creativity and exploiting the managerial talent. The name emphasises the equality and the advertising campaign used employees from both organisations to stress the friendly nature.

Mazur (2000) reports that unfortunately a number of former Chrysler executives started to leave, disgruntled as Daimler executives began to dominate matters.

All members of an organisation, management and employees, are intertwined with the corporate personality; they are one and the same. The spirit and vigour with which all members of an organisation embody and articulate the mission are, according to Topalian (1984), a means by which the identity is shaped. The personality is embodied in the way the organisation carries out its business, the logic of its activities, the degree of persistence and aggression it displays in the markets in which it operates and the standards that are expected of all stakeholders.

The personality is embodied in the way the organisation carries out its business, the logic of its activities, the degree of persistence and aggression it displays in the markets in which it operates and the standards that are expected of all stakeholders.

Corporate personality is the totality of the characteristics which identify an organisation. Consider the values held by organisations such as easyJet, HSBC, Railtrack, Tesco and Oxfam. Not only are the images different but so are the values and the personalities.

The BBC and Channel 5 are interesting organisations to consider from a personality perspective. The BBC is a mature organisation where stability and security have long been regarded as important characteristics. However, these are now regarded by some as impediments to progress and innovation. Channel 5 is young and vibrant, where programme quality is measured differently to the BBC and where innovation is seen as an important part of challenging the rules of standard broadcasting.

Corporate personality is what an organisation actually is.

Corporate identity

The second element in the image process is corporate identity. This is the formation of the cues by which stakeholders can recognise and identify the organisation. Many organisations in recent years have chosen to pay more attention to their identity and have tried to manage these cues more deliberately.

Corporate identity – on-line banking

Many financial services organisations have begun to offer on-line banking. The chance to reduce costs and reach new customer groups has been a major force behind this development. What is interesting, however, is that many have chosen to rebrand their on-line offering and create a separate identity.

The Halifax uses 'If', the Cooperative Bank 'Smile' and Prudential 'Egg'. Abbey National chose to uses the name 'Cahoot' in order to reach a more affluent customer, one who research shows would not normally bank with Abbey National. The disguise of the on-line brand identity therefore enables organisations to use communications to be directed to particular customer segments without having to overcome the negative values associated with the parent brand.

Identity is a means by which the organisation can differentiate itself from other organisations. Bernstein (1984) makes an important point when he observes that all organisations have an identity, whether they like it or not. Some organisations choose to deliberately manage their identities, just as individuals choose not to frequent particular shops or restaurants, drive certain cars or wear specific fabrics or colours. Other organisations take less care over their identities and the way in which they transmit their identity cues, and as a result confuse and mislead members of their networks and underperform in the markets in which they operate.

According to Olins (1989), management of the identity process can communicate three key ideas to its audiences. These are what the organisation is, what it does and how it does it. Corporate identity is manifested in four ways. These can be interpreted as the products and services that the organisation offers, where the offering is made or distributed, how the organisation communicates with stakeholders and, finally, how the organisation behaves (Olins, 1990).

These are what the organisation is, what it does and how it does it.

The marked development of the corporate brand has been noticeable in recent years. Organisations have used it as a means of differentiating their products from competitors' products and have recognised the power of the characteristics which delineate one organisation from another. These characteristics are embodied by the organisation's personality, values and culture. The corporate brand is a means of presenting these characteristics to various audiences, such as financial markets, suppliers, employees, channel network partners, trade unions, competitors and customers.

Industry brands – Association of British Insurers

Just as organisations can develop brands, so can an industry. For example, It was announced in 1999 that a consortium of pensions providers had been formed under the banner of the Association of British Insurers, to launch a £15 million advertising campaign in an attempt to rebuild the image of the industry following the prolonged public visibility of the pension misselling scandal that had cost the industry over £13 billion.

Bawden (1999) comments that the rectification process involved a six-month period consulting various stakeholder groups such as the government regulators, consumer groups and life/pension providers in order to explore issues concerning the quality and transparency of various product offerings. This is an important part of the process as the industry was anticipating a period of substantial change, caused by industry consolidation (the Prudential is industry leader and only has an 8% share), the launch of stakeholder pensions and an increasing need for pension providers to become more efficient. The advertising campaign needed to build on a credible base otherwise, instead of clarifying, it would further confuse consumers and restrict growth in the sector.

There are three broad types of identity cues used by organisations, especially in the development of corporate brands; these are symbolism, behaviour and communication (Birkigt and Stadler, 1986). Symbolism refers to the visual aspect and concerns the logo, letterhead and overall appearance of the design aspect associated with the company. The use of symbolism enables a level of harmonisation to be achieved by bringing together all of the identity cues.

There are three broad types of identity cues used by organisations, especially in the development of corporate brands; these are symbolism, behaviour and communication.

Corporate branding and names

The constituent parts of a corporate brand are many and varied. One interpretation suggests that a brand consists of the following variables: reputation, product and service performance, product brand and customer portfolio and networks in the sense of positioning (Knox and Maklan, 1998). Another interpretation is that each brand is perceived with varying degrees of intensity depending upon the level of involvement customers have with the brand itself. According to Kunde (2000), brands can range from a product base where there is little value other than the name, through to a corporate concept brand where there is a strong and consistent relationship between the consumers, the company and the brand. At the highest level is brand religion where the brand is paramount for consumers, a belief or a religion that enables a range of other products to be introduced within the same religious environment. He quotes

The name of an organisation is a strong corporate cue as it is often people's first contact with the organisation.

Body Shop, Harley-Davidson and Coca-Cola. What is noticeable about this approach is the importance attached to the internal culture and the need to balance the internal and external positioning, a view echoed throughout contemporary corporate branding literature and one thoroughly endorsed and supported in this text.

The name of an organisation is a strong corporate cue as it is often people's first contact with the organisation.

Mergers – BAE Systems

When British Aerospace and Marconi Electronic Systems merged in May 1999 the name and the visual identity of the new company, which was to be the third largest aerospace and defence company in the world, were important decisions.

The brand identifiers had to build on the strength of the two companies yet at the same time there was a need to signal change to both the employees and other relevant external stakeholders. The word British was extremely powerful and, although the name Marconi was not available, the new name, BAE Systems, represented an evolutionary rather than a revolutionary change. According to Mazur (2000), this represents a more practical approach bearing in mind the strength of equity and position that both companies had in the market place. A revolutionary approach to the visual identity was possible to represent the increased global presence of the new company.

Names used in the telecommunications sector were for a long time dominated by purely descriptive functionally orientated names. In 1994 this started to change when Wolff Olins created the Orange brand for Hutchinson Telecom. Orange offered instant differentiation which also reflected the 'different' service being offered for the first time. Owning a 'colour' offered a sense of exclusivity and allowed for a number of creative advertising opportunities. Goldfish, the name given to the British Gas discount card also allowed for immediate differentiation and an identity that challenged the norms for the sector (Murphy, 1999).

Corporate repositioning – HP Bulmer

HP Bulmer changed its name and redesigned its logo in an effort to reposition itself as a broader drinks company (brands such as Amstel lager, Schnapper, Zoensky and Vapour) and not just a cider-only maker (Scrumpy Jack, Strongbow and Woodpecker brands).

The behavioural aspect is largely concerned with the way in which employees and managers interact with one another and, more importantly, with external members of the organisation. The tone of voice used and the actions and consideration of customer needs by employees are often represented within a customer service policy, which is as an important part of an organisation's interface with various stakeholder groups.

Communication is used to inform stakeholders quickly of episodes concerning products and the organisation. This is normally achieved through the use of visual and verbal messages. However, a broad use can be seen in communicating not only values but also the direction the organisation is heading and notable traits that the organisation wishes to inform its audiences of. For example, in the UK Volvos were seen as very safe but very dull cars driven by people who were similarly uninteresting. Communication was used to convey interest and excitement without the loss of the stable and important 'safe' attribute.

The steward of the corporate brand is responsible for the consistency of the brand, in terms of the way it is presented, and for the way in which external members develop their images of the organisation.

When considering the development of a corporate brand, the stewardship dimension needs also to be considered. This refers to the degree of importance that a company places on the development and maintenance of a corporate brand. The steward of the corporate brand is responsible for the consistency of the brand, in terms of the way it is presented, and for the way in which external members develop their images of the organisation. The former chairman of British Airways, Bob Ayling, might be accused of not stewarding the British Airways brand appropriately, as manifest in the inconsistency of the management of the visual identity and falling corporate performance. Vision and responsibility for this function often reside with 'the chairman but many companies who successfully take care of their corporate image also have one communications professional charged with the task' (Ferguson, 1996), operating at a very senior level within the organisation.

Questionable stewardship – Barclays Bank

The CEO of Barclays Bank decided in the summer of 2000 to announce closures to the branch network (retail outlets). One of the problems with this was that the closures affected many rural communities and attracted a great deal of hostile publicity and negative media comment. This should have been anticipated and measures put in place to ameliorate the damage. Unfortunately the bank authorised an advertising campaign to run at exactly the same time. The problem was that the corporate branding campaign was national and it focused on functional positioning issues, namely the size of the bank.

The timing was unfortunate as the credibility of the messages was lost in the welter of negative comment about the branch closures. Questionable timing may have resulted in a negative impact on the bank's reputation.

Much of this is an external perspective of identity, whereas much of the organisational behaviour literature sees identity as embedded within the organisation, with employees. Employees are members who sense identity and who are responsible for projecting their group identity to non-members, those outside the organisation. Identity develops through feelings about what is central, distinctive and enduring (Albert and Whetten, 1985) about the character of the organisation, drawn from the personality (see Chapter 7 for greater detail).

Corporate identity is the way the organisation presents itself to its stakeholders.

Corporate image

The third and final element is corporate image. This is the perception that different audiences have of an organisation and results from the audience's interpretation of the cues presented by an organisation. As Bernstein (1984) says, 'the image does not exist in the organisation but in those that perceive the organisation'. This means that an organisation cannot change its image in a directly managed way, but it can change its identity. It is through the management of its identity that an organisation can influence the image held of it.

For an image to be sustainable, the identity cues upon which the image is fashioned must be based on reality and reflect the values and beliefs of the organisation.

The image held of an organisation is the result of a particular combination of a number of different elements, but is essentially a distillation of the values, beliefs and attitudes that an individual or organisation has of the focus organisation. The images held by members of the distribution network, for example, may vary according to their individual experiences, and will almost certainly be different from those which management thinks exists. This means that an organisation does not have a single image, but may have multiple images.

For an image to be sustainable, the identity cues upon which the image is fashioned must be based on reality and reflect the values and beliefs of the organisation.

Images can be consistent, but are often based upon a limited amount of information. Images are prone to the halo effect, whereby stakeholders shape images based upon a small amount of information. The strategic credibility of Microsoft may be based largely on the image of Bill Gates rather than the current financial performance of Microsoft and the actual strategies being pursued by the organisation. Stakeholders extrapolate that Bill Gates has a high reputation for business success, therefore, anything to do with Bill Gates is positive and likely to be successful.

Corporate images are shaped by stakeholder interpretations of the identity cues they perceive at an individual level. These cues are the identity signals transmitted by organisations, either deliberately planned and timed or accidental, often unknown to the organisation and very often unwelcome. Planned corporate communications reflected through symbolism, communication and behaviour are accompanied by unplanned communications such as those generated by competitors, through word of mouth and the personal experiences and memories of the individual (Cornelissen, 2000).

Corporate image is what stakeholders perceive the organisation to be.

Corporate reputation

A deeper set of images constitute what is termed corporate reputation. This concept refers to an individual's reflection of the historical and accumulated impacts of previous identity cues, fashioned in some cases by near or actual transactional experiences. It is much harder and takes a lot longer to change reputation, whereas images may be influenced quite quickly. The latter is more transient and the former more embedded.

A deeper set of images constitute what is termed corporate reputation.

A strong reputation is considered strategically important for three main reasons: as a primary means of differentiation when there is little difference at product level, as a support facility during times of turbulence and as a measure of corporate value

(Greyser, 1999). An even more tangible impact of a strong reputation is the effect on a company's share price, perhaps as much as 15% (Cooper, 1999).

In a survey reported by Gray (2000) the importance of a company's reputation was regarded by 1005 CEOs consulted to be either important or very important. Fombrun (1996) claims that in order to build a favourable reputation four attributes need to be developed. These are credibility, trustworthiness, reliability and responsibility. Using these criteria it may be possible to speculate about the reputation developed by a company such as Nokia, the mobile phone manufacturer. Credibility is established through its range of products, which are perceived to be of high quality and branded. Trustworthiness has been developed through attention to customer service and support. Reliability and consistency have been achieved by setting and adhering to particular standards of quality, and responsibility is verified through a strong orientation to service and values manifested through the company's strong product development and innovation policy.

Damaged reputation

McDonald's, British Airways, Microsoft, Nike, Coca Cola and Perrier are just some of the leading global brands that have been subject to media or judicial investigation. As a result of being in the public spotlight, their corporate reputation might be questioned, spoof Web sites created and doubt expressed about their integrity and well being.

Many of these brands represent a benchmark for marketing performance. Using highly recognisable visual identity cues (e.g. 'Golden Arches', 'National Flags', packaging or unique logos) consistently throughout the world, these brands are normally associated with high standards of service, good value for money and are widely available. To help maintain their identity, huge sums are spent each year on advertising, public relations and relevant in-house training and support.

Despite their overall and continued marketing success, it would appear that the reputation of corporate brands can be tarnished. However, it is the strength of the brand, management's flexibility and willingness to be open and transparent with inquisitive publics that can protect reputation in the long run.

Reputation itself is developed through a number of variables. Greyser (1999) suggests that the key drivers are competitive effectiveness, market leadership, customer focus, familiarity/favourability, corporate culture and communications. It is the combination of these elements that drives corporate reputation. However, he states that the most important dimension that impacts on reputation is the relationship between expectation and action. Whether this be at corporate level or at product/brand level, the brand promise must be delivered if reputation is to be enhanced, otherwise damage to the corporate reputation is most likely.

Strategy and corporate identity/image

It is taken for granted that measurements of the perceptions that consumers have of brands and offerings are taken periodically. This practice varies with each organisation and industry, but the overall tendency is to take such measurements on an *ad hoc* basis. As well as measuring the strength of perception of the organisation's offerings, measurements should also be taken of the perceptions that stakeholders have of the organisation. It may be that the marketing communications have to realign perceptions of the organisation before new offerings can be launched successfully.

In Figure 16.3, the perceptions that customers have of four recruitment companies are presented. The axes used show the levels of awareness and attitude towards the service provided by each of the companies, and for the

It may be that the marketing communications have to realign perceptions of the organisation before new offerings can be launched successfully.

sake of discussion each company is depicted in one of the four quadrants. Recruitment company A is in the strongest position and its communications should be aimed at maintaining its current position. Recruitment company B is liked just as much as A, but only known to a limited audience. Work needs to be undertaken to improve levels of awareness by reaching a larger number of stakeholders. Recruitment company C, to those that are aware of it, is seen as a poor organisation, but fortunately only a few know about it. Management's task is to bring about improvements to their offering and delay informing stakeholders until the level of service is satisfactory. Recruitment company D is seen to suffer from poor service delivery and everyone knows about it. Management's task is to lower the level of awareness, or not actively increase it, and put right the service offering before seeking stakeholder attention.

This depiction is obviously a simplification, as corporate image is multidimensional (Dowling, 1986) and there is no single indicator that can adequately reflect the corporate personality. As different stakeholders will inevitably have different images, the measurement of corporate image is made difficult. Spector (1961) found that there are six main factors that account for the main dimensions that people use to articulate their image of an organisation. These are:

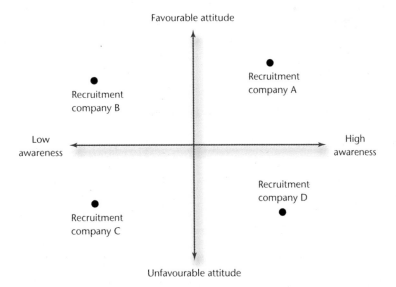

Figure 16.3   Images held by stakeholders of four recruitment companies. Adapted from Barich and Kotler (1991) by permission of the publisher. Copyright 1991 by the Sloan Management Review Association. All rights reserved.

- dynamic – pioneering, attention getting, active, goal orientated;
- cooperative – friendly, well liked, eager to please;
- business – wise, shrewd, persuasive, well organised;
- character – ethical, reputable and respectable;
- successful – financial performance, self-confidence;
- withdrawn – aloof, secretive, cautious.

Spector points out that strength in one particular dimension may not be adequate, as the standard by which respondents make their judgements may be based upon an ideal or the dimension may be of little importance or significance.

Various models have been developed to provide a visual interpretation of the elements involved in corporate identity (Kennedy, 1977; Dowling, 1986; Abratt and Shee, 1989; Stuart, 1999). These models reflect the development of the subject and the growing integrative nature of corporate identity within an organisation's overall strategy. One such framework, presented by Markwick and Fill (1997) and entitled the corporate identity management process (CIMP) (Figure 16.4), depicts the three main elements of the process as identified by Abratt and Shee (1989): corporate personality, corporate

In order for management to be able to use such a model, there must be understanding of the linkages between the components.

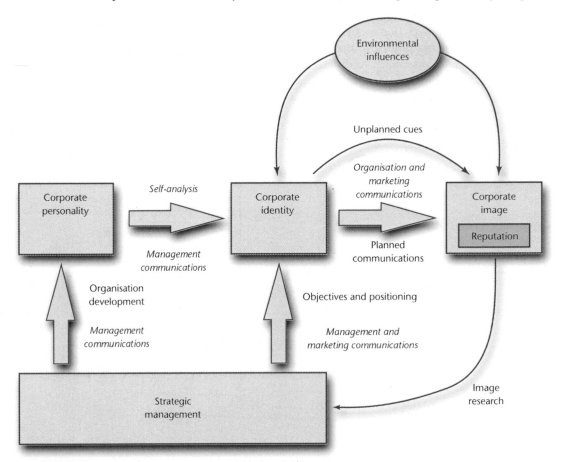

Figure 16.4 The corporate identity management process.

identity and corporate image. In order for management to be able to use such a model there must be understanding of the linkages between the components. Just as the linkages in the value chain determine the extent of competitive advantage that may exist, so the linkages within the corporate identity process need to be understood in order to narrow the gap between reality and perception.

Identity and strategy – Iceland

Iceland's recent 27% profit increase helped it to outperform competitors in the UK supermarket sector. There are many reasons for this growth but one of them was Iceland's quick decision to ban genetically modified ingredients in its own brands. This action was openly applauded by Friends of the Earth and earned Iceland a distinct position (and lead) over the main four supermarkets on this issue.

Subsequent campaigns have attempted to build on this advantage by repositioning the brand. Following research that indicated that many people thought that the supermarket chain Iceland only sold frozen foods, the company decided it needed to communicate its strategy more clearly.

Part of this has been achieved through the company's innovative and pathfinding efforts at home delivery services and the adoption of a new informal approach to its advertising. This involved in-store displays as well as externally orientated TV campaigns designed to communicate price and product information. In addition, it changed its name to Iceland.co.uk to reflect their new multichannel capabilities.

Iceland is trying to convey that it is a contemporary and innovative company. Taking a modern and upbeat approach to advertising will rub off on consumers' perceptions.

Adapted from various sources including McLuhan (1999) and Jardine (2000).

To assist with the linking process, van Riel's (1995) composition of corporate communication is used. These are marketing, management and organisational communications.

The first linkage is to transpose, through self-analysis, the corporate personality so that management, or those responsible for the management of the corporate identity, have a realistic perception of the corporate personality. This can be assumed to be what management thinks the personality is and the principal method is through management communication.

The second linkage is between corporate identity and the corporate image. In order that stakeholders are able to perceive and understand the organisation, the corporate identity is projected to them. The identity can be projected with orchestrated cues, planned and delivered to a timed schedule, or it can be projected as a series of random, uncoordinated events and observations. In virtually all cases, corporate identity cues are a mixture of the planned (e.g. literature, telephone style and ways of conducting business) and the unplanned (e.g. employees' comments, media views and product failures). The principal linkages are through organisation and marketing communications.

All organisations communicate all the time; everything they make, do, say or do not say is a form of communication. The totality of the way the organisation presents itself, and is visible, can be called its identity (Olins, 1990). Corporate image is how stakeholders actually perceive the identity. It is, of course, unlikely that all stakeholders will hold the same image at any one point in time. Owing to the level of noise and the different experiences stakeholders have of an organisation, multiple images of an organisation are inevitable (Dowling, 1986). It is important that organisations monitor these images to ensure that the (corporate) position is maintained.

All organisations communicate all the time; everything they make, do, say or do not say is a form of communication.

The third linkage is between the image that stakeholders have of an organisation and the corporate strategy formulation and implementation processes that an organisation adopts. This research-based linkage provides feedback and enables the organisation to adjust its personality and its identity, thus consequently affecting the cues presented to stakeholders. Image research is an important method of linking back into the strategy process.

The cues used to project the corporate identity are many and varied; some are controllable and others beyond the reach of management. These cues include the logo and letterheads, the way employees speak of the organisation, the buildings and architecture, the perception of the ability of the organisation to fulfil its obligations, its technical skills, prices, dress style, competitor communications, word of mouth and the way the telephone is answered, for example. Of all these and the many others, however, research needs to determine those attributes that key stakeholders perceive as important.

Having determined the important attributes, stakeholders should be asked to evaluate how well the organisation rates on each of them and how well it performs on each attribute in comparison with competitors. Figure 16.5 sets out the possible results of such research along two dimensions, the importance of the attribute to the stakeholder and the perceived performance of the organisation against the attribute.

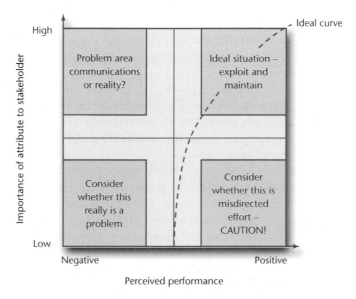

Figure 16.5   A two-dimensional attribute perception matrix. From Markwick (1993); used with kind permission.

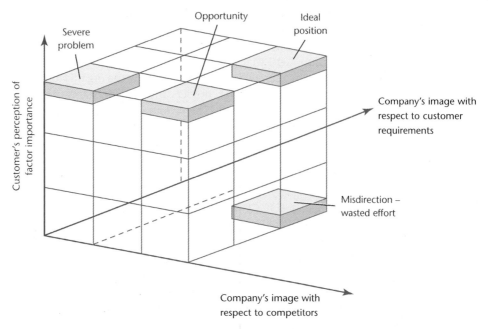

Figure 16.6   A three-dimensional attribute perception matrix. From Markwick (1993); used with kind permission.

It can be seen that the ideal position lies to the right of the curve, and communication strategy should be aimed at achieving such a position. By introducing a third dimension, an evaluation of relative competitors against the same attributes, it is possible to determine a number of strategies that could lead to sustainable competitive advantage.

Stakeholder images can also be determined on three dimensions: the importance of attributes, organisational performance against the attributes and performance with respect to competitors on the same attributes. A three-dimensional perception matrix (Figure 16.6) draws out the significant points. The ideal position occurs when high customer and competitor ratings are recorded for important attributes. When the attribute has a low level of importance it may be that the organisation's effort is misdirected, and management should reduce the effort spent on developing this image or seek alternative markets where this attribute has higher levels of importance. The worst position occurs when the organisation underperforms with respect to the customers' requirements and the competition on an attribute that is important. A change of strategy is required.

Effort should be concentrated on developing either corporate identity or personality in areas where the customer rating is poor and competitor rating is high on a factor that is important.

This model reveals that, by understanding the strength of images held by key stakeholders across attributes that are important to them, corrective action may be required to the personality and cues presented to stakeholders as part of the identity process. Strategic development therefore can result from an understanding of the images held about an organisation by its stakeholders.

Therefore, for the CIMP framework to be complete, management is required to analyse and interpret the research data and then use management and marketing communications either to develop the personality or to provide adjusted corporate identity cues for positioning and goal-setting purposes.

It may be concluded that corporate identity is not a peripheral tool to be used *ad hoc* but is a component that is central to the strategic management process. It should be used regularly by managers to understand how the organisation is being interpreted and understood by different stakeholders and to understand the essence of the organisation and whether the symbolic, behavioural and communication cues are contextually appropriate.

Network conflict

Corporate personality is a key part of the corporate image process. Just as individuals have personalities and behave in different ways, so organisations have personalities (or characteristics) and display a variety of behaviour pat-

Just as individuals have personalities and behave in different ways, so organisations have personalities (or characteristics) and display a variety of behaviour patterns.

terns. Organisational behaviour in the collective form is partially a reflection of the events and accumulated experiences of the organisation. Part of the experience is the conflict encountered between members of the network. Successful corporate communications recog-

nise conflict to be endemic. Conflict exists within each organisation and it also exists within the relationships that an organisation develops with its various stakeholders. While accepting that conflict need not be dysfunctional, organisations should not only seek ways of understanding the nature of any conflict but also attempt to reduce the level of any counterproductive conflict that may arise.

Transactional analysis (TA), developed by Berne (1966), provides a convenient and easy framework with which to understand the nature of conflict and indicates how conflict might be avoided or reduced in particular situations. TA also classifies behaviour into one of three groupings, each reflecting a particular state or source within the personality.

As seen in Chapter 3, Freudian theory suggests that the *ego* plays a central role in understanding personality. The ego represents reality and attempts to control the *id* and the *superego*. TA uses this psychoanalytical base to identify three ego states, each of which is roughly equivalent to the Freudian concepts. All three states are thought, by some, to exist within people, but one state may dominate. The three ego states are as follows:

1. *Child (id)*
   This state is characterised by very immature behaviour. The behaviour is either submissive and conforming or insubordinate and emotional. Overall, an impulsive behaviour dominates.

2. *Adult (ego)*
   A rational and cool-headed approach to problems is likely to lead to logical choices being made. This behaviour is generally referred to as mature and is regarded as fair and objective.

3. *Parent (superego)*
   In this state behaviour is observed to be protective or critical. It is characterised by the need to establish boundaries or the parameters by which others can operate. Dominance and the setting of standards prevail.

Each ego state is composed of a series of playbacks or recordings derived from real experiences. The parent and child states are based upon experiences during the first five years of life. Everything a child's parents do and say is used by the child to develop a unique set of characteristics which will be used to form the future parent from within the child. The parent role can be 'critical' or 'nurturing'; both roles are taught (see Table 16.2). The adult role is thought to originate from the ability of the individual to discard the child and parent roles and to think in a rational and objective manner.

Here, the critical assumption is that an organisation can possess these three ego

Table 16.2   A classification of ego states

Ego state	Description	Derivation	Classification	Behaviour and verbal clues
Parent	Feeling what is proper, right and wrong. Provides discipline and protection. Dogma and control are evident.	First 5 years of life from external stimuli. Mainly parental stimuli. A recording of imposed unquestioned events.	*Critical parent* Critical, prejudicial, moralising or punitive *Nurturing parent* Nurturing, protective, sympathetic and comforting	Pointed finger – arms folded Head shaking – foot tapping Sighing – always, never, remember you ought to know better Pat on shoulder Consoling sound There, there, you poor thing, try again, don't worry
Adult	Gathering information. Evaluation, decision making in objective terms. Can review and monitor parent and child 'tapes'.	Begins to emerge at around 10 months old when the infant's capacity to see things in addition to the taught parent concepts and the feeling child concept.	That part of the individual that is rational and logical. This requires stating things and reasons before acting.	Postures indicating interest listening and thinking. Why, what, where, who, how, alternatives, possible, probable, practical, feasible
Child	Part of the personality preserved from childhood. Reactions through emotions, angry, frightened, loving, carefree, adventurous, trusting and curious.	During first 5 years a recording of internal events takes place. The feelings experienced as an infant could only be expressed as emotions.	*Natural* behaviour dictated by feelings. Impulsive, inquisitive, curious, affectionate, playful. Also fearful, self-centred and aggressive. *Adapted* toned-down behaviour to make it more acceptable to others.	Tears, tempers, tantrums, shoulder shrugging Look at me, nobody loves me, that's mine, can't, want, whoopee Giggling, teasing, flirting, pointing, whining Please, thank you, I wish, I'll try, I don't care, I don't know

Source: Walker and Bird (1984); used with kind permission.

states rooted within a corporate personality. In individuals, these ego states can be observed in the gestures, tone of voice, expressions and reactions to others in our environment. Organisations can also be observed to gesticulate (Ratners, Asda), use particular styles (tones) of communication (Perrier, Peugeot, Marks & Spencer) and react in different ways to particular stimuli (Hanson, Lonrho, Glaxo). Note the way in which, for example, Tesco, Body Shop, NatWest, Virgin Atlantic and Boots express themselves and how the perceptions held of these organisations are a reflection of the reader's perception of each organisation's history and development.

Transactions

When a communication takes place, a response is expected. The nature of these responses or *transactions* can be classified as complementary or crossed transactions.

Complementary transactions are achieved when a message sent from one particular ego state is reciprocated with a message from the same or expected ego state. For example, an outward adult message might be, 'the system appears to have broken down again'. An adult message in response might be 'yes, because we have received too many orders in the last week'.

Complementary transactions are achieved when a message sent from one particular ego state is reciprocated with a message from the same or expected ego state.

Crossed transactions are the source of a great deal of organisational conflict and occur when the message sent from a particular ego state is returned by a message from an unexpected ego state. For example, an outbound child message might be 'I wish the system wouldn't keep breaking down all the time'. A parent response could be 'don't worry, it will be put right soon'. Crossed transactions mean that the intended communication has failed to be successfully decoded and can be regarded as ineffective.

TA can be used to understand interpersonal relationships better and its most obvious deployment is through direct selling, in terms of the promotion mix. However, there are a number of opportunities to use TA to understand the behaviour of organisations as they interact and communicate with their various stakeholders. Conflict is endemic within networks, and organisations may utilise TA as a useful means of observing and interpreting the actions of members, especially those of the channel leader.

There are a number of opportunities to use TA to understand the behaviour of organisations as they interact and communicate with their various stakeholders.

Transactional analysis is useful as a means of understanding interpersonal relationships, as a means of developing new personal constructive behaviour patterns and as a means of understanding the way organisations communicate with their employees. An extension of this tool is to examine the manner in which organisations communicate with other organisations or stakeholders. Practical interpretations of TA are more easily observed in the specialist field of crisis management.

For example, Perrier, the mineral water brand leader, can be seen to display particularly good transactions with its UK stakeholders. It has been argued that because Perrier lets each market handle the problem of contaminated water in its own way, consumers were getting different advice in different markets (Jones, 1994). However, once the contamination had been proved, there followed a slight hesitancy, presumably as it grasped the potency of the situation facing the company. It then transmitted a series of adult messages to its stakeholders, withdrawing all stocks from all worldwide locations. The response of distributors and retailers was equally adult, as they adhered to the demands of Perrier. It could also be argued that the response of their customers was equally adult, because Perrier soon recovered a large part of its European market share. Perrier was taken over by Nestlé, an indication of possible undervaluation and potential profitability within Perrier and the mineral water market.

An example of poor transactions can be observed in the Hatfield rail crash. When the accident happened, the communications that followed from Railtrack managers were at times contradictory and confusing. At one stage the public was informed that the track would be closed for a few days, then weeks and then months. The CEO wanted to resign and was forced by different stakeholders to stay, which he did, only to go a few months later. The nationwide track inspection and relaying programme that followed (parent behaviour) slowed train journey times, drove passengers away from rail travel and made Railtrack a centre piece for news programmes and news-papers for many weeks. In contrast, the chairman of British Midland Airways (now British Midland International) was quickly on the scene of the accident when a plane crashed on the M1 motorway, with over 40 fatalities. The chairman's prompt appearance, acceptance of his organisation's involvement and con-cern for the victims and relatives can be interpreted as adult behaviour in transactional terminology. His actions were paramount in enabling the public to forgive British Midland and to ensure the continuity of the company.

TA provides a useful, if simple, insight into the form of the communications that exists between any two organisations or between an organisation and a range of stakeholders.

Transactional analysis can be used to interpret the behaviour patterns of organis-ations, and if the observed behaviour is diagnosed as inappropriate a strategy can be developed to correct matters. TA provides a useful, if simple, insight into the form of the communications that exist between any two organisations or between an organis-ation and a range of stakeholders.

Organisations that appear to have a disproportionate number of crossed transac-tions will want to design a communications strategy that seeks to correct this type of imbalance. Likewise, those organisations that can be termed leaders will want to 'stroke' (a unit of recognition in TA language) certain other organisations in the net-work as often as possible, in order that their relationship be maintained and enhanced, which, in theory, can lead to improved performance. Stroking can be seen in the form of increased discounts, seminars, joint promotional activities and various forms of corporate hospitality, aimed mainly at those individuals who work at the boundary of participant organisations.

Specialised networks embracing all key stakeholders

There are some messages that need to be distributed across all stakeholder networks, such as those proclaiming technological advances, business acquisitions and contracts won. It is also apparent that communication flows do not change radically over the short term. On the contrary, they become established and regularised through use. This allows for the emergence of specialised communication networks (Chapter 2). Furthermore, it is common for networks to be composed of subnetworks, overlaying each other. The complexity of an organisation's networks is such that unravelling each one would be dysfunctional, however, an understanding of the main forms of special-ised network provides an opportunity to examine the content of the message carried.

Harold Guetzkow (1965) wrote a landmark paper on the nature of communications within organisations. Much of his work can be interpreted in the context of interorganisational and group communications. He identified five major types of network, based upon the content of the messages each network carries:

1. *Authority networks*

   These carry information in a unidirectional form, from higher to lower levels within the performance network. Authority networks are usually found within a VMS but can also be observed in non-integrated channels where the authority of the channel leader is such that procedures such as those for ordering, advertising, discounting and personal selling can be prescribed.

2. *Information exchange networks*

   In non-integrated relationships, information must flow throughout the network if coordination and the maintenance of the independent status of the members are to be maintained. This may be informal, but in most channel situations the network is formal and routinised. For example, professional and trade associations (e.g. the Association of British Pharmaceutical Industry or the Federation of Master Builders) often provide their members with information about the 'business' or the particular environment within which they operate, often compiled from information generated by the membership.

   > *In non-integrated relationships, information must flow throughout the network if coordination and the maintenance of the independent status of the members are to be maintained.*

3. *Task-expertise networks*

   These are typified by experts who cross over different hierarchical levels in the quest for a solution to a problem common to the market. The flow is bidirectional, as information has to be exchanged and disseminated at the conclusion. Examples include sales representatives selling complex offerings which require explanation and technical support on both a pre- and post-sales basis. Advertising and PR agencies and market research consultancies supply expert information and are members of the support network rather than the performance network.

4. *Friendship networks*

   Friendships may emerge as interaction through common activities develops. Those operating at the boundary of the organisation and dealing with others within the network may be able to provide information that otherwise was officially unavailable. Conferences often allow members on the same level of the channel to exchange information through a common bond of friendship.

5. *Status networks*

   Messages may also be perceived to assign prestige to individuals and to the organisation they represent. Status may be determined by regulating who initiates and receives particular messages, and the messages themselves tend to be informal and symbolic.

Communication managers need to consider the specialised networks that may exist and develop those that are of potential benefit. Highly specialised networks may emerge to resolve particular issues and may keep out messages of friendship and loyalty. The development of communities through new media is a reflection of these networks, a contemporary interpretation of the same conceptual idea.

There are costs associated with communication in these networks. These costs may be direct, in the form of dealer conferences and house magazines. Costs may also be indirect in nature. For example, the views of particular retailers or manufacturers' representatives may go unheard or unreported. These views might be critical to the development of particular markets and hence be of strategic importance.

An examination of the communication networks, perhaps through a channel-wide communication audit, will reveal the need to develop communication networks appropriate to the needs of each individual organisation and the performance network as a whole.

Summary

Communication strategies need to encompass the communication needs of all those other stakeholders, those other constituencies who might influence the organisation or be influenced by it. These approaches are referred to as the profile strategy and so complete the 3Ps for communication, push, pull and profile.

Profile strategies are essentially concerned with the communication dialogue about the organisation itself rather than its products and/or services. The focus rests with the corporate body itself, who it is, what it is, what it is seeking to do and how it is important to other stakeholders.

At the root of this strategic approach is the notion of corporate identity. Organisations project themselves (as they want to be seen/understood) through a series of cues. These are then interpreted by stakeholders and used to create an image of the organisation. This corporate image may or may not be a correct interpretation of the organisation but this perception is an important one and must be treated seriously. Reputations develop from the image and can be seen to feed back to the corporate personality and impact upon the way members of an organisation think about themselves and determine what is central, distinctive and enduring.

Profile strategies are an important part of communication strategy and should be regarded as an integral part of any integrated marketing communications approach (Chapter 19) that might be developed.

Review questions

1. Define corporate communications. What is a profile strategy?
2. Explain what a corporate brand is. How does it differ from a product brand?
3. What are the main facets of corporate personality?
4. Describe the personality or defining characteristics of five different organisations. What are their distinctive differences?
5. Prepare brief notes explaining what corporate identity is. Set out the differences between personality and identity.
6. Suggest ways in which planned and unplanned corporate identity cues are presented to stakeholders. Use an organisation with which you are familiar to illustrate your answer.
7. What is corporate image and how does it differ from corporate identity?
8. Draw the CIMP model, paying particular attention to the linkages between the components.

9. Discuss the view that there is nothing intrinsically different between corporate image and reputation.

10. List the main features of transactional analysis. How might this approach assist marketing communications?

MINI CASE

This mini case was written by Hilary Wright, Senior Research Executive at Taylor Nelson Sofres. The author would like to acknowledge the contribution of Chris Goard, Global Marketing Director, TNS.

Taylor Nelson *Sofres*

Merging organisations

Organic growth and rapid expansion through acquisition has positioned Taylor Nelson *Sofres* (TNS) as the fourth largest market information company in the world. The truly global nature of the company is reflected in its offerings of continuous and customised research and analysis, in key specialist sectors, in over 80 countries. A total commitment to a client focus ensures their continued success.

Taylor Nelson *Sofres* was formed in December 1997 by the merger of two of the world's leading market information groups, the British company Taylor Nelson AGB and the largest research group in France, *Sofres*. The immense challenge was not only to capitalise on the advantages that would result from the merger but also to embrace the diversity of cultures coexisting in the new company while working to create an identity that reflected a truly harmonised business. It was important to make the necessary internal changes in order that the organisation's claims be credible.

Primarily the TNS name had to be introduced worldwide. A new visual identity, mainly the logo, was designed to reflect the equal importance of the two merged companies by placing the names on one level, a coming together of Taylor Nelson and *Sofres*. The simplicity and clarity of design, including the style of font used, communicated TNS's intent to position itself as a 'one-stop' company, providing solutions for all geographical and techno-

logical research needs. The colours chosen respected the interpretations of the language of colours; in China for example, red represents luck and happiness and blue, serenity. See Plate 16.1.

Once agreed by the TNS board, the new logo was applied to all stationery, electronic and other sites. There was still flexibility, however, to allow for local variations, for example, in France the logo is traditionally placed on the left-hand side of letterheads, while in other countries the right-hand side is normal. Business cards were printed in English on one side and the local language on the reverse. TNS also recognised the importance of local brand continuity in the global marketplace and hence business cards included not only the TNS name but also the sector specialism or the local brand name for that product or service. The NIPO brand in Holland is so integrated and ingrained in the customer's mind that it is also used generically as the word for research; replacing this name would obviously have had detrimental consequences for TNS. Consideration had to be given to peripheral issues, such as stock control of stationery and signage of the TNS name on the front and inside of the office buildings. These had to be changed from the original company name to TNS, and provision had to be made to obtain planning permission to carry out these alterations in various countries.

TNS was very much aware of the historical and cultural pressures it had to confront and negate in the communication of a consistent set of messages to its existing and new audiences. To help encourage a smooth transition, standard letters were sent out to all clients in all countries detailing the new company name and reinforcing the consistency and high quality of products and services already established. Personalised letters from the chairman of TNS were forwarded to the managing directors of key clients, emphasising the recognition of the importance of a client orientation.

Internally, country and sector managing directors were fully briefed so they could broadcast the appropriate information to employees. The high-tech environment in which TNS operates enabled the rapid dissemination of the details needed to launch the new corporate identity and so develop the corporate brand. The information could be downloaded from the FTP site on the Intranet, ensuring that all countries received timely and consistent information, which could then be taken to a local designer to incorporate local adaptations if necessary.

It took only 6–8 months to introduce the new organisational brand to 150 offices and 52 countries, although this is not a true reflection of the complexity of the challenge and a measure of the organisational and planning ability of those involved. To remain in the FTSE 200, and sustain considerable continued growth as announced in March 2001, are both tangible evidence of the undisputed success of the TNS campaign.

Mini-case questions

1. Taylor Nelson *Sofres* reflects a balanced naming strategy. What might have been the alternatives and the consequences of a different naming strategy?
2. How might a corporate branding strategy help Taylor Nelson *Sofres* in the future?
3. To what extent did the new company consider aspects of internal marketing communications?
4. Comment on the likely personality of TN*Sofres*? Apart from the logo, what other visual identity cues should it use?
5. Discuss the flexible branding approach adopted by Taylor Nelson *Sofres* when meeting local country needs. Do you think this approach might strengthen or dilute the corporate brand?

References

Abratt, R. and Shee, P.S.B. (1989) A new approach to the corporate image management process. *Journal of Marketing Management*, **5**(1), pp. 63–76.

Albert, S. and Whetten, D.A. (1985) Organisational identity. In *Research in Organisational Behaviour* (eds L.L. Cummings and B.M. Straw). Greenwich, CT: JT Press.

Balmer, J.M.T. (1998) Corporate identity and the advent of corporate marketing. *Journal of Marketing, Management*, **14**(8), pp. 963–96.

Barich, H. and Kotler, P. (1991) A framework for marketing image management. *Sloan Management Review*, **94** (Winter), pp. 94–104.

Bawden, T. (1999) Can advertising fix pensions industry? *Marketing Week*, 8 July, pp. 18–19.

Berne, E. (1966) *Games People Play: The Psychology of Human Relationships*. London: André Deutsch.

Bernstein, D. (1984) *Company Image and Reality: A Critique of Corporate Communications*. London: Holt, Rinehart & Winston.

Birkigt, K. and Stadler, M.M. (1986) Corporate identity. In van Riel (1995).

Cooper, A. (1999) What's in a name? *Admap*, **34**(6), pp. 30–2.

Cornelissen, J. (2000) Corporate image: an audience centred model. *Corporate Communications: an International Journal*, **5**(2), pp. 119–25.

Cowlett, M. (2000) Buying into brands. *PR Week*, 24 November, p. 13.

Dowling, G.R. (1986) Measuring your corporate images. *Industrial Marketing Management*, **15**, pp. 109–15.

Dowling, G.R. (1993) Developing your company image into a corporate asset. *Long Range Planning*, **26**(2), pp. 101–9.

Ferguson, J. (1996) The image. *Communicators in Business*, **9** (Summer), pp. 11–14.

Fombrun, C. (1996) *Reputation: Realising Value from the Corporate Image*. Cambridge, MA: Harvard Business School Press.

Gorb, P. (1992) The psychology of corporate identity. *European Management Journal*, **10**(3), (September), pp. 310–13.

Gray, R. (2000) The chief encounter. *PR Week*, 8 September, pp. 13–16.

Greyser, S.A. (1999) Advancing and enhancing corporate reputation. *Corporate Communications: an International Journal*, **4**(4), pp. 177–81.

Guetzkow, H. (1965) Communications in organisations. In *Handbook of Organisations* (ed. J.G. March). Chicago, IL: Rand McNally.

Ind, N. (1992) *The Corporate Image: Strategies for Effective Identity Programmes*. London: Kogan Page.

Jardine, A. (1999) McDonald's still facing a McLibel backlash. *Marketing*, 16 September, p. 15.

Jardine, A. (2000) Iceland rebrand to build online sales. *Marketing*, 23 March, p. 1.

Jones, H. (1994) Nightmare on high street. *Marketing Week*, 16 September, pp. 28–30.

Kennedy, S. (1977) Nurturing corporate images. *European Journal of Marketing*, **11**(3), pp. 120–64.

Knox, S. and Maklan, S. (1998) *Competing on Value. Bridging the Gap Between Brand and Customer Value*. London: Financial Times.

Kunde, J. (2000) *Corporate Religion*. London: Financial Times.

Leuthesser, L. and Kohli, C. (1997) Corporate identity: the role of mission statements. *Business Horizons*, **40**(3) (May–June), pp. 59–67.

Markwick, N. (1993) Corporate image as an aid to strategic development. Unpublished MBA project, University of Portsmouth.

Markwick, N. and Fill, C. (1997) Towards a framework for managing corporate identity. *European Journal of Marketing*, **31**(5/6), pp. 396–409.

Mazur, L. (2000) Anatomy of a new identity, *Marketing*, 16 March, p. 22.

McLuhan, R. (1999) Iceland's new strategy proves popular with consumers. *Marketing*, 1 April, p. 24.

Michalczyk, I. (1999) HP Bulmer in global image relaunch. *Marketing*, 9 December, p. 4.

Murphy, C. (1999) The real meaning behind the name. *Marketing*, 14 October, p. 31.

Olins, W. (1989) *Marketing*, 12 April, pp. 21–4.

Olins, W. (1990) *Corporate Identity: Making Business Strategy Visible Through Design*. London: Thames & Hudson.

van Riel, C.B.M. (1995) *Principles of Corporate Communication*. Hemel Hempstead: Prentice Hall.

Schein, E.H. (1985) *Organisational Culture and Leadership*. San Francisco, CA: Jossey-Bass.

Spector, A.J. (1961) Basic dimensions of the corporate image. *Journal of Marketing*, 25 October, pp. 47–51.

Stuart, H. (1999) Towards a definitive model of the corporate identity management process. *Corporate Communications: an International Journal*, **4**(4), pp. 200–7.

Topalian, A. (1984) Corporate identity: beyond the visual overstatements. *International Journal of Advertising*, **3**, pp. 55–62.

Walker, A.K. and Bird, A.M. (1984) *The First Principles of Medical Advertising*. Warner Lambert International, internal publication.

Wright, D.(1997) Comment: Halifax facts. *Sunday Times*, Money, 10 August, p. 2.

17

Marketing communications across borders

The management of marketing communications for audiences domiciled in two or more countries is haunted by the dilemma of whether to send the same message to all regions or adapt it to meet the needs of local markets, or do a little bit of them both.

AIMS AND OBJECTIVES

The aim of this chapter is to examine the impact that cross-border business strategies might have on marketing communications agencies and advertising strategies.

The objectives of this chapter are:

1. To consider the development and variety of organisations operating across international borders.

2. To appraise different aspects of culture as a key variable affecting marketing communications.

3. To examine the media as a further important variable that can influence marketing communications strategy.

4. To discuss the adaptation vs. standardisation debate about marketing communication messages.

5. To explore the ways in which advertising agencies have developed to meet the international communication requirements of their clients.

Introduction

For organisations the differences between operating within home or domestic markets as compared with overseas or international markets are many and varied. Most of these differences can be considered within an economic, cultural, legal, technological and competitive framework. If the core characteristics of a home market (such as prices, marketing channels, finance, knowledge about customers, legislation, media and competitors) are compared with each of the same factors in the international markets which an organisation might be operating in, then the degree of complexity and uncertainty can be illuminated easily. Management might be conversant with the way of doing business at home, but, as they move outside their country/regional borders areas which represent their domain of knowledge, understanding and to some extent security, so levels of control decline and risk increases.

The goal of this chapter is to consider some of the issues that impact upon marketing communications when operating across international borders.

The objective of this chapter is not to consider these particular characteristics, as time and space restrict scope. Readers interested in these issues are recommended to consult some of the many international marketing or business texts that are available. The goal of this chapter is to consider some of the issues that impact upon marketing communications when operating across international borders. To do this it is first necessary to consider the various environments and types of organisations that operate away from their home markets.

Types of cross-border organisation

Organisations can be regarded as international, multinational, global or transnational (Keegan, 1989; Bartlett and Ghoshal, 1991) and each form is a reflection of their structure and disposition towards its chosen markets (see Table 17.1).

International organisations evolve from national organisations whose origins are to serve national customers using domestic or 'home-grown' resources. Some of these organisations, either by accident or by design, begin to undertake a limited amount of work 'overseas'. They begin to become international, first by deploying their domestically orientated marketing mix and then later by adapting it to the needs of the new local 'overseas' market. This adaption phase signals the commencement of a *multinational strategy*. What distinguishes these organisations is that they regard the world (or their parts of it) as having discrete regions. Each country/area reports to a world head office, and performance is normally geared to meet financial targets.

International organisations evolve from national organisations whose origins are to serve national customers using domestic or 'home-grown' resources.

Organisations at this stage in the evolutionary process are referred to as *global*. This is characterised by centralised decision-making, where, unlike in multinational companies, the similarities as well as the differences of each country/area are sought. Customers are seen on a global rather than a country/area basis.

Transnational organisations are an extension of global organisations.

Transnational organisations are an extension of global organisations. These sophisticated organisations seek to develop advantages based on efficien-

Table 17.1 Organisational frameworks

International organisations	These organisations see their overseas operations as appendages or attachments to a central domestic organisation. The marketing policy is to serve customers domestically and then offer these same marketing mixes to other countries/areas.
Multinational organisations	These organisations see their overseas activities as a portfolio of independent businesses. The policy is to serve customers with individually designed country/area marketing mixes.
Global organisations	These organisations regard their overseas activities as feeders or delivery tubes for a unified global market. The policy is to serve a global market with a single, fundamental marketing mix.
Transnational organisations	These organisations regard their overseas activities as a complex process of coordination and cooperation. The environment is regarded as one where decision-making is shared in a participatory manner. The policy is to serve global business environments using flexible global resources to formulate different global marketing mixes.

Source: Based on Bartlett and Ghoshal (1991) and de Mooij (1994).

cies driven by serving global customers. Using technology as a key part of the infrastructure, networks allow resources to be globally derived in response to local requirements.

Anholt (2000), among others, suggests that in recent years a new type of transnational organisation has emerged. Primarily as a result of the Internet these organisations are conceived and born as global brands and therefore do not experience the slow development and evolution as suggested in the previous framework. These new *universal* brands, owned by either a global parent or a small independent operator, often from start-up, transcend established patterns by either minimising or negating

These new universal *brands, owned by either a global parent or a small independent operator, often from start-up, transcend established patterns by either minimising or negating the formal distribution channels.*

the formal distribution channels. Dell computers, Microsoft and search engines such as Yahoo and Excite all require a global market and have emerged in the last decade of the 20th century. What characterises these new organisations is that they are generally smaller, faster and more adaptable than the established organisations. They might have a global business but some of them operate with a single office, are based in third-world nations or are simply small global businesses in their own right.

Organisations are far from static, and, as domestic markets may stagnate and technology and communication opportunities in particular develop, so opportunities contract and expand. A further configuration reflects the need to be efficient and flexible in the organisation's use of materials and resources. The use of strategic alliances and outsourcing arrangements complements this goal, and network organisations, spanning the globe, emerge.

Appreciating the different types of worldwide organisation is important, not just from a structural perspective but also for the formulation and implementation of business strategy. In addition to this, other issues concerning the products, markets and the marketing communications used by these organisations also surface.

Key variables affecting international marketing communications

There are a large number of variables that can impact upon the effectiveness of marketing communications which cross international borders. Many of these are controllable by either local or central management. However, there are a large number that are uncontrollable, and these variables need to be carefully considered before communications are attempted. The following variables (culture and media) are reviewed here because of their immediate and direct impact on organisations and their communication activities.

Culture

The values, beliefs, ideas, customs, actions and symbols that are learned by members of particular societies are referred to as culture. The importance of culture is that it provides individuals with identity and the direction of what is deemed to be acceptable behaviour. Culture is acquired through learning. If it were innate or instinctual, then everyone would behave in the same way. Human beings across the world do not behave uniformly or predictably. Therefore different cultures exist, and from this it is possible to visualise that there must be boundaries within which certain cultures, and hence behaviours and lifestyles, are permissible or even expected. These boundaries are not fixed rigidly, as this would suggest that cultures are static. They evolve and change as members of a society adjust to new technologies, government policies, changing values and demographic changes, to mention but a few dynamic variables.

Cultural changes – the impact on euromale

With changes to expectations about a job for life, women's increasingly independent financial and social lifestyle and media debates concerning the role of men in society, it is not surprising that international marketing communications targeted at men are unlikely to be based on common attitudes, values and beliefs. Research by RDSi revealed, for example, the following.

Italian men are comfortable in their relationships with women, unless they are their superiors at work. The family is very important with men aspiring to beautiful wives, beautiful children and a beautiful home. Therefore, aspirational advertisements are favoured and scenes depicting family life are approved.

Spanish men are judged to have low morale, partly as a result of the country's relatively recent move towards democracy and the high levels of unemployment when compared with the rest of Europe. The family is an important unit and with it come high levels of respect for the older generation. Cross-generation advertisements that reflect bonding and family ties are well received. There is still a strong macho theme in society with men seeking to prove themselves.

German men see these changes as a challenge and one that needs a disciplined approach. The family is high on their list as something to be openly valued but, unlike the Italians and the French, they are uncertain about how to achieve this as it conflicts with the German work ethic.

Frenchmen are the most self-assured of all European males. They are relaxed and confident about the changing role of women in society and see opportunities to change themselves. There are some poorer sections of French society that do resent the changes and resort to displays of masculinity to reassert themselves.

British males retain a US-style work ethic and on the surface are comfortable with the changes in society. Underneath, however, the research suggests that they are in denial and cites the successful lads' magazines (e.g. *Loaded*, *FHM*) as evidence. This complexity, when combined with the most sophisticated advertising literacy and cynicism, makes it difficult to communicate with British males.

Adapted from Davies (2000).

Culture is passed from generation to generation. This is achieved through the family, religion, education and the media. These conduits of social behaviour and beliefs serve to provide consistency, stability and direction. The extent to which the media either move society forward or merely reflect its current values is a debate that reaches beyond the scope of the book. However, there can be no doubt as to the impact that the media have on society and the important part that religion plays in different cultures around the world.

Culture is passed from generation to generation. This is achieved through the family, religion, education and the media.

Culture has multiple facets, and those that are of direct relevance to marketing communications are the values and beliefs associated with *symbols*, such as language and aesthetics, *institutions* and *groups*, such as those embracing the family, work, education, media and religion, and finally *values*, which according to Hofstede *et al.* (1990) represent the core of culture. These will be looked at in turn.

Symbols

Language, through both the spoken and the non-spoken word, permits members of a society to enter into dialogue and to share meaning. Aesthetics, in the form of design and colour, forms an integral part of packaging, sales promotions and advertising. Those involved in personal selling must be aware of the symbolic impact of formal and informal dress codes and the impact that overall personal appearances and gestures, for example, when greeting or leaving people, may have on people in different cultures. Advertisers need to take care that they do not infringe a culture's aesthetic codes when designing visuals or when translating copy into the local language.

Institutions and groups

The various institutions which help form the fabric of societies and particular cultures provide a means by which culture is communicated and perpetuated through time. These groups provide the mechanisms by which the process of socialisation occurs. Of these groups, the family plays an important role. The form of the *family* is evolving in some Western cultures, such that the traditional family unit is declining and the

Colour

Colours must be treated with care depending on the particular country where communications are being conducted. Griffin (1993) uses the colour of flowers to illustrate this point. Purple flowers are associated with death and unhappiness in Brazil; white lilies have this association in Canada, Great Britain and Sweden, white and yellow lilies in Taiwan and yellow lilies in Mexico. Yellow flowers stand for infidelity in France and disrespect for a woman in the (ex) Soviet Union.

number of single-parent families is increasing. In many developing economies the extended family, with several generations living together, continues to be a central stable part of society. Marketing communication messages need to reflect these characteristics. The impact and importance of various decision-makers need to be recognised and the central creative idea needs to be up to date and sensitive to the family unit.

Work patterns vary across regions: not all cultures expect a 9-to-5 routine. This is breaking down in the UK as delayering pressurises employees to work increased hours, while in Asia-Pacific Saturday morning work is the norm.

Literacy levels can impact heavily on the ability of target audiences to understand and to ascribe meanings to marketing communication messages. The balance between visual and non-visual components in messages and the relative complexity of messages should be considered in the light of the education levels that different countries and regions have reached. In addition to these factors, some target audiences in more developed economies have developed a high level of advertising sophistication. The meaning given to messages is in some part a reflection of the degree to which individuals understand commercial messages and what the source seeks to achieve. This high level of interaction with messages or advertising literacy suggests that advertisers need to create a dialogue with their audiences that recognises their cognitive processing abilities and does not seek to deceive or misinform.

> Literacy *levels can impact heavily on the ability of target audiences to understand and to ascribe meanings to marketing communication messages.*

Religion has always played an important part in shaping the values and attitudes of society. Links between religion and authority have been attempted based on the highly structured nature of religion and the influence that religion can play in the family, forming the gender decision-making roles and nurturing the child-rearing process. While the results of research are not conclusive, there appears to be agreement that religion plays an important part in consumer buying behaviour and that marketing communications should take into account the level of religious beliefs held by the decision-maker (Delner, 1994).

Similarly, mass communication technologies provide audiences with improved opportunities to understand and appreciate different religious beliefs and their associated rituals and artifacts, so care needs to be taken not to offend these groups with offensive or misinformed marketing communications.

Values

One of the most important international and culturally orientated research exercises was undertaken by Hofstede (1980, 1991). Using data gathered from IBM across 53

International messages – TicTac

The 1990s advertising for the TicTac brand, owned by Ferrero, has been judged to be of similar dubious quality to that of its sister brands Ferrero Rocher and Kinder Surprise (Watts, 2000). Much of Ferrero's advertising has been based on a pan-European advertising approach, as per their infamous Ferrero Rocher and Kinder Surprise advertising. For much of the 1990s TicTac European advertising was based upon the use of German models acclaiming the virtues of just 2 calories per sweet (Watts, 2000).

The mint category in which TicTac operates has been rejuvenated by the entry of Smint and its rather unorthodox advertising. Polo, an established competitor, began to exploit the 'hole' in its adverting and with Trebor promoting its smaller mints the market has developed and become more contemporary. TicTac was beginning to be left behind and its European approach was clearly not working. Watts quotes James Lowther (chairman of M&C Saatchi) who says that 'doing a campaign that reaches all markets is not a very successful idea. In order to find something that doesn't displease, you end up reducing the things you can do to the lowest common denominator'.

countries, Hofstede's research has had an important impact on our understanding of culture (Hickson and Pugh, 1995).

From this research, several dimensions of culture have been discerned. The first of these concerns the individualist/collectivist dimension. It is suggested that individualistic cultures emphasise individual goals and the need to empower, to progress and to be a good leader. Collectivist cultures emphasise good group membership and participation. Consequently, difficulties can arise when communications between these two types of culture have meanings ascribed to them that are derived from different contexts. To avoid the possible confusion and misunderstanding, an adapted communication strategy is advisable.

It is suggested that individualistic cultures emphasise individual goals and the need to empower, to progress and to be a good leader.

In addition to these challenges, comprehension (ascribed meaning) is further complicated by the language context. In high-context languages information is conveyed through who is speaking and their deportment and mannerisms. Content is inferred on the basis that it is implicit: it is known and does not need to be set out. This is unlike low-context languages, where information has to be detailed and 'spelled out' to avoid misunderstanding. Not surprisingly, therefore, when (marketing) communications occur across these contexts, inexperienced communicators may be either offended at the blunt approach of the other (of the low-context German or French, for example) or intrigued by the lack of overt information being offered from the other (from the high-context Japanese or Asians, for example).

A further cultural dimension concerns the role that authority plays in society. Two broad forms can be identified. In high-power-distance cultures, authority figures are important and guide a high proportion of decisions that are made. In low-power-distance cultures, people prefer to use cognitive processing and make reasoned

A further cultural dimension concerns the role that authority plays in society.

decisions based on the information available. What might be deduced from this is that expert advice and clear, specific recommendations should be offered to those in high-power-distance cultures, while information provision should be the goal of marketing communications to assist those in low-power-distance cultures (Zandpour and Harich, 1996).

People in different cultures can exhibit characteristics that suggest they feel threatened or destabilised by ambiguous situations or uncertainty. Those cultures that are more reliant on formal rules are said to have high levels of uncertainty avoidance.

Different countries are more receptive to messages that have high or low levels of logical, rational and information-based appeals (think). Other countries might be more receptive to psychological and dramatically based appeals (feel).

They need expert advice, so marketing communications that reflect these characteristics and are logical, clear and provide information in a direct and unambiguous way (in order to reduce uncertainty) are likely to be more successful.

From the adaptation/standardisation perspective, this information can be useful in order to determine the form of the most effective advertising messages. Zandpour and Harich used these cultural dimensions, together with an assessment of the advertising industry environment in each target country. The results of their research suggest that different countries are more receptive to messages that have high or low levels of logical, rational and information-based appeals (think). Other countries might be more receptive to psychological and dramatically based appeals (feel).

International variations – regulations

Advertising of toys is not permitted in Sweden at all and is banned until 22.00h in Greece. In France all alcohol advertisements are banned, while in the Czech Republic drink can be shown but it cannot be poured, nor can advertisements show people enjoying the product. In Mexico the restrictions state that food must be visible, whereas the Costa Ricans are allowed to see a glass being filled or the drink being poured, but not both.

Tobacco advertising is about to be banned across countries in the EU.

Pet food advertisements are banned in Lithuania before 23.00h. The reason for this strict ruling is that food is scarce and this type of commercial could be considered offensive to humans.

Media

The rate of technological change has had a huge impact on the form and type of media that audiences can access. However, media availability is far from uniform, and the range and types of media vary considerably across countries. These media developments have been accompanied by a number of major structural changes to the industry and the way in which the industry is regulated. Many organisations (client brands, media and agencies) have attempted to grow through diversification and the development of international networks (organic growth and alliances), and there has been an increase in the level of concentration as a few organisations/individuals have begun to own and hence control larger proportions of the media industry. For example, Rupert Murdoch, Ted Turner, Time-Warner, Bertelsmann and Silvio Berlusconi now have substantial cross-ownership holdings of international media. This concentration is partly the result of the decisions of many governments to deregulate their control over the media and to create new trading relationships. As a result, this cross-ownership of the media (television, newspapers, magazines, cable, satellite, film, publishing, advertising, cinema, retailing, recorded music) has created opportunities for client advertisers to have to go to only one media provider, who will then provide access to a raft of media across the globe. For example, the recent Time-Warner/AOL merger takes the concentration and cross-industry collaboration a stage further as positions for future markets are adopted. This facility, known as one-stop shopping, has been available in North America for some time, and was attempted by Saatchi & Saatchi and WPP in the 1980s from a European base, but it is only in the 1990s that this opportunity has been offered elsewhere.

Deregulation has had a profound impact on media provision in nearly all parts of the world. In Korea, for example, the number of daily newspapers has grown from 60 in 1988 to 125 in 1996, while the number of television channels has grown from three to four terrestrial channels plus 26 cable services and one satellite broadcaster (Kilburn, 1996).

Table 17.2 sets out some of the more general worldwide trends in advertising media. The net impact of all these changes has been principally the emergence of satellite television and cable provision and the development of the international consumer press.

Cross-border communication strategy

The degree to which organisations should adapt their external messages to suit local or regional country requirements has been a source of debate since Levitt (1983) published his landmark work on global branding. The standardisation/adaptation issue is unlikely to be resolved yet is an intuitively interesting and thought-provoking subject. The cost savings associated with standardisation policies are attractive and, when these are combined with the opportunity to improve message consistency, communication effectiveness and other internally related efficiencies such as staff morale, cohesion and organisational identity, the argument in favour of standardisation seems

---

Table 17.2   General trends in worldwide media

- Electronic media expenditures have grown at the expense of print.
- The worldwide adspend on newspapers has fallen considerably.
- The number of general-interest magazines has fallen and the number of specialist-interest magazines has grown.
- The growth of satellite facilities has helped generate the development of television and cable networks.
- On-line adspend is increasing faster than for any other medium.
- Television programming and distribution have become more important.
- Cinema capacity is beginning to outstrip demand.
- Out-of-home media, in particular outdoor and alternative new media (e.g. ambient), have grown significantly.

difficult to renounce. However, in practice there are very few brands that are truly global. Some, such as McDonald's, Coca-Cola and Levi's are able to capitalise upon the identification and inherent brand value that they have been able to establish across cultures. The majority of brands lack this depth of personality, and because individual needs vary across cultures so enterprises need to retune their messages in order that their reception is as clear and distinct as possible.

The arguments in favour of adapting messages to meet the needs of particular local and/or regional needs are as follows:

1. Consumer needs are different and vary in intensity. Assuming there are particular advertising stimuli that can be identified as having universal appeal, it is unlikely that buyers across international borders share similar experiences, abilities and potential either to process information in a standardised way or to ascribe similar sets of meanings to the stimuli they perceive. Ideas and message concepts generated centrally may be inappropriate for local markets.

2. The infrastructure necessary to support the conveyance of standardised messages varies considerably, not only across but often within broad country areas.

3. Educational levels are far from consistent. This means that buyers' ability to give meaning to messages will vary. Similarly, there will be differing capacities to process information, so that the complexity of message content has to be kept low if universal dissemination is to be successful.

4. The means by which marketing communications are controlled in different countries is a reflection of the prevailing local economic, cultural and political conditions. The balance between voluntary controls through self-regulation and state control through legislation is partly a testimony to the degree of economic and political maturity that exists. This means that what might be regarded as acceptable marketing communication activities in one country may be unacceptable in another. For example, cold calling is not permissible in Germany and, although not popular with either sales personnel or buyers, is allowed in The Netherlands and France.

5. Local management of the implementation of standardised, centrally determined messages may be jeopardised because of a lack of ownership. Messages crafted by local 'craftsmen' to suit the needs of local markets may receive increased levels of support and motivation.

Just as the arguments for adaptation appear convincing at first glance, then so do those in favour of standardisation:

1. Despite geographical dispersion, buyers in many product categories have a number of similar characteristics. This can be supported by the various psychographic typologies that have been developed by advertising agencies for their clients. As brand images and propositions are capable of universal meaning, there is little reason to develop a myriad of brand messages.

2. Many locally driven campaigns are regarded as being of poor quality, if only because of the lack of local resources, experiences and expertise (Harris, 1996). It is better to control the total process and at the same time help exploit the opportunities for competitive advantage through shared competencies.

3. As media, technology and international travel opportunities impact upon increasing numbers of people, so a standardised message for certain offerings allows for a strong brand image to be developed.

4. Just as local management might favour local campaigns, so central management might prefer the ease with which they can implement and control a standardised campaign. This frees local managers to concentrate on managing the campaign and removes from them the responsibility of generating creative ideas and associated issues with local advertising agencies.

5. Following on from this point is one of the more enduring and managerially appealing ideas. The economies of scale that can be gained across packaging, media buying and advertising message creation and production can be enormous. In addition, the prospect of message consistency and horizontally integrated campaigns across borders is quite compelling. Buzzell (1968) argued that these economies of scale would also improve levels of profitability.

Standardisation – Ford

Ford unveiled its new 'roadblocks' campaign through a dominance media strategy launch. The two-minute ad was shown in 40 countries at the same time, literally. At 21.00h on 1 November 1999, every commercial station in the target countries showed the £9.4 million campaign. The ad featured seven of the company's brands (Ford, Volvo, Mazda, Jaguar, Lincoln, Mercury and Aston Martin) and depicted the way the brands featured in people's lives all round the world. So as to present the Ford brand as 'human', consumer orientated and not just a faceless, arrogant conglomerate, it depicted different ethnic groups greeting each other and all using Ford products in a variety of situations. Rosier (1999) also claims that the ad was a sign that global marketing initiatives can drive the creative content even at a domestic level.

Fielding (2000) and Hite and Fraser (1988) argue that the evidence indicates that, although organisations pursued standardisation strategies in the 1970s, the trend since then has been towards more local adaptation. Harris makes the point that, although the operation of a purely standardised programme is considered desirable, there is no evidence to suggest that standardisation actually works. There appears to have been little research to compare the performance of advertising that has been developed and implemented under standardisation policies with that executed under locally derived communications.

However, while a few organisations do operate at either end of the spectrum, the majority prefer a contingency approach. This means that there is a degree of standardisation, where for example creative themes, ideas and campaign planning are driven centrally and other campaign elements such as language, scenes and models are adapted to the needs of the local environment. The cosmetic manufacturer L'Oréal distributes its Studio Line of hair care products aimed at 18–35 year olds across 50 countries. 'These are the same products with the same formulation with the same attitudinal message of personal choice' (Sennett, in Kaplan, 1994). All the advertisements have the same positioning intentions, which are developed centrally, but the executions (featuring different hairstyles) are produced locally to reflect the different needs of different markets. It is too easy to consider the internationalisation debate in terms of packaged goods companies whereas other sectors have approached the task in different ways. Bold (2000) refers to pharmaceutical companies that have generally made the product the centre of their communication strategy, not brands. Drugs are launched in different countries using different names and different strategies targeted at the medical professionals. He comments that while this approach was prevalent the structure of pharmaceutical companies tended to be nation-focused even to the extent that there would be separate regionalised budgets. The merger and consolidation activity together with the rapid rise in patient involvement in health care (e.g. AIDS) has resulted in the formation of centralised marketing departments, the development of multinational brands.

The reasons for some form of standardisation are two-fold. First, there is an increasing need for improved levels of internal efficiency (and accountability) in terms of the use of resources. Secondly, there is an increasing awareness of the benefits that standardised advertising may have on organisational identity, employee morale and satisfaction. The pressure to make cost savings and to develop internal efficiencies, therefore, appears to override the needs of the market.

However, those who argue in favour of standardisation need to be aware that the information content will often need to be correspondingly low. Mueller (1991) observes that the greater the amount of information the greater the opportunity for buyers to discriminate among alternative purchases.

There is an increasing need for improved levels of internal efficiency (and accountability) in terms of the use of resources.

Conversely, the emphasis with uninformative advertising is to use imagery and indirect (peripheral) cues. Multinational organisations prepare individual marketing mixes for individual countries/areas. Products and prices will be different, so comparisons are difficult. Likewise, key attributes will vary across countries/areas, so this means that organisations need to decide whether high levels of standardisation and low levels of information are preferred to adapted campaigns with higher levels of information content.

The criterion by which organisations should decide whether to adapt or standardise their marketing (communications) activities is normally the impact that the different strategies are likely to have on profit performance (Buzzell, 1968). The basis for these financial projections has to be a suitably sensitive segmentation analysis based on a layering of segment information. Country-only or arbitrary regional analysis is

Adaptation – Guinness

When Guinness appointed AMV and Saatchi and Saatchi as its two creative agencies (reducing the number of roster agencies substantially) the decision was made in recognition that the brand's heritage and promotional requirements were essentially two-fold.

Tylee (2001) explains that in the relative sophistication of Europe and the USA the brand is perceived as a premium product supported by very emotionally led advertising reflecting years of development. In Africa and other parts of the world, the brand established itself originally because it was able to be shipped long distances and still be drinkable. Now, Guinness is a mass market brand and is supported in Africa by a James Bond character, Michael Power, a black all-action hero.

Guinness recognises the need to utilise different creative approaches in respect of market perceptions.

unlikely to be suitable. Cross-cultural and psychographic data need to be superimposed to provide the richness upon which to build effective communications.

Organisations rarely decide on a polarised strategy of total adaptation or complete standardisation. In practice, a policy of 'glocalisation'

In practice, a policy of 'glocalisation' seems to be preferred.

seems to be preferred. Under this approach, organisations develop standard messages centrally but expect the local country areas to adapt them to meet local cultural needs by adjusting for language and media components. There are, of course, variations on this theme. For example, head office might decide on the strategic direction and thrust of the campaign and leave the local country management to produce its own creatives.

The international promotional mix

International public relations

International public relations differs from domestically related activities only in the sense that it seeks to build cultural, geographical and linguistic bridges between stakeholders outside the country of origin. As if to continue

Public relations wherever practised needs to be based on a willingness and propensity to share information.

the foregoing debate, the issues remain about whether to standardise communications or adapt them to meet local needs. One complication to this approach concerns the development and prevalence of trading blocs and the degree to which individuals within these blocs retain notions of national identity. This in turn will influence the relationships formed between stakeholder groups.

Public relations wherever practised needs to be based on a willingness and propensity to share information, to be prepared to adjust one's own position in the light of feedback, to be ethical in one's own behaviour.

Packaging

Product packaging fulfils two main functions. One is to protect the product so that the customer can consume the product in pristine condition at all times. The second function concerns the marketing communication needs and its potential impact on the purchase decision process. Packaging, especially in consumer markets for purchase decisions which generate low levels of involvement, need to be protective (due to possibly longer distribution chains and variations on temperature/climate) and be persuasive in such a way that it reinforces the positioning requirements and the other activities of the promotional mix. Research by Berg-Weitzel and van de Laar (2000) states quite emphatically that a nation's culture has repercussions for the design of its packaging and if standardised packaging is decided upon then a neutral design should be pursued. If the decision is to adapt, then local aspects of design should be 'exploited to gain the consumer's confidence'. Colour, shape and language issues need to be carefully considered whether the decision is to standardise of localise packaging design.

Trade shows and exhibitions

This is a much underestimated aspect of marketing communications and in an international dimension is of great significance. The benefits for organisations attending trade fairs are basically the same whether they be domestic or international events. What is significant, however, is that exhibitions are important, especially in the b2b market, for building and maintaining relationships with customers and members of the marketing channel (horizontally and vertically). In an international arena where the cultural backgrounds of visitors and exhibitors may be very diverse, it is essential that not only is attendance made but the visibility be high and hospitality compatible with the local environment and those of other significant visitors.

Exhibitions are important, especially in the b2b market, for building and maintaining relationships with customers and members of the marketing channel.

Personal selling

As to personal local customs, culture, language and product attribute determine that a localised approach to personal selling techniques and content is vital and that a standardised approach selling across international markets is for the vast majority of organisations a non-starter. Having said that, an international sales effort can be organised and managed with a degree of standardisation. There are four main approaches, which can be either used in sequence or simultaneously as conditions permit.

The first approach, mainly applicable for small organisations beginning to operate in international markets, enables them to use spare domestic capacity. They use a sales force that is based in the home market and which either has some international responsibilities or operates abroad exclusively. This requires the sales personnel not only to be fully conversant with the entire product range but also to understand the countries, organisations and cultures in which they seek to operate. If only from a time and expense perspective there are strong limitations to the extent to which this approach can be realistically expected to work.

A second approach requires the use of manufacturers' representatives and agents. These organisations provide local knowledge of both competitors and culture which can cut considerably the length of time necessary to enter a new market. However, there are problems associated with the commitment and bias of such agents and the level of control that management can retain. For example, agents are paid on a commission-only basis and their allegiance to a product/manufacturer is thin, such that their desire to sort out local problems of logistics, finance or product operation is questionable.

A third approach is to establish a marketing channel and appoint distributors and dealers in the target country/regions. This allows management a greater level of control but it does incur greater levels of management time and commitment to the international trade channel and the associated training if the strategy is to be successful.

The fourth and final approach is to establish a dedicated sales force in each of the country/regions. This is expensive and although control is considerably improved it is an approach only adopted once a market presence has been well established.

International sponsorship

Sponsorship, whether it be in a domestic (Serie A football in Italy) or an international (World Cup 2002) context, enables support of the public relations activity either by providing a means to meet key customers or members of the marketing channel in an informal way or by improving awareness and attitudes towards the sponsor. In addition, sponsorship has an impact on the quality of relationships with a variety of stakeholders. Relations with employees, governments and local communities can all be enhanced through understanding and sympathetic alignment with the sponsor's position regarding their social responsibilities, ethical stance and overall role as a corporate citizen (Owusu-Frimpong, 2000).

It is not surprising that the costs associated with sponsorship activities vary according to the scale (size and duration) of the activities and the size of the audience. Global brands need sponsorship on an international basis in order to reinforce their market presence and to support and reinforce the other aspects of the promotional mix. Integrated marketing communications in an international context needs to use advertising (to make aware and to reinforce brand values), public relations (to provide understanding, interest and goodwill), sponsorship (to be seen to be involved) and personal selling (to enable and drive customer action) if a brand is to be established.

Direct marketing

Most of the points concerning domestic direct marketing apply equally on the international stage. It would appear that there are four main factors that need to be considered:

1. Language is an important factor as most people prefer to receive (and give) communications in their own first language. The focus organisation needs to consider translation costs, (including time), list availability and making judgements about tone, humour and indeed what the most appropriate language might be.

2. The second factor is media availability. There may be wide variances in the range and quality of the media in the country/regions that it wishes to trade in. The quality and effectiveness of the telephone and postal services, the coverage of cable and satellite channels, the significance of magazines and the readership of the national, regional and local press all need to be carefully considered when developing an international direct marketing campaign.

3. The third factor to consider is the quality and breadth of the services and infrastructure necessary to support an international campaign. The quality of mailing lists, databases and supporting agencies need to be carefully reviewed before committing to an international DM campaign.

4. The quality of management control is the final international factor to be considered. Most campaigns of this nature need to be controlled centrally by the focus organisation and/or their direct marketing agency. This centralised approach is important in the light of the needs for integration, control of costs and data management. There may be conditions which allow for the development of a decentralised approach where by the planning and implementation of these direct campaigns are delegated to local management.

The centralised and decentralised positions are at two ends of a spectrum. Many organisations adopt a mid position, with strategy and direction being determined centrally and the tactics and implementation issues determined locally.

The role of the Internet

The Internet has an important role to play for those organisations considering internationalisation or those who have already achieved transnational status. Hamill and Gregory (1997) found that smaller organisations view the Internet as a tool to enable them to develop network communications, sales promotion and market intelligence activities.

The Internet has an important role to play for those organisations considering internationalisation or those that have already achieved transnational status.

The Internet provides global market access for all organisations and each needs a strategy to determine the role of its Web site and how it will interact with the organisation's current established distribution and communication strategies.

International advertising agencies

Just as many organisations have sought to expand internationally, so many advertising agencies have attempted to grow with their clients. This process has gathered speed in the 1980s and 1990s, with varying levels of success. By trying to mirror client/brand needs and by expanding operations over increased geographic areas, organisations have experienced many financial and management challenges. These challenges have been met with varying degrees of success. The consequences of this 'natural' development are that aspects such as the structure of the industry, the configuration and work patterns of constituent agencies, the relationships between clients and advertisers and the form of advertising messages that are developed and given meaning by target audiences and agencies alike have evolved.

Agency development overseas

Operating overseas is not a recent phenomenon for advertising agencies. This strategy has been established for many decades. There are three primary routes that agencies have taken to secure international growth. These are *organic growth* through the creation of overseas subsidiaries, *acquisitive growth* through the purchase of established indigenous agencies and finally *cooperative growth*, where agencies collaborate through the formation of networks and strategic alliances.

Organic growth requires the setting up of subsidiary offices in selected regions or countries. Costs and management can be controlled, but the relatively slow speed of development has deterred many from this approach.

Organic growth *requires the setting up of subsidiary offices in selected regions or countries.*

Acquisitive growth, involving the merger with or purchase of advertising agencies already operating in the required market, is attractive because it is possible to use the skills and established contacts of local managers. However, these overseas operations are relatively inflexible and can incur considerable overheads as well as high initial purchase costs. *Cooperative growth* through strategic alliances and partnerships, often as part of global networks, can appear to be a more flexible and efficient approach to meeting a client's international marketing communications requirements. One of the potential problems with this approach is that the level of control over local actions can be reduced, but the reduced costs and increased speed of set-up and delivery make this an attractive option.

A further variation of this method of expansion is the formation of networks of independent agencies. By contributing to a central financial fund, so giving the network a formal legal status, agencies are able to work together and provide flexibility for their clients.

International agency networks can provide clients with a number of advantages. Primarily these focus on two main areas: resource utilisation and communication effectiveness.

Resource utilisation

1. Clients and agencies help each other by avoiding costly duplication of message development work and media buying.

2. Economies of scale can reduce costs for both parties.

3. By centralising decision-making, management has increased control over the direction of campaigns and their implementation such that clients have a single main point of contact.

4. Special resources and scarce creative expertise is made available to a client globally.

Communication effectiveness

1. Creative ideas from all parts of the network can be shared and, if a largely adaptive strategy is followed, good ideas can be replicated elsewhere. Good creative ideas are rare, so by using an international agency these highly prized gems can used to the client's benefit worldwide.

2. Internal communications are improved by a common infrastructure and management information system.

3. By using a single agency, operating across many markets, feedback and market analyses can be standardised (process, timing and format), thus facilitating common reporting and fast feedback of audience and competitor actions.

Freeman (1996) argues that, as manufacturers are re-evaluating the way in which they approach their customers, changes are also being brought about at business-to-business advertising agencies. Rapid technological advances in communications, global marketing of brands, shorter purchase decision-making cycles and heightened competition are forcing agencies to re-evaluate their internal organisation and communications strategies. This, he suggests, has already led to a number of mergers with larger organisations and internal reorganisation to better handle clients' needs.

These developments have impacted on the pitching process. When WPP agreed a deal to manage the Boots global account, the decision was made between Martin Sorrell and Steve Russell, the respective CEOs of the two organisations. The agenda, to create a unified brand and save money (White, 2000) is clear and understandable. However, the process by which the agreement was reached signalled some concern for other agencies. As a result of this 'boardroom' deal, many roster agencies (e.g. OMD) lost substantial billings and did not have an opportunity to defend their business, even though their client had, at marketing manager levels, been more than satisfied with the relationship.

Agency growth

The expansion of advertising agencies away from domestic markets is essentially an investment decision in which normal return on investment criteria need to be determined. Such decisions can be based upon the relative size of competitive advantage that an expanded operation might generate. Multinational agencies (MNAs) might be able to develop key advantages, such as size, access to capital, the loyalty given to them by multinational advertisers, their knowledge and skill, and their ability to use their foreign locations to service regional markets (West, 1996). Some of the growth has been motivated by the need to meet the expanding international requirements of clients. Kim (1995) cites Procter & Gamble's entry into eastern Europe and the subsequent opening of offices in the same area by its adverting agency, Leo Burnett. Anholt (2000) refers to Lintas's development on the back of Unilever's growth. Offensive and defensive business strategies, to either capitalise on or counter competitor moves, can also be regarded as prime motivating factors.

A further explanation lies with the motivations of individual managers, or agency theory. This perspective suggests that managers seek growth in order to fulfil personal needs rather than those that may be in the best interests of the organisation. These advantages nevertheless have little distinguishing power if the MNA itself is unable to coordinate its activities and lever its resources to provide client benefits of speed, creativity and media purchasing power.

Some implications of international growth

One of the current dilemmas facing clients and agencies is that through consolidation the number of agencies capable and interested in international work is declining. At the same times the volume of work available is expanding as a greater number of clients seek to develop internationally. Indeed, the work is fragmenting and hence the value of individual pieces of work is getting smaller. As Anholt (2000) states quite succinctly, 'Global clients are getting more numerous, smaller and spending less, as global agencies are getting fewer, bigger and charging more'. What this means is that the something has to change, probably in the way agencies think and act towards global business opportunities and the way in which they implement strategies and involving more local creative experience to satisfy client needs.

Many advertisers have been comfortable with the way in which advertising agencies have attempted to build European and international networks to complement their own global branding initiatives. There is some evidence, however, that this one-stop shopping approach is not entirely satisfactory (*Economist*, 1996). Some client organisations want access to a range of creative teams and also want the benefits of consolidation at the same time. The response of some MNAs has been to reorganise internally. Many of the megamergers between major agency networks have resulted in further structural changes as agencies shed accounts that cause conflicts of interest. Those clients caught up in the restructuring and consequent consolidation of the industry may well regard themselves as unwitting participants.

The relatively new position of worldwide account director (Farrell, 1996) is an attempt to coordinate and control the global accounts of clients such as IBM and Reebok who have centralised their international advertising activities. Another role that has emerged is that of the worldwide creative director (Davies, 1996). This pos-

Developing internationally – Samsung Electronics Company

Samsung Electronics is a major Korean business organisation which was founded in 1969. Because of the nature and size of the Korean market, Samsung's principal activities were export-focused from the beginning, so the time spent developing in domestic markets was not typical of many organisations in developed Western economies.

International stage

OEM-branded exporting dominated Samsung's business activities, as this provided a convenient and less risky form of rapidly improving export volumes and cash flow. Until 1977 an export department was responsible for routine matters of shipping and courting foreign buyers. From this date an international department was created, as a more sophisticated approach was adopted, to perform market research, some product development and overseas demand forecasting. Several foreign branches were created to encourage communication with foreign buyers, and full-scale export marketing communications, with advertising, sales promotions and exhibitions, were commenced.

Corporate messages sought to establish the size and capabilities of Samsung and were targeted at importers and OEM manufacturers. Product-based messages emphasised particular brands and were targeted at distributors and dealers in the USA, Europe, Asia, the Middle East and Central and South America.

However, the product range that Samsung offered evolved during this period so that the locus moved from televisions, radios and cassette players to microwaves and VCRs. This shift meant that Samsung had to adjust the messages it conveyed in order that the company be perceived as technologically progressive. To accomplish this, it adopted a corporate identity programme.

Multinational stage

This signalled the commencement of the multinational stage in Samsung's development. The message was developed centrally and the same message (standardisation) was then communicated throughout all of the markets in which Samsung was active.

Trade restraints imposed by many economies led to a change in the organisation's corporate strategy. Market penetration could now only be achieved by setting up subsidiary companies in the markets in which it wished to operate. This meant that nationals with local knowledge were required to head each of these new SBUs.

The OEM emphasis gave way to own-branded exports, and, in order to support the local distribution channels and dealers, provincial marketing communications began to proliferate. Head office developed and implemented corporate communication messages and local offices (and agencies) developed product-based communications. Problems were encountered when attempting to harmonise the company awareness campaign with the vagaries of media availability in some of the markets. The 'low-cost, high-quality' message was now targeted at consumers rather than dealers, but difficulties were encountered in getting access to appropriate media. The net result of this was that uncoordinated promotional work ensued, which was relatively ineffective in achieving its goals.

Global stage

Samsung needed to change its corporate strategy, as it was unable to continue competing on a low-cost basis, mainly because of competitors' relocation of their production facilities and the increasing labour costs in Korea. By reducing the OEM activity and promoting its own high-quality brands, Samsung was better positioned to achieve one its goals of becoming one of the world's top five electronics companies.

Corporate profitability had fallen despite increased sales revenues. The company strategy highlighted the need to coordinate its activities across the group and to reduce duplication and unnecessary investments.

The group's promotional activities were also overhauled. A coordinated global corporate and brand identity programme was established with the goal of allowing its global consumers to differentiate Samsung. Korean advertising agencies were internationalising themselves either through the establishment of overseas offices or by entering into alliances with other agencies that gave them access to global networks.

Transnational stage

It is perhaps too early to establish whether a move to transnational status has been accomplished, but it seems that Samsung might be evolving toward this form.

Adapted from Cho *et al.* (1994).

ition, it is suggested, has developed directly from clients' expectations for their agency networks to mirror their own global branding drives and management structures. But, as Martin (1996) points out, as these worldwide creative directors are invariably appointed with no department or resources and are inclined to meet resistance from local management teams, the position appears to be irrelevant and impotent.

Media planning has become increasingly difficult, as not only has the provision of media services in particular regions (e.g. Asia) expanded rapidly but at the same time there have been major social changes. Kilburn (1996) reports that, in Taiwan, Ogilvy & Mather and J. Walter Thompson have formed The Media Partnership from their media buying operations, thus providing increased buying power for their clients in what is effectively a fragmented market.

Agency structures are evolving and adapting to the needs of their environments.

Agency structures are evolving and adapting to the needs of their environments. The traditional perspective of control by head office executives over the work of local network agencies, either by a disproportionate level of standardisation policies or by rather inflexible procedures that put bureaucratic needs before market requirements, is changing. Instead of control, coordination is one of the keys to competitive advantage in MNA/agency relationships. The one factor that distinguishes transnational organisations applies equally to advertising agencies. As Banerjee (1994) suggests, agency decision-making concerning the development of major multicountry brands will need to be collaborative in the future as 'agency power structures evolve to better reflect emerging revenue geographies'.

Stages of cross-border advertising development

Cho *et al.* (1994) propose a framework whereby the type of advertising deployed can be considered in the context of the stage of internationalisation that organisations have reached. Based upon studies of Korean firms, the authors propose that the advertising strategy is (or should be) a direct reflection of the marketing and business strategies employed. Therefore:

Domestic marketing	=	Domestic advertising
Export marketing	=	Export advertising
Multinational marketing	=	Multinational advertising
Global marketing	=	Global advertising

From this, and utilising the information about international development, it is possible to establish the key characteristics and strategies associated with each stage of international growth (Table 17.3).

Summary

As organisations saturate domestic markets and seek growth opportunities overseas, so they meet new challenges and embark upon fresh strategies. Organisations operating across a number of international and/or regional borders evolve through international, multinational, global and transnational phases and forms. The differentiating characteristics appear pronounced and convincing as growth drivers impel development.

Table 17.3 Strategies associated with international advertising development

	Home	International	Multinational	Global	Transnational
Advertising stage	Domestic	Export	Multinational	Global	Transnational
Key message	Product or corporate	Product and brand	Corporate and brand	Corporate and brand	Corporate and/or brand
Management	Standardisation	Standardisation	Standardisation and adaptation	Regional adaptation	Global adaptation
Management structure/support	Centralised	Centralised	Decentralised	Grouped centralisation	Network
Agency	Domestic	Domestic	Domestic and foreign local	Global	Transnational network

Two of the main variables that impact upon the marketing communications deployed by organisations across these different forms are culture and the media. Culture is a composite of a number of elements, ranging from symbols such as language, groups and education, through values represented in language context and power distance.

The media are also significant drivers which have been influenced by both technological drivers and political initiatives to deregulate and open up accessibility.

The strategies used to communicate with cross-border audiences focus upon either standardisation or total adaptation to the needs of the local audience. While the debate is interesting and practice varied, the evidence suggests that a mixture of the two approaches, glocalisation, is the preferred practice of many global and transnational organisations.

Advertising agencies have had to respond to the initiatives driven by their clients. Global advertising agency development has taken a variety of forms, however, there appears to be a match between the marketing strategies pursed by client organisations and the consequent advertising strategies to support them.

Review questions

1. There are four types of organisation reflecting their structure and disposition to their markets. Name them and their key characteristics.

2. Prepare some brief notes explaining how culture impacts upon an organisation's marketing communications.

3. Select two countries of your choice. Compare the significance of cultural symbols and provide examples of how these are used.

4. Explain high- and low-context languages.

5. Discuss how deregulation of media ownership has affected marketing communications.

6. You have been asked to make a presentation to senior managers on the advantages and disadvantages of standardising the marketing messages delivered for your brand throughout the world. Prepare notes for each of the slides you will use.

7. Evaluate the different ways in which advertising agencies can grow.

8. International advertising agencies provide resource utilisation and communication effectiveness as their main advantages. Explain the detail associated with these two characteristics.

9. Determine the four stages of cross-border advertising development.

10. What are the key differences between each of the these four stages?

◼ MINI CASE

This mini case was written by Clifford Conway, Senior Lecturer in Marketing at Brighton University.

International promotion

Globalisation and culture

Levitt (1983) was one of the first authors to suggest that the world is becoming a global marketplace where consumers have similar and universal needs and that companies need to standardise their marketing mix strategies to gain the resulting economies of scale and therefore competitive advantage.

The opposite of a global strategy is the local or adaption strategy. Unilever's household cleaner Jif was marketed in Europe under different brand names, e.g. Cif in France. Although this allows for greater sensitivity to local markets, it leads to problems of costs and coordination, which makes a global, standardised strategy appear very attractive.

The following vignettes and examples, however, will indicate that a standardised promotional strategy can be problematic and that culture in particular can be a major stumbling block. (Read Agrawal (1995) for a fuller debate concerning standardisation or adaption in advertising.)

(A) A major UK snack food firm decided to launch its products, e.g. Scotch eggs, black pudding, pork pies and Cornish pasties as picnic snacks, etc. into the Lebanon during the Christmas period in 2000. Although this was Ramadan, it was thought that people would be very hungry in the evenings.

The Lebanon, a country whose capital was once reputed to be the Paris of the Middle East, was thought to be a prime target with its warm climate through the year and mixed ethnic groupings, suggesting a cosmopolitan environment.

Using the same brand name as in the UK, 'Snack-U-Like'™, it was proposed to advertise and promote this product to young men and women (18–30) using the strapline 'Snack and have fun'. Using the British commercial featuring a beach scene, the British actors are seen wearing conservative bathing costumes. As pretend couples, the actors could be seen playing and having a fun time because of the convenience offered by the snack foods. In the background could be heard the famous Cliff Richard song 'Summer holiday' from the 1960s.

The product did not sell well and the product range and advertising campaign were withdrawn.

(B) The CEO for the 'Snack-U-Like'™ food range decided to send his top selling sales representative, Ms James, to Japan, to negotiate sales contracts with leading food retailers. The product ranges are national British food icons and it was felt that, as the Japanese love Scotch whisky, Burberry cloths and books by the Brontë sisters, these food icons would also become a success.

On arrival in Tokyo, Ms James, using the equivalent of Kompass, makes appointments for the following week to meet with the CEO of Japan's leading food retailers.

On making her first appointment she does not meet the CEO but his commercial manager. Undeterred, she produces one of her English business cards and immediately files the reciprocated one. Unsure of the business etiquette, she shook hands but did not bow, and then handed over an expensive gift intended for the CEO.

Ms James then goes through her normal sales pitch in English and at the end produces a contract for both parties to sign; at this point she is told that only the CEO has authority to sign such contracts and that they would be in contact shortly.

Ms James never heard from this potential Japanese customer.

(C) In 1989 Benetton launched its 'United

colours of Benetton' poster campaign. In France the campaign won an award for creativity but in the USA the posters (a man dying from AIDS and an image of a black and white man shackled together) had to be withdrawn because of complaints from civil rights and Christian leaders.

(D) The Vauxhall Nova failed in Spanish-speaking countries, the Volvo 444 failed in Chinese-speaking countries and the name Matsushita had to be changed to Panasonic for the US market.

The above vignettes and examples suggest that a global, standardised promotion strategy can be problematic. A useful compromise is to take the 'glocal' approach: think global but act local (a term first coined by Akio Morita, the founder of Sony). Standardise where possible, adapt where necessary. The key to successful promotion is good research, know the market.

Mini-case questions

1. Read and critique the Levitt (1983) article; what issues did he get right and where have his propositions fallen down?
2. In the example cited in vignette A, why did the campaign fail?
3. In vignette B, what recommendations would you make to Ms James to help improve her sales success?
4. For vignette C, why can creativity in one market be commended but in another vilified?
5. Why did the brand names fail in vignette D and what recommendations would you suggest in choosing a new brand name that could be used globally?

References

Agrawal, M. (1995) Review of a 40-year debate in international advertising: practitioner and academician perspectives to the standardization/adaptation issue. *International Marketing Review*, **12**(1), pp. 26–48.

Anholt, S. (2000) Updating the international advertising model. *Admap*, (June), pp. 18–21.

Banerjee, A. (1994) Transnational advertising development and management: an account planning approach and a process framework. *International Journal of Advertising*, **13**, pp. 95–124.

Bartlett, C. and Ghoshal, S. (1991) *Managing Across Borders: The Transnational Solution*. Cambridge, MA: Harvard Business School Press.

Berg-Weitzel van den, L. and Laar van de, R. (2000) Local or global packaging. *Admap* (June), pp. 22–5.

Bold, B. (2000) Unlocking the global market. *PR Week*, 11 August, pp. 13–14.

Buzzell, R. (1968) Can you Standardise multinational marketing? *Harvard Business Review*, **46** (November/December), pp. 102–13.

Cho, D.-S., Choi, J. and Yi, Y. (1994) International advertising strategies by NIC multinationals: the case of a Korean firm. *International Journal of Advertising*, **13**, pp. 77–92.

Davies, J. (1996) The rise of the super-creative. *Campaign*, 1 November, p. 18.

Davies, J. (2000) Euroman: warrior or wimp? *Campaign*, 15 October, p. 39.

Delner, N. (1994) Religious contrast in consumer decision behaviour patterns: their dimensions and marketing implications. *European Journal of Marketing*, **28**(5), pp. 36–53.

Economist (1996) A passion for variety. *Economist*, 30 November, pp. 68–71.

Farrell, G. (1996) Suits: the world is their ad oyster. *Adweek*, **37**(8), pp. 29–33.

Fielding, S. (2000) Developing global brands in Asia. *Admap*, (June), pp. 26–9.

Freeman, L. (1996) Client-driven change alters agency strategies. *Advertising Age – Business Marketing*, **81**(2), pp. 1–20.

Griffin, T. (1993) *International Marketing Communications*. London: Butterworth Heinemann.

Hamill, J. and Gregory, K. (1997) Internet marketing in the Internationalisation of UK SMEs. *Journal of Marketing Management*, **13**, pp. 9–28.

Harris, G. (1996) International advertising: developmental and implementational issues. *Journal of Marketing Management*, **12**, pp. 551–60.

Hickson, D.J. and Pugh, D.S. (1995) *Management Worldwide*. London: Penguin.

Hite, R.E. and Fraser, C. (1988) International advertising strategies of multinational corporations. *Journal of Advertising Research*, **28** (August/September), pp. 9–17.

Hofstede, G. (1980) *Culture's Consequences: International Differences in Work Related Values*. Sage.

Hofstede, G. (1991) *Cultures and Organisations*. London: McGraw-Hill.

Hofstede, G., Neuijen, B., Ohayv, D.D. and Sanders, G. (1990) Measuring organisational cultures: a qualitative and quantitative study across twenty cases. *Administrative Science Quarterly*, **35**(2), pp. 286–316.

Kaplan, R. (1994) Ad agencies take on the world. *International Management* (April), pp. 50–2.

Keegan, W.J. (1989) *Global Marketing Management*. Englewood Cliffs, NJ: Prentice Hall.

Kilburn, D. (1996) Asia rising. *Adweek*, **37**(34), pp. 22–6.

Kim, K.K. (1995) Spreading the net: the consolidation process of large transnational advertising agencies in the 1980s and early 1990s. *International Journal of Advertising*, **14**, pp. 195–217.

Levitt, T. (1983) The globalization of markets. *Harvard Business Review* (May/June), pp. 92–102.

Martin, M. (1996) How essential is the role of a worldwide creative director? *Campaign*, 9 February, p. 45.

de Mooij, M. (1994) *Advertising Worldwide*. Hemel Hempstead: Prentice Hall.

Mueller, B. (1991) An analysis of information content in standardised vs. specialised multinational advertisements. *Journal of International Business Studies* (First Quarter), pp. 23–39.

Owusu-Frimpong, N. (2000) The theory and practice of sponsorship in international marketing communications. In *The Handbook of International Marketing Communications* (ed. S.O. Moyne). Oxford: Blackwell.

Rosier, B. (1999) Ford to 'roadblock' the world in TV campaign. *Marketing*, 28 October, p. 4.

Tylee, J. (2001) AMV and Saatchis prepare to meet over Guinness. *Campaign*, 12 January, p. 23.

Watts, J. (2000) Tic Tac looks to UK agencies to get a fresher image. *Campaign*, 25 August, p. 24.

West, D.C. (1996) The determinants and consequences of multinational advertising agencies. *International Journal of Advertising*, **15**(2), pp. 128–39.

White, J. (2000) Can agencies survive clients' global expansion? *Campaign*, 27 October, p. 24.

Zandpour, F. and Harich, K. (1996) Think and feel country clusters: a new approach to international advertising standardization. *International Journal of Advertising*, **15**, pp. 325–44.

18

Interactive communication strategy

The development of the Internet and related digital technologies has brought sweeping changes to the way in which organisations can conduct business and, in particular, the role marketing communications are expected to undertake. The interactivity and rapid two-way communications enabled by technology require the development of new strategies and a fresh understanding of what customers might need.

AIMS AND OBJECTIVES

The aim of this chapter is to explore some of the strategic issues concerning the utilisation of the Internet as part of an organisation's overall approach to marketing communications. Consideration is given to both the interorganisational and consumer sectors. It is recommended that this chapter be read in conjunction with Chapter 25.

The objectives of this chapter are:

1. To clarify understanding of the Internet and the distribution and communication opportunities it represents.

2. To explain how the communication process is considered to work in the Internet environment.

3. To appreciate the variety of business models and Internet strategies that have evolved.

4. To examine the characteristics of the business-to-business and business-to-consumer eCommerce models and to introduce related issues concerning marketing communications.

5. To consider branding in association with dotcom companies.

6. To explore strategic implications on the Internet on the retail sector.

7. To examine issues relating to interactive communication strategies.

Introduction

The Internet comprises of millions of computers, thousands of networks, and it is still growing. These are linked together in such a way that users can search for, utilise and access information provided by others. The World Wide Web (WWW) provides a user-friendly, multimedia interface to this vast network and easy ways to search for, retrieve and file specific information.

The Internet provides a wide variety of activities, which include electronic mail, global information access and retrieval systems, discussion groups, multiplayer games and file transfer facilities, all of which are helping to not only transform the way we think about marketing communications but is also impacting on business strategy, marketing channel structures, interorganisational relationships and the configuration of the marketing communications mix.

However, the Internet impacts upon marketing in two main ways: distribution and communication. The first concerns distribution and marketing channels. The Internet provides a new more direct route to customers, which can either replace or supplement current distribution arrangements. The second element concerns the Internet as a communication medium. It provides a means of reaching huge new audiences and enabling the provision of vast amounts of information. The WWW represents the multimedia component, providing facilities such as full-colour graphics, sound and video (Berthon *et al.*, 1996). These two elements, distribution and communication, combine as eBusiness and eCommerce to provide benefits for both buyers and sellers.

The Internet impacts upon marketing in two main ways: distribution and communication.

The WWW can be considered as a network within which there are a number of nodes, called Web sites. These sites are created and maintained by organisations and individuals who wish to participate in Internet activities with the expectation that they can benefit (often profitably) from such participation. Web sites are intended to be visited by those browsing the Internet, and once visited the opportunity to interact and form a dialogue increases rapidly. The commercial attractiveness of a Web site is based around the opportunities to display product and company information, often in the form of catalogues, as a corporate identity cue and for internal communications, to generate leads, to provide on-screen order forms and customer support at both pre- and post-purchase points and to collect customer and prospect information for use within a database or as a feedback link for measurement and evaluative purposes. The principal benefits of an Internet presence are set out in Table 18.1. The list of benefits is quite extensive and far ranging. From low barriers to entry for those developing Web sites and the attraction of considerably lower transaction costs to improved collaboration and better business relationships and enhanced customer satisfaction, the Internet provides opportunities for considerable development.

It is relatively inexpensive to create a site and, of course, depends upon the level of required site complexity.

It is relatively inexpensive to create a site and, of course, depends upon the level of required site complexity. Domain name registration can cost as little as £10 for two years, Web site design (50 pages) may cost £2,500 while hosting and registering costs average out at around £250, although this can vary widely. The attractiveness of these costs is that they are the same for all participants; there is an equality of entry costs. Also, because

Table 18.1   Benefits of an Internet presence

- Considerably reduced transaction costs
- Opportunities for growth and innovation
- Improved competitive position
- Encouragement of cooperative behaviour
- Stimulates review of business and marketing strategies
- Enhances communications with customers
- Can improve corporate image and reputation
- Information about customers improved
- Enhanced measurement and evaluation of customer interaction
- Customer service developed

of the nature of the mediated environment, no one Web site can gain a communication advantage over others as the share of voice (see Chapter 11) remains (essentially) the same. However, it is possible for some Web site owners to gain preferential positions (seedings) in the listings displayed when a keyword search is activated. Higher positions can be achieved by ensuring that keywords are to be found at the top of each page, or by increasing the number of hits on the site. Not only can the competitive position be improved but the collaborative aspect of an organisation's business activities can be reconsidered and developed. In some cases it is possible to pay a premium price in order to have a top spot or by using a specialist Web seeding service better list placing can be achieved (McLuhan, 2000).

It was believed that there were 10.6 million adults, or 25% of the adult population, on-line in the UK according to internet consultants NUS (Lord, 1999). Murphy (2000) claims that 88% of organisations are connected to the Internet. In the UK, 50% of the population are ABC1 who also account for 74% of Internet users. This leads to the conclusion that Internet audiences are well educated, achieve above-average earnings and are socially active. Lord claims that 55% of Internet users receive tertiary education and earn in excess of £30k.

The significance of these figures is that on-line advertising represents less than 0.3% of the total UK advertising expenditure.

Estimates of UK on-line advertising spend vary from £23 million by *Marketing Week* to £50 million in 1999 (Fletcher Research, cited by Woolgar, 1999). The significance of these figures is that on-line advertising represents less than 0.3% of the total UK advertising expenditure, although the rate of growth will outstrip that of overall advertising as on-line advertising reached £100 million in 2000.

Communication characteristics of the WWW

The dialogue that marketing communications seeks to generate with customers and stakeholders is partially constrained by an inherent time delay based upon the speed at which responses are generated by the participants in the communication process. Technological advances now allow participants to conduct marketing communication-based 'conversations' at electronic speeds. The essence of this speed attribute is that it allows for interactively based communications, where enquiries are responded to more or less instantly.

Table 18.2   A comparison of new and traditional media

Traditional media	New media
One to many	One-to-One and Many-to-Many
Greater monologue	Greater Dialogue
Active provision	Passive Provision
Mass marketing	Individualised
General need	Personalised
Branding	Information
Segmentation	Communities

The differences between traditional and new media are set out in Table 18.2. The interesting aspect is that the Internet is a medium that provides an opportunity for real dialogue with customers. With traditional media the tendency is for monologue or at best delayed and inferred dialogue. One of the first points to be made about these new interactive communication facilities is that the context within which marketing communications occurs is redefined. Traditionally, dialogue occurs in a context which is familiar (relatively) and which is driven by providers who deliberately present their messages through a variety of communication devices into the environments that they expect their audiences may well pass or recognise. Providers implant their messages into the various environments of their targets. Yuan *et al.* (1998) refer to advertising messages being 'unbundled', such as direct marketing, which has no other content, or 'bundled' and embedded with other news content such as television, radio and Web pages with banner ads. Perhaps more pertinently, they refer to direct and indirect on-line advertising. Direct advertising is concerned with advertising messages delivered to the customers (email) while indirect advertising is concerned with messages that are made available for customers to access at their leisure (Web sites).

The Internet is a medium that provides an opportunity for real dialogue with customers.

Direct advertising is concerned with advertising messages delivered to the customers (email) while indirect advertising is concerned with messages that are made available for customers to access at their leisure (Web sites).

With interactive communications, providers become relatively passive. Their messages are presented in an environment that requires targets to use specific equipment to actively search them out. The roles are reversed, so that the drivers in the new context are active information seekers, represented by the target audience (members of the public and other information providers such as organisations), not just the information providing organisations.

A further development resulting from the use of new technology in marketing communications is the target of the communication activity. Interactivity, as stated above, has increased in speed, but interactivity can occur not only between people as a result of a message conveyed through a particular medium but also with machines or cyberspace. As Hoffman and Novak (1996) state, people interactivity is now supplemented by machine interactivity. This means that the dialogue that previously occurred *through* machines now occurs *with* the equipment facilitating the communication exchanges (see Figure 18.1).

These authors refer to the work of Steuer (1992), who suggests that the principal

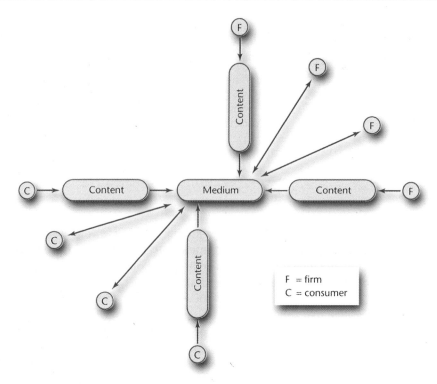

Figure 18.1 A model of marketing communications in a hypermedia computer-mediated environment. From Hoffman and Novak (1996); reprinted with permission from the *Journal of Marketing*, published by the American Marketing Association.

relationship is with what is referred to as a *mediated environment* and not between sender and receiver. This is important, as it is the potential of all participants in the communication activity to mediate or influence the environment (especially the message content) in which the dialogue occurs that makes interactive marketing communications so dynamic and such a radically revolutionary new promotional medium.

There has been considerable media attention given to the development and potential of interactive services. However, the reality is that only a very small proportion of the public has become immersed in these mediated environments, measured in terms of advertising space sold, usage and attitude research, and the number of transactions undertaken interactively. The development of interactive services may well be best served by the identification of those most likely to adopt such services and who will encourage others in their social orbits to follow their actions. This strategy would require communication with innovators and early adopters to speed the process of adoption (Rogers, 1983). This is quite crucial, as the infrastructure and associated heavy costs require an early stream of cash flows (Kangis and Rankin, 1996). The cost of equipment and time taken to learn and utilise interactive services does represent a barrier to adoption. These barriers might be substantial depending upon the background characteristics, education, personality, propensity to take risk and willingness to develop new skills and patterns of behaviour. This reinvention process can take individuals varying mounts of time to accomplish and hence impact on the speed of adoption.

The reality is that only a very small proportion of the public has become immersed in these mediated environments.

Business models and eCommerce

Ecommerce, the electronic buying and selling of goods and services, either in a b2b or b2c context provides potentially huge benefits for participants. The essential attraction for sellers is that a global market becomes available and transaction costs are reduced. For buyers, search convenience combined with lower prices make eCommerce a compelling option.

There are a number of eCommerce or business models that can be identified operating over the WWW. The range of business models includes the following:

eRetail (demand-led buying opportunities for the public);

eMalls (demand-led collection of eRetail 'shops' who seek common synergies);

ePurchase (demand-led buying and selling for businesses);

eProcurement (supply-led services for the purchase of materials and equipment);

eService providers (supply-led provision of specialty business services);

eAuction (demand- and supply-orientated bidding processes for both consumers and organisations);

eCollaboration (demand and supply orientation for mutual benefit).

Other dotcom models include what are known colloquially as ' clicks' and 'bricks & clicks' operations. 'Bricks & clicks' operations refer to organisations that retain a physical presence (high street or business park) and on-line facilities are added either to reach discrete segments/new markets or as a supplement to the current distribution and communication facilities. The 'clicks' model refers to dedicated Internet brands (e.g. bol.com, lastminute.com) that only have a virtual presence. Following initial enthusiasm in the late 1990s hundreds of dotcoms were formed but it is expected that a large percentage of these will fail. However, long-established businesses are adding dotcom facilities to their business and promotional activities. There are several implications for marketing communications and branding activities for both of these two types of Internet operations and these will be examined later.

A number of hybrid business formats have emerged.

It is not surprising, therefore, that out of this complexity of formats and styles, markets and customer needs, a number of hybrid business formats have emerged, principally to meet the needs of the new electronic marketplace.

Business strategy and new technologies – Blockbuster

The development of broadband technology demonstrates the impact that the digital evolution can have in terms of channel structure and the strategic shift that organisations need to make in order to remain competitive.

Films are traditionally marketed first through cinemas, then through video releases and then finally through television (as video on demand, then pay-for channels and then terrestrial services). The full financial potential is realised through this channel structure. The development of digital technologies and Internet facilities offers certain advantages to film studios but it is not necessarily to their advantage to cut out these intermediaries. For example, not all films are successful and it is sometimes necessary to go 'straight to video' in which case the video rental store plays a significant part in the marketing channel.

Broadband services enable people to see films on-line, whenever and wherever they want. For organisations such as Blockbuster video rental stores this development posed a major threat. With 65 million cardholders and 6,300 stores worldwide (Oliver, 2000) the company needed to anticipate the changes in supply and demand. Blockbuster's response was to change the fundamental purpose or mission of the organisation and become a leisure and entertainment company, to be an overall entertainment provider for the home. The development of eCommerce facilities has been a key part of their strategy.

Central to this strategy was the non-exclusive digital download and video streaming rights agreement with the film studio MGM and independent film operator AtomFilms. This enables Blockbuster to showcase selected films on its Web site (*www.blockbuster.co.uk*). (This first step may lead to agreements with other studios and may well prove attractive to other entertainment-based companies that might enter into partnership deals.)

The Web site also enables people to purchase CDs, DVDs, games as well as the core product, videos. In addition, Blockbuster has used interactive technologies to provide a higher level of customer personalisation in the services they offer. For example, its 'Blockbuster Recommends' facility suggests films to customers based upon their previous selections or a list of films rated *I hate it* or *I like it*. Another example of the personalisation approach is the facility to suggest films to match the mood of the viewer. For example, if someone is feeling depressed then it may suggest a Gene Wilder film. All of these changes have been supported with a substantial off-line advertising campaign to inform current customers of the changes and to remind them of the Blockbuster proposition and values, to attract and persuade potential new customers to visit the site or a local store and finally to reposition the brand by differentiating it from it previous position and its main competitors.

Effectively, the company has revised its strategy to accommodate changes in the environment, implemented the necessary changes to its offering and then rebranded itself to reposition itself in the home entertainment business.

Adapted from Oliver (2000).

However, despite the complexities associated with formats and services provided, there are two main models. One concerns interorganisational communications and transaction activity, referred to as business-to-business (b2b). The other concerns activities with consumers and is referred to as business-to-consumer (b2c). In the USA the development of b2c is much further advanced than it is in Europe, where the emphasis has been on b2b. These two models will now be looked at in turn but readers are advised that references to other aspects of Internet based communications are made throughout the book.

Internet strategies

The function and speed of development of Internet facilities within organisations is a function of many factors, such as the size and core skills of the organisation (it is easier for an IT organisation than a transport organisation to develop eCommerce facilities), the nature of the product offering and the market and competitor conditions. It cannot, therefore, be concluded that there is a fixed pathway for the development and incorporation of the Internet within an organisation, nor should there be one as the flexibility and adaptability to meet individual organisational requirements needs to be retained.

It is this technology factor, more than any other, that has done so much to accelerate moves towards integrated marketing communications.

However, it is useful to understand the basic types of on-line facilities in order to appreciate the strategic thinking that needs to be undertaken. The Internet can become an integral part of the way a business operates, the way it sees it future and the way others see it, and not just be used to supplement the organisation's promotional programme. Having said that, it is this technology factor, more than any other, that has done so much to accelerate moves towards integrated marketing communications and to encourage managers to consider the totality of their activities rather than focus on an individual aspect.

Bickerton *et al.* (1998) suggest that there three main stages to the development and implementation of the Internet within organisations: presentation, interaction and representation, and van Doren *et al.* (2000) and others present a four-stage model. What is consistent among these and the other interpretations is that the spectrum of Internet opportunities range from the use of the Internet as a:

shop window (I would like to look at what you have to offer) through to

enquiry (may I know more about that one please) to a fully

interactive engagement (I would like to buy that one and have it delivered please) to one which is

fully integrated or embedded with the business systems and procedures of partner organisations.

In this last phase the transactional activities between organisations are routinised and embedded in the relationship and business processes. The phases are set out in Table 18.3

These phases of development need to be considered alongside the technological platform that the organisation wishes to operate. Essentially the Internet provides Web site access for everyone. However, an Extranet platform enables an organisation to restrict access to a number of selected organisations/people. For example, end-user customers, intermediaries and suppliers all might use an Extranet to provide benefits that all can share and through which the host might develop competitive advantage. An Intranet platform enables the use of the same browser-based technology but access is restricted to the employees of an organisation.

An Extranet platform enables an organisation to restrict access to a number of selected organisations/people.

The strategic choice of platform requires consideration of the communities with which the organisation wishes to interact. The management of these communities is

Table 18.3   Internet utilisation – development phases

Phase	Explanation	Technological/organisational involvement	Departments involved
Presentation or 'shop window' – look what we have to offer	Web site projects name and identity of organisation and displays products and services	Low – externally managed Web site – Internet	Marketing, IT, external Web agency
Enquiry '...and contact us to find out more'	Presentation still important but site now permits registration, email enquiries and limited interrogation	Medium – externally managed Web site, staff access to email – Internet and possibly Intranet	Marketing, IT, external Web agency, sales or call centre staff.
Interaction – 'buy on-line and we will deliver'	Stronger two-way communication is established and full interaction is enabled	High – requires security and invoicing; logistics to convert on-line order to standard order systems – Internet and Intranet	Marketing, IT, sales, accounts, dedicated process staff
Embeddedness – Web is fully integrated with business systems and procedures of partner organisations	Web integrates all business activities throughout the organisation, suppliers and customers	Full integrated ordering, supply, marketing, sales, invoicing, delivery and customer services – Internet, Intranet and Extranet	All staff and external partners

then necessary in order to ensure optimum usage and the development of suitable relationships. Management need to encourage communities to grow and to interact with one another and this requires that users be empowered, encouraged to innovate and be reviewed on a regular basis. Rather like a gardener, one of the first stages in the process is the planting stage where the rules and regulations of the community and the way in which they should interact are agreed. The next stage concerns the nurturing of plants and this involves monitoring development and taking expert action in the light of events. Pruning is a necessary activity in order to encourage growth, so management need to be prepared to remove particular communities should they threaten the interests of the wider group.

Business-to-business

In b2b markets organisational buying behaviour is more complex than that observed in consumer markets. This is because of the increased number of people involved in the decision-making process and the nature of the relationships between individuals and organisations. As a result of this and other factors, marketing communications in the b2b market are traditionally characterised by the predominance of personal selling and relatively little use of advertising (see Chapter 15). In fact, it is the complete reversal of consumer-based promotional activity (b2c) where mass media based communications have tended to be the most important route through to the target audience (see Chapters 14 and 15).

The advantages of the Internet and digital technologies in a b2b context are numerous and as Lancioni *et al.* (2000) state the use of the Internet in supply chain management is not only increasing very quickly but it can provide managers with fast, accurate information which is critical for flexibility and adaptation to changing market conditions. Some of the more prominent advantages are that:

1. communication can be faster, more timely, accurate and with up-to-date information;

2. costs can be lowered and transactions made more effective and efficient;

3. relationships with intermediaries can be renewed, new and revised types of intermediary introduced to add value;

4. levels of customer satisfaction can be improved and channel issues resolved more quickly;

5. the communication system can provide more accurate and clearer information owing to less noise and ambiguity;

6. exit barriers can be installed to protect key intermediaries;

7. the communication mix (and budget) can be used far more productively (e.g. the sales force can spend more time in front of higher-value customers).

One of the principal reasons for using the Internet as a distribution channel and communication medium between organisations is that it can drastically improve productivity. Electronic commerce saves transaction time, lowers costs and shortens the time between order and delivery. Digitally based communications can improve the accuracy of the information provided and so provide a good measure of the effectiveness of marketing communication activities. However, off-line communications are going to still be important and these new communication formats should be considered as an addition to rather than a substitution for current marketing communications. For example, the collection of data for use through on- and off-line sources can be deployed to improve direct marketing activities, to target sales promotions so as to provide real and valued incentives and even benefit public relations activities by placing suitable material on the Web pages. Therefore, productivity measures apply to marketing communications on and off-line.

The use of the Internet in supply chain management is not only increasing very quickly but it can provide managers with fast, accurate information which is critical for flexibility and adaptation to changing market conditions.

The set-up costs associated with the Internet although not excessive require careful examination and consideration, especially when it is expected that channel partners will need to reconsider their strategies and relationships. Careful strategic consideration needs to be given to the new relationships that will develop and some of the exit and entry barriers that some digital technologies might impose or instigate should conditions change. Internet access for smaller business partners may be restricted and they may prefer to continue having face-to-face contact with the sales force. This should be respected and the marketing communications mix formulated carefully so as to move these types of organisations gradually to new forms of communications.

The use of the Internet can enhance corporate reputation, if used appropriately.

The use of the Internet can enhance corporate reputation, if used appropriately. Web site management and brand behaviour influence the way dotcoms are perceived and strongly influence the relationship between two organisations and the likelihood that a return visit will be made. The importance of trust and commitment has been established in traditional business trading conditions. These remain important factors but through eCommerce part of the trust in a relationship is delegated to the performance and capability of the technology used. Customer satisfaction arises through commitment which needs to be fostered through the development of trust and an electronic trading relationship.

Communication costs can also be considerably reduced. Just as sales literature and demonstration packs take time to prepare, even longer to change/update and are quite expensive with a great deal of wastage, brochure ware on the Web site is fast, easily accessible and adaptable. One step further into Web site development is the collection of names and addresses, response to email questions and the provision of rich data for the sales force. If developed further, transactional Web sites enable routine orders to be processed quickly and at a lower cost. This can free up the sales force to visit established customers more often, open more new accounts and manage those accounts that are strategically important, more attentively.

There will also be some legal and information security issues that need to be addressed in order to reduce any risk to business partners. This is part of the development and maintenance of profitable relationships and marketing communications has an important role to play in the development of these relationships by reducing perceived risk and uncertainty. Marketing communications also needs to provide clarity and fast, pertinent and timely information in order that decisions can be made. Through marketing communications (and operational efficiencies and political contingencies) the development of loyalty between organisations might be observed. By targeting information and customising messages for the right people within a partner organisation, via an Extranet for example, the development of loyalty through trust and commitment might be possible. Regularised, balanced communication which is embedded within the operational interactions between organisations is much more likely to lead to higher levels of customer (intermediary) satisfaction than when absent. The need to reduce the frequency and intensity of conflict that is inevitable in interorganisational relationships is paramount. It has already been established (Chapter 15) that the propensity to share information and to provide higher rather than lower volumes of information is perceived as an indicator of high quality (and therefore satisfying) communication. The Internet is an ideal resource for enabling these events to happen and in doing so bind partner organisations closer.

Marketing communications also needs to provide clarity and fast, pertinent and timely information in order that decisions can be made.

Business-to-consumer

Using the Internet to communicate directly with consumers and encourage them to enter into financial exchanges has been an enticing goal for most businesses operating in this sector. The speed at which this sector has grown (outside of the USA) has not been as rapid or as profitable as first thought, evidenced by commentator predictions in 1999 and the failure of most dotcom brands to achieve profitability and some that have collapsed. Indeed, there are a number of far-ranging b2c issues, beyond the scope of this text, concerning fraud, morality, education, family life and the nature and purpose of the current and future retail environments (e.g. the configuration and use of the high street).

There are about 6 million UK interactive consumers according to Whitely (2000) and they are skewed towards higher disposable incomes (£25,000 plus) and the ABC categories. Books, music, travel and computer products make up the top purchase categories. Books and music represent low-involvement purchases and low perceived risk, so the distribution (and price) advantages of the WWW dominate. Travel and computer equipment represent high involvement and high perceived risk so the search (and price) facilities of the WWW dominate buyer's use and selection.

Books and music represent low-involvement purchases and low perceived risk, so the distribution (and price) advantages of the WWW dominate.

Whitely's report goes on to state that 31% of respondents (who had bought products over the WWW) claimed that they had first heard of the site through a recommendation made by a friend or relative (active seekers), 20% by surfing (passive seekers) and only 15% mentioned off-line media communications and only 6% through on-line advertisements. What this means is that word-of-mouth communications and the role and influence of opinion formers and especially opinion leaders (see Chapter 2) are critical to supporting interactive communications and exchanges.

Business to consumer – Unilever

Unilever is typical of organisations that are using on-line communications as a back-up to off-line communications. The whole communication package is integrated and in part designed to reduce large marketing communication budgets. In 1998 the company spent £234 million on advertising of which £179 million was on television (Rosier, 1999). New media is seen as a way of reducing these amounts and at the same time reach a wider audience. Another strategy has been to design Web sites from a user's perspective rather than that of the producer.

Dotcom branding

Branding in eCommerce is about developing and sustaining a valuable relationship with consumers. Breen (1999) argues that dotcom brands are stronger if:

1. There is an overall communications strategy.
2. It is not expected to establish consumer relationships through a single Web site visit. The development of a personalised pathway for continued dialogue, such as that used by Amazon.com which sends regular emails to customers about the status of their purchases and details of potentially interesting offers, is important.
3. A record is kept of the changing needs and interests of their consumers.
4. Attempt to be seen as a trustmark, not a trademark.
5. They try to integrate relationship building activities with the real world. For example, financial services broker Charles Schwab opens 70% of its accounts in branches where there is a face-to-face based relationship from which account

details are put on-line. The feeling that there is a personal element to the on-line relationship appears to add comfort and security.

Relationships, needs and continuity – Birds Eye Fish Fingers

A pan-European site for the Birds Eye fish fingers was designed to boost the brand among 9–11 year olds, the age period when fish finger products are dropped in favour of other foods. The site consists of animated characters and games which visitors are encouraged to use in order to complete an on-line mission. By registering details, children could receive emails informing them when a new mission became available to play. These additional missions are added periodically in a bid to encourage dialogue and build relationships with the brand.

The Web site provides a focus for the brand identity and it is the experience consumers have with a site which determines whether a site will be revisited. The Web site acts as a prime means of differentiating on-line brands and those that fail to develop differential advantage will probably learn that visitors are only one click away from leaving a site (Oxley and Miller, 2000). These commentators refer to a site's 'stickiness' and ability to retain visitors which in turn can increase advertising rate card costs. However, as they point out, a long visit does not necessarily mean that the experience was beneficial as the site may try to facilitate customer transactions quickly, or enable them to find the information they need without difficulty; in other words, reduced levels of stickiness may be appropriate in some circumstances. All dotcom branding activities need to extend across all key consumer contact points, in both off-line and on-line environments. Active and passive seekers using the Internet generally exhibit goal-directed behaviour and experiential motivations Goal-directed behaviour that is satisfied is more likely to make people want to return to a site. Therefore, it can be concluded (broadly) that satisfying experiential motivations makes people stay.

The Web site acts as a prime means of differentiating on-line brands.

Developing the brand – Pepperami

The launch of a spoof Web site was part of a strategy to get closer to the Pepperami customer base (Rosier, 2000). Through the use of interactive components the goal was to get site visitors more involved with the brand. First there is a fictitious site hijacking on entry to the site and second the site has photos, video, sound clips and downloads which perpetuates the cult style identity of the brand.

Sales promotion activities are used to solicit visitor details. In return for completing a questionnaire a sound activated Fanimal Pepperami toy can be claimed (www.pepperami.com).

Retailing and ecommerce

Retailers are faced with particular problems which concern the amount of property/freehold they possess and the as-yet unknown pattern of consumer shopping behaviour in the light of eCommerce channels. The Arcadia Group (owns Dorothy Perkins, Wallis, Top Shop, etc.) has made a significant attempt to make its own name synonymous with on-line shopping through the development of Zoom, an on-line shopping mall. Some people might think that retailers should dispose of their fixed assets and move into the Internet or perhaps reconfigure their store layouts. In most cases the optimum solution is to develop a multichannel solution whereby a range of media and experiences are offered to consumers. So, some prefer the Internet, some traditional shopping, some will use interactive TV and some will prefer catalogue shopping. This approach puts customers' needs first by determining their preferred marketing channels and also enables organisations to reconfigure their cost structures.

The Arcadia Group (owns Dorothy Perkins, Wallis, Top Shop, etc.) has made a significant attempt to make its own name synonymous with on-line shopping through the development of Zoom, an on-line shopping mall.

What may happen is that shopping activities become divided into categories which reflect particular channel options. So, routine, unexciting purchases may be consigned to on-line and interactive channels, and the more explorative, stimulating and perhaps socially important purchases are prioritised for shopping expeditions. Stores will need to adapt themselves to provide more value than the current product focus. Related benefits and enhanced services will be important to provide differentiation and attraction. For example, the bookstore Ottakers provides coffee bars and comfortable seating, an environment in which customers are encouraged to relax and consider their possible purchases. Larger stores and main stream brands will need to establish themselves as 'destination' stores where the attraction for consumers is bound by excitement, entertainment and a brand experience. Jardine (1999) reports that in some destination stores it is possible to test ride mountain bikes in an 'authentic outdoor environment', to attend cookery classes in supermarkets or perhaps shrink fit your own Levi jeans by taking a dip in a store bathtub.

In the USA these types of store are now relatively common and experience shows that high street shopping is not about to die but take a revised shape, form and role. Mercedes has a cafe on the Champs-Élysées in Paris but its role is to remind, differentiate and bring the brand into peoples consciousness away from the traditional frame of reference. There is no persuasion as cars cannot be bought (or sold), but the brand is reinforced.

Fulfilment

Fulfilment of customer orders is absolutely imperative if a repeat visit to a site is to be encouraged. There is still a great deal of uncertainty as to what constitutes an acceptable delivery period but as with conventional retailing the provision of shoddy, substandard, damaged or incomplete goods is unacceptable. Fulfilment expectations are also raised because the on-line experience placing the order is characteristically convenient, quick, efficient and this is then projected by the consumer onto all consequent order-

Fulfilment of customer orders is absolutely imperative if a repeat visit to a site is to be encouraged.

processing activities. Email is often used to acknowledge orders and to advise of despatch. If this should be delayed, however, consumers may perceive this as a failure of part of the fulfilment exercise.

However, order fulfilment often requires the cooperation of outsourcing suppliers such that stock is not stored on site but in a warehouse at a distant location. According to Gray (2000), this is a key decision for organisations moving from a conventional trading environment to a multichannel approach. Should warehousing and fulfilment be outsourced or kept in-house? Even if the decision is to undertake fulfilment in-house, slim stocking still requires suitable systems to enable suppliers to replenish stock quickly.

Clicks & bricks vs clicks

Competitive advantage in the book retailing sector appears to lie with retailers from the bricks & clicks sector. The advantage that Borders.com and Barnesandnoble.com have over their clicks-only competitors is that they have a tangible means by which customers can return books, a facility which Amazon and others have yet to provide. Rushe (2000) believes that Amazon needs to develop a partnership with an off-line retailer in order to provide the credibility and reassurance that customers appear to want.

Eretailers need delivery partners and there is evidence that new providers who are able to deliver at times and locations (e.g. work addresses) convenient to consumers will be able to gain a foothold in the marketplace. In other words, the rise of b2c eCommerce has brought about a restructuring of the delivery and fulfilment sector to meet the changing needs of customers.

On-line security and trust

Technology is available to provide virtually secure on-line transactions and despite the relatively small amount of on-line crime there is a strong consumer perception that on-line transactions are not safe, even though many of these same people willingly give their credit card details over the telephone to complete strangers. As an eRetailer, one of the tasks marketing communications has to undertake is the provision of a strong level of consumer reassurance or reduced levels of perceived risk associated with on-line shopping.

As an eRetailer, one of the tasks marketing communications have to undertake is the provision of a strong level of consumer reassurance or reduced levels of perceived risk associated with on-line shopping.

Thomas (2000) suggests that there are a number of things that can be done to provide such reassurance. These are:

1. Strong off-line brands immediately provide recognition and an improved level of security although care needs to be taken to convince audiences that the operator's on-line work is as effective as that of the off-line brand.

2. Ensure that the Web pages where sensitive data are stored are hosted on a secure

server. Use the most up-to-date security facilities and then tell consumers the actions you have taken to create a feel-good association and trust with the on-line brand. It is also worthwhile listing any physical, tangible addresses the company might have in order that consumers feel they are dealing with a modern yet conventional business.

3. Provide full contact details, fax, telephone, postal addresses and the names of people they can refer to. Again, this enables a level of personalisation and may soften the virtual atmosphere for those hesitant to immerse in on-line transactions.

4. Provide an opportunity for the consumer to lock into the on-line brand by registering and subscribing to the site. Many organisations offer an incentive such as a free email newsletter or introductory offer.

5. By satisfying criteria associated with transparency, security and customer service it is possible to earn accreditation or cues which signal compatibility and compliance. The Academy of Internet Commerce operates a best practice called the Academy Seal of Approval. The logo appears on the site and when clicked provides a full text of the charter itself, a powerful form of reducing functional and financial risk.

6. Post-purchase communications are just as important in the on-line as well as the off-line environment. Email acknowledgement of an order provides reassurance that the company actually exists and prompt (immediate next day) delivery or, if on extended delivery, an interim progress report (email) will provide confidence. On-line order tracking is now quite common, so that it is possible to see the exact location of an order.

Consumers contemplating on-line purchases are effectively trading off the variety and sensory experiences of high street shopping against the convenience and money saved by shopping off-line. It is therefore important to ensure that the on-line experience is perceived to be secure and rewarding in other ways. Central to this is the establishment of trust, because those interactive facilities that are trusted and deliberately managed to reduce risk will be differentiated as a superior offering compared with those that are perceived to be less trustworthy (Morrison and Firmstone, 2000).

Interactive communications strategy

While the ability to reach customers directly, avoiding channel intermediaries and reducing transaction costs is attractive, strategies must be decided upon for attracting customers to a Web site (or TV-based 'shop'). Reliance on on-line communications alone is too limiting and unlikely to be successful so a combination of off-line and on-line communications is necessary to attract sufficient traffic.

The variety of off-line communications used by organisations varies according to their budgets and their overall strategy. Many dotcoms used television and outdoor advertising to promote not only the Web site but, more importantly for them, the brand name to drive shareholder interest as these new entities sought stock market listings. As a result of this activity, outdoor advertising spend grew substantially in 1999. Sponsorship is also used to promote Web site addresses as well as a host of corporate literature such as

The variety of off-line communications used by organisations varies according to their budgets and their overall strategy.

company reports, brochures, calling cards and letterheads. On-line communications vary from banner ads and pop-ups to viral marketing and public relations. However, research indicates that the most important factor that drives first-time visits is word of mouth and recommendations by significant others. In other words, people are more disposed to having their Web site behaviour directed by those they trust rather than risk time and effort seeking information based on communications that lack inherent credibility.

The balance between off-line and on-line generated traffic will also vary depending upon the nature of the brand itself. If a brand is being developed by a bricks and mortar company as an additional distribution and communications channel, but there is to be no visible tie to the parent company (Egg and Prudential), then the off-line branding development will need to be considerable. However, if the brand is to be tied in closely to the current channels (e.g. Argos), the initial branding can be constrained to converting current customers to the new product and to stimulating word-of-mouth recommendations, a much lower communications investment.

However, whatever the reason or branding strategy used to generate traffic, thought should be given to capitalising on the facilities to personalise the experience through the use of underlying data capture, storage, retrieval and processing abilities of integrated technologies. The ability to start with some knowledge of a customer's preferences, previous purchases, his or her already secure financial details and delivery address, for example, should be a major source of advantage. In addition, the interactive communications strategy needs to be thought through all points of customer interaction. Many companies have addressed the need to capture customers and even extract critical personal information but have failed to think through the total process and consider how the behaviour of the company communicates attitudes and degree of care. The use of email to confirm receipt and despatch details of a customer's order goes a long way to developing trust and positive customer attitudes, but unless the whole fulfilment exercise is compatible (and fulfilling), the whole of the investment in the front end of the exercise will be wasted.

The use of email to confirm receipt and despatch details of a customer's order goes a long way to developing trust and positive customer attitudes.

Summary

The growth of the Internet has been astonishing in recent years and represents the major form of interactive marketing communications. Interactivity through machines with people is now complemented with interactivity with machines. The Internet has two main elements, distribution and communication, and when these are applied together ecommerce opportunities, together with Internet marketing, provide opportunities to transform the way business is conducted, shape the relationships between organisations and provide consumers with increased search convenience, lower prices and access to a wealth of information.

The Internet is changing the way marketing communications are used by organisations and there may be a reduced reliance on above-the-line spend. It may be that the initial surge of investment and media interest in dotcom organisations and associated activities will be seen as merely symptomatic of the scramble to establish norms, commercial trading rules and leadership positions in a new and unknown environment. The establishment of the Internet has led many organisations to reconsider the pattern and format of their marketing communications strategies and some have not only taken the opportunity to reconfigure just the way they communicate with their target audiences but also enabled their customers to reconfigure the way they interact with their preferred suppliers.

Perhaps above all else, this technology has spurred the development of integrated marketing communications as organisations are forced to reconsider their communication strategies (Chapter 19).

Review questions

1. Prepare brief notes explaining how interactive and traditional communications differ.
2. Draw the Hoffman and Novak model of communications in a hypermedia computer-mediated environment.
3. List a range of eCommerce business models.
4. What are the primary differences between b2b and b2c eCommerce models?
5. Explain each of the four stages (phases) of Internet development in an organisation.
6. Discuss the use of Extranets and Intranets as a means of developing relationships with significant stakeholders.
7. Identify the factors that need to be considered by an established high street fashion retailer when considering whether to set up an ecommerce facility.
8. Identify and explain means by which security and trust might be established in order to encourage consumers to trade using the Internet.
9. Write brief notes explaining how the use of the Internet might assist an organisation's branding strategy.
10. Explain the role of off-line communications as part of an Internet communications strategy.

MINI CASE

This mini case as written by Mike Molesworth, Senior Lecturer in Marketing at Bournemouth University.

Greydia

Greydia.com is a Guernsey-based Web retailer specialising in imported DVDs and CDs (although DVDs account for over 85% of sales value). North American DVDs make up its core range and these are often released several months before the European version. For example, *Pitch Black* was released on DVD in the US two weeks before its cinema release in the UK, over a year before the planned European DVD release date.

Imported DVD films need specially converted DVD players to work. For consumers this means getting UK DVD players converted by a third party (not the retailer or the manufacturer). Information on how to do this can often be found on the Web, for example, in newsgroups. Imported CDs will work on any CD player. US DVDs and CDs are frequently cheaper than their UK equivalents but this is not true when compared with European retail prices. Perhaps as a result, 89% of Greydia's sales are from the UK.

Greydia buys its products from a range of retailers and wholesalers in the USA and Canada rather than from film and music distributors who are naturally unwilling to aid the grey import market. This often involves expensive trips to the USA to negotiate on bulk purchase of product. Although Greydia has established relationships with a number of suppliers, the nature of the grey import business means that supply can occasionally be difficult.

Greydia sells these products to consumers in Europe via mail order. UK-based retailers would not be able to sell owing to legal (censorship) restrictions. This gives Greydia significant competitive advantages – early release dates for many DVD films and CDs and lower prices. Low taxes in the Channel Islands also increase potential profit margins and offset increased postage charges to customers (Greydia sells products postage free).

Greydia has been trading for just over three years (February 2001) and has been profitable for the last two years – a very different situation from most eTailers. The management puts this down to the competitive advantages identified above and to a realistic business model that focused on profitable trading from the outset. Turnover now stands at £1,150,000 (end 2000) with a gross profit of £180,000.

To date Greydia has spent only a modest budget on promotions consisting of a £10,000 on-line banner campaign at the start of trading which lasted for the first year. This campaign was based on movie-related sites known to the staff at Greydia (actually most banners were purchased via a network of friends and friends of friends). It purchased the campaign direct. After the first year Greydia spent very little on promotion, amounting to the occasional banner ad and some small classified ads in movie-related magazines such as *Empire*. Greydia's strategy, if it could be called that, has been to rely on the loyalty of existing customers and word of mouth to gain new customers.

A significant amount of time and money has been spent on its own Web site and the 'back end' support systems. The site records visitor IP

address information automatically and requires user registration before ordering, capturing valuable consumer data. Invoicing has been fully automated and the site allows on-line order tracking. Significant investment has been made in site and transaction security. The site also has a search engine facility, an order history facility and will recommend films based on previous purchases. There is also an email-based general enquiry form. For the coming year new developments are planned including a chat room, a customer review section and content in French and German (currently the site is entirely in English). However, taking stock of the last year, the management of Greydia notices that sales are stagnant and may even be going into decline (see Table 18.4).

Table 18.4   Greydia sales trends

Quarter	Sales (£)	Average order value (£)
2000/4	325,000	29.48
2000/3	294,000	25.65
2000/2	245,000	22.14
2000/1	286,000	24.31
1999/4	335,000	25.51
1999/3	295,000	20.34
1999/2	245,000	20.15
1999/1	236,000	21.21

This may be due to an increase in competition over that time. The sales trend is particularly worrying given the increases in on-line shoppers and the increases in DVD ownership over the same period. This has made the management question future activities.

Stephen Toulmin, the director of the company, feels that the business is still viable, but is worried that the business is not attracting enough new customers. His background (and the backgrounds of the other three staff at Greydia) is in IT and he therefore feels that the company lacks the marketing communications skills required to develop an effective communications strategy.

Stephen has asked you, his old university friend, to offer advice.

Mini-case questions

1. From the evidence presented and from what you know of Internet trends, explain what you think may be happening to Greydia's business? You may consider the value of *diffusion* theory in your analysis.
2. In the light of growing competition, assess the degree to which Greydia can maintain its competitive advantages.
3. Assess the stage of Web evolution the company is at currently. What would it need to do to further integrate the Web within the business?
4. Critically evaluate the nature of the interactive functions that are currently on the site and that are proposed for the coming year. Assess the likely impact of these and other functions on consumer behaviour. Which functions do you think most need to be included and why?
5. Discuss the communication issues raised by the case. What does Greydia need to communicate and to whom?
6. Evaluate the on-line and off-line communication tools available to Greydia. What sort of communications campaign, if any, would you recommend? Identify objectives for your campaign and try to give specific details of tactical elements.

Acknowledgement

The author would like to acknowledge the thoughtful and critical contribution provided by Mike Molesworth, Bournemouth University, in the development of this chapter.

References

Berthon, P., Pitt, L.F. and Watson, R.T. (1996) Re-surfing W3: research perspectives on marketing communications and buyer behaviour on the Worldwide Web. *International Journal of Advertising*, **15**, pp. 287–301.

Bickerton, P., Bickerton, M. and Simpson-Holley, K. (1998) *Cyberstrategy*. Oxford: Butterworth-Hienemann.

Breen, B. (1999) Builder stronger internet identities. *Marketing*, 16 September, pp. 25–6.

van Doren, D.C., Fechner, D.L. and Green-Adelsberger, K. (2000) Promotional strategies on the World Wide Web. *Journal of Marketing Communications*, **6**, pp. 21–35.

Gray, R. (2000) E-tail must deliver on web promises. *Marketing*, 2 March, p. 37.

Hoffman, D.L. and Novak, P.T. (1996) Marketing in hypermedia computer-mediated environments: conceptual foundations. *Journal of Marketing*, **60** (July), pp. 50–68.

Jardine, A. (1999) Traditional retailers face their high noon. *Marketing*, 16 September, pp. 22–23.

Kangis, P. and Rankin, K. (1996) Interactive services: how to identify and target the new markets. *Journal of Marketing Practice: Applied Marketing Science*, **2**(3), pp. 44–67.

Lancioni, R.A., Smith, M.F. and Oliva, T. A. (2000) The role of the Internet in supply chain management. *Industrial Marketing Management*, **29**, pp. 45–56.

Lord, R. (1999) The Web audience. *Campaign Report*, 28 May, p. 10.

McLuhan, R. (2000) Search for a top ranking. *Marketing*, 19 October, p. 47.

Morrison, D.E. and Firmstone, J. (2000) The social function of trust and implications of e-commerce. *International Journal of Advertising*, **19**, pp. 599–623.

Murphy, D. (2000) IT decision makers put faith in the net. *Marketing*, 6 April, p. 31.

Oliver, R. (2000) Will broadband kill the video store? *Revolution*, 8 March, pp. 36–9.

Oxley, M. and Miller, J. (2000) Capturing the consumer: ensuring website stickiness. *Admap* (July/August), pp. 21–4.

Rogers, E.M. (1983) *Diffusions of Innovations*, 3rd edn. New York: Free Press.

Rosier, B (1999) The future of FMCG.com. *Marketing*, 21 October, pp. 30–2.

Rosier, B. (2000) Pepperami's Fanimal to star in 'spoof' web site. *Marketing*, 21 September, p. 12.

Rushe, D. (2000) Amazon loses to offline rivals. *Sunday Times*, 10 December, p. 4.

Steuer, J. (1992) Defining virtual reality: dimensions determining telepresence. *Journal of Communication*, **42**(4), pp. 73–93.

Thomas, R. (2000) How to create trust in the net. *Marketing*, 2 March, p. 35.

Whitely, J. (2000) Understanding the online buyer. *Admap* (July/August), pp. 14–16.

Woolgar, T. (1999) Web audit. *Campaign*, 30 October, pp. 3–4.

Yuan, Y., Caulkins, J.P. and Roehrig, S. (1998) The relationship between advertising and content provision on the Internet. *European Journal of Marketing*, **32**(7/8), pp. 677–87.

Integrated marketing communications

Integrated marketing communications are more likely to occur when organisations attempt to enter into a coordinated dialogue with their various internal and external audiences. The communication tools used in this dialogue and the messages conveyed should be internally consistent with the organisation's objectives and strategies. The target audiences should perceive the communications and associated cues as coordinated, likeable and timely.

AIMS AND OBJECTIVES

The aims of this chapter are to explore the concept of integrated marketing communications with a view to appreciating the complexities associated with this relatively new strategic approach.

The objectives of this chapter are:

1. To introduce integrated marketing communications (IMC) and establish a need for this new concept.

2. To understand the possible meanings that lie behind IMC.

3. To illustrate the breadth and depth of IMC as applied to organisations.

4. To explain the manner in which the marketing mix communicates.

5. To consider how the structures and frameworks of advertising agencies might need to change so that they are better able to work with IMC.

6. To appraise the reasons for the development of IMC and the main drivers propelling its growth.

7. To set out some of the main reasons why IMC is resisted and how such resistance might be best overcome.

Introduction

Promotional tools have often been regarded by practitioners and academics as separate, individualistic techniques that offer particular benefits for buyers. Through the use of each promotional tool, clients were able to achieve impacts or effects *on* buyers and only each particular tool was able to achieve these impacts. Consequently, clients were required to deal with a variety of functionally different and independent organisations in order to communicate with their various audiences.

As a result, clients and suppliers of the promotional tools saw specialisation as the principal means to achieve communication effectiveness. This resulted in a proliferation of advertising agencies and the development of sales promotion houses. Public relations specialists stood off from any direct association with marketing. Personal selling had already evolved as a discrete function within organisations. This specialist approach was further emphasised by the development of trade associations and professional management groups (for example, the Institute of Practitioners in Advertising (UK) and the Institute of Sales Promotion (UK)) which seek to endorse, advance, protect and legitimise the actions of their professions and members. One of the results of this individualistic perspective and functional development of the marketing communications industry has been the inevitable opposition to the desire for change driven by clients. Improvements and new approaches to create and sustain a dialogue with buyers are now central requirements. The structural inadequacies of the marketing communication industry have restrained the means by which client organisations can achieve their marketing and marketing communication objectives.

This specialist approach was further emphasised by the development of trade associations and professional management groups.

The structural inadequacies of the marketing communication industry have restrained the means by which client organisations can achieve their marketing and marketing communication objectives.

It is interesting that the rapid development of direct marketing initiatives since the second half of the 1980s and the impact the Internet has made have coincided with a move towards what has become regarded as integrated marketing communications (IMC). A further significant development has been the shift in marketing philosophies, from transaction to relationship marketing, as introduced in Chapter 1. These will be considered later.

IMC has emerged partially as a reaction to the structural inadequacies of the industry and the realisation by clients that their communication needs can (and should) be achieved more efficiently and effectively than previously. In other words, just as power has moved from brand manufacturers to multiple retailers and in many cases to consumers, so some power is shifting from agencies to clients.

While the origins of IMC might be found in the prevailing structural conditions and the needs of particular industry participants, an understanding of what IMC is or should be is far from being resolved and is evolving as the industry matures.

What does integration mean?

The trend away from traditional communication strategies, based largely on mass communication delivering generalised messages, to one based more on personalised, customer-orientated and technology-driven approaches, is referred to as integrated marketing communications. Duncan and Everett (1993) recall that this new (media) approach has been referred to variously as *orchestration, whole egg* and *seamless communication*. More recent notions involve the explicit incorporation of corporate communications, reflected in titles such as integrated marketing and integrated communications. See Cornelissen (2000).

However defined, the development is marked by an increased realisation that multidisciplinary approaches are required to achieve marketing and business objectives. To that end the synergistic benefits are perceived as not only achievable but also desirable.

One of the more popular and intrinsically satisfying views of IMC is that the messages conveyed by each of the promotional tools should be harmonised in order that audiences perceive a consistent set of messages. An interpretation of this perspective, at one level, is that the key visual triggers (design, colours, form and tag line) used in advertising should be replicated across the range of promotional tools used, including POP and the sales force. At another level it is the integration of some of the promotional tools. One such combination is the closer alliance of advertising with public relations. Increasing audience fragmentation means that it is more difficult to locate target audiences and communicate with them in a meaningful way. By utilising the power of public relations to get advertisements talked about (e.g. the Wonderbra £300,000 media campaign generating £5 million media equivalents through public relations) so a form of communications consistency, or integration to some, becomes possible. A further interpretation, at a deeper level, is that the theme and set of core messages used in any campaign should be determined initially and then deployed across the promotional mix (sometimes referred to as synergy). One of the differences is the recognition that mass media advertising is not always the only way to launch consumer or business-to-business promotional activities, and that a consideration of the most appropriate mix of communication forms might be a better starting point when formulating campaigns. An alternative perspective of IMC is provided by Duncan and Moriarty (1998) who state quite challengingly that stakeholders (including customers) automatically integrate brand messages. This suggests that as long as the gaps between messages are acceptable then management's task is to manage the process and seek to narrow these gaps that stakeholders may perceive.

> *One of the more popular and intrinsically satisfying views of IMC is that the messages conveyed by each of the promotional tools should be harmonised in order that audiences perceive a consistent set of messages.*

What runs through both these approaches is the belief that above-the-line and below-the-line communications need to be moulded into one cohesive bundle, from which tools can be selected and deployed as conditions require.

> *Above-the-line and below-the-line communications need to be moulded into one cohesive bundle.*

It was determined earlier that marketing communications success is not determined solely by the activities or use of the promotional tools. The elements of the marketing mix, however configured, also communicate (Smith, 1996). The price and associated values, the product, in terms of the quality, design and tangible attributes, the manner and efficiency of the service delivery people and where and how it is made available, for example the location, retailer/dealer reputation and overall service quality (Bucklin, 1966) are brand identity cues with which recipients develop images and through time may shape brand reputations.

Communication through the marketing mix

The target marketing process requires the development and implementation of a distinct marketing mix to meet the requirements of the selected target markets. The elements are mixed together in such a way that they should meet the needs of the target segment. Each element of the marketing mix has a variable capacity to communicate (Figure 19.1).

Product

A product is more than its physical components. It represents the potential to satisfy a range of conscious and unconscious customer needs. Products consist of a combi-

A product is more than its physical components. It represents the potential to satisfy a range of conscious and unconscious customer needs.

nation of physical and service elements, and the balance between the two will vary. At one extreme, for example, a Waterman pen provides tangible attributes of grip and writing facilities. However, it also possesses a further dimension which is the prestige and status that such a pen bestows (or is thought to bestow) upon the owner. In contrast, the owner of a common disposable pen would normally only perceive the tangible aspects of the pen's writing facilities.

Offerings therefore consist of tangible and intangible attributes. The marketing communication task is to ensure that the perception of the offering and/or the organisation is the desired one. One of the most important aspects of perception, in this context, is that of perceptual cues. These are the means by which individual judgements are made about products and organisations.

Intrinsic cues are related to the physical characteristics of the offering. These may be size, colour, flavour or shape. Very often these cues are used to make judgements about quality. When Guinness attempted to redesign its label, tests revealed that

Summary

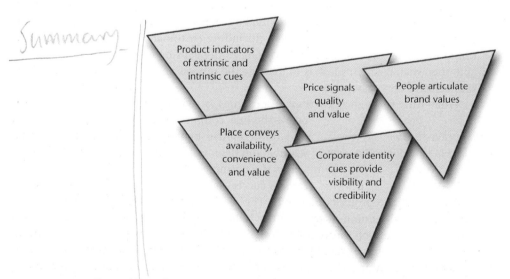

Figure 19.1   The marketing mix communicates.

Guinness drinkers were unable to distinguish the bottles with the new round label from all the other bottles on the shelves. The cue for ordering a Guinness had been removed, and so was the new design.

Extrinsic cues have normally been concerned with price, store image and the manufacturer. Retail outlets have their own images, and these influence the perception of the offerings they carry. One way of providing consistency is the use of own-label products.

In a similar way, consumers make judgements about offerings based on the perception of the retail outlets where it is available. Organisations (including manufacturers) who are perceived positively will generate higher levels of stakeholder confidence (especially consumer confidence). This can lead to an earlier acceptance of new products in comparison with those organisations whose image is

Marketing communications need to establish favourable images to build confidence and to facilitate the spread of positive word-of-mouth communications.

neutral or worse. Marketing communications need to establish favourable images to build confidence and to facilitate the spread of positive word-of-mouth communications from opinion formers and leaders. Furthermore, research shows that offerings that are heavily promoted are perceived as higher in quality than those that are not advertised or promoted and consumers prefer to buy advertised brands, particularly if they have been recommended through personal communications as well.

Price

Marketing communications have the responsibility of informing the target audience about the price of an offering. This can be undertaken via advertising, personal selling and sales promotion activity, or through in-store merchandising and packaging-based communications. Buyers may concern themselves with price, but this is used in combination with other cues, such as the shape, size, smell and colour, to determine a perception of the value that the offering represents. Price is an important contributor to perceived value. Is an expensive offering overpriced, or does it represent exceptional value and bestow high status upon those who are seen to have purchased the product? The answer to this type of question depends upon a number of factors, including the level of disposable income available to the buyer, the perception by the buyer of competitive offerings and the changing expectations of buyers.

Price can prevent purchase because the potential buyer may be unable or unwilling to enter into the exchange process. The stated price may also be seen as too low, and so represent low value and hence low quality. Decision-making by buyers in unfamiliar markets is often based upon price. For

Decision-making by buyers in unfamiliar markets is often based upon price.

example, the first purchase of a camera or a power tool can be anchored on the relative prices of each of the offerings being considered. Price can, therefore, be a major cue in the purchase decision process.

The pricing strategy needs to be reflected in the communications undertaken by the organisation. The prominence that price receives depends on a large number of factors (target audience, level of involvement and attitude to risk, complexity and technicality of the offering and the importance of price in the decision-making process), but it should be sensitive to the expectations of the target audience and the positioning strategy.

People

As the service element becomes increasingly important as a means of differentiating organisations and their product offerings, so the value employees bring to the customer/company interface becomes a vital aspect of the marketing mix.

The significance of internal marketing communications has been explored earlier in Chapter 7 and so will not be repeated here. However, the impact that people make or bring to the marketing communication process is substantial in terms of organisational identity issues and the projection of corporate identity cues.

Place

The use of intermediaries to make available products and services to members of the target market has been discussed earlier (Chapters 10 and 15). These organisations, which cooperate to achieve their business goals, represent a significant target audience for all involved in the marketing channel system.

Communication activities need to be coordinated and synchronised in such a way that the best possible impact is derived from an organisation's attempt to communicate effectively. When companies launch new products, for example, and make promises to customers through pull-based communications, it is essential that the product is made available through the supply chain. If customers are unable to buy or see the product, then the credibility of the product is damaged and competitors are given a window of opportunity to take the initiative in the newly identified and exposed market. For marketing communications it is very important to have adequate levels of stock in the distribution system at the launch of a new offering, and to achieve that requires a coherent set of formal and informal internal and external communication networks.

Communication activities need to be coordinated and synchronised in such a way that the best possible impact is derived from an organisation's attempt to communicate effectively.

As discussed earlier, the customer's perception of the store, point of purchase or the other organisations in the performance channel will affect the attitudes and purchase behaviour of customers. It is important at this point to appreciate what the marketing communications planner needs to do:

1. Liaise with channel members to ensure that stock is available.

2. Be aware of the needs of channel members who may require the support of your organisation's marketing communications. This will be stated in the marketing plan.

3. Provide consistency for all communications used in the channel.

4. Understand and act in accordance with the communications strategy.

5. Ensure that all members of the organisation understand, support and are empowered to implement the concept. The use of internal marketing communications is important to ensure that the blend of internal and external communications is appropriate.

6. Coordinate actions with any main agencies involved with the communications programme.

This brief look at the marketing strategy serves to remind us that the communications plan can only be successfully developed if the key factors within the marketing plan are clearly identified and developed. It can therefore be established that IMC cannot be achieved just by saying the same message through a variety of promotional tools; the marketing mix is also a strong communicator.

The communications plan can only be successfully developed if the key factors within the marketing plan are clearly identified and developed.

If marketing communications are to be used effectively, then there is a need to communicate aspects of the direction in which the organisation intends moving and how it intends to achieve this. In other words, the business philosophy and its aims and objectives, often expressed formally through mission and vision statements (Chapter 5), need to be communicated to particular audiences in a way that is synchronised and coordinated with the organisation's other communication endeavours.

Table 19.1 sets out the main elements that need to be considered and managed when developing IMC. The breadth and depth of these elements suggests that the organisation as a whole needs to accommodate many changes and that IMC is not just a matter of transmitting uniform marketing communications messages.

The internal/external dimension of integration

Following on from Chapter 14 it might be concluded that branding provides a form of integration. This means that the internal organisation issues need to be sufficiently coordinated so that the brand is perceived externally as consistent and uniform. However, this proposition is based on the view that a brand is prepared and delivered for a single target audience and we are only too aware of audience fragmentation and media splintering. This suggests that audience sizes are shrinking which means that in many situations a single audience is no longer economically viable. Brands therefore, need to appeal to a number of different audiences (White, 2000) and to do this it is necessary to develop brands that appeal to diverse consumer groups. White refers to these new brands as 'chameleon' brands which are characterised by their ability to adapt to different situations (audiences and media) yet retain a core proposition that provides a form of continuity and recognition. For example, a dress made by Stella McCartney can be seen by the owner as beautiful and comfortable, by a guest at a party as ostentatiously outrageous and by a friend as a product of clever design and marketing. All three might have developed their attitudes through different sources (e.g. different print media, fashion shows,

Brands therefore, need to appeal to a number of different audiences.

Table 19.1   Elements involved in integrating marketing communications

Promotional mix	Above-the-line and below-the-line
Marketing mix	Price, product, people, place and promotion
Business strategy	Philosophy, objectives and mission, content
Outsourced providers	Agencies, production and material suppliers, fulfilment houses
The organisation	Employees and management, whether located at HO, SBUs, departments or overseas divisions

boutiques, word of mouth) but all agree that the brand has a common set of values and associations that are important to each of them.

The presentation of chameleon brands requires high levels of integration, a need to develop a series of innovative messages based around a core proposition. The use of a single ad execution needs to be replaced by multiple executions delivered through a variety of media. This means that the audience are more likely to be surprised or reminded of the brand (and its essence) through a series of refreshingly interesting ads, so raising the probability that the likeability factor (see Chapter 20) will be strengthened, along with the brand and all relevant associations.

IMC is regarded by some as a means of using the tools of the promotional mix in a more efficient and synergistic manner. To some extent this is true but IMC requires a deeper understanding of how and where messages are created. At a strategic level, IMC has at its roots the overall business strategy of the organisation. Using Porter's (1980) generic strategies, if a low-cost strategy (e.g. Asda) is being pursued, it makes sense to complement the strategy by using messages that either stress any price advantage that customers might benefit from or at least do not suggest extravagance or luxury. If using a differentiation focus strategy (e.g. Waitrose), price should not figure in any of the messages and greater emphasis should be placed on particular attributes that enable clear positioning.

The next major issue concerns the recognition that IMC cannot be sustained unless it is supported by all customer facing employees. It is better still that all employees adopt a customer focus and 'live' the brand. While this

The next major issue concerns the recognition that IMC cannot be sustained unless it is supported by all customer facing employees.

can be partially achieved through the use of training courses and in-house documentation (including electronic forms), this usually requires a change of culture and that means a longer-term period of readjustment and the adoption of new techniques, procedures and ways of thinking and behaving.

Once the internal reorientation has begun (not completed), it is possible to take the message to external audiences. As long as they can see that employees are starting to act in different ways and do care about them as customers and do know what they are talking about in support of the products and services offered, then it is likely that customers (and other stakeholders) will be supportive. IMC is about blending internal and external messages so that there is clarity, consistency and reinforcement of the organisation's (or brand's) core proposition. There is no right way (or formula) to establish IMC but there is a need to recognise that it is a developmental exercise and that it has strategic origins as well as strategic outputs.

Moving to a customer focus – Variable Life

When Variable Life became part of a larger financial services organisation in the mid-1990s it embarked on a programme of change and development. Indeed, the purchase was intended to provide greater capitalisation to enable Variable Life to grow.

The overall aim for Variable Life was to become a customer- rather than task-focused organisation. To help achieve this, a series of projects was developed but a major tenet was that change had to be achieved internally before the message was taken externally, otherwise there was a real danger that the claim would lack credibility. Other contextual elements were that the company held rather traditional values, was structured hierarchically and the resultant culture and values stifled development. Communication was one way and staff began to boycott the internal communications because they felt they were being overloaded. One of the problems was that too much information, in a variety of inappropriate media, was presented rather like a wave. This meant that each individual had to wade in and find information that was pertinent to them. This was time consuming, exasperating and inefficient.

A review of the role of internal communications led to the belief that it should be perceived as a means of enabling the different projects to achieve their goals, as a way of providing the right information at the right time and as a way of demonstrating to staff that change was happening. In other words, internal communications had both a strategic and a tactical role to fulfil.

Instead of a linear process, a circular communication process was introduced which incorporated more face-to-face communications, explanations about why things were being done/changed and opportunities to discuss proposals. A new redesigned and company content orientated magazine was introduced, the email system was overhauled such that only relevant information was sent through, managers were retrained and the internal television facilities were revised to be more pacey and emotive. All of the communication methods were interlinked so that one reinforced another and each either provided a means of either providing information for change to be implementated or demonstrated how change was happening either through examples of best practice or behaviours that others could adopt. All these are known to be crucial aspects of successful internal communication programmes.

The external communication programme was then developed in order to deliver the new customer-focused values to the market place. The first campaign featured young people who represented their target market and all were depicted as having busy and diverse lifestyles and who represented the brand 'Variable Life'. The message that Variable Life is there to look after your financial matters regardless of your lifestyle was a strong feature of the campaign.

What this brief case history demonstrates is that integrated marketing communications needs to involve the whole organisation, that it blends internal and external communications, in that order and it is strongly identified with the strategy and direction of the organisation.

From this exploration it is now possible to offer a definition of IMC, bearing in mind that there is no single form of IMC that can be identified:

> *IMC is the management process associated with the strategic development, delivery and dialogue of consistent, coordinated messages, that stakeholders perceive as reinforcing core brand propositions.*

This definition serves to encapsulate the two-way nature of IMC, that external and internal communications need to blend together and reinforce simple messages and that IMC can be interpreted either at a promotional mix level or at the positioning or business strategy level, depending upon the stage of IMC development an organisation has reached.

Reasons for the development of IMC

The explosion of interest in IMC has resulted from a variety of drivers. Generally they can be grouped into three main categories: those drivers (or opportunities) that are market based, those that arise from changing communications, and those that are driven from opportunities arising from within the organisation itself. These are set out in Table 19.2.

The opportunities offered to organisations that contemplate moving to IMC are considerable and it is somewhat surprising that so few organisations have been either willing or able to embrace the approach. One of the main organisational drivers for IMC is the need to become increasingly efficient. Driving down the cost base enables managers to improve profits and levels of productivity. By seeking synergistic advantages

One of the main organisational drivers for IMC is the need to become increasingly efficient.

through its communications and associated activities and by expecting managers to be able to account for the way in which they consume marketing communication resources, so integrated marketing communications becomes increasingly attractive. At the same time, organisation structures are changing more frequently and the need to integrate across functional areas reflects the efficiency drive.

From a market perspective, the predominant driver is the reorientation from transaction-based marketing to relationship marketing. The extension of the brand personality concept into brand relationships (Hutton, 1996) requires a customer

---

Table 19.2 Drivers for IMC

Organisational drivers for IMC
- Increasing profits through improved efficiency
- Increasing need for greater levels of accountability
- Rapid move towards cross-border marketing and the need for changing structures and communications
- Coordinated brand development and competitive advantage
- Opportunities to utilise management time more productively
- Provide direction and purpose for employees

Market-based drivers for IMC
- Greater levels of audience communications literacy
- Media cost inflation
- Media and audience fragmentation
- Stakeholders' need for increasing amounts and diversity of information
- Greater amounts of message clutter
- Competitor activity and low levels of brand differentiation
- Move towards relationship marketing from transaction-based marketing
- Development of networks, collaboration and alliances

Communication-based drivers for IMC
- Technological advances (Internet, databases, segmentation techniques)
- Increased message effectiveness through consistency and reinforcement of core messages
- More effective triggers for brand and message recall
- More consistent and less confusing brand images
- Need to build brand reputations and to provide clear identity cues

---

consideration in terms of asking not only 'What do our customers want?' but also 'What are their values, do they trust us and are we loyal to them?' By adopting a pos-

By adopting a position designed to enhance trust and commitment, an organisation's external communications need to be consistent and coordinated.

ition designed to enhance trust and commitment (Morgan and Hunt, 1994) an organisation's external communications need to be consistent and coordinated, if only to avoid information overload and misunderstanding.

From a communication perspective, the key driver is to provide a series of triggers by which buyers can understand the values a brand stands for and a means by which they can use certain messages to influence their activities. By differentiating the marketing communications, often by providing clarity and simplicity, advantages can be attained. The adage 'What does advertising do to people?' is no longer viable (Lannon, 1996). The question to be asked, she says, is 'What do people do *with* advertising?' (marketing communications).

Integration – Häagen-Dazs

Häagen-Dazs demonstrated the effective use of IMC when it entered the UK market. Ice-cream was traditionally a seasonal children's food, and the market had experienced little growth or innovation. The business strategy adopted was to create a new market segment, one that has become referred to as the super-premium segment.

The positioning intention was to present Häagen-Dazs as a luxury, fashion-orientated food for adults. To achieve the business goals, the entire marketing mix was coordinated: the product reflected high quality, the high price induced perceived quality and the distribution in the launch was through up-market restaurants in prestige locations and five-star hotels where Häagen-Dazs was the only branded ice-cream on the menu.

The promotional campaign used celebrities from many walks of life as opinion leaders to create a word-of-mouth ripple effect. The quality of the media used and messages themselves reflected the same quality theme. The brand has since become firmly established and, although the arrival of Ben & Jerry's and other up-market brands has increased competition and rivalry, the brand remains distinctive and continues to use an integrated approach to its communications.

An integrated approach should attempt to provide a uniform or consistent set of messages. These should be relatively easy to interpret and to assign meanings. This enables target audiences to think about and perceive brands within a consistent context and so encourage behaviour as expected by the source. Those organisations that try to practise IMC understand that buyers refer to and receive messages about brands and companies from a wide range of information sources. Harnessing this knowledge is a fundamental step towards enhancing marketing communications.

To finalise this section, it seems useful to itemise the advantages and disadvantages associated with IMC. These are set out in Table 19.3. General opinion suggests that the advantages far outweigh the disadvantages and that increasing numbers of organisations are seeking to improve their IMC resource. As stated earlier, technology,

Table 19.3 Advantages and disadvantages of IMC

Advantages of IMC
- Provides opportunities to cut communication costs and/or reassign budgets
- Has the potential to produce synergistic and more effective communications
- Can deliver competitive advantage through clearer positioning
- Encourages coordinated brand development with internal and external participants
- Provides for increased employee participation and motivation
- Has the potential to cause management to review its communication strategy
- Requires a change in culture and fosters a customer focus
- Provides a benchmark for the development of communication activities
- Can lead to a cut in the number agencies supporting a brand

Disadvantages of IMC
- Encourages centralisation and formal/bureaucratic procedures
- Can require increased management time seeking agreement from all involved parties
- Suggests uniformity and single message
- Tendency to standardisation might negate or dilute creative opportunities
- Global brands restricted in terms of local adaptation
- Normally requires cultural change from employees and encourages resistance
- Has the potential to severely damage a brand's reputation if incorrectly managed
- Can lead to mediocrity as no single agency network has access to all sources of communication expertise

especially in the form of the Internet, has provided great impetus for organisations to review their communications and to implement moves to install a more integrated communication strategy.

Managing the implementation of IMC

The development and establishment of IMC by organisations has not been as widespread as the amount of discussion around the subject has been. Recent technological advances and the benefits of the Internet and related technologies have meant that organisations have had a reason to reconsider their marketing communications and have re-evaluated their approach. Whatever route taken, the development of IMC requires change, a change in thinking, actions and expectations. The changes required to achieve IMC are large and the barriers are strong. What can be observed are formative approaches to IMC and that organisations have experimented and tried out various ideas within their resource and cultural contexts.

The development and establishment of IMC by organisations has not been as widespread as the amount of discussion around the subject has been.

As with many aspects of change, there is nearly always resistance to the incorporation of IMC, and, if sanctioned, only partial integration has been achieved. This is not to say that integration is not possible or has not been achieved, but the path to IMC is far from easy and the outcomes are difficult to gauge with great confidence. However, it is the expectation (what level of IMC) that really matters, as it signals the degree of change that is required.

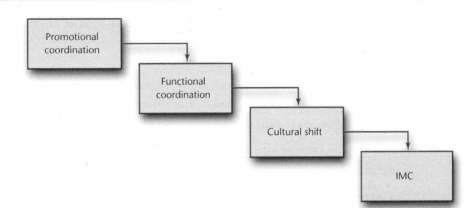

Figure 19.2   An incremental approach to the establishment of IMC.

It seems logical that moves towards the establishment of IMC must be undertaken in steps: an incremental approach (Figure 19.2). What has been achieved so far can be recognised as forms of coordination. Different organisations have coordinated various aspects of their communications activities. The majority have focused upon their promotional activities and have tried to bring together their communications to provide consistency and thematic harmonisation.

Therefore, it seems that the starting point in the move towards IMC is at the level of the promotional mix. From *promotional coordination*, progress through to *functional coordination* seems likely, where different parts of the organisation are introduced to the notion of internal marketing relationships and where internal marketing communications plays an important part of the process.

The next stage is characterised by the organisation moving towards a strong(er) customer orientation. This requires a *cultural shift* of values and beliefs, whereby organisational and brand identity issues become paramount. This can only be implemented at this stage, as the internal systems, procedures and employee mind set need to be in place if the strategy is to be credible to customers and other stakeholders.

The next stage is characterised by the organisation moving towards a strong(er) customer orientation.

In order for these incremental stages to be undertaken and completed satisfactorily, managers must be clear and agreed about what it is they wish to achieve and communicate their intent to all that it involves, both inside and outside the organisation.

One of the key issues encouraging the establishment of IMC has been the willingness of some public relations practitioners to move closer to the marketing department. As Miller and Rose (1994) comment, the previously held opposition to integration by public relations practitioners has begun to dissolve as the more enlightened agencies see it as 'a reality and a necessity'.

Developing IMC – identifying resistance to integration

Resistance to change is partly a reflection of the experiences and needs of individuals for stability and the understanding of their environments. However, it is also a reflection, again, of the structural conditions in organisations and industry, which have helped determine the expectations of managers and employees.

Eagle and Kitchen (2000) set out four principal areas or themes concerned with barriers to IMC programmes:

Power, coordination and control issues

Client skills, centralisation/organisation and cultural issues

Agency skills/talent and overall time/resource issues

Flexibility/modification issues

While these provide a useful general overview, the following represent some of the more common, more focused reasons for the resistance to the incorporation of IMC.

Financial structures and frameworks

Resistance through finance-led corporate goals, which have dominated industry performance and expectations, has been particularly significant. The parameters set around it and the extent to which marketing communications are often perceived as a cost rather than an investment have provided a corporate environment where the act of preparing for and establishing integrative activities is disapproved of at worst or room for manoeuvre restricted at best. Furthermore, the period in which promotion activities are expected to generate returns works against the principles of IMC and the time needed for the effects to take place.

Opposition/reluctance to change

The attitudes and opinions of staff are often predictable in the sense that any move away from tried and proven methods to areas which are unknown and potentially threatening is usually rejected. Change has for a long time been regarded with hostility and fear, and as such is normally resisted. Our

Any move towards IMC therefore represents a significantly different approach to work.

apparent need for stability and general security has been a potent form of resistance to the introduction of IMC. This is changing as change itself becomes a familiar aspect of working life. Any move towards IMC therefore represents a significantly different approach to work, as not only are the expectations of employees changed but so also are the working practices and the associated roles with internal customers and, more importantly, those providing outsourcing facilities.

Traditional hierarchical and brand management structures

Part of the reluctance to change is linked with the structure and systems inherent in many organisations. Traditional hierarchical structures and systems are inflexible and slow to cope with developments in their fast-adapting environments. These structures stifle the use of individual initiative, slow the decision-making process and encourage inertia. The brand management system, so popular and appropriate in the 1970s and early 1980s, focuses upon functional specialism, which is reflected in the horizontally and vertically specialised areas of responsibility. Brands now need to be managed by flexible teams of specialists, who are charged with responsibilities and the resources necessary to coordinate activities across organisations in the name of integration.

Attitudes and structure of suppliers and agencies

One of the principal reasons often cited as a barrier to integration is the relationship that clients have with their agencies, and in particular their advertising agencies. Generally, advertising agencies have maintained their traditional structures and methods of operating, while their clients have begun to adapt and reform themselves. The thinking behind this is that advertising agencies have tried to maintain their dominance of mass advertising as the principal means of brand development. In doing so they seek to retain the largest proportion of agency fee income, rather than having these fees diluted as work is allocated below the line (to other organisations). The establishment of IMC threatens the current role of the main advertising agencies. This is not to say that all agencies think and act in this way. They do not, as witnessed by the innovative approaches to restructuring and the provision of integrated resources for their clients by agencies such as St Lukes. So, while clients have seen the benefits of integrated marketing communications, their attempts to achieve them have often been thwarted by the structures of the agencies they need to work with and by the attitudes of their main agencies.

The establishment of IMC threatens the current role of the main advertising agencies.

Perceived complexity of planning and coordination

The complexity associated with integrating any combination of activities is often cited as a means for delaying or postponing action. Of greater significance are the difficulties associated with coordinating actions across departments and geographic boundaries. IMC requires the cooperation and coordination of internal and external stakeholder groups. Each group has an agenda which contains goals that may well differ from or conflict with those of other participants.

For example, an advertising agency might propose the use of mass media to address a client's needs, if only because that is where its specialist skills lie. However, direct marketing might be a more appropriate approach to solving the client's problem, but because there is no established mechanism to coordinate and discuss openly the problem/solution, the lead agency is likely to have its approach adopted in preference to others.

Implementing change – overcoming the restraints

The restraints that prevent the development of IMC need to be overcome. Indeed, many organisations that have made significant progress in developing IMC have done so by instigating approaches and measures that aim to reduce or negate the impact of the barriers that people put up to prevent change. The main approaches to overcoming the barriers are as follows.

Adopting a customer-focused philosophy

The adoption of a customer-focused approach is quite well established within marketing departments. However, this approach needs to be adopted as an organisation-wide approach, a philosophy that spans all departments and which results in unified cues to all stakeholders. In many cases, agencies need to adopt a more customer-orientated approach and be able and willing to work with other agencies, including those below the line.

Training and staff development programmes

A move towards IMC cannot be made without changes in the expectations held by employees within the client and agency sectors. Some of the key processes that have been identified as important to successful change management need to be used. For example, the involvement and participation of all staff in the process is in itself a step to providing motivation and acceptance of change when it is agreed and delivered.

The involvement and participation of all staff in the process is in itself a step to providing motivation and acceptance of change when it is agreed and delivered.

Appointing change agents

The use of change agents, people who can positively affect the reception and implementation of change programmes, is important. As IMC should span an entire organisation, the change agent should be a senior manager, or preferably director, in order to signal the importance and speed at which the new perspective is to be adopted. Some organisations have experimented with the appointment of a single senior manager who is responsible for all internal and external communications.

Planning to achieve sustainable competitive advantage

In order to develop competitive advantages, some organisations have restructured by removing levels of management, introduced business reprocessing procedures and even set up outsourcing in order that they achieve cost efficiencies and effectiveness targets. Prior to the implementation of these delayering processes, many organisations were (and many still are) organised hierarchically.

As Brown (1997) rightly states, the emergence and establishment of IMC will only have a real chance of success once the industry matures, becomes market orientated and leaves behind issues concerning client–agency complications and in many cases traditional brand management systems, most designed to prevent the development of synergies or shared knowledge. What is required therefore is a restructuring and redesignation of who manages and this requires a planned approach. It is unlikely that current systems, processes, procedures and structures will suffice; a planned approach to enabling IMC can be an important step.

Finally, total IMC is achieved when all external agencies, outsourcing providers and partners work with the organisation in such a way that customers perceive consistency in the promises and actions the organisation makes.

Finally, total *IMC* (integration of all marketing and corporate communications) is achieved when all external agencies, outsourcing providers and partners work with the organisation in such a way that customers perceive consistency in the promises and actions the organisation makes and are satisfied with the organisation's attempts to anticipate and satisfy customer needs and the results that they seek from their relationships with the brand or organisation.

Agency structures and IMC

In order for messages to be developed and conveyed through an integrated approach, the underlying structure supporting this strategy needs to be reconsidered. Just as the structure of the industry had a major impact on the way in which messages were developed and communicated as the industry developed, so the structural underpinning needs to adapt to the new and preferred approaches of clients in the 1990s and the new millennium.

The use of outside agencies that possess skills, expertise and purchasing advantages which are valued by clients is not new and is unlikely to change. However, the way in which these outsourced skills are used and how they are structured has been changing. Aspects of client–agency relationships are important and are considered in Chapter 11. What is important for this part of the text is a consideration of the way in which organisations who provide outsourcing facilities and contribute to a client's IMC can be configured to provide optimal servicing and support. Gronstedt and Thorsen (1996) suggest five ways in which agencies could be configured to provide integrated marketing communications. The research is centred upon US-based advertising agencies, so, while not immediately transferable to the European, Asian or other regional markets, their proposals provide a base from which other agencies might evolve in other geographic markets.

The models are presented in Figure 19.3, and although the authors acknowledge

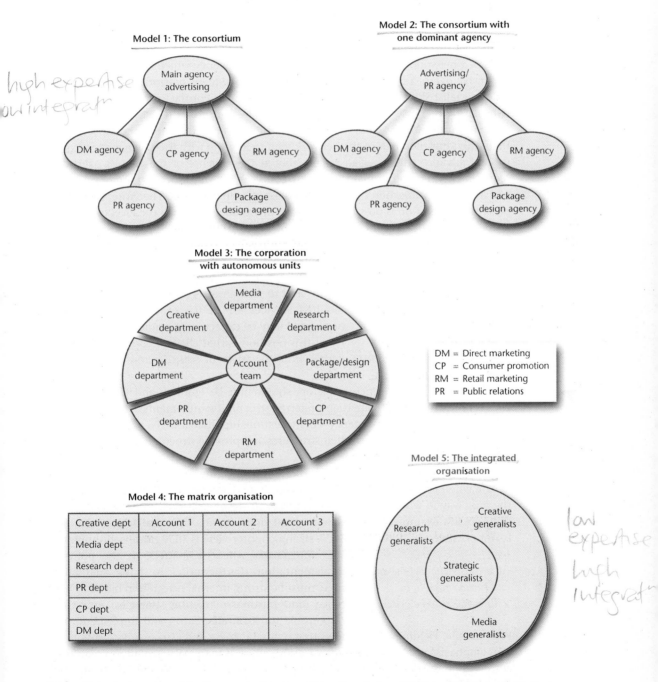

Figure 19.3   An overview of the five agency structures. From Gronstedt and Thorson (1996); used with kind permission.

The forms denote a continuum, at one end of which is a highly centralised organisation that can provide a high level of integration for a variety of communication disciplines.

that a mix of forms could be identified, one particular form tended to dominate each agency. The forms denote a continuum, at one end of which is a highly centralised organisation that can provide a high level of integration for a variety of communication disciplines. Staffed by generalists with no particular media bias, these organisations are structured according to client needs, not functional specialisms. Total integration is offered at the expense of in-depth and leading-edge knowledge in new and developing areas.

At the other end of the continuum are those providers who group themselves in the form of a network. Often led by a main advertising agency which has divested itself of expensive overheads, the independent yet interdependent network players each provide specialist skills under the leadership of the main contractor agency. One of the two main weaknesses associated with this model concerns the deficiency associated with communications across the players in the network. This horizontal aspect means that individual members of the network tend to identify with their own area of expertise and advance their specialism, possibly at the expense of the client's overriding requirements. The other main weakness concerns the transitory or temporary nature of a member organisation's involvement within such networks. Therefore, the level of potential integration is possibly weakest in this model, although the level of expertise available to clients is highest at this end of the continuum.

One of the essential points emerging from this research is that there seems to be a trade-off between levels of integration and the expertise provided by different agencies.

There seems to be a trade-off between levels of integration and the expertise provided by different agencies.

Clients who want to retain control over their brands and to find an integrated agency where all the required services are of the exact level and quality demanded may be expecting too much. The inevitability of this position is that clients may choose to select marketing communication expertise from a variety of sources, and the integrated agency may well lose out.

Furthermore, environmental factors should not be ignored, and it may be that clients in the future will state their preferred structural requirements at the pitching or client briefing stage of the agency–client relationship. Increasingly, agencies may well be required to mix and match their structures and provide structural flexibility to meet the varying needs of their clients.

A further point concerns global branding and the standardisation/adaptation debate when considered in the light of IMC. One argument is that standardisation is the only way in which IMC can be achieved. However, as it is generally accepted that there are few examples of truly standardised global brands, does that suggest that IMC is not possible for global brands? A strong counter-view is that glocalisation encourages integration where it matters, at the point of implementation. Furthermore, to have adaptation, there must be strong internal integration between head office (and business/marketing strategies) and those responsible for local adaptation and implementation.

For IMC to succeed, a consistent core message and local or regional flavour need to be delivered if such a difference is to be overcome.

For example, Fielding (2000) shows that many Japanese and Korean advertising messages emphasise product-related information, whereas many Western brands require an emphasis on the development of brand personality and character. For IMC to succeed, a consistent core message and local or regional flavour need to be delivered if such a difference is to be overcome.

Client structures and IMC

The final aspect to be considered in IMC concerns the structure of the client organisation. The hierarchical structures common in many organisations in the period up to 1970s have been subject to attack. In search of survival in recession and increasing profits and dividends in times of plenty, organisations have sought to restructure and realign themselves with their environment. Hierarchies delivered a management structure that delegated authority in compartmentalized units. The brand management

The restructuring process has resulted in organisations that are delayered and leaner.

system that accompanied this structural approach provided a straitjacket and gave only partial authority to incumbents. At the same time, responsibility for pricing, channel management, personal selling and public relations activities was split off and allocated to a number of others. It follows from this that the likelihood of internal integration has been hampered by the structure of the organisation and the way in which structural units were assembled.

The restructuring process has resulted in organisations that are delayered and leaner. This means that the gap between senior management and those within the operating core (Mintzberg, 1996) is both smaller and now capable of sustaining viable internal communications that are truly two way and supportive.

Increasingly organisations are operating in overseas or cross-border markets. For a deeper account of the issues concerning international marketing communications, readers are referred to Chapter 17. However, as organisations develop structurally, from international to multinational to global and transnational status, so the need to coordinate internally and to integrate internal communications becomes ever more vital to sustain integrated marketing communications (Grein and Gould, 1996). Internal marketing (Chapter 7) is becoming more popular with clients (and agencies) as it is realised that employees are important contributors to corporate identity programmes and invaluable spokespersons for the products they market. Internal communications can help not only to inform and remind/reassure but also to differentiate employees in the sense that they understand the organisation's direction and purpose, appreciate what the brand values are and so identify closely with the organisation as a whole. This is a form of integration from which marketing communications can benefit.

Charities and IMC – NSPCC

This campaign, which sought to stop cruelty to children, had a number of integrated communication characteristics. The ambitious targets, range of activities and the huge number of people involved needed an integrated marketing communications campaign to make it succeed.

To start with there was a range of stakeholders involved: police, parents, teachers, businesses, agencies, the media and, of course, children. All needed to be part of the communications.

The strategy was based around two main phases. The first was a strong pull campaign directed at the public and designed to raise awareness of child cruelty and the second step was action orientated. In parallel there was a strategy designed to communicate with businesses in order to generate funds, goodwill and support.

The overall profile of the organisation (NSPCC) was also to be raised and communications needed to ensure that the integrity of the organisation and those associated with it was maintained. In addition, all communications had to be consistent. The promotional mix used to create a dialogue with the public used public relations, TV, posters, field marketing, direct marketing, direct mail, telemarketing and a Web site.

In the first phase, public relations were used at the initial stages of the campaign to help create awareness. Public address systems at railway stations and airports were used as a reminder mechanism.

A national TV campaign, supported by posters, broke soon after the public relations in order to raise awareness and provoke the question within each individual, 'what can I do?' The message strategy was very emotional and used strong imagery to create shock and attention.

The heavy TV campaign looked to generate 600 TVRs, 85% coverage at 7.1 OTSs. The supporting poster campaign used 48 sheets on 3,500 sites designed to deliver 55% coverage with 21 OTSs. Initial enquiries in response to this wave of communications were handled by an automated telemarketing bureau.

In the second phase the aim was to provide the public with an answer to the question that the advertising had provoked, namely to sign the pledge and/or volunteer as a donor or fundraiser. An envelope picked up on the TV creative treatment repeating as a subdued background motif the image of nursery wallpaper with a teddy bear covering its eyes with its paws: 'Don't close your eyes to cruelty to children'. This was to be delivered to 23 million postboxes, as a doordrop campaign.

It was thought that the doordrop letter addressed as 'Dear Householder' might offend established donors. To avoid this, 160,000 best donors were sent an early warning letter in advance of the campaign breaking in order to get their support. Another million received personal letters just ahead of the doordrop. It was expected that the bulk of enquires would come from the doordrop action and these were to be handled through personal telemarketing responses (inbound). The Web site was also adapted in order that it would be able to accept pledges.

In addition to this, the campaign utilised a call-to-action weekend with volunteers manning 2000 sites around the country, including most city centres, to remind and raise cash donations.

The promotional mix used to communicate with businesses involved sponsorship, direct mail/information pack and the Internet. Sponsorship deals were made available enabling businesses to align themselves more closely with the campaign. Microsoft has been closely involved with the NSPCC for a number of years and it acted as a prime mover, encouraging other businesses to pledge their support. The advertising for the campaign was sponsored by Microsoft. Other sponsorship and cause-related marketing packages were detailed in a toolkit distributed to other major organisations. Direct mail was also used to encourage businesses to make donations and electronic communications were used to promote pledges on-line.

At this stage it appears that the coordinated promotional plan enabled a simple yet hard-hitting message to be conveyed to a substantial part of the nation. The publicity derived from the above-the-line work and the rigorous nature of the below-the-line activities suggest that many of the objectives have been achieved. However, results declared in December 2000 showed that in its first year, of the £75 million budget, less than half was spent on child-related services, suggesting to some that the Full Stop campaign was more about brand building.

Adapted from Goften (1999) and Day (2000).

Integrated marketing communications are more likely to occur when organisations attempt to enter into a coordinated dialogue with their various internal and external audiences. The communication tools used in this dialogue and the messages conveyed should be internally consistent with the organisation's objectives and strategies. The target audiences should perceive the communications and associated cues as coordinated, likeable and timely.

Integrated marketing communications means different things to different people. However, if it is to be a significant development for organisations then the term should embrace the marketing mix, the promotional mix, internal communications and all those outsourced providers who contribute to the overall marketing communication process. As Figure 19.4 demonstrates, all of these elements should be linked to the overall purpose of the organisation, normally encapsulated and framed in the strategy, philosophy and mission of the organisation.

Summary

The development of IMC can be seen as resulting naturally from two main factors. The first concerns the way in which the tools of the promotional mix have been deployed. Their use, in the past, has been largely singular in that they have been departmentalised and managed, internally and externally, as separate and independent items. By combining tools and enabling the communication strengths of one tool to reinforce those of another, target audiences are more likely to benefit, along with the organisation.

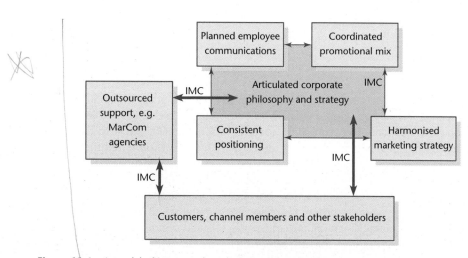

Figure 19.4   A model of integrated marketing communications.

Second, and following on from this first point, has been the drive for business efficiency and increased effectiveness. IMC offers opportunities to improve effectiveness and deliver messages in a more productive manner. Now that a genuine mixture of tools can be assembled, many managers can see IMC as a way of putting right a number of problems across the organisation, many of them structural or communication orientated.

While the concept of IMC is attractive, the development of the approach in practical terms has to date not been very encouraging. There has been a great deal of debate and some attempt to coordinate the content and delivery of marketing communication messages. Most organisations have yet to achieve totally integrated marketing communications; only partial or coordinated levels of activity have so far been achieved.

Review questions

1. Discuss the main reasons for the development of IMC.

2. Prepare brief notes setting out what IMC means.

3. Write a definition of IMC and prepare notes for a colleague explaining how the elements of the McCarthy marketing mix communicate.

4. Explain with the aid of a rough diagram how different agency structures can be developed to accommodate IMC.

5. What are the principal reasons for the development of IMC?

6. List the main drivers for the growth of IMC.

7. Appraise the main reasons offered for the failure of organisations to develop IMC.

8. What is the incremental approach to establishing IMC?

9. Evaluate the view that IMC is principally an internal marketing tool.

10. Prepare the outline for an essay arguing whether IMC is a strategic approach or just a means to correct internal operational difficulties and to reduce media costs.

MINI CASE

CoServe Engineering

CoServe is a privately owned civil engineering company, employing approximately 2,500 people worldwide. The company specifies, designs, implements and services the development of major civil engineering projects in a variety of vertical market sectors. The company has recently embarked upon a new business strategy, partly as a response to changing market and competitive conditions and partly because of a need to grow the business.

Traditionally, the industry is characterised by market exchanges. A client developed a project requirement, put it to competitive tender and those that submitted the best value-for-money bid were appointed to the design of the project. The problem with this approach is that the appointed civil engineering company had limited input to the original requirement specification and as soon as the project was completed, its involvement was terminated and it was effectively discarded. Perhaps even more importantly, the margins earned on such projects are notoriously slim, so, in order to grow the business, higher margins needed to be generated.

The new strategy is based upon a relationship marketing approach, referred to by CoServe as the 3C approach: clients, culture and commercialisation. These are all interlinked but this strategy refers to a change in direction from a purely engineering/product focus to one which centres on client needs and their total project requirements. The name CoServe is new and replaces the previous company name which was based on the name of founders of the original company.

The company now views each project as a commercial activity and all employees must adopt increased levels of commercial awareness (e.g. project risk assessment, the importance of working within budget and invoicing on time). In addition, CoServe now offers a total engineering service. Rather than provide just a civil engineering design service that represented the original core business, the emphasis is now based upon providing added value by shifting the offering both upstream and downstream. Therefore, CoServe now provides three connected offerings:

(A) The front-end work which involves undertaking the planning and risk analysis work for its clients.
(B) The core work which is about the design and build aspect of the project.
(C) The tail-end work which is essentially facilities management.

This added value, competitive strategy seeks to free clients from the whole range of tasks associated with the development of major civil engineering projects. This should allow them to concentrate upon their core business of retailing, ferry transport, road development/ maintenance or railway infrastructure management.

There are two significant benefits. The first is the substantially higher margins that the front- and tail-end work attracts. The second concerns the reduced 'resource' wastage by being able to help accurately define the client problem at the earliest possible stage in the project life cycle.

In order to develop and implement this strategy, CoServe had to evolve a new skills mix and to do this it either bought or formed alliances with companies that had the skills it required.

While this might sound reasonably straightforward, CoServe has had to address further issues. These concern the development of a suitable commercial culture for the established employees plus the grafting on of the newly acquired employees into the CoServe culture, including values and corporate philosophy. A further issue concerns the way the company presented itself (and the new strategy) to its clients and other interested stakeholders.

The level of communication frequency between client and CoServe varies across the life of a project. There is a great deal of communication at the outset of a project as the brief is determined by all parties. As the project moves to the design phase, the level of communication tends to subside. However, once the build phase is reached, communication activity reaches its greatest level of intensity, if only because a third party, a contractor, is now involved and required to interpret the design and specification previously agreed by client and CoServe. Any communication analysis in project-based engineering work needs to take account of the critical issue of timescales. Projects always run tight on their deadlines, and hence interorganisational, and even intraorganisational, communication levels intensify in an attempt to resolve on-site problems as quickly as possible.

Through this increased familiarity with a client's business and the reciprocal act of the client trusting CoServe with sensitive company information, the newly formed partnerships enable CoServe to become more knowledgeable and better acquainted with its partners' needs and the types of problems it is required to resolve.

CoServe has implemented a strategy that

seeks to develop a relational marketing strategy through the development of strong client relationships (partnering). Through the new offer of added value services immediately upstream and downstream from the typical infrastructure consultancy services offered, the company hopes to be able to lock in clients, improve margins and improve company performance for its shareholders.

Personal contact is the most significant communication tool used in the development and maintenance of client relationships.

This mini case is based on a real organisation but the names and identity have been changed to provide anonymity.

Mini-case questions

1. Explain how the change in corporate strategy has impacted on CoServe's communication strategy.
2. Identify the drivers for the development of an integrated marketing communications strategy at CoServe.
3. Explain the role of internal marketing communications at CoServe and its contribution to an integrated strategy.
4. Formulate a promotional mix for CoServe as it might be at the end of the mini case.
5. To what extent is it possible to identity the IMC stages of development at this company?

References

Brown, J. (1997) Impossible dream or inevitable revolution: an exploration of integrated marketing communications. *Journal of Communication Management*, **12**(1), pp. 70–81.

Bucklin, (1966) *A Theory of Distribution Channel Structure*. Berkeley, CA: IBER Publications.

Cornelissen, J. (2000) Integration in communication management: conceptual and methodological considerations. *Journal of Marketing Management*, **16**, pp. 597–606.

Day, J. (2000) A time for gifts. *Marketing Week*, 14 December, pp. 22–5.

Duncan, T. and Everett, S. (1993) Client perceptions of integrated marketing communications. *Journal of Advertising Research*, **3**(3), pp. 30–9.

Duncan, T. and Moriarty, S. (1998) A communication-based marketing model for managing relationships. *Journal of Marketing*, **62** (April), pp. 1–13.

Eagle, L. and Kitchen, P. (2000) IMC, brand communications, and corporate cultures. *European Journal of Marketing*, **34** (5/6), pp. 667–86.

Fielding, S. (2000) Developing global brands in Asia. *Admap* (June), pp. 26–9.

Goften, K. (1999) NSPCC aims to convert abuse anger into cash. *Marketing*, 25 March, pp. 37–8.

Grein, A.F. and Gould, S.J. (1996) Globally integrated communications. *Journal of Marketing Communications*, **2**, pp. 141–58.

Gronstedt, A. and Thorsen, E. (1996) Five approaches to organise an integrated marketing communications agency. *Journal of Advertising Research* (March/April), pp. 48–58.

Hutton, J.G. (1996) Integrated relationship-marketing communications: a key opportunity for IMC. *Journal of Marketing Communications*, **2**, pp. 191–9.

Lannon, J. (1996) Integrated communications from the consumer end. *Admap* (February), pp. 23–6.

Miller, D.A. and Rose, P.B. (1994) Integrated communications: a look at reality instead of theory. *Public Relations Quarterly* (Spring), pp. 13–16.

Mintzberg, H. (1996) *The Strategy Process*, European edn. Englewood Cliffs, NJ: Prentice Hall.

Morgan, R.M. and Hunt, S.D. (1994) The commitment–trust theory of relationship marketing. *Journal of Marketing*, **58** (July), pp. 20–38.

Porter, M.E. (1980) *Competitive Strategy: Techniques for Analyzing Industries and Competitors*. New York: Free Press.

Smith, P. (1996) Benefits and barriers to integrated communications. *Admap* (February), pp. 19–22.

White, R. (2000) Chameleon brands: tailoring brand messages to consumers. *Admap*, (July/August), pp. 38–40.

part 4

Applications and methods of marketing communications

Chapters 20–31

The tools of the marketing communication mix and associated media

20

Advertising: how it might work

An attempt to understand how advertising might work must be cautioned by an appreciation of the complexity and contradictions inherent in this commercial activity. Understanding how advertising might work with its rich mosaic of perceptions, emotions, attitudes, information and patterns of behaviour is nothing short of the quest for the holy grail.

AIMS AND OBJECTIVES

The aims of this chapter are to explore the different views about how advertising might work and to consider the complexities associated with understanding how clients can best use advertising.

The objectives of this chapter are:

1. To consider the role advertising plays in both consumer and business-to-business markets.

2. To examine the strengths and weaknesses of the sequential models of how advertising works.

3. To introduce the principal frameworks by which advertising is thought to influence individuals.

4. To appraise the strong and weak theories of advertising.

5. To explain cognitive processing as a means of understanding how people use advertising messages.

6. To discuss the contribution that the elaboration likelihood model can make to comprehending how motivation and attitude change can be brought together.

7. To present a composite model of how advertising might work.

Introduction

The purpose of an advertising plan is to provide the means by which appropriate messages are devised and delivered to target audiences who then act in appropriate ways. This may be to buy a product, to enquire about a product or simply memorise a single aspect for future action. Guidelines for the content and delivery of messages are derived from an understanding of the variety of contexts in which the messages are to be used. For example, research might reveal a poor brand image relative to the market leader, or the different or changing media habits of target consumers. The nature of the messages and the problems to be addressed will be specified in the promotional objectives and strategy.

An advertising plan is composed, essentially, of three main elements:

1. The message, or what is to be said.
2. The media, or how the message will be conveyed.
3. The timing, or manner in which the message will be carried.

This chapter is concerned with an exploration of how advertising might work and introduces a number of concepts and frameworks that have contributed to our understanding. The next chapter considers the content of the advertising message, or what is to be said. Chapter 22 looks briefly at the media used to carry messages but focuses upon the third issue (media planning or the timing and scheduling of the selected media). Those readers interested in the different types of media should visit the companion Web site for this book at *www.booksites.net/fill*. Issues concerning the measurement and evaluation of advertising are considered in Chapter 31.

Role of advertising

The role of advertising in the promotional plan is an important one. Advertising, whether it be on an international, national, local or direct basis, is important, as it can influence audiences by informing or reminding them of the existence of a brand, or alternatively by persuading or helping them differentiate a product or organisation from others in the market.

Advertising can influence audiences by informing or reminding them of the existence of a brand, or alternatively by persuading or helping them differentiate a product or organisation from others in the market.

Advertising can reach huge audiences with simple messages that present opportunities to allow receivers to understand what a product is, what its primary function is and how it relates to all the other similar products. This is the main function of advertising: to communicate with specific audiences. These audiences may be consumer or organisation based, but wherever they are located, the prime objective is to build or maintain awareness of a product or an organisation.

Management's control over advertising messages is strong; indeed, of all the elements in the promotional mix, advertising has the greatest level of control. The message, once generated and signed off by the client, can be transmitted in an agreed manner and style and at times that match management's requirements. This means that, should the environment change unexpectedly, advertising messages can be 'pulled' immediately. For example, if a campaign to encourage rail travel had been planned for November 2000, it would have had to have been pulled in October following the Hatfield rail crash and the subsequent difficulties experienced by Railtrack, train operators, the government and, of course, the travelling public. Lying low allowed management to concentrate on dealing with the consequences of the accident, the problems related to the track and the associated publicity of the event and the subsequent track replacement programme caused, rather than the negative effects that the advertising would have caused had it been transmitted.

Advertising costs can be regarded in one of two ways. On the one hand, there are the absolute costs, which are the costs of buying the space in magazines or newspapers or the time on television, cinema or radio. These costs can be enormous, and they impact directly on cash flow. For example, the rate card cost of a full-page (mono) advertisement in the *Daily Mail* was £31,500 (July 2001) and a prime spot on *Coronation Street* for 30 seconds would cost £140,000 (station average price, as at April 2001).

On the other hand, there are the relative costs, which are those costs incurred to reach a member of the target audience with the key message. So, if an audience is measured in hundreds of thousands, or even millions on television, the cost of the advertisement spread across each member of the target audience reduces the cost per contact significantly. This aspect is developed further in Chapter 22.

The main roles of advertising are to build awareness, induce a dialogue (if only on an internal basis) and to (re)position brands, by changing either perception or attitudes. The regular use of advertising, in cooperation with the other elements of the communication mix, can be important to the creation and maintenance of a brand personality. Indeed, advertising has a significant role to play in the development of competitive advantage. In some consumer markets advertising is a dominant form of promotion. Advertising can become a mobility barrier, deterring exit and, more importantly, deterring entry to a market by organisations attracted by the profits of the industry. Many people feel that some brands sustain their large market shares by sheer weight of advertising; for example, the washing powder brands of Procter & Gamble and Unilever.

The main roles of advertising are to build awareness, induce a dialogue (if only on an internal basis) and to (re)position brands, by changing either perception or attitudes.

Advertising can create competitive advantage by providing the communication necessary for target audiences to frame a product. By providing a frame or the perceptual space with which to pigeonhole a product, target audiences are able to position an offering relative to their other significant products much more easily. Therefore advertising can provide the means for differentiation and sustainable competitive advantage. It should also be appreciated, however, that differentiation may be determined by the quality of execution of the advertisements, rather than through the content of the messages.

Advertising can also be regarded as an anchor for many integrated campaigns. Normally, it is necessary to use advertising to build awareness and to develop brands. Indeed, the explosion in numbers of dotcom businesses and the flurry of stock market flotations that many sought in 1999 were largely driven by the use of some television and print advertising but a huge amount of outdoor 48- and 96-sheet poster work, trying to raise awareness of the dotcom brands and drive traffic to their Web sites. In addition, public relations and sales promotions are more effective when advertising is used to raise initial awareness and shape attitudes respectively.

Advertising in the business-to-business market is geared, primarily, to providing relevant factual information upon which 'rational' decisions can be made. Regardless of the target audience, all advertising requires a message and a carrier to deliver the message to the receiver. This text will concentrate on these two main issues, while acknowledging the wider role that advertising plays in society.

How does advertising work?

For a message to be communicated successfully, it should be targeted at the right audience, capable of gaining attention, understandable, relevant and acceptable. For effective communication to occur, messages should be designed that fit the cognitive capability of the target audience and follow 'the' model of how advertising works. Unfortunately, there is no such single model, despite years of research and speculation by a great many people. However, from all of the work undertaken in this area, a number of views have been expressed, and the following sections attempt to present some of the more influential perspectives.

For effective communication to occur, messages should be designed that fit the cognitive capability of the target audience.

Sequential models

Various models have been developed to assist our understanding of how these promotional tasks are segregated and organised effectively. Table 20.1 shows some of the better-known models.

Table 20.1 Sequential models of advertising

Processing	Aida sequence[a]	Hierarchy of effects sequence[b]	Information sequence[c]
		Awareness	Presentation ↓
Cognitive		↓	Attention ↓
	Attention ↓	Knowledge ↓	Comprehension ↓
	Interest	Liking ↓	Yielding
Affective	↓	Preference ↓	↓
	Desire	Conviction	Retention
Conative	↓	↓	↓
	Action	Purchase	Behaviour

[a] Strong (1925). [b] Lavidge and Steiner (1961). [c] McGuire (1978).

Aida

Developed by Strong (1925), the AIDA model was designed to represent the stages that a salesperson must take a prospect through in the personal selling process. This model shows the prospect passing through successive stages of attention, interest, desire and action. This expression of the process was later adopted loosely as the basic framework to explain how persuasive communication, and advertising in particular, was thought to work.

Hierarchy of effects models

An extension of the progressive staged approach advocated by Strong emerged in the early 1960s. Developed most notably by Lavidge and Steiner (1961), the hierarchy of effects models represent the process by which advertising was thought to work and assume that there is a series of steps a prospect must pass through, in succession, from unawareness to actual purchase. Advertising, it is assumed, cannot induce immediate behavioural responses; rather, a series of mental effects must occur with fulfilment at each stage necessary before progress to the next stage is possible.

The information processing model

McGuire (1978) contends that the appropriate view of the receiver of persuasive advertising is as an information processor or cognitive problem solver. This cognitive perspective becomes subsumed as the stages presented reflect similarities with the other hierarchical models, except that McGuire includes a retention stage. This refers to the ability of the receiver to retain and understand information which is valid and relevant. This is important, because it recognises that marketing communication messages are designed to provide information for use by a prospective buyer when a purchase decision is to be made at some time in the future.

It recognises that marketing communication messages are designed to provide information for use by a prospective buyer when a purchase decision is to be made at some time in the future.

Difficulties with the sequential approach

For a long time the sequential approach was accepted as the model upon which advertising was to be developed. However, questions arose about what actually constitute adequate levels of awareness, comprehension and conviction and how it can be determined which stage the majority of the target audience has reached at any one point in time.

The model is based on the logical sequential movement of consumers towards a purchase via specified stages. The major criticism is that it assumes that the consumer moves through the stages in a logical, rational manner: learn, then feel and then do. This is obviously not the case, as anyone who has taken a child into a sweet shop can confirm. There has been a lot of research that attempts to give an empirical validation of some of the hierarchy propositions, the results of which are inconclusive and at times ambiguous (Barry and

The major criticism is that it assumes that the consumer moves through the stages in a logical, rational manner: learn, then feel and then do.

Howard, 1990). Among these researchers is Palda (1966), who found that the learn–feel–do sequence cannot be upheld as a reflection of general buying behaviour and provided empirical data to reject the notion of sequential models as an interpretation of the way advertising works.

The sequential approach sees attitude towards the product as a prerequisite to purchase, but as discussed earlier (Chapter 3) there is evidence that a positive attitude is not necessarily a good predictor of purchase behaviour. What is important, or more relevant, is the relationship between attitude change and an individual's intention to act in a particular way (Ajzen and Fishbein, 1980). Therefore, it seems reasonable to suggest that what is of potentially greater benefit is a specific measure of attitude *towards* purchasing or *intentions* to buy a specific product. Despite measurement difficulties, attitude change is considered a valid objective, particularly in high-involvement situations.

A great deal of time and money must be spent on research, determining what needs to be measured. As a result, only large organisations can utilise the model properly: those with the resources and the expertise to generate the data necessary to exploit this approach fully.

All of these models share the similar view that the purchase decision process is one in which individuals move through a series of sequential stages. Each of the stages from the different models can be grouped in such a way that they are a representation of the three attitude components, these being cognitive (learn), affective (feel) and conative (do) orientations. This could be seen to reflect the various stages in the buying process, especially those that induce high involvement in the decision process but do not reflect the reality of low-involvement decisions.

Advertising frameworks

Hall (1992) and O'Malley (1991) have suggested that there are four main advertising frameworks (Figure 20.1):

1. *The sales framework*
   This framework, orientated mainly to direct response work, is based on the premise that the level of sales is the only factor that is worth considering when measuring the effectiveness of an advertising campaign. This view holds that all advertising activities are aimed ultimately at shifting product – generating sales. Advertising is considered to have a short-term direct impact on sales. This effect is measurable and, while other outcomes might also result from advertising, the only important factor is sales. On sales alone will the true effect of any advertising be felt.

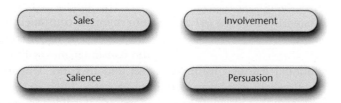

Figure 20.1   Four advertising frameworks.

2. *The persuasion framework*

The second framework assumes advertising to work rationally, because messages are capable of being persuasive. Persuasion is effected by gradually moving buyers through a number of sequential steps. These hierarchy of effects models assume that buyer decision-making is rational and can be accurately predicted. As discussed earlier, these models have a number of drawbacks and are no longer used as the basis for designing advertisements, despite great popularity in the 1960s and 1970s.

Persuasion is effected by gradually moving buyers through a number of sequential steps.

3. *The involvement framework*

Involvement-based advertisements work by drawing members of the target audience into the advertisement and eliciting a largely emotional response. Involvement with the product develops as a consequence of involvement with the advertisement. Yellow Pages developed a highly successful series of television commercials that centred upon a fictional character called J.R. Hartley. This elderly gentleman was shown using Yellow Pages as a means of resolving a number of problems and served to provide warmth and character which involved people not only with J.R. Hartley but also helped establish brand values.

Another example of this approach can be observed in the Nescafé Gold Blend coffee advertisements. During the late 1980s and early 1990s, UK viewers witnessed the development of a relationship between an aspirational couple with a mutual liking for the Gold Blend brand of coffee. Each advertisement, which presents particular events in the development of the couple's relationship, was eagerly looked forward to by an involved and often obsessive audience. By involving the target in the drama, the brand became part of the involvement, a crucial part of each of the ritualistic playlets. Later in the decade the couple were reincarnated as a younger couple and presented in a more adventurous context. Again, the theme was romance, which was allowed to unfold over a series of different advertisements.

By involving the target in the drama, the brand became part of the involvement, a crucial part of each of the ritualistic playlets.

4. *The salience framework*

This interpretation is based upon the premise that advertising works by standing out, by being different from all other advertisements in the product class. The launch of Radion, a soap powder that used the twin propositions of cleaning and removing odours, was remarkable because of its ability to 'shout' at the audience through the use of lurid colours and striking presentations. Tango (a canned drink) was repositioned using strikingly different, zany (and interactive) messages. Pot Noodle drew attention through presentation techniques based upon a seemingly unprofessional and off-the-wall domestic camcorder production. Alternative examples of salience advertising are the Tosh campaign by Toshiba (O'Malley, 1991) and the Benson and Hedges Silk Cut campaigns (Hall, 1992).

Acceptance of the persuasion and salience frameworks is based on the assumption that the audience are active, rational problem solvers and are perfectly capable of discrimination among brands and advertisements. Furthermore, the models bring to attention two important points about people and advertising. Advertisements are capable of generating two very clear types of response: a response to the featured product

Advertisements are capable of generating two very clear types of response: a response to the featured product and a response to the advertisement itself.

and a response to the advertisement itself. As will be seen later in this chapter, the cognitive responses that people make when exposed to advertisements and the elaboration likelihood model (ELM) are important means of understanding how different motivations affect decision-making.

The explanations offered to date are all based on the premise that advertising is a potent marketing force, one that is persuasive and which is done *to* people. More recent views of advertising theory question this fundamental perspective. Prominent among the theorists are Jones, McDonald and Ehrenberg, some of whose views will now be presented. Jones (1991) presented the new views as the strong theory of advertising and the weak theory of advertising.

The strong theory of advertising

All the models presented so far are assumed to work on the basis that they are capable of affecting a degree of change in the knowledge, attitudes, beliefs or behaviour of target audiences. Jones refers to this as the strong theory of advertising, and it appears to have been universally adopted as a foundation for commercial activity.

According to Jones, exponents of this theory hold that advertising can persuade someone to buy a product that they have never previously purchased. Furthermore, continual long-run purchase behaviour can also be generated. Under the strong theory, advertising is believed to be capable of increasing sales at the brand and class levels. These upward shifts are achieved through the use of manipulative and psychological techniques, which are deployed against consumers who are passive, possibly because of apathy, and are generally incapable of processing information intelligently. The most appropriate theory would appear to be the hierarchy of effects model, where sequential steps move buyers forward to a purchase, stimulated by timely and suitable promotional messages.

The weak theory of advertising

Increasing numbers of European writers argue that the strong theory does not reflect practice. Most notable of these writers is Ehrenberg (1988, 1997), who believes that a consumer's pattern of brand purchases is driven more by habit than by exposure to promotional messages.

The framework proposed by Ehrenberg is the awareness–trial–reinforcement (ATR) framework. Awareness is required before any purchase can be made, although the elapsed time between awareness and action may be very short or very long. For the few people intrigued enough to want to try a product, a trial purchase constitutes the next phase. This may be stimulated by retail availability as much as by advertising, word-of-mouth or personal selling stimuli. Reinforcement follows to maintain awareness and provide reassurance to help the customer to repeat the pattern of thinking and behaviour and to cement the brand in the repertoire for occasional purchase activity. Advertising's role is to breed brand familiarity and identification (Ehrenberg, 1997) .

A consumer's pattern of brand purchases is driven more by habit than by exposure to promotional messages.

Following on from the original ATR model (Ehrenberg, 1974), various enhancements have been suggested. However, Ehrenberg added a further stage in 1997, referred to as the nudge. He argues that some consumers can 'be nudged into buying the brand more frequently (still as part of their split-loyalty repertoires) or to favour it more than the other brands in their consideration sets'. Advertising need not be any different from before; it just provides more reinforcement that stimulates particular habitual buyers into more frequent selections of the brand from their repertoire.

Building credibility – Playstation

As if to demonstrate the role of advertising, Playstation uses a variety of communications in order to build credibility and to maintain its strong position in the youth market. Advertising's role is just to hold a consistent position and even then it is not TV but brand name association with Skate Parks, the provision of equipment to clubs and societies which then distribute flyers with the Playstation logo, all of which encourages sampling and new user experiences. Word-of-mouth, endorsement and association are far more powerful forms of generating credibility in certain markets than reliance on traditional advertising.

According to the weak theory, advertising is capable of improving people's knowledge, and so is in agreement with the strong theory. In contrast, however, consumers are regarded as selective in determining which advertisements they observe and only perceive those which promote products that they either use or have some prior knowledge of. This means that they already have some awareness of the characteristics of the advertised product. It follows that the amount of information actually communicated is limited. Advertising, Jones continues, is not potent enough to convert people who hold reasonably strong beliefs that are counter to those portrayed in an advertisement. The time available (30 seconds in television advertising) is not enough to bring about conversion and, when combined with people's ability to switch off their cognitive involvement, there may be no effective communication. Advertising is employed as a defence, to retain customers and to increase product or brand usage. Advertising is used to reinforce existing attitudes not necessarily to drastically change them.

Advertising is employed as a defence, to retain customers and to increase product or brand usage. Advertising is used to reinforce existing attitudes not necessarily to drastically change them.

Unlike the strong theory, this perspective accepts that when people say that they are not influenced by advertising they are in the main correct. It also assumes that people are not apathetic or even stupid, but capable of high levels of cognitive processing.

In summary, the strong theory suggests that advertising can be persuasive, can generate long-run purchasing behaviour, can increase sales and regards consumers as passive. The weak theory suggests that purchase behaviour is based on habit and that advertising can improve knowledge and reinforce existing attitudes. It views consumers as active problem solvers.

These two perspectives serve to illustrate the dichotomy of views that has emerged about this subject. They are important because they are both right and they are both wrong. The answer to the question 'How does advertising work?' lies somewhere between the two views and is dependent upon the particular situation facing each advertiser. Where elaboration is likely to be high if advertising is to work, then it is most likely to work under the strong theory. For example, consumer durables and financial products require that advertising urges prospective customers into some form of trial behaviour. This may be a call for more information from a sales representative or perhaps a visit to a showroom. The vast majority of product purchases, however, involve low levels of elaboration, where involvement is low and where people select, often unconsciously, brands from an evoked set.

New products require people to convert or change their purchasing patterns. It is evident that the strong theory must prevail in these circumstances. Where products become established their markets generally mature, so that real growth is non-existent. Under these circumstances, advertising works by protecting the consumer franchise and by allowing users to have their product choices confirmed and reinforced. The other objective of this form of advertising is to increase the rate at which customers reselect and consume products. If the strong theory were the only acceptable approach, then theoretically advertising would be capable of continually increasing the size of each market, until everyone had been converted. There would be no 'stationary' markets.

Considering the vast sums that are allocated to advertising budgets, not only to launch new products but also to pursue market share targets aggressively, the popularity and continued implicit acceptance of the power of advertising suggest that a large proportion of resources is wasted in the pursuit of advertising-driven brand performance. Indeed, it is noticeable that during the mid-to late 1980s organisations were increasingly switching resources out of advertising into sales promotion activities. There are many reasons for this (Chapter 23), but one of them concerns the failure of advertising to produce the expected levels of performance: to produce market share. The strong theory fails to deliver the expected results, and the weak theory does not apply to all circumstances. Reality is probably a mixture of the two.

Cognitive processing

Reference has already been made to whether buyers actively or passively process information. In an attempt to understand how information is used, cognitive processing tries to determine 'how external information is transformed into meanings or patterns of thought and how these meanings are combined to form judgements' (Olsen and Peter, 1987).

By assessing the thoughts (cognitive processes) that occur to people as they read, view or hear a message, an understanding of their interpretation of a message can be useful in campaign development and evaluation (Wright, 1973; Greenwald, 1968). These thoughts are usually measured by asking consumers to write down or verbally report the thoughts they have in response to such a message. Thoughts are believed to be a reflection of the cognitive processes or responses that receivers experience and they help shape or reject a communication.

By assessing the thoughts that occur to people as they read, view or hear a message, an understanding of their interpretation of a message can be useful in campaign development and evaluation.

Researchers have identified three types of cognitive response and have determined how these relate to attitudes and intentions. Figure 20.2 shows these three types of

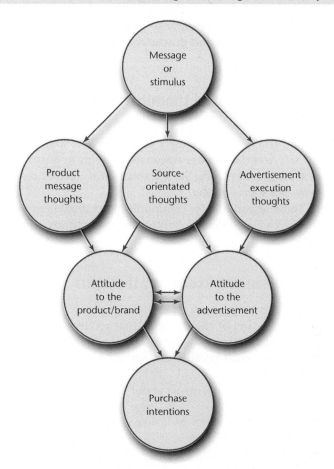

Figure 20.2   A cognitive processing model. Adapted from Lutz *et al.* (1983); used with kind permission.

response, but readers should appreciate that these types are not discrete; they overlap each other and blend together, often invisibly.

Product/message thoughts

These are thoughts which are directed to the product or communication itself. Much attention has been focused upon the thoughts that are related to the message content. Two particular types of response have been considered: counter-arguments and support arguments.

A counter-argument occurs when the receiver disagrees with the content of a message. According to Belch and Belch (1990), 'The likelihood of counter-argument is greater when the message makes claims that oppose the beliefs or perceptions held by the receiver. Not surprisingly, the greater the degree of counter-argument, the less likely the message will be accepted. Conversely, support-arguments reflect acceptance and concurrence with a message. Support-arguments, therefore, are positively related to message acceptance.' Use of the social value groups, discussed in Chapter 5, can provide important

Two particular types of response have been considered: counter-arguments and support arguments.

input to this aspect of message generation. Communications planners should ensure that advertisements and general communications encourage the generation of support arguments.

Source-orientated thoughts

A further set of cognitive responses is those aimed at the source of the communication. This concept is closely allied to that of source credibility (Chapter 2), where, if the source of the message is seen as annoying or distrustful, there is a lower probability of message acceptance. Such a situation is referred to as source derogation; the converse as a source bolster.

Those responsible for communications should ensure, during the context analysis, that receivers experience bolster effects to improve the likelihood of message acceptance.

Advertisement execution thoughts

This relates to the thoughts an individual may have about the advertisement or message itself. Many of the thoughts that receivers have are not product related but are emotionally related towards the message itself. Understanding these feelings and emotions is important because of their impact upon attitudes towards the advertisement and the offering.

People make judgements about the quality of advertisements and the creativity, tone and style in which an advertisement has been executed, and, as a result of their experiences and perception, form an attitude towards the advertisement. Some suggest that attitudes towards the advertisement can be transferred to the product. An increasing proportion of advertisements appeal to feelings and emotions, as many researchers believe that attitudes towards both the advertisement and the product should be encouraged.

People make judgements about the quality of advertisements and the creativity, tone and style in which an advertisement has been executed.

Emotion in advertising

The preceding material, if taken at face value, suggests that advertising only works by people responding to advertising in a logical, rational and cognitive manner. It also suggests that people only take out the utilitarian aspect of advertising messages (cleans better, smells fresher) This is obviously not true and there is certainly a case for arguing the case for the role of emotion and the power of the affective component in the cognitive, affective and conative circle of attitudinal disposition (Chapter 3). It should also be remembered that advertised brands are not normally new to consumers as they have some experience of the brand whether that be through use or just through communications. This experience affects their interpretation of advertising as memories have already been formed.

The role of feelings in the way advertisements work suggests a consumerist interpretation of how advertising works rather than the rational which is much more a researchers' interpretation (Ambler, 1998). Consumers view advertising in the con-

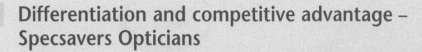

Differentiation and competitive advantage – Specsavers Opticians

Specsavers Opticians broke the mould of price-led competition in the UK opticians market by adopting a more expressive approach to their advertising. Using well-known endorsers, people who either use vision creatively (an artist) or think deeply and develop inner vision about high level physics and associated activities, they helped change the way the brand was perceived and differentiate themselves from their competitors. See the mini case at the end of this chapter and Plates 20.1 and 20.2.

Feelings and emotions play an important role in advertising especially when advertising is used to build awareness levels and brand strength.

text of their experience of the category and memories of the brand. Aligned with this approach is the concept of likeability where the feelings evoked by advertising trigger and shape attitudes to the brand and attitudes to the advertisement (Vakratsas and Ambler, 1999).

Feelings and emotions play an important role in advertising especially when advertising is used to build awareness levels and brand strength.

Elaboration likelihood model

What should be clear from the preceding sections is that neither the purely cognitive nor the purely emotional interpretation of how advertising works is realistic. In effect it is probable that both have an important part to play in the way advertising works, but the degree of emphasis swings according to the context within which the advertising is expected to work.

One approach to utilise both these elements has been developed by Petty and Cacioppo (1983). The ELM has helped to explain how cognitive processing, persuasion and attitude change occur when different levels of

The ELM has helped to explain how cognitive processing, persuasion and attitude change occur when different levels of involvement are present.

involvement are present. Elaboration refers to the extent to which an individual needs to develop and refine information necessary for decision-making to occur. If an individual has a high level of motivation or ability to process information, elaboration is said to be

high. If an individual's motivation or ability to process information is poor, then his or her level of elaboration is said to be low. The ELM distinguishes two main cognitive processes, as depicted in Figure 20.3.

Under the central route the receiver is viewed as very active and involved. As the level of cognitive response is high, the ability of the advertisement to persuade will depend upon the quality of the argument rather than executional factors. For example, the purchase of a consumer durable such as a car or washing machine normally requires a high level of involvement. Consequently, potential customers would be expected to be highly involved and willing to read brochures and information about the proposed car or washing machine prior to demonstration or purchase. Their

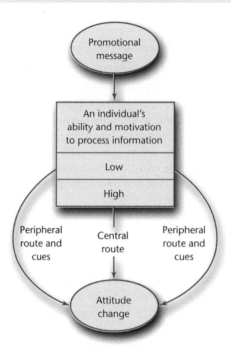

Figure 20.3 The elaboration likelihood model. Based on Aaker *et al.* (1992).

decision to act would depend upon the arguments used to justify the model as suitable for the individual. For the car purchase these might include the quiet engine, environmentally friendly catalytic converter, the relatively excellent consumption and other performance indicators, together with the comfort of the interior and the effortless driving experience. Whether the car is shown as part of a business executive's essential 'kit' or the commercial is flamboyant and rich will be immaterial for those in the central route.

Under the peripheral route, the receiver is seen to lack the ability to process information and is not likely to engage cognitive processing. Rather than thinking about and evaluating the message content, the receiver tends to rely upon what have been referred to as 'peripheral cues', which may be incidental to the message content. Twinings use peripheral cues to attract attention to their brand. See Plate 20.3.

Rather than thinking about and evaluating the message content, the receiver tends to rely upon what have been referred to as 'peripheral cues', which may be incidental to the message content.

In low-involvement situations, a celebrity may serve to influence attitudes positively. This is based upon the creation of favourable attitudes towards the source rather than engaging the viewer in the processing of the message content. For example, Gary Lineker has been used as a celebrity spokesperson to endorse Walkers crisps. The power of Gary Lineker would be more important as a major peripheral cue (more so than the nature of the product) in eventually persuading a consumer to try the brand or retaining current users. Think crisps, think Gary Lineker, think Walkers. Where high involvement is present, any celebrity endorsement is of minor significance to the quality of the message claims.

Communication strategy should be based upon the level of cognitive processing that the target audience is expected to engage in and the route taken to affect attitu-

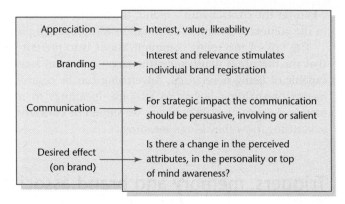

Figure 20.4   The alphabetical model of advertising. Adapted from Prue (1998); used with kind permission.

dinal change. If the processing level is low (low motivation and involvement), the peripheral route should dominate and emphasis needs to be placed on the way the messages are executed and on the emotions of the target audience (Heath, 2000). If the central route is expected, the content of the messages should be dominant and the executional aspects need only be adequate.

Prue (1998) presents a framework entitled the alphabetical model, based upon the premise that advertising should be interpreted from a customer orientation. His model is an attempt to return to the simplicity inherent in the AIDA and other sequential models. See Figure 20.4. This is not so much a theory as a rather wide depository for all known interpretations of how advertising might work.

A cognitive–association model of advertising

Depending upon their level of elaboration, buyers are capable problem solvers. They can be regarded as active information processors (to varying degrees) in all product categories. Advertising is a convenient and often cost-effective way of conveying information about brands to people, who then have an opportunity to reappraise their understanding of the brand and its related elements. This information is processed internally and is used to update their knowledge about the brand as they see it and possibly the generic category of products ('Oh, Hoovers can now have a hose that coils itself automatically').

Our understanding of perception suggests that people organise filtered and selected stimuli according to the context of their current situation and their past experiences.

Therefore marketing communication messages need to be consistent in order that people can organise information about a brand in the same way as they processed the information the last time they perceived the stimuli.

Therefore marketing communication messages need to be consistent in order that people can organise information about a brand in the same way as they processed the information the last time they perceived the stimuli. Now, the stimulus need not be just an advertisement: it could be any element of the promotional or marketing mix, in particular the brand itself. Therefore the presence of either the product or the communication may act as a stimulus. It is not surprising that integrated marketing communications require that whatever the contact with a brand, the message should be the same and be expected in the context with which information was processed previously.

The task of marketing communications is to present key messages in such a way that the meanings that people (the target audience) ascribe to them are relevant and capable of being memorised. Advertising can be regarded as a potentially powerful means of enabling buyers to attribute meanings to messages they receive about brands. As Lannon (1992) argues, we should be concerned with what people do *with* advertising, how they assign meaning.

Triggers, memory and brand associations

So far in this chapter, a number of issues have been presented which, taken independently, are interesting but lack overall coherence and direction. These will now be brought together in an attempt to offer a general framework of how advertising might work.

Before proceeding any further, readers are advised that this question, 'How does advertising work?', is as complex as the question posed by Duckworth (1995): 'How does literature work?' Think about it and describe how literature works to yourself or to a friend. Has the question any inherent validity? The same may said of advertising, and what follows is an attempt to pull together some of the strands of thought presented earlier. No formula is presented or intended, just a few ideas about the interrelationships between concepts, ideas and current research.

Advertising should be considered as a marketing (communications) tool that is used by people in one of two main ways, depending upon the context in which the message, the brand and the individual interact. Advertising messages normally pass individuals unobserved. Those that are remembered contain particular characteristics (Fletcher, 1994; Brown, 1991). These would

'Significance' means that the message is meaningful, relevant and is perceived to be suitably credible.

appear to be that the product must be different or new, that the way the advertisement is executed is different or interesting and that the message proclaims something that is personally significant to the individual in their current context. The term 'significance' means that the message is meaningful, relevant (e.g. the individual is actually looking to buy a new car or is going to buy breakfast cereals tomorrow) and is perceived to be suitably credible. These three characteristics can be tracked from the concept of ad likeability (Chapter 21) which researchers have isolated as the only meaningful indicator of the success of an advertisement.

Advertising characteristics

To be successful it is necessary for advertising to:

■ Present a new product or a product that is substantially different from the other products in the category.
■ Be interesting and stimulating.
■ Be personally significant.

The net effect of these characteristics might be that any one advertisement may be *significantly valuable* to an individual.

The strong theory of advertising may be regarded as the most applicable framework for *new brands* or those which proclaim something that is perceived to be significantly different. There is evidence that short-term sales effects can be correlated with advertising associated with these brands (Jones, 1995; McDonald, 1997). Consumers may be intrigued and interested enough to want to try the brand at the next purchase opportunity. For these people there is a high level of personal relevance derived from the message, and attitude change can be induced to convince them that it is right to make a purchase. For them the advertisement is significantly valuable and as a result may well generate a purchase decision which, from a market perspective, will drive a discernible sales increase. It may be that many of the brands that win advertising effectiveness awards fall into this category.

> *The net effect of these characteristics might be that any one advertisement may be significantly valuable to an individual.*

However, the vast majority of advertisements are about products that are not new or which are unable to proclaim or offer anything substantially different. These messages are either ignored or, if interest is aroused, certain parts of the message are filed away in memory for use at a later date. The question is, if parts are filed away, which parts are filed and why and how are they retrieved?

The weak theory suggests that advertising is really used to defend purchase behaviour. Advertising provides a rationale or explanation for why consumers (cognitive processors) have bought a brand and why they should continue buying it. Normally, advertising does not persuade – it simply reminds and reassures consumers. Or, to put it another way, consumers use advertising to remind themselves of preferred brands or to reassure themselves of their previous (and hence correct) purchase behaviour.

> *Consumers use advertising to remind themselves of preferred brands or to reassure themselves of their previous (and hence correct) purchase behaviour.*

Consumers, particularly in fast-moving consumer goods (FMCG) markets, practise repertoire buying based on habit, security, speed of decision-making and to some extent self-expression. The brands present in any single individual repertoire normally provide interest and satisfaction. Indeed, advertising needs to ensure that the brand remains in the repertoire or is sufficiently interesting to the consumer that it is included in a future repertoire. Just consider the variety of advertising messages used by mobile phone operators, such as Cellnet, One-

Cadbury's Flake

Brown (1991) reports about research concerning ads for Cadbury's Flake. This chocolate bar crumbles easily when bitten. An advertisement was devised which depicted the bar being eaten by three different people in three different contexts. The first was a secretary, who collected the crumbs in the wrapping paper. The second was a man on a train, who collected the crumbs on a plate, and the third was a small boy, who used a straw to suck up the crumbs. Each character was shown for 10 seconds, but in the tracking studies that followed it was the small boy who was recalled most, in disproportion to the time of the message exposure. See Figure 20.5.

to-One, Vodafone and Orange. These are continually updated and refreshed using particular themes which are visually engaging.

Advertising that is interesting, immediately relevant or interpreted as possessing a deep set of personal meanings (all subsequently referred to as likeable; see Chapter 21) will be stored in long-term memory (Chapter 3). As research shows repeatedly, only parts of an advertisement are ever remembered – those parts which are of intrinsic value to the recipient and are sometimes referred to as 'the take-out'. The Brown (1991) example provides suitable evidence of this phenomenon.

This selectivity, or message take-out, is referred to as the *creative magnifier* effect. Figure 20.5 illustrates the effect that parts of a message might have on the way a message is remembered.

The implication of this is that advertising works best through the creation of interest and likeable moments, from which extracts are taken by consumers and stored away in memory. Interest is generated through fresh relevant ideas where the brand and the messages are linked together in a meaningful and relevant way. This in turn allows for future associations to be made, linking brands and advertising messages in a positive and experiential way.

Advertising is used to trigger brand associations and experiences for people, not only when seated in front of a television but also when faced with product purchase decisions. Seventy per cent of low-value FMCG purchase decisions are said to be made at the point of purchase. Advertising can be used to trigger brand associations, which in turn are used to trigger advertising messages or, rather, 'likeable' extracts.

> *Advertising is used to trigger brand associations and experiences for people.*

This last point is of particular significance because advertising alone may not be sufficient to trigger complete recall of brand and advertising experiences. The brand, its

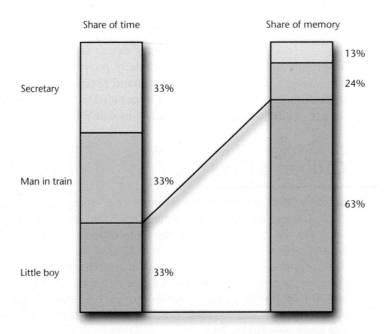

Figure 20.5   The creative magnifier. From Brown (1991); used with kind permission.

Advertising alone may not be sufficient to trigger complete recall of brand and advertising experiences. The brand, its packaging, sales promotion, outdoor media and POP all have an important role to play in providing consistency and interest and prompting recall and recognition.

packaging, sales promotion, outdoor media and POP all have an important role to play in providing consistency and interest and prompting recall and recognition. Integrated marketing communications is important, not just for message take-out or likeable extracts, but also for triggering recall and recognition and stimulating brand associations.

The model presented in Figure 20.6 attempts to bring together those elements that influence the way in which advertising might be considered to work. Stimuli act upon levels of elaboration, which in turn determine levels of cognitive processing. Likeable extracts are taken out of the messages and stored for future use. Advertising messages and/or brand experiences then allow for these extracts to be recalled. This impacts on the attitude to the brand and towards the advertisement, which affects purchase intentions. Therefore brands and advertising work together: one is capable of reinforcing the other and triggers are required to action the process and to reinforce previous behaviour.

For advertisements to be effective, they must be likeable (interesting, meaningful and relevant to the brand and the target audience) and therefore must be contextually compatible with the target audience and the brand.

Summary

Through time, a variety of models has been presented, each of which attempts to explain how advertising works. AIDA and sequential models, such as the hierarchy of

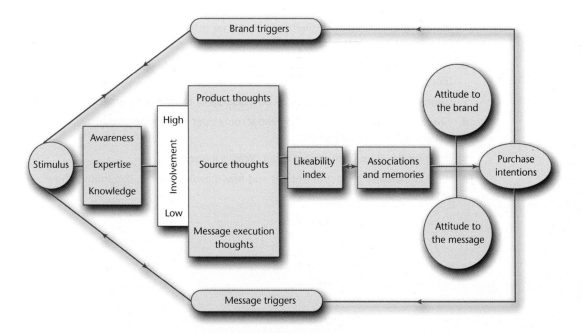

Figure 20.6   A cognitive association model of advertising/brand relationships.

effects approach, were for a long time the received wisdom in this area. Now they are regarded as quaint but out of date, for a number of hard-hitting reasons.

With the development of our understanding of cognitive processing, feelings, like-ability and elaboration, so new views of advertising have gathered pace and increased acceptance. At the same time, many writers have become sceptical of advertising's power to persuade consumers to change their purchasing habits. When brands are per-ceived to have some credible value, perhaps because they are new, then advertising might be considered to work under the strong theory.

One of the new views is that advertising should be regarded as a means of defend-ing customers' purchase decisions and for protecting markets, not building them. Reality suggests that the majority of advertising cannot claim to be of significant value to most people. Those messages that are of value are normally dissected so that only parts of the message are extracted and stored for future use. Messages or extracts of messages can be recalled or released from long-term memory when triggered by an association, such as new incoming advertising messages or brand experiences. Advertising and brands should be regarded as elements which need to work together if advertising is to be successful and brands are to survive.

Review questions

1. Explain the role that advertising plays within marketing communications.

2. Write brief notes outlining the difference between absolute and relative costs.

3. Name three sequential models of how advertising is thought to work and evaluate the ways in which they are considered to work.

4. Which element in McGuire's model separates it from other similar models?

5. What are the essential differences between the involvement and salience frameworks of advertising? Find four advertisements (other than those described in the text) that are examples of these two approaches.

6. Write a short presentation explaining the differences between the strong and weak theories of advertising.

7. Cognitive processing is thought to be made up of three main elements. Name them.

8. Give examples of peripheral and central route cues to attitude change using the elaboration likelihood model.

9. Describe the creative magnifier effect. Why is it important?

10. What is the likely impact of triggers and brand associations in determining how advertising works?

▋MINI CASE

This mini case was written by Selina Bichard, Group Communications Manager, Specsavers Optical Group.

'Artist' and 'physicist'

Specsavers Opticians

Specsavers Opticians are the UK market leaders in retail optics, with 25% share of the market by volume and 20% by value. Their main competitors are national chains such as Dolland and Aitchison, Vision Express, Leighton's and Boots, while there are a large number of independent, family-owned businesses. Specsavers Opticians have attained their strong position through their 'value for money' proposition and their strong commitment to marketing.

Sector advertising has tended to focus on price-led discounts and two-for-one sales promotions. Dolland and Aitchison use celebrity actor Burt Reynolds and a two-for-one offer, Boots offer two-for-one and a Joanna Lumley voice-over while Vision Express use their CEO and similar discounts. Specsavers Opticians wanted to distance themselves from this approach and find a more meaningful professional market position.

The campaign was commissioned specifically to support the Specsavers Opticians brand value of professionalism and to raise awareness of the importance of eyecare. With a long purchasing cycle (two years plus) and a low-value product, it is essential to stimulate demand for services and products; in retail optics product purchase is usually the result of a new prescription obtained during an eye examination. So although opticians make their money in the retail side of their operation, the opportunity to do so is not released until the professional side of the business has been addressed. While price-led advertising will attract customers already actively seeking to purchase in the eyecare market at the time, this campaign serves to encourage consumers to consider the importance of eyecare – i.e. to bring them back into the market.

The bulk of their marketing promotions are price led, as may be expected of their position in the market, but there is another significant factor. Opticians provide a professional service as well as a retail product and the two are more likely to be perceived as contradictory rather than as a natural partnership.

With a healthcare message, the campaign could not be overtly commercial, but had to attract and hold viewers' attention in the brash and busy medium of the TV commercial break. By using well-known and respected figures working in fields where their vision is crucial, Specsavers Opticians was able to convey the eyecare message in a thought-provoking way without resorting to the didacticism inherent in most 'good health' TV advertising, and in a visually interesting way that would stand out in the clutter of TV commercial messages.

The first commercial featured the famous wildlife artist David Shepherd, was highly visual and made the obvious connection between sight and the visual arts. The second, featuring Professor Stephen Hawking, reflected the two different meanings of the word vision – eyesight and the inner 'vision' that is an essential tool of the theoretical physicist. In both commercials, the focus is on the benefits of good eyesight.

Neither commercial was strongly branded; the logo and strapline appear only on the final frames. They were not heavily supported in stores, but linked to other promotional activity through ubiquitous use of the strapline. Interviews with David Shepherd and Professor Hawking appeared in *VIEW*, Specsavers Opticians' customer magazine.

The TV campaigns ran in two bursts per year, in early spring and autumn, during the 'shoulder months' between offer-led promotions of the winter, when people have more time to shop, and product-led promotions of the summer, when protection from the sun is a key consumer interest.

The campaign has succeeded in raising awareness of the importance of eyecare and has reinforced and enhanced Specsavers Opticians' reputation as caring, professional opticians.

See Plates 20.1 and 20.2

Mini-case questions

1. Does the Specsaver Opticians campaign better illustrate the strong or the weak theory of advertising? Why?
2. Position fashion spectacles and work-wear spectacles on the FCB framework (Chapter 12).
3. Discuss the view that rather than use advertising to inform about price discounts, it might be more effective to just use sales promotion activities.
4. To what extent does this campaign help or hinder cognitive processing? Does it matter?
5. Identify possible brand triggers (and possibly 'take-outs') resulting from these ad executions.

References

Aaker, D.A., Batra, R. and Myers, J.G. (1992) *Advertising Management*, 4th edn. Englewood Cliffs, NJ: Prentice Hall.

Ajzen, I. and Fishbein, M. (1980) *Understanding Attitudes and Predicting Social Behaviour*. Englewood Cliffs, NJ: Prentice Hall.

Ambler, T. (1998) Myths about the mind: time to end some popular beliefs about how advertising works. *International Journal of Advertising*, **17**, pp. 501–9.

Barry, T. and Howard, D.J. (1990) A review and critique of the hierarchy of effects in advertising. *International Journal of Advertising*, **9**, pp. 121–35.

Belch, G.E. and Belch, M.A. (1990) *An Introduction to Advertising and Promotion Management*. Homewood, IL: Richard D. Irwin.

Brown, G. (1991) *How Advertising Affects the Sales of Packaged Goods Brands*. Warwick: Millward Brown Publications.

Duckworth, G. (1995) How advertising works, the universe and everything. *Admap* (January), pp. 41–3.

Ehrenberg, A.S.C. (1974) Repetitive advertising and the consumer. *Journal of Advertising Research*, **14** (April), pp. 25–34.

Ehrenberg, A.S.C. (1988) *Repeat Buying*, 2nd edn. London: Charles Griffin.

Ehrenberg, A.S.C. (1997) How do consumers come to buy a new brand? *Admap* (March), pp. 20–4.

Fletcher, W. (1994) The advertising high ground. *Admap* (November), pp. 31–4.

Greenwald, A. (1968) Cognitive learning, cognitive response to persuasion and attitude change. In *Psychological Foundations of Attitudes* (eds A. Greenwald, T.C. Brook and T.W. Ostrom). New York: Academic Press.

Hall, M. (1992) Using advertising frameworks. *Admap* (March), pp. 17–21.

Heath, R. (2000) Low involvement processing. *Admap* (April), pp. 34–6.

Jones, J.P. (1991) Over-promise and under-delivery. *Marketing and Research Today* (November), pp. 195–203.

Jones, J.P. (1995) Advertising exposure effects under a microscope. *Admap* (February), pp. 28–31.

Lannon, J. (1992) Asking the right questions – what do people do with advertising? *Admap* (March), pp. 11–16.

Lavidge, R.J. and Steiner, G.A. (1961) A model for predictive measurements of advertising effectiveness. *Journal of Marketing* (October), p. 61.

Lutz, J., Mackensie, S.B. and Belch, G.E. (1983) Attitude toward the ad as a mediator of advertising effectiveness. *Advances in Consumer Research X*. Ann Arbor, MI: Association for Consumer Research.

McDonald, C. (1997) Short-term advertising effects: how confident can we be? *Admap* (June), pp. 36–9.

McGuire, W.J. (1978) An information processing model of advertising effectiveness. In *Behavioral and Management Science in Marketing* (eds H.L. Davis and A.J. Silk). New York: Ronald/Wiley.

Olsen, J.C. and Peter, J.P. (1987) *Consumer Behaviour*. Homewood, IL: Richard D. Irwin.

O'Malley, D. (1991) Sales without salience? *Admap* (September), pp. 36–9.

Palda, K.S. (1966) The hypothesis of a hierarchy of effects: a partial evaluation. *Journal of Marketing Research*, **3**, pp. 13–24.

Petty, R.E. and Cacioppo, J.T. (1983) Central and peripheral routes to persuasion: application to advertising. In *Advertising and Consumer Psychology* (eds L. Percy and A. Woodside). Lexington, MA: Lexington Books.

Prue, T. (1998) An all-embracing theory of how advertising works? *Admap*, (February), pp. 18–23.

Strong, E.K. (1925) *The Psychology of Selling*. New York: McGraw-Hill.

Vakratsas, D. and Ambler, T. (1999) How advertising works: what do we really know? *Journal of Marketing*, **63**, (January), pp. 26–43.

Wright, P.L. (1973) The cognitive processes mediating the acceptance of advertising. *Journal of Marketing Research*, **10** (February), pp. 53–62.

21

Advertising messages and creative approaches

The context in which people receive and interpret advertising messages must be considered thoroughly if the effectiveness of a communication is to be maximised. Ensuring that the right balance of information and emotions is achieved and that the presentation of the message is appropriate for the target audience represents a critical part of the creative process for the advertising agency and the client.

AIMS AND OBJECTIVES

The aim of this chapter is to consider some of the ways in which advertising messages can be created by focusing on some of the principal aspects of message construction.

The objectives of this chapter are:

1. To show how messages can be constructed to account for the context in which they are to be received.

2. To examine the use of emotions and feelings in advertising messages.

3. To explore the advantages and disadvantages of using spokespersons in message presentation.

4. To consider how advertising messages might be best presented.

5. To suggest how informational and transformational motives can be used as tactical tools in an advertising plan.

Introduction

Whether advertising converts people into becoming brand-loyal customers or acts as a defensive shield to reassure current buyers, and whether central or peripheral cues are required, there still remains the decision about the nature and form of the message to be conveyed: the creative strategy.

In practice, the generation of suitable messages is derived from the creative brief. For the sake of discussion and analysis, four elements will be considered. These concern the *balance*, the *structure*, the perceived *source* and the *presentation of the message* to the target audience.

The balance of the message

It is evident from previous discussions that the effectiveness of any single message is dependent upon a variety of issues. From a receiver's perspective, two elements appear to be significant: first, the amount and quality of the information that is communicated, and, second, the overall judgement that each individual makes about the way a message is communicated.

This suggests that the style of a message should reflect a balance between the need for information and the need for pleasure or enjoyment in consuming the message. Figure 21.1 describes the two main forms of appeal. Messages can be product orientated and rational or customer orientated and based upon feelings and emotions.

It is clear that when dealing with high-involvement decisions, where persuasion occurs through a central processing route, the emphasis of the message should be on the information content, in particular, the key attributes and the associated benefits. This style is often factual and product orientated. If the product evokes low-involvement decision-making, then the message should concentrate upon the images that are created within the mind of the message recipient. This style seeks to elicit an emotional response from receivers.

With high-involvement decisions, where persuasion occurs through a central processing route, the emphasis of the message should be on the information content, in particular, the key attributes and the associated benefits.

There are, of course, many situations where both rational and emotional messages are needed by buyers in order to make purchasing decisions.

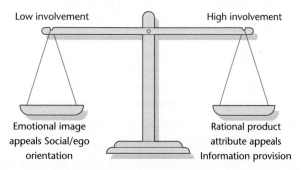

Figure 21.1   The balance of emotions and information provision.

Message style – salon brands

Salon brands of haircare products, such as Paul Mitchell, Fudge and Tigi, are distributed through hair salons and use the credibility that consumers bestow upon their 'regular' hairdressers as an important means to judge salon brands. Consumers delegate decision responsibilities to their professional.

Decisions about salon brands are made as a result of interpreting both rational and emotional messages. Rational messages are driven by the superior quality of the product and the finished about product quality, the strength of the relationship held with their hairdresser and the diagnosis that hairdressers provide. Emotional messages are derived from the packaging, the quality of the relationship with the hairdresser and the imagery associated with the relative exclusivity that salon brands afford. Younger buyers perceive increased 'shower cred' and older customers perceive indulgence and a treat factor.

Likeability

An issue that has been gaining increasing attention since the beginning of the 1990s concerns the level of likeability that an advertisement generates. Likeability is important, because learning and attitude change may be positively correlated with the degree to which consumption of the message is enjoyed. This means that the greater the enjoyment, the greater the exposure to the message and the lower the probability that the message will be perceptually zapped.

Likeability is important, because learning and attitude change may be positively correlated with the degree to which consumption of the message is enjoyed.

Biel (1990) found that changes in product preferences were considerably improved when receivers had 'liked the commercial a lot'. This compares with those who were less enthusiastic or neutral towards the advertisement. Haley (1990) reported that advertisements that create a belief that the product is excellent and where messages that are liked are commercially more successful. In other words, a message that is well liked will sell more product than a message that fails to generate interest and liking.

This begs the question, 'what makes a message liked?' Obviously, the receiver must be stimulated to become interested in the message. Having become emotionally engaged, interest can only be sustained if the credibility of the advertisement can also be maintained. The style of the message should be continued, in order that the context of the message does not require the target audience to readjust their perception. This is particularly important for low-involvement messages, where receivers have little or no interest. If the weak theory is adopted, then 'liked' advertisements will tend to be those for whom the receiver has prior experience or exposure. Messages that are well liked appear to consist of the following components (du Plessis, 1998):

1. The advertisement needs to be entertaining. This usually means that the advertisement is new and people are curious.

2. People like advertisements with which they can identify and which show them in a good light.

3. People appear to like advertisements that refer to products that are new, that tell them how the products might be useful to them and which show them how to use products.

Otherwise, perceptual selection will ensure that messages for products of which the target has no experience, or which the target has no interest in, will be screened out regardless of the quality or the likeability of the communication.

The likeability level that an advertisement achieves is not the sole reason or measure of an advertisement's success or effectiveness.
The likeability level that an advertisement achieves is not the sole reason or measure of an advertisement's success or effectiveness (Joyce, 1991). Research from The Netherlands suggests that interest is also an important and interrelated factor. Stapel (1991) strongly suggests that advertisers should make their messages interesting, as this will probably lead to liking and overall effectiveness. However, likeability and associated interest are new and interesting contributions that need to be considered when the style of an advertising message is determined.

Message consistency – BMW

When BMW (GB) was first established in 1979 it replaced a distributor which had sold a range of performance cars. The business goal was to treble sales volumes to 40,000 cars a year and to maintain the high margins.

The advertising strategy was to build on the core brand values and move the perception of BMW cars from one of *performance* to one of *reward*. The line 'Ultimate Driving Machine' was first used in 1979 and has been used to underline the BMW brand since then. A consistent tone of voice was adopted whereby the advertising messages are always factually correct and removed from other types of glamour car advertising. Because of the need to focus on the technological strengths and benefits of BMW, a policy not to include any people in the advertisements was developed. The reasoning is that people are fallible, whereas BMW technology is not.

Robin Wight at WCRS, the advertising agency responsible for the continued success of BMW in the UK, leads what is referred to as a 'product interrogation' team each year. The team visits the factory and tries to uncover from the engineers new information and developments about BMW technology.

He recalls a time when he spent half a day trying to understand why six-cylinder engines were smoother than those with four cylinders. The exasperated engineer was finally asked how he would convince his next-door neighbour not to buy a Mercedes (arch rival) but a BMW. He thought for a while and then said that he would place a glass of water on both engines. When revving the Mercedes the glass would not move but the imperfections in the balance of the engine would destabilise the water in the glass. No matter how much he revved the BMW, the water would not move.

Wight arrived back in London and tested the claim. It worked. Within 15 minutes the 'Shaken, not stirred' advertisement was created (see Plate 21.1).

Adapted from publicity materials kindly provided by BMW (1994) and Broadbent (1994)

Message structure

An important part of message strategy is the consideration of the best way of communicating the key points, or core message, to the target audience without encountering objections and opposing points of view. The following are regarded as important structural features which shape the pattern of a message.

Conclusion drawing

Should the message draw a firm conclusion for the audience or should people be allowed to draw their own conclusions from the content? Explicit conclusions are, of course, more easily understood and stand a better chance of being effective (Kardes, 1988). However, it is the nature of the issue, the particular situation and the composition of the target audience that influence the effectiveness of conclusion drawing (Hovland and Mandell, 1952). Whether or not a conclusion should be drawn for the receiver depends upon the following:

1. *The complexity of the issue*
   Healthcare products, central heating systems and personal finance services, for example, can be complex, and for some members of the target audience their cognitive ability, experience and motivation may not be sufficient for them to draw their own conclusions. The complexity of the product requires that messages must draw conclusions for them. It should also be remembered that even highly informed and motivated audiences may require assistance if the product or issue is relatively new.

2. *The level of education possessed by the receiver*
   Better-educated audiences prefer to draw their own conclusions, whereas less educated audiences may need the conclusion drawn for them because they may not be able to make the inference from the message.

3. *Whether immediate action is required*
   If urgent action is required by the receiver, then a conclusion should be drawn very clearly. Political parties can be observed to use this strategy immediately before an election.

4. *The level of involvement*
   High involvement usually means that receivers prefer to make up their own minds and may reject or resent any attempt to have the conclusion drawn for them (Arora, 1985).

One- and two-sided messages

This concerns whether the cases for and against an issue or just that in favour are presented to an audience. Messages that present just one argument, in favour of the product or issue, are referred to as one-sided. Research indicates that one-sided messages are more effective when receivers favour the opinion offered in the message and when the receivers are less educated.

One-sided messages are more effective when receivers favour the opinion offered in the message and when the receivers are less educated.

Two-sided messages, where the good and bad points of an issue are presented, are more effective when the receiver's initial opinion is opposite to that presented in the message and when they are highly educated. Credibility is improved and two-sided messages tend to produce more positive perceptions of a source than one-sided messages (Faison, 1961).

Order of presentation

Further questions regarding the development of message strategy concern the order in which important points are presented. Messages which present the strongest points at the beginning use what is referred to as the *primacy* effect. The decision to place the main points at the beginning depends on whether the audience has a low or high level of involvement. A low level may require an attention-getting message component at the beginning. Similarly, if the target has an opinion opposite to that contained in the message, a weak point may lead to a high level of counter-argument.

A decision to place the strongest points at the end of the message assumes that the *recency* effect will bring about greater levels of persuasion. This is appropriate when the receiver agrees with the position adopted by the source or has a high positive level of involvement.

The order of argument presentation is more relevant in personal selling than in television advertisements.

The order of argument presentation is more relevant in personal selling than in television advertisements. However, as learning through television is largely passive, because involvement is low and interest minimal, the presentation of key selling points at the beginning and at the end of the message will enhance message reception and recall.

Source of the message

The importance of source credibility was established during the discussion of communication theory in Chapter 2. The effect of source credibility on the effectiveness of the communication, and in particular the persuasiveness of a message, should not be underestimated. The key components of source credibility are, first, the level of perceived expertise (how much knowledge the source is thought to hold) and the personal motives the source is believed to possess. What degree of trust can be placed in the source concerning the motives for communicating the message in the first place? No matter what the level of expertise, if the level of trust is questionable, credibility will be adversely affected.

Establishing credibility

Credibility can be established in a number of ways. One simple approach is to list or display the key attributes of the organisation or the product and then signal trustworthiness through the use of third-party endorsements and the comments of satisfied users.

Trustworthiness and expertise, the two principal aspects of credibility, can be developed by using a spokesperson.

A more complex approach is to use referrals, suggestions and association. Trustworthiness and expertise, the two principal aspects of credibility, can be developed by using a spokesperson or organisation to provide testimonials on behalf of the sponsor of the advertisement. Credibility, therefore, can be established by the initiator of the advertisement or by a messenger or spokesperson used by the initiator to convey the message.

Credibility established by the initiator

The credibility of the organisation initiating the communication process is important. An organisation should seek to enhance its reputation with its various stakeholders at every opportunity. However, organisational credibility is derived from the image, which in turn is a composite of many perceptions. Past decisions, current strategy and performance indicators, level of service and the type of performance network members (e.g. high-quality retail outlets) all influence the perception of an organisation and the level of credibility that follows.

One very important factor that influences credibility is branding. Private and family brands in particular allow initiators to develop and launch new products more easily than those who do not have such brand strength. Brand extensions (such as Mars ice-cream) have been launched with the credibility of the product firmly grounded in the strength of the parent brand name (Mars). Consumers recognise the name and make associations that enable them to lower the perceived risk and in doing so provide the platform to try the new product.

The need to establish high levels of credibility also allows organisations to divert advertising spend away from a focus upon brands to one that focuses upon the organisation. Corporate advertising seeks to adjust organisation image and to build reputation.

Credibility established by a spokesperson

People who deliver the message are often regarded as the source, when in reality they are only the messenger. These people carry the message and represent the true source or initiator of the message (e.g. manufacturer or retailer). Consequently, the testimonial they transmit must be credible. There are four main types of spokesperson: the expert, the celebrity, the chief executive officer and the consumer.

The expert has been used many times and was particularly popular when television advertising first established itself in the 1950s and 1960s. Experts are quickly recognisable because they either wear white coats and round glasses or dress and act like 'mad professors'. Through the use of symbolism, stereotypes and identification, these characters (and indeed others) can be established very quickly in the minds of receivers and a frame of reference generated which does not question the authenticity of the message being transmitted by such a person. Experts can also be users of products, for example, professional photographers endorsing cameras, secretaries endorsing word processors and professional golfers endorsing golf equipment (Exhibit 21.1).

Experts can also be users of products, for example, professional photographers endorsing cameras, secretaries endorsing word processors.

Entertainment and sporting celebrities have been used increasingly in the 1990s, not only to provide credibility for a range of high-involvement (e.g. Angus Deayton for Barclaycard and Marianne Faithfull for Virgin Atlantic, see Plate 21.2) and low-involvement decisions (e.g. David Beckham for Brylcream) but also to grab the attention of people in markets where motivation to decide between competitive products may be low. The celebrity enables the message to stand out among the clutter and noise that typify many markets. It is also hoped that the celebrity and or the voice-over will become a peripheral cue in the decision-making process: Joanna Lumley for Boots Opticians and AOL email, Gary Lineker for Walkers Crisps and Heather Lockyear for L'Oréal.

Exhibit 21.1   Sir Richard Branson being used to endorse APA. Picture kindly supplied by APA. Photograph by Steve Pike.

Walkers Crisps

Walkers Crisps have embarked upon a series of campaigns that have incorporated a consistent communications mix. The objective was to revive and reposition the brand, and this has been achieved using television and Gary Lineker as the central spokesperson to appeal to both adults and teenagers.

Lineker has been a consistent element throughout all the campaigns and is presented and perceived as a cheeky but fun endorser for the brand. Advertisements with a number of related spokespersons, such as Paul Gascoigne and the Spice Girls, have been mixed with messages with unrelated spokespersons, such as everyday people and even a nun. These campaigns have been used to promote sales promotions such as competitions, from which a tremendous amount of PR media coverage has been generated.

The market has grown by 11%, but Walkers have achieved growth of 21%. They have revived their brand, achieved market leadership and profitability and repositioned themselves as the number one snack food brand in the UK through the use of IMC.

There are some potential problems which advertisers need to be aware of when considering the use of celebrities. First, does the celebrity fit the image of the brand and will the celebrity be acceptable to the target audience? Consideration also needs to be

Does the celebrity fit the image of the brand and will the celebrity be acceptable to the target audience?

given to the longer-term relationship between the celebrity and the brand. Should the lifestyle of the celebrity change, what impact will the change have on the target audience and their attitude towards the brand? Witness the separation of the (then) England football coach, Glenn Hoddle, and his wife, and the consequent termination of the Weetabix advertisement set around the family breakfast table.

This matching process can be used to change brand attitudes as well as reinforce them. BT wanted to change the attitude that men had to telephone calls. Rather than being just the bill payer and the gatekeeper of calls to other members of the family, the role Bob Hoskins had was to demonstrate male behaviour and to present a solution that was acceptable to all members of the family. Attitudes held by men towards the telephone and its use changed significantly as a result of the campaign, partly because Hoskins was perceived as a credible spokesperson, someone with whom men could identify and feel comfortable.

The second problem concerns the impact that the celebrity makes relative to the brand. There is a danger that the receiver remembers the celebrity but not the message or the brand that is the focus of the advertising spend. The celebrity becomes the hero, rather than the product being advertised. Summers (1993) suggests that the Cinzano advertisements featuring Joan Collins and Leonard Rossiter are a classic example of the problem: 'The characters so dwarfed the product that consumers may have had trouble recalling the brand'.

Issues such as brand development can also be impeded when identification by an audience with the celebrity is strong. Sony had to fade audiences away from its association with John Cleese by using a Robot/Cleese lookalike for a period.

Richard Branson is used to promote Virgin Financial products and Victor Kiam 'so liked the razor that he bought the company' (Remington). Here, the CEO openly promotes his company. This form of testimonial is popular when the image of the CEO is positive and the photogenic and on-screen characteristics provide for enhanced credibility. Bernard Mathews has established authenticity and trustworthiness with his personal promotion of Norfolk Roasts. See also Chapter 7 and the concept of strategic credibility.

The final form of spokesperson is the consumer. By using consumers to endorse products, the audience is being asked to identify with a 'typical consumer'. The identification of similar lifestyles, interests and opinions allows for better reception and understanding of the message. Consumers are often depicted testing similar products, such as margarine and butter. The Pepsi Challenge required consumers to select Pepsi from Coca-Cola through blind taste tests. By showing someone using the product, someone who is similar to the receiver, the source is perceived as credible and the potential for successful persuasion is considerably enhanced.

Sleeper effects

The assumption so far has been that high credibility enhances the probability of persuasion and successful communication. This is true when the receiver's initial position is opposite to that contained in the message.

When the receiver's position is favourable to the message a moderate level of credibility may be more appropriate.

When the receiver's position is favourable to the message, a moderate level of credibility may be more appropriate.

Whether source credibility is high, medium or low is of little consequence, according to some researchers (Hannah and Sternthal, 1984). The impact of the source is believed to dissipate after approximately six weeks and only the content of the message is thought to dominate the receiver's attention. This sleeper effect (Hovland *et al.*, 1949) has not been proved empirically, but the implication is that the persuasiveness of a message can increase through time. Furthermore, advertisers using highly credible sources need to repeat the message on a regular basis, in order that the required level of effectiveness and persuasion be maintained (Schiffman and Kanuk, 1991).

Presentation of the message

The presentation of the promotional message requires that an appeal be made to the target audience. The appeal is important, because unless the execution of the message appeal (the creative) is appropriate to the target audience's perception and expectations, the chances of successful communication are reduced.

There are two main factors associated with the presentation. Is the message to be dominated by the need to transmit product-orientated information or is there a need to transmit a message which appeals predominantly to the emotional senses of the receiver? The main choice of presentation style, therefore, concerns the degree of factual information transmitted in a message against the level of imagery thought necessary to make sufficient impact for the message to command attention and then be processed.

The main choice of presentation style, therefore, concerns the degree of factual information transmitted in a message against the level of imagery thought necessary to make sufficient impact for the message to command attention.

There are numerous presentational or executional techniques, but the following are some of the more commonly used appeals.

Appeals based upon the provision of information

Factual

Sometimes referred to as the 'hard sell', the dominant objective of these appeals is to provide information. This type of appeal is commonly associated with high-involvement decisions where receivers are sufficiently motivated and able to process information. Persuasion, according to the ELM, is undertaken through the central processing route. This means that advertisements should be rational and contain logically reasoned arguments and information in order that receivers are able to complete their decision-making processes.

Slice of life

As noted earlier, the establishment of credibility is vital if any message is to be accepted. One of the ways in which this can be achieved is to present the message in such a way that the receiver can identify immediately with the scenario being presented. This process of creating similarity is used a great deal in advertising and is referred to as slice-of-life advertising. For example, many washing powder advertisers use a routine that depicts two ordinary women (assumed to be similar to the target receiver), invariably in a kitchen or garden, discussing the poor results

One of the ways in which this can be achieved is to present the message in such a way that the receiver can identify immediately with the scenario being presented.

BA don't give a Shiatsu.

UpperClass Free onboard massage.   virgin atlantic

achieved by one of their washing powders. Following the advice of one of the women, the stubborn stains are seen to be overcome by the focus brand.

The overall effect of this appeal is for the receiver to conclude the following: that person is like me; I have had the same problem as that person; he or she is satisfied using brand X, therefore, I too will use brand X. This technique is simple, well tried, well liked and successful, despite its sexist overtones. It is also interesting to note that a number of surveys have found that a majority of women feel that advertisers use inappropriate stereotyping to portray females roles, these being predominantly housewife and mother roles.

Demonstration

A similar technique is to present the problem to the audience as a demonstration. The focus brand is depicted as instrumental in the resolution of a problem. Headache remedies, floor cleaners and tyre commercials have traditionally demonstrated the pain, the dirt and the danger respectively and then shown how the focus brand relieves the pain (Panadol), removes the stubborn dirt (Flash) or stops in the wet on a coin (or edge of a rooftop – Continental tyres). Whether the execution is believable is a function of the credibility and the degree of life-like dialogue or copy that is used.

Comparative advertising

Comparative advertising is a popular means of positioning brands. Messages are based upon the comparison of the focus brand with either a main competitor brand or all competing brands, with the aim of establishing superiority. See Exhibit 21.2. The comparison may centre upon one or two key attributes and can be a good way of entering new markets. Entrants keen to establish a presence in a market have little to lose by comparing themselves with market leaders. However, market leaders have a great deal to lose and little to gain by comparing themselves with minor competitors.

Channel crossings

When the Channel tunnel was opened it was necessary for Eurotunnel to provide a series of benefits to encourage consumers to rationalise their use of the tunnel in preference to the established ferry crossing. A series of messages was used, one of which was to suggest that the EuroStar service reduced the travel time to get to France; another was to suggest through a poster depicting a rough sea, that Eurostar was smooth and free of sea-sickness discomfort. The ferry operators responded with messages that showed the ferry crossing to be an integral part of a holiday experience and that the ferry was like a mini cruise, with all the attendant feelings associated with that type of holiday.

Appeals based upon emotions and feelings

Appeals based on logic and reason are necessary in particular situations. However, as products become similar and as consumers become more aware of the range of available products, so the need to differentiate becomes more important. Increasing numbers of advertisers are using messages which seek to appeal to the target's emotions and feelings, a 'soft sell'. Cars, toothpaste, toilet tissue and mineral water often use emotion-based messages to differentiate their products.

There are a number of appeals that can be used to solicit an emotional response from the receiver. Of the many techniques available, the main ones that can be observed to be used most are fear, humour, animation, sex, music, and fantasy and surrealism.

Fear

Fear is used in one of two ways. The first type demonstrates the negative aspects or physical dangers associated with a particular behaviour or improper product usage.

The threat of social rejection or disapproval if the focus product is not used.

Drink driving, life assurance and toothpaste advertising typify this form of appeal. The second approach is the threat of social rejection or disapproval if the focus product is not used. This type of fear is used frequently in advertisements for such products as anti-dandruff shampoos and deodorants and is used to support consumers' needs for social acceptance and approval.

Fear appeals need to be constrained, if only to avoid being categorised as outrageous and socially unacceptable. There is a great deal of evidence that fear can facilitate attention and interest in a message and even motivate an individual to take a particular course of action: for example, to stop smoking. Fear appeals are persuasive, according to Schiffman and Kanuk (1991), when low to moderate levels of fear are induced. Ray and Wilkie (1970), however, show that should the level of fear rise too much, inhibiting effects may prevent the desired action occurring. This inhibition is caused by the individual choosing to screen out, through perceptive selection, messages that conflict with current behaviour. The outcome may be that individuals deny the existence of a problem, claim there is no proof or say that it will not happen to them.

Humour

The use of humour as an emotional appeal is attractive because it can draw attention and stimulate interest. A further reason to use humour is that it can put the receiver in a positive mood. Mood can also be important, as receivers in a positive mood are likely to process advertising messages with little cognitive elaboration (Batra and Stayman, 1990). This can occur because there is less effort involved with peripheral rather than central cognitive processing, and this helps to mood protect. In other words, the positive mood state is more likely to be maintained if cognitive effort is avoided. Yellow Pages have used humour quietly to help convey the essence of their brand and to help differentiate it from the competition (see Plate 21.3).

It is also argued that humour is effective because argument quality is likely to be high. That is, the level of counter-argument can be substantially reduced. Arguments against the use of humour concern distraction from the focus brand, so that while attention is drawn, the message itself is lost. With the move to global branding and standardisation of advertising messages, humour does not travel well. While the level and type of humour are difficult to gauge in the context of the processing abilities of a domestic target audience, cultural differences seriously impede the transfer of jokes around the world. Visual humour (lavatorial, Benny Hill type approaches) is more universally acceptable (Archer, 1994) than word-based humour, as the latter can get lost in translation without local references to provide clues to decipher the joke. Humour, therefore, is a potentially powerful yet dangerous form

Cultural differences seriously impede the transfer of jokes around the world.

of appeal. Haas (1997) reports that UK advertising executives have significantly higher confidence in the use of humour than their US counterparts, but concludes that 'humour is a vague concept and that its perception is influenced by many factors'. These factors shape the context in which messages are perceived and the humour conveyed.

Animation

Animation techniques have advanced considerably in recent years, with children as the prime target audience. However, animation has been successfully used in many adult-targeted advertisements, such as those by Schweppes, Compaq, Tetley Tea, Direct Line Insurance and the Electricity Board. The main reason for using animation is that potentially boring and low-interest/involvement products can be made visually interesting and provide a means of gaining attention. A further reason for the use of animation is that it is easier to convey complex products in a way that does not patronise the viewer.

Tax returns – self-assessment

In the two-year period leading to the introduction of self-assessment, the Inland Revenue had to raise awareness of the new system and encourage the self-employed and higher-rate tax payers, in particular, to keep tax records and meet particular deadlines for the submission of the new-style tax returns.

Exhibit 21.3 Hector the Tax Inspector – animated character used to reduce perceived risk and increase awareness of the self-assessment programme. Picture reproduced with the kind permission of the Inland Revenue.

Tax matters are normally assumed to instil feelings of panic and fear and so it was decided to use an animated personality, Hector, as an approachable tax inspector as a device to create impact. A campaign that used TV, press, direct mail and a variety of ambient media helped drive awareness of self-assessment from 26% in 1995 to 99% of the self-employed in 1997 and 96% of higher-rate tax payers in November 1997.

Since self-assessment was introduced, Hector's role is to remind the self-employed about tax-related deadlines, provide continuity and reduce levels of fear and panic. Awareness levels now run at 95% for the self-employed and 96% in the higher-rate tax payers group.

Hector was retired in January 2001 to reflect the Revenue's more modern business approach and its strategic diversity as an organisation and as a service provider. See Exhibit 21.3.

Materials kindly supplied by the Inland Revenue

Sex

Sexual innuendo and the use of sex as a means of promoting products and services are both common and controversial. Using sex as an appeal in messages is excellent for gaining the attention of buyers. Research shows, however, that it often achieves little else, particularly when the product is unrelated. Therefore, sex appeals normally work well for products such as perfume, clothing and jewelry but provide for poor effectiveness when the product is unrelated, such as cars, photocopiers and furniture. Häagen-Dazs premium ice-cream entered the UK market using pleasure as central to the message appeal. This approach was novel to the product class and the direct, natural relationship between the product and the theme contributed to the campaign's success.

Using sex as an appeal in messages is excellent for gaining the attention of buyers.

The use of sex in advertising messages is mainly restricted to getting the attention of the audience and, in some circumstances, sustaining interest. It can be used openly, as in various lingerie, fragrance and perfume advertisements, such as WonderBra and Escape, sensually, as in the Häagen-Dazs and Cointreau campaigns, and humorously in the Locketts brand.

Music

Music can provide continuity between a series of advertisements can and also be a good peripheral cue. A jingle, melody or tune, if repeated sufficiently, can become associated with the advertisement. Processing and attitudes towards the advertisement may be directly influenced by the music. Music has the potential to gain attention and assist product differentiation. Braithwaite and Ware (1997) found that music in advertising messages is used primarily either to create a mood or to send a branded message. In addition, music can also be used to signal a lifestyle and so communicate a brand identity through the style of music used.

Many advertisements for cars use music, partly because it is difficult to find a point of differentiation (*Independent*, 18 October 1996), and music is able to draw attention, generate mood and express brand personality (e.g. Rover, BMW, Nissan Micra, Peugeot, Renault).

Some luxury and executive cars are advertised using commanding background music to create an aura of power, prestige and affluence, which is combined with strong visual images in order that an association be made between the car and the environment in which it is positioned. There is a contextual juxtaposition between the car and the environment presented. Readers may notice a semblance of classical conditioning, where the music acts as an unconditioned stimulus. Foxall and Goldsmith (1994) suggest that the stimulus elicits the unconditioned emotional responses that may lead to the purchase of the advertised product.

Some luxury and executive cars are advertised using commanding background music to create an aura of power, prestige and affluence.

Fantasy and surrealism

The use of fantasy and surrealism in advertising has grown partly as a result of the increased clutter and legal constraints imposed on some product classes. By using fantasy appeals, associations with certain images and symbols allow the advertiser to focus attention on the product. The receiver can engage in the distraction offered and become involved with the execution of the advertisement. If this is a rewarding experience it may be possible to affect the receiver's attitudes peripherally. Readers may notice that this links to the earlier discussion on 'liking the advertisement'.

By using fantasy appeals, associations with certain images and symbols allow the advertiser to focus attention on the product.

Finally, an interesting contribution to the discussion of message appeal has been made by Lannon (1992). She reports that consumers' expectations of advertisements can be interpreted on the one hand as either literal or stylish and on the other as serious or entertaining, according to the tone of voice. This approach vindicates the view that consumers are active problem solvers and willing and able to decode increasingly complex messages. They can become involved with the execution of the advertisement and the product attributes. The degree of involvement (she argues implicitly) is a function of the motivation each individual has at any one moment when exposed to a particular message.

Advertisers can challenge individuals by presenting questions and visual stimuli that demand attention and cognitive response. Guinness challenged consumers to decode a series of advertisements which were unlike all previous Guinness advertisements and, indeed, all messages in the product class. The celebrity chosen was dressed completely in black, which contrasted with his blonde hair, and he was shown in various time periods, past and future, and environments that receivers did not expect. He was intended to represent the personification of the drink and symbolised the individual nature of the product. Audiences were puzzled by the presentation and many rejected the challenge of interpretation. 'Surfer' and 'Bet on Black' are more recent Guinness campaigns which seek to convey the importance and necessity to wait (for the drink to be poured properly). To accomplish this, it portrays a variety of situations in which patience results in achievement.

Advertisers can challenge individuals by presenting questions and visual stimuli that demand attention and cognitive response.

When individuals respond positively to a challenge, the advertiser can either provide closure (an answer) or, through surreal appeals, leave the receivers to answer the questions themselves in the context in which they perceive the message. One way of achieving this challenging position is to use an appeal that cognitively disorients the receiver (Parker and Churchill, 1986). If receivers are led to ask the question 'What is

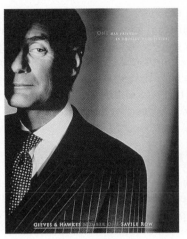

Exhibit 21.4
A series of print advertisements designed to challenge readers by encouraging the question 'what is going on here?' Picture reproduced with kind permission of Gieves and Hawkes.

going on here?' their involvement in the message is likely to be very high. See Exhibit 21.4 for an excellent example of a print advertisement for Gieves and Hawkes that deliberately seeks to stimulate the reader to ask the question 'What is this?' Benetton consistently raises questions through its advertising. By presenting a series of messages that are socially disorientating, and for many disconcerting, Benetton continually presents a challenge that moves away from involving individuals into an approach where salience and 'standing out' predominates. This high-risk strategy, with a risk of rejection, has prevailed for a number of years.

The surrealist approach does not provide or allow for closure. The conformist approach, by contrast, does require closure in order to avoid any possible counter-arguing and message rejection. Parker and Churchill argue that, by leaving questions unanswered, receivers can become involved in both the product and the execution of the advertisement. Indeed, most advertisements contain a measure of rational and emotional elements. A blend of the two elements is necessary and the right mixture is dependent upon the perceived risk and motivation that the target audience has at any one particular moment.

The message appeal should be a balance of the informative and emotional dimensions. Furthermore, message quality is of paramount importance. Buzzell (1964) reported that 'Advertising message quality is more important than the level of advertising expenditure'. Adams and Henderson Blair (1992) confirm that the weight of advertising is relatively unimportant, and that the quality of the appeal is the dominant factor. However, the correct blend of informative and emotional elements in any appeal is paramount for persuasive effectiveness.

The message appeal should be a balance of the informative and emotional dimensions.

Advertising tactics

The main creative elements of a message need to be brought together in order for an advertising plan to have substance. The processes used to develop message appeals need to be open but systematic.

The level of involvement and combination of the think/emotional dimensions that receivers bring to their decision-making processes are the core concepts to be considered when creating an advertising message. Rossiter and Percy (1997) have devised a deductive framework which involves the disaggregation of the emotional (feel) dimension to a greater degree than that proposed by Vaughn (1980) (see Chapter 12 for details). They claim that there are two broad types of motive that drive attitudes towards purchase behaviour. These are informational and transformational motives and these will now be considered in turn.

Informational motives

Individuals have a need for information to counter negative concerns about a purchase decision. These informational motives are said to be negatively charged feelings. They can become positively charged, or the level of concern can be reduced considerably, by the acquisition of relevant information.

Motive	Possible emotional state
Problem removal	Anger – relief
Problem avoidance	Fear – relaxation
Incomplete satisfaction	Disappointment – optimism
Mixed approach–avoidance	Guilt – peace of mind
Normal depletion	Mild annoyance – convenience

Transformational motives

Promises to enhance or to improve the user of a brand are referred to as transformational motives. These are related to the user's feelings and are capable of transforming a user's emotional state, hence they are positively charged. Three main transformational motives have been distinguished by Rossiter *et al.* (1991):

Motive	Possible emotional state
Sensory gratification	Dull – elated
Intellectual stimulation	Bored – excited
Social approval	Apprehensive – flattered

Various emotional states can be associated with each of these motives, and they should be used to portray an emotion that is appropriate to the needs of the target audience.

One of the key promotion objectives, identified earlier, is the need to create or improve levels of awareness regarding the product or organisation. This is achieved by determining whether awareness is required at the point of purchase or prior to purchase. Brand recognition (at the point of purchase) requires an emphasis upon visual stimuli, the package and the brand name, whereas brand recall (prior to purchase) requires an emphasis on a limited number of peripheral cues. These may be particular copy lines, the use of music or colours for continuity and attention-getting frequent use of the brand name in the context of the category need, or perhaps the use of strange or unexpected presentation formats.

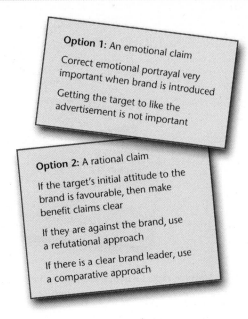

Figure 21.2   Message tactics where there are high involvement and informational motives. Based on Rossiter and Percy (1997); used with kind permission.

Advertising tactics can be determined by the particular combination of involvement and motives that exist at a particular time within the target audience. If a high-involvement decision process is determined, with people using a central processing route, then the types of tactics shown in Figures 21.2 and 21.3 are recommended by Rossiter and Percy (1997). If a low-involvement decision process is determined, with the

Advertising tactics can be determined by the particular combination of involvement and motives that exist at a particular time within the target audience.

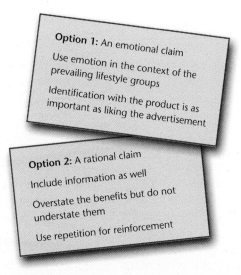

Figure 21.3   Message tactics where there are high involvement and transformational motives. Based on Rossiter and Percy (1997); used with kind permission.

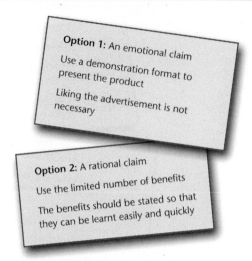

Figure 21.4 Message tactics where there are low involvement and informational motives. Based on Rossiter and Percy (1997); used with kind permission.

target audience using a peripheral processing route, then the types of tactics shown in Figures 21.4 and 21.5 are recommended.

The Rossiter–Percy approach provides for a range of advertising tactics that are orientated to the conditions that are determined by the interplay of the level of involvement and the type of dominant motivation. These conditions may only exist within a member of the target audience for a certain time. Consequently, they may change and the advertising tactics may also have to change to meet the new conditions. There are two main points that emerge from the work of Rossiter and Percy. The first is that all messages should be designed to carry both rational, logical information and emotional stimuli, but in varying degrees and forms. Second, low-involvement conditions require the use of just one or two benefits in a message, whereas high-involvement

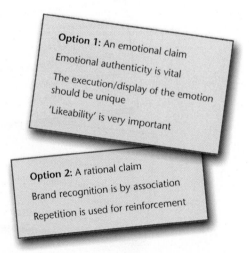

Figure 21.5 Message tactics where there are low involvement and transformational motives. Based on Rossiter and Percy (1997); used with kind permission.

conditions can sustain a number of different benefit claims. This is because persuasion through the central processing route is characterised by an evaluation of the alternatives within any one product category.

Summary

Advertising has an important role to play in most promotional plans. It is used primarily to build awareness and to usher in the other tools of the mix. The tasks that advertising is expected to achieve will have been set out in the promotional objectives and they will require communication with target consumers and organisational buyers.

Advertising is normally regarded as a tool that can persuade and change the behaviour of individuals, but there are a growing number of researchers who believe that its prime use is to defend loyal customers from the attacks of competitor products, by reinforcing attitudes.

The design and assembly of advertising messages is crucially important. Through establishment of a good realm of understanding, messages can be created in such a way that they stand a far greater opportunity of building a dialogue between members of the target audience and the brand. By appreciating the underlying emotions of the target buyer and the motivations which drive attitudes and purchase intentions, the balance and the pattern they assume can be shaped in such a way that they lead to effective advertising.

Review questions

1. Describe each of the four elements needed to create promotional messages.
2. Discuss what is meant by the term 'balance' when applied to an advertising message.
3. How might an understanding of conclusion drawing assist the development of an advertising message?
4. What is 'likeability' when applied to advertising?
5. Select five print advertisements and comment on the nature and extent to which the order of presentation features in each of them.
6. Why do advertisers use spokespersons in their advertising?
7. Find examples of each type of spokesperson.
8. What are the main types of appeal that are used by advertisers?
9. Find examples of advertising messages for each of the main appeals identified.
10. Explain the difference between informational and transformational motivations.

MINI CASE

This mini case was written by Dr Mary Carberry, Senior Lecturer in Marketing at the University of Portsmouth.

Brand revival

Bally

Retailers agree luxury footwear creates some of fashion's most loyal customers. Shoes may make the man, but customers spending between $250 and $1,000 and beyond for footwear are not going to limit their discretionary income and discriminating taste to their feet.

The UK retail footwear market underwent several years of stagnation during the 1990s. However, as a result of the strong UK economy, the demand for high-quality shoes has opened the opportunity for diversifying into a niche-orientated footwear market, where the market growth is expected to be around £6.6 billion between 1999 and 2003 (Keynote, 1999). UK manufacturers such as C & J Clark and R. Griggs, although producing footwear for the general market, cannot compete with the style gurus of Gucci, Louis Vitton and Bally.

Company history

'Bally', founded in 1851 by Carl Franz Bally, was originally a family ribbon business. During a trip to Paris, Carl purchased several pairs of handmade shoes for his wife. While identifying the marketing potential for such products he also recognised the limitations of handmade shoes and so he developed the first mechanised shoe-manufacturing technique. The company flourished and by 1864 the company's annual turnover was $100 million. Global expansion quickly followed to the extent that by 1880 the company was selling across Europe, the Middle East and Americas. In 1882 the doors opened to its first store on London's fashionable New Bond Street. Like many other companies, the world depression during the 1930s affected sales but after the Second World War Bally enjoyed a revival in its fortunes. The 1970s saw some major changes in the company with international distribution diversifying into handbags and other leather goods. Furthermore, ownership moved from the Bally family in 1977 tc Werner K. Rey, a Swiss inventor who only possessed the majority stake in Bally for nine months before he sold his shares to the Oerlikon-Buhrle Group – principally known as Swiss armaments manufacturers. During this ownership the 'Bally' brand quickly became diluted through inappropriate licensing agreements and improper distribution. The net effect of this brand mismanagement was that by 1998, the company was making a loss in the region of 100 million Swiss francs per annum.

Seeking to reverse this decline, Texas Pacific Group (TPG) bought Bally for $200 million in 1999, with a strategy to streamline company operations and give the 150 year old Swiss footwear brand a huge jolt of youthful sex appeal. Crucial to this strategy, Bally hired designer Scott Fellows and his hand-picked management team to mastermind the brand's transformation. The management team quickly identified that their competition was not the middle market, which Bally had previously targeted, but high-class brand players such as Gucci and Louis Vitton. Both Gucci and Louis Vitton provide offerings in handbags, other leather goods, ready-to-wear clothing, etc. and are the byword for luxury.

Gucci, in particular, typified 'luxury' through its brand image which was built around the architecture of its stores, which can be seen both in its advertising and clothing, allowing the brand to speak to a global consumer.

As part of TPG's revival brand strategy for Bally just about every detail from the company's merchandising to the latest ad campaign was revised and, like other revived brands, Bally took a good look at its past before designing its future.

The branding strategy

TPG had decided to move the Bally brand from fancy goods and to return it to the luxury goods sector on a par with Gucci and Louis Vitton (part of LVMH). The new management quickly identified Bally's weaknesses: the disparate, fragmented product assortment of several thousand product offerings, lack of quality control and increasingly ageing clientele. During 1999 sweeping internal measures were undertaken by the management resulting in 1,000 job cuts worldwide, including selling their third manufacturing plant in Norwich, England, to the management, 100 Bally-owned stores being closed and deliveries to 1,600 retail outlets which did not live up to the new image suspended. The result was that the product assortment for 2001 had been scaled down to around 300 items and the company had a network of 280 retail stores and 1,080 wholesale doors opened worldwide.

The repositioning strategy employed by the Bally management team followed the shoes-to-leather-to-collection formula successfully employed by other companies such as Gucci (which took four years to reduce the number of licences for its products), however, the time frame set for the brand turnaround was only four years. The first stage in the repositioning strategy was to create a range of leather accessories partly because of the fashion strategy being followed but mainly for fast sales to overcome the current company deficit, Scott Fellows' rationale being that 'we want to follow in the footsteps of the company's history and so become the Armani of the leather business'.

As part of Bally's new brand image, TPG refurbished and upgraded all of the retail outlets, combining the modern minimalist style of the store furnishings with Swiss wooden panelling on the walls and floors. A decision was also made to provide the clientele with an identical assortment of merchanise worldwide. Previously, Bally operated at a local level in all its international markets with the Bally brand image and marketing support altering between countries, for example, the brand was seen as high class in America and middle market in the UK. The essence of the new brand strategy was the deployment of the new logo, corporate colours red, brown, beige and white playing a significant role in store design, and the new luxury price point of £200–£500.

The product range itself involved the redesign of their leather accessories (travel bags, computer bags, etc.) and the creation of a clothing collection. These product ranges were test marketed during 2000 with the major product launch to the public occurring in the autumn of 2001. Bally's new target segment were young high earners and they were depicted in various repositioning campaigns using 'hyper-realistic photos', a similar strategy to that of to their main competitors, Gucci and Louis Vitton.

As with all fashion collections, retail outlets purchase their ranges 12 months in advance. Thus, the fact that Bally has had to adjust its price point for the men's wear autumn 2001 collection indicates that all is not running smoothly in its new repositioning strategy.

Mini-case questions

1. How might Bally establish brand credibility? If a spokesperson is to be used, who might that be?
2. Apply and evaluate the ideas concerning the *balance*, *structure*, perceived *source* and the *presentation of the message* to Bally and its desired new position.
3. Many companies are taking on board 'act global, think local'. Is this appropriate for the luxury accessory market? Do you think the global marketing and branding strategy employed by Bally is appropriate?
4. Visit the Bally, Gucci and Louis Vitton Web sites. Prepare a list of similarities and differences between these luxury brands. Can Bally really be seen as a luxury global brand in comparison with its major competitors?

   http://www.ballyswiss.com/
   http://www.gucci.com/
   http://www.lvmh.com/

References

Adams, A.J. and Henderson Blair, M. (1992) Persuasive advertising and sales accountability. *Journal of Advertising Research*, **32**(2) (March/April), pp. 20–5.

Archer, B. (1994) Does humour cross borders? *Campaign*, 17 June, pp. 32–3.

Arora, R. (1985) Consumer involvement: what it offers to advertising strategy. *International Journal of Advertising*, **4**, pp. 119–30.

Batra, R. and Stayman, D.M. (1990) The role of mood in advertising effectiveness. *Journal of Consumer Research*, **17** (September), pp. 203–14.

Biel, A. (1990) Love the ad. Buy the product? *Admap* (September), pp. 35–40.

Braithwaite, A. and Ware, R. (1997) The role of music in advertising. *Admap* (July/August), pp. 44–7.

Broadbent, T. (1994) *How 15 years of consistent advertising helped BMW treble sales without losing prestige*. IPA Advertising Effectiveness Awards. London: WCRS.

Buzzell, R. (1964) Predicting short-term changes in market share as a function of advertising strategy. *Journal of Marketing Research*, **1**(3), pp. 27–31.

Faison, E.W. (1961) Effectiveness of one-sided and two-sided mass communications in advertising. *Public Opinion Quarterly*, **25** (Fall), pp. 468–9.

Foxall, G.R. and Goldsmith, R.E. (1994) *Consumer Psychology for Marketing*. London: Routledge.

Haas, O. (1997) Humour in advertising. *Admap* (July/August), pp. 14–15.

Haley, R.I. (1990) Final report of the Copy Research Validity Project. Advertising Research Foundation Copy Research Workshop, July.

Hannah, D.B. and Sternthal, B. (1984) Detecting and explaining the sleeper effect. *Journal of Consumer Research*, 11 September, pp. 632–42.

Hovland, C.I. and Mandell, W. (1952) An experimental comparison of conclusion drawing by the communicator and by the audience. *Journal of Abnormal and Social Psychology*, **47** (July), pp. 581–8.

Hovland, C.I., Lumsdaine, A. and Sheffield, F.D. (1949) *Experiments on Mass Communication*. New York: Wiley.

Joyce, T. (1991) Models of the advertising process. *Marketing and Research Today* (November), pp. 205–12.

Kardes, F.R. (1988) Spontaneous inference processes in advertising: the effects of conclusion omission and involvement on persuasion. *Journal of Consumer Research*, **15** (September), pp. 225–33.

Keynote Report (1999) Clothing and Footwear (UK), March.

Lannon, J. (1992) Asking the right questions – what do people do with advertising? *Admap* (March), pp. 11–16.

Parker, R. and Churchill, L. (1986) Positioning by opening the consumer's mind. *International Journal of Advertising*, **5**, pp. 1–13.

du Plessis, E. (1998) Advertising likeability. *Admap* (October), pp. 34–6.

Ray, M.L. and Wilkie, W.L. (1970) Fear: the potential of an appeal neglected by marketing. *Journal of Marketing*, **34** (January), pp. 54–62.

Rossiter, J.R. and Percy, L. (1997) *Advertising and Promotion Management*, 2nd edn. New York: McGraw-Hill.

Rossiter, J.R., Percy, L. and Donovan, R.J. (1991) A better advertising planning grid. *Journal of Advertising Research* (October/November), pp. 11–21.

Schiffman, L.G. and Kanuk, L. (1991) *Consumer Behaviour*, 4th edn. Englewood Cliffs, NJ: Prentice Hall.

Stapel, J. (1991) Like the ad . . . but does it interest me? *Admap* (April), pp. 30–1.

Summers, D. (1993) Dangerous liaisons. *Financial Times*, 18 November, p. 12.

Vaughn, R. (1980) How advertising works: a planning model. *Journal of Advertising Research*, **20**(5), pp. 27–33.

Useful or supporting Internet site addresses

http://www.ballyswiss.com/

http://www.keynote.com/

http://strategis.gc.com/

22

Media and media planning – delivering the message

Media planning is essentially a selection and scheduling exercise. The selection refers to the choice of media vehicles to carry the message on behalf of the advertiser. Scheduling refers to the number of occasions, timing and duration that a message is exposed, in the selected vehicles, to the target audience.

AIMS AND OBJECTIVES

The aims of this chapter are to introduce the fundamental elements of media planning and to set out some of the issues facing media planners.

The objectives of this chapter are:

1. To explain the role of the media planner and to highlight the impact of media and audience fragmentation.

2. To examine the key concepts used in media selection: reach and cover, frequency, duplication, rating points and CPT.

3. To provide an understanding of how learning and forgetting by individuals affect the selection and use of media vehicles.

4. To appreciate the concept of repetition and the debate concerning effective frequency and recency planning.

5. To understand the concepts of effectiveness and efficiency when applied to media selection decisions.

6. To introduce media source effects as an important factor in the selection and timing of advertising in magazines and television programmes.

7. To explore the different ways in which advertisements can be scheduled.

Introduction

Once a message has been created and agreed, a media plan should be determined. The aim of the media plan is to devise an optimum route for the delivery of the promotional message to the target audience. This function is normally undertaken by specialists, either as part of a full service advertising agency or as a media independent whose sole function is to buy air time or space from media owners (e.g. television contractors or magazine publishers) on behalf of their clients, the advertisers. This traditional role has changed since the mid-1990s, and many media independents now provide consultancy services, particularly at the strategic level, plus planning and media research and auditing services.

Media departments are responsible for two main functions. These are to 'plan' and to 'buy' time and space in appropriate media vehicles. There is a third task – to monitor a media schedule once it has been bought – but this is essentially a subfunction of buying. The planner chooses the target audience and the type of medium, while the buyer chooses programmes, frequency, spots and distribution, and assembles a multi-channel schedule (Armstrong, 1993). In the past the media planner has been pre-eminent, but the role of the buyer is changing. Some feel the role of the buyer is in the ascendancy, but there are others who feel that the role is capable of increased automation and that many software packages now fulfil many functions of the media buyer. Such a move has implications for the type of person recruited. In the USA, for example, many housewives have been recruited on a part-time basis to do many parts of the traditional media planner's job.

Media planning is essentially a selection and scheduling exercise. The selection refers to the choice of media vehicles to carry the message on behalf of the advertiser.

Media planning is essentially a selection and scheduling exercise.

Scheduling refers to the number of occasions, timing and duration that a message is exposed, in the selected vehicles, to the target audience. However, there are several factors that complicate these seemingly straightforward tasks. First, the variety of available media is huge and rapidly increasing. This is referred to as media fragmentation. Second, the characteristics of the target audience are changing equally quickly. This is referred to as audience fragmentation. Both these fragmentation issues will be discussed later. The job of the media planner is complicated by one further element: money. Advertisers have restricted financial resources and require the media planner to create a plan that delivers their messages not only effectively but also efficiently.

Three sets of decisions need to be made about the choice of media, vehicles and schedules.

The task of the media planner, therefore, is to deliver advertising messages through a selection of media which match the viewing and/or reading habits of the target audience at the lowest possible cost. In order for these tasks to be accomplished, three sets of decisions need to be made about the choice of media, vehicles and schedules.

Media

Decisions about the choice of media are complex. While choosing a single one is reasonably straightforward, choosing media in combination and attempting to generate synergistic effects is far from easy. Advances in IT have made media planning a much faster, more accurate process, one which is now more flexible and capable of adjusting to fast-changing market conditions.

Organisations use the services of a variety of media so that they can deliver their planned messages to target audiences. Of the many

Organisations use the services of a variety of media so that they can deliver their planned messages to target audiences.

available media, six main classes can be identified. These are broadcast, print, outdoor, new, in-store and other media classes. Within each of these classes there are particular media types. For example, within the broadcast class there are television and radio, and within the print class there are newspapers and magazines.

Within each type of medium there are a huge number of different media vehicles which can be selected to carry an advertiser's message. For example, within UK television there are the terrestrial networks (Independent Television Network, Channel 4 and Channel 5) and the satellite (BSkyB) and cable (NTL) networks. In print, there are consumer- and business-orientated magazines and the number of specialist magazines is expanding rapidly. These specialist magazines are targeted at particular activity and interest groups, such as *Amateur Photographer*, *Golf World* and the infamous *Bungee Jumpers' Gazette*. This provides opportunities for advertisers to send messages to well-defined homogeneous groups which improves effectiveness and reduces wastage in communication spend. There are, therefore, three forms of media: classes, types and vehicles (Table 22.1).

One of the key tasks of the marketing communications manager is to decide which combination of vehicles should be selected to carry the message to the target audience. First, it is necessary to consider briefly the main characteristics of each media type in order that media planning decisions can be based upon some logic and rationale. The fundamental characteristics concern the costs, delivery and audience profile associated with a communication.

Costs

One of the important characteristics that need to be considered is the costs that are incurred using each type of medium. There are two types of cost: absolute and relative.

Absolute costs are the costs of the time or space bought

Relative costs are the costs of contacting each member of the target audience.

in a particular media vehicle. These costs have to be paid for and directly impact upon an organisation's cash flow. Relative costs are the costs of contacting each member of the target audience. Television, as will be seen later, has a high absolute cost, but, because messages are delivered to a mass audience, when the absolute cost is divided by the total number of people receiving the message the relative cost is very low.

Ability to communicate a message

The way in which an advertiser's message is conveyed to the target audience varies

Table 22.1   Summary chart of the main forms of media

Class	Type	Vehicles
Broadcast	Television	*Brookside, Friends*
	Radio	*Virgin 1215, Classic FM*
Print	Newspapers	*Sunday Times, The Mirror, The Mail*
	Magazines	
	Consumer	*Cosmopolitan, FHM, Woman*
	Business	*The Grocer, Plumbing News*
Outdoor	Billboards	96 and 48 sheet
	Street furniture	Adshel
	Transit	London Underground, taxis, hot-air balloons
New media	Internet	Web sites, email, Intranet
	Digital television	ONdigital
	Teletext	SkyText, Ceefax
	CD-ROM	Various: music, educational, entertainment
In store	Point of purchase	Bins, signs and displays
	Packaging	The *Coca Cola* contour bottle
Other	Cinema	Pearl and Dean
	Exhibitions	Ideal Home, The Motor Show
	Product placement	FedEx in Castaway
	Ambient	Litter bins, golf tees, petrol pumps
	Guerrilla	Flyposting

across media types. Certain media, such as television, are able to use many communication dimensions, and through the use of sight, sound and movement can generate great impact with a message. Other types of media have only one dimension, such as the audio capacity of radio. The number of communication dimensions that a media type has will influence the choice of media mix. This is because certain products, at particular points in their development, require the use of different media in order that the right message be conveyed and understood. A new product, for example, may require demonstration in order that the audience understands the product concept. The use of television may be a good way of achieving this. Once understood, the audience does not need to be educated in this way again and future messages need to convey different types of information which may not require demonstration, so radio or magazine advertising may suffice.

Audience profile

The profile of the target audience (male, female, young or old) and the number of people within each audience that a media type can reach are also significant factors in media decisions. For example, 30% of adults in the socioeconomic grade A read the *Sunday Times*. Only 4% of the C2 group also read this paper. Messages appropriate to the A group would be best placed in the *Sunday Times* and those for the C2 group transmitted through the *News of the World*, which 34% of the C2 group read. It is important that advertisers use media vehicles that convey their messages to their target markets with as little waste as possible.

The characteristics of each medium are summarised in Table 22.2. It can be seen

Table 22.2 A summary of media characteristics

Type of media	Strengths	Weaknesses
Print		
Newspapers	Wide reach High coverage Low costs Very flexible Short lead times Speed of consumption controlled by reader	Short lifespan Advertisements get little exposure Relatively poor reproduction, gives poor impact Low attention-getting properties
Magazines	High-quality reproduction which allows high impact Specific and specialised target audiences High readership levels Longevity High levels of information can be delivered	Long lead times Visual dimension only Slow build-up of impact Moderate costs
Television	Flexible format, uses sight, movement and sound High prestige High reach Mass coverage Low relative cost so very efficient	High level of repetition necessary Short message life High absolute costs Clutter Increasing level of fragmentation (potentially)
Radio	Selective audience, e.g. local Low costs (absolute, relative and production) Flexible Can involve listeners	Lacks impact Audio dimension only Difficult to get audience attention Low prestige
Outdoor	High reach High frequency Low relative costs Good coverage as a support medium Location orientated	Poor image (but improving) Long production time Difficult to measure
New media	High level of interaction Immediate response possible Tight targeting Low absolute and relative costs Flexible and easy to update Measurable	Segment specific Slow development of infrastructure High user set-up costs Transaction security issues
Transport	High length of exposure Low costs Local orientation	Poor coverage Segment specific (travellers) Clutter
In-store POP	High attention-getting properties Persuasive Low costs Flexible	Segment specific (shoppers) Prone to damage and confusion Clutter

that each of the types of media has a variety of characteristics that will help or hinder the communication of an advertiser's message. In addition to this, each media vehicle will have a discrete set of characteristics that will also influence the way in which messages are transmitted and received.

McLuhan (1966) said that the medium is the message. He went on to say that the medium is the massage, as each medium massages the recipient in different ways and so contributes to learning in different ways. For example, Krugman (1965) hypothesised that television advertising washes over individuals. He said that viewers, rather than participate actively with television advertisements, allow learning to occur passively. In contrast, magazine advertising requires active participation if learning is to occur.

Newspapers enable geographically based target audiences to be reached. The tone of their content can be controlled, but the cost per target reached is high. Each issue has a short lifespan, so for positive learning to occur in the target audience, a number of insertions may be required.

Each issue has a short lifespan, so for positive learning to occur in the target audience, a number of insertions may be required.

A large number of magazines contain specialised material which appeals to particular target groups. These special-interest magazines (SIMs) enable certain sponsors to reach interested targets with reduced wastage. General-interest magazines (GIMs) appeal to a much wider cross-section of society, to larger generalised target groups. The life of these media vehicles is generally long and their 'pass along' readership high. It should not be forgotten, however, that noise levels can also be high owing to the intermittent manner in which magazines are often read and the number of competing messages from rival organisations.

Magazine Launch – *Glamour*

When *Glamour* was launched in March 2001, the new publication from Condé Nast received huge marketing communications support. This included a £4.5 million campaign featuring television, print, outdoor and cinema. In addition, public relations generated a huge amount of publicity about the A5 'handbag-sized' format.

Part of the rationale for the radically different size was not only the success experienced in the USA and Italy where the format has been successful for over seven years but also the trend towards miniaturisation (Walkmans, mobile phones) and the fashion appeal that the smaller size might represent. In addition, however, is the high impact the smaller size has in standing out on the shelves of newsagents amongst the clutter of the established, larger heavyweight competitors.

Television reaches the greatest number of people, but although advertisers can reach general groups, such as men aged 16–24 or housewives, it is not capable of reaching specific groups and incurs high levels of wastage. This blanket coverage offers opportunities for cable and satellite entrepreneurs to offer more precise targeting, but for now television is a tool for those who wish to talk to mass audiences. Television is expensive from a cash flow perspective but not in terms of the costs per target reached.

Radio offers a more reasonable costing structure than television and can be utilised to reach particular geographic audiences. For a long time, however, this was seen as its only real strength, particularly when its poor attention span and non-visual dimensions are considered. Research in the 1990s, however, indicates that it is not destined to remain the poor relation to television, as radio has been shown to be capable of generating a much closer personal relationship with listeners, witnessed partly by the success of Classic FM and Virgin 1215, than is possible through posters, television or print.

The interesting point about outdoor and transit advertising is that exposure is only made by the interception of passing traffic. Govoni *et al.* (1986) make the point that such interception represents opportunistic coverage. Consequently the costs are low, at both investment and per contact levels.

The use of direct marketing has grown in recent years, as technology has developed and awareness has increased. The precise targeting potential of direct mail and its ability to communicate personally with target audiences is impressive. In addition, the control over the total process, including the costs, remains firmly with the sponsor.

Vehicle selection

Increasingly, organisations are required to prove how advertising adds value to the bottom line. While this is not a new question, it is one that is being asked more often and in such a way that answers are required. As advertisers attempt to demonstrate effectiveness, contribution and return on investment, questions concerning the choice of media, how much should be spent on message delivery and how are financial resources to be allocated in a multichannel environment increasingly haunt senior managers.

Media decisions have become significantly more important and certainly more visible areas attracting management attention in the late 1990s and early years of the new millennium. For example, Brech (1999) reports that companies such as Scottish Courage need to make choices about the split between the Internet, mass media, digital TV and consumer press. Companies such as BT, Ikea and ScottishPower need to use media strategically in order that they reach the right audience, in the right context, at the right time and at an acceptable cost. To help organisations achieve these goals a variety of approaches have been adopted. For example, New PHD is retained by BT to advise about strategic (media) planning and budget allocation. However, Zenith Media implement decisions for press and radio and the Allmond Partnership manages TV and cinema while Outdoor Connections handle poster buying. This division provides objectivity, reduces partisan approaches and can deliver more effective media plans. Cost per response is certainly one way of measuring effectiveness but the communication impact, or share of mind, is also important. There has also been a move away from volume of media to one where media decisions are made by looking at media in the context of the brand's total communications.

Companies need to make choices about the split between the Internet, mass media, digital TV and consumer press.

There has also been a move away from volume of media to one where media decisions are made by looking at media in the context of the brand's total communications.

A further problem facing clients and media concerns the integrated media experience. For a long time, some organisations have used above-the-line media to reach audiences of 20 million people. With fragmented media it is difficult to generate consistent levels and types of impact. Increasingly media management is being outsourced so there are fewer in-house areas of expertise. All this means that, to forge appropriate solutions, advertisers and media agencies need to work closely together so that the relationship becomes so close that it acts more as an extension to the marketing department.

Decisions regarding which vehicles are to carry an advertiser's message depend upon an understanding of a number of concepts: reach and coverage, frequency, gross rating points, effective frequency, efficiency and media source effects.

Media planning concepts

Reach and coverage

Reach refers to the percentage of the target audience exposed to the message at least once during the relevant time period. Where 80% of the target audience has been exposed to a message, the figure is expressed as an '80 reach'.

Coverage, a term often used for reach, should not be confused or used in place of reach. Coverage refers to the size of a potential audience that might be exposed to a particular media vehicle. For media planners, therefore, coverage (the size of the target audience), is very important. Reach will always be lower than coverage, as it is impossible to reach 100% of a target population (the universe).

Building reach within a target audience is relatively easy as the planner needs to select a range of different media vehicles. This will enable different people in the target audience to have an opportunity to see the media vehicle. However, a point will be reached when it becomes more difficult to reach people who have not been exposed. As more vehicles are added, so repetition levels (the number of people who have seen the advertisement more than once) also increase.

As more vehicles are added, so repetition levels also increase.

Frequency

Frequency refers to the number of times a member of the target audience is exposed to a media vehicle (not the advertisement) during the relevant time period. It has been stated that targets must be exposed to the media vehicle, but to say that a target has seen an advertisement simply because they have been exposed to the vehicle is incorrect. For example, certain viewers hop around the channels as a commercial break starts. This has been referred to as 'channel grazing' by Lloyd and Clancy (1991). Individuals have different capacities to learn and to forget, and how much of a magazine does a reader have to consume to be counted as having read an advertisement? These questions are still largely unanswered, so media planners have adopted an easier and more consistent measure: opportunities to see (OTS).

This is an important point. The stated frequency level in any media plan will always be greater than the advertisement exposure rate. The term OTS is used to express the reach of a media vehicle rather than the actual exposure of an advertisement. However, a high OTS could be generated by either a large number of the target audience being exposed once (high reach) or a small number being exposed several times (high frequency).

This then raises the first major issue. As all campaigns are restricted by time and budget limitations, advertisers have to trade off reach against frequency. It is impossible to maximise both elements within a fixed budget and set period of time.

To launch a new product, it has been established that a wide number of people within the target audience need to become aware of the product's existence and its salient attributes or benefits. This means that reach is important, but, as more and more people become aware, so more of them become exposed a second, third or fourth time, perhaps to different vehicles. At the outset, frequency is low and reach high, but as a campaign progresses so reach slows and frequency develops. Reach and frequency are inversely related within any period of time, and media planners must know what the objective of any campaign might be: to build reach or frequency.

Reach and frequency are inversely related within any period of time, and media planners must know what the objective of any campaign might be: to build reach or frequency.

Gross rating point

To decide whether reach or frequency is the focus of the campaign objective, a more precise understanding of the levels of reach and frequency is required. The term 'gross rating point' (GRP) is used to express the relationship between these two concepts. GRPs are a measure of the total number of exposures (OTS), generated within a particular period of time. The calculation itself is simply reach × frequency:

$$\text{reach} \times \text{frequency} = \text{gross rating point}$$

Media plans are often determined on the number of GRPs generated during a certain time period. For example, the objective for a media plan could be to achieve 450 GRPs in a burst (usually four or five weeks). However, as suggested earlier, caution is required when interpreting a GRP, because 450 GRPs may be the result of 18 message exposures to just 25% of the target market. It could also be an average of nine exposures to 50% of the target market.

Rating points are used by all media as a measurement tool, although they were originally devised for use with broadcast audiences. GRPs are based on the total target audience (e.g. all women aged 18–34, or all adults) that might be reached, but a media planner needs to know, quite rightly, how many GRPs are required to achieve a particular level of effective reach and what levels of frequency are really required to develop effective learning or awareness in the target audience. In other words, how can the effectiveness of a media plan be improved?

Effective frequency

There are a number of reasons why considering the effectiveness of a media plan has become more important. First, there is the combination of media and audience fragmentation and rising media costs. Second, there are short-termism, increased managerial accountability and intensifying competition. This last point about competition refers to the media planning industry itself and the restructuring and concentration of media buying points (centralisation) in response to clients' globalisation strategies and their need for more cost-effective ways of buying media.

Frequency refers to the number of times members of the target audience are exposed to the vehicle. It says nothing about the quality of the exposures and whether any impact was made. Effective frequency refers to the number of times an individual needs to be exposed to an advertisement before the communication is effective. Being exposed once or possibly twice is unlikely to affect the disposition of the receiver. But the big question facing media planners is, how many times should a message be repeated for effective learning to occur? The level of effective frequency is generally unknown, but there has been some general agreement following work by Krugman (1972) that, for an advertisement to be effective (to make an impact), a target should have at least three OTS. The first exposure provokes a 'What is this?' reaction, the second reaction is 'What does this mean to me?' The reaction to the third is 'Oh I remember' (du Plessis, 1998). More than 10 will be ineffective and a waste of resources. The level of three was determined by messages that first provide understanding, second provide recognition and third actually stimulate action.

Frequency refers to the number of times members of the target audience are exposed to the vehicle.

Determining the average frequency partially solves the problem. This is the number of times a target reached by the schedule is exposed to the vehicle over a particular period of time. For example, a schedule may generate the following:

10% of the audience is reached ten times ($10 \times 10 = 100$)

25% of the audience is reached seven times ($25 \times 7 = 175$)

65% of the audience is reached once ($65 \times 1 = 65$)

Total $= 340$ exposures

Average frequency $= 340/100 = 3.4$

This figure of average frequency is misleading because different groups of people have been reached with varying levels of frequency. In the example above, an average frequency of 3.4 is achieved but 65% of the audience is reached only once. This means that the average frequency, in this example, may lead to an audience being underexposed.

Members of the target audience do not buy and read just one magazine or watch a single television programme. Consumer media habits are complex, although distinct patterns can be observed, but it is likely that a certain percentage of the target audience will be exposed to an advertisement if it is placed in two or more media vehicles. Those who are exposed once constitute unduplicated reach. Those who are exposed to two or more are said to have been duplicated. Such overlapping of exposure, shown in Figure 22.1, is referred to as duplicated reach.

Consumer media habits are complex, although distinct patterns can be observed.

Duplication provides an indication of the levels of frequency likely in a particular schedule, so media plans need to specify levels of duplicated and unduplicated reach. Duplication also increases costs, so if the objective of the plan is unduplicated reach, duplication brings waste and inefficiency.

Nevertheless, it is generally agreed that a certain level of GRPs is necessary for awareness to be achieved and that increased GRPs are necessary for other communication effects to be achieved. These levels of GRPs are referred to as weights, and the weight a campaign has reflects the objectives of the campaign. For example, a burst designed to achieve 85% coverage with eight OTS would make a 680 rating, which is

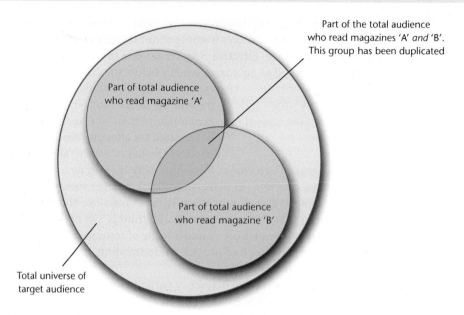

Part of the total audience who read magazines 'A' *and* 'B'. This group has been duplicated

Part of total audience who read magazine 'A'

Part of total audience who read magazine 'B'

Total universe of target audience

Figure 22.1 Duplication.

considered to be heavy. Such high ratings are often associated with car launches and, for example, products that are market leaders in their class, such as Nescafé. An average rating would be one set to achieve a 400 rating, through 80% coverage and five OTS over the length of a five-week period.

Readers might be interested to know that, at deseasonalised prices, each 100 rating points cost an advertiser around £330,000. That means that an average five-week burst set to achieve 400 rating points will cost approximately £1.5 million, just for the broadcast time. These figures relate to an all-adult audience. If the target was all men, then the figure would rise to nearer £500,000 for each 100 ratings. Production costs and commissions need to be added to this figure.

Our understanding about how learning works can assist the quest for effective frequency levels. The amount of learning in individuals increases up to a certain point,

Table 22.3 A television laydown for a national burst

	3–9 January	10–16 January	17–23 January	24–30 January	Total (including satellite)
London	125	100	100	86	411
Central	125	100	100	77	402
Granada	125	112	111	111	459
North	125	100	100	68	393
STV	125	125	115	115	480
HTV	125	100	100	53	378
Meridian	125	100	100	47	372
Anglia	125	100	100	48	373
WCTV	125	100	100	41	366
Border	125	100	100	72	397
Grampian	125	118	100	100	443

where further exposure to material adds little to our overall level of knowledge. The same applies to the frequency level and the weightings applied to exposures. Table 22.3 shows the spread of weights for a burst bought by a major advertiser. The ratings are spread in such a way that greater weight is 'laid down' at the beginning of the campaign, to get attention, and in some areas (WCTV) the weight in week 4 is only 33% of the first week's activity.

The figures that coverage and reach provide only show the numbers of people who are exposed to the vehicle. Effective reach measures those that are aware of the message. This ties in with the previous discussion on effective frequency levels. Essentially, media planners recognise that effective advertising requires that, in addition to the other aspects of advertising planning, a single transmission (reach) of an advertisement will be unproductive (Naples, 1979; Krugman, 1975). A minimum of two exposures and a reach threshold of 45% of the target audience are required for reach to be regarded as effective (Murray and Jenkins, 1992).

Recency planning

A new perspective to counter the effective frequency model has emerged from the USA. This is known as recency planning, and has developed at a time when the weak theory of advertising has started to gain greater acceptance as the most acceptable general interpretation of how advertising works. It is also more generally accepted that advertising is not the powerful marketing tool that it was once thought to be (Jones, 1990) and that the timing and presentation of advertising messages need to be reconsidered in the light of the way the advertising is currently thought to work.

If it is accepted that consumer decision-making is more heavily influenced by running out of particular products (opening empty fridges and store cupboards) rather than exposure to advertising messages that are repeated remorselessly, then it follows that advertising needs to be directed at those people who are actually in the market and prepared to buy (Ephron, 1997).

Advertising needs to be directed at those people who are actually in the market and prepared to buy.

As many fast-moving consumer goods products are purchased each week, Jones (1995) argues that a single exposure to an advertising message *in the week* before a purchase is to be made is more important than adding further messages and so increasing frequency. Recency planning considers reach to be more important than frequency.

The goal of this new approach is to reach those few consumers who are ready to buy (in the market). To do this the strategy requires reaching as many consumers as possible in as many weeks as possible (as far as the budget will extend).

This requires a lower weekly weight and an extended number of weeks to a campaign. Advertising budgets are not cut; the fund is simply spread over a greater period of time. According to Ephron, this approach is quite different from effective frequency models and quite revolutionary; see Table 22.4.

This approach has been greeted with a number of objections. It has not been accepted universally and has not been widely implemented in the UK market at the time of writing.

Gallucci (1997), among others, rejects the notion of recency planning because effectiveness will vary by brand, category and campaign. He claims that reaching 35%

Table 22.4   The differences between effective frequency and recency planning

Recency planning model	Effective frequency model
Reach goal	Frequency goal
Continuity	Burst
One-week planning cycle	Four-week planning cycle
Lowest cost per reach point	Lowest cost per thousand
Low ratings	High ratings

Source: Adapted from Ephron (1997).

of a cola market (Indonesia) once a week will not bring about the same result as reaching 65% four times a week.

The development of banner advertising on the Internet raises interesting questions concerning effective frequency in new media. Is the frequency rate different and if so how many times is exposure required in order to be effective? Research into this area is in infancy and no single accepted body of knowledge exists. Broussard (2000) reports that, in a limited study concerning the comparison of a direct response and a branding-based campaign in the Internet, the lowest cost per lead in the direct response campaign was achieved with low frequency levels. Results from the branding campaign suggest that up to seven exposures were necessary to improve brand awareness and knowledge of product attributes.

The development of banner advertising on the Internet raises interesting questions concerning effective frequency in new media.

The debate concerning the development of recency planning and effective frequency will continue. What might be instrumental to the outcome of the debate will be a better understanding of how advertising works and the way buyers use advertising messages that are relevant to them.

Media usage and attitudes

Research from a variety of sources (e.g. CIA MediaLab reported by Beale, 1997) consistently reveals that a large proportion of the population (50% plus) has a negative attitude towards advertising. Advertising is seen by this large body of people as both intrusive and pervasive. Beale's work led to the development of a four-part typology of personality types based upon respondents' overall attitudes towards advertising. Through an understanding of the different characteristics, it is possible to make better (more informed) decisions about the most appropriate media channels to reach target audiences; see Table 22.5.

It is common for advertisers and media planners to discuss target markets in the context of heavy, medium, light and non-users of a product. It is only now that consideration is being given to the usage levels of viewers and readers. Zenith Media have determined that TV audiences can be categorised as heavy, medium and light users based upon the amount of time they spend watching television. Table 22.6 presents a breakdown of the general categories, where the amount of time spent viewing can be seen to vary considerably between the summer and winter periods.

One of the implications of this approach is that if light users consume so little tele-

Plate 13.1 Harveys Bristol Cream. The relaunch of Harveys Bristol Cream involved the use of blue glass, often synonymous with quality glass from the area. The bottle was also reshaped to provide positive images. For a fuller account see Chapter 13, page 329. Picture reproduced with the kind permission of Harveys and Allied Domecq.

Plate 14.1 JCB. The Dancing Diggers are an important part of the company's publicity strategy. See Chapter 14, page 354. Picture reproduced with the kind permission of JCB.

Plate 15.1 Reebok.   Use of trade advertising to inform and remind dealers. See Chapter 15, page 375. Picture reproduced with the kind permission of Reebok International Ltd.

Plate 16.1 Taylor Nelson Sofres.   A new visual identity was designed to reflect the equal importance of the two merged companies by placing the names on one level, a coming together of Taylor Nelson and Sofres. See Chapter 16, page 408. Picture and material used with the kind permisiion of Taylor Nelson Sofres.

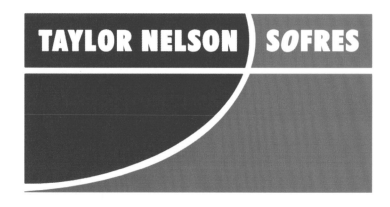

Plate 20.1 and 20.2 Specsavers Opticians. Using people known for the way they use their sight, Specsavers Opticians delivered differentiation and added value to the market. Plate 20.1 (above right) shows the artist David Shepherd; Plate 20.2 (below right) shows the physicist Stephen Hawkings. See Chapter 20, page 497 and the mini case on page 505. Pictures and material reproduced with the kind permission of Specsavers Opticians.

Spring into
life
with a brisk,
full-bodied tea

ENGLISH
BREAKFAST

www.twinings.com

There's more to tea with **TWININGS**

Plate 20.3 Twinings. Through the use of peripheral cues, Twinings have been able to enrich the way their brand is perceived while at the same time improve the level of awareness. See Chapter 20, page 498. Picture reproduced with the kind permission of Twinings.

Plate 21.1 BMW. Shaken not stirred. This BMW is a classic advertisement which portrays comparative product attributes, originality and message consistency. See Chapter 21, page 511. Picture reproduced with the kind permission of BMW and WCRS.

Plate 21.2 Virgin Atlantic and Marianne Faithfull. The use of celebrities to help endorse and support a brand can be a significant element in an individual's brand choice criteria. Marianne Faithful was used by Virgin Atlantic to convey messages about the overall Virgin Atlantic brand. See Chapter 21, page 514. Picture reproduced with the kind permission of Virgin Atlantic Ltd.

Plate 21.3 Yellow Pages. Mistletoe. The gentle use of humour is exemplified by Yellow Pages. See Chapter 21, page 519. Picture reproduced with the kind permission of Yellow Pages.

It's because they're not afraid

to get their hands filthy.

To eat the paste.

To use a hammer as a brush.

To break something just to see how it works.

And to start with the impossible,

which is where grownups usually stop.

Just a few of the things we're keeping in mind

as we invent the new hp.

Want to come along?

www.hp.com

Plate 26.1 HP invent. As part of the process of preparing for the future, Hewlett Packard used corporate advertising to reaffirm corporate values, with staff and major stakeholders. See Chapter 26, page 638. Picture reproduced with the kind permission of Hewlett Packard Ltd.

Plate 28.1 Direct Line telephone. The red telephone identifies Direct Line, one of the first to establish direct marketing as its principal form of marketing communications. See Chapter 28, page 679. Picture reproduced with the kind permission of Direct Line Insurance.

Plate 30.1 GEMPLUS exhibition stand. An exhibition stand designed to convey product attributes and the drug's main point of differentiation. See Chapter 31, page 719. Picture reproduced with the kind permission of GEMPLUS Ltd.

Plate 30.2 Coca-Cola contour bottle. Packaging is an important aspect of marketing communications in many sectors. Depicted here is the Coca-Cola bottle with its unique (and well-protected) shape. See Chapter 30, page 722. Coca-Cola is a registered trade mark of the Coca-Cola Company. This image has been reproduced with the kind permission of the Coca-Cola Company.

Table 22.5   Advertising attitudes for media determination

Cynics (22%)	Enthusiasts (35%)
This group perceives advertising as a crude sales tool. They are resentful and hostile to advertisements, although they are more likely to respond to advertisements placed in relevant media.	Enthusiasts like to get involved with advertising and creativity is perceived as an important part of the process. Apart from newspapers, which are regarded as boring, most types of media are acceptable.
Ambivalents (22%)	**Acquiescents (21%)**
While creativity is seen as superfluous and irrelevant, Ambivalents are more disposed to information-based messages or those that promise cost savings. The best advertisements are those that use media that reinforce the message.	As the name suggests, this group of people has a reluctant approach to advertising. This means that they see advertising as unavoidable and an inevitable part of their world. Therefore, they are open to influence through a variety of media.

Source: Adapted from Beale (1997). Used with kind permission.

vision, then perhaps it is not worthwhile trying to communicate with them and resources should be directed to the medium and heavy user groups. The other side of the argument is that light users are very specific in the programmes that they watch, therefore, it should be possible to target messages at them and so use a heavy number of GRPs. Questions still remain about the number of ratings necessary for effective reach in each of these categories.

The question concerning how many rating points should be purchased was addressed by Ostrow (1981). He said that, rather than use average frequency, a decision should be made about the minimum level of frequency necessary to achieve the objectives and then maximise reach at that level. Ostrow (1984) suggested that consideration of the issues set out in Table 22.7 would also assist.

The traditional approach of using television to reach target audiences to build awareness is still strong. For example, Procter & Gamble, Lever Brothers, Nestlé, Kellogg's and British Telecom all spend in excess of 75% of their budgets on television advertising. However, there are signs that some major advertisers are moving slowly from a dominant above-the-line approach to a more integrated and through-the-line

Table 22.6   Usage patterns of television consumption (Zenith Media)

	Minutes spent watching TV[a] per day
Winter	
Heavy	195–500+
Medium	106–200
Light	Less than 100
Summer	
Heavy	150–500+
Medium	60–150
Light	Less than 60

[a]ITV + CH4.

Table 22.7   Issues to be considered when setting frequency levels

	Low frequency	High frequency
Marketing issues		
Newness of the brand	Established	New
Market share	High	Low
Brand loyalty	Higher	Lower
Purchase and usage cycle times	Long	Short
Message issues		
Complexity	Simple	Complex
Uniqueness	More	Less
Image versus product sell	Product sell	Image
Message variation	Single message	Multiple messages
Media plan issues		
Clutter	Less	More
Editorial atmosphere	Appropriate	Not appropriate
Attentiveness of the media in the plan	Holds	Fails to hold
Number of media in the plan	Less	More

Source: Adapted from Ostrow (1981); used with kind permission.

approach as a more effective way of delivering messages to target audiences. Nescafé now uses 48-sheet posters and Unilever, traditionally a heavy user of television, has begun to use radio and posters as support for its television work.

Efficiency

All promotional campaigns are constrained by a budget. Therefore a trade-off is required between the need to reach as many members of the target audience as possible (create awareness) and the need to repeat the message to achieve effective learning in the target audience. The decision about whether to emphasise reach or frequency is assisted by a consideration of the costs involved in each proposed schedule or media plan.

All promotional campaigns are constrained by a budget.

There are two main types of cost. The first of these is the *absolute cost*. This is the cost of the space or time required for the message to be transmitted. For example, the cost of a full-page single-insertion colour advertisement, booked for a firm date in *The Sunday Times*, is £75,600 (July 2001). Cash flow is affected by absolute costs.

In order that an effective comparison be made between media plans the *relative costs* of the schedules need to be understood. Relative costs are the costs incurred in making contact with each member of the target audience.

Traditionally, the magazine industry has based its calculations on the cost per thousand people reached (CPT). The original term derived from the print industry is CPM, where the 'M' refers to the Roman symbol for thousand. This term still has limited use but the more common term is CPT:

$$CPT = \text{space costs (absolute)} \times 1{,}000/\text{circulation}$$

The newspaper industry has used the milline rate, which is the cost per line of space per million circulation.

Broadcast audiences are measured by programme ratings (USA), and television audiences in the UK are measured by television ratings or TVRs. They are essentially the same in that they represent the percentage of television households who are tuned to a specific programme. The TVR is determined as follows:

Broadcast audiences are measured by television ratings or TVRs.

$$\text{TVR} = \text{number of target TV households tuned into a programme} \times 100/\text{total number of target TV households}$$

A single TVR, therefore, represents 1% of all the television households in a particular area who are tuned into a specific programme.

A further approach to measuring broadcast audiences uses the share of televisions that are tuned into a specific programme. This is compared with the total number of televisions that are actually switched on at that moment. This is expressed as a percentage and should be greater than the TVR. Share, therefore, reveals how well a programme is perceived by the available audience, not the potential audience.

The question of how to measure relative costs in the broadcast industry has been answered by the use of the rating point or TVR. Cost per TVR is determined as follows:

$$\text{cost TVR} = \text{time costs (absolute costs)}/\text{TVR}$$

Intra-industry comparison of relative costs is made possible by using these formulae. Media plans which only involve broadcast or only use magazine vehicles can be evaluated to determine levels of efficiency. However, members of the target audience do not have discrete viewing habits; they have, as we saw earlier, complex media habits which involve exposure to a mix of media classes and vehicles. Advertisers respond to this mixture by placing advertisements in a variety of media, but have no way of comparing the relative costs on an inter-industry basis. In other words, the efficiency of using a *News at Ten* television slot cannot be compared with an insertion in the *Economist*. Attempts are being made to provide cross-industry media comparisons, but as yet no one formula has yet been provided that satisfies all demands. The television and newspaper industries, by using CPT in combination with costs per unit of time and space respectively, have attempted to forge a bridge which may be of use to their customers.

Members of the target audience do not have discrete viewing habits; they have, as we saw earlier, complex media habits which involve exposure to a mix of media classes and vehicles.

Finally, some comment on the concept of CPT is necessary, as there has been speculation about its validity as a comparative tool. There are a number of shortcomings associated with the use of CPT. For example, because each media class possesses particular characteristics, direct comparisons based on CPT alone are dangerous. The levels of wastage incurred in a plan, such as reaching people who are not targets or by measuring OTS for the vehicle and not the advertisement, may lead to an overestimate of the efficiency that a plan offers.

Similarly, the circulation of a magazine is not a true representation of the number of people who read or have an opportunity to see. Therefore, CPT may underestimate the efficiency unless the calculation can be adjusted to account for the extra or pass-along readership that occurs in reality. Having made these points, media buyers in the UK continue to use CPT

CPT may underestimate the efficiency unless the calculation can be adjusted to account for the extra or pass-along readership that occurs in reality.

and cost per rating point (CPRP) as a means of planning and buying time and space. Target audiences and television programmes are priced according to the ratings they individually generate. The ratings affect the cost of buying a spot. The higher the rating, the higher the price to place advertisements in the magazine or television programme.

Media source effects

CPT is a quantitative measure, and one of its major shortcomings is that it fails to account for the qualitative aspects associated with media vehicles. Before vehicles are selected, their qualitative aspects need to be considered on the basis that a vehicle's environment may affect the way in which a message is perceived and decoded.

An advertisement placed in one vehicle, such as *Cosmopolitan*, may have a different impact upon an identical audience to that obtained if the same advertisement is placed in *Options*. This differential level of 'power of impact' is caused by a number of source factors, of which the following are regarded as the most influential:

1. Vehicle atmosphere – editorial tone, vehicle expertise, vehicle prestige.
2. Technical and reproduction characteristics – technical factors, exposure opportunities, perception opportunities.
3. Audience and product characteristics – audience/vehicle fit, nature of the product.

Vehicle atmosphere

Editorial tone
This refers to the editorial views presented by the vehicle and the overall tone of the material contained. Understandably, some clients do not want to be associated with particular television shows or certain specialist magazines that are characterised by sex or violence.

Vehicle expertise
Magazines and journals can reflect a level of expertise and represent source credibility. Readers who regard particular magazines, especially some of the consumer SIMs (e.g. *Golf Monthly*), business-to-business magazines (e.g. *Fire & Rescue*) and academic journals (e.g. *Harvard Business Review*), as important sources of credible information are more relaxed and open to persuasion.

Vehicle prestige
The message strategy adopted for each advertisement should be appreciated, as this can have a strong effect upon the scheduling. The prestige of a vehicle is important to some products, especially when targeted at audiences where vehicle status is important, for example *Country Life*. Transformational advertisements have been shown to be more effective in prestige-based vehicles than in expertise-based vehicles (and vice versa for information-based advertisements).

Technical and reproduction characteristics of a vehicle

Technical factors
The technical characteristics of the vehicle, such as its visual capability, may influence the impact of the message. The use of colour, movement and sound may be necess-

ary for the full effectiveness of a message to be realised. Other messages may need only a more limited range of characteristics, such as sound. For example, the promotion of inclusive tour holidays benefits from the communication of an impression (photograph/drawing) of the destination resort. This is important, as each destination needs to be differentiated, in the minds of the target audience, from competing destinations.

Exposure opportunities

The possibility that an advertisement will be successfully exposed to the target increases as more consideration is given to the likelihood of successful communication. Each vehicle has a number of time slots or spaces that provide opportunities for increased exposure. The back pages of magazines or facing matter often command premium advertising rates, just as prime time spots or film premieres on television always generate extra revenue for the television contractors.

The back pages of magazines or facing matter often command premium advertising rates, just as prime time spots or film premieres on television always generate extra revenue for the television contractors.

Perception opportunities

Being exposed to the message does not mean that the message is perceived. A reader may not perceive an advertisement when searching for the next page of an article. Similarly, a car driver may not 'hear' a radio message because his or her attention may be on a passing car or a strange engine noise. The solution is to use strong attention-gaining materials, such as loud or distinctive music or controversial headlines. In addition, new imaginative ways of attracting attention are being developed. Car dealers have used incentives to attract audiences to test drive a car and receive vouchers for a free video film or have free subscriptions to particular magazines.

Audience/product characteristics

Audience/vehicle fit

The media plan should provide the best match between the target market and the audience reached by the vehicles in the media schedule. The more complex the target market description or consumer profile, the greater the difficulty of matching it with appropriate vehicles. Weilbacher (1984) argues that media evaluation based on product usage may be better than using demographics and psychographics. These may be inappropriate and inefficient when matching markets with audiences. As advertising is directed at influencing consumer behaviour, product usage is a more logical measure of media evaluation. This view is supported by media planners targeting heavy, medium and light users.

This perspective contrasts with the view of Rothschild (1987). He sees demographic and psychographic factors as being relatively stable and enduring factors, and thus as suitable influences upon the media selection decision. By contrast, the dynamic factors (those that vary within an individual with respect to brand choice, purchase behaviour and time of adoption between products) are seen as being more suitable for influencing media strategy.

Nature of the product

In addition to this, consideration needs to given to the nature of the product itself. Audiences have particular viewing patterns, therefore, it does not make sense to advertise when it is known that the target audience is not watching (for example, promoting children's sweets late at night or photocopiers in consumer interest magazines).

Prime television spots such as *Coronation Street* or major sporting occasions such as the Olympic Games will attract many major competitive brands. It may be wise to avoid competing for time and look for other suitable programmes.

Vehicle mood effects

The mood that a vehicle creates can also be an important factor. Aaker *et al.* (1992) report on the work of a number of studies in this area. These suggest that food advertisements using transformational appeals are more effective when placed in situation comedies than in thrillers and mystery programmes. Adverts for analgesics work better in both adult westerns and situation comedies (Crane, 1964).

Vehicle-related source effects need to be considered as support for the quantitative work undertaken initially.

These qualitative, vehicle-related source effects need to be considered as support for the quantitative work undertaken initially. They should not be used as the sole reason for the selection of particular media vehicles, if only because they are largely subjective.

Scheduling

This seeks to establish when the messages are transmitted in order that the media objectives be achieved at the lowest possible cost. The first considerations are the objectives themselves. If the advertising objectives are basically short term, then the placements should be concentrated over a short period of time. Conversely, if awareness is to be built over a longer term, perhaps building a new brand, then the frequency of the placements need not be so intensive and can be spread over a period so that learning can occur incrementally.

The second consideration is the purchasing cycle. We have seen before that the optimum number of exposures is thought to be between three and 10, and this should occur within each purchasing cycle. This, of course, is only really applicable to packaged goods, and is not as applicable to the business-to-business sector. However, the longer the cycle, the less frequency is required.

The longer the cycle, the less frequency is required.

The third consideration is the level of involvement. If the objective of the plan is to create awareness, then when there is high involvement few repetitions will be required compared with low-involvement decisions. This is because people who are highly involved actively seek information and need little assistance to digest relevant information. Likewise, where there is low involvement, attitudes develop from use of the product, so frequency is important to maintain awareness and to prompt trial.

Finally, the placement of an advertisement is influenced by the characteristics of the target audience and their preferred programmes. By selecting compatible 'spots', message delivery is likely to improve considerably.

Timing of advertisement placements

The timing of placements is dependent upon a number of factors. One of the overriding constraints is the size of the media budget and the impact that certain placement patterns can bring to an organisation's cash flow. Putting cost to one side, many researchers have identified and labelled different scheduling patterns. Govoni *et al.* (1986), Sissors and Bumba (1989), Burnett (1993) and Kotler (1997) all suggest different approaches to scheduling. Figure 22.2 and the following are presented as a synthesis of the more common scheduling options.

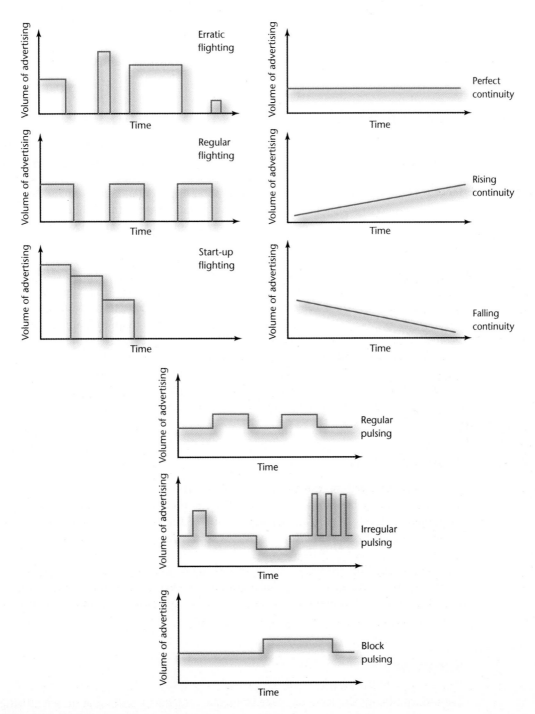

Figure 22.2   Media scheduling patterns.

Continuity patterns

Continuous patterns involve regular and uniform presentation of the message to the target audience. Over the long term, a continuous pattern is more appropriate for products and services where demand is crisis led, e.g. plumbing, or where there is a long purchase cycle. These continuous patterns are often used for mature products, where reminder advertising is appropriate. A rising pattern is used when activity centres around a particular event, such as the FA Cup Final, the Olympic Games or a general election. A fading pattern may follow an initial burst to launch a new product or to inform of a product modification.

Flighting patterns

Flighting allows advertisers the opportunity to spread their resources across a longer period of time. This may improve the effectiveness of their messages. A flighting pattern may be appropriate in situations where messages need to reflect varying demand, such as that experienced by the retail sector throughout the year. Flighting is also adopted as a competitive response to varying advertising weights applied by rivals. These schedules are used for specific events, such as support for major sales promotions and responses to adverse publicity or one-off market opportunities.

Flighting allows advertisers the opportunity to spread their resources across a longer period of time.

Flighting patterns can also be used in short and often heavy periods of investment activity. Because of the seasonality of the product (e.g. for inclusive tour operators), advertising at other times is inappropriate and a waste of resources. This approach can also be used to respond quickly to a competitor's potentially damaging actions, to launch new products or to provide unique information, such as the announcement of a new organisation as a result of merger activity, or to promote information about a particular event such as an impending share offer.

Flighting patterns can also be used in short and often heavy periods of investment activity.

Pulsing patterns

Pulsing seeks to combine the advantages of both the previous patterns. As a result it is the safest of all the options, but potentially the most expensive. It allows advertisers to increase levels of message activity at certain times of the year, which is important for times when sales traditionally increase, as with car sales at the beginning of August.

Whereas flighting presents an opportunity for individuals to forget messages during periods of no advertising, pulsing helps to prevent the onset of forgetting, to build high levels of awareness and to provide a barrier that holds back competitor attack.

Summary

The task of buying the time or space in media vehicles in order that an advertising message be carried to a target audience appears seductively straightforward. It is not.

It is complicated by a number of factors, ranging from the size and dispersion of the target audience to the increasing number and variety of available media. These factors are referred to as audience and media fragmentation, which bring both benefits to and difficulties for media planners and advertisers. For example, it is easier to target more specialised and compact target audiences using new and specialised media. However, audience profiles are changing rapidly and there is little control information about these audiences that allows advertising funds to be allocated 'properly' (Meuller-Heumann, 1992).

Another major difficulty, increasing in its importance, is the question of how many times a message must be repeated before an impression, awareness or learning occurs. The search for effective frequency continues, particularly by product class. However, it is generally accepted that three exposures are necessary as a minimum and 10 as a maximum.

Decisions regarding the media cannot be made in isolation from the qualitative factors associated with each vehicle. Known as vehicle source effects, these are concerned with the quality of the vehicle in terms of its atmosphere, technical aspects and audience/product fit.

The final task concerns the timing or scheduling of advertisements. As with most things in life, timing is of the essence. Scheduling calls for subjectivity and, while there are numerous quantitative measures to assist decision-making, media planning is essentially about management making judgements about where best to place its client's messages to maximise their effectiveness and the efficiency of the spend.

Review questions

1. What are the main tasks facing media planners?

2. If the rate at which information decays within individuals is known, then the task of the media planner is simply to place messages at suitable intervals in the path of decay. Discuss.

3. Draw a typical learning curve and then explain interference theory.

4. Why is it important that a media planner knows whether reach or frequency is the main objective of a media plan?

5. Why are frequency levels so important? Explain the concept of effective frequency.

6. How does recency planning differ from effective frequency?

7. What is a TVR and how does it relate to GRPs?

8. How is CPT flawed as a measure of media efficiency?

9. Write a brief report outlining the principal characteristics of media source effects.

10. What are the main ways in which media plans can be scheduled?

MINI CASE

This mini case was written by Julie Tinson, Marketing Lecturer at Bristol Business School.

Material for this mini case was supplied by Manning Gottlieb Media and used with their kind permission.

thetrainline.com

Background

In February 1999 the Trainline telephone rail ticket service went on-line and thetrainline.com business was unveiled. Between February and September 1999 thetrainline.com service was offered to Virgin Train customers through Virgin Train's own marketing. This acted as an invaluable 'soft' launch allowing testing and evaluation of the site and business potential.

On 1 October 1999 the business was launched to the public, giving consumers the opportunity to enquire about any train journey in the UK and then to book the tickets there and then on-line.

The task

Thetrainline.com is an on-line business selling direct communicating solely through advertising (and PR). Crucial to its success was the building of its brand to develop a successful on-line national business and deliver predetermined targets for both site registrations and ticket sales (volume and value). The business was to be conducted not through the sale of additional rail travel but through switching the method of purchase and behaviour (not an easy task).

Factors for and against success

Success for this brand was not guaranteed. Rife dotcom confusion, evident market clutter and growing cynicism among the public did not ensure development of the business or the brand. In addition the commerce targets for the business were hugely ambitious given a brand that was unknown and a desired outcome of changing consumer behaviour. Security issues for on-line purchases were also a consideration.

However, thetrainline.com had a sensible and clearly understood brand name and proposition. There was no competition and a growing Internet-enabled audience. With the backing of Virgin and Stagecoach and an impressive on-line business and service synergy, the critical success factors for launching this brand were in place.

Media strategy

The strategy was simply to launch the site and brand among the target audience and then maintain and build awareness continuously thereafter. This was on the bold premiss that awareness, confidence and understanding would automatically generate registrations and bookings. As an unknown brand (and a dotcom brand) the task was not only to create a brand but also to create reassurance among the audience that Thetrainline.com is a credible, safe and long-term on-line business.

After significant levels of investment and 11 months of advertising a positive return on the investment was achieved (a fact not shared by the majority of dotcom brand launches).

The target audience

Broad target was rail-users owning a PC mainly used for the Internet. This subdivided into commuters, business and leisure.

Role of media

The choice of media and implementation of the campaign was two-fold. Essentially it was to provide consumers with ongoing reassurance that the business offered a credible, safe and reliable service. The following tools were used specifically for this purpose: television, roadside posters, taxi sides, liveried taxis, bus sides, banners, bridge sites, on-line and newspapers

Secondly, the message had to be relevant to all members of the target audience, connecting with and influencing consumers when they are experiencing rail travel or in a position to plan journeys and buy tickets. Radio, Adrail, London Underground, newspapers (*Metro*), special builds, station floors and on-line advertising were all used to this end.

Each element of the plan complemented the whole with no one media channel requiring excessive weight.

Media channel strategy

After initial launch bursts, the campaign switched to a 50 TVR a week constant drip nationally using 20 second ads. These ran on the key days of Saturday–Tuesday only to push home use and maximise early week office use.

Use of taxis and buses (upweight London) rotated alternately, maintaining a constant outdoor presence. In addition liveried taxis, special builds/banners, special sites built at Paddington and King's Cross and the use of the biggest ever UK banner were used to maximise target audience and media attention. A constant presence on Adrail packages rotating six sheets for two weeks, then 48 sheets for two weeks, was designed to keep activity fresh and visible.

Tailored campaigns in core newspapers allowed both specific targeting and integration.

Different space sizes were used per paper with a constant presence, for example, the back-page strip in *Metro* and 5×1 box ad in *Telegraph* next to the crossword.

Summary

The launch of thetrainline.com was an unrivalled success in the dotcom market with 1.4 million registered users and 45% prompted brand awareness achieved. It also demonstrated a positive return on investment within 12 months of open trading and is preparing for a variety of NPD to extend the business and the brand in the future. Specific media were selected to target audience groups to reassure them and give a motive to use and this activity directly and measurably influenced bookings. The media strategy has thus demonstrably been instrumental in thetrainline.com's success.

Mini-case questions

1. How might external factors have influenced this campaign?
2. What media strategy may be employed in the event of increased on-line competition?
3. How might increased competition affect share of voice?
4. What are the strategic implications of subdividing the target audience and how might this shape the choice of media vehicle?
5. What are the critical success factors relating to media planning for building dotcom brands?

References

Aaker, D., Batra, R. and Myers, J.G. (1992) *Advertising Management*, 4th edn. Englewood Cliffs, NJ: Prentice Hall.

Armstrong, S. (1993) The business of buying: time, lads, please. *Media Week*, 3 September, pp. 26–7.

Beale, C. (1997) Study reveals negativity towards ads. *Campaign*, 28 November, p. 8.

Brech, P. (1999) When the media buck stops with you. *Media Week*, 19 November, pp. 22–3.

Broussard, G. (2000) How advertising frequency can work to build online effectiveness. *International Journal of Market Research*, **42**(4), pp. 439–57.

Burnett, J. (1993) *Promotion Management*. New York: Houghton Mifflin.

Crane, L.E. (1964) How product, appeal, and program affect attitudes towards commercials. *Journal of Advertising Research*, **4** (March), p. 15.

Ephron, E. (1997) Recency planning. *Admap* (February), pp. 32–4.

Gallucci, P. (1997) There are no absolutes in media planning. *Admap* (July/August), pp. 39–43.

Govoni, N., Eng, R. and Galper, M. (1986) *Promotional Management*. Englewood Cliffs, NJ: Prentice Hall.

Jones, P. (1990) Advertising: strong or weak force? Two views an ocean apart. *International Journal of Advertising*, 9(3), pp. 233–46.

Jones, P. (1995) *When Ads Work: New Proof that Advertising Triggers Sales*. New York: Simon & Schuster, The Free Press/Lexington Books.

Kotler, P. (1997) *Marketing Management: Analysis, Planning, Implementation and Control*, 9th edn. Englewood Cliffs, NJ: Prentice Hall.

Krugman, H.E. (1965) The impact of television advertising: learning without involvement. *Public Opinion Quarterly*, **29** (Fall), pp. 349–56.

Krugman, H.E. (1972) How potent is TV advertising. Cited in du Plessis (1998).

Krugman, H.E. (1975) What makes advertising effective? *Harvard Business Review* (March/April), pp. 96–103.

Lloyd, D.W. and Clancy, K.J. (1991) CPMs versus CPMis: implications for media planning. *Journal of Advertising Research*, 31(4) (August/September), pp. 34–44.

McLuhan, M. (1966) *Understanding Media: The Extensions of Man*. New York: McGraw-Hill.

Mueller-Heumann, G. (1992) Market and technology shifts in the 1990s: market fragmentation and mass customisation. *Journal of Marketing Management*, **8**, pp. 303–14.

Murray, G.B. and Jenkins, J.R.G. (1992) The concept of effective reach in advertising. *Journal of Advertising Research*, **32**(3) (May/June), pp. 34–42.

Naples, M.J. (1979) *Effective Frequency: The Relationship Between Frequency and Advertising Effectiveness*. New York: Association of National Advertisers.

Ostrow, J.W. (1981) What level frequency? *Advertising Age* (November), pp. 13–18.

Ostrow, J.W. (1984) Setting frequency levels: an art or a science? *Marketing and Media Decisions*, **24**(4), pp. 9–11.

Du Plessis, E. (1998) Memory and likeability: keys to understanding ad effects. *Admap* (July/August), pp. 42–6.

Rothschild, M.L. (1987) *Marketing Communications*. Lexington, MA: D.C. Heath.

Sissors, J.Z. and Bumba, L. (1989) *Advertising Media Planning*, 3rd edn. Lincolnwood, IL: NTC Business Books.

Weilbacher, W. (1984) *Advertising*. New York: Macmillan.

23

Sales promotion

Sales promotion seeks to offer buyers additional value as an inducement to generate an immediate sale. These inducements can be targeted at consumers, distributors, agents and members of the sales force. Sales promotions can form an important part of the communication mix and are often of strategic importance to number 3 and 4 brands in fast-moving consumer goods markets.

AIMS AND OBJECTIVES

The aim of this chapter is to consider the nature and role of sales promotion and to appraise its position within the marketing communications mix.

The objectives of this chapter are:

1. To explain the role of sales promotion in the promotional mix.
2. To discuss the reasons for the increased use of sales promotions.
3. To examine the way in which sales promotions are considered to work.
4. To appraise the value of this promotional tool.
5. To discuss the nature of loyalty programmes and issues associated with customer retention.
6. To appreciate how sales promotions can be used strategically.

Introduction

One of the main tasks of advertising is to develop awareness in the target audience. The main task of sales promotion is to encourage the target audience to behave in a particular way, usually to buy a product. These two tools set out to accomplish tasks at each end of the attitudinal spectrum: the cognitive and the conative elements. Just as advertising seeks to work over the long term, sales promotion can achieve short-term upward shifts in sales.

Sales promotion seeks to offer buyers additional value, as an inducement to generate an immediate sale. These inducements can be targeted at consumers, distributors, agents and members of the sales force. A whole range of network members can benefit from the use of sales promotion.

Sales promotion seeks to offer buyers additional value, as an inducement to generate an immediate sale.

This promotional tool is traditionally referred to as below-the-line expenditure, because, unlike advertising, there are no commission payments from media owners with this form of communication. The promotional costs are borne directly by the organisation initiating the activity, which in most cases is a manufacturer or producer. There are a number of reasons why sales promotions are used, and some of them are set out in Table 23.1.

There are many sales promotion techniques, but they all offer a direct inducement or an incentive to encourage receivers of the promotional messages to buy a product sooner rather than later. The inducement (for example, price-offs, coupons, premiums) is presented as an added value to the basic product and is intended to encourage buyers to act 'now' rather than later. Sales promotion is used, there-

Sales promotion is used, therefore, principally as a means to accelerate sales.

Table 23.1 Reasons for the use of sales promotions

■ *Reach new customers.*	They are useful in securing trials for new products and in defending shelf space against anticipated and existing competition.
■ *Reduce distributor risk.*	The funds that manufacturers dedicate to them lower the distributor's risk in stocking new brands.
■ *Reward behaviour.*	They can provide rewards for previous purchase behaviour.
■ *Retention.*	They can provide interest and attract potential customers and in doing so encourage them to provide personal details for further communications activity.
■ *Add value.*	Can encourage sampling and repeat purchase behaviour by providing extra value (superior to competitors' brands) and a reason to purchase.
■ *Induce action.*	They can instill a sense of urgency among consumers to buy while a deal is available. They add excitement and interest at the point of purchase to the merchandising of mature and mundane products.
■ *Preserve cash flow.*	Since sales promotion costs are incurred on a pay-as-you-go basis, they can spell survival for smaller, regional brands that cannot afford big advertising programmes.
■ *Improve efficiency.*	Sales promotions allow manufacturers to use idle capacity and to adjust to demand and supply imbalances or softness in raw material prices and other input costs, while maintaining the same list prices.
■ *Integration.*	Provide a means of linking together other tools of the promotional mix.
■ *Assist segmentation.*	They allow manufacturers to price discriminate among consumer segments that vary in price sensitivity. Most manufacturers believe that a high-list, high-deal policy is more profitable than offering a single price to all consumers. A portion of sales promotion expenditures, therefore, consists of reductions in list prices that are set for the least price-sensitive segment of the market.

fore, principally as a means to accelerate sales. The acceleration represents the short-ened period of time in which the transaction is completed relative to the time that would have elapsed had there not been a promotion. This action does not mean that an extra sale has been achieved.

Sales promotions can be targeted, with considerable precision, at particular audiences. There are three broad audiences to whom sales promotions can be targeted. These are consumers, members of the distribution or channel network, and the sales forces of both manufacturers and resellers. It should be remembered that the accuracy of these promotional tools means that many subgroups within these broad groups can be reached quickly and accurately.

Sales promotions targeted at employees

GKN Westland Aerospace saved £5 million as part of a total quality management programme which was supported by a voucher scheme (Kingfisher Vouchers, using B&Q, Comet and Woolworths retailers).

GKN's old scheme was based around a suggestion box and involved 15% of staff (Miller, 2000a). The revised scheme involves 85% of the 1500 staff. By personalising the incentives, every member of staff has a real choice of reward.

The role of sales promotion has changed significantly over recent years. At one time, the largest proportion of communications budgets was normally allocated to advertising. In many cases advertising no longer dominates the communication budget and sales promotion has assumed the focus of the communications spend, for reasons that are described below. This is particularly evident in consumer markets that are mature, have reached a level of stagnation, and where price and promotion work are the few ways of inducing brand switching behaviour.

Short-termism

The short-term financial focus of many industrialised economies has developed a managerial climate geared to short-term performance and evaluation, over periods as short as 12 weeks. To accomplish this, communication tools are required that work quickly and directly impact upon sales. Many see this as leading to an erosion of the brand franchise.

Managerial accountability

Following on from the previous reason is the increased pressure upon marketing managers to be accountable for their communications expenditure. The results of sales promotion activities are more easily justified and understood than those associated with advertising. The number of coupons returned for redemption and the number of bonus packs purchased can be calculated quickly and easily, with little room for error or misjudgement. Advertising, however, cannot be so easily measured in either the short or the long term. The impact of this is that managers can relate the promotional expenditure to the bottom line much more comfortably with sales promotion than with advertising.

Brand performance

Technological advances have enabled retailers to track brand performance more effectively. This in turn means that manufacturers can be drawn into agreements that promulgate in-store promotional activity at the expense of other more traditional forms of mass media promotion. Barcode scanners, hand-held electronic shelf-checking equipment and computerised stock systems facilitate the tracking of merchandise. This means that brand managers can be held responsible much more quickly for below-par performance.

Brand expansion

As brand quality continues to improve and as brands proliferate on the shelves of increasingly larger supermarkets, so the number of decisions that a consumer has to make also increases. Faced with multiple-brand decisions and a reduced amount of time to complete the shopping expedition, the tension associated with the shopping experience has increased considerably over the last decade.

As brands proliferate on the shelves of increasingly larger supermarkets, so the number of decisions that a consumer has to make also increases.

Promotions make decision-making easier for consumers: they simplify a potentially difficult process. So, as brand choice increases, the level of shopping convenience falls. The conflict this causes can be resolved by the astute use of sales promotions. Some feel that the cognitive shopper selects brands that offer increased value, which makes decision-making easier and improves the level of convenience associated with the shopping experience. However, should there be promotions on two offerings from an individual's repertoire then the decision-making is not necessarily made easier.

Competition for shelf space

The continuing growth in the number of brands launched in the 1980s and 1990s and the fragmentation of consumer markets mean that retailers have to be encouraged to make shelf space available. Sales promotions help manufacturers win valuable shelf space and assist retailers to attract increased levels of store traffic and higher utilisation of limited resources.

The credibility of this promotional tool is low, as it is obvious to the receiver what the intention is of using sales promotion messages. However, because of the prominent and pervasive nature of the tool, consumers and members of the trade understand and largely accept the direct sales approach. Sales promotion is not a tool

The credibility of this promotional tool is low.

that hides its intentions, nor does it attempt to be devious (which is not allowed, by regulation).

The absolute costs of sales promotion are low, but the real costs need to be evaluated once a campaign has finished and all redemptions received and satisfied. The relative costs can be high, as not only do the costs of the premium or price discount need to be determined, but also the associated costs of additional transportation, lost profit, storage and additional time spent organising and administering a sales promotion campaign need to be accounted for.

Sales promotions – UK car market

In the UK car market sales promotions have usually been used to drive customers to the dealerships. However, the retail landscape for car buyers is changing enormously following numerous stories, parliamentary comment and news media observation that car prices in the UK are 10–15% higher than in continental Europe.

In addition to the pressure to reduce prices, the opportunities and marketing channels (Internet driven) for purchasing new cars has expanded considerably. Therefore, the primary role for sales promotions now appears to be one of presenting the car to the customer in the channel environments that customers are more likely to inhabit (Miller, 2000b). It would appear that sales promotions are being used as a strategically and integrated tool to develop brands

In its favour, sales promotion allows for a high degree of control. Management is able to decide just when and where a sales promotion will occur and also estimate the sales effect. Sales promotions can be turned on and off quickly and adjusted to changed market conditions. The intended message is invariably the one that is received, as there is relatively little scope for it to be corrupted or damaged in transmission.

Sales promotion plans: the objectives

The objectives of using this tool are sales orientated and are geared to stimulating buyers either to use a product for the first time or to encourage use on a routine basis.

One objective of sales promotion activity is to prompt buyers into action, to initiate a series of behaviours that result in long-run purchase activity. These actions can be seen to occur in the conative stage of the attitudinal set. They reflect high or low involvement, and indicate whether cognitive processing and persuasion occur via the central or peripheral routes of the ELM (Chapter 20). If the marketing objectives include the introduction of a new product or intention to enter a new market, then the key objective associated with low-involvement decisions and peripheral route processing is to stimulate trial use as soon as possible. When high-involvement decisions and central route processing are present, then sales promotions need to be withheld until a suitable level of attitudinal development has been undertaken by public relations and advertising activities.

The main objective of sales promotion activity is to prompt buyers into action, to initiate a series of behaviours that result in long-run purchase activity.

If a product is established in a market, then a key objective should be to use sales promotions to stimulate an increase in the number of purchases made by current customers and to attract users from competing products (Figure 23.1). The objectives, therefore, are either to increase consumption for established products or to stimulate trial by encouraging new buyers to use a product. Once this has been agreed then the desired trial and usage levels need to be determined for each of the target audiences. Before discussing these aspects, it is necessary first to review the manner in which sales promotions are thought to influence the behaviour of individuals.

Involvement

	High	Low
New product or market	Withold sales promotion	Use sales promotion to stimulate trial
Established product or market	Non-loyals – use for switching Loyals – use carefully	Non-loyals – use sales promotions to attract for trial Loyals – use sales promotion to reward for increased usage

Figure 23.1 A sales promotion objectives grid.

Increasing usage and supporting sponsorship – Daz

As part of a campaign to increase market penetration and loyalty, an integrated marketing communications campaign was launched in the late summer of 2000. Core to the campaign was sponsorship of the TV programme *Emmerdale*. This was supported by an on-pack promotion which itself had been promoted through advertisements in national tabloids and TV weeklies, Web site support, POP and on-pack devices.

The promotion itself required customers to match symbols found on the on-pack gamecard with clothing symbols that were broadcast as part of the *Emmerdale* credits. To find out how much they had won, customers with matching symbols were required to phone a free hot-line. The campaign was very successful with volume share increasing over 11% in the short term.

An overview of how sales promotions work

If the overriding objectives of sales promotions are to accelerate or bring forward future sales, the implication is that a behavioural change is required by the receiver for the sales promotion to be effective. The establishment of new behaviour patterns is the preferred outcome. If sales promotions are to work over the longer term, that is to bring about repeat purchase behaviour, then the new behaviour patterns need to be learned and adopted on a permanent basis.

If sales promotions are to work over the longer term, that is to bring about repeat purchase behaviour, then the new behaviour patterns need to be learned and adopted on a permanent basis.

This is a complex task, and is referred to by behaviourists as shaping. The behaviourist's view is advocated, for example, by Rothschild and Gaidis (1981). They suggest that by breaking the overall task into its constituent parts, a series of smaller sequential tasks can be learned. When the successive actions are aggregated, the new desired pattern of behaviour emerges. This view emphasises the impact of external stimuli in changing the behaviour of people.

The cognitive view of the way sales promotions operate is based on the belief that consumers internally process relevant information about a sales promotion, including those of past experiences, and make a reasoned decision in the light of the goals and objectives that individuals set for themselves.

The ELM suggests that individuals using the peripheral route will only consider simplistic cues, such as display boards and price reduction signs, for example. Individuals using the central route of the ELM have a higher need for information and will develop the promotional signal to evaluate the relative price and the salient attributes of the promoted product before making a decision (Inman *et al.*, 1990).

The main difference between the views of the behaviourists and those of the cognitive school of thought is that the former stress the impact of externally generated stimuli, whereas the latter recognise the complexity of internal information processing as the most significant element.

Loyalty and retention programmes

The growth of loyalty programmes has been a significant promotional development in recent years. One of the more visible schemes was the ClubCard offered by Tesco, which has been partly responsible for Tesco ousting Sainsbury's as the number one supermarket in the UK. Sainsbury's initial response was to publicly reject loyalty cards, but some 18 months later it launched its Reward Card.

Loyalty schemes have been encouraged through the use of swipe cards. Users are rewarded with points each time a purchase is made. This is referred to as a 'points accrual programme', whereby loyal users are able to build up the necessary points, which are stored (often) on a card, and 'cashed in' at a later date for gifts or merchandise. The benefit for the company supporting the scheme is that the promised rewards motivate customers to accrue more points and in doing so increase their switching costs, effectively locking them into the loyalty programme and preventing them from moving to a competitor brand.

Recent technological developments mean that smart cards (a card that has a small microprocessor attached) can record enormous amounts of information, which is updated each time a purchase is made.

Not only have loyalty schemes for frequent flyers (e.g. BA Executive Club and Virgin Freeway) been very successful, but the cards are also used to track individual travelers. Airlines are able to offer cardholders particular services, such as special airport lounges and magazines; the card through its links to a database also enables a traveller's favourite seat and dietary requirements to be offered. In addition, the regular accumulation of air miles fosters continuity and hence loyalty, through which business travellers reward themselves with leisure travel.

The potential number of applications for smart cards is tremendous. However, just like swipe cards the targeting of specific groups of buyers can be expected to become more precise and efficient and it is also easier to track and target individuals for future promotional activities.

Christopher (1997) claims that it can cost a company as much as five times extra to obtain a new customer than to retain an existing one. Customer retention is a bedrock for sustained profitable performance. Perhaps the attention being given to loyalty and retention issues is misplaced because marketing is about the identification, anticipation and satisfaction of customer needs (profitably). If these needs are being met properly it might be reasonable to expect that customers would return anyway, reducing the need for overt 'loyalty' programmes. The demise of Safeway's ABC loyalty card suggests that their investment did not provide a competitive advantage and did not differentiate the supermarket sufficiently to drive profits and provide shareholder value.

Customer retention is a bedrock for sustained profitable performance.

There is an argument that these schemes are important not because of the loyalty aspect but because the programme allows for the collection of up-to-date customer information and then the use of the data to make savings in the supply chain. It is suggested that Tesco have saved over £500 million through the use of their customer data (Jardine, 2000). However, one of the main logistical problems concerns the management and analysis of the huge volumes of data collected. Some organisations use less than half the data they collect and then it can be argued that the data actually used can be bought in at a much lower cost than these loyalty schemes cost to run. There are a proliferation of loyalty cards, reflecting the increased emphasis upon keeping customers rather than constantly finding new ones. Whether loyalty is being developed by encouraging buyers to make repeat purchases or whether the schemes are merely sales promotion techniques that encourage extended and consistent purchasing patterns is debatable. Customer retention is a major issue and a lot of emphasis has been given to loyalty schemes as a means of achieving retention targets.

Loyalty at one level can be seen to be about increasing sales volume, that is, fostering loyal purchase behaviour. High levels of repeat purchase, however, are not necessarily an adequate measure of loyalty, as there may be a number of situational factors determining purchase behaviour, such as brand availability (Dick and Basu, 1994).

At another level loyalty can be regarded as an attitudinal disposition.

At another level, loyalty can be regarded as an attitudinal disposition. O'Malley (1998) suggests that customer satisfaction has become a surrogate measure of loyalty. However, she points out that there is plenty of evidence to show that many satisfied customers buy a variety of brands and that polygamous loyalty, as suggested by Dowling and Uncles (1997), may be a better reflection of reality.

At whichever level of loyalty, customer retention is paramount and neither behavioural nor attitudinal measures alone are adequate indicators of true loyalty. O'Malley suggests that a combination of the two is of greater use and that the twin parameters relative attitudes (to alternatives) and patronage behaviour (the recency, frequency and monetary model), as suggested by Dick and Basu, when used together offer more accurate indicators of loyalty.

The need to develop suitable attitudes and behaviours lies at the heart of loyalty programmes. It is about the provision and use of information, skilful segmentation and the development of appropriate relationships. The Sharwood's example goes some way to illustrate this point.

Using interactive competitions – Sharwood's Asian Foods

As part of a strategy to develop and maintain the position of the Sharwood's brand of Asian foods (www.sharwoods.com), the organisation used a £5 million above-the-line television campaign as part of their strategy to build a more engaging brand. This has included its first investment in interactive digital television. Via banner advertising on the NTL digital platform consumers were directed to a microsite to participate in an interactive competition to win two Virgin flights and one of 10,000 money off coupons for Sharwood's products. The promotion not only developed an extensive database for use in future emarketing but added value through entertainment and built the brand in a lighthearted, involving context. See Exhibit 23.1

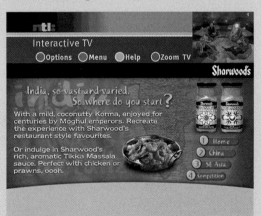

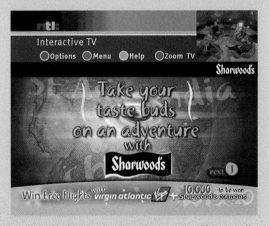

Exhibit 23.1   Sharwood's brand development using an interactively based sales promotion campaign. Picture reproduced with the kind permission of Centura Foods Ltd.

Material kindly provided by Caroline Clarke, Senior Brand Manager, Sharwood's.

Types of loyalty

The concept of loyalty has attracted much research attention if only because of the recent and current popularity of this approach. Table 23.2 represents some of the more general types of loyalty that can be observed.

Table 23.2   Types of loyalty

Emotional loyalty	This is a true form of loyalty and is driven by personal identification with real or perceived values and benefits.
Price loyalty	This type of loyalty is driven by rational economic behaviour and the main motivations are cautious management of money or financial necessity.
Incentivised loyalty	This refers to promiscuous buyers: those with no one favourite brand who demonstrate through repeat experience the value of becoming loyal.
Monopoly loyalty	This class of loyalty arises where a consumer has no purchase choice owing to a national monopoly. This, therefore, is not a true form of loyalty.
Inertia	This final form of loyalty arises when a buyer is disinclined to move between brands for whatever reason.

Loyalty can be interpreted as a pyramid or as a ladder (Figure 23.2). These gradu-ation schemes suggest that consumers are capable of varying degrees of loyalty. This type of categorisation has been questioned by a number of researchers. Fournier and Yao (1997) doubt the validity of the pyramid and Baldinger and Rubinson (1996) sup-port the idea that consumers work within an evoked set and switch between brands. This view is supported on the grounds that many consumers display elements of curiosity in their purchase habits, enjoy variety and are happy to switch brands as a result of marketing communication activities and product experience.

There is little evidence to support the notion that sales promotions, and in par-ticular the use of premiums, are capable of encouraging loyalty, whether that be defined as behavioural and/or attitude. 'The notion of hard core loyals is fast becom-ing extinct' (Yim and Kannan, 1999) as the proliferation of brands has led customers to prefer to actively select from a repertoire of favourite brands, each of which serves to satisfy slightly different needs.

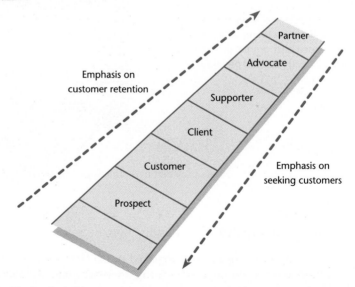

Figure 23.2   The loyalty ladder.

The value of sales promotions

The increasing proportion of budgets being allocated to sales promotions has prompted concern about the costs and effects of these activities. It might be reasonable to expect that the sales curve following a sales promotion would look like that depicted in Figure 23.3. An upward shift in demand is, however, unrealistic, particularly in mature markets. Extra stock is being transferred to consumers, and therefore they have more than they require for a normal purchase cycle.

The increasing proportion of budgets being allocated to sales promotions has prompted concern about the costs and effects of these activities.

The graph shown in Figure 23.4 is more likely to occur, with sales falling in the period when consumers are loaded with stock and temporarily removed from the market. A third scenario is shown in Figure 23.5. Promotional activity does not take place in a vacuum with new products: competitors will be attracted and some customers lost to competitive offerings; in mature markets, non-loyals will take advantage

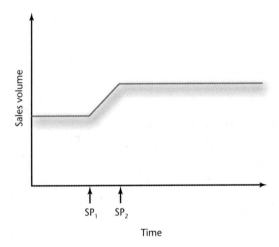

Figure 23.3   Expected response to a sales promotion event: SP_1 is the start of the event; SP_2 is the end.

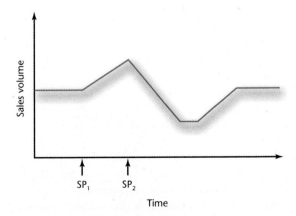

Figure 23.4   Realistic response to a sales promotion event: SP_1 is the start of the event; SP_2 is the end.

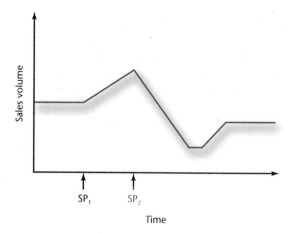

Figure 23.5 Destructive effect of competitive sales promotions.

of the sales promotion and then revert to competitors' sales promotions when they re-enter the market. The result is that overall demand for the product may be reduced owing to the combined effects of competitive promotional activity.

Sales promotions incur a large number of hidden costs. It was stated earlier that the cost of a sales promotion is thought to be relatively low but, as Buzzell *et al.* (1990) and others have demonstrated, there are a host of other indirect costs that must be considered. Manufacturers, for example, use promotional deals to induce resellers to buy stock at a promotional price, in addition to their normal buying requirements. The additional stock is then held for resale at a later date, at regular retail prices. The effect of this forward buying on the costs of the reseller can be enormous. Buzzell *et al.* point out that the promotional stock attracts higher interest charges, storage costs, expenses associated with the transfer of stock to different geographical areas of the organisation and the costs associated with keeping normal and promotional stock separate. When these are added to the manufacturer's forward buying costs, it is probable, they conclude, that the costs outweigh the benefits of the sales promotion exercise.

These activities suggest that the relationship between the members of the network is market orientated rather than relational. However, many of these extra costs are unknown, and the resellers are unaware of the costs they are absorbing as a result of the deal. In the future, resellers and manufacturers should work together on such promotions and attempt to uncover all the costs involved to ensure that the exercise is successful for both parties.

Not only the short-term costs associated with a sales promotion but also the long-term costs must be evaluated. Jones (1990) refers to this as the double jeopardy of sales promotions. He argues that manufacturers who participate extensively in short-term sales promotions, mainly for defensive reasons, do so at the expense of profit. The generation of sales volume and market share is at the expense of profit. The long-term effects are equally revealing. As the vast majority of sales promotions are temporary price reductions (TPRs), the opportunity to build a consumer franchise, where the objective is the development of brand identity and loyalty, is negated. Evidence shows that as soon as a sales promotion is switched off, so any increased sales are also terminated until the next promotion. The retaliatory effect that TPRs have on competitors does nothing to stabilise what Jones calls volatile demand, where the only outcome, for some products, is decline and obscurity.

Sales promotions can lead consumers to depend upon the presence of a promotion before commitment to a purchase is made. If the preferred product does not carry a coupon, premium or TPR, then they may switch to a competitor's product that does offer some element of increased value. A related issue concerns the speed at which sales promotions are reduced following the introduction of a new product. If the incentives are removed too quickly, it is probable that consumers will have been unable to build a relationship with the product. If the incentives are sustained for too long, then it is possible that consumers have only identified a product by the value of the incentive, not the value of the product itself. The process by which a sales promotion is removed from a product is referred to as fading, and its rate can be crucial to the successful outcome of a product launch and a sales promotion activity.

> *Sales promotions can lead consumers to depend upon the presence of a promotion before commitment to a purchase is made.*

The strategic use of sales promotions

For a long time sales promotions have been regarded as a short-term tactical tool whose prime purpose is to encourage customers to try a brand or to switch brands (within their repertoire) attracted by the added value of the sales promotion. Indeed, Papatia and Krishnamurthi (1996) claim that coupons can actively promote switching behaviour and so reduce levels of loyalty. As discussed earlier what happens after a sales promotion activity finishes is debatable. Some claim that once a promotion is withdrawn satisfied customers will return to the brand unsupported by a sales promotion, but supported by other elements of the marketing communications mix: in particular advertising, to maintain awareness of the brand and its values, direct marketing, to provide personal attention and the opportunity to take immediate action, and public relations to sustain credibility and relevance.

By way of contrast it can be argued that sales promotion serves to discount a brand, either directly through price-based reductions or indirectly through coupons and premiums. Customer alignment is to the deal rather than to the brand itself. This serves to lower expectations of what a brand stands for and what it is capable of delivering. So, once a sales promotion is removed, the normal price is perceived as representing inferior value and so repeat purchase behaviour is deterred.

> *It can be argued that sales promotion serves to discount a brand, either directly through price-based reductions or indirectly through coupons and premiums.*

However, despite these less than positive views, some writers (Davis, 1992; O'Malley, 1998) argue that sales promotions have a strategic role to play in the promotional mix. Traditionally they have been viewed as short-term tactical tools which can be used offensively to induce the trial of new products, or defensively for established products to retain shelf space and consumers. Sales promotions that do not work as intended may have been used to support inappropriate products or may have been devised without adequate planning. An example of the latter issue may be the Hoover free flights misjudgement and the associated over-subscription that followed the launch of that particular sales promotion activity. There can be no doubt that sales promotions orientated to consumer deals and TPRs, in particular, do little to contribute to the overall strategy adopted for an organisation or even a product.

One of the consequences of competitive sales promotions, especially in consumer markets, is the spiral effect that retaliatory actions can have on each organisation. A sales promotion 'trap' develops when competitors start to imitate each other's activities, often based upon price reductions. This leads eventually to participants losing profitability and consumers losing value and possibly choice as some products are forced to drop out of the market.

A sales promotion 'trap' develops when competitors start to imitate each other's activities, often based upon price reductions.

With the development of relationship marketing and the move towards integrated marketing communications has been the realisation that employees are an important target audience. There is a strong need to motivate the workforce and sales promotion activities have an important role to play. However, employee incentives need to made accessible to everyone and not just a few (such as the sales force). This means that rewards need to be more broadly spread and there needs to be choice. Vouchers, for example, enable the prize winner to make a choice based on their circumstances and they are easier to administer than many of the other types of reward. Incentive schemes should be designed in such a way that they do not fall into the trap of creating winners and losers which can be the case when for example, the top 20 in a scheme win a prize, which effectively creates 80 losers out of every 100 employees.

Many schemes are based around product prizes, typically electrical goods. However, for many people these are no longer attractive (or sufficiently motivating) as rewards. Virgin vouchers provide activity-based rewards where there is an experience which gives the recipient a memory. Activities such as hot-air ballooning, sky diving, visits to the theatre or to health farms appeal to a wide cross-section of people.

The true strategic effect of sales promotion activities can only be achieved if they are coordinated with the other activities of the promotional mix, and this requires planning. In particular, the complementary nature of sales promotion and advertising should be exploited through the use of common themes and messages, timing, targeting and allocation of resources (in particular budgets). Sales promotions that are planned as a sequence of predetermined activities, reflecting the promotional requirements of a product over the longer term, are more likely to be successful than those sales promotions that are simply reactions to competitors' moves and market developments.

Integrated sales promotions – Kellogg's

Kellogg's entered into an on-pack promotion to donate a minimum of £500,000 to the charity Childline. Under the Kellogg's strapline Helping Kids Grow, consumers sent six tokens from Kellogg's cereal packs in return for a three-track CD. Consumers could select three tracks from a list of 10. For every CD requested, Kellogg's donated 30p to Childline, and, for a submission of tokens and no CD, Kellogg's donated £1. The record company BMG was enlisted as it had recording rights to a wide range of artists.

The cereal packs together with leaflets, dedicated Web site and direct mail to 30,000 teachers all helped to raise awareness of the ways in which children at risk could help themselves. A TV campaign was used to support the promotion and the music artists, ad agency and fulfilment houses all gave their time and services free of charge. The important aspect of this promotion is that Kellogg's was able to associate itself with a cause and at the same time underline its own proposition of healthy eating and care for others (Clarke, 2000).

The strategic impact of sales promotions is best observed when they are designed or built into a three- to four-year plan of promotional activities, coordinated with other promotional tools and integrated with the business strategy.

The manner in which many of the loyalty programmes are managed signals a move from pure sales promotion to direct marketing. The integration of these two approaches has become necessary in order that the advantages of both are realised. This does raise an interesting conflict, in that sales promotion is essentially a short-term tool, and direct marketing needs to work over the long term. The former is product orientated (albeit giving added value to consumers) and often orientated to mass audiences, whereas the latter is based upon developing a personal dialogue (Curtis, 1996).

A further strategic issue concerns the use of joint promotions with other leading brands. With the intention of promoting the health aspects of its oil for frying purposes, Goldenfields rapeseed oil joined up with Morphy Richards to offer a two-tier campaign. The first involved 20 stainless steel fat fryer prizes in return for coupons from the oil bottle label and the second was a health farm prize and a further 20 fat fryers (Clarke, 2001). By twinning brand names increased promotional impact can assist both partners. However, there is a danger that such a pairing will be short lived, and hence the strategic perspective may be limited.

A further strategic issue concerns the use of joint promotions with other leading brands.

Finally, the huge sums of money involved in some of the mainstream loyalty or reward-based programmes suggest that these should be seen as longer-term promotional investments. As the return will spread over many years, a medium-term perspective may be more appropriate rather than a short-term view based on a sales 'blip'.

Summary

Sales promotions now command the lion's share of the promotional budget. This is because it has been proved that they are very effective as a communication tool with consumers, members of the performance network and the sales force. The range of techniques and methods used to add value to offerings is enormous, but there are growing doubts about the effectiveness and profitability associated with some sales promotions.

In comparison with advertising and public relations, many of the sales promotion techniques are easier to evaluate, if only because the number of variables is smaller and they are easier to isolate. Having said this, there is a lack of effective sales promotion measurement and control. This often leads to a short-term focus. Retailers are the same, except for the evaluation on a pre- and post-test basis of their own-brand promotions. Store traffic, sales volume and consumer attitude studies prevail.

Sales promotions have a strategic role to play, particularly when they are used to complement the other activities in the promotional mix. By attempting to develop a consistent theme to a promotional plan, sales promotions can follow advertising's awareness-building activities with a series of messages that continue the theme already established. Success is much more likely when consumers are invited to take advantage of a promotion for a product that they not only are aware of but are conscious of through recent promotional messages.

▪ Review questions

1. Why is sales promotion referred to as a below-the-line promotional tool?

2. What are the purposes of using sales promotion and why has it assumed such a large share of promotional expenditure?

3. Write a brief note explaining how shaping works.

4. Identify the major differences between the behavioural and the cognitive explanations of how sales promotions work.

5. Does sales promotion have a strategic or a tactical role to play in the promotional mix?

6. Write brief notes outlining some of the issues associated with loyalty programmes and customer retention initiatives.

7. How would you advise a newly appointed assistant brand manager on the expected outcomes of a sales promotion programme? (Choose any sector/industry of your choice.)

8. Find three examples of sales promotion activity and determine the extent to which they are strategic or tactical.

9. What is the value of joint sales promotion activities?

10. How might use of technology assist strategic brand development?

▪ MINI CASE

This mini case was written by Geraldine McKay, Senior Lecturer in Marketing at the University of Staffordshire.

Esporta Health

Developing and keeping relationships

Esporta Health and Fitness run more than 30 premium sport and leisure clubs. With over 120,000 members they plan further expansion, in both the UK and Europe. Esporta's new club in Madrid has more than 9,000 existing members – a problem if they all use the club at the same time.

The number of clubs is expected to grow by 50% in the next two years. This will require increased membership targets along with objectives which are 'focused on improving membership loyalty and increasing spend per head'. At present, the average member is 34 years old, with a slight female bias. Most join as part of a couple or family. Members pay a one–off joining fee, alongside a monthly or yearly subscription. There are subscription rates for different categories of members including off peak, over 55s, and children. Hostage marketing commits joiners to a minimum of one year's membership.

Sales promotion has an important role and clubs are encouraged to run a number of creative schemes to fulfil a number of different objectives. Some schemes are available nationally, others are devised at local or regional level, stimulating activity when local conditions demand. Promotions may be reactive, e.g. to counter the affects of a competitor, others more proactive. Success is measured in the short and long term and the database is used to record members' responsiveness to offers. New members are encouraged to use the club and take part in special competitions, offering them more of a chance to win prizes, the more activities they become involved in.

Price promotions (discounts on joining fees, not subscriptions) are used but free gift offers (free case of wine, free colour television, the chance to stay at a villa in Spain, sports towels, etc.) generate interest. Cash incentives are popular – one scheme gave £50 cash to each member who successfully recommended a friend. Free trials are offered (via the Internet site) so that potential members can experience the facilities and service. At Christmas, vouchers offering '12 days of fitness' for a friend of a member are mailed. Although much of the promotion is short term, it is very important to retain members. Recruitment promotion must not alienate the existing clientele. A scheme to foster loyalty among existing members is the 'Gold' membership category for those who have stayed with the club over two years. This offers a slightly lower monthly subscription rate along with other member benefits such as discounts on a range of complementary products like car hire, sports clothing and physiotherapy. The Esporta wine club has been launched. Gold members get free entry to many social events held in the club.

With so many promotions being used by the clubs, there could be a problem with confusion and fatigue. Staff must keep up to date with the latest incentives and invent fresh promotions to meet targets.

Health club marketing raises many unique issues. Intelligent use of tactical and strategic sales promotion by Esporta will continue to benefit the clubs and their members.

Mini-case questions

1. What is meant by strategic and tactical sales promotion?
2. How might technology be used to enhance sales promotion activity by Esporta?
3. Can sales promotion encourage 'emotional' loyalty at Esporta and why should they consider this?
4. Why is it important to encourage use of the club's facilities by its members?
5. What are the issues that need to be considered by Esporta when designing and implementing a new sales promotion programme?
6. What methods of sales promotion would you suggest to fulfil the following objectives:
   (a) database building;
   (b) member recruitment;
   (c) encouraging involvement;
   (d) retention.

References

Baldinger, A. and Rubinson, J. (1996) Brand loyalty: the link between attitude and behaviour, *Journal of Advertising Research*, **36**(6) (November–December), pp. 22–34.

Buzzell, R.D., Quelch, J.A. and Salmon, W.J. (1990) The costly bargain of trade promotion. *Harvard Business Review* (March/April), pp. 141–9.

Christopher, M. (1997) *Marketing Logistics*. London: Butterworth-Heinemann.

Clarke, A. (2000) Kellogg's in CD push for childline. *Promotions and Incentives*, October, pp. 28–30.

Clarke, A. (2001) Finger on the pulse. *Promotions and Incentives*, (February), pp. 41–4.

Curtis, J. (1996) Opposites attract. *Marketing*, 25 April, pp. 28–9.

Davis, M. (1992) Sales promotions as a competitive strategy. *Management Decision*, **30**(7), pp. 5–10.

Dick, A.S. and Basu, K. (1994) Customer loyalty: toward an integrated framework. *Journal of the Academy of Marketing Science*, **22**(2), pp. 99–113.

Dowling, G.R. and Uncles, M. (1997) Do customer loyalty programmes really work? *Sloan Management Review* (Summer), pp. 71–82.

Fournier, S. and Yao, J.L. (1997) Reviving brand loyalty: a reconceputalisation within the framework of consumer–brand relationships. *International Journal of Research in Marketing*, **14**(5), pp. 451–72.

Inman, J., McAlister, L. and Hoyer, D.W. (1990) Promotion signal: proxy for a price cut? *Journal of Consumer Research*, **17** (June), pp. 74–81.

Jardine, A. (2000) Why loyalty's not as simple as ABC. *Marketing*, 18 May, p. 19.

Jones, P.J. (1990) The double jeopardy of sales promotions. *Harvard Business Review* (September/October), pp. 145–52.

Miller, R. (2000a) Rewarding staff is a matter of choice. *Marketing*, 10, February, pp. 27–8.

Miller, R. (2000b) Car pricing battles boost promotions. *Marketing*, 13 July, p. 29.

O'Malley, L. (1998) Can loyalty schemes really build loyalty? *Marketing Intelligence and Planning*, **16**(1), pp. 47–55.

Papatia, P. and Krishnamurthi, L. (1996) Measuring the dynamic effects of promotions on brand choice. *Journal of Marketing Research*, **33**, pp. 20-35.

Rothschild, M.L. and Gaidis, W.C. (1981) Behavioural learning theory: its relevance to marketing and promotions. *Journal of Marketing Research*, **45**(2), pp. 70–8.

Yim, C.K. and Kannan, P.K. (1999) Consumer behavioural loyalty: a segmentation model and analysis. *Journal of Business Research*, **44**(2), pp. 75–92.

24

Sales promotion techniques

The range and sophistication of the main sales promotion techniques reflect the variety of audiences, their needs and the tasks that need to be accomplished. By adding value to the offer and hoping to bring forward future sales, these techniques provide a source of competitive advantage, one that is invariably short rather than long run.

AIMS AND OBJECTIVES

The aim of this chapter is to consider the nature and characteristics of the main sales promotion tools and techniques.

The objectives of this chapter are:

1. To examine the sales promotional techniques used by manufacturers to influence resellers.

2. To examine the sales promotional techniques used by manufacturers to influence consumers.

3. To examine the sales promotional techniques used by resellers to influence consumers.

4. To examine the sales promotional techniques used by manufacturers to influence the sales force.

5. To clarify the particular objectives sales promotions seek to satisfy.

Introduction

As established in the previous chapter, sales promotions seek to offer buyers additional value, as an inducement to generate an immediate sale. These inducements

Sales promotions seek to offer buyers additional value, as an inducement to generate an immediate sale.

can be targeted at consumers, distributors, agents and members of the sales force. A whole range of network members can benefit from the use of sales promotion. The purpose of this chapter is to consider each of the principal sales promotion techniques.

The techniques considered in this chapter attempt to reflect the range and variety of techniques that are used to add value and induce a sale sooner rather than later. The nature and characteristics of the target audiences mean that different techniques work in different ways to achieve varying objectives. Therefore, consideration is given to the range of tasks that need to be accomplished among the following audiences: resellers, consumers and the sales force.

Sales promotions: manufacturers to resellers

Manufacturers and retailers see sales promotions as important devices to encourage trials among non-users and stimulate repeat purchase among users. Retailers prefer in-store promotions (push) instead of promotions aimed at consumers (pull) strategies. This has implications for the promotional mixes deployed by manufacturers.

Objectives for new products: trial

For manufacturers launching new products, the main marketing objective is to establish distribution. This is because the use of awareness advertising at the launch of a new product is pointless unless the product is available for consumers to purchase at retail outlets. Therefore, a distribution network needs to be set up in anticipation of consumer demand. The task of marketing communications is to encourage resellers to distribute a new product and to establish trial behaviour.

Objectives for established products: usage

Sales of established products need to be maintained and encouraged. The active support and participation of resellers is crucial. One of the main objectives of manufacturers is to develop greater exposure for their products; this means motivating distributors to allocate increased shelf space to a product thereby (possibly) reducing the amount of shelf space allocated to competitors. The task of marketing communications, therefore, is to encourage resellers to buy and display increased amounts of the manufacturer's products and establish greater usage.

It is an interesting point that the trial objective for retailers is to increase the number of new customers visiting a store. The usage objective aims to increase levels of store loyalty and the overall number of visits made by current customers. In the same way that manufacturers seek to establish brand loyalty, so retailers seek to build store loyalty.

The usage objective aims to increase levels of store loyalty and the overall number of visits made by current customers.

Resellers (in particular, retailers) and manufacturers have conflicting objectives. Manufacturers want to increase the amount of shelf space and attention paid to their products, whereas resellers want to increase the numbers of people using the store; they want to develop store traffic.

Methods

The main type of sales promotion used to motivate trade customers is an *allowance*. Allowances can take many forms, some of the more common ones being buying, count and recount, buy-back allowances, merchandising and promotional allowances. Trade allowances are a means of achieving a short-term increase in sales.

The main type of sales promotion used to motivate trade customers is an allowance.

They can be used defensively to protect valuable shelf space from aggressive competitors. By offering to work with resellers and providing them with extra incentives, manufacturers can guard territory gained to date.

Buying allowances

The most common form of discount is the buying allowance. In return for specific orders between certain dates, a reseller will be entitled to a refund or allowance of x% off the regular case or carton price. The only factor that the reseller must consider is the timing of the order. Manufacturers often use these sales promotions so that they coincide with a main buying period, reducing risk to the distributor.

For the manufacturer, these types of allowances can lead to an increase in the average size of orders, which in turn can utilise idle capacity and also prevent competitors securing business at their expense. This technique can also be used to encourage new stores to try the manufacturer's products or to stimulate repeat usage (restocking).

Count and recount allowances

Manufacturers may require resellers to clear old stock before a new or modified product is introduced. One way this can be achieved is to encourage resellers to move stock out of storage and into the store. The count and recount method provides an allowance for each case shifted into the store during a specified period of time.

The arithmetic for this transaction is as follows:

opening stock + purchases − closing stock = stock entitled to receive the agreed allowance

This technique can also be used to prevent a store becoming out of stock, and as such is essentially a usage-only technique. If a promotional campaign is to be launched, count and recount can prevent stock-out, loss of custom and wastage of promotional resources.

Buy-back allowances

Buy-backs can be used to follow up count and recount promotions. Under this scheme, the purchases made after the count and recount scheme (up to a maximum of the count and recount) are entitled to an allowance to encourage stores to replenish their stocks (with the manufacturer's product and not that of a competitor). By definition this is a usage-only technique.

Merchandise allowances

The previous three methods require the exchange of money, in the form of either a credit or a cash refund. Merchandising allowances benefit resellers by providing extra goods for which no payment is required. These free goods are only delivered if a reseller's order reaches a specific size. The benefit to

Merchandising allowances benefit resellers by providing extra goods for which no payment is required.

the manufacturer is that the administrative and transportation costs for the allowance are very low and are tied to those associated with the costs of the regular order.

For resellers, the incentive is that they can earn above-average profits with the free units. Manufacturers use this type of allowance to generate trials and to open up new distributors. However, this sales promotions technique needs the support of other activities, such as advertising, to provide security and confidence before potential resellers commit themselves to a new product.

Advertising allowances

Advertising allowances can be made if resellers can show that they have undertaken a promotional campaign featuring a manufacturer's product. A percentage allowance is given against a reseller's purchases during a specified period of time. This is a useful technique in stimulating trial by new stores. By weighting the allowances, resellers can be encouraged to take stock and create shelf space for new products.

Dealer listings are advertisements and notices that identify resellers and the range of products that each carries. Issued by manufacturers to help consumers locate their nearest store, they are effective in generating store traffic and for providing source credibility.

A further refinement of the advertising allowance is a scheme which involves the collaboration of a reseller so that an advertising campaign can be jointly funded.

The scheme involves the collaboration of a reseller so that an advertising campaign can be jointly funded.

Instead of providing an allowance against product purchases, an allowance is provided against the cost of an advertisement or campaign. Govoni *et al.* (1986) suggest that there are two forms of cooperative advertising, vertical and horizontal:

1. *Vertical advertising allowances*

   In vertical advertising, a manufacturer agrees to contribute to the reseller's campaign. A common approach is for a retailer to take out a full-page newspaper advertisement in which a number of different products are highlighted. Each manufacturer then contributes a share of the total cost, proportionate to its space/share of the advertisement. This omnibus approach is popular, as costs are shared and store traffic (usage) can be considerably improved. In addition to these benefits, manufacturers will invariably provide materials, such as artwork and schedules, to assist the promotion and coordinate the activities with their national campaigns.

   Direct mail is used increasingly, as lower unit costs and low wastage (relative to the mass appeal of advertising) encourage resellers to devote more time and resources to this form of promotion.

2. *Horizontal advertising allowances*

   In horizontal advertising, competitors join together to promote the product class and so stimulate primary demand. This form of promotion is often organised and controlled by a trade association. For example, the Milk Marketing Board's award-winning promotion of the home delivery service served to inform and remind people that the doorstep delivery service provided a range of benefits on behalf of relatively small delivery services who individually could not have undertaken the campaign and reached their target audiences so effectively.

Retailers have participated in horizontal programmes, but are normally reluctant to do so for competitive reasons. Retailers stocking products which have a territorial franchise associated with them are more willing to participate; the Southern Ford Dealers programme is a good example of retailer collaboration.

There are, of course, advantages and disadvantages with advertising allowance schemes. The manufacturer is able to buy more space, or time, for each pound spent on advertising, because the spend is often made at local, not national rates. A further factor in their favour is that the scheme encourages those who do not use advertising to participate.

Advertising allowances can also induce new resellers to become distributors when the objective is trial.

Finally, advertising allowances can also induce new resellers to become distributors when the objective is trial.

One of the main drawbacks concerns the cooperative aspect of the allowance arrangements. Resellers are able to assume control over the process and this can lead to circumstances where inappropriate messages and media are used. Furthermore, fraudulent claims have been submitted for advertising that either did not take place or duplicated a previous claim. This lack of control can lead to conflict, and the very scheme that was designed to foster collaborative behaviour can degenerate into a conflict of opinion and a deterioration in reseller/manufacturer relationships. It is interesting to observe that the organisations in the network that have the responsibility for distributing the manufacturer's products are the same ones which may (theoretically) be penalised by their supplier (Grey, as cited in Govoni *et al.* 1986), following abuse of sales promotions.

Hostaging

Hostaging is a process whereby a retailer/reseller is able to exert power over a manufacturer in order to pressurise or force it into providing trade promotions on a more or less continual basis. A less dependent firm may use influence strategies, such as requests and information exchange (Anderson and Narus, 1990). In contrast, the more dependent firm should seek to add value (or reduce costs) to the exchange for the partner firm, at a relatively small cost to itself.

Hostaging is a process whereby a retailer/reseller is able to exert power over a manufacturer in order to pressurise or force it into providing trade promotions on a more or less continual basis.

The more dependent firm in a working relationship needs to protect its transactions-specific assets by taking various actions, such as close bonding with end-user firms. Strategies to avoid 'hostaging' would include reducing the frequency of trade deals, converting trade spending into advertising and consumer promotions, and focusing on differentiating the brand with less reliance on price (Blattberg and Neslin, 1990).

Other forms of sales promotions aimed at resellers

There are a number of other techniques that can be used to achieve sales promotion objectives. These include dealer contests, which should be geared to stimulating increased usage. By encouraging resellers to improve their performance, growth can be fostered and the reseller's attention focused on the manufacturer's products, not those of the competition. Motivation and the provision of information are necessary at the launch of new products and at the beginning of a new selling season. To assist these objectives, dealer conventions and meetings are used extensively, often in conjunction with a dealer contest. The informal interaction between the focus organisation and its resellers that these events facilitate can be an invaluable aid to the development and continuance of good relations between the two parties and, of course, at a horizontal level between resellers.

Many manufacturers provide extensive training and support for their resellers. This is an important communications function, especially when products are complex or subject to rapid change, as in the IT markets. Such coordination means that a stronger relationship can be built and manufacturers have greater control over the messages that the reseller's representatives transmit. It also means that the switching costs of the reseller are increased, since the training and support costs will be incurred again if a different supplier is adopted. Coordination through training and support can be seen as a form of marketing communications.

Many manufacturers provide extensive training and support for their resellers.

Personal selling is an important tool used to persuade buyers, the objective being to ensure that the reseller follows the guide of the manufacturer. As products become more similar and as channel power becomes concentrated in the retail sector, so resellers are able to select products from a variety of suppliers and determine the most appropriate sales promotions necessary for the markets in which they operate. This means that manufacturers can no longer assume control over members of the performance network, and they must find different ways of accessing the sales force of their distributors.

Marketing communications between manufacturers and resellers are vitally important. Sales promotions play an increasingly important role in the coordination between the two parties. Resellers look for sales promotions to support their own marketing initiatives. Supplier selection decisions depend in part upon the volume and value of the communications support. In other words, will supplier X or Y provide the necessary level of promotional support, either within the channel or direct to the consumer?

Sales promotions: resellers to consumers

Objectives

There are two overall objectives that retailers wish to achieve. The first is to promote the store as a brand. Growth at the retail level can be achieved by generating store traffic and increasing the number of people who become store (brand) loyal. This, as stated previously, is the equivalent to the *generation of trial*. To do this they need to communicate with those who are store switchers and non-store-users. Therefore, store image advertising is undertaken by retailers and is executed away from the store. The aim is to convert switchers and non-loyals into store-loyal customers.

In an attempt to increase usage, marketing communications are orientated to shifting particular stock at particular times.

The second main objective, according to a study undertaken by Blattberg *et al.* (1981), is to transfer stock and its associated costs from the retailer's shelves to the cupboards and refrigerators of consumers. In an attempt to increase usage, marketing communications, and sales promotion activity in particular, are orientated to shifting particular stock at particular times. This means that turnover is increased (and targets are reached) and shelves are cleared to receive new products.

Methods

Sales promotion by retailers is normally tied to the activities of manufacturers, but some price-off techniques are retailer driven. Joint advertising and sales promotion in the local press combine to attract customers to the store. However, as discussed earlier, many of these advertising campaigns are cooperative exercises and so cannot be classed as retailer sales promotions. The attention-getting devices of in-store displays are normally regarded as merchandising, in that they are geared to gaining attention, not moving product.

Promotions that do occur in store, regardless of origin, appear to affect non-store loyals to a greater extent than store loyals. Rossiter and Percy (1987) report the work of a Nielsen study in which sales promotions in supermarkets were tracked and sales correlated with the degree of store loyalty. The main finding was that non-store-loyals recorded a 20-fold increase in sales following the promotion, whereas store loyals increased their sales by a factor of only 10.

Sales promotions: manufacturers to consumers

Objectives

Manufacturers use sales promotions to communicate with consumers because they can be a cost-effective means of achieving short-term increases in sales. The objectives are to stimulate trial use by new users or to increase product usage among those customers who buy the product on an occasional or regular basis.

The importance of stimulating trial use cannot be underestimated.

The success of any new offering is partly dependent on the number of consumers encouraged to try the product in the first place and partly upon the number who repurchase the product at a later point in the purchase cycle. The importance of stimulating trial use cannot be underestimated. Through the use of coupons, sampling and other techniques (see below), sales promotions have become an important element in the new product launch and introduction processes.

Sales promotions to stimulate trial – Butlins

In an attempt to reposition itself as a short-break leisure destination, Butlins used a new Web site to offer vouchers to its mainly C1 and C2 audience, entitling them to a free day pass to experience the refurbished and new-look resorts.

In markets that are mature, sales growth can only be realistically achieved by encouraging users of competitive products to switch their allegiance.

In addition to trial, organisations need to encourage consumers to repurchase products. In markets that are mature, sales growth can only be realistically achieved by encouraging users of competitive products to switch their allegiance. This can be achieved by offering them superior benefits and added value. Attracting non-users is an alternative route, but this requires convincing them, first, that they have a need for the product class and, second, that they should try the promoted product. A more productive approach is to find new uses for the product. For example, breakfast cereals have been promoted as nourishing snacks, suitable for consumption at different times of the day. Dairies have distributed recipe books where many of the meals use milk as a prime ingredient.

Trade promotions – Mars

One of the problems faced by Mars Confectionery has been its rival's (Walls) dominance of ice-cream freezer cabinets in the independent sector. Most shops have only enough space for one cabinet and that, historically, has been Walls. A promotion was targeted at familiarising customers with the location of Mars freezers and its product range. The 'Find a Freezer' game required consumers to locate Mars freezers in 6,000 outlets. Freezers were given a name sticker and the Capital FM radio station invited listeners to find them in return for cash and Mars merchandise rewards.

Just as sales promotions are used to attract customers of competing products, so competitors use sales promotions to counter-attack and defend their markets. Sales promotions, sometimes in combination with advertising, must be used to defend a customer base from competitive attacks. By using bonus packs (extra product), price-offs, competitions and coupons to encourage increased usage, customers can be loaded with stock, effectively removing them from the market for a period longer than the normal purchase cycle.

The second reason is the need to transfer the cost of stock from the reseller to the consumer, boosting revenue and clearing the way for new products with better margins.

There are two prime reasons for using sales promotions with consumers. The first is to collaborate with resellers in an attempt to defend the shelf space or franchise. This helps build a close and supportive relationship and also creates a mobility barrier that has to be overcome by competitive organisations. The second reason is the need to transfer the cost of stock from the reseller to the consumer, boosting revenue and clearing the way for new products with better margins.

Methods for encouraging new users to try a product

There are three main approaches to encourage new customers to try a product for the first time: sampling, coupons and a range of consumer deals.

Sampling

When a product is introduced, whether it be a new product category or an improved or modified product, sampling is one of the most effective sales promotion techniques available. For decisions that evoke low involvement, where there is little thought or elaboration undertaken by the consumer, attitudes are confirmed as a result of product experience. It makes sense, therefore, to provide a risk-free opportunity for consumers to test a product.

It makes sense, therefore, to provide a risk-free opportunity for consumers to test a product.

Samples are very often free miniature versions of the actual product and can be used to win new customers and to protect a customer base. Samples can take the form of demonstrations, trial size packs that have to be purchased or free use for a certain period of time. The recent offers by car manufacturers to allow purchasers to return their cars after a four-week period if not satisfied provide a good example of a high-involvement decision where attitudes are formed prior to trial and are used to confirm a purchase decision. The use of scented page folds in women's magazines to demonstrate new scents and perfumes is an innovative and interesting example of making trial easier. Previously, the only method of testing perfume was through the use of samplers, available on the counters in cosmetic departments of retail outlets. Marketing communications and sales promotions in particular were aimed at enticing people to the store. Using scent folds means that it is easier for consumers to try a perfume. A far greater number of people can try a new scent, while the reader's attention can be focused on the accompanying advertisement. Readership and recall scores increase remarkably.

Softone samples – Phillips Lighting

In order to introduce the new range of Softone light bulbs to a newer, younger audience, Phillips Lighting used a two-stage sampling approach. Utilising a door-to-door approach, the first phase consisted of the delivery of a questionnaire to collect database material and to ask which colour of bulb the householder would like to receive. The following day, phase 2 kicked in with the collection of the questionnaire and the delivery of the appropriate colour bulb (so avoiding the problem of delivering a glass product through a letterbox too small to accept it).

Awareness rose to 82%, 10% of targeted households requested a sample and from the 1,100,000 questionnaires that were completed, Phillips was able to pinpoint innovators, early adopters and early majority individuals and use these data to roll the campaign out nationwide, and in doing so substantially reduce its costs and improve its efficiency and effectiveness.

Sampling is expensive. Of all the available sales promotion techniques, the costs associated with sampling are the largest. To offset the high cost, the potential rewards can be equally dramatic, especially if the audience is familiar with or predisposed to the product class, and if the sample has some superior benefits. Sampling is best undertaken when the following apply:

Sampling is expensive.

1. Advertising alone is unable to communicate the key benefits.
2. The product has benefits that are superior to its competitors and which are clearly demonstrable.
3. Competitive attacks require loyal customers to be reminded of a product's advantages. A further use occasion of sampling is to introduce the product to customers of competitive products, in an effort to encourage them to switch.

Apart from the size, mass and degree of perishability associated with the physical characteristics, the main constraints concern the number of people who are required to receive the samples and when they are to receive them: the timing of the trial. Samples are often distributed to consumers free of charge, with the twin goals of introducing the product to new users and hopefully encouraging them to switch brands. In addition to this, sampling provides an ideal opportunity to gather valuable market research data from the field.

However, some retailers prefer miniature products which customers are expected to purchase. This approach encourages consumers to use the sample, and because they paid for it they will be likely to use it. For the retailer, this approach provides a margin in part compensation for the risk associated with any stock purchased in advance and for the floor or shelf space allocated for the trial.

Rossiter and Percy have compiled a table (Table 24.1) which sets out the main sampling media.

Table 24.1 Eight methods of distributing samples

	Uses	Limitations
Door to door	■ Virtually any product can be delivered in this way	■ Most expensive means of sampling ■ Problem with leaving perishables if occupant absent ■ Illegal in some areas
Direct mail	■ Best for small, light products that are non-perishable	■ Rising postal costs
Central location	■ Best for perishables such as food, or when personal demonstration is required	■ If in-store, same offer must be made to all retailers (Robinson–Patman Act) ■ Usually involves cost of sales training ■ If in public place, may be illegal in some areas
Sample pack in stores	■ Best method for attracting retail support, because retailers sell the packs at a premium unit price	■ Requires retail acceptance like any other new product ■ May necessitate special production for trial sizes
Cross-product sampling in or on pack	■ Good for low-cost sampling of a manufacturer's other products	■ Trial limited to users of 'carrier' product ■ Restricted to large products
Co-op package distribution	■ Good for narrow audiences such as college students, military personnel, brides	■ Little appeal to trade
Newspaper or magazine distribution	■ Relatively low-cost method of sample distribution for flat or pouchable products	■ Seem to be regarded by media vehicle recipients as 'cheap' and are often disregarded, resulting in less trial than with other sampling methods ■ Obviously limited to certain product types
Any of above with coupon	■ Increases post-sample trial rate by using purchase incentive	■ Additional cost of coupon handling

Source: Rossiter and Percy (1987); used with permission.

Coupons

Coupons are a proven method by which manufacturers can communicate with consumers and are a strong brand-switching device. They may be distributed via resellers or directly to consumers. Coupons are vouchers or certificates which entitle consumers to a price reduction on a particular product. The value of the reduction or discount is set and the coupon must be presented when purchasing the product. The objective therefore, is to offer a price deal, a discount off the full price of the product. Retailers and wholesalers act as agents for manufacturers by allowing consumers to redeem the value of coupons from them at the point of purchase. They in turn recover the cost of the deal, the value of the coupon, from the manufacturer.

Coupons provide precision targeting of price-sensitive customers, without harming those regular customers who are prepared to pay full price.

Coupons provide precision targeting of price-sensitive customers, without harming those regular customers who are prepared to pay full price. In reality, however, some coupons are redeemed by regular product users, and their use reduces margins unnecessarily. The level of perceived risk experienced by new users can be reduced through the use of coupons. Users of competitive products can also be encouraged to try the product, so coupons can be effective for product introductions and established products in stable markets.

Smart-shoppers are those consumers who feel some exclusivity and control as a result of using coupons to try new brands. They receive a psychological and economic benefit. While retailers like coupons because they merely switch the brand bought and so do not lose a sale, manufacturers are less keen, as they consider they may lose out. The evidence suggests that consumers tend to revert to their pre-coupon preferred brand after redemption of the coupon (Kahn and Louie, 1990).

This form of sales promotion allows management to set a specific period of time in which a promotion is to run. This in turn allows the other elements of the promotional mix to be integrated. For example, advertising can be used to create awareness, and print media can then be used to display a coupon for the reader to cut out for redemption at the next purchase opportunity. When attempting to generate trial, advertising must be used to create awareness, since a coupon for an unknown product will be totally ineffective and usually discarded by consumers. Personal selling can be timed to inform resellers of a forthcoming coupon offer and give time for shelves to be fully stocked when the campaign breaks. Unfortunately, it is difficult to estimate when and how many coupons will be redeemed. There are certain guides developed through experience and a redemption rate of between 3% and 5% can be considered good. The variance, however, can be marked, and the promotional cost of a stock-out can be considerable.

Couponing is an expensive activity.

Couponing is an expensive activity. Not only has the face value of the coupons to be considered, but the production and distribution costs must also be accounted for. General Mills, the US food group, decided to reduce the number of coupons it issues on the grounds that it sees them as a waste of money (Tomkins, 1994). At 2% redemption, the cost in terms of time, print and distribution costs plus the face value of the coupon itself means that the exercise was costing General Mills money. It has moved back to an 11% price reduction on its products instead. Many organisations, like General Mills, consider that a saving of 30% in the promotional budget and a cut in the price on the shelf is a better and more profitable way to do business. This approach is sometimes referred to as everyday low prices (EDLP).

There are three primary ways in which coupons can be distributed:

1. Consumer direct distribution allows management to focus the coupons upon particular target audiences. Coupons can be sent through the post, delivered on a door-to-door basis or with new media delivered via a Web site. This last approach works through use of a smart card inserted into a PC which can then receive the downloaded coupon, which the user can then present to a retailer (either bricks or clicks) for redemption.

   Some manufacturers are collaborating with other manufacturers (non-competitive) to distribute coupons on a joint basis.

   An average redemption rate of 6% makes this one of the more effective methods of distributing coupons, although a major disadvantage is that its costs are increasing. Consequently, some manufacturers are collaborating with other manufacturers (non-competitive) to distribute coupons on a joint basis.

2. Media direct distribution allows management to gain a broad level of exposure for a product. Free-standing inserts are a popular way of distributing coupons. These are separate sheets containing a number of different coupons. This contrasts with the normal method of printing the coupon in a newspaper or magazine. However, the redemption rates of this second approach are low because of the short life of such media vehicles, particularly newspapers, and the extra effort required by readers to cut out and store the coupon until the next purchase opportunity arises.

   Various alternative methods have been developed in response to the need to find novel ways of attracting readers' attention. On-page coupons can be found in magazines coupled with an advertisement. Pop-ups are coupons printed on card and bound into a magazine. Finally, tip-ins are coupons glued to the cover of a magazine.

3. Package direct distribution generates the highest redemption rates of all the methods available. By inserting (in) or imprinting (on) coupons on the packaging of a product (in/ons), distribution costs can be minimised. However, coupons distributed in this way only reach users; they fail, therefore, to reach non-users.

   Package direct distribution generates the highest redemption rates.

Instant coupons are an effective point-of-purchase incentive which allow purchasers literally to rip the coupon off the package for redemption at the check-out. This can generate very high levels of redemption and is administratively easier to manage than price deals, as the latter require the active participation of the reseller.

Coupons that are redeemable off the next purchase of the same item are referred to as bounce-back coupons. Coupons which are redeemable against different products are referred to as cross-ruff coupons. These are particularly effective in encouraging consumers to try other products in a manufacturer's product range. Soap, frozen foods and breakfast cereals are product ranges where this couponing approach has been successful.

Over 200 million coupons are issued each year in the UK and this represents a great deal of business activity. Fulfilment houses undertake the work for brand managers, acting as brokers for the issuers and retailers who accept them. Manufacturers outsource coupon work, if only because it is so labour intensive. New software systems threaten to replace some of this work, especially the tracking of vouchers, which can be undertaken in house.

Many technological advances, and in particular the use of barcode scanners, present opportunities for manufacturers and retailers to use couponing more effectively. Fraudulent use of coupons can be cut considerably and checkout speeds increased.

This technology has the potential to monitor an individual customer's purchases, establish buying patterns and dispense coupons to users of competitive products at the checkout.

More importantly, however, this technology has the potential to monitor an individual customer's purchases, establish buying patterns and dispense coupons to users of competitive products at the checkout. This will lead inevitably to the identification of those customers who use coupons more frequently and the development of coupon user profiles. Manufacturers will also gain by the reduced distribution costs and the reduction in time spent handling coupons. One such system is called Catalina.

The Catalina system, which claims a redemption rate of 6–8%, was developed in the USA and Asda became one of the first UK users which, after an initial proving period, installed the system in all of its UK stores. Somerfield also used the system extensively. Catalina claims a number of advantages for both manufacturers and retailers. For manufacturers it provides for exclusivity, as only one manufacturer per product category can be installed. For retailers the overall incentive is that the system encourages return visits and increases store traffic, and volume grows.

Catalina and other similar systems provide money-off coupons plus the opportunity to deliver a variety of messages to specific shoppers. In addition, it is possible to provide incentives to the right target customers to encourage participation in research exercises. Sampling opportunities increase as well. Asda uses the system to target those customers most likely to use free telephone numbers in order to receive a free sample of a new/other product or hear a pre-recorded message. This is referred to as *confined target advertising*, or in other words a blend of sales promotion, direct marketing and advertising.

A more recent initiative concerns machines that dispense coupons but at the POP not POS. In other words, by providing coupons at the point a purchase decision is

By providing coupons at the point a purchase decision is made, at the shelf and not after the decision, at the till, a greater uplift in sales is to be expected.

made, at the shelf and not after the decision, at the till, a greater uplift in sales is to be expected. One such facility, The Instant Coupon Machine allows consumers to withdraw a paper coupon, for either a single or group of brands, and redeem them at the till or use at a later date. Sales increases of up to 60% were reported by companies taking part in some of the trials (Mathews, 1999).

Consumer deals

These forms of sales promotion are only effective in the short term. They are not used to build consumer franchises or brand personalities. Their function is to bring about a short-term increase in sales by moving the product from the shelves of the reseller to the homes of consumers. They can encourage trial behaviour by new users and also stimulate repurchase by existing users. The techniques are as follows.

Price-offs

By far the simplest technique is to offer a direct reduction in the purchase price with the offer clearly labelled on the package or point of purchase display. These are simply referred to as 'price-offs'. A minimum reduction of 15% appears to be required for optimal effect (Della Bitta and Monroe, 1980). Others suggest that this figure varies

Research indicates that consumers are sceptical of price deals, in particular those concerning price-offs.

according to the store and the type of brand under consideration. Research indicates that consumers are sceptical of price deals, in particular those concerning price-offs. This may result in individuals discounting the discounts (Gupta and Cooper, 1992).

Train Offers

Following the Hatfield rail crash in the UK and the consequent rail inspections and track relaying programme by Railtrack, which is responsible for the track systems and infrastructure, a huge number of rail travellers reverted to other forms of transport. In an effort to encourage these lapsed customers back to the rail network, the various rail operating companies (which provide the trains and services) entered into a massive sales promotion campaign to incentivise people to use the train network.

Some operators gave away boxes of chocolates, some gave heavily discounted weekends in London and Virgin offered £10 million in the form of price reductions over a one-month period. Virgin referred to it as 'The worlds biggest train offer', and Benady and Barrett (2001) draw similarities to the British Airways 'World's biggest offer' in the early 1990s, in the attempt to revive air travel after the Gulf War and fear of terrorism.

The mere presence of a price-off for those with a low need for elaboration, regardless of the value of the sales promotion, appears to be sufficient to bring about a change in an individual's disposition towards the promoted product (Inman *et al.*, 1990). They suggest that it is theoretically possible to bring about an increase in sales from those with a low need for information simply by placing a promotional display without actually reducing the price.

In a study by AC Nielsen (reported by Miller, 1997) of consumer attitudes towards price-offs and sales promotions, five different types of people were identified. These are set out in Table 24.2.

Whatever the decision regarding the value of the price-off, the entire price reduction should be carried by the manufacturer, as the retailer must be continually motivated and a reduction in margin will be adversely received. Retailers see price deals as a necessary activity to stimulate short-term sales. Manufacturers regard price deals as effective when tied into media advertising.

Bonus packs

Bonus packs offer more product for the regular pack price. They provide direct impact at the point of purchase, and this, combined with the lure of lower unit costs and extra value, means that this is a popular technique with consumers and manufacturers. However, resellers do not gain from bonus packs: there is no additional margin and extra shelf space is required.

Refunds and rebates

Refunds and rebates are used to invite consumers to send in a proof of purchase and in return receive a cash refund. These are very effective in encouraging the trial of new products and have proved exceptionally popular with consumer durables (rebate) as

Table 24.2   Five types of customers and their attitude towards sales promotion

Branded EDLP seekers (19%)
This group has a restricted income but is brand loyal. These customers, therefore, look around for the best deal they can get for their preferred brand. In their search for everyday low prices they ignore coupons and money-off promotions.

Low price fixture ferrets (23.3%)
Again, income is restricted in this group, which is mainly populated by young families. They are very budget conscious and are store rather than product loyal. They like promotions and are quick to switch brands.

Promotion junkies (18.4%)
These people are referred to as professional shoppers because of their desire to seek out bargains. They have zero loyalty and are keen to tell their contacts of their shopping successes. They are a hazard to both manufacturers and retailers.

Stockpilers (21%)
These shoppers are loyal to both manufacturers and retailers. They have no income difficulties and are happy to buy up large quantities of their preferred brands, regardless of the costs. Of the five types of shopper, these are the second most promotionally active, as they search for bargains but they do not switch brands for promotional reasons.

Promotionally oblivious (18.3%)
This group is totally unaware of any promotions. Described as rather old-fashioned, this group is not interested in pursuing low prices. Therefore, these customers will buy a preferred brand regardless of the existence of a promotion and so represent a reliable group of buyers.

Source: Miller (1997). Used with kind permission.

well as fast-moving consumer goods (FMCG) (refunds). The process of redeeming refunds may evoke negative feelings, as consumers do not like the trouble and inconvenience associated with claiming refunds and, when combined with the negative perception that consumers have of manufacturers who offer such rebates, the conclusion has to be that any redemption procedure should be clear, simple and easy to implement.

Methods for encouraging increased consumption – usage

There are two main ways in which sales promotions can be used to encourage increased usage: premiums (direct and self-liquidating) and contests and sweepstakes.

Premiums

Premiums are items of merchandise that are offered free or at a low cost. Premiums are used as a direct incentive to motivate people to purchase a specific product. The premium merchandise is used to add value to the product and represent an advantage over competitor products. Finding suitable low-cost premiums for the adult market, however, is difficult, as a poor premium may deter people from buying the product. Consumers are required to show proof that a purchase has been made. However, Internet facilities now allow consumers to collection digital currencies which can be redeemed for gifts or discounts. MyPoints is one such retention system and is supported by a variety of mainstream retailers such as

Premiums are items of merchandise that are offered free or at a low cost.

Boots, Kingfisher Group, Virgin and Argos. Witthaus (2000) reports, however, that instead of points being awarded in return for purchases made, points can be collected as a result of accepting advertising, either by visiting an advertiser's site or by accepting emails. An added point of differentiation is that MyPoints can be redeemed either on-line or by visiting the bricks and mortar store. This system appears to recognise that a large number of people prefer (understand) high street shopping and provides a gradual transfer rather than impose a totally dedicated on-line shopping experience and reward.

Premiums are used to increase sales by attracting repeat buyers, stimulating impulse purchase and brand-switching behaviour, and to offset competitor moves.

Premiums are used to increase sales by attracting repeat buyers, stimulating impulse purchase and brand-switching behaviour, and to offset competitor moves. There are two main forms of premium: direct and self-liquidating.

Direct premiums are provided for the consumer at the point of purchase. They are free of charge and require the consumer to do nothing other than buy the package. The premium merchandise may be attached to the product as an on-pack premium. This can result in improving the shelf display, which is attractive to resellers as it presents an instant stimulus–response opportunity to potential buyers. Unfortunately, on-packs take up extra space, and this can mean increased labour in shelf replenishment. The extra costs involved with packaging also need to be taken into account when designing on-pack premiums.

Gillette UK attempted to switch users of competitive shaving products by offering free gel with its disposable razors. Blister packaging makes for an attractive, attention-getting display and provides an incentive for consumers to receive a free product.

Premium merchandise that is packaged inside the product is referred to as an in-pack premium. This obviously saves space and reduces costs for the manufacturer, as there is virtually no requirement to change the packaging. Breakfast cereals have traditionally used this approach.

In contrast to direct premiums, *self-liquidating* premiums require consumers to contribute to the cost of the incentive. Manufacturers seek only to cover their costs and, by buying the premium merchandise in volume, can offer the merchandise at prices considerably below the regular retail price.

The effectiveness of self-liquidating premiums is not as strong as that of direct premiums because they do not provide the same impact. There is a time delay between awareness of the offer and the reward, often a matter of weeks. Consequently, the

Mail-in premiums – Pepsi and Robbie Williams

Robbie Williams wrote a track which was used in a television advertisement. Consumers collect 25 ring pulls for a CD-ROM of an exclusive track, plus backstage footage, an interview with RW, and a screensaver. The ring pulls are redeemable at HMV stores and by mail order. Fulfilment rates are equivalent to number 8 in the charts.

Dunmore (2000) reports that the Pepsi Web site features audio and video clips of the ad, with a chance to win RW concert tickets in exchange for an email address and personal details.

redemption rate for these types of sales promotion is very low (0.1%). They can be used to stimulate resellers and create attention in the market, and they can deflect attention from competitor brands. Proposed new regulations from the EU threaten the abolition of self-liquidating premiums.

Manufacturers can also offer mail-in premiums to customers if they send several proofs of purchase. The premium is technically free to the customer and the multiple purchases that are stimulated generate revenue, take stock off the shelves and take customers out of the market for a period of time because they are loaded with stock.

Contests and sweepstakes

A contest is a sales promotion whereby customers compete for prizes or money on the basis of skills or ability. Entry requires a proof of purchase and winners are judged against a set of predetermined criteria. Completing the line 'I like XXX because . . .', writing one-line slogans, suggesting names, and drawing posters and pictures are some of the more common contests used to involve consumers with products.

A sweepstake is a sales promotion technique where the winners are determined by chance and proof of purchase is not required. There is no judging and winners are drawn at random. A variant of the sweepstake is a game which also has odds of winning associated with it. Scratchcards have become very popular games, mainly because consumers like to participate and winners can be instantly identified.

A sweepstake is a sales promotion technique where the winners are determined by chance.

Sweepstakes are more popular than contests because they are easier to enter and, because there is no judging, administration is less arduous and less expensive. Both contests and sweepstakes bring excitement and attention to campaigns, and if the contest or sweepstake is relevant, both approaches can bring about increased consumer involvement with the product.

Great care and preparation must be put into contests and sweepstakes. Because of the legal implications and requirements of these sales promotions, many organisations contract the event to organisations that specialise in such activities.

Sales promotions: the sales force

Just as consumers and resellers benefit from the motivation provided by sales promotions, so members of the sales force can benefit too. To stimulate performance, sales promotions can be directed at the sales force of either the manufacturer or the reseller. Incentives such as contests and sales meetings are two of the most used motivators.

Contests

Contests have been used a great deal, and if organised and planned properly can be very effective in raising the performance outcomes of sales teams. By appealing to their competitive nature, contests can bring about effective new product introductions, revive falling sales, offset a rival's competitive moves and build a strong customer base. To do this, contests must be fair, so that participants have a roughly equal chance of being successful, and the winners should not be those who have high-density and high-potential territories. A further consideration is the duration of the contest: too short and the full effects may not be realised; make it too long and interest and support for the incentive may wane.

Sales meetings

Sales meetings provide an opportunity for management to provide fresh information to the sales force about performance, stock positions, competitor activities, price deals, consumer or reseller promotions, and new products. Sales training exercises can be introduced and short product training sessions can often be included. These formal agenda items are supplemented by the informal ones of peer reassurance and competitive stimulus, as well as information exchange and market analysis. Meetings can be held annually, quarterly, monthly or at local level on a weekly basis. The time that representatives are off territory needs to be considered, but generally such meetings are of benefit to people who spend the greater part of their working week away from the office, at the boundary of the organisation.

Other sales promotion aids

Brochures are a sales promotion that can be used to assist consumers, resellers and the sales forces. Apart from the ability of the brochure to impart factual information about a product or service, brochures and sales literature stimulate purchase and serve to guide decisions. For service-based organisations, the brochure represents a temporary tangible element of the product. Inclusive tour operators, for example, might entice someone to book a holiday, but consumption may take place several months in the future. The brochure acts as a temporary product substitute and can be used to refresh expectations during the gestation period and remind significant other people of the forthcoming event (Middleton, 1989). Just as holiday photographs provide opportunities to relive and share past experiences, so holiday brochures serve people to share and enjoy pre-holiday experiences and expectations. Consumption of inclusive tours, therefore, can be said to occur at the booking point, and the brochure extends or adds value to the holiday experience.

The brochure represents a temporary tangible element of the product.

Sales literature can trigger awareness of potential needs. As well as triggering awareness, sales literature can be useful in explaining technical and complex products. For example, leaflets distributed personally at DIY stores can draw attention to a double-glazing manufacturer's products. Some prospective customers may create an initial impression about the manufacturer, based on past experiences triggered by the literature, the quality of the leaflet and the way it was presented. The leaflet acts as a cue for the receiver to review whether there is a current need and, if there is, then the leaflet may be kept longer, especially where high involvement is present; value is thus added to the purchase experience.

Financial services companies use sales literature at various stages in the sales process. Mailers are used to contact prospective customers, corporate brochures are used to provide source credibility, booklets about the overall marketplace are left with clients after an initial discussion and product guides and brochures are given to customers after a transaction has been agreed. To help prevent the onset of cognitive dissonance, a company magazine is sent soon after the sale and at intermediate points throughout the year to cement the relationship between client and company.

An increasingly important and expensive approach is to license a TV cartoon character from the Simpsons, Rugrats or South Park or a cyber person such as Lara Croft who was used by Lucozade. These characters are used to attract the attention of children and provide the parental agreement necessary for a purchase to be made. There are, of course, issues concerning consistency of brand values and the need to prevent competitors using the same or similar characters to support their brands. It is also argued that apart from a short-term sales increase there is a residual sales increase following promotions utilising these prime characters, especially if the promotion is based upon a free gift or the chance to win an instant gift.

These characters are used to attract the attention of children and provide the parental agreement necessary for a purchase to be made.

Character licensing is used strategically to build brands. Murphy (1999) reports how Disney has long-term contracts with McDonald's and Nestlé which grant them first refusal on tie-ins to new films. Warner Bros and Cadbury's have established a similar arrangement.

Summary

The range of techniques and methods used to add value to offerings is enormous but there are growing doubts about the effectiveness and profitability associated with some sales promotions.

Sales promotions used by manufacturers to communicate with resellers are aimed at encouraging resellers to either try new products or purchase more of the ones they currently stock. To do this, trade allowances, in various guises, are the principal means.

Sales promotions used by resellers (largely retailers) to influence consumers are normally driven by manufacturers, although some price deals and other techniques are used to generate store traffic. The majority of sales promotions are those used by manufacturers to influence consumers. Again, the main tasks are to encourage trial or increased product purchase. A range of techniques, from sampling and coupons to premiums and contests and sweepstakes, are all used with varying levels of success.

Review questions

1. Explain the objectives that manufacturers might have when encouraging resellers to take more product.
2. List the main sales promotion methods used by manufacturers and targeted at consumers.
3. Evaluate the allowance concept.
4. Consider whether hostaging is conducive to relationship marketing.
5. Collect four examples of sampling and determine whether you feel they were effective in achieving their objectives.
6. Name five different methods of distributing samples.
7. How can coupons be used to reduce levels of perceived risk?

8. Which of the two forms of premiums is generally regarded as the less successful and why do you think this is?

9. What role does the sales brochure play in marketing communications?

10. Consider the view that the sales force does not require incentivising through sales promotion as it is motivated sufficiently through other means.

MINI CASE

Denby Toiletries

Richard Littlejohn was delighted when he was invited to join Denby Toiletries, as marketing and sales director. He was already one of three national line sales managers for a leading FMCG food organisation and he was ambitious to take full responsibility for the sales and marketing of a single company.

Denby Toiletries

Denby Toiletries offer two main brands, 'Caress', a soap in toilet- and bath-size packages, and 'Splash' a shower gel. Both brands are distributed throughout the UK. The recommended retail price for a Caress toilet bar is 88p. This places the brand in the upper third by price, among the quality brands, although some soaps are considerably more expensive. The Splash brand has been positioned in a similar way in the top third.

Group net turnover was about £9.2 million last year, giving Denby Toiletries less than 2% of the national market. Littlejohn calculated that in real terms Denby's sales appear to have been decreasing around 5% per annum over the past four years. Nevertheless, the Caress brand is widely recognised and the firm made a profit before tax of 4% on sales last year. The Caress brand had been sold for over 50 years and has a good sound quality image, appealing to AB women in the grey market (50+ year olds), with above-average disposable incomes. Distribution is through the independent sector, not supermarkets. The Splash shower gel was launched in 1994 but has failed to establish a strong position in the market. It is seen by supermarket buyers as a third-rate product and,

so far, they have failed to list it, let alone devote shelf space to it.

Both the Caress and the Splash brands are targeted at the independent sector (high street chemists, retail chains) and most are serviced through wholesalers. Very large chains are able to buy direct from Denby. During the Second World War, Denby had been forced to use general manufacturers' representatives working on commission to cover its accounts. Thereafter, Denby never fully returned to an employee sales force. The firm now operates through a field marketing organisation in six regions, although its own sales director covers a seventh – London West – operating from the head office at Ealing. Representatives work on 2% commission for all orders from their regions, including national, wholesale and retail chains who purchase for delivery to other regions.

Research

When he arrived at Denby, Littlejohn was confident he could change the situation by repositioning both brands. He is on first-name terms with many of the buyers for national supermarket and retail chains, comes into frequent contact with them to arrange special deals and promotions, and has entertained and been 'out on the town' with a number of them.

One of Littlejohn's first actions on joining his new company was to meet the current advertising agency, Parsons, Smith and Brown (PSB). The agency commissioned a series of research activities including a study of the representation of the Denby brands in different outlets and its share of the market through those outlets. The results confirmed that Caress (and to a lesser extent Splash) had a strong presence in the independent chemist sector, have a very poor share of the grocery outlets and little representation through the major multiples.

Even more revealing were PSB's findings about people's attitudes towards the Caress and Splash brands. Research indicated that while a substantial market existed for the Caress brand (for those who wished to reward themselves with a luxury soap), a new segment was emerging for technology-based products. The target market appears to be characterised by ABC1 women, aged 18–35 who have busy careers and who pursue modern lifestyles. This group wants a soap product that has a highly technical formulation, provides reassurance and protection for sensitive skin, and hints at some expression of the user's awareness of environmental issues.

Several competitors had an SOV double that of Caress but Littlejohn has said that he is not impressed with the advertising strategies being used to increase market share. He referred to the heavy advertisers as 'adland's puppets'. These strategies were based on highly emotional messages where differentiation was based upon self-indulgence and reward. Littlejohn believed that to achieve market share customers wanted added value, a tangible reason to buy.

Virtually all housewives buy toilet soap and some 9% – disproportionately grouped in the 35–44 age bracket – were classified as heavy users. To get at these heavy users, PSB argued there was no substitute for brand advertising. Littlejohn recognised the argument but favoured trying to reach occasional users of both Caress and competitor brands. He believed an emphasis was needed on below-the-line work and in particular sales promotion, merchandising and packaging.

The Nurella brand

Littlejohn's idea is to withdraw Splash from the market, continue with Caress and launch a soap brand as Nurella. A new shower gel should then follow, to be called 'Nurella Protein Plus', thus extending the Nurella brand. Littlejohn saw Nurella positioned as a scientifically, hi-tech, modern and credible brand. Access to supermarket shelves should be possible with Nurella, as long as Denby was prepared to invest in a promotional campaign to support the multiple grocers. Meanwhile, the Caress brand would be unaffected and so the risk to Denby, he reasons, is limited to the possible loss of the current volume of Splash sales through the independent sector.

Mini-case questions

1. Do you believe Littlejohn can build the Caress and Nurella brands without using advertising?
2. If Littlejohn is to use sales promotion, which techniques do you advise he uses? Why?
3. Who might be the target audiences for the sales promotions?
4. If asked whether premiums or sampling would be appropriate to support the Caress brand, what would be your answer and why?
5. What role might advertising play if sales promotions are to dominate the promotional strategy?

References

Anderson, J.C. and Narus, J.A. (1990) A model of distributor firm and manufacturer firm working partnerships. *Journal of Marketing*, **54** (January), pp. 42–58.

Benady, D. and Barrett, L. (2001) Virgin terrain. *Marketing Week*, 18 January, pp. 28–9.

Blattberg, R.C. and Neslin, S.A. (1990) *Sales Promotion: Concepts, Methods and Strategies.* Englewood Cliffs, NJ: Prentice Hall.

Blattberg, R.C., Eppen, G.D. and Lieberman, J. (1981) A theoretical and empirical evaluation of price deals for consumer nondurables. *Journal of Marketing*, 5(1), pp. 116–29.

Della Bitta, A.J. and Monroe, K.B. (1980) A multivariate analysis of the perception of value from retail price advertisements. In *Advances in Consumer Research*, Vol. 8 (ed. K.B. Monroe). Ann Arbor, MI: Association for Consumer Research.

Dunmore, T (2000) Can net music help sell your products? *Marketing*, 14 September, p. 39.

Govoni, N., Eng, R. and Gaper, M. (1986) *Promotional Management*. Englewood Cliffs, NJ: Prentice Hall.

Gupta, S. and Cooper, L.G. (1992) The discounting of discounts and promotion brands. *Journal of Consumer Research*, **19** (December), pp. 401–11.

Inman, J., McAlister, L. and Hoyer, D.W. (1990) Promotion signal: proxy for a price cut? *Journal of Consumer Research*, **17** (June), pp. 74–81.

Kahn, B.E. and Louie, T.A. (1990) Effects on retraction of price on brand choice behaviour for variety seeking and last purchase-loyal-consumers. *Journal of Marketing Research*, **18** (August), pp. 279–89.

Mathews, V. (1999) Return of the instant promotion, *Financial Times*, 30 April.

Middleton, V.T.C. (1989) *Marketing in Travel and Tourism*. Oxford: Heinemann.

Miller, R. (1997) Does everyone have a price? *Marketing*, 24 April, pp. 30–3.

Murphy, C. (1999) Using cartoons to build brands. *Marketing*, 24 June, pp. 25–6.

Rossiter, J.R. and Percy, L. (1987) *Advertising and Promotion Management*. New York: McGraw-Hill.

Tomkins, R. (1994) Time to cut it out. *Financial Times*, 21 April, p. 25.

Witthaus, M. (2000) Baiting the buy. *Marketing Week*, 16 November, pp. 71–3.

25

On-line marketing communications

The use of the Internet as a means of communicating with specific audiences is becoming an increasingly important aspect of contemporary marketing communications. The role of the Web site and the deployment of the promotional tools, on-line, has now to be considered an integral part of an organisation's overall communication activity.

AIMS AND OBJECTIVES

The aim of this chapter is to explore some of the essential characteristics of the Internet as a medium for marketing communications.

The objectives of this chapter are:

1. To explore issues concerning the management of Web sites.

2. To examine Web site characteristics and to understand their strengths and weaknesses.

3. To compare the content and potential of traditional media with Web sites.

4. To understand Web site visitor behaviour and to consider its impact on Web site design.

5. To examine the primary techniques and issues relating to advertising on-line.

6. To consider some of the issues relating to the way in which each of the tools of the promotional mix can be deployed on-line.

7. To introduce developing interactive technologies and their impact on marketing communications.

Introduction

Issues relating to marketing communications strategy on the Internet were considered in Chapter 18. This chapter follows on and explores some of the more pertinent issues associated with Web site characteristics and considers the degree to which each of the promotional tools can be deployed on-line.

Web sites are the cornerstone of Internet activity for organisations, regardless of whether they are operating in the b2b or b2c sectors and whether the purpose is merely to offer information or provide fully developed embedded ecommerce (transactional) facilities. The characteristics of a Web site can be crucial in determining the length of stay, activities undertaken and the propensity for a visitor to return to the site at a later time. When the experience is satisfactory, then both the visitor and the Web site owner might begin to take on some of the characteristics associated with relationship marketing.

The characteristics of a Web site can be crucial in determining the length of stay, activities undertaken and the propensity for a visitor to return to the site at a later time.

To understand the characteristics associated with Web site interaction, consideration will first be given to their strengths and weaknesses, then the issues associated with the development of a Web site will be identified and then finally the processes involved in attracting and managing Web site activity will be examined.

Characteristics of Web sites

Web sites can be used for a variety of purposes but essentially they are either product orientated or corporate orientated. Product-orientated Web sites aim to provide product-based information such as brochureware, sales-based enquiries, demonstrations and endorsements through to on-line transactions and ongoing technical support as the main activities.

Corporate-orientated Web sites aim to provide information about the performance, size, prospects, financial data and job opportunities relating to the organisation. They also need to relate to issues concerning the ethical expectations and degree of social responsibility accepted by the company, if only to meet the needs of prospective investors and employees. The demarcation is not necessarily as clear cut as this might suggest but the essence of a site's orientation is to a large extent derived from the organisation's approach to branding.

Corporate-orientated Web sites aim to provide information about the performance, size, prospects, financial data and job opportunities.

The strengths and weaknesses of Web site facilities are set out in Table 25.1; however, it should be remembered that these are generalised comments and that some organisations have attended to these issues and have been able to develop the strengths and negate some of the weaknesses such that their Web sites are particularly attractive, user friendly and encourage repeat visits.

Strengths

Any WWW user can create a Web site, consisting of a home page and a number of linked pages. Business pages can carry advertising, product catalogues, descriptions, pricing, special offers, press releases – all forms of promotional material. They can link

Table 25.1   Strengths and weaknesses of Web site based communications

Strengths	Weaknesses
Quick to set up and easy to maintain	Slow access and page downloading speeds
Flexibility	Huge variability in Web site design and user
Variety of information	friendliness
High level of user involvement	Unsolicited email
Potentially high level of user convenience	Security and transaction privacy issues
(and satisfaction)	Relatively poor Internet penetration across
Range of service facilities	UK households
Global reach and equal access opportunities	Inconsistent fulfilment standards (information
Open all hours – reduced employment costs	only to on-line transactions)
Very low relative costs (per person reached)	Variability and speed of technology provision
Can provide cost efficiencies in terms of	Lack of regulation concerning content and
marketing research	distribution
	On-line search time costs prohibitive for many
	users

to on-line order pages, so that potential customers can order directly, or to email facilities for requesting further information or providing feedback. Consumer interest and activity can be monitored easily, allowing for timely market research, rapid feedback and strategy adaptation.

Barriers to entry are low, it is relatively inexpensive to create/maintain a site and share of voice is theoretically equal for all participants although in practice this is clearly not the case. Large organisations can buy banner ads and have a better chance of appearing in the first few results presented by search engines. Good design can add to brand appeal and recognition.

Good design can add to brand appeal and recognition.

Potential customers actively seek products and services, which is both time and cost effective from a company's point of view, and indicative of positive attitudes, perception and involvement. Channel communications can also be swift and supportive. Coverage is global, without the need for huge investment or expensive staff to be employed around the clock. Savings can be made in advertising budgets, travel, postage and telephone costs. Different time zones no longer matter in the virtual environment and language barriers are less of an issue. However, it has been suggested that cultural and language issues have been partly responsible for the relatively slow take-up of the Internet through PCs, which is in essence a geographic and cultural variance in the process of diffusion (Curtis, 2000).

Weaknesses

Some of the disadvantages are that the speed of access, page location and loading are still too slow for many users, especially from home PCs. Potential customers are easily put off by slow or unreliable connections and this frustration can result in negative images of the company or product. Poorly designed Web sites, that confuse rather than clarify, also leave a lasting poor impression, one which deters a return visit.

Unsolicited email is extremely annoying to many users and may be counterproductive. The worries over the security of financial details and transactions on line, while not discouraging people from seeking information, may still be a barrier to full eCommerce. Fulfilment issues, principally delivery problems (such as long delays), wrong items, incorrect billing, plus the associated inconvenience of returning products or otherwise seeking resolution may deter repeat purchase.

It is interesting to note that the UK supermarket chain Somerfield announced in June 2000 that it was closing its Web site and three associated distribution centres. A spokesman said on the radio that this operation had been 'a distraction'. While this is potentially true, consideration must be given to the marketing strategy and the overall context, internal resources, audience requirements, available computing and telecommunications facilities, prior to the design and build of any marketing Web site.

Some regard eCommerce as transactional Web sites or extended enterprises but it is more to do with information/communication management and the impact on relationships. eCommerce should be aimed at building new relationships with established customers and providing potential customers with a reason to change. The idea that eCommerce provides process efficiencies is correct but these features need to be transformed into benefits for customers.

eCommerce should be aimed at building new relationships with established customers and providing potential customers with a reason to change.

Web site development

The advantages and disadvantages of Web site ownership are set out in Table 25.1. However, many of the disadvantages are technological matters which even at the time of going to press have been or are in the process of being remedied, such is the speed at which this marketing communication medium is developing.

Many of the frameworks proposed for developing a Web site on the Internet have several deficiencies (Morgan, 1996). In an attempt to overcome these shortcomings, the framework developed by Ong (1995) and presented by Morgan (Figure 25.1) is reproduced here not as a universal panacea for Web site creation but as a recognition of its attempt to overcome some of the difficulties inherent in this activity and to demonstrate the breadth of thought and vision that needs to be accommodated when developing (and reviewing) an organisation's Web presence.

Just as integrated marketing communications should have a strong link with corporate and marketing strategy, this framework requires consideration of the marketing strategy and the overall context within which the Web site is to be developed and operated. Internal resources, audience requirements, country or regional telecommunications facilities have all to be evaluated prior to the design and build of the Web site itself.

However, the development of a Web site should not be undertaken without first understanding the processes and expectations of Internet users. By understanding the needs of users, management can then set appropriate objectives and an overall strategy which is coherent in terms of the users' experience in both the virtual and real worlds, through speedy, accurate, timely and courteous fulfilment activities.

Web sites – visitor behaviour

It is possible to deconstruct users' Web site behaviour into a number of discrete activities. However, the resultant list would be far too complex to be of any practical assistance. People who use the Internet have been categorised into the following groups by Lewis and Lewis (1997):

It is possible to deconstruct users' Web site behaviour into a number of discrete activities.

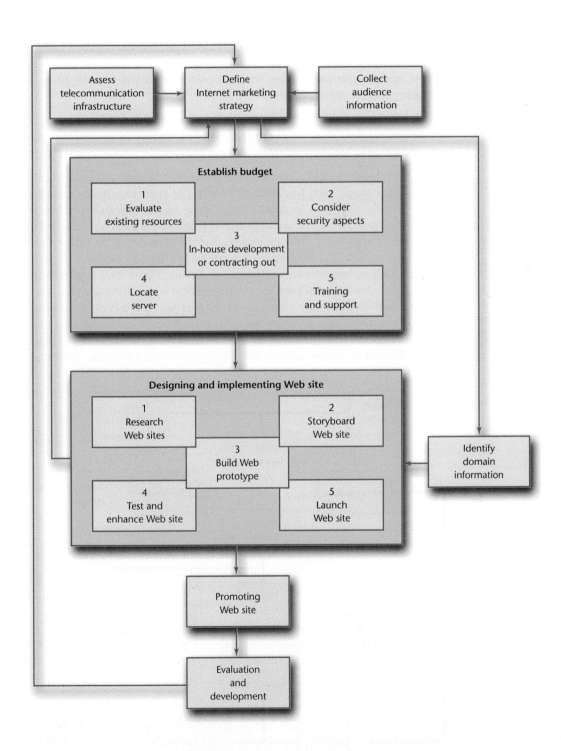

Figure 25.1   A framework for developing a site on the WWW. From Ong (1995); used with kind permission.

Directed information seekers: experienced users who know what information they require and where to find it.

Undirected information seekers: inexperienced users (generally) who surf looking for information or who browse for leisure and pleasure.

Directed buyers: experienced users who are on-line with the express intention of purchasing specific goods/services.

Bargain hunters: users in search of free offers and sizeable discounts.

Entertainment seekers: users whose intentions are primarily to exploit sales promotions and competition opportunities and use chat rooms.

The design of Web sites should account for the needs of these different types of user and also the different stages each has reached in terms of their experience in using the Internet, their stage in the adoption process (see Chapter 2) and different stages users have reached in the buying process. For the purposes of the rest of this text, reference is made to two broad categories, active (goal directed) and passive (experiential) information seekers. Figure 25.2 depicts a process framework which describes the path that visitors follow when visiting a Web site.

The design of Web sites should account for the needs of these different types of user.

The initial goal is to generate awareness of the Web site and this needs to be understood in the knowledge that there are many Web users who have no interest in a particular (your) Web site and those that do are said to have a potential interest. The task is therefore to drive awareness levels among those who might find the site useful.

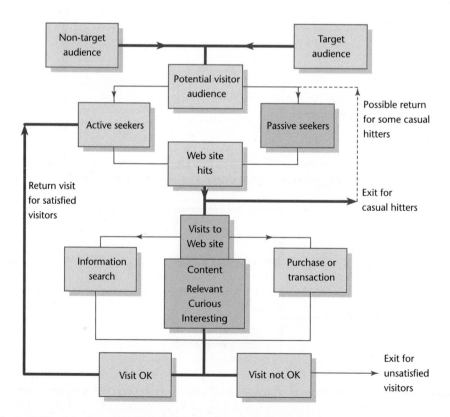

Figure 25.2   A framework depicting Web site visitor behaviour.

The second phase is to encourage the potential segment to actually visit the site. The problem is that there are two types of information seeker, passive and active. Passive seekers have no intention of hitting any particular site, whereas active seekers do have the express intention of visiting a particular site. Part of the communication strategy must therefore be geared to facilitating active seekers and attracting passive information seekers.

The next phase is to ensure that active seekers, once on the Web site, are able to find the information they need quickly and efficiently so that they are inclined to revisit. This entails good site access and, once found, good site design so that navigation is easy, simple and fast. This normally means that the design of the site is simple and is user, rather than technologically, orientated. Passive information seekers on the other hand need to be made curious and stimulated to want to know more about the site and the products and services available. Here the objective is to convert hitters into visitors. A site registration book, supported perhaps with sales promotion devices, or a site design that is sufficiently intriguing may allow these goals to be met. Research (Oxley and Miller, 2000) suggests that there are three main elements that strongly influence the perceived quality of a Web site visit. These are all content orientated and refer to whether the site material is relevant to the needs of the visitor, the degree to which the content (and design) encourages curiosity to explore the site and whether the content is presented in an interesting way. These three points correlate strongly with the idea of 'likeability', that advertising effectiveness improves when an individual assigns significant value (represented by relevance, curiosity and interest) to any particular advertisement (Chapter 20). Therefore, the main factors that might influence the way an individual perceives a Web site, may be similar to the way they process and evaluate advertising.

Advertising effectiveness improves when an individual assigns significant value (represented by relevance, curiosity and interest) to any particular advertisement.

The Internet as a medium for marketing communications

An initial, yet small, study undertaken by Bush *et al.* (1998) in the b2b sector found that advertisers perceived the Internet to be an important part of their future marketing communications activities. The Internet was seen as a primary means of providing product information but there were doubts about its ability to deliver competitive advantage and whether it could offer suitable levels of privacy, security and measures of advertising effectiveness.

A further study undertaken by Leong *et al.* (1998) attempted to compare Internet users' perceptions of the effectiveness of the Internet with the traditional media. This supported the results of the previous research, namely that the Internet is excellent at conveying detailed product based information. The main outcomes are highlighted in Table 25.2.

What needs to be taken from this work is that the Internet is not a panacea for a manager's marketing communications problems. It is just a new, different means of communication which should be integrated into the marketing communications mix. Web sites can complement other media and, as stated earlier, there is plenty of evidence that marketers are using off-line media to drive on-line traffic. Off-line communications are used to raise site awareness and interest amongst a wide audience and to

Table 25.2 Comparison of information content

Web sites/Internet	Traditional media
Good at providing rational product-based information	Better at conveying emotional brand values
More efficient as costs do not increase in proportion to the size of the target audience	Costs are related to usage
Better at prompting customer action	Less effective for calling to action except point-of-purchase and telemarketing
Effective for short-term product-orientated brand action goals and long-term corporate identity objectives	Normally associated with building long-term values
Poor at generating awareness and attention	Strong builders of awareness
Poor at managing attitudes	Capable of changing and monitoring attitudes
Measures of effectiveness weak and/or in the process of development	Established methodologies, if misleading or superficial (mass media); direct marketing techniques are superior
Dominant orientation – cognition	Dominant orientation – emotion

provide them with the site address. Once at the Web site, in-depth product information can be exchanged for customer-specific details to refresh the database and fuel future communication activity. It is this holistic perspective of the new media that should be developed.

Promoting a Web site – thetrainline.com

Thetrainline.com is a pre-pay ticket specialist owned by both Virgin Travel and Stagecoach. The web site (www.thetrainline.co) provides a timetable search facility, a shopping basket facility for buying a number of tickets in the same site visit, a favourite journey feature to store details of frequent trips (and tickets) and a facility to store to credit card details.

A £21 million budget has been used to convey the simple message of jumping the queue or 'book over the net and avoid the station queues'. An integrated promotions mix helped raise awareness and prompt people to visit the site. The marketing communications mix consisted mainly of outdoor advertising (around stations and unconventional locations), radio, three national TV bursts, limited email and a roadshow distributing leaflets and demonstrating how to use the Web site. As a result of a £50,000 prize draw, run for eight weeks, registrations rose by 14%. Within 10 months of launch thetrainline.com brand had 47% spontaneous awareness, 1.4 million registered users and a turnover of over £2.5 million per week. This represents two-and-a-half times more revenue than the average train operator's ticket sales.

Traditional marketing communications strategies employ a mix of tools and normally an emphasis is put on one type of promotional device depending on the context. Broadly it has been the norm to weight advertising over the other tools, when dealing with consumer markets, and to weight personal selling when operating in the b2b sector. This reflects advertising's ability to raise awareness and develop brands and personal selling's prime skill at provoking behavioural action and closing orders. These general approaches have begun to be relaxed as audience and media fragmentation gathers speed and new ways of doing business (e.g. eCommerce) are developed. The prime benefit of the Internet, as a hybrid medium, is that it is good at all of these activities but not as good for any one task as a single promotional tool might be.

The Internet provides a complementary facility to the other marketing communication tools.

Interestingly, it excels as a part of the communication and decision-making process that the established promotional tools fail to properly address, namely the search for and retrieval of information pertinent to purchase behaviour. It might be said, therefore, that the Internet provides a complementary facility to the other marketing communication tools and as such should be used with, and not instead of, the established means of marketing communication.

The next section considers the role of each of the main tools of the promotional mix, when used in an on-line context.

On-line advertising

In order to drive traffic to a Web site, advertisements are bought and placed on other Web sites. Through careful analysis it is possible to place the ads on sites where it is thought that members of the target market will pass and not only see the advertisements but also be prompted to click the banner and be taken to the advertiser's own corporate site. The most common form of ads are referred to as banner ads (see below), but as technology and marketing knowledge improves so more sophisticated versions of the banner ad have evolved. Some of these are outlined below.

In comparison with traditional media, the Internet provides an interesting contrast. Space (or time) within traditional media is limited and costs rise as demand for the limited space/time increases. On the Internet, space is unlimited so absolute costs remain very low and static, while relative costs plummet as more visitors are recorded as having been to a site. Another aspect concerns the focus of the advertising message. Traditionally advertisers tend to emphasise the emotional rather than information aspect, particularly with low-involvement categories. On the Internet the prime objective of customers is to seek information and so the emotional aspect of advertising messages tends to have a lower significance. As branding becomes a more important aspect of Internet activity, it is probable that there will be a greater use of emotions, especially when the goal is to keep people at a Web site, rather than when driving them to it.

Apart from the obvious factor that the Internet provides interactive opportunities that traditional media cannot provide, it is important to remember that OTS are generally driven by customers rather than by the advertiser who interrupts viewing or reading activities. People drive the dialogue at a speed that is convenient to them; they are not driven by others.

Advertising, and indeed all promotional activity on the Internet, needs to be planned and managed in just the same way as with traditional media. Setting suitable goals is part of this process and Cartellieri *et al.* (1997) provide a useful set of objectives in this context:

Delivering content: click through to a corporate site which provides more detailed information (e.g. health advice).

Enabling transactions: a direct response that leads to a sale (e.g. easyJet)

Shaping attitudes: development of brand awareness (e.g. start-up situations)

Soliciting response: encouraging interaction with new visitors (building market share)

Improving retention: reminding visitors and seekers of the organisation (developing reputation and loyalty).

The final comment to be made before examining some of the WWW advertising techniques is that management not only have greater opportunities to control the position and placement of advertisements but also can change the advertising much more quickly than is possible with traditional media. The goals outlined above indicate the framework within which advertising needs to be managed.

Banner ads

These are the dominant form of paid-for communication on the Web. Fifty-five per cent of all Web ads are banner ads which are responsible for 96% of all Internet ad awareness. Banner ads use a link through to an advertiser's chosen destination and therefore can act as a gateway to other Web sites but are also effective in their own right. Banner ads are linked to key words submitted by a seeker into a search engine. The ad should therefore be strategically positioned to catch the optimum, or even greatest, traffic flow. Certain product groups such as computer-related products represent 56% of all banner ads, whereas financial products account for only 7%. An extension of the banner concept is e*banners. These allow for media-rich content which enables a depth of material and even ecommerce transactions. Therefore banners are said to signpost and e*banners provide action.

Banner ads use a link through to an advertiser's chosen destination.

The aim of the banner ad is to attract attention and stimulate interest but the problem is that click-through rates are low, some reports suggest just 4%, which leads to the question about whether banner ads are worthwhile. Briggs and Hollis (1997) found that click-through rates are determined by five main factors; see Table 25.3.

An interesting outcome from the Briggs and Hollis work was that banner ads are an important and effective form of communication. Making allowances for the scope of their research, click-through was seen as unnecessary for the development of brand awareness and even the development of brand attitudes.

Table 25.3 Determinants for click-through

Source of predisposition	Factor
Audience related	Innate tendency to click through
Audience related	Immediate relevance of product
Audience related	Pre-existing source appeal (product or organisation)
Advertising related	Immediate relevance of the message
Advertising related	Level of curiosity generated by the banner

Source: Briggs and Hollis (1997). Used with kind permission.

Pop-up ads

Instead of transferring users to an orthodox Web site, banner ads can also be used to transfer users to an interactive site based upon games or a competition. These games provide entertainment and seek to develop user involvement and an incentive to return to the site at a later date. In addition, data can be captured about the user in order to refine future marketing offers. These ads can be saved for later use and are therefore more adaptable and convenient than interstitial ads which appear as users move between Web sites and cannot be controlled by the user.

Superstitials or interstitials

Also known as transitional on-line ads, these appear during the time when pages are being downloaded. They are intended to appear as a relief to the boredom that might set in when downloading can take a long time. In that sense they are not regarded as intrusive but supportive. One of the first of these was run by British Airways with a three-second media rich advertisement which was triggered when users clicked on either the travel or the business link on the *The Times* homepage. In turn there was a link to the British Airways Web site.

Micro sites

This type of site is normally product or promotion specific and is often run as a joint promotion with other advertisers. Creating a separate site avoids the difficulty of directing traffic to either of the joint partners' sites. Micro sites are much less expensive to set up than the traditional site and are particularly adept at building awareness as click-throughs to micro sites are higher than through just banners.

Micro sites are much less expensive to set up than the traditional site.

Email

Email can be used with high levels of frequency which is important when building awareness. It is extremely cost effective in that each message costs less than a penny (Groften, 2000). Email communications are easily customised, enabling tailored messages for different segments. Brands such as www.FT.com send out customised messages to 14 different sectors and Groften reports that this is likely to increase. Email is also a part of direct marketing (see below).

Rich media banner ads

The essential difference between regular and rich media banner ads is that the latter allow for significantly more detailed and enhanced messages to be communicated to the target audience. Video, and other more visitor-engaging material, provide depth and interest. Millward Brown argue that the media-rich banner ads are highly effective mainly because the medium enhances the message.

Off-line media

In the late 1990s it was a common strategy to use TV advertising to build awareness and provide information about the Web site address. This TV approach cost £11 million

Experience and research suggest that newspaper ads, magazines, word of mouth and on-line ads are far more effective in driving Web site traffic.

in 1999 but in 2000 this figure fell 25% (McCawley, 2000). This was partly due to a fall in the number of dotcom flotations and some bad publicity following the failure of some high-profile organisations such as boo.com. However, experience and research suggest that newspaper ads, magazines, word of mouth and on-line ads are far more effective in driving Web site traffic.

On-line sales promotions

In principle these have been used either to attract and retain customers or as a way of providing interest and involvement with the brand by encouraging return visits. In reality price deals and competitions have been the main tools used. Bol.com used a viral campaign to announce a three-hour window in which it offered spectacular discounts. The information spread quickly, thousands of new customers registered and Bol had a huge number of new names and addresses on its database.

Virtual sales promotions are generally cheaper than hard copy versions but to date it appears that WWW sales promotions have not been used to develop brand differentiation or added value. The issue is, of course, that sales promotions are normally used to bring forward future sales, to provide a reason to buy now. On the Internet this motivation does not exist in the same way and for many people the only reason to use the Internet is to find information and to compare prices. Sales promotions need to be reinvented in such a way that they perform a slightly different role to their more established cousins.

Web site price deals – Asda

Asda is set to launch a price war on the Web with a new service allowing users to hunt for the cheapest on-line prices for books, CDs and other goods.

Rosier and Jardine (1999) report that users will be able to look at prices for a range of goods from different retailers within the site, using so-called 'shopping-agent' technology. By allowing comparison, Asda will be able to discount and establish itself as the cheapest.

This service will enhance and complement the company's strategy to be seen as a competitively priced retailer and supporting its positioning as 'Permanently lower prices'. Other eRetailers, such as Amazon and Bol, have tended to use speed and convenience rather than price as the key attribute.

McLuhan (2000) refers to Amazon who email occasional users offering them a £3 voucher which is instantly redeemable and of immediate value. Beenz is a cyber currency which can be collected at a number of sites and then 'cashed' in for goods at other sites. Honda used Beenz to encourage test drives but the real value of Beenz collection is questioned by McLuhan as all that is involved is site registration. iPoints works in much the same way but the major difference is that these points can only be accessed at one appointed trader in each sector. This offers competitive advantage and the benefit of horizontal cooperation between iPoints traders (e.g. database knowledge). However, these currency collection devices (similarities to old-fashioned green shield stamps) serves only to foster 'site grazing' for Web points and are hardly a suitable way to develop brand values. They are also in danger of being abused through the development of automated software designed to scan and collect points by cheating.

On-line direct marketing

The most obvious form of direct marketing on the Internet is email. However, direct marketing has an important part to play off-line to drive site traffic. Interestingly, advertising was the primary off-line tool used to drive traffic but following the reassessment and consolidation of dotcom growth at the beginning of 2000, direct marketing (and direct mail in particular) appears to have taken on the mantle as primary traffic generator. It does this in one of two main ways. The first way is to launch a teaser campaign appealing to people's innate curiosity or, second, the direct mail piece is part of a sales promotion campaign where the promise of a reward lures people to the Web site. Figure 25.3 sets out the main roles that email direct marketing is best accomplishing.

In order to utilise this potency, by far the most influential aspect of email is what is referred to as viral marketing. This works on the principle that brand-based email messages are conveyed to a small part of the target audience and the content is sufficiently humorous, interesting or persuasive that the receiver is compelled to send it on to a friend. Felix pet food used this approach so that recipients ended up with cartoon cats walking around their screens. This is effectively word-of-mouth (word-of-mouse) communication and as such has very high credibility and penetration.

This is effectively word-of-mouth (word-of-mouse) communication and as such has very high credibility and penetration.

Another approach is to identify affinity groups. Given the increasingly goal-directed nature of much Web use, communicating to people through an affinity site can be more cost effective that trying to bring people to your site. Many on-line retailers sell via other sites, using the visitors of that site and the relationship that those visitors have with the site content.

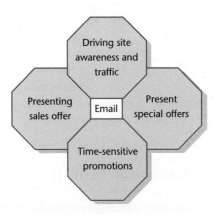

Figure 25.3   Four keys tasks for email direct marketing.

Mail combination – British Airways

Using direct mail and email British Airways ran a promotion that achieved a staggering 20% response rate. The opportunity to win one of 500 travel prizes to a variety of destinations was communicated via direct mail to one million members of its Executive Club and Travel Service. Miller (2000) reports that these mail shots were then followed up by email messages which resulted in one in five recipients visiting the Web site. Everyone one who took part by completing the questionnaire was awarded 50 air miles so everyone derived something from the campaign.

While the potential through email advertising and communications is high and often quite legitimate when a user has registered his/her email address at a particular site, the risk of being accused of sending spam or junk mail is equally high as it is perceived as unethical and intrusive. The development of permission marketing has brought about a change in perspective as contemporary approaches are now based upon communication with people who have already agreed to receive such marketing communications, very often agreed when registering at a site.

On-line public relations

The use of public relations on the Internet, and Extranets in particular, is claimed by many as a viable and active part of the promotional mix. The claim is that Web site hosts become media owners in the sense that they are free to publish materials and information without recourse to the origin. The problem is that the information they present or convey (on behalf of themselves) has not been influenced by an independent third party, such as an opinion former, and may be no more than brochureware. However, the role is more complex because the Web site assumes the role of the fax machine, with press releases posted so that those interested can view (at their discretion and initiative) and then enter into a dialogue into order to expand on the information provided.

Other forms of public relations are more easily observable. Sponsorship activity is an important part of on-line marketing communications, whether it be a partnership deal or direct sponsorship of a site. Web sites can also play an important role in terms of crisis management. In the event of an organisational crisis or disaster, up-to-date information can be posted quickly either providing pertinent information or directing visitors to off-line facilities should it be appropriate.

Sponsorship activity is an important part of on-line marketing communications.

On-line personal selling

Face-to-face personal communications over the Internet for the purposes of buying and selling remain the one part of the promotional mix that the Internet cannot address. Increasingly video conferencing (see later) does provide this facility but costs and logistics limit the practical application of this tool to conferencing and non-sales meetings. The Internet is an impersonal medium and as such does not allow for direct personal communication. The recognition of this limitation should direct management attention to the use of the Internet as a complementary role within the promotional mix. However, it has been determined that the Internet can impact upon sales performance indirectly through sales management activities (Avlonitis and Karayanni, 2000). They describe how managing and analysing data can refine segmentation and customer classification schemes, allowing sales people to spend more time on core activities.

The Web site remains at the core of Internet marketing and eCommerce activities and therefore it is important to attempt to evaluate a site's overall effectiveness if progress and goals are to be achieved. Many researchers have formulated methodologies and techniques to achieve this (e.g. Dreze and Zurfryden, 1997; Evans and King, 1999) and this topic is explored in greater detail in Chapter 31. However, a Web site does appear to have particular general parameters that need to be in position if the site is to be successful. These parameters concern access to the page (and ease of initial location), the technical specification of the page (e.g. page loading times) and the design and content in order that seekers can complete their visit goals as quickly and inefficiently as possible, yet be stimulated in order to want to return another time.

Interactive communications

Technological advances have made possible a range of other interactive communication opportunities. Stress so far has been placed on the Internet, but there have been many other imaginative and exciting developments and applications. One area where interactivity has been subject to experimentation is television, and some of the organisations that have experimented with interactive messages most notably are Chicken Tonight, Dove, Mazda and Tango.

Among the most important is the development of digital broadcasting and the opportunities for interactive television. Digital television and interactive services are two related but different facilities. Digital services will arrive well before fully interactive services become commercially feasible.

Some believe that digital TV will overtake the Internet in terms of revenue by around 2003 or 2004 (Rosen, 1997). One of the biggest factors accelerating the consumer use of digital TV will be the entertainment possibilities that the Internet will struggle to provide. It is thought by many that digital TV will stimulate growth in home shopping. Digital TV will impact on home shopping, but probably not to the extent that many popular writers assume. Research suggests that at this stage of development, rather than take an increasing proportion of total retail sales, growth in home shopping via digital television will be mainly at the expense of traditional mail order (Wade and McKechnie, 1998).

Digital TV will impact on home shopping, but probably not to the extent that many popular writers assume.

There are a series of home shopping experiments being conducted by a variety of retailers. Perhaps most notably the dominant supermarkets have invested heavily in this area, and if successful the likely impact could be significant. Home

Interactive TV – Unilever

Unilever ran the first UK interactive TV ad for its Chicken Tonight brand, endorsed by the ex-footballer and emerging entertainer Ian Wright. According to Reid (2001), the ad provoked response rates 70% higher than those normally associated with DRTV.

The next major phase of the Unilever interactive strategy was to run two (digital) spots for its brands Coleman's and Olivio spread. Each interactive ad offered click-throughs to the company's portal, Creative Kitchen, containing all of the company's food brands.

shopping represents a change in buyer behaviour which may affect a range of ancillary activities. Transport and storage location facilities will need to be adjusted, and there could be alterations to employment patterns and the support and training necessary to augment new processes and procedures. It is unlikely that the retailers' high street presence will diminish significantly, as many consumers derive important entertainment and social interaction satisfaction by actively shopping.

The financial services sector can be expected to undergo further change as home banking in particular becomes a secure and more convenient transaction context. Entertainment possibilities will be even more attractive, as interactive games and interactive viewing through pay per view, video on demand and time shifting (which is, as Rosen points out, the option to view yesterday's programmes today) become easily accessible.

The new technology and the new communication infrastructure will give increasing numbers of people the opportunity to experience interactive marketing communications and the new media. This may impact upon their expectations and bring changes to the way in which people lead their lives.

Grofton (2000) reports about intuitive software which monitors a visitor's movement around a site, stores it and then adjusts the site to meet the preferred pattern each time that visitor enters the site. The implications for targeting advertising are enormous. However, despite all these developments, it appears that Cohen (1995) was quite

At the beginning of the 21st century on-line profitability remains elusive to most pioneer virtual traders.

prophetic when he commented that there was 'great uncertainty as to the level of consumer demand'. In 1995 technology and demand were uncertain but even at the beginning of the 21st century on-line profitability remains elusive to most pioneer virtual traders. Continually media reports are upbeat about potential demand but simultaneously downbeat when reporting usage and interactive shopping revenues. The reality must be that technological advance and changes in buyer behaviour are more severely lagged than originally realised. While some consumers are ready and eager to take advantage of the new opportunities, many are not and the process of diffusion needs to move forward in order that an increasing proportion of customers have the means and motivation to participate in the interactive environments.

Video conferencing

There are currently two main types of video conferencing systems, PC based and room based.

PC-based, or desktop, systems are suitable for a small number of people, for short time periods. The cameras are usually fixed focus, with small field capability, and viewing screens are also small. Transmission speeds are limited by modem and telephone line capabilities. An advantage is that software applications and files can be shared and viewed jointly.

Room-based systems use large, sophisticated (pan–tilt–zoom) cameras and wide TV screens. More people can participate. Transmission via ISDN (integrated services digital network), including satellite links, facilitates better picture/sound quality. Sessions have to be pre-booked and are costlier than PC based (*source*: www.videocom.co.uk, 7 July 2000).

Video conferencing can be used in marketing communications for research (audience polling), product promotion/launch, training, employee and/or channel member briefings and sales negotiations. The advantages of videoconferencing include speed and convenience as travel costs are minimised and potential reduction in message ambiguity as there is joint and simultaneous viewing of materials and instant feedback.

One of the disadvantages is that all participants have to be available at the same time, which can be difficult across time zones. The connections are not always reliable and room time slots often cannot be extended beyond the original booking. Some people are uneasy in front of cameras, which may impair effectiveness.

Interactive television

Another important technological development is digital broadcasting and the opportunities for interactive television, not least because there are still more televisions than computers in homes. Indeed, with keyboard or voice input to TV, some predict that this will be more significant for consumer interactivity than the Internet. Digital television has been likened to direct marketing but this is a restricted view because digital television needs to fulfil a range of broader marketing tasks that are currently satisfied by current television advertising (Iremonger, 2000).

Digital television and interactive services are two related but different facilities. Digital television is now a reality, but full interactivity has yet to be delivered to the majority of the population. Potential advantages are consumer familiarity, the full-screen, high-quality sound and picture format, fast channel and picture/text 'hopping', combining entertainment and shopping.

Disadvantages include the current high cost of the sets to consumers and of broadcasting for companies. Also, it cannot deal with individual customers until TV-based email is widely established. Penetration rates will rise as analogue services in the UK are to be phased out by 2010.

Digital services provide many benefits for consumers, one of which will be the opportunity to screen out current intrusive advertising. Interactive advertising will be more focused, integrated and consistent, advertising that will be driven by consumers deciding which advertisements they want to watch, when and how long they will stay involved. The creative possibilities will be extensive but in order to retain audiences it will become increasingly important to develop creative ideas based upon a sound understanding of the target audience and their interactive and buying patterns. Currently, on

Digital television and interactive marketing communications are unlikely to thrive isolated from other methods of communication.

UK teletext there are pages about holiday bargains, which direct potential users to the Internet (www.tele-text.co.uk/holidays) where they will find a searchable database, plus weather reports, resort reviews and advice. This service claims a choice of preferred operators, competitive pricing, confidence – full financial protection, up-to-date offers and human interaction at the point of sale. It states that in the future, customers will be able to access the full functionality of the Web site via digital TV and/or mobile phone. The point is that digital television and interactive marketing communications are unlikely to thrive isolated from other methods of communication. Just as on-line facilities need off-line drivers, and just as bricks and clicks appear to be a more profitable format than just clicks, so an integrated perspective is required if digital television and interactive advertising are to be successful.

Mobile phones

WAP phones (wireless application protocol) have an Internet browser facility as well as offering email and text information services. The key advantage of this mobile commerce (mCommerce) is that it offers flexibility in terms of sending and receiving messages which PC-based communications cannot offer. As a result, messages can be not only location specific but also time specific, for example a message sent when someone is in a town centre at lunch time, promoting a café, restaurant or shop. Mobile phones have a far higher penetration than PC users and greater potential. However, the growth in WAP usage in 2000 has not been as great as expected, mainly because of the text input facilities. In Japan, WAP usage far exceeds PC usage and has been positioned away from the Internet Internet sites have to design/develop information displays especially for phones, and this is in its infancy at the moment.

However, Virgin, for one, is offering 'mobile shopping' from ordinary mobile phones with a range of electrical goods, travel, music, videos, games, wines and insurance, with independent data on product quality, performance and value for money. It promises overnight delivery for items in stock and 'around 7 days' if they have to be ordered. The service uses the 'One 2 One' network in the UK, and can hook up to one of 150 networks in 79 countries abroad (www.virgin.com/mobile). Billing procedures and facilities allow for integrated payment system for goods and services.

To conclude and summarise, marketing communications with business partners will improve through increased efficiency and effectiveness, which in turn will be reflected in the nature and quality of the relationships, and made manifest in overall performance.

Improved trust, commitment and a higher propensity to share information must lead to increased business performance. The development of the Internet-based communications is a strategic decision, one that needs to be thought through in turns of

Improved trust, commitment and a higher propensity to share information must lead to increased business performance.

the impact it will have on the way we and our partners do business. This in turn will require significant changes in the way we currently communicate and do business in the b2b market.

Summary

The development and maintenance of a Web site as part of an organisation's overall marketing communications activities is now well established and is virtually standard and expected practice. While the quality and 'stickiness' of Web sites is inevitably quite variable, they do provide another communication point with stakeholders. Web sites may be simple points of contact between users and an organisation or they may be complex systems embedded into two or more organisations allowing for the high levels of commercial exchange. Web sites can disguise the size and stature of the host organisation and they can enable all organisations to reach global audiences. What this means is that organisations large and small are now able to compete on more (but not totally) equal terms.

Web sites are dynamic in nature in that they can be developed through different phases reflecting different levels of capability and user interaction. Just as Web sites vary in user friendliness and capabilities, so the behaviour of site visitors is variable and every attempt should be made to accommodate their varying needs.

All the tools of the promotion mix can be deployed, to a greater or lesser extent, on-line. Advertising, through a variety of techniques, is a prime method of on-line communication but all the tools are able to fulfil particular on-line roles. Off-line communications are also important, particularly for driving visitors to Web sites.

Other forms of interactive communications, and in particular digital television services, are beginning to provide new forms of entertainment, shopping and banking facilities as well as marketing communications opportunities. In the longer term fully interactive services will bring increased leisure and entertainment facilities to a greater number of people and new opportunities for advertisers through interactive advertisements.

Review questions

1. List five and strengths and five weaknesses attributed to Web sites.
2. Identify the different categories of Internet users. What are the principal characteristics of each type of user?
3. Prepare brief notes explaining the different phases of Web site visitor behaviour.
4. Explain how the communication capability of a Web site compares with traditional media.
5. Discuss the validity of the five goals suggested by Cartellieri *et al.* as a necessary part of Web site design.
6. What is the role of the Web site in terms of marketing communications? Explain four types of on-line advertising.
7. Find three examples of on-line sales promotions and evaluate their effectiveness.
8. To what extent are on-line public relations just on-line advertising?
9. Write a report examining the use of email on-line as a form of marketing communications. Find examples to support the points you make.
10. The development of Web sites has been a feature of recent organisational communications for reaching members and non-members. Prepare short notes

outlining the problems in developing such sites and argue the case for developing a Web site for a manufacturer of household electrical goods, a Premier League football club and a department store.

MINI CASE

On-line communications for Sunny Cottage Holidays

Sunny Cottage Holidays (SCH) was considering its marketing communications and trying to determine how best to communicate with its different audiences. The company operates in the holiday cottage market and until now employed traditional processes and procedures to attract business.

Fifty-eight per cent of demand for rented holiday cottages is concentrated in the A, B and C1 social groups. Very often customers want an independent family holiday rather than be part of a group. The notion of 'escaping to the countryside' for a short break is significant for those holidaying out of season in rented cottages. For those holidaying in the main summer months, the prime reasons for renting a cottage, apart from the geographic scenery, appear to be the informality associated with these types of holidays and the wide range of activities available to families of all ages. Some 94% of bookings are for periods of four or more nights in the period from June to September. The purchase decision process is inevitably one of high involvement and based upon high levels of trust.

The Agents' view

Cottage owners require bookings and to assist them they choose to undertake their own marketing, to use an agent or to use a combination of the two methods. When using an agent (such as Sunny Cottage Holidays), responsibility for marketing properties and managing bookings passes to the agent who receives a 20% commission for each successful booking.

Agents such as Sunny Cottage Holidays need to market themselves to cottage owners (to develop a portfolio) and to customers in order to obtain revenue and profit on the cottages they rent out.

An agent's attractiveness to property owners is related to its ability to be seen to be active in securing bookings and to the development of an image with which property owners are happy to be associated. Focused geographic markets permit advertising in the local press, in local authority guides and in Tourist Information Centres (TICs). Word-of-mouth and participation at local exhibitions are further important means of developing visibility. By instigating a system to check the standards of accommodation, agents demonstrate their concern for and orientation to quality and tourist satisfaction.

Agents also use advertising to encourage property owners to place their accommodation with them in order that they secure bookings on their behalf. Both placements and bookings are generated partly through advertising in such publications as the *Exchange and Mart*, *Dalton's Weekly*, the *Sunday Times*, the *Observer*, and a variety of provincial newspapers and travel magazines.

The Tourist Board view

One of the roles of the Regional Tourist Board (RTB) is to encourage people to visit and take their holidays in the area and to encourage the provision and improvement of tourist amenities and facilities. The RTBs accomplish these aims by, in broad terms, providing financial assistance to certain tourism projects, by investing in promotional activities and by providing advisory and information services. TICs and tourist information points (TIPs) are vital supporting elements of the tourism industry. TIPs are unmanned information points, whereas TICs are usually staffed and provide tourists with authoritative information and assist them with their arrangements associated with their visit.

The RTB inspects tourist accommodation at the request of owners and managers. Accommodation that reaches the necessary standard is said to be 'verified' and described as such in its publications. Verification is justified on the grounds that it helps to protect consumer interests by giving customers a greater guarantee of appropriate standards. It also provides a potential advantage to scheme participants in that the endorsement is seen to be granted by a third party who has no pecuniary interest in the accommodation. Finally, it is claimed that the system helps to advance improvements in the quality of accommodation offerings.

The customer view

The primary purchasing procedure is based around a colour brochure, mailed to customers by agents and/or cottage owners. These colour brochures are traditionally large and require customers to identify their preferred cottages by thumbing through pages of photographs of cottages, categorised by first geographical area and then size of accommodation. Most photographs were taken of the exterior of the cottages, although some of the more expensive or desirable properties have some interior views. The limited descriptive text is normally supported by a coding system in order to provide some comparative measure of quality and content. To determine the price of renting a cottage for a week, reference had to be made to particular price bands which are correlated with different weeks of the year. The next step is to telephone Sunny Cottage Holidays to find out whether the identified and preferred cottage is available in the week(s) required.

Sunny Cottage Holiday's view

SCH is considering the way it communicates with its customers as it feels there are certain problems associated with the way it currently does business, for example the high cost of producing the colour brochures, the long lead times involved in changing and updating them combined with the wastage involved in mailing to people who may not be actively interested in renting a holiday cottage. The call centre is perceived as an important part of the process and is effective in both clarifying information for customers and building trust through 'personal' contact. However, SCH believes that there is a more effective and efficient way of using its marketing communications and providing customers with a more customer-friendly communication process.

This mini case was compiled from a variety of sources and is not meant to suggest good or bad management practice.

Mini-case questions

1. Explain the benefits SCH might experience from developing a Web site.
2. How might SCH drive traffic to the Web site?
3. Write brief notes about how customers might benefit from an on-line brochure. Compare this with the characteristics of the purchase process associated with the traditional paper-based brochure.
4. Suggest ways in which the Web site might be used to communicate with customers who have purchased at least one holiday from SCH.
5. Set out a revised promotional mix for SCH based upon the utilisation of on-line communications.

References

Avlonitis, G.J. and Karayanni, D. (2000) The impact of Internet use of business-to-business marketing. *Industrial Marketing Management*, **29**, pp. 441–59.

Briggs, R. and Hollis, N. (1997) Advertising on the web: is there response before click-through? *Journal of Advertising Research* (March/April), pp. 33–45.

Bush, A.J., Bush, V. and Harris, S. (1998) Advertiser perceptions of the Internet as a marketing communications tool. *Journal of Advertising Research* (March–April), p. 17.

Cartellieri, C., Parsons, A., Rao, V. and Zeisser, M. (1997) The real impact of Internet advertising. *McKinsey Quarterly*, **3**, pp. 44–63.

Chaffey, D., Meyer, R., Johnston, K. and Ellis-Chadwick, F. (2000) *Internet Marketing*. London: Pearson Education.

Cohen, R. (ed.) (1995) Interactive demand is not as high as believed. *Precision Marketing*, 25 September, p. 8.

Curtis, J. (2000) Can Japan wipe out? *Revolution*, 13 December, pp. 41–4.

Dreze, X. and Zurfryden, F. (1997) Testing web site design and promotional content. *Journal of Advertising Research* (March/April), pp. 77–91.

Evans, J.R. and King, V.E. (1999) Business-to-business marketing and the world wide web: planning, managing and assessing web sites. *Industrial Marketing Management*, **28**, pp. 343–58.

Groften, K. (2000) Have you got permission? *Marketing*, 22 June, pp. 28–9.

Iremonger, M. (2000) Interactive TV is much more than just a direct marketing tool. *Revolution*, 6 December, p. 33.

Leong, E.F.K., Huang, X. and Stanners, P.J. (1998) Comparing the effectiveness of the web site with traditional media. *Journal of Advertising Research* (September–October), pp. 44–50.

Lewis, H. and Lewis, R. (1997) Give your customers what they want. Cited in Chaffey *et al.* (2000).

McCawley, I. (2000) Are TV ads a waste of dot-com money? *Marketing Week*, 31 August, p. 12.

McLuhan, R. (2000) A lesson in online brand promotion. *Marketing*, 23 March, pp. 31–2.

Miller, R. (2000) How DM can drive traffic to your site. *Marketing*, 12 October, p. 43.

Morgan, R.F. (1996) An Internet marketing framework for the World Wide Web (WWW). *Journal of Marketing Management*, **12**, pp. 757–75.

Ong, C.P. (1995) Practical aspects of marketing on the WWW. MBA Dissertation, University of Sheffield, UK.

Oxley, M. and Miller, J. (2000) Capturing the consumer: ensuring website stickiness, *Admap*, (July/August), pp. 21–4.

Reid, A. (2001) Unilever continues to defy the skeptics over digital tv spots. *Campaign*, 16 February, p. 18.

Rosen, E.M. (1997) Digital TV will soon overtake the Internet. *Revolution* (July), pp. 6–7.

Rosier, B. and Jardine, A. (1999) Asda set to launch Web site price war. *Marketing*, 14 October, p. 1.

Wade, N. and McKechnie, S.A. (1998) The impact of digital television: will it change our shopping habits? Working paper presented at the 3rd International Conference on Marketing and Corporate Communications.

Useful or supporting Web site addresses

www.thetrainline.com

www.easycottages.com

www.ft.com

26

Public relations

Public relations is a management activity that attempts to shape the attitudes and opinions held by an organisation's stakeholders. Through dialogue with these stakeholders the organisation may adjust its own position and/or strategy. Therefore, there is an attempt to identify with, and adjust an organisation's policies to, the interests of its stakeholders. To do this it formulates and executes a programme of action to develop mutual goodwill and understanding. Profile communication strategies make substantial use of public relations when developing understanding about who they are and what their intentions are.

AIMS AND OBJECTIVES

The aim of this chapter is to explore public relations in the context of promoting organisations and their products.

The objectives of this chapter are:

1. To discuss the role of public relations in the communications mix.

2. To clarify the differences between corporate public relations and marketing public relations.

3. To highlight the main audiences to which public relations activities are directed.

4. To provide an overview of some of the main tools used by public relations.

5. To appreciate the development and significance of corporate advertising.

6. To examine the nature and context of crisis management.

7. To determine the manner in which public relations complements the other tools of the promotional mix.

Introduction

The shift in the degree of importance given by organisations to public relations over recent years is a testimony to its power and effectiveness. An increasing number of organisations are now recognising that the role that public relations can play in the external and internal communications of organisations is a tool for use by all organisations, regardless of the sector in which they operate. Therefore, all organisations in the public, hybrid, not-for-profit and private sectors can use this tool to raise visibility, interest and goodwill.

Traditionally, public relations has been a tool which dealt with the manner and style with which an organisation interacted with its major 'publics'. It sought to influence other organisations and individuals by public relations, projecting an identity that would affect the image that different publics held of the organisation. By spreading information and improving the levels of knowledge that people held about particular issues, the organisation sought ways to advance itself in the eyes of those it saw as influential. This approach is reflected in the definition of public relations provided by the Institute of Public Relations: 'Public Relations practice is the planned and sustained effort to establish and maintain goodwill and mutual understanding between an organisation and its publics'. Another definition has been provided by delegates attending a world convention of public relations associations in 1978, entitled the Mexican Statement: 'Public Relations is the art and social science of analysing trends, predicting their consequences, counselling organisations' leadership and implementing planned programmes of action which will serve both the organisation's and the public interest' (Public Relations Educational Trust, 1991). A more recent and practitioner-orientated definition from Bruning and Ledingham (2000) is that public relations is the management of relationships between organisations and its stakeholders (publics).

By spreading information and improving the levels of knowledge that people held about particular issues, the organisation sought ways to advance itself in the eyes of those it saw as influential.

The main issues expressed by both these definitions are that PR is concerned with the development and communication of corporate and competitive strategies. Public relations provides visibility for an organisation, and this in turn, it is hoped, allows it to be properly identified, positioned and understood by all of its stakeholders. What these definitions do not emphasise or make apparent is that public relations should also be used by management as a means of understanding issues from a stakeholder perspective. Good relationships are developed by appreciating the views held by others and by 'putting oneself in their shoes'.

Through this sympathetic and patient approach to planned communication, a dialogue can be developed which is not frustrated by punctuated interruptions (anger, disbelief, ignorance and objections). Public relations is a management activity that attempts to shape the attitudes and opinions held by an organisation's stakeholders. It attempts to identify its policies with the interests of its stakeholders and formulates and executes a programme of action to develop mutual goodwill and understanding.

Public relations is a management activity that attempts to shape the attitudes and opinions held by an organisation's stakeholders.

Characteristics of public relations

Public relations should, therefore, be a planned activity, one that encompasses a wide range of events. However, there are a number of characteristics that single out this particular tool from the others in the promotional mix. Public relations does not require the purchase of airtime or space in media vehicles, such as television or magazines. The decision on whether an organisation's public relations messages are transmitted or not rests with those charged with managing the media resource, not the message sponsor. Those that are selected are perceived to be endorsements or the views of parties other than management. The outcome is that these messages usually carry greater perceived credibility than those messages transmitted through paid media, such as advertising.

The degree of trust and confidence generated by public relations singles out this tool from others in the promotional mix as an important means of reducing buyers' perceived risk. However, while credibility may be high, the amount of control that management is able to bring to the transmission of the public relations message is very low. For example, a press release may have been carefully prepared in-house, but as soon as it is passed to the editor of a magazine or newspaper, a possible opinion former, all control is lost. The release may be destroyed (highly probable), printed as it stands (highly unlikely) or changed to fit the available space in the media vehicle (almost certain, if it is decided to use the material). This means that any changes will not have been agreed by management, so the context and style of the original message may be lost or corrupted.

While credibility may be high, the amount of control that management is able to bring to the transmission of the public relations message is very low.

The costs associated with public relations also make this an important tool in the promotional mix. The absolute costs are minimal, except for those organisations that retain an agency, but even then their costs are low compared with those of advertising. The relative costs (the costs associated with reaching members of the target audiences) are also very low. The main costs associated with public relations are the time and opportunity costs associated with the preparation of press releases and associated literature. If these types of activity are organised properly, many small organisations could develop and shape their visibility in a relatively inexpensive way.

A further characteristic of this tool is that it can be used to reach specific audiences, in a way that paid media cannot. With increasing media fragmentation and finer segmentation (customisation) of markets, public relations represents a cost-effective way of reaching such markets and audiences.

This tool can be used to reach specific audiences, in a way that paid media cannot.

The main characteristics of public relations are that it represents a very cost-effective means of carrying messages with a high degree of credibility. However, the degree of control that management is able to exert over the transmission of messages can be limited.

Publics or stakeholders?

The first definition of public relations quoted earlier used, as indeed does most of the public relations industry, the word *publics*. This word is used traditionally to refer to the various organisations and groups with which a focus organisation interacts. So far, this text has referred to these types of organisation as *stakeholders*. 'Stakeholders' is a term used increasingly in the field of strategic management, and as public relations is essentially concerned with strategic issues, the word 'stakeholders' is used in this text to provide consistency and to reflect the strategic orientation and importance of this promotional tool.

The stakeholder concept has been discussed earlier, at great length, in Chapter 10. Various networks of stakeholders were identified, with each network consisting of members who are orientated towards supporting the focus organisation either in an indirect way or directly through the added-value processes.

For the purposes of this chapter it is useful to set out who the main stakeholders are likely to be. Stakeholder groups, it should be remembered, are not static and new groups can emerge in response to changes in the environment. The main core groups, however, tend to be the following.

Employees

The employees of an organisation have already been established as major stakeholders. In an internal context, employees represent a major source of word-of-mouth communications. It has long been established that employees need to be motivated, involved and stimulated to perform their tasks at a high level. Their work as external communicators is less well established, but their critical role in providing external cues as part of the corporate identity programme was discussed earlier.

Employees represent a major source of word-of-mouth communications.

Shareholders

Shareholders require regular information to maintain their continued confidence in the organisation and to prevent them changing their portfolios and reducing the value of the organisation.

Suppliers

Suppliers need to be informed of the strategies being pursued by the focus organisation, if they are to be able to provide continuity and a quality service.

Financial groups

In addition to the shareholders, there are those individuals who are either potential shareholders or those who advise shareholders and investors. These represent the wider financial community but who nevertheless have a very strong influence on the stature, strength and value that an organisation has. Financial analysts need to be supplied with information in order that they be up to date with the activities and performance outcomes of organisations, but also need to be advised of developments within the various markets that the organisation operates.

Organisations attempt to supply analysts with current information and materials about the organisation and the markets in which they are operating, to ensure that the potential and value of publicly quoted organisations is reflected in the share price. The

Public relations is an important form of communication in that it can create and shape relationships.

success of any further attempts to increase investment and to secure any necessary capital will be determined by the confidence that the financial community has in the organisation. Public relations is an important form of communication in that it can create and shape relationships. By developing confidence in this way, the perception of risk held by investors can be lowered, funds are released and new products are developed and launched.

Media

The relationships that organisations develop with the media are extremely important. Of all the media, the press is the most crucial, as it is always interested in newsworthy items and depends to a large extent on information being fed to it by a variety of corporate press officers. Consequently, publicity can be generated for a range of organisational events, activities and developments.

Community

The local community is often the target of public relations activities because of its proximity and the influence that local citizens may have on an organisation. By attempting to keep it informed and by trying to develop a spirit of goodwill and mutual understanding, the local community can be encouraged to identify more strongly with the focus organisation. For example, it is possible to establish an environment within which an initiative to expand plant capacity will be received favourably and supported by the local community, rather than encountering public protests and hostility.

Local authorities and the government

The power and influence held by local authorities cannot be underestimated. For example, their willingness to grant planning permission for the capacity extension mentioned above will reflect the attitudes and relationships between the two parties. Organisations should seek to work with, rather than against, these stakeholder groups. As a result, public relations should be aimed at informing local authorities of their strategic intentions and seeking ways in which the objectives of both parties can be satisfied.

Public relations should be aimed at informing local authorities of their strategic intentions and seeking ways in which the objectives of both parties can be satisfied.

Where local authorities interpret legislation and frame the activities of their citizens and constituent organisations, the government determines legislation and controls the activities of people and organisations across markets. This control may be direct or indirect, but the power and influence of government are such that large organisations and trade associations seek to influence the direction and strength of legislation, because any adverse laws or regulations may affect the profitability and the value of the organisation. Recent initiatives by the UK government to reduce the length of time that new drugs are protected by patent were severely contested by representatives from drug manufacturers and their trade association, the Association of British Pharmaceutical Industries. Despite a great deal of lobbying, the action was lost, and now manufacturers have only eight years to recover their investment before other manufacturers can replicate the drug.

Customers

This stakeholder group is often the target of public relations activities, because although members of the public may not be current customers, the potential they represent is important. The attitudes and preferences towards the organisation and its products may be unfavourable, in which case it is unlikely that they will wish to purchase the product or speak positively about the organisation. By creating awareness and trust, it is possible to create goodwill and interest, which may translate into purchase activity or favourable word-of-mouth communications.

A framework of public relations

Communications with such a wide variety of stakeholders need to vary to reflect different environmental conditions, organisational objectives and form of relationship. Grunig and Hunt (1984) have attempted to capture the diversity of public relations activities through a framework. They set out four models to reflect the different ways in which public relations is, in their opinion, considered to work. These models, based on their experiences as public relations practitioners, constitute a useful approach to understanding the complexity of this form of communication. The four models are set out in Figure 26.1.

	Model			
Characteristic	*Press agentry/publicity*	*Public information*	*Two-way asymmetric*	*Two-way symmetric*
Purpose	Propaganda	Dissemination of information	Scientific persuasion	Mutual understanding
Nature of communication	One-way; complete truth not essential	One-way; truth important	Two-way; imbalanced effects	Two-way; balanced effects
Communication model	Source ⟶ Rec.*	Source ⟶ Rec.*	Source ⇄ Rec.* Feedback	Group ⇄ Group
Nature of research	Little; 'counting house'	Little; readability, readership	Formative; evaluative of attitudes	Formative; evaluative of understanding
Leading historical figures	P.T. Barnum	Ivy Lee	Edward L. Bernays	Bernays, educators, professional leaders
Where practised today	Sports, theatre, product promotion	Government, not-for-profit associations, business	Competitive business; agencies	Regulated business; agencies
Estimated percentage of organisations practising today	15%	50%	20%	15%

Figure 26.1 Models of public relations. From Grunig and Hunt (1984); used with kind permission.
* Receiver.

The press agentry/publicity model

The essence of this approach is that communication is used as a form of propaganda. That is, the communication flow is essentially one way, and the content is not bound to be strictly truthful as the objective is to convince the receiver of a new idea or offering. This can be observed in the growing proliferation of media events and press releases.

The public information model

Unlike the first model, this approach seeks to disseminate truthful information. While the flow is again one way, there is little focus on persuasion, more on the provision of information. This can be best seen through public health campaigns and government advice communications in respect of crime, education and health.

The two-way asymmetric model

Two-way communication is a major element of this model. Feedback from receivers is important, but as power is not equally distributed between the various stakeholders and the organisation, the relationship has to be regarded as asymmetric. The purpose remains to influence attitude and behaviour through persuasion.

The purpose remains to influence attitude and behaviour through persuasion.

The two-way symmetric model

This represents the most acceptable and mutually rewarding form of communication. Power is seen to be dispersed equally between the organisation and its stakeholders and the intent of the communication flow is considered to be reciprocal. The organisation and its respective publics are prepared to adjust their positions (attitudes and behaviours) in the light of the information flow. A true dialogue emerges through this interpretation, unlike any of the other three models, which see an unbalanced flow of information and expectations.

A true dialogue emerges through this interpretation, unlike any of the other three models, which see an unbalanced flow of information and expectations.

The model has attracted a great deal of attention and has been reviewed and appraised by a number of commentators (Miller, 1989). As a result of this and a search for excellence in public relations, Grunig (1992) revised the model to reflect the dominance of the 'craft' and the 'professional' approaches to public relations practices. That is, those practitioners who utilise public relations merely as a tool to achieve media visibility can be regarded as 'craft' orientated. Those organisations whose managers seek to utilise public relations as a means of mediating their relationships with their various stakeholders are seen as 'professional' practitioners. They are considered to be using public relations as a longer-term and proactive form of planned communication. The former see public relations as an instrument, the latter as a means of conducting a dialogue.

These models are not intended to suggest that communication planners should choose among them. Their use and interpretation depend upon the circumstances that prevail at any one time. Organisations use a number of these different approaches to manage the communication issues that exist between them and the variety of different stakeholder audiences with whom they interact. However, there is plenty of evidence to suggest that the press/agentry model is the one most used by practitioners and that the two-way symmetrical model is harder to observe in practice.

In addition, it is important to remember that the shift to a relationship management perspective effectively alters the way public relations is perceived and practised by organisations. Instead of trying to manipulate audience opinion so that the organisation is of primary importance, the challenge is to use symbolic visual communication messages with behaviour such that the organisation–audience relationship improves for all parties (Ehling, 1992). What follows from this is a change in evaluation, from measuring the decimation of messages to one that measures audience influence and behavioural and attitudinal change or, as Bruning and Ledingham (2000) put it succinctly, from outputs to outcomes.

The challenge is to use symbolic visual communication messages with behaviour such that the organisation–audience relationship improves for all parties.

Structure and form of public relations

It can be seen that public relations can be involved with a range of organisational issues. This may be seen as a reflection of the potency of this form of communication. It is more than just a means of influencing other stakeholders through propaganda and/or publicity-based activities. Public relations can be used to mediate the different relationships that an organisation has with its environment and can perform a number of valuable roles, such as counsellor, diplomat and arbiter (Pieczka, 1996). For this to happen a number of environmental conditions need to exist, such as equitable information flows, a managerial predisposition to treat incoming information in an unbiased and apolitical manner, that the power bases throughout the information network are equally dispersed and that the level of connectedness is relatively stable and suitable. If these conditions prevail then public relations may be able to perform the role of a communication conduit for internal and external stakeholders more effectively than under adverse conditions.

The role that public relations should assume and its structural position within an organisation have become increasingly complex and debatable. Traditionally, public relations has been regarded as a function that reports directly to the CEO. Control over the activities of public relations is direct and the purpose is to convey appropriate information about the corporate entity and to create goodwill and understanding with other stakeholders. To that end, public relations was seen as separate to and distinct from marketing. A publication by the Public Relations Educational Trust (1991) declares that 'PR is NOT Marketing'. The substantiation for this is based on an interpretation of marketing, one that is strictly profit orientated. This does not reflect reality, as self-help groups and organisations such as the NHS and charities would not be able to practise marketing if such a narrow perspective was supported.

The role that public relations should assume and its structural position within an organisation have become increasingly complex and debatable.

Kotler and Mindak (1978) set out five ways in which organisations can manage the marketing and public relations functions. These are depicted in Figure 26.2. It can be seen that the structural relationship of marketing and public relations can range from

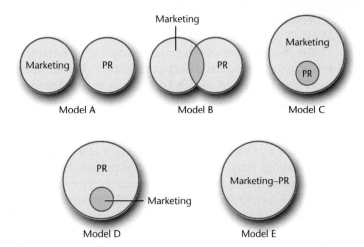

Figure 26.2   Relationships between marketing and public relations. From Kotler and Mindak (1978); used with kind permission.

the traditional view, where they are separate and totally unconnected, fulfilling different roles, through various other forms where one subsumes the other, to model E. Here, both share an equal and mutually supportive relationship. In this form, both recognise the need to segment markets and to provide different satisfactions. Each function needs the support of the other and both have similar needs in terms of understanding the attitudes, perceptions and awareness held by each market or stakeholder. Internal conflict is effectively reduced, and this in turn facilitates the transmission of consistent, positive and coordinated messages to all stakeholders.

Kotler and Mindak highlight these key relationships well, but the models can also be used to depict the development of public relations and marketing in organisations. For example, local authorities have for a long time had a public relations department, but only recently have they begun to appoint marketing managers in response to their changing responsibilities, environments and new competitive orientation. Hospitals are having to focus on market needs rather than the needs of internal experts. Many are increasing the level of public relations activities and are also introducing marketing as a distinct function, partly to assist the necessary change in culture.

Many private sector organisations are making a transition from model C to model D or E, depending upon their experiences and organisational culture, market environments and the perspective of the CEO and senior management team towards the roles of public relations and marketing.

Corporate public relations and marketing public relations

Many writers and organisations are now challenging the traditional view of public relations. The marketing dimension of public relations has been developed considerably in recent years. This is a response to media rates increasing ahead of inflation, media and markets becoming increasingly fragmented and marketing managers seeking more effective communication mixes. As a result, public relations is being used actively to support and reinforce other elements of the communications mix (Kitchen, 1991).

The development of integrated marketing communications has helped bring marketing and public relations closer together. The advantage of utilising a number of tools together is that through coordination message impact is improved. One of the best examples of this is the Wonderbra campaign by Playtex. It is estimated that the poster campaign was enhanced by £50 million worth of 'extra' media coverage based on the stories and publicity generated by the programme (Barrett, 1997).

It was established earlier (Chapter 10) that a performance network consists of those organisations (stakeholders) who directly influence or are influenced by the value-added processes of the focus organisation. They can engage in relational exchanges and often seek to develop long-term collaborative relationships. The support network consists of those organisations who influence and are influenced by the value-adding processes in an indirect way. They tend to engage in market exchanges which encourage a short-term perspective.

Both these networks require public relations, but in different ways. The support network needs public relations to help build and sustain goodwill between members and to create relationships which acknowledge the direction and intent of the strategy being pursued by each of them. This requires the work of a more traditional approach to public relations. The performance network needs public relations to sustain an environment where there is not only goodwill but also collaboration and trust, one where the satisfaction of particular target segments is the goal of all members. This requires a marketing orientation where there is a greater emphasis on the need to achieve certain levels of profitability as a result of meeting and satisfying customer needs.

Bearing these points in mind and recalling the professional and craft designations set out previously, it is not surprising that two types of public relations have begun to emerge: corporate public relations and marketing public relations. Corporate public relations, according to Cutlip *et al.* (1985), is 'a function of management seeking to identify, establish and maintain mutually beneficial relationships between an organisation and the various publics on whom its success and failure depend'. They define marketing public relations as 'not only concerned with organisational success and failure but also with specific publics: customers, consumers and clients with whom exchange transactions take place'.

This dichotomy is not intended to suggest that these are mutually exclusive forms of public relations, since they are not, and, as Kitchen and Proctor (1991) rightly point out, they are mutually interactive. The use of corporate communications has an effect similar to that of ink being injected into a bottle of water: the diffusion produced can assist all parts of an organisation and its stakeholders, whether they be in the performance or support networks. Similarly, public relations at the product level can have an immediate effect upon the goodwill and perspective with which stakeholders perceive the whole organisation.

For example, an airline opening a new route and using marketing PR (MPR) activities focused on customers in the hinterland of each destination will impact on both the product and the airline as a whole. Further examples of MPR can be observed by companies installing 'carelines' that can be used by customers to contact (to seek advice and complain) about aspects of the company's products and

Further examples of MPR can be observed by companies installing 'carelines' that can be used by customers to contact (to seek advice and complain) about aspects of the company's products and services.

Marketing public relations – Jersey potatoes

As part of the preparations for the launch of the new season's crop of Jersey potatoes to its main market, the UK, Hammond Communications research uncovered a case of potato rustling on the island. They discovered that not only was poaching a current problem for farmers but they were unaware of the extent of the problem.

By referring to the potatoes as 'brown gold' and using the television detective Bergerac (John Nettles) to organise a 'Spud Watch' with local farmers an event was staged. The resultant photocall and subsequent interviews were covered by BBCTV News 24, Channel 5 News, GMTV, seven national and 31 regional daily newspapers and three national radio stations.

Adapted from PR Awards 2000

services. The telephone number, which can be made visible on posters, receipts, catalogues, advertisements and shopping bags, serves to feed negative and positive aspects and through the use of data analysis can assist the development of new products and services. Indeed, Burger King have used this to develop new menus and merchandising items.

The net impact of either approach has to be reflected in the performance of the organisation, and for many that is the profitability of the unit. The identification of these two forms of public relations does not mean that this approach is a widely used practice. Indeed, at this stage only a minority of organisations recognise the benefits that this approach can bring. However, as an increasing number of organisations, in a variety of sectors, are expanding their use of PR, so more sophisticated approaches are likely to emerge, aimed at improving product, corporate and overall performance and satisfaction levels.

Objectives of a public relations plan

It can be seen that the main broad objectives of public relations activities are to provide visibility for the corporate body and support for the marketing agenda at the product level. The promotional objectives, established earlier in the plan, will have identified issues concerning the attitudes and relationships stakeholders have with an organisation and its products. Decisions will have been made to build awareness and to change perception, preferences or attitudes. The task of the public relations plan is to provide a series of programmes that develop and enhance some of the identity cues used by stakeholders to develop their image of the organisation and its products.

Public relations can be used to address issues identified within the support and performance networks. These will be concerned with communications that aim to develop positive attitudes and dispositions towards the organisation and generally concern strategic issues. Public relations can also contribute to the marketing needs of the organisation and will therefore be focused at the product level in the performance network and on consumers, seeking to change

PR can be used to address issues identified in the support and performance networks.

attitudes, preferences and awareness levels with respect to products and services offered. Therefore a series of programmes is necessary: one to fulfil the corporate requirements and another to support the marketing of products and services.

Public relations and repositioning – Heinz Salad Cream

Cowlett (2000) reports that established food brands need to be refreshed and repositioned on a regular basis in order to be of value to successive generations. Heinz Salad Cream, for example, is a brand that has been around for over 85 years and was generally perceived as a salad dressing preferred mainly by the older generation. Many adults have not even tried it as they have been brought up using mayonnaise.

Rather than discontinue the brand, Heinz decided to reposition the product by introducing it to a new generation of young adults and surrounding it with a new set of associations and brand values. This was accomplished using public relations, advertising, radio and in-store promotions in concert with the Web site. A launch event using Denise van Outen and Graham Norton was used to generate media attention and through sponsorship of a comedy tour, tasting opportunities were increased among the target audience.

Whether public relations is being used in the performance, support or consumer markets, the development of levels of awareness held by particular audiences is crucial. Similarly, public relations should be used to build credibility, to motivate members of the networks and to minimise overall costs of communication.

Cause-related marketing

One major reason for the development of public relations and the associated corporate reputation activities has been the rise of cause-related marketing (CRM), which over the last six years in particular has been a significant influence as many brand owners have become aware of the need to be perceived as credible, responsible and ethically sound. Developing a strong and socially orientated corporate reputation has become a major form of differentiation in many markets where price, quality and tangible attributes are relatively similar. Being able to present their corporate brands as contributors to the wider social framework, a role beyond that of simple profit generators, has enabled stronger positive positions to be achieved.

Developing a strong and socially orientated corporate reputation has become a major form of differentiation in many markets where price, quality and tangible attributes are relatively similar.

One of the methods used by brands is CRM. This is a commercial activity by which profit orientated and not-for-profit organisations form partnerships to exploit, for mutual benefit, their association in the name of a particular cause.

The benefits from a properly planned and constructed campaign accrue to all participants. CRM helps improved corporate reputation, enables product differentiation and appears to contribute to improved customer retention through enhanced sales. In essence, CRM is a means by which relationships with stakeholders can be developed effectively. As organisations outsource an increasingly larger part of their business activities and as the stakeholder networks become more complex, so the need to be perceived as (and to be) socially responsible becomes a critically important dimension of an organisation's image.

Cause-related marketing – Tesco

Tesco's computers for schools campaign required customers to collect vouchers which they then gave to schools. The schools then redeemed them for computing and related equipment.

It is estimated that the programme has put over £50 million worth of information equipment into schools, or one per school, and redemption rates were recorded at over 65% (Adkins, 1999). According to the marketing director at Tesco, 'the growing importance of building customer loyalty, enhancing the brand and providing added value as a differentiator, plus the benefit that can be gained through cause related marketing, increasingly validates it . . .'.

A public relations programme consists of a number of planned events and activities that seek to satisfy communication objectives. The following represent some of the broad tools and techniques associated with public relations, but it should be noted that the list is not intended to be comprehensive.

Public relations methods and techniques

An organisation's corporate identity is those activities that reflect, to a large extent, the personality of an organisation (see Chapter 16). Public relations provides some of the deliberate cues which enable stakeholders to develop images and perceptions by which they understand and recognise organisations.

The range of public relations cues or methods available to organisations is immense. Different organisations use different permutations in order that they can communicate effectively with their stakeholders. For the purposes of this text a general outline is provided of the more commonly used methods.

Public relations cues are largely visual, whereas those provided by sales promotion, for example, may appeal to a broad range of senses, such as taste, touch and sight.

Public relations cues are largely visual.

Kitchen and Moss (1995) report how a number of fast-moving consumer goods companies in the UK have categorised the tools used in both these types of public relations. For these organisations, media and sports sponsorships, publicity and sales promotion tie-ups constitute the core activities of marketing public relations. Corporate public relations activities revolve around corporate publicity, issues management, public affairs, lobbying, financial/investor relations and corporate advertising. This demarcation should not be regarded as typical or indeed desirable, but it serves as a useful means of understanding the focus of these two types of public relations. What also emerges is a profound recognition of the need to integrate the various communication activities, which itself requires objective and coordinated management attention.

Book launch – Harry Potter

The launch date of the eagerly awaited fourth book in the Harry Potter series was announced in February 2000, a full five months before actual publication. During this period, J.K. Rowling, the author, suggested that there not be any reviews of the book, in an attempt keep secret the plot of the new story.

When the launch was made the author undertook an eight-day book-signing tour and to do this she conducted her tour of the UK by steam engine which was painted and branded the Hogswarts Express, as per one of the character's journeys in previous books (Bold, 2000).

In May, prior to the launch, *The Times*, following an invited pitch of all national newspapers, had an exclusive interview with the author. In a novel sales promotion event, each bookshop was sent 'golden tickets' which it could distribute in any way (e.g. competitions), enabling children to have their copy of the book signed on the train itself.

The launch achieved massive publicity, not only in the UK but also in Australia, the USA and Canada. Advance book orders reached £5 million and a huge number of bookshops ran out of stock.

No further attempt is made in this book to segregate the cues used by organisations for either marketing or corporate public relations. The main reason for this is that there is no useful benefit from such a subdivision. Cues are interchangeable and can be used to build credibility or to provide visibility for an organisation. It is the skill of the public relations practitioner that determines the right blend of techniques. The various types of cue are set out in Table 26.1.

Cues are interchangeable and can be used to build credibility or to provide visibility for an organisation.

While there is general agreement on a definition, there is a lower level of consensus over what constitutes public relations. This is partly because the range of activities is diverse and categorisation problematic. The approach adopted here is that public relations consists of a range of communication activities, of which publicity and event management appear to be the main ones used by practitioners. There are also other activities which are derived from public relations, as follows:

- lobbying (out of personal selling and publicity);
- sponsorship (out of event management and advertising);
- corporate advertising (out of corporate public relations and advertising);
- crisis management (which has developed out of issues management, a part of corporate public relations);
- investor relations (out of issues management and publicity).

Table 26.1   Cues used by PR to project corporate identity

Cues to build credibility	Cues to signal visibility
Product quality	Sales literature and company publications
Customer relations	Publicity and media relations
Community involvement	Speeches and presentations
Strategic performance	Event management
Employee relations	Promotional messages
Crisis management skills	Media mix
Third-party endorsement	Design (signage, logo, letterhead)
Perceived ethics and environmental awareness	Dress codes
Architecture and furnishing	Exhibitions/seminars
	Sponsorships

Publicity

The quality of the relationship between an organisation and the media will dramatically affect the impact and dissemination of news and stories released by an organisation. The relationships referred to are those between an organisation's public relations manager and the editor and journalists associated with both the press and the broadcast media.

Press releases

The press release is a common form of media relations activity. A written report concerning a change in the organisation is sent to various media houses for inclusion in the media vehicle as an item of news. The media house may cover a national area, but very often a local house will suffice. These written statements concern developments in the organisation, such as promotions, new products, awards, prizes, new contracts and customers. The statement is deliberately short and written in such a style that it attracts the attention of the editor. Further information can be obtained if it is to be included within the next publication or news broadcast.

The press release is a common form of media relations activity.

Press conferences

Press conferences are used when a major event has occurred and where a press release cannot convey the appropriate tone or detail required by the organisation. Press conferences are mainly used by politicians, but organisations in crisis (e.g. accidents and mergers) and individuals appealing for help (e.g. police requesting assistance from the public with respect to a particular incident) can use this form of communication. Press kits containing a full reproduction of any statements, photographs and relevant background information should always be available.

Interviews

Interviews with representatives of an organisation enable news and the organisation's view of an issue or event to be conveyed. Other forms of media relations concern bylined articles (articles written by a member of an organisation about an issue related to the company and offered for publication), speeches, letters to the editor, and photographs and captions.

Media relations can be planned and controlled to the extent of what is sent to the media and when it is released. While there is no control over what is actually used, media relations allow organisations to try to convey information concerning strategic issues and to reach particular stakeholders.

Events

Control over public relations events is not as strong as that for publicity. Indeed, negative publicity can be generated by other parties, which can impact badly on an organisation by raising doubts about its financial status or perhaps the quality of its products.

Three main event activity areas can be distinguished: product, corporate and community events.

Three main event activity areas can be distinguished: product, corporate and community events.

1. *Product events*

   Product-orientated events are normally focused upon increasing sales. Cookery demonstrations, celebrities autographing their books and the opening of a new store by the CEO or local MP are events aimed at generating attention, interest and sales of a particular product.

2. *Corporate events*

   Events designed to develop the corporate body are often held by an organisation with a view to providing some entertainment. These can generate a lot of local media coverage, which in turn facilitates awareness, goodwill and interest. For example, events such as open days, factory visits and donations of products to local events can be very beneficial.

3. *Community events*

   These are activities that contribute to the life of the local community. Sponsoring local fun runs and children's play areas, making contributions to local community centres and the disabled are typical activities. The organisation attempts to become more involved with the local community as a good employer and good member of the community. This helps to develop goodwill and awareness in the community.

The choice of events an organisation becomes involved with is critical. The events should have a theme and be chosen to satisfy objectives established earlier in the communications plan. See Chapter 27 for an example of sponsorship of local community events.

▇ Lobbying

The representation of certain organisations or industries within government is an important form of public relations work. While legislation is being prepared, lobbyists provide a flow of information to their organisations to keep them informed about events (as a means of scanning the

Lobbyists provide a flow of information to their organisations to keep them informed about events.

environment), but they also ensure that the views of the organisation are heard in order that legislation can be shaped appropriately, limiting any potential damage that new legislation might bring.

Moloney (1997) suggests that lobbying is inside public relations as it focuses on the members of an organisation who seek to persuade and negotiate with its stakeholders in government on matters of opportunity and or threat. He refers to in-house lobbyists (those members of the organisation that try to influence non-members) and hired lobbyists contracted to complete specific tasks.

His view of lobbying is that it is one of 'monitoring public policy-making for a group interest; building a case in favour of that interest; and putting it privately with varying degrees of pressure to public decision makers for their acceptance and support through favourable political intervention'.

The pharmaceutical industry has been actively lobbying the EU with respect to legislation on new patent regulations and to the information that must be carried in any promotional message. The tobacco industry is well known for its lobbying activities, as is ICI and many other organisations.

Corporate advertising

In an attempt to harness the advantages of both advertising and public relations, corporate advertising has been seen by some as a means of communicating more effectively with a range of stakeholders. The credibility of messages transmitted through public relations is high, but the control that management has over the message is limited. Advertising, however, allows management virtually total control over message dispersion, but the credibility of these messages is usually low. Corporate advertising is the combination of the best of advertising and the best of public relations.

Corporate advertising has been seen by some as a means of communicating more effectively with a range of stakeholders.

Corporate advertising, that is advertising on behalf of an organisation rather than the products or services of the organisation, has long been associated with public relations rather than the advertising department. This can be understood in terms of the origins and former use that organisations made of corporate advertising (Figure 26.3). The first major period was the 1960s, when institutional advertising became prominent. According to Stanton (1964), the primary task of institutional advertising was to create goodwill. The next period was the 1970s, when corporate image

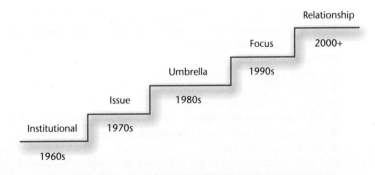

Figure 26.3   The development of corporate advertising.

advertising became popular. During this decade, organisations used issue and advo-cacy advertising as a means of promoting political and social ideas in an attempt to generate public support for the position adopted by an organisation.

During the 1980s, which witnessed a large number of mergers and takeovers, there was an increase in the use of umbrella advertising. Organisations used the name of the organisation as a broad banner, under which a range of products and services were promoted. As discussed previously, there has been a movement towards the incorpo-ration of products and services in the use of public relations. This is reflected in the use of corporate advertising in the 1990s. Although the generation of goodwill con-tinues to be a dominant theme, there is also a need to focus upon organisations as dis-crete units. As many organisations de-layer and return to core business activities, so there is a need to focus communications on what they do best. Such focusing also enables them to reduce advertising expenditure on products because of increased media costs.

Corporate advertising – Vauxhall

Vauxhall is trialling corporate advertising because it is felt its marque lacked per-sonality. No cars are shown but instead the message tries to develop the relation-ship between its company and a customer. Targeted at the young adult market it focuses on innovative aspects (anti-lock brakes) and being the first to make all its cars able to take unleaded petrol (Barrett, 1999).

Corporate advertising provides some opportunity for organisations to achieve these objectives. However, the main purpose of corporate advertising appears to be the pro-vision of cues by which stakeholders can identify and understand an organisation. This is achieved by presenting the personality of the organisation to a wide range of stakeholders, rather than presenting particular functions or products that the organis-ation markets. Schumann *et al.* (1991) conclude that a number of US studies indicate that the first goal of corporate advertising is to enhance the company's reputation and the second is to provide support for the promotion of products and services. Table 26.2 sets out the six most important goals that executives see corporate advertising as responsible for satisfying.

Table 26.2 Goals of corporate advertising

- Enhance corporate reputation
- Improve credibility
- Provide a point of differentiation
- Support for products and services
- Attract higher-quality employees
- Underpin shareholder value
- Easier access to new markets and suppliers
- Advocacy of a position
- Public communication of the company's social and environmental actions

---

Reasons for the use of corporate advertising

The need to improve and maintain goodwill and to establish a positive reputation among an organisation's stakeholders has already been mentioned. These are tasks that need to be undertaken consistently and continuously, with the aim of building a reputational reservoir. In addition, however, there are particular occasions when organisations need to use corporate advertising:

These are tasks that need to be undertaken consistently and continuously, with the aim of building a reputational reservoir.

- during change and transition;
- when the organisation has a poor image;
- for product support;
- recruitment;
- repositioning;
- advocacy or issues.

Change

When an organisation experiences a period of major change, perhaps the transition before, during and after a takeover or merger, corporate advertising can be used in a variety of ways. The first is defensively, to convince stakeholders, particularly shareholders, of the value of the organisation and of the need not to accept hostile offers; second to inform and to advise of current positions; finally to position any 'new' organisation that may result from the merger activity. The sale of shares in lastminute.com in 1999 was preceded by a burst of corporate advertising designed to raise awareness and to build stature and authority. This was intended to raise credibility and hence ensure a good take-up of the share offer.

Poor image

Corporate advertising can also be used to correct any misunderstanding that stakeholders might have of corporate reality (Reisman, 1989). For example, financial analysts may believe that an organisation is underperforming, but reality indicates that performance is good. As we have seen before, this can be a result of poor communication, and through corporate advertising the organisation can correct such misunderstandings and help establish strategic credibility with the financial community and other stakeholders.

Product support

Corporate advertising can also assist the launch of new products. The costs normally associated with a launch can be lowered, and it is feasible to assume, although difficult to measure, that the effectiveness of a product launch can be improved when corporate advertising has been used to establish good reputational equity.

Corporate advertising can also assist the launch of new products.

Recruitment

Corporate advertising is used to recruit employees by creating a positive and attractive image of the organisation. The development of source credibility, in particular trust, is fundamental, and through the process of identification individuals can become attracted to the notion of working for a particular organisation and are stimulated to seek further information.

Recruitment – the police force

In order to recruit sufficient numbers for the police force, M & C Saatchi used a self-selection process. The purpose of the exercise was not to generate a volume of enquiries but to attract the right type of person and in effect reduce the ratio of enquiries to recruits. In the past too many people failed to follow through with their enquiries when they found out not only what the job entailed but what the rewards and conditions of employment were like. Until this campaign, police recruitment was managed on a local-force basis. This approach broke with the local approach and went national.

The approach adopted asks potential recruits the question 'could you?' Using a series of characters believed to be perceived by the public as highly credible and of high esteem, (Patsy Palmer from *EastEnders*, a Falklands war hero, Simon Weston, and the ex-footballer John Barnes, representing females, bravery and ethnic minorities) they enlarge on what is required in the job, namely to break the news of a death, protect a drug dealer's girlfriend or face a gang of thugs . . . and they all say that they could not do it (Newland, 2000).

Repositioning

Organisations periodically undergo self-review which may lead to repositioning. Hewlett-Packard launched its 'Invent' campaign as part of a process of preparing stakeholders for the future. The campaign sought to take the company back to its roots, its original ideology 'the rules of the garage' in which the founders first developed the organisation and the values that are part of the corporate philosophy. The campaign sought to encourage invention and to legitimise exploration and risk taking, remembering, of course, that the HP way determines how employees work and that the customer defines whether the job is well done. See Plate 26.1.

Organisations can be repositioned by the activities of competitor organisations. New products, new corporate messages, an improved trading performance or the arrival of a new CEO and the implementation of a new strategy can displace an organisation in the minds of its different stakeholders. This may require an adjustment by the focus organisation to re-establish itself. The Pepsi Challenge, referred to earlier, effectively dislodged Coca-Cola from its position as brand leader and led to a stream of product adjustments and messages from Coca-Cola aimed at repositioning itself.

Advocacy

The reasons presented so far for the use of corporate advertising are strongly related to image. A further traditional reason for the use of this tool is the opportunity for the organisation to inform its stakeholders of the position or stand that it has on a particular issue. This is referred to as advocacy advertising. Rather than promoting the organisation in a direct way, this form of corporate advertising associates an organisation with an issue of social concern, which public relations very often cannot achieve alone.

This form of corporate advertising associates an organisation with an issue of social concern.

The organisation can be seen as a brand in much the same way as products and services are branded. Just as a product-based brand can be tracked, so can the corporate entity be tracked for levels of awareness, attitudes and preferences held by stakeholders.

Crisis management

A growing and important part of the work associated with public relations is crisis management. At one time, when a crisis such as a threat of takeover or workplace accident struck an organisation, the first stakeholders to be summoned by the CEOs were merchant bankers. Today the public relations consultant is first through the door. The power of corporate and marketing communications is beginning to be recognised and appreciated. Indeed, the astute CEO summons the public relations consultant in anticipation of crisis, on the basis that being prepared is a major step in diffusing the energy with which some crises can affect organisations.

Crises are emerging with greater frequency as a result of a number of factors. The first, according to Ten Berge (1991), concerns the rise of consumer groups (e.g. Greenpeace) and their ability to investigate and publicise the operations and policies of organisations. The second is that the age of instant communication, facilitated by electronic media, means that information can be disseminated throughout the world within 30 minutes of an event occurring. Third, the rate at which technology is advancing has brought about crises such as those associated with transportation systems and aircraft disasters. Human error is also a significant factor, often associated with the rate of technological change. Fourth, the climate is also changing substantially in certain parts of the world, and this can bring disaster to those who lie in the wake of natural disturbances. Finally, the economic environment is also changing as the Western world currently experiences growth and high levels of employment and countries in the developing world follow a fluctuating path of revitalisation and competition that has brought some organisations and industries in the west to collapse (e.g. UK shipbuilding).

Crises are emerging with greater frequency as a result of a number of factors.

Figure 26.4 describes organisational crises in the context of two key variables. On the horizontal axis is the degree to which management has control over the origin of the crisis. Is the origin of the crisis outside management's control, such as an earthquake, or is it within its control, such as those crises associated with poor trading results? The vertical axis reflects the potential impact that a crisis might have on an organisation. All crises, by definition, have a potential to inflict damage on an organisation. However, some can be contained, perhaps on a geographic basis, whereas others have the potential to cause tremendous damage to an organisation, such as those experienced through product tampering and environmental pollution.

Is the origin of the crisis outside management's control?

The increasing occurrence of crises throughout the world has prompted many organisations to review the manner in which they anticipate managing such events, should they be implicated. It is generally assumed that those organisations that take the care to plan in anticipation of disaster will experience more favourable outcomes than those that fail to plan. Quarantelli (1988) reports that there is only a partial correlation between those that plan and those that experience successful outcomes. He attributes this to

There is only a partial correlation between those that plan and those that experience successful outcomes.

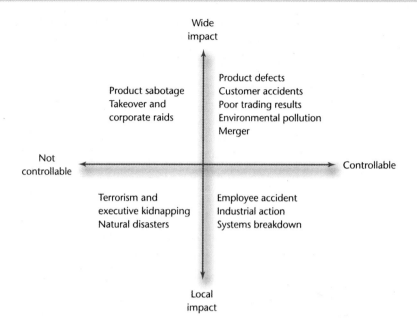

Figure 26.4   An organisational crisis matrix.

the fact that only some of the organisations that take care to prepare do so in a professional way. Poor planning can only deliver poor results.

The second reason concerns the expectations of those who design and implement
crisis plans. It is one thing to design a plan; it is entirely another to implement it.
Crisis planning is about putting into position those elements that can effect speedy
outcomes to the disaster sequence. When a crisis strikes, it is the application of con-
tingency-based tactics by all those concerned with the event that will determine the
strength of the outcome.

Crisis phases

The number of phases through which a crisis passes varies according to author and the
management model they are proposing. For example, Penrose (2000) mentions
Littlejohn's six-step model, Fink's audit, Mitroff's portfolio planning approach and
Burnett's crisis classification matrix. However, for the sake of clarification a four-phase
framework will be adopted here: scanning, pre-impact, impact and readjustment
phases. It should be remembered that the duration of each phase can vary considerably, depending upon the nature of the crisis and the manner in which management
deals with the events associated with the crisis.

The first period is referred to as the scanning phase. Good strategic management
demands that the environment be scanned on a regular basis to detect the first signs
of significant change. Organisations that pick up signals that are repeated are in a
better position to prepare for disaster than those that do not scan the environment.

*Those that fail to scan are often taken by
surprise and have to react with less time and
control to manage the events that hit them.*

Penrose reports that those who perceive the impact of
a crisis to be severe or very damaging and plan accordingly tend to achieve more successful outcomes. Those
that fail to scan are often taken by surprise and have to

react with less time and control to manage the events that hit them. Even if they do pick up a signal, many organisations not only ignore it but also attempt to block it out (Pearson and Mitroff, 1993). It is as if management is attempting to deny the presence of the signals in order that any stability and certainty they may have could continue.

Many of the signals detected during the scanning phase wither and die. Some gather strength and develop with increasing force. This pre-impact phase is characterised by increasing activity and preparation in anticipation of the crisis, once its true nature and direction have been determined. Much of the activity should be geared to training and the preparation and deployment of crisis teams. The objective is not to prevent the crisis but to defuse it as much as possible, to inform significant stakeholders of its proximity and possible effects, and finally to manage the crisis process.

The impact phase is the period when the 'crisis breaks out' (Sturges *et al.*, 1991). Management is tested to the limit and if a plan has been developed it is implemented with the expectation of ameliorating the damage inflicted by the crisis. One method of reducing the impact is to contain or localise the crisis. By neutralising and constraining the event, it is prevented from contaminating other parts of the organisation or stakeholders. Pearson and Mitroff suggest that the containment of oil spills and the evacuation of buildings and aircraft are examples of containment and neutralisation. Through the necessity to talk to all stakeholders, management at this point will inevitably reveal its attitude towards the crisis event. Is its attitude one of genuine concern for the victims and stakeholders? Is the attitude consistent with the expectations that stakeholders have of the management team? Alternatively, is there a perception that management is making lame excuses and distancing itself from the event, and is this consistent with expectations?

The readjustment phase refers to the recovery and realignment of the organisation and its stakeholders to the new environment, once the deepest part of the crisis has passed. The essential tasks are to ensure that the needs of key stakeholders can still be met and, if they cannot, to determine what must be done to ensure that they can be. For example, continuity of product supply is critically important. This may be achieved by servicing customers from other locations.

Common characteristics of this phase are the investigations, police inquiries, public demonstrations, court cases and media probing that inevitably follow major crises and disasters.

Common characteristics of this phase are the investigations, police inquiries, public demonstrations, court cases and media probing that inevitably follow major crises and disasters. The manner in which an organisation handles this fall-out and tries to appear reasonable and consistent in its approach to such events can have a big impact on the perception that other stakeholders have of the organisation.

The rate at which organisations readjust is partly dependent upon the strength of the image held by stakeholders prior to the crisis occurring. If the organisation had a strong reputation then the source credibility attributed to the organisation will be high. This means that messages transmitted by the organisation would be received favourably and trusted. However, if the reputation is poor, the effectiveness of any marketing communications is also going to be low. The level of source credibility held by the organisation will influence the speed with which stakeholders allow an organisation to readjust and recover after a crisis.

The level of source credibility held by the organisation will influence the speed with which stakeholders allow an organisation to readjust and recover after a crisis.

Sales promotion crisis – McDonald's

In January 1999 McDonald's launched a buy-one, get-one free sales promotion event on Big Macs, as part of its celebration of 25 years in the UK. The problem was that it did not expect (or plan correctly for) the demand that the promotion stimulated. Demand at some locations was eight times over normal and those customers that could not get into the overcrowded restaurants were turned away, especially when restaurants ran out of burgers and began issuing vouchers.

Television advertising had been used to draw attention to the offer and, although it was eventually suspended, a large number of complaints were made to the company and to the Independent Television Commission.

McDonald's response was to apologise through full-page advertisements in the national press, claiming that they had expected demand to double. However, the 'McBungle' (Rushe, 1999) cost McDonald's in terms of its reputation, defections to Burger King, the increased media costs and having to pay staff time-and-a-half as recompense for the stress they had been put under.

Adapted from Rushe (1999) and Darby (1999)

Crisis for on-line brands

The development of the Internet has appeared to have forced many organisations to reconsider the significance of corporate reputation as part of their communication strategies. With so much information available instantaneously about each organisation it is important that brands that have gone on line be transparent and open in the way they communicate. The problem is that they are prone to attack from a variety of stakeholders. There are customers who have gripes, and there are others who despise the company on trading, moral and ethical stances. There are others who enjoy the fun of the chase. Hollingworth (2000) lists the areas of attack in Table 26.3.

It is important that brands that have gone on-line be transparent and open in the way they communicate.

Who is affected by crisis events? When a crisis hits an organisation, many different stakeholders are vulnerable to the repercussions. Pearson and Mitroff suggest that stakeholders may perceive the focus organisation adopting a particular role. This role may be as a hero, villain or even protector. Figure 26.5 depicts some of the roles that the focus organisation might be cast in; in much the same way, stakeholders themselves might be cast in a role that reflects the perception of the focus organisation. It is interesting to monitor the ascribed roles and to see whether stakeholders actually fulfil their designated role or perhaps another when crisis strikes. Perhaps a move from rescuer to enemy is not uncommon.

The importance of this perspective is that attention has to be focused on the different organisations, not just the one on which the crisis has had immediate

Table 26.3   Forms of cyber attack

Method	Explanation
Cyber squatting	By registering and setting up domain names similar to established brand names, an attempt is made to mislead (gone out of business signs), misdirect (send them to other sites) or exploit (extract personal details) users.
Anti-corporate sites	Sometimes referred to as 'suck sites', these attempt to niggle large corporations (e.g. Mcspotlight) to extend their complaint or gripe.
Distributed denial of service	A DDOS attack comprises several hijacked computers simultaneously feeding information requests to a single site. This causes it to slow down or deny access.
Firewall attack	The defence shield surrounding a site becomes insecure and the host prone to data loss, misuse and corruption.
IP and Web spoofing	These sites look and feel just like the master site. However, the intention may be to use the customer data fraudulently, to spy on the host site or just present a nuisance factor.
Direct/indirect site attacks	There are number of forms of attack which vary from the indirect form by changing the style of the site text (e.g. to a biblical style) or by using Post-it style notes (e.g. 'Will never use this xxxx service again') to the more direct approach such as rewriting the Web pages in real time and changing the prices.
Email	This is a potential problem for organisations – cyber harassment, defamation and the spread of viruses by email are unfortunately quite common.
Password capture	Entering networks with fake identities is a problem for companies as data destruction, corruption and misuse can seriously undermine customer confidence.

Source: Hollingworth (2000); used with kind permission.

Figure 26.5   Crisis roles for stakeholders. From Pearson and Mitroff (1993); used with kind permission.

The organisation that has a crisis plan of value is one that has considered the impact upon its stakeholders.

impact. The stakeholder net is wide and the sensitivity among cohesive groups in particular can be acute. The organisation that has a crisis plan of value is one that has considered the impact upon its stakeholders.

Integration of public relations in the promotional mix

Public relations has two major roles to play within the communications programme of an organisation. These are the development and maintenance of corporate goodwill and the continuity necessary for good product support.

Its task is to provide a series of cues by which the stakeholders can recognise, understand and position the organisation in such a way that the organisation builds a strong reputation.

The first is the traditional role of creating goodwill and stimulating interest between the organisation and its various key stakeholders. Its task is to provide a series of cues by which the stakeholders can recognise, understand and position the organisation in such a way that the organisation builds a strong reputation. This role is closely allied to the corporate strategy and the communication of strategic intent.

Creating brand visibility – Slazenger

Slazenger, a manufacturer of cricket bats, was not an official sponsor of the Cricket World Cup in 1999 but decided to forge a link between its sponsored players, the World Cup and its own handcrafted cricket bats. The result would be to position Slazenger as the premier cricket equipment brand.

Various activities were undertaken, one of which was to paint the bats used by the England players the colour (blue) of their kit and another to smuggle a giant inflatable branded blue bat into England matches, which invaded the pitch at the end of each game. Just before the first appearance of the blue bats, the International Cricket Council announced a decision banning them. PR agency Shine contacted Sky News which held the rights and secured comment from Ian Botham supporting the bats. A press release on the ban resulted in 16 positive articles in the national press, delivered 143 media hits and sales increased by 34% (Hiscock, 2000).

The second role of public relations is to support the marketing of the organisation's products and services, and its task is to integrate with the other elements of the pro-motional mix. Public relations and advertising have complementary roles. For example, the launch of a new product commences not with advertising to build awareness in target customers but with the use of public relations to inform editors and news broadcasters that a new product is about to be launched. This news material can be used within the trade and consumer press

Its task is to integrate with the other elements of the promotional mix.

before advertising occurs and the target buyers become aware (when the news is no longer news). To some extent this role is tactical rather than strategic, but if planned, and if events are timed and coordinated with the other elements of the promotional mix, then public relations can help build competitive advantage.

Summary

Public relations, whether orientated primarily to product support or to the development of corporate goodwill, plays an important role within the communications mix. According to Haywood (1991), public relations can support marketing in a number of ways, from improving awareness and projecting credibility to the creation of direct sales leads and motivating the sales force and members of the performance network.

By providing all stakeholders with cues by which they can develop an image of an organisation, public relations enables organisations to position themselves and provide stakeholders with a means of identifying and understanding an organisation. This may be accomplished inadvertently through inaction or deliberately through a planned presentation of a variety of visual cues. These range from publicity through press releases to the manner in which customers are treated, products perform, events are managed and expectations are met.

Finally, the area referred to as crisis communications management has grown in significance during recent years. Public relations plays an important role in preparing for and constraining the impact of a crisis and re-establishing an organisation once a crisis has passed.

By creating campaigns targeted at individual stakeholders, or at least identifying the needs of the performance network as separate from those of the support network, the effects intended at the outset can be measured at the close of different campaigns.

Review questions

1. Define public relations and set out its principal characteristics.
2. Using an organisation of your choice, identify the main stakeholders and comment on why it is important to communicate with each of them.
3. Highlight the main objectives of using public relations.
4. What is the difference between corporate public relations and marketing public relations? Is this difference of importance?
5. Write a brief paper describing the main methods of publicity.
6. Why do you think an increasing number of organisations are using sponsorship as a part of their promotional mix?
7. Suggest occasions when corporate advertising might be best employed.
8. Identify the main phases associated with crisis management.
9. What roles might stakeholders adopt when a crisis occurs?
10. Discuss the view that public relations can only ever be a support tool in the promotional mix.

This mini case was written by Gary Warnaby, Lecturer at Salford University, and Dominic Medway, Department of Retailing and Marketing, The Manchester Metropolitan University.

Promoting town centre retailing

The real shopping experience

In the UK over the last 30 years an increasing amount of retail sales have occurred in 'off-centre' retail outlets (i.e. located on 'greenfield' and 'brownfield' sites outside traditional retail areas in town centres). Off-centre retailing varies from stand-alone supermarkets/superstores and retail parks, which arguably complement town centre retailing by satisfying consumer demand for bulky and convenience items, to regional shopping centres (RSCs), which closely replicate the retail offer of town centres, often in a more pleasant, safe and controlled environment. This development of off-centre retailing has raised issues relating to the future 'vitality and viability' of town centres. Partly in response to such concerns, the concept of town centre management has emerged as a means of helping individual towns to achieve a competitive edge by involving key urban stakeholders in coordinating the management of the public realm and better satisfying the aspirations of all town centre users.

In 1995 planning permission was granted to build the Trafford Centre RSC on the outskirts of Manchester in the North-West of England. Its potential impact on surrounding town centres was huge. Accordingly, member towns of the Association of Town Centre Management in the North-West commissioned a report to evaluate this impact. It made sobering reading: four towns could potentially lose over 20% of their retail sales and a further 10 could lose 10–19% if they did nothing to counter the threat. These figures, when published, created much interest (somewhat sensationalised) in local and regional media and encouraged towns in the North-West to collaborate in developing a PR-led awareness campaign to emphasise the positive aspects of shopping in town centres.

The campaign adopted the strapline 'Town Centres – the Real Shopping Experience' and had a total budget of £15,000–20,000, much less than the promotional budgets of retailers within the Trafford centre and, indeed, of the Trafford Centre itself. In view of this potential for a 'David and Goliath' struggle, it was decided to adopt a positive campaign tone, emphasising the benefits of town centre shopping rather than trying to 'knock' the Trafford centre *per se*.

The campaign began in May 1998, five months before the Trafford Centre opened, with an event in Manchester to announce the formation of the North West Towns' Consortium (NWTC), comprising 28 towns in the region. This involved a press conference at which 27 town centre managers were present, each wearing a T-shirt displaying their own town's name. This provided a photo opportunity which was exploited by moving the T-shirt-clad town centre managers around so that each one appeared to the front of the group, thus generating a series of targeted photos which could be disseminated to localised media in each town centre.

In July 1998 the PR campaign itself was officially launched at Manchester Town Hall. This generated much media coverage, including regional TV and radio, and copy in a wide range of regional and local newspapers. Press releases were also tailored to exploit the specific local media interest around the North-West. Between the July launch and the next natural peak of the campaign, the opening of the Trafford Centre in September 1998, Meredith Thomas, a Manchester-based PR consultancy appointed by the NWTC, acted as a central point through which newsworthy items from individual town centre managers taking part in the campaign were developed and disseminated. This policy proved to be effective in maintaining the campaign's momentum over the summer of 1998.

On Saturday 5 September 1998, the weekend before the opening of the Trafford Centre, many of the partner towns in the NWTC had a 'Shop Local' day. Publicity for this event was generated in individual town centres through the use of T-shirts, stickers, balloon releases, etc. Eccles also had a 'Family Fun' day in the town centre, as did the towns of Blackburn, Burnley and Bolton. As well as creating many photo opportunities, these activities helped create a 'buzz' about town centres the weekend before the Trafford Centre opened.

The actual opening of the Trafford Centre generated much media coverage. For three evenings up to the opening, the Granada TV regional news programme did special reports from town centres under the theme 'Shopping Centred', in which members of the NWTC were featured. On the opening day itself BBC regional news programmes were broadcast from the Trafford Centre. A frenetic day in terms of media relations activity ensued, involving a range of regional and national broadcast and print media. Given the amount of media activity undertaken by various individuals involved in the campaign, the importance of them delivering a coherent message was vital. As a result, all the NWTC representatives interviewed on broadcast media kept to a tightly defined 'script', accentuating the positives of town centres.

While not a measure of the true impact of the campaign, the potential value of the media coverage generated can be gauged in terms of equivalent values. It has been calculated that coverage of the launch of the NWTC, the launch of the actual campaign and the coverage around the opening of the Trafford Centre would have cost in the region of £850,000 if bought at commercial advertising rates. While such figures may appear impressive on the surface, the true measure of the campaign's effectiveness needs to be judged in terms of its impact on shopping patterns within the various towns in the region. Evidence suggests that the original estimated losses of retail trade have not materialised. Of course, these deflection figures were based on the premise that the towns concerned would not respond to the threat posed by the Trafford Centre and this was certainly not the case. As 'The Real Shopping Experience' campaign has demonstrated, the NWTC has been very proactive, and successful, in its attempts to raise the profile of the region's town centres, thereby directly countering the threat from the Trafford Centre.

Mini-case questions

1. Why was the adoption of a positive campaign tone, emphasising the attractions of town centres, an appropriate move?
2. What was the key role of the public relations consultancy in the campaign?
3. Why were effective media relations so important for this campaign?
4. How could the success of the campaign be evaluated?
5. Overall, why do you think that the main emphasis of 'The Real Shopping Experience' campaign focused on public relations?

References

Adkins, S. (1999) The wider benefits of backing a good cause. *Marketing*, 2 September, pp. 20–1.

Barrett, P. (1997) A marriage of PR and ads. *Marketing*, 30 October, p. 15.

Barrett, L. (1999) Vauxhall car-free TV ad focuses on customers. *Marketing*, 30 September, p. 4.

Bold, B. (2000) Bloomsbury casts spell for Potter sequel. *PR Week*, 21 July, p. 22.

Bruning, S.D. and Ledingham, J.A. (2000) Perceptions of relationships and evaluations of satisfaction: an exploration of interaction. *Public Relations Review*, **26**(1), pp. 85–95.

Cowlett, M. (2000) Cooking up a recipe for long-term success. *PR Week*, 16 August, p. 8.

Cutlip, S., Center, A.H. and Broom, G.J. (1985) *Effective Public Relations*. Englewood Cliffs, NJ: Prentice Hall.

Darby, I. (1999) Big Mac blunder hits McDonalds. *Marketing*, 7 January, p. 1.

Ehling, W.P. (1992) Estimating the value of public relations and communication to an organisation. In *Excellence in Public Relations and Communication Management* (eds J.E. Grunig, D.M. Dozier, P. Ehling, L.A. Grunig, F.C. Repper and J. Whits), pp. 617–38. Hillsdale, NJ: Lawrence Erlbaum.

Grunig, J. (ed.) (1992) *Excellence in Public Relations and Communications Management*. Hillsdale, NJ: Lawrence Erlbaum.

Grunig, J. and Hunt, T. (1984) *Managing Public Relations*. New York: Holt, Rineholt & Winston.

Haywood, R. (1991) *All About Public Relations*, 2nd edn. Maidenhead: McGraw-Hill.

Hiscock, J. (2000) PRCA Awards 2000. *Marketing*, 7 September, pp. 34–5.

Hollingworth, C. (2000) Cyber–Attack, Communications Directors Forum, June.

Kitchen, P.J. (1991) Developing use of PR in a fragmented demassified market. *Marketing Intelligence and Planning*, 9(2), pp. 29–33.

Kitchen, P.J. and Moss, D. (1995) Marketing and public relations: the relationship revisited. *Journal of Marketing Communications*, 1, pp. 105–19.

Kitchen, P.J. and Procter, R.A. (1991) The increasing importance of public relations in FMCG firms. *Journal of Marketing Management*, 7, pp. 357–70.

Kotler, P. and Mindak, W. (1978) Marketing and public relations. *Journal of Marketing*, 42 (October), pp. 13–20.

Miller, G. (1989) Persuasion and public relations: two 'Ps' in a pod. In *Public Relations Theory* (eds C. Botan and V. Hazelton). Hilldale, NJ: Lawrence Erlbaum.

Moloney, K. (1997) Government and lobbying activities. In *Public Relations: Principles and Practice* (ed. P.J. Kitchen). London: International Thomson Press.

Newland, F. (2000) Can this campaign strengthen the thin blue line? *Campaign*, 8 September, p. 28.

Pearson, C.M. and Mitroff, I. (1993) From crisis prone to crisis prepared: a framework for crisis management. *Academy of Management Executive*, 7(1), pp. 48–59.

Penrose, J.M. (2000) The role of perception in crisis planning. *Public Relations Review*, 26(2), pp. 155–71.

Pieczka, M. (1996) Public opinion and public relations. In *Critical Perspectives in Public Relations* (eds. J. L'Etang and M. Pieczka). London: International Thomson Business Press.

Public Relations Educational Trust (1991) *The Place of Public Relations in Management Education*. London: Institute of Public Relations.

Quarantelli, E.L. (1988) Disaster crisis management: a summary of research findings. *Journal of Management Studies*, 25(4), pp. 373–85.

Reisman, J. (1989) Corporate advertising in disguise. *Public Relations Journal* (September), pp. 21–7.

Rushe, D. (1999) How McDonald's bit off more than it could chew. *Sunday Times*, 10 January, p. 6.

Schumann, D.W., Hathcote, J.M. and West, S. (1991) Corporate advertising in America: a review of published studies on use, measurement and effectiveness. *Journal of Advertising*, 20(3), pp. 35–56.

Simms, J. (2000) Into a web of danger. *Marketing*, 28 September, pp. 38–9.

Stanton, W.J. (1964) *Fundamentals of Marketing*. New York: McGraw-Hill.

Sturges, D.L., Carell, B.J., Newsom, D.A. and Barrera, M. (1991) Crisis communication management: the public opinion node and its relationship to environmental nimbus. *SAM Advanced Management Journal* (Summer), pp. 22–7.

Ten Berge, D. (1991) Planning for crisis: how to cope with the wolf at the door. *European Management Journal*, 9(1), pp. 30–5.

27

Sponsorship

Sponsorship is a commercial activity, whereby one party permits another an opportunity to exploit an association with a target audience in return for funds, services or resources. Organisations are using sponsorship activities in a variety of ways to generate awareness, brand associations and to cut through the clutter of commercial messages.

AIMS AND OBJECTIVES

The aims of this chapter are to introduce and examine sponsorship as an increasingly significant form of marketing communications.

The objectives of this chapter are:

1. To appreciate the variety and different forms of sponsorship activities.
2. To understand the reasons why sponsorship has become an important part of the promotional mix.
3. To provide an insight into the main characteristics of this form of communication.
4. To consider where in the promotional mix sponsorship may be best associated.
5. To explore ways in which sponsorship can be best evaluated.

Introduction

It was mentioned earlier that an organisation should contribute to the local community with a view to being seen as participative, caring and more involved with local affairs. The degree of control that can be levied against this type of activity is limited once a commitment has been made. By adopting a more commercial perspective, some organisations have used sponsorship, particularly of sports activities, as a means of reaching wider target audiences. Sponsorship can provide the following opportunities for the sponsoring organisation:

1. Exposure to particular audiences that each event attracts in order to convey simple awareness-based brand messages.

2. To suggest to the target audiences that there is an association between the sponsee and the sponsor and that by implication this association may be of interest and/or value.

3. To allow members of the target audiences to perceive the sponsor indirectly through a third party and so diffuse any negative effects associated with traditional mass media and direct persuasion.

4. Sponsorship provides sponsors with the opportunity to blend a variety of tools in the promotional mix and use resources more efficiently and arguably more effectively.

From this it is possible to define sponsorship as a commercial activity, whereby one party permits another an opportunity to exploit an association with a target audience in return for funds, services or resources.

It is necessary to clarify the distinction between sponsorship and charitable donations. The latter are intended to change attitudes and project a caring identity, with the main returns from the exercise being directed to society or the beneficiaries. The beneficiaries have almost total control over the way in which funds are used. When funds are channelled through a sponsorship the recipient has to attend to the needs of the sponsor by allowing it access to the commercial associations that are to be exploited, partly because they have a legal arrangement, but also to ensure that the exchange becomes relational and longer term; in other words, there is repeat purchase (investment) activity. The other major difference is that the benefits of the exchange are intended to accrue to the participants, not society at large.

To suggest to the target audiences that there is an association between the sponsee and the sponsor and that by implication this association may be of interest and/or value.

The development of sponsorship as a communication tool has been spectacular since the early 1990s. This is because of a variety of factors, but among the most important, according to Meenaghan (1991), are the government's policies on tobacco and alcohol, the escalating costs of advertising media, the proven ability of sponsorship, new opportunities due to increased leisure activity, greater media coverage of sponsored events and the recognition of the inefficiencies associated with the traditional media. In addition to this list of drivers can be added regulations and technology. The ITC have acted to restrict the nature and form of programme (or broadcast) sponsorship. However, a recent relaxation in the regulations has allowed for the development of this type of sponsorship. The reference to technology concerns systems such as TiVo which allow users to skip over advertising breaks (and eventually block them out altogether). Should these machines achieve strong consumer penetration then the sponsorship credits could become more important than advertising in achieving brand presence (Table 27.1).

It has been suggested that the rapid worldwide development of sponsorship is such that it is now seen as a standardised method of communicating a brand name (Witcher *et al.*, 1991). This form of communication has certainly gained popularity, but not to the extent of standardisation. Sponsorship remains a communication tool, part of the promotional mix, but as with other tools it needs to be used with a pur-

Table 27.1   Growth and development of sponsorship

Increased media coverage of events
Relaxation of government and industry regulations
Increased incidence of sponsorship event supply (and demand)
Relationship orientation and association between sponsorship participants
Positive attitude change toward sponsorship by senior management
Awareness and drive towards integrated marketing communications
Increasing rate of other media costs
Need to develop softer brand associations and to reach niche audiences

Sponsorship provides a further tool which, to be used effectively, needs to be harnessed strategically.

pose and as part of an integrated communications approach. In other words, sponsorship provides a further tool which, to be used effectively, needs to be harnessed strategically. For example, many companies and brands originating in South-East Asia and Pacific regions have used sponsorship as a means of overseas market entry in order to develop name or brand awareness (e.g. Panasonic, JVC and Daihatsu).

Timed sponsorship – watches

Many watch manufacturers have developed associations with particular sports personalities or sporting events. The main goals of these sponsorships have been to develop brand awareness, associations and favourable values. The following examples are just some of the associations that have been developed between particular events and watch manufacturers (Balfour, 2000):

Motor racing

The TAGHeuer brand has been associated with precision technology and Grand Prix motor racing for a long time.

Omega sponsors Michael Schumacher, the World Racing Champion (2000).

Chopard makes the Mille Liglia chronograph at the time of the road race and presents one to all competitors.

Water sports

Omega promotes its Seamaster in association with the America's Cup.

Cartier and Alfred Dunhill promote their watches through water polo events.

Football

Tissot sponsors Michael Owen, the Liverpool and England footballer.

The Bregeut Type XX Aéronavale watch was used in association with the Football France promotion in 1998.

Aviation

Breitling has developed an association with aviation.

In addition, many sponsorships have survived recessionary periods. This may be because of the two- to three-year period that each sponsorship contract covers and the difficulty and costs associated with terminating such agreements. It may also be because of the impact that sponsorship might have on the core customers that continue to buy the brand during economic downturns. Easier targeting through sponsorship can also assist the reinforcement of brand messages. Readers are reminded of the weak theory of advertising (Chapter 20), and it may be that sponsorship is a means of defending a market and of providing additional triggers to stimulate brand recall/recognition.

Easier targeting through sponsorship can also assist the reinforcement of brand messages.

Sponsorship objectives

There are both primary and secondary objectives associated with using sponsorship. The primary reasons are to build awareness, developing customer loyalty and improving the perception (image) held of the brand or organisation. Secondary reasons are more contentious, but generally they can be seen to be to attract new users, to support dealers and other intermediaries and to act as a form of staff motivation and morale building (Reed, 1994).

Sponsorship is normally regarded as a communications tool used to reach external stakeholders. However, if chosen appropriately sponsorship can also be used effectively to reach internal audiences. Care is required because different audiences transfer diverse values (Grimes and Meenaghan, 1998). According to Harverson (1998), one of the main reasons IT companies sponsor sports events is that this form of involvement provides opportunities to 'showcase' their products and technologies, in context. Through application in an appropriate working environment, the efficacy of a sponsor's products can be demonstrated. The relationship between sports organisers and IT companies becomes reciprocal as the organisers of sports events need technology in order for the events to run. Corporate hospitality opportunities are often taken in addition to the brand exposure that the media coverage provides. EDS claims that it uses sponsorship to reach two main audiences, customers (and potential customers) and potential future employees. The message it uses is that the EDS involvement in sport is sexy and exciting.

A further interesting point arises from a view of a company sponsor through time. Meenaghan (1998) suggests that, at first, the sponsor acts as a donor, through the pure exchange of money in order to reach an audience. The next stage sees the sponsor acting as an investor, where, although large sums of money may well be involved, the sponsor is now actively involved and is looking for a return on the investment made. The third stage is reached when the sponsor assumes the role of an impresario. Now the sponsor is vigorously involved and seeks to control activities so that they reflect corporate/brand values and so assist the positioning process.

Following on from this is the issue about whether sponsorship is being used to support a product or the organisation. Corporate sponsorships, according to Thwaites (1994), are intended to focus upon developing community involvement, public awareness, image, goodwill and staff relations. Product- or brand-based sponsorship activity is aimed at developing media coverage, sales leads, sales/market share, target market awareness and guest hospitality. What is important is that sponsorship is

Sponsorship is not a tool that can be effective in a stand-alone capacity.

not a tool that can be effective in a stand-alone capacity. The full potential of this tool is only realised when it is integrated with some (all) of the other tools of the promotional mix. The implementation of integrated marketing communications is further encouraged and supported when sponsorship is an integral part of the mix in order to maximise the full impact of this communication tool (see Chapter 29).

Interpretations about how sponsorship might work are varied but assuming a cognitive orientation sponsorship works through associations that consumers make with a brand (which will be an accumulation of previous advertising and other promotional activities) and the event being supported. In addition, consumers make a judgement based upon the fit between the event and sponsorship such that the greater the degree of compatibility the more readily acceptable the sponsorship will be.

If a behavourist orientation is used to explain how sponsorship works, then the sponsorship will be perceived as a reinforcement of previous brand experiences. An event generates rewards by reminding individuals of pleasurable brand experiences. However, this assumes that individuals have previous brand experience and fails to explain adequately how sponsorship works when launching new products.

Generally, sponsorship plays a supporting or secondary role in the communication mix of many organisations and is not an important source of corporate information. This is largely because the communication impact of sponsorship is limited because sponsorship only reinforces previously held corporate (or product) images (positive or negative) rather than changing them (Javalgi *et al.*, 1994). It is also suggested that the only significant relationship between sponsorship and corporate image occurs where there has been direct experience of the brand. This in turn raises questions about whether sponsorship should be used to influence the image of the product category and its main brands in order to be of any worthwhile affect (Pope and Voges, 1999).

Generally, sponsorship plays a supporting or secondary role in the communication mix of many organisations and is not an important source of corporate information.

Types of sponsorship

It is possible to identify particular areas within which sponsorship has been used (Table 27.2). These areas are sports, programme/broadcast, the arts, and others which encompass activities such as wildlife/conservation and education. Out of all of these, sport has attracted most attention and sponsorship money.

Table 27.2   Long-term trends in UK sponsorship market by sector, 1980–2000

	Sports (£m)	Arts (£m)	Broadcast (£m)	Other (£m)	Total (£m)
1980	30	3	–	2	35
1985	125	22	–	20	167
1990	223	35	7	16	281
1993	250	50	60	26	386
1996	302	80	99	38	519
2000*	400	160	180	60	800

Source: Mintel.
* estimated.

Table 27.3   The relative size of sponsorship

	1998	1999
UK sports sponsorship	353m	377m
UK arts sponsorship	115m	142m
Value of Millennium Dome sponsorship		160m

Source: Ipos-RSL Sportscan, and Arts and Business.

One of the more notable sponsorships in recent years has been that of the Dome. Troubled by low visitor attendance, strong public opinion and political intrigue this financial fiasco serves to illustrate the size and relative dynamics associated with sponsorships of this scale (Table 27.3). Major zone sponsors of the Dome each agreed to £12 million support but as Darby (2000) suggests, they may have since reconsidered the value of their investments in the light of the poor publicity the Dome has attracted. However, one of the difficulties facing sponsors is the low number of high-profile properties that are available for sponsorship support. One possible solution is that some sponsors will create their own sponsorship properties, simply because of the powerful impact of successful sponsorship.

Sports sponsorship

Sports activities have been very attractive to sponsors, partly because of the high media coverage they attract. Sport is the leading type of sponsorship, mainly for the following reasons:

1. Sport has the propensity to attract large audiences, not only at each event but more importantly through the media that attach themselves to these activities.

2. Sport provides a simplistic measure of segmentation, so that as audiences fragment generally, sport provides an opportunity to identify and reach often large numbers of people who share particular characteristics.

3. Visibility opportunities for the sponsor are high in a number of sporting events because of the duration of each event (e.g. the Olympics or the FIFA World Cup).

Carling's recent sponsorship of the football Premier League and the Nationwide Building Society's sponsorship of the Football League has been motivated partly by the attraction of large and specific target audiences with whom a degree of fit is considered to exist. The constant media attention enables the sponsors' names to be disseminated to distant audiences, many of them overseas.

The constant media attention enables the sponsors' names to be disseminated to distant audiences.

Marshall and Cook (1992) found that event sponsorship (e.g. the Olympics or the Ideal Home Exhibition) is the most popular form of sponsorship activity undertaken by organisations. This was followed by team, league and individual support.

Golf has attracted a great deal of sponsorship money, mainly because it has a global upmarket appeal and generates good television and press coverage. Golf clubs are also well suited for corporate entertainment and offer the chance of playing as well as watching. Volvo has sponsored the European Golf Championship for the period

Sports sponsorship – sailing

Ellen MacArthur's second place in the Vendée Globe solo round-the-world yacht race that ended in February 2001 resulted in considerable media exposure for her main sponsor, the Kingfisher Group, after whom her boat was named. The Group's recent purchase of several French companies, France being a country enthusiastic about sailing, meant that the heroism and media interest in MacArthur's achievement was extremely high.

Kingfisher's investment of £2 million was easily recouped if the strong positive media coverage was correctly valued at about £50 million media equivalents. However, as Hill (2001) reports, the overall success of the sponsorship lay in the supporting promotional campaign.

1996–2000 for £20 million. Johnny Walker has put £11 million into the game throughout the world (Wighton, 1995). Toyota supports the World Matchplay Championship at Wentworth each year because the tournament fits into a much wider promotion programme. Toyota used to support the World Matchplay Championship at Wentworth each year because the tournament fitted into a much wider promotion programme. Toyota dealers sponsored competitions at their local courses, with qualifiers going through to a final at Wentworth. The winner of that played in the pro-am before the World Matchplay. Toyota incorporated the tournament into a range of incentive and promotional programmes and flew in top distributors and fleet customers from around the world. In addition the environment was used to build customer relationships.

Sports event sponsorship – Rugby World Cup

The 1999 Rugby World Cup was sponsored by Visa, South African Airways, Guinness, Ford, BT, Xerox, Lloyds TSB, and Coca Cola. Darby (1999) reports that each sponsor paid £2 million for logo and signage rights to the third largest sporting event in the world. Sponsors were promised an audience of 3 billion and 3 million live spectators. Guinness put in a further £4 million to sponsor ITV's coverage of the event – sales rose by 15% during the World Cup – and a further £16 million to a marketing programme to ensure long-term brand benefit.

Programme sponsorship

While becoming established in North America in the 1980s, television programme sponsorship has only began to receive serious attention in the UK in the late 1990s. The market is worth around £180 million (estimates vary) in 2000 and is growing, partly because of a relaxation by the Independent Television Commission (ITC) in the regulations. However, the visibility that each sponsor is allowed has been strictly controlled to certain times and before, during the break and after each programme with the credits. The ITC has now relaxed its rules governing the sponsorship of TV programmes. Allen (2000) reports that while it is still not intended that sponsors influence the content or scheduling of a programme so as to affect the editorial independence and responsibility of the broadcaster, it is now permissible to allow the sponsor's product to be seen along with the sponsor's name in bumper credits and to allow greater flexibility in terms of the use of straplines. There is a requirement on the broadcaster to ensure that the sponsored credit is depicted in such a way that it cannot be mistaken as a spot advertisement.

It is now permissible to allow the sponsor's product to be seen along with the sponsor's name in bumper credits.

So, Hedburg (2000) gives the example of Nescafé sponsoring *Friends* and shows a group of people sitting on a sofa and drinking coffee and of *Coronation Street* sponsor Cadbury, which presents a whole chocolate street and chocolate characters.

Masthead programming, where the publisher of a magazine such as *Amateur Photographer* sponsors a programme in a related area, such as *Photography for Beginners*, is generally not permitted, although the regulations surrounding this type of activity are being relaxed.

There are a number of reasons why programme sponsorship is appealing. First, it allows clients to avoid the clutter associated with spot advertising. In that sense it creates a space or mini-world in which the sponsor can create awareness and provide brand identity cues unhindered by other brands. Second, it represents a cost-effective medium when compared with spot advertising. It is expected that the cost of programme sponsorship will increase as the value of this type of communication is appreciated by clients (Fry, 1997). Third, the use of credits around a programme offers opportunities for the target audience to make associations between the sponsor and the programme.

Research by the Bloxam Group suggests that for a sponsorship to work there needs to be a linkage between the product and the programme. Links that are spurious, illogical or inappropriate are very often rejected by viewers. For example, Summers (1995) argues that 'Tango's sponsorship of the youth programme *The Word* was regarded as about right but the Prudential's link with *Film on Four* was not seen to link at all well'.

Programme sponsorship – Kellogg's

Kellogg used broadcast sponsorship to launch a new cereal, Crispix. It used an association with a new, and at the time unproven, prime-time programme, *Kids Say the Funniest Things*. Crawford (1999) reports that the ITV programme ran immediately before *Coronation Street*, which has been the channel's highest rating programme. The only previous sponsorship was in 1994 when the Frosties brand was linked to the series *Gladiators*.

The integrated launch involved television, press and poster advertising to compete in an increasingly competitive market, which is also characterised by a decline in the number of people eating cereals or even breakfast at home.

The same research suggests that viewers claim to own their favourite programmes. Therefore sponsors should acknowledge this relationship and act accordingly, perhaps as a respectful guest, and not intrude too heavily on the programme. They should certainly resist any active participation in the programme. 'If Pop Larkin starts asking for a cup of Tetley, then that's not right', claims Summers, and product placement issues begin to confuse matters.

Programme sponsorship is not seen as a replacement for advertising; indeed, the argument that sponsorship is not a part of advertising is demonstrated by the point that many sponsors continue with their spot advertising when running major sponsorships.

Programme sponsorship is not seen as a replacement for advertising.

Cadbury's sponsorship of the premier UK soap opera, *Coronation Street*, which began in 1996, is reported to have cost £10 million each year, when all the additional promotional activities and requirements are considered. The linkage established between the two parties (Cadbury and *Coronation Street*) exemplifies the view about the relationship and the linkages. 'The best sponsorships are those where there is an equivalence of stature between the two partners', according to Richard Frost, Cadbury's head of public relations. Research indicates that those aware of the sponsorship regarded the chocolate and the company more positively than those unaware of the linkage. Cadbury was also awarded higher marks for being up to date and a supporter of the local community (Smith, 1997).

Arts sponsorship

Arts sponsorship has been very successful in the 1980s and 1990s, as responsibility for funding the arts in the UK has shifted from the government to the private sector and business in particular. Growth has slowed down, partly because of the increasing need to justify such investments, partly because of the increasing opportunities to reach target audiences and also because it is difficult to engage in these very visible activities when profits are declining and company restructuring activities are of greater concern to those being made redundant or being displaced.

Arts sponsorship, according to Thorncroft (1996), began as a philanthropic exercise, with business giving back something to the community. It was a means of developing corporate image and was used extensively by tobacco companies as they attempted to reach their customer base. It then began to be appreciated for its corporate hospitality opportunities: a cheaper, more civilised alternative to sports sponsorship, and one that appealed more to women.

Music sponsorship – Wella

Sponsorship at music festivals is certainly not new but according to McCormack (2000) brand managers now realise the potential by being imaginative and creative and by bringing some added value to an event. For example, Wella provided a styling tent as a sponsor at a V2000 event for those attending the event. Orange provided a chill-out area at the Glastonbury festival, where people could recharge their mobile phones.

Many organisations sponsor the arts as a means of enhancing its corporate status and as a means of clarifying its name. Another important reason why organisations use sponsorship is to establish and maintain favourable contact with key business people, often at board level, together with

Many organisations sponsor the arts as a means of enhancing its corporate status and as a means of clarifying its name.

other significant public figures. Through related corporate hospitality, companies can reach substantial numbers of their targeted key people.

NTL use the benefits of sponsorship to enhance the corporate body, to increase awareness of the company and to change part of the corporate image. Others use sponsorship to influence image and awareness factors at the brand level, such as 7-Up, Foster's and Budweiser (Meenaghan, 1998).

Most recently, sponsorship has been used to reach specific groups of consumers. Beck's, part of Scottish & Newcastle Breweries, has used sponsorship to position the brand as an upmarket beer for free-spending young professionals. To accomplish this, exhibitions by avant-garde artists such as Gilbert and George and Damien Hirst have been supported (Thorncroft, 1996).

Community sponsorship – Royal & SunAlliance

Royal & SunAlliance has many commercial offices around the UK, but one of the more substantial is located in Horsham, West Sussex. It is by far the town's largest employer, with over 2,000 staff. For some time sections of the local community were alienated against the organisation despite the provision of considerable financial support. It transpires that one of the major reasons for the negative feelings stems from the huge building programme when the main campus building was developed in the town centre. The scale of the work was so large that the layout of the town centre was radically altered.

Royal & SunAlliance decided that it was important to generate positive, warmer feelings towards the organisation. So, in addition to the financial assistance, the company now provides practical support, targeted where the community informs the company that it is most needed:

■ *Photocopying*: charity newsletters, church magazines event programmes, information leaflets, posters and publicity material for events.

■ *Design*: production of artwork for small groups.

■ *Hosting*: provision of meeting, lecture and function rooms which are not used by the company during the weekends or evenings. Staff act as hosts and ushers as necessary.

■ *Catering*: in-house facilities to support the hosting activities above.

■ *Professional advice*: business advice delivered to voluntary groups through attendance at local committees.

■ *Raffle prizes*: gifts surplus to the requirements of the direct marketing division are donated to charities for raffles to raise funds.

■ *Minibuses*: company minibuses are used regularly to support local events, such as sponsored walks, students' educational trips and taking disabled children to swimming galas.

■ *Town centre events*: major town events, such as festivals, Christmas decorations and the biennial Arts Fanfare, are rigorously supported, as are the local churches, schools, Chamber of Commerce and local health and emergency services.

■ *Staff support*: the staff themselves are actively involved in voluntary activities in and around Horsham, and again the company seeks to support its employees in these pursuits.

The change from finance provider to resource facilitator appears to have had a major impact on the attitudes held by the community towards Royal & SunAlliance in Horsham. A corporate image study will be undertaken shortly to measure the degree of change. This use of sponsorship and public relations activities has been used to the benefit of all concerned and it seems that a positive dialogue has resulted in mutual understanding and goodwill.

Information kindly supplied by Ann Seabrook, Community Liaison Manager for Royal & SunAlliance in Horsham

The sponsorship of the arts has moved from being a means of supporting the community to a sophisticated means of targeting and positioning brands. Sponsorship, once part of corporate public relations, has developed skills which can assist marketing public relations.

These three main forms of sponsorship, sports, arts and programme, are not mutually exclusive and use of one does not necessarily prevent use of either of the others.

These three main forms of sponsorship, sports, arts and programme, are not mutually exclusive.

NTL sponsor four major English and Scottish football teams to achieve brand awareness, particularly in areas in which they seek to develop the cable services. NTL also undertake programme sponsorship and work with *Who Wants to be a Millionaire*. This helps to develop brand values and may be more cost effective than spot advertising, especially at peak times. In addition to these two major sponsorships, NTL also support the MacMillan Cancer Relief fund, perhaps to present a more caring or balanced identity for its various audiences. However, because of targeting issues many organisations find it more efficient to use one major form of sponsorship, supported by a range of secondary sponsorship activities.

Other forms of sponsorship

It has been argued that there is little opportunity to control messages delivered through sponsorship, and far less opportunity to encourage the target audiences to enter into a dialogue with sponsors. However, the awareness and image opportunities can be used by supporting either the local community or small-scale schemes. Whitbread has been involved in supporting school programmes, environmental developments and other locally orientated activities because that is where its customers are based. Volkswagen wanted to be associated with the motoring environment rather than just the motorist. To help achieve this goal it sponsored the jackets worn by road-crossing wardens (lollipop people) so that the local authority was free to use the money once spent on uniforms on other aspects of road safety (Walker, 1995).

Brands sought to leverage each other and achieve greater efficiencies and impact through association with each other.

A fresh form of sponsorship emerged in 1997 as brands sought to leverage each other and achieve greater efficiencies and impact through association with each other. For example, Cable & Wireless (C&W) supported Barnardos in its campaign to increase awareness of current issues, generate funds and redefine the image held of the charity. C&W provided the funds for the TV campaign and in return had a credit at the end of the commercial. The integrated campaign included radio, newspapers, direct marketing and leaflets in each of the 320 Barnardos shops. C&W had previously involved Barnardos in its own launch through direct response advertisements and also sponsored a major report published by Barnardos about child care. Its has stated its intention to become involved with local community projects (Campbell, 1997).

The majority of sponsorships, regardless of type, are not the sole promotional activity undertaken by the sponsors. They may be secondary and used to support above-the-line work or they may be used as the primary form of communication but supported by a range of off-screen activities, such as sales promotions and (in particular) competitions.

This section would not be complete without mention of the phenomenon called 'ambush marketing'. This occurs when an organisation deliberately seeks an association with a particular event but does so without paying sponsorship fees. Such hijacking is undertaken with the purpose of influencing the audience to the extent that they believe the ambusher is legitimate. According to Meenaghan (1998), this can be achieved by overstating the organisation's involvement in the event, perhaps through major promotion activity using theme-based advertising or by sponsoring the media coverage of the event.

The role of sponsorship in the promotional mix

Whether sponsorship is a part of advertising, sales promotion or public relations has long been a source of debate. It is perhaps more natural and comfortable to align sponsorship with advertising. Since awareness is regarded as the principal objective of using sponsorship, advertising is a more complementary and accommodating part of the mix. Sales promotion from the sponsor's position is harder to justify, although from a sponsee's perspective the value-added characteristic is interesting. The more traditional home for sponsorship is public relations (Witcher *et al.*, 1991). Sponsees, such as a football team, a racing car manufacturer or a theatre group, may be adjudged to perform the role of opinion former. Indirectly, therefore, messages are conveyed to the target audience with the support of significant participants who endorse and support the sponsor. This is akin to public relations activities.

The more traditional home for sponsorship is public relations.

Hastings (1984) contests that advertising messages can be manipulated and adapted to changing circumstances much more easily than those associated with sponsorship. He suggests that the audience characteristics of both advertising and sponsorship are very different. For advertising there are viewers and non-viewers. For sponsorship there are three groups of people that can be identified. First there are those who are directly involved with the sponsor or the event, the active participants. Second is a much larger group, consisting of those who attend sponsored events, and these are referred to as personal spectators. The third group is normally the largest, and comprises all those who are involved with the event through various media channels; these are regarded as media followers.

To demonstrate the potential sizes of these groups, an analysis of the sponsorship of Formula 1 racing suggests that there are approximately 3.5 million people who attended the 1995 Grand Prix championship races (active participants) and 330 million people (media followers) who saw television coverage of each race, in 160 countries (Priddy, 1997).

Sponsorship is better able to generate awareness and a wider set of product-related attributes than advertising.

Exploratory research undertaken by Hoek *et al.* (1997) suggests that sponsorship is better able to generate awareness and a wider set of product-related attributes than advertising can when dealing with non-users of a product, rather than users. There appears to be no discernible difference between the impact that these two promotional tools have with users.

The authors claim that sponsorship and advertising can be considered to work in approximately the same way if the ATR model developed by Ehrenberg (1974) is adopted (Chapter 20). Through the ATR model, purchase behaviour and beliefs are considered to be reinforced by advertising rather than new behaviour patterns being established. Advertising fulfils a means by which buyers can meaningfully defend their purchase patterns. Hoek *et al.* regard this approach as reasonably analogous to sponsorship. Sponsorship can create awareness and is more likely to confirm past behaviour than prompt new purchase behaviour. The implication, they conclude, is that, while awareness levels can be improved with sponsorship, other promotional tools are required to impact upon product experimentation or purchase intentions.

While awareness levels can be improved with sponsorship, other promotional tools are required to impact upon product experimentation or purchase intentions.

It was suggested earlier that one of the opportunities that sponsorship offers is the ability to suggest that there is an association between the sponsee and sponsor which may be of value to the message recipient. This implies that there is an indirect form of influence through sponsorship. This is supported by Crimmins and Horn (1996), who argue that the persuasive impact of sponsorship is determined in terms of the strength of links that are generated between the brand and the event that is sponsored.

These authors claim that sponsorship can have a persuasive impact and that the degree of impact that a sponsorship might bring is as follows:

$$\frac{\text{persuasive}}{\text{impact}} = \frac{\text{strength}}{\text{of link}} \times \frac{\text{duration of}}{\text{the link}} \times \left(\frac{\text{gratitude felt due}}{\text{to the link}} + \frac{\text{perceptual change}}{\text{due to the link}} \right)$$

The strength of the link between the brand and the event is an outcome of the degree to which advertising is used to communicate the sponsorship itself. Sponsors that failed to invest in advertising during the games have been shown to be far less successful in building a link with the event than those who chose to invest.

The *duration of the link* is also important. Research based on the Olympic Games shows that those sponsors who undertook integrated marketing communications long before the event itself were far more successful than those who had not. The use of mass media advertising to communicate the involvement of the sponsor, the use of event graphics and logos on packaging, and the creative use of promotional tie-ins and in-store event-related merchandising facilitated the long-term linkage with the sponsorship and added value to the campaign.

Gratitude exists if consumers realise that there is a link between a brand and an event. Sixty per cent of US adults said that they 'try to buy a company's product if they support the Olympics'. They also stated that 'I feel I am contributing to the Olympics by buying the brands of Olympic sponsors'.

Perceptual change occurs as a result of consumers being able to understand the relationship (meaning) between a brand and an event. The sponsor needs to make this clear, as passive consumers may need the links laid out before them. The link between a swimwear brand and the Olympics may be obvious, but it is not always the case. Crimmins and Horn describe how VISA's 15% perceived superiority advantage over MasterCard was stretched to 30% during the 1992 Olympics and then settled at 20% ahead one month after the games finished. The perceptual change was achieved through the messages that informed audiences that VISA was the one card that was accepted for the Olympic Games; American Express and MasterCard were not accepted.

Sponsorship may bring advantages if care is taken to invest in communications long before and during the event to communicate the meaning between the brand and the event, which will leverage gratitude from a grateful audience.

This research, while only based upon a single event, indicates that sponsorship may bring advantages if care is taken to invest in communications long before and during the event to communicate the meaning between the brand and the event, which will leverage gratitude from a grateful audience.

Summary

Sponsorship of events, activities and organisations will continue to grow in significance, if only because of its effectiveness and value as a tool of marketing communications relative to the other tools in the mix. Organisations believe that sponsorship allows them access to specific target audiences and enhances their corporate image (Marshall and Cook, 1992). Other areas will become subject to sponsorship such as the development of television programme sponsorship (for example, the weather forecasts by Portman Building Society on Meridian and Tulip Computers on Sky).

There seems little doubt that the introduction of new products and brands can be assisted by the use of appropriate sponsorships. Indeed, it appears that sponsorship, in certain contexts, can be used to prepare markets for the arrival and penetration of new brands.

The evaluation of sponsorship arrangements poses a problem in that measurement is little better than that used for advertising. However, the impact and approach that sponsorship can have suggest that the two tools should be used together, coordinated, if not integrated, to develop awareness and strong brand associations and triggers. There is a warning, and that concerns the degree to which sponsorship is capable of changing purchase behaviour through persuasion. Organisations considering the use of sponsorship as a means of directly impacting upon the bottom line are likely to be disappointed. Other tools are required to stimulate behaviour; sponsorship alone is not capable of persuading target audiences to behave differently.

Review questions

1. What are the main opportunities that sponsorship opens up for organisations?
2. Why has sponsorship become such a major promotional tool in the 1990s?
3. If the objective of using sponsorship is to build awareness (among other things), then there is little point in using advertising. Discuss this view.

4. Name four types of sponsorship.

5. Why is sport more heavily sponsored than the arts or television programmes?

6. Chose eight sporting events and name the main sponsors. Why do you think they have maintained their associations with the events?

7. Consider five television programmes which are sponsored and evaluate how viewers might perceive the relationship between the programme content and the sponsor.

8. How might sponsorship have a persuasive impact on its target audiences? What is the formula used to measure this impact?

9. Explain the role of sponsorship within the promotional mix.

10. How might sponsorship develop in the future?

MINI CASE

This mini case was written by Graham Hughes, Senior Lecturer at the Leeds Business School.
Adapted from a paper submitted by Ben Leonard of Advertising Principles to the IPA Area Advertising
Effectiveness Awards 1999. Used with kind permission.

Seven Seas

Programme sponsorship

Programme sponsorship can provide significant benefits for companies. Introductory and commercial-break credits come at times when viewers are likely to be paying close attention as their 'selected' programme is about to start or pause or has just ended. It could be argued that this kind of targeting is more focused than the relatively more random nature of advertising space booking. Of major importance in establishing TV programme sponsorship is to clearly identify the sponsor's brand with that of the audience for the programme.

A prime example of this audience identification can be seen by examining the sponsorship of the popular Channel 4 quiz show *Countdown* by Seven Seas cod liver oil. Research had shown Seven Seas that existing and new cod liver oil users were switching on to own-label products because the core brand message – 'relieving joint pain and stiffness' – was losing resonance. A new media strategy based on the *Countdown* programme sponsorship was developed in order to counter these trends.

Seven Seas built the cod liver oil brand and has always maintained a brand leadership position.

From 1996, however, two significant market trends emerged: firstly, leakage from the market of existing regular, heavier brand users, significantly women aged 55 plus; secondly there was a slow-down in the recruitment of users.

The key marketing objective set for 1999–2000 was to halt the decline in brand share by addressing the brand resonance issue among core target audience. This required refreshing and contemporising the brand image. Key image attributes such as modernity, excitement and a feeling of being 'of the moment' were identified as being part of the target audience's mindset.

From a communications perspective, traditional and non-traditional media options were considered. Research had confirmed that the core target audience was notoriously difficult to influence via traditional above-the-line advertising as they tend to be habitual, have entrenched opinions and view brand advertising with a high degree of cynicism. Non-traditional media solutions were therefore sought.

These included broadcast TV programme sponsorship and a review was undertaken to find a suitable 'vehicle' which provided 'brand fit, audience targeting and exploitability'. This resulted in the selection of Channel 4's *Countdown* quiz show. The audience profile provided an excellent 'fit' – 59% female, 71% aged 55 plus, 35% ABC1, 44% C1/C2 and offered 3.6 million individual impacts per annum (BARB, September 1998).

One of the difficulties of broadcast sponsorship of this kind is that by definition it means buying into an 'existing property'. In addition to seeking brand exposure, there is an element that might be described as 'brand image transference'. *Countdown* had already developed its own image and identity through its presenters, Richard Whiteley and Carol Vorderman. What was the core audience perception of them and are they likely to behave in a way that might be detrimental to the brand? A risk/benefit analysis of these issues suggested that the *Countdown* property was low risk in these terms.

The Seven Seas Tin Man icon has been a consistent part of the brand advertising since 1983 and there was a strong and positive association with the cod liver oil brand itself. It was therefore decided to incorporate the Tin Man into the sponsorship by showing him laying the conundrum game during the credits. In delivering the benefit message of pain and stiffness relief, answers to the questions set were based on brand benefits such as joint flexibility and suppleness.

In measuring the effectiveness, a decision was taken not to run any additional marketing communication activity throughout the sponsorship period. This was done in an attempt to isolate movements in consumer awareness and image measures. Pre-activity measures were taken in research by Millward Brown in order to establish awareness levels. Awareness ratings against an index of pre versus peak activity showed startling results (Table 27.4).

After a period of no growth, sales value of Extra High Strength Cod Liver Oil showed an

Table 27.4 Advertising awareness: Seven Seas cod liver oil

Activity	Index: peak vs. pre-sponsorship
TV	131
Magazine advertisement	58
In store	29
Newspaper	71

uplift indexing at 163 from the sponsorship launch and 174 year on year. In addition, share growth indexed at 103 in June 1999 compared with June 1998. Both sales and share uplift came from existing, regular and heavy users and significantly from new recruits. The broadcast sponsorship had clearly done something which differentiated the brand that had not been achieved using traditional above-the-line communications.

Mini-case questions

1. Identify some further examples of TV programme sponsorship. What is the relationship between the programmes and the target audiences?
2. Suggest some potential TV programme sponsorships. Why would these be appropriate in terms of communicating with the target audiences?
3. For one of these proposals undertake a risk/benefit analysis of the issues involved in associating the brand values with the values of the programme.
4. Can you identify further suggestions for evaluating the effectiveness of TV programme sponsorships?
5. Should TV programme sponsorship be used alongside or instead of traditional above-the-line advertising? Discuss with examples.

References

Allen, D. (2000) TV sponsorship rules are eased. *Media Week*, 14 April, p. 3.

Balfour, M. (2000) Precision technology delivered in record times. *Financial Times*, 25 March.

Campbell, L. (1997) C&W underpins Barnardos ads. *Marketing*, 30 October, p. 4.

Crawford, A.-M., (1999) Kellogg's £4m launch uses TV tie-in. *Marketing*, 21 October, p. 5.

Crimmins, J. and Horn, M. (1996) Sponsorship: from management ego trip to marketing success. *Journal of Advertising Research* (July/August), pp. 11–21.

Darby, I (1999) Is it worth sponsoring rugby? *Marketing*, 4 November, p. 15.

Darby, I. (2000) Dome raises doubts on sponsorship value. *Marketing*, 20 January, p. 15.

Ehrenberg, A.S.C. (1974) Repetitive advertising and the consumer. *Journal of Advertising Research*, **14** (April), pp. 25–34.

Fry, A. (1997) Keeping the right company. *Marketing*, 22 May, pp. 24–5.

Grimes, E. and Meenaghan, T. (1998) Focussing commercial sponsorship on the internal corporate audience. *International Journal of Advertising*, **17**(1), pp. 51–74.

Harverson, P. (1998) Why IT companies take the risk. *Financial Times*, 2 June.

Hastings, G. (1984) Sponsorship works differently from advertising. *International Journal of Advertising*, **3**, pp. 171–6.

Hedburg, A., (2000) Bumper crop. *Marketing Week*, 19 October, pp. 28–32.

Hill, A. (2001) On the crest of a sponsorship wave. *PR Week*, 23 February, p. 9.

Hoek, J., Gendall, P., Jeffcoat, M. and Orsman, D. (1997) Sponsorship and advertising: a comparison of their effects. *Journal of Marketing Communications*, **3**, pp. 21–32.

Javalgi, R.G., Traylor, M.B., Gross, A.C. and Lampman, E. (1994) Awareness of sponsorship and corporate image: an empirical investigation. *Journal of Advertising*, **24** (June), pp. 1–12.

Marshall, D.W. and Cook, G. (1992) The corporate (sports) sponsor. *International Journal of Advertising*, **11**, pp. 307–24.

McCormack, D. (2000) Music festivals grow up. *PR Week*, 18 August, p. 11.

Meenaghan, T. (1991) The role of sponsorship in the marketing communications mix. *International Journal of Advertising*, **10**, pp. 35–47.

Meenaghan, T. (1998) Current developments and future directions in sponsorship. *International Journal of Advertising*, **17**(1), pp. 3–28.

Pope, N.K.L. and Voges, K.E. (1999) Sponsorship and image: a replication and extension. *Journal of Marketing Communications*, **5**, pp. 17–28.

Priddy, P. (1997) An analysis and evaluation of tobacco sponsorship in motor sport, with a focus towards Formula One Grand Prix motor racing. Unpublished dissertation (BA (Hons) Business Studies), University of Portsmouth.

Reed, D. (1994) Sponsorship. *Campaign*, 20 May, pp. 37–8.

Smith, A. (1997) UK sponsors look to US. *Financial Times*, 24 March, p. 16.

Summers, D. (1995) Sponsors' careful link with TV. *Financial Times*, 2 March, p. 14.

Thorncroft, A. (1996) Business arts sponsorship: arts face a harsh set of realities. *Financial Times*, 4 July, p. 1.

Thwaites, D. (1994) Corporate sponsorship by the financial services industry. *Journal of Marketing Management*, **10**, pp. 743–63.

Walker, J.-A. (1995) Community service. *Marketing Week*, 20 October, pp. 85–90.

Wighton, D. (1995) The FT guide to golf: the price of playing. *Financial Times*, 20 July, p. xxvii.

Witcher, B., Craigen, G. Culligan, D. and Harvey, A. (1991) The links between objectives and functions in organisational sponsorship. *International Journal of Advertising*, **10**, pp. 13–33.

28

Direct marketing

Direct marketing is a strategy used to create a personal and intermediary-free dialogue with customers. This should be a measurable activity and it is very often media based, with a view to creating and sustaining a mutually rewarding relationship. The development and use of direct marketing principles by a variety of organisations are testimony to the power of this personal form of communication.

AIMS AND OBJECTIVES

The aim of this chapter is to explore the characteristics of direct marketing and to develop an understanding of interactive marketing communications.

The objectives of this chapter are:

1. To introduce and define direct marketing.
2. To consider the reasons behind the growth and development of this new marketing communications tool.
3. To examine the relationship of direct brands and direct-response media and their role within the marketing communications mix.
4. To appreciate the significance of the database in direct marketing.
5. To identify and consider different direct-response media.
6. To consider the value of integrating the activities of direct marketing with other elements of the mix.

Introduction

From previous discussions about relational and marketing exchanges (Chapters 1 and 10), it should be apparent that the long-term goal of most organisations is to build a long-term relationship with each of their customers. Most of the tools of the promotional mix address mass audiences. Advertising communicates with large audiences and primarily seeks to provide certain information, affect emotions and frame intentions when the next purchase opportunity arises. Advertising is not capable of talking personally to individual customers, nor is it used to generate personal responses. Furthermore, those who choose to use advertising are constrained by the page sizes, paper types, fonts and style or the available spots, the skill of the media planner and the programmes that are available.

Sales promotions are designed to generate an immediate sale, but the information is not stored or used in such a way that a relationship is deliberately created and sustained. Public relations seeks to develop favourable interest and goodwill by piggybacking on other media. Personal selling is certainly founded upon the need to establish long-term personal relationships. However, the range of tasks that the sales force is expected to complete means that only a small percentage of its time can be focused upon generating an immediate response. Personal selling is expensive and there is variable control over the messages that are transmitted by individual members of the sales force.

In addition to these promotional tool deficiencies, the distribution element of the marketing mix was the last to receive attention. Faced with an increasing lack of product/service differentiation and margins being eroded through price competition, the marketing channel was ripe for investigation and review. It became clear that many cost advantages could be achieved through a more direct approach to the market. This meant sidelining or avoiding expensive intermediaries (channel network members) and providing opportunities to improve quality and service provision. For these main reasons, direct marketing has developed and flourished in recent years.

It became clear that many cost advantages could be achieved through a more direct approach to the market.

The role of direct marketing

Initially direct mail was the main tool, but technological advances, most notably the development of information technology and, in particular, the database, have introduced a range of other media that can be used to communicate effectively with individual customers. Indeed, all the elements of the promotional mix can be used with direct marketing to support and build meaningful relationships with consumers and members of the various stakeholder networks.

Direct marketing, therefore, is a term used to refer to all media activities that generate a series of communications and responses with an existing or potential customer. Early on there was considerable debate about the term 'direct marketing' itself. It was often referred to as direct mail or as 'curriculum marketing, dialogue marketing, personal marketing and database marketing' (Bird, 1989). This proliferation of terms reflects the range of activities that are undertaken in an attempt to prompt a response from a customer. Terminology has settled in favour of direct marketing, and this broad approach will be adopted here.

Direct marketing is a strategy used to create and sustain a personal and intermediary-free dialogue with customers, potential customers and other significant stakeholders.

Direct marketing is a strategy used to create and sustain a personal and intermediary-free dialogue with customers, potential customers and other significant stakeholders. This should be a measurable activity and

Call to action – Baileys

Direct Marketing's ability to provoke action is demonstrated by Baileys appointing a direct marketing agency, Craik Jones, to encourage more frequent drinking of its product.

Research indicated that Baileys was perceived as a special occasion drink but in order to drive future growth this perception needed to be changed. By presenting the drink as one that can be consumed on different, more informal occasions and by developing the database into a resource that can be used to support a number of campaigns across various communication channels, it was intended to reposition the drink and achieve the organisation's goals. Targeted, individual special offers, celebratory free gifts and providing advice about general promotions would also be possible as part of the move towards CRM. The budget for this was set at £500,000 but the above-the-line spend was also increased by 40% to support the brand.

Adapted from Kleinman (2000)

it is very often media based. There are a number of important issues associated with this definition. The first is that the activity should be measurable. That is, any response(s) must be associated with a particular individual, a particular media activity and a particular outcome, such as a sale or enquiry for further information. The second issue concerns the rewards that each party perceives through participation in the relationship. The customer receives a variety of tangible and intangible satisfactions. These include shopping convenience, time utility and the satisfaction and trust that can develop between customers and a provider of quality products and services when the customers realise and appreciate the personal attention they appear to be receiving.

Underpinning the direct marketing approach are the principles of trust and commitment, just as they support the validity of the other promotional tools. If a meaningful relationship is to be developed over the long term and direct marketing is an instrumental part of the dialogue, then the pledges that the parties make to develop commitment and stability are of immense importance (Ganesan, 1994).

Underpinning the direct marketing approach are the principles of trust and commitment.

Indeed, the concept of establishing trust is vital if relational exchanges are to be developed. Trust is a multidimensional construct (Morgan and Hunt, 1994) and the need to ensure that it is recognised and accepted by parties where direct marketing is used is highly important (Fletcher and Peters, 1997).

The direct marketer derives benefits associated with precision target marketing and minimised waste, increased profits and the opportunities to provide established customers with other related products, without the huge costs of continually having to find new customers. In addition, direct marketing represents a strategic approach to the market. It actively seeks to remove channel intermediaries, reduce costs, and improve the quality and speed of service for customers, and through this bundle of attributes presents a new offering for the market, which in itself may provide competitive advantage. First Direct, Virgin Direct

Direct marketing represents a strategic approach to the market.

and the pioneer, Direct Line, all provide these advantages, which have enabled them to secure strong positions in the market.

Types of direct brand

Direct marketing is assumed to refer to direct promotional activity, but this is only part of the marketing picture. Using direct-response media in this way is an increasingly common activity used to augment the communication activities surrounding a brand and to provide a new dimension to the context in which brands are perceived.

In addition to these promotional advantages there are two main types of direct brands: *pedigree direct* brands and *hybrid direct* brands (Foster, 1996). These reflect their origins in the sense that the pedigree direct brand is developed to deliberately exploit a market-positioning opportunity. Hybrid direct brands are essentially the same except that the brand heritage is rooted in traditional distribution channels, which may well continue to be a route to market used in parallel to the direct route. Therefore, as Foster points out, the main difficulty facing the hybrid direct brand is the organisational culture: its context and heritage. With these brands there is a generally accepted approach to the market and commonality as to the way things should be done. Even the systems and processes associated with the intermediary-based approach are established and need to be altered to meet the needs of a new type of customer.

There are two main types of direct brands: pedigree direct brands and hybrid direct brands.

However, there is further difficulty, which lies with the image that the customer base and other stakeholders have of the hybrid direct brand. It represents a change from the frame in which stakeholders expect to see the brand. Care therefore needs to be taken with the marketing communications to ensure that the transition is carried out in such a way that the credibility of the brand is maintained.

From this review it is possible to view direct marketing as part of one the following types (Figure 28.1). These are not hierarchical in the sense that there has to be progression from one type to another. They are reflections of the way different organisations use direct marketing and the degree to which the tool is used strategically.

Type 1: complementary tool

At this level, direct-response media are used to complement the other promotional activities used to support a brand. Their main use is to generate leads and to some extent awareness, information and reinforcement. For example, financial services companies, tour operators and travel agents use DRTV to stimulate enquiries, loans and bookings, respectively.

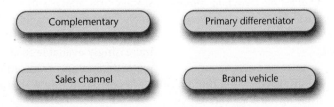

Figure 28.1 Types of direct marketing.

Type 2: primary differentiator

They are used to provide a distinct point of differentiation from competitor offerings.

Rather than be one of a number of promotional tools, at this level direct-response media are the primary form of communication. They are used to provide a distinct point of differentiation from competitor offerings. They are the principal form of communication. In addition to the type 1 advantages they are used to cut costs, avoid the use of intermediaries and reach finely targeted audiences (for example, book, music and wine clubs).

Type 3: sales channel

A third use for direct marketing and telemarketing in particular concerns its use as a means of developing greater efficiency and as a means of augmenting current services. By utilising direct marketing as a sales tool, multiple sales channels can be used to meet the needs of different customer segments and so release resources to be deployed elsewhere and more effectively. This idea is developed further later in this chapter.

Type 4: brand vehicle

At this final level, brands are developed to exploit market space opportunities.

At this final level, brands are developed to exploit market space opportunities. These may be the pedigree or hybrid brands identified earlier (for example, Direct Line, Virgin Direct and Eagle Star Direct). The strategic element is most clearly evident at this level. Indeed, the entire organisation and its culture are orientated to the development of customer relationships through direct marketing activities.

The growth of direct marketing

There can be little doubt that, of all the tools in the marketing communications mix, direct marketing has experienced the most growth in the last 10 years. The reasons for this growth are many and varied, but two essential drivers behind the surge in direct marketing have been technological advances and changing buyer lifestyles and expectations. These two forces for change demonstrate quite dramatically how a change in the context can impact on marketing communications.

Growth driver 1: technology

Technology has enabled the collection, storage and analysis of customer data to become relatively simple, cost effective and straightforward.

Rapid advances in technology have heralded the arrival of new sources and forms of information. Technology has enabled the collection, storage and analysis of customer data to become relatively simple, cost effective and straightforward. Furthermore, the management of this information is increasingly available to small businesses as well as the major blue chip organisations. Computing costs have plummeted, while there has been a correspondingly enormous increase in the power that technology can deliver.

The technological surge has in turn stimulated three major developments. The first

Table 28.1 Advances in technology

Data capture and collection
  Scanners, smart cards, loyalty schemes, marketing research
Information processing
  Database marketing
Communication and interaction
  Greater precision in segmentation and targeting effectiveness, direct mail, telemarketing and decline in traditional media consumption/effectiveness

concerns the ability to capture information, the second to process and analyse it and the third to represent part or all of the information as a form of communication to stimulate dialogue and interaction to collect further information (Table 28.1).

Organisations have been able to make increasing use of technological developments within marketing communications. Indeed, all areas of the mix have benefited as new and more effective and efficient processes and methods of communication evolve. Advances in technology are responsible for the demise of some traditional forms of communication. For example, the impact of mass communications and advertising in particular as a single device has diminished in favour of a more personalised and integrated approach to communications, enabled by technology. This gives the ability to target potential customers much more precisely at lower cost.

Advances in technology are responsible for the demise of some traditional forms of communication.

Growth driver 2: changing market context

The lifestyles of people in western European and North American societies, in particular, have evolved and will continue to do so. Generally, the brash phase of *selfishness* in the 1980s gave way to a more caring, society-orientated *selflessness* in the 1990s. The start of the 21st century suggests that a *self- awareness* lifestyle might predominate and be reflected in brand purchase behaviour and a greater emphasis on long-term value and different brand values. Continued fragmentation of the media and audiences requires finely tuned segmentation and communication devices. Direct marketing offers a solution to this splintering and micro market scenario and addresses some of the changing needs of management, namely for speed of response and justification for the use and allocation of resources (Table 28.2).

Direct marketing offers a solution to this splintering and micro market scenario.

Table 28.2 Changing market context

Lifestyles and expectations
  Inner directedness, pluralism, individualism
Fragmentation
  Audience, media
Management requirements
  Costs, accountability, competition, speed of response

The role of the database

At the hub of successful direct marketing activities is the database. A database is a collection of files held on a computer that contain data that can be related to one another and which can reproduce information in a variety of formats. Normally the data consist of information collected about prospects and customers which are used to determine appropriate segments and target markets and to record responses to communications conveyed by the organisation. A database therefore plays a role as a storage, sorting and administrative device to assist direct and personalised communications: a dialogue propagator.

Age and lifestyle data are important signals of product usage. However, there will

Age and lifestyle data are important signals of product usage.

be attitudinal variances between people in similar groups demanding further analysis. This can, according to Reed (2000), uncover clues concerning what the direct mail piece should look like. So, older customers do not like soft colours and small type and sentences should not begin with 'and' or 'but'.

Direct marketing – Tesco

The UK grocery market leader Tesco now uses its database, in which it holds detailed information about its customers' purchases, as a pivotal part of its marketing communications activities. The database holds information about its customers that it can mine and then target sales promotions, advertising and direct marketing communications. For example, each quarter it sends out a statement to its 10 million regular Clubcard users and includes promotional vouchers and coupons mirroring each customer's purchases. As a result, there are 100,000 different promotional messages reflecting the preferences and buying habits of customers rather than the supermarket's desire to sell particular products (Marsh, 2001).

This demand-led approach has strengthened Tesco's position in the market. In 2000, the number of in-store promotions fell from 700 to just 200, reflecting the need to provide for those who are price sensitive.

Increasingly, the information stored is gathered from transactions undertaken with customers, but on its own this information is not enough and further layering of data is required. The recency/frequency/monetary (RFM) model provides a base upon which lifestyle data, often bought in from a list agency, can be used to further refine the information held. Response analysis requires the

The database now consists of several layers of information (Figure 28.2) whereby traditional segmentation data can be fused with transactional data.

identification of an organisation's best customers, and then another layer of data can be introduced which points to those that are particularly responsive to direct mail or mail order (Fletcher, 1997). It is the increasing sophistication of the information held in databases that is enabling more effective targeting and communications. The database now consists of several layers of information (Figure 28.2) whereby traditional segmentation data, which set out customer profiles, can be fused

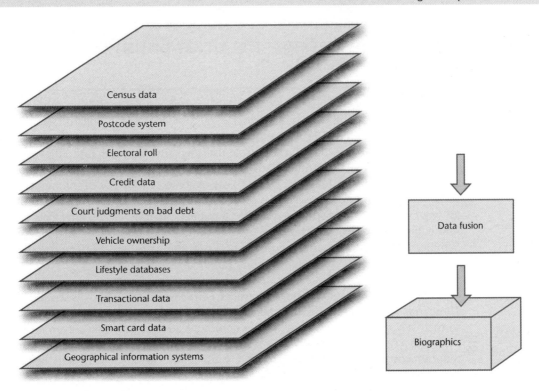

Census data

Postcode system

Electoral roll

Credit data

Court judgments on bad debt

Vehicle ownership

Lifestyle databases

Transactional data

Smart card data

Geographical information systems

Data fusion

Biographics

Figure 28.2   Layers of database marketing. From Evans (1998); used with kind permission.

with transactional data so that biographics (Evans, 1998) emerges as a potent new approach to developing a dialogue with individual customers.

It is through the use of the database that relationships with participants can be tracked, analysed and developed. Some tobacco companies, in anticipation of the total media ban, have invested in sales promotion activities to generate information about their heavy users, in order that they can move over to a direct marketing approach when tobacco advertising becomes illegal.

Databases provide the means by which a huge range of organisations, large and small, can monitor changes in customer lifestyles and attitudes, or, in the business-to-business sector, the changing form of the interorganisational relationships and their impact on other members in the network as well as the market structure and level of competitive activity (Gundach and Murphy, 1993).

However, there are a number of tensions associated with the use of the database. For example, customers have varying tolerances regarding the level of privacy that a database can exploit. The tolerance or thresholds (Goodwin, 1991) vary according to the information itself, how it was collected and even who collected it. The information exists on a database very often because a customer entered into a transaction. The business entity that received the information as part of a transaction has a duty to acknowledge the confidential nature of the information and the context in which it was collected before selling the details to a third party or exploiting the information to the detriment of the individual who provided it in the first place. Breaking privacy codes and making unauthorised disclosures of personal details lay open the tenuous relationship an organisation thinks it has with its 'loyal' customers.

Database marketing – the Great British Bollard Company

The simple yet successful use of a database as part of a direct marketing campaign is demonstrated by the launch of 'Ferrocast' by the Great British Bollard Company (GBBC) and reported by Gardiner and Quinton (1998). GBBC had developed a new traffic bollard that provide a high level of user benefits. UK local authorities were identified as the main customer base and direct marketing was seen as the most cost-efficient means of reaching buyers. Lists of three or four key decision-makers within each local authority were developed from the *Municipal Year Book* and the list was cleaned using telephone research. A market database of 200 architects and 400 engineers was constructed and used as the basis of a direct mail campaign. Samples were produced and used in response to enquiries and as demonstration units for the sales director when meeting potential customers.

Analysis of the database indicated that there were certain specifiers and key decision-makers who would never consider Ferrocast or the GBBC as a supplier. These individuals were labelled 'traditionalists' and were flagged on the database so that they did not receive any further communications from GBBC, even if they moved to a new local authority. This saved sending out unwanted communications, reduced costs, improved targeting and subsequent calling activity and helped develop corporate reputation by focusing on potential customers.

Adapted from Gardiner and Quinton (1998)
Used with kind permission

Direct-response media

The choice of media for direct marketing can be very different from those selected for general advertising purposes. The main reason for using direct-response media is that direct contact is made with prospects and customers in order that a direct response is solicited and a dialogue stimulated or maintained. In reality, a wide variety of media can be used, simply by attaching a telephone number or response card. However, if broadcast media such as television and radio are the champions of the general advertiser, their adoption by direct marketers in the UK has been relatively slow. Direct mail, telemarketing and door-to-door activities are the main direct-response media, as they allow more personal, direct and evaluative means of reaching precisely targeted customers.

Direct mail, telemarketing and door-to-door activities are the main direct-response media.

Direct mail

The largest direct-response media expenditure is direct mail, which grew by 6% in the year ending October 2000 (Ridgeway, 2000). Direct mail refers to personally addressed advertising that is delivered through the postal system. It can be personalised and targeted with great accuracy, and its results are capable of precise measurement.

The generation of enquiries and leads together with the intention of building a personal relationship with customers are the most important factors contributing to the growth of direct mail. However, the intention to build loyalty is not reflected in the statistics as Ridgeway reports that mailings appear to be focused on customer acquisition, not retention. Other factors include the increased market and media fragmentation, which have combined to reduce the overall effectiveness of general advertising. Direct mail can be expensive, at anything between £250 and £500 per 1,000 items dispatched. It should, therefore, be used selectively and for purposes other than creating awareness.

Expenditure on direct mail advertising increased rapidly in the late 1980s. Despite a slight dip in 1990, adspend on direct mail has continued to increase and demands an increasing proportion of advertisers' budgets. In 1992, £945 million was spent on direct mail, equating to 11% of total promotional expenditure (DMIS, 1993). By 2000, direct mail volumes have increased so that they account for nearly half of the overall letterbox

Direct mail volumes have increased so that they account for nearly half of the overall letterbox.

(DMIS, 2000) and 15% of total promotional expenditure (Ridgeway, 2000). However, Day (2000) reports that levels of opening and reading of direct mail items have fallen with 75% opened and 53% read. So, the volumes sent out have increased but response rates have fallen and as reported by Reed (2000) 'we mail the customer until they give in'. In other words, this persistent approach to marketing is used to overcome a failure in segmentation and targeting.

Organisations in the financial services sectors are the main users of this medium and the financial health of the sector is dependent to a large extent on some of the major financial services companies maintaining their spend on direct mail. However, an increasing number of other organisations are experimenting with this approach, as they try to improve the effectiveness of their promotional expenditure and reduce television advertising costs. The growth in consumer-based direct mail activities has outstripped that of the business-to-business sector. The number of direct mail items sent to consumers has increased considerably in comparison with the b2b sector.

Telemarketing

The prime qualities of the telephone are that it provides for interaction, is flexible and permits immediate feedback and the opportunity to overcome objections, all within the same period of communication. Other dimensions of telemarketing include the development and maintenance of customer goodwill, allied to which is the increasing need to provide high levels of customer service. Telemarketing also allows organisations to undertake marketing research and is highly measurable and accountable in that the effectiveness can be verified continuously and call rates, contacts reached and the number and quality of positive and negative responses are easily recorded and monitored.

Growth in telemarketing activity in the business-to-business sector has been largely at the expense of personal selling. The objectives have been to reduce costs and to utilise the expensive sales force and their skills to build on the openings and leads created by telemarketing and other lead generation activities.

Growth in telemarketing activity in the business-to-business sector has been largely at the expense of personal selling.

Calls can be categorised as outbound when organisations contact buyers directly, urging them to buy, asking them to provide research information or trying to interest them in the product or service so that they are prepared to buy or receive a further call or personal visit.

Telemarketing – Alton Towers

The brand development of Oblivion, the world's first vertical drop roller coaster, at Alton Towers incorporated the use of telemarketing. Gray (1999) reports that a special telephone number was set up for a promotion aimed at the young adult market. A mocking voice explained the ride to callers, goading and daring callers to try the ride:

> Pilots can experience black-out, grey-out or even red-out; Oblivion may be enough for some people to experience what is commonly known as a cop-out.
> If you decide not to, no one will consider it a weakness or a lack of nerve. Honest.

Callers were challenged to book a special time slot by transferring within the same call to live telemarketers at Alton Towers or Telecom Potential. Branding was extended to the queue for the ride with a series of TV monitors showing the face behind the sneering voice, and still goading consumers towards the ride.

Inbound calls are those received by organisations in response to direct-response advertisements, which, for example, use 0345 or 0800 numbers.

All of these activities can be executed by personal selling, but the speed, cost, accuracy and consistency of the information solicited through personal visits can often be improved upon by telemarketing. The complexity of the product will influence the degree to which this medium can be used successfully. However, if properly trained professional telemarketers are used, the sales results, if measured on a call basis, can outperform those produced by personal selling.

Generally there are three main ways in which telemarketing can be approached. These are canned, framed and customised. The first approach, the *canned call*, occurs when the caller follows a prepared script, often regardless of the interjections of the receiver. The same 'canned call' is presented to all in the caller's hit list, regardless of their needs and product knowledge. This rather crude approach can be quite sophisticated, as computer software prepares scripts which 'branch', as in a decision tree, to respond to a prospect's different answers (Roberts and Berger, 1989). A variation of this approach is the use of interactive voice response. This enables organisations to respond quickly to incoming calls with the use of technology and remove the expense of a human operator. Data and information can be collected quickly and efficiently and calls can be routed around the organisation to the appropriate department (e.g. customer service, sales or fault reporting), so cutting queues and waiting times. However, the downside of this is that customers who are rerouted and then end up in a lengthy queue listening to background music often fail to appreciate, at that moment, the benefits of new technology.

The second approach is the *framed call*. This is similar to a semistructured interview, where the caller has a number of topics that need to be covered but the order and the style in which the issues are dealt with are immaterial.

The *customised call* is the telephone version of a personal sales presentation. Undertaken by professionally trained callers, the conversation is tuned to the needs of the receiver, not those of the caller. When the call is completed, regardless of whether an order has been placed, recipients replace the handset feeling satisfied that they have used their time appropriately and in full expectation that they will receive further calls.

To assist outbound callers, predictive dialling software has been shown to increase efficiency. This tool enables engaged lines, no response and answering machines to be avoided (ignored), thus allowing operators to spend an increased proportion of their time talking to potential customers rather than wasting time dialling and listening to telephones ringing. Estimates vary, but now operators can talk for 45 minutes in every hour, compared with 25 minutes before the development of predictive dialling facilities (Cook, 1997).

To assist outbound callers, predictive dialling software has been shown to increase efficiency.

The costs of telemarketing are high: for example, £10 to reach a decision-maker in an organisation. When this is compared with £1.50 for a piece of direct mail or £100+ for a personal sales call to the same individual, it is the effectiveness of the call and the return on the investment that determines whether the costs are really high.

Carelines

Another reason to use telemarketing concerns the recent development of carelines. Many manufacturers use call centres to enable customers to make contact to complain, seek advice or make suggestions regarding product or packaging development. The previous letter-based mechanism did not encourage customer response especially when research by Sitel (McLuhan, 2000) found that 98% of customers switched brands rather than complain. Telephone and email contact encourages greater contact and the chance to talk to customers because it is easier and quicker to implement. The majority of the careline calls are not about complaints but seek advice or help about products. Food manufacturers can provide cooking and recipe advice, cosmetic and toiletries companies can provide healthcare advice and application guidelines while white goods and service-based organisations can provide technical and operational support.

Manufacturers use call centres to enable customers to make contact to complain, seek advice or make suggestions regarding product or packaging development.

Telephone and email contact encourages greater contact and the chance to talk to customers because it is easier and quicker to implement.

Carelines are essentially a post-purchase support mechanism which facilities market feedback and intelligence gathering. They can warn of imminent problems (product defects), provide ideas for new products or variants and of course provide a valuable method to reassure customers and improve customer retention levels. Call operators, or agents as many of them are now being called, have to handle calls from a variety of new sources, Web, email, interactive TV and mobile devices, and it is appreciated that many are more effective if they have direct product experience. Instant messaging channels enable on-line shoppers to ask questions which are routed to a call centre for response. Sales conversion ratios can be up by 40–50% and costs are about £1 to answer an inbound question, compared with £3.5 by phone (Murphy, 2000). Also, the instant messaging can be changed to email (or nothing) depending upon available resources.

Expenditure on telemarketing increased rapidly in the late 1980s and early 1990s, but this rapid growth then subsided. Some organisations began undertaking their outbound calls themselves rather than using tele-agencies to do the work on their behalf but as technology improved outsourcing resumed normal growth. In recent years the telemarketing sector has experienced huge growth. There were signs of oversupply in the market and so there is huge pressure on costs and margins.

As the application of digital technologies gathered pace so telemarketing and call centres became threatened. Rather than persist in a potentially declining business activity, call centres repositioned themselves so that they could provide multimedia support services such as eCRM, Internet and even email management. The accent is now on strategic partnership to assist clients develop customer relationships and this is helping to sustain annual sector growth of 40% (McLuhan, 2000).

The accent is now on strategic partnership to assist clients develop customer relationships.

While the Internet has provided further growth opportunities, the Internet will take on a number of the tasks currently the preserve of telemarketing bureaux. Web sites may enable product information and certain support advice to be accessed without the call centre costs and focus attention on other matters of concern to the customer. Chat room discussions, collaborative browsing and real-time text conversations are options to help care for customers in the future. However, it is probably the one-to-one telephone dialogue between customer and the agent that will continue to provide the satisfaction and benefits for both parties.

Inserts

Inserts are media materials that are placed in magazines or direct mail letters. These not only provide factual information about the product or service but also enable the recipient to respond to the request of the direct marketer. This request might be to place an order or post back a card for more information, such as a brochure.

Inserts have become more popular, but their cost is substantially higher than a four-colour advertisement in the magazine in which the insert is carried. Their popularity is based on their effectiveness as a lead generator, and new methods of delivering inserts to the home will become important to direct mailing houses in the future. Other vehicles, such as packages rather than letter mail, will be become important. For example, BT has commissioned Colleagues, a major direct mail organisation, to provide inserts to be delivered with new telephone directories.

Print

There are two main forms of direct response advertising through the printed media: first, catalogues and, second, magazines and newspapers.

Catalogues mailed direct to consumers have been an established method of selling products for a long time. Mail order organisations such as Freeman's, GUS and Littlewood's have been successfully exploiting this form of direct marketing for a long time. Organisations such as Scotcade, Innovations and Kaleidoscope have successfully used mini-catalogues, but instead of providing account facilities and the appointment of specific freelance agents, their business transactions are on a cash-with-order basis.

Catalogues mailed direct to consumers have been an established method of selling products for a long time.

Business-to-business marketers have now begun to exploit this medium, and organisations such as IBM now use catalogues, partly to save costs and partly to free valuable sales personnel so that they can concentrate their time selling into larger accounts.

Direct response advertising through the press is similar to general press advertising except that the advertiser provides a mechanism for the reader to take further action.

The mechanism may be a telephone number (call free) or a coupon or cut-out reply slip requesting further information.

Door to door

This delivery method can be much cheaper than that of direct mail as there are no postage charges to be accounted for. However, if the costs are much lower, so are the response rates. Responses are lower because door-to-door drops cannot be personally addressed like direct mail, even though the content and quality can be controlled in the same way.

Avon Cosmetics and Betterware are traditionally recognised as professional practitioners of door-to-door direct marketing. Other organisations, such as the utility companies (gas, electricity and water), are using door-to-door to create higher levels of market penetration. For more information on this see Chapter 30.

Radio and television

Of the two main forms discussed earlier, radio and television, the former is used as a support medium for other advertising, often by providing enquiry numbers. Television has greater potential because it can provide the important visual dimension, but it is not used a great deal in the UK for direct marketing purposes. One of the main reasons for this has been the television contractors' attitude to pricing.

The industry has experienced a period of great change.

However, the industry has experienced a period of great change and has introduced greater pricing flexibility, and a small but increasing number of direct marketeers have used the small screen successfully, mainly by providing freephone numbers for customers. Direct Line, originally a motor insurance organisation, has been outstanding in its use of television not only to launch but also to help propel the phenomenal growth of a range of related products (see Plate 28.1).

The Internet and new media

The explosion of activity around new media and the Internet has been quite astonishing in recent years and represents the major form of interactive marketing communications. The development of digital television services will herald the birth of a new form of interactivity during the first 10 years of the new century as analogue services are withdrawn. Initially home shopping and banking facilities will be attractive to those whose lifestyles complement the benefits offered by the new technology. In the longer term fully interactive services will bring increased leisure and entertainment opportunities to a greater number of people. A much fuller consideration of interactive communications can be found in Chapters 18 and 25.

Initially home shopping and banking facilities will be attractive to those whose lifestyles complement the benefits offered by the new technology.

■ Integration and direct marketing

This brief review of the media used in direct marketing activities has tended to present them as separate, independent resources. Increasingly, successful direct marketing

Increasingly, successful direct marketing programmes are using these media in combination, as a team of complementary tools.

programmes are using these media in combination, as a team of complementary tools. Many organisations, regardless of whether their marketing activities are orientated solely to direct marketing or not, are using direct-response media to support and supplement their other promotional activities (Emerick, 1993; Gardiner and Quinton, 1998).

Other organisations are using integrated direct marketing, which Eisenhart (1990) identified as 'the orchestration of various direct marketing vehicles so that they work together in a synergistic fashion'. An example of this orchestration might be the dispatch of a direct mailing using a well-qualified list followed by contacting addresses through a telemarketing programme within 24 hours of the mailer arriving. In some cases, response rates have doubled by using telemarketing in this way.

Some doubt whether organisations can justify the cost and the administrative and managerial implications of complex integrated direct campaigns. Advocates of the approach claim that each contact with a prospect helps to create a wave effect, with response rates increasing at each contact.

Some doubt whether organisations can justify the cost and the administrative and managerial implications of complex integrated direct campaigns.

There can be little doubt that direct-response media will be used increasingly in the future as organisations realise its power and overcome built-in resistance to the direct approach. As general media rates continue to increase ahead of inflation, and as managers seek new ways of providing evidence of their astute use of marketing and, in particular, promotional resources, so direct-response media will play an increasingly important role in the marketing activities of a large number of organisations. However, commitment to the direct route or to a combination of general and direct-response media means that organisations must ensure that they are transmitting a consistent or complementary message through each medium used.

Supporting the sales force

In an effort to increase the productivity of the sales force and to use their expensive skills more effectively, direct marketing has provided organisations with an opportunity to improve levels of performance. In particular, the use of an inside telemarketing department is seen as a compatible sales channel to the field sales force.

Direct marketing has provided organisations with an opportunity to improve performance.

The telemarketing team can accomplish the following tasks: they can search for and qualify new customers, so saving the field force from cold calling; they can service existing customer accounts and prepare the field force should they be required to attend to the client personally; they can seek repeat orders from marginal or geographically remote customers, particularly if they are low-unit-value consumable items; finally, they can provide a link between network members which serves to maintain the relationship, especially through periods of difficulty and instability. Many organisations prefer to place orders through telesales teams, as it does not involve the time costs associated with personal sales calls. The routine of such orders gives greater efficiency for all concerned with the relational exchange and reduces costs.

Direct mail activities are also becoming more important in areas where personal contact is seen as unnecessary or where limited field sales resources are deployed to

Direct mail activities are also becoming more important in areas where personal contact is seen as unnecessary or where limited field sales resources are deployed to key accounts.

key accounts. As with telesales, direct mail is often used to supplement the activities of the field force. Catalogue and electronic communications such as fax can be used for accounts which may be regarded as relatively unattractive.

All of these activities free the field sales force to increase their productivity and to spend more time with established customers or those with high profit potential.

Multiple-channel selling

A number of different sales channels have been identified and many organisations, in their search to reduce costs, are trying to restructure their sales operations in an attempt to fit the expected needs of their stakeholders. Restructuring has often taken the form of introducing multiple sales channels with the simple objective of using less

Table 28.3 Comparison of four types of sales channel

Sales channel	Knowledge of customer needs/requirments	Direct access to customers	Time/customer	Cost/contact
Key account Coordinated sales and support activities to one or a few customers representing high-volume annual purchases	Very high level of understanding of needs/requirements	Access typically concentrated at headquarters location, and with different individuals within customer organisation	Calls are typically frequent and long	Very high because of length of contact and number of contacts within customer organisation
Field salesperson Field salesperson responsible for several customers/prospects assigned on the basis of geographical area, product scope or market scope	High to medium level of understanding (highest when needs are similar across customer base)	Face-to-face contact with assigned accounts; may include team-selling activities	Call patterns vary but are typically shorter than key account calls	High to medium depending on call duration
Telemarketing Assignment of large number of customers/prospects to a salesperson who contacts accounts by phone	Medium to low level of understanding	Access by telephone and electronic support	Calls are relatively short: frequency may vary according to buying/serving patterns	Low relative to face-to-face contact
Electronic mail contact Customers/prospects contacted by computer, fax or mail	Low level of understanding unless purchasing is routine repurchase of standard items	Contacts indirect	Direct contact is not involved	Very low indirect contact costs

Source: Cravens *et al.* (1991); used with kind permission.

expensive channels to complete selling tasks that do not require personal, face-to-face contact, as discussed in Cravens *et al.* (1991). These authors have presented a comparison of four types of sales channel mentioned above; see Table 28.3.

Using a matrix, accounts can be categorised according to their potential attractiveness and the current strength of the relationship between two organisations (Figure 28.3). A strong relationship, for example, is indicative of two organisations engaged in mutually satisfying relational exchanges. A weak relationship suggests that the two parties have no experience of each other or, if they have, that it is not particularly satisfying. If there have been transactions, it may be that these can be classified as market exchange experiences. Attractiveness refers to the opportunities a buying organisation represents to the vendor: how large or small the potential business is in an organisation.

For reasons of clarity, these scales are presented as either high or low, strong or weak. However, they should be considered as a continuum, and with the use of some relatively simple evaluative criteria accounts can be positioned on the matrix and strategies formulated to move accounts to different positions, which in turn necessitate the use of different sales channel mixes.

Using the approach of Cravens *et al.* (1991), appropriate sales channels are superimposed on the matrix so that optimum efficiency in selling effort and costs can be managed (Figure 28.4). Accounts in section 1 vary in attractiveness, as some will be assigned key account status. The others will be very important and will require a high level of selling effort, which has to be delivered by the field sales force. Accounts in section 2 are essentially prospects because of their weak relationship but high attractiveness. Selling effort should be proportional to the value of the prospects: high effort for good prospects and low for the others.

As the relationship becomes stronger, so field selling takes over from telesales.

All the main sales channels should be used, commencing with direct mail to identify prospects, telesales for qualification purposes, field sales force selling directed at the strong prospects and telesales for the others. As the relationship becomes stronger, so field selling takes over from telesales. If the relationship weakens, then the account may be discontinued and selling redirected to other prospects.

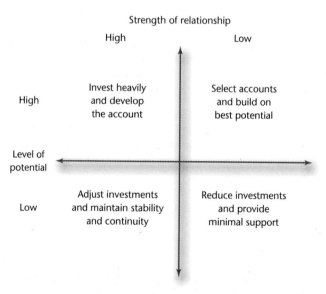

Figure 28.3 Account investment matrix.

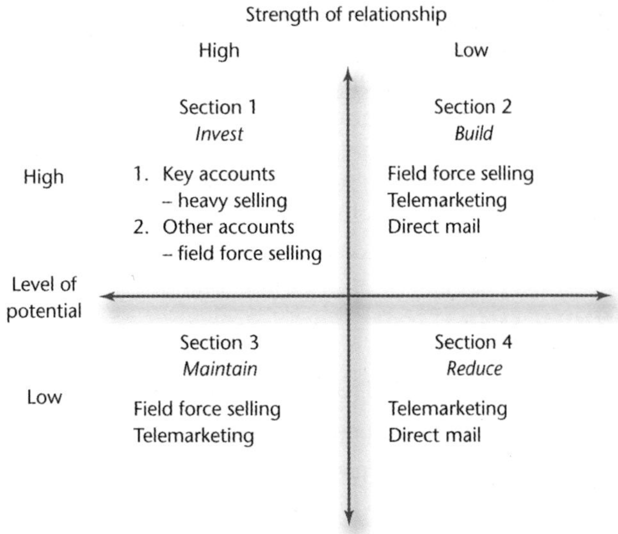

Strength of relationship

	High	Low
	Section 1 *Invest*	Section 2 *Build*
High	1. Key accounts – heavy selling 2. Other accounts – field force selling	Field force selling Telemarketing Direct mail
Level of potential		
Low	Section 3 *Maintain* Field force selling Telemarketing	Section 4 *Reduce* Telemarketing Direct mail

Figure 28.4   Sales channel mix allocation. Adapted from Cravens *et al.* (1991).

Accounts in section 3 are not particularly attractive and, although the relationship is strong, there are opportunities, according to Cravens *et al.*, to switch the sales channel mix by reducing, but not eliminating, the level of field force activity and to give consideration to the introduction of telesales for particular accounts. Significant cost reductions can be achieved with these types of accounts by simply reviewing the means and reasoning behind the personal selling effort. Accounts in section 4 should receive no field force calls, the prime sales channels being telesales, direct mail and catalogue selling.

Establishing a multiple sales channel strategy based on the matrix suggested above may not be appropriate to all organisations. For example, the current level of performance may be considered as exceeding expectations, in which case there is no point in introducing change. It may be that the costs and revenues associated with redeployment are unfavourable and that the implications for the rest of the organisation of implementing the new sales channel approach are such that the transition should be either postponed or rejected.

Costs can be reduced through the introduction of a multiple sales channel approach and levels of customer satisfaction and the strength of the relationship between members of the network can be improved considerably.

However, experience has shown, according to LaForge *et al.* (1985) that costs can be reduced through the introduction of a multiple sales channel approach and that levels of customer satisfaction and the strength of the relationship between members of the network can be improved considerably.

Summary

Direct marketing is a relatively new approach which, through the use of direct-response media and database support, permits the generation and feedback of messages with individual customers. The overarching objectives are to build and sustain a mutually rewarding relationship with each customer, reduce media costs and improve effectiveness and measurement.

The use of direct marketing has grown considerably in the 1990s and will undoubtedly continue to grow during the first decade of the next century. For some organisations their whole marketing approach has been built around the direct concept (e.g. financial services), whereas for others the approach needs to be used to complement their use of the other tools in the promotional mix.

Review questions

1. Set out a definition of direct marketing and consider the key words in the definition.

2. Explain the differences between direct-response media and direct marketing.

3. Direct-response media have many advantages over general mass advertising. What are they and why is this form of promotional communication increasing so quickly?

4. What are the different levels of direct marketing? What is the fundamental difference between levels?

5. Evaluate the main drivers behind the growth of direct marketing. How might these drivers change in the future?

6. Discuss the role of the database as the hub of marketing communications.

7. Telemarketing has become an integral feature of the promotional mix for reaching consumer and business-to-business markets. Why is this and what particular features of telemarketing attract clients?

8. Identify and then evaluate three different media for delivering direct-response communications.

9. Find two examples of organisations using carelines. Comment on their effectiveness.

10. Explain why direct marketing activities should be integrated with other elements of the promotional mix.

MINI CASE

This mini case was written by Shena Mitchell, Senior Lecturer in Marketing at the University of Portsmouth.

Mu Mu Café Bar

Direct marketing

The projected figures for direct marketing transactions in the UK, for the year 2001, are estimated at £10 billion, which reflects the continued growth and significance of this marketing communications tool. An important feature for consideration for direct marketers is the new Data Protection Act 1998, which was fully implemented in October 2001 and goes significantly further than the UK Data Protection Act 1984. The following list provides examples of some of the changes.

Data subjects must give their express permission to the firm; the onus will be on the firm to seek the consent of the data subject and provide them with full details of all the intended disclosure.

All records will be subject to control – paper records are exempt.

Profiling the consumers will be severely restricted.

The transfer of data to countries outside the European Community that do not have equally stringent data protection laws will be forbidden.

Blanket list swapping between organisations will not be allowed.

The practical impact of the Data Protection Act 1998, will depend to some extent on the way in which it is interpreted and implemented. However, it will have an impact on most, if not all, organisations in some way or another. One of the aims of the Act is to protect consumers from feeling threatened by organisations that intrude upon their privacy. In addition, it offers consumers more control over their personal, financial and medical data.

Located in a south-coast town, the Mu Mu Café Bar started trading as an Italian pasta bar in 1998, offering mainly pasta and wines from around the world to its mainly young and trendy business executive market. The Bar has a cosmopolitan feel, with a minimalist approach to décor creating a fashionable and modern environment, with subdued lighting and modern music. The food is basic, yet served in an extravagant style, on oversized large white plates and the atmosphere is 'busy' and 'bubbly' during weekends. The Bar's unique selling points are that it opens early in the morning, serves a good English breakfast to complement its Italian menu, has good facilities for children, the staff are well trained and, although there is limited parking, it is suitably located for its target market.

Because of a drastic drop in turnover since Christmas, the manager of the Mu Mu Café Bar has decided to offer 'two for the price of one', in a hope to increase sales. Rather than sending a blanket mail drop to the whole of the local area, the manager wants to send promotional information to a list of carefully selected existing and new customers. A database has been built up over the last three years, yet consent for contact has not been given by each individual customer.

One major change in Schedule 2 of the Data Protection Act 1998 is that it requires the consumer to be proactive and consent by 'opting in' to contact. This has caused the manager a serious dilemma in her marketing communications strategy, as, although it is assumed that the existing database is built on legitimate reasons and therefore can be used legally, new customers will need to give consent prior to any formal contact.

Not wanting to be prosecuted under the Data Protection Act 1998, the manager decided that she would need to get express consent from the Bar's consumers. The Act allows organisations to request consent in an initial contact, but no further contact can be made until the consumer has responded with his or her consent. Non-response is deemed as non-consent.

Mini-case questions

1. How would you advise the owner of the Mu Mu Café Bar about managing this shift of control to the consumer?
2. What restriction is the new Act likely to impose on identifying new customers and segmenting and targeting approaches?
3. How can organisations such as Mu Mu Café Bar recruit new customers?
4. What are the major strategic marketing communication decisions that need to be made?
5. Are these decisions any different from those which would be taken by other organisations?

References

Bird, D. (1989) *Commonsense Direct Marketing*, 2nd edn. London: Kogan Page.
Cook, R. (1997) The future of telemarketing. *Campaign*, 20 June, pp. 27–8.

Cravens, D.W., Ingram, T.N. and LaForge, R.W. (1991) Evaluating multiple channel strategies. *Journal of Business and Industrial Marketing*, **6**(3/4), pp. 37–48.

Day, J. (2000) Battle for mats and minds. *Marketing Week*, 14 September, pp. 42–3.

DMIS (1993) *Letterbox Fact File*. Bristol: Direct Mail Information Service.

DMIS (2000) *Letterbox Fact File*. Bristol: Direct Mail Information Service.

Eisenhart, T. (1990) Going the integrated route. *Business Marketing* (December), pp. 24–32.

Emerick, T. (1993) The multimedia mix. *Direct Marketing* (June), pp. 20–2.

Evans, M. (1998) From 1086 and 1984: direct marketing into the millennium. *Marketing Intelligence and Planning*, **16**(1), pp. 56–67.

Fletcher, K. (1997) External drive. *Marketing*, 30 October, pp. 39–42.

Fletcher, K.P. and Peters, L.D. (1997) Trust and direct marketing environments: a consumer perspective. *Journal of Marketing Management*, **13**, pp. 523–39.

Foster, S. (1996) Defining the direct brand. *Admap* (October), pp. 33–6.

Ganesan, S. (1994) Determinants of long-term orientation in buyer–seller relationships. *Journal of Marketing*, **58** (April), pp. 1–19.

Gardiner, P. and Quinton, S. (1998) Building brands using direct marketing – case study. *Marketing Intelligence and Planning*, **16**(1), pp. 6–11.

Goodwin, C. (1991) Privacy: recognition of a consumer right. *Journal of Public Policy & Marketing*, **10**(1), pp. 149–66.

Gray, R. (1999) Using the voice at the end of the line. *Marketing*, 16 September, pp. 29–30.

Gundach, G.T. and Murphy, P.E. (1993) Ethical and legal foundations of relational marketing exchanges. *Journal of Marketing*, **57** (October), pp. 93–4.

Kleinman, M. (2000) Baileys database task awarded to Craik Jones. *Marketing*, 24 August, p. 16.

LaForge, R.W., Cravens, D.W. and Young, C.E. (1985) Improving sales force productivity. *Business Horizons* (September/October), pp. 50–9.

Marsh, H. (2001) Dig deeper into the database goldmine. *Marketing*, 11 January, pp. 29–30.

McLuhan, R. (2000) How a complaint can offer insights. *Marketing*, 3 August, pp. 25–6.

Morgan, R.M. and Hunt, S.D. (1994) The commitment–trust theory of relationship marketing. *Journal of Marketing*, **58** (July), pp. 20–38.

Murphy, D. (2000) Call centres ponder price of technology. *Marketing*, 14 September, pp. 43–4.

Reed, D. (2000) Too much, too often. *Marketing Week*, 12 October, pp. 59–62.

Ridgeway, J. (2000) DirectWatch in 2000. *Marketing*, 21 December, pp. 24–5.

Roberts, M.L. and Berger, P.D. (1989) *Direct Marketing Management*. Englewood Cliffs, NJ: Prentice Hall.

29

Personal selling

This form of marketing communication involves a face-to-face dialogue between two persons or by one person and a group. Message flexibility is an important attribute, as is the immediate feedback that often flows from use of this promotional tool.

AIMS AND OBJECTIVES

The aims of this chapter are to examine personal selling as a promotional tool and to consider management's use of the sales force.

The objectives of this chapter are:

1. To consider the different types, roles and tasks of personal selling.
2. To determine the strengths and weaknesses of personal selling as a form of communication.
3. To explore the ways in which personal selling is thought to work.
4. To establish the means by which management can organise a sales force.
5. To compare some of the principal methods by which the optimum size of a sales force can be derived.
6. To introduce the concept of multiple sales channels.
7. To discuss the future role of the sales force.

Introduction

The traditional image of personal selling is one that embraces the hard sell, with a brash and persistent salesperson delivering a volley of unrelenting persuasive messages at a confused and reluctant consumer. Fortunately, this image is receding quickly as the professionalism and breadth of personal selling become more widely recognised and as the role of personal selling becomes even more important in the communications mix.

Personal selling activities can be observed at various stages in the buying process of both the consumer and business-to-business markets. This is because the potency of personal communications is very high, and messages can be adapted on the spot to meet the requirements of both parties. This flexibility, as we shall see later, enables objections to be overcome, information to be provided in the context of the buyer's environment and the conviction and power of demonstration to be brought to the buyer when the buyer requests it.

The potency of personal communications is very high, and messages can be adapted on the spot to meet the requirements of both parties.

Personal selling is different from other forms of communication in that the transmitted messages represent, mainly, dyadic communications. This means that there are two persons involved in the communication process. Feedback and evaluation of transmitted messages are possible, more or less instantaneously, so that these personal selling messages can be tailored and be made much more personal than any of the other methods of communication.

Using the spectrum of activities identified by the hierarchy of effects, we can see that personal selling is close enough to the prospective buyer to induce a change in behaviour. That is, it is close enough to overcome objections, to provide information quickly and to respond to the prospects' overall needs, all in the context of the transaction, and to encourage them directly to place orders.

Types of selling

One way of considering the types of personal selling is to examine the types of customer served through this communication process (Govoni *et al.*, 1986):

1. *Performance network*

This involves selling offerings onward through a particular channel network to other resellers. They in turn will sell the offering to other members who are closer to the end-user. For example, computer manufacturers have traditionally distributed their products through a combination of direct selling to key accounts and through a restricted number of dealers, or value-added resellers. These resellers then market the products (and bundle software) to their customers and potential customer organisations.

One way of considering the types of personal selling is to examine the types of customer served through this communication process.

2. *Industrial*

Here the main type of selling consists of business-to-business marketing and requires the selling of components and parts to others for assembly or incorporation within larger offerings. Goodman manufactures car radio systems and sells them to Ford, which then builds them into its cars as part of the final product offering.

3. *Professional*

This type of selling process requires ideas and offerings to be advanced to specifiers and influencers. They will in turn incorporate the offering within the project(s) they are developing. For example, a salesperson could approach an architect to persuade him or her to include the alarm system made by the salesperson's organisation within the plans for a building that the architect has been commissioned to design.

4. *Consumer*

This form of personal selling requires contact with the retail trade and/or the end-user consumer.

It will be apparent that a wide range of skills and resources is required for each of these types of selling. Selling to each of these types of customer requires different skills; as a result, salespersons usually focus their activities on one of these types.

The role of personal selling

The major questions that need to be addressed when preparing a communications plan are 'What will be the specific responsibilities of personal selling?' and 'What role will it have relative to the other elements of the mix?'

What role will it have relative to the other elements of the mix?

Personal selling is the most expensive element of the communications mix. The average cost per contact can easily exceed £100 when all markets and types of businesses are considered. It is generally agreed that personal selling is most effective at the later stages of the hierarchy of effects or buying process, rather than at the earlier stage of awareness building. Therefore, each organisation should determine the precise role the sales force is to play within the communication mix.

The role of personal selling is largely one of representation. In business-to-business markets sales personnel operate at the boundary of the organisation. They provide the link between the needs of their own organisation and the needs of their customers. This linkage is absolutely vital, for a number of reasons that will be discussed shortly, but without personal selling communication with other organisations would occur through electronic or print media and would foster discrete closed systems.

Many authors consider the development, organisation and completion of a sale in a market exchange-based transaction to be the key part of the role of personal selling.

The degree of expertise held by the salesperson may be high.

Sales personnel provide a source of information for buyers so that they can make the right purchase decisions. In that sense they provide a good level of credibility, but they are also perceived, understandably, as biased. The degree of expertise held by the salesperson may be high, but the degree of trustworthiness will vary, especially during the formative period of the relationship, unless other transactions with the selling organisation have been satisfactory. Once a number of transactions have been completed and product quality established, trustworthiness may improve.

As the costs associated with personal selling are high, it is vital that sales staff are used effectively. To that end, organisations are employing other methods to decrease the time that the sales force spends on administration, travel and office work and to maximise the time spent in front of customers, where they can use their specific selling skills.

The amount of control that can be exercised over the delivery of the messages through the sales force depends upon a number of factors. Essentially, the level of control must be regarded as low, because each salesperson has the freedom to adapt messages to meet changing circumstances as negotiations proceed. In practice, however, the professionalism and training that members of the sales force receive and the increasing accent on measuring levels of customer satisfaction mean that the degree of control over the message can be regarded, in most circumstances, as very good, although it can never, for example, be as high as that of advertising.

Message control – hay fever

It can be argued that members of the sales team must be free to adapt messages at the point of delivery because individual clients are themselves different and have different needs and requirements. Lloyd (1997) believes that, when selling to doctors, medical representatives enter into conversations that are appropriate for individual doctors.

An example concerns two products manufactured by Schering-Plough. They have two hay fever products (one nasal and the other an oral antihistamine), and sales representatives are expected to decide which to present (in detail) to doctors, based upon the representatives' knowledge and experience of each individual doctor's preferences and the needs of his or her patients.

This flexibility is framed within the context of the product strategy. Decisions that impact upon strategy are not allowed. There is freedom to adapt the manner in which products are presented, but there is no freedom for the sales representatives to decide the priority of the products to be detailed.

Strengths and weaknesses of personal selling

There are a number of strengths and weaknesses associated with personal selling. It is interesting to note that some of the strengths can in turn be seen as weaknesses, particularly when management control over the communication process is not as attentive or as rigorous as it might be.

Strengths

Dyadic communications allow for two-way interaction, which, unlike the other promotional tools, provides for fast, direct feedback. In comparison with the mass media, personal selling allows for the receiver to focus attention on the salesperson, with a reduced likelihood of distraction or noise.

Dyadic communications allow for two-way interaction.

There is a greater level of participation in the decision process by the vendor than in the other tools. When this is combined with the power to tailor messages in response to the feedback provided by the buyer, the sales process has a huge potential to solve customer problems.

Weaknesses

One of the major disadvantages of personal selling is the cost. Costs per contact are extremely high, and this means that management must find alternative means of communicating particular messages and improve the amount of time that sales personnel spend with prospects and customers. Reach and frequency through personal selling are always going to be low, regardless of the amount of funds available.

Costs per contact are extremely high, and this means that management must find alternative means of communicating particular messages.

Control over message delivery is very often low, and, while the flexibility is an advantage, there is also the disadvantage of message inconsistency. This in turn can lead to confusion (a misunderstanding perhaps with regard to a product specification), the ramifications of which can be enormous in terms of cost and time spent by a variety of individuals from both parties to the contract.

The quality of the relationship can, therefore, be jeopardised through poor and inconsistent communications.

When personal selling should be a major part of the promotional mix

In view of the role and the advantages and disadvantages of personal selling, when should it be a major part of the communications mix? The following is not an exhaustive list, but is presented as a means of considering some of the important issues: complexity, network factors, buyer significance and communication effectiveness.

Complexity

Personal selling is very important when there is a medium to high level of relationship complexity. Such complexity may be associated either with the physical characteristics of the product, such as computer software design, or with the environment in which the negotiations are taking place. For example, decisions related to the installation of products designed to automate an assembly line may well be a sensitive issue. This may be due to management's attitude towards the operators currently undertaking the work that the automation is expected to replace. Any complexity needs to be understood by buyer and seller in order that the right product is offered in the appropriate context for the buyer. This may mean that the buyer is required to customise the offering or provide assistance in terms of testing, installing or supporting the product.

Personal selling is very important when there is a medium to high level of relationship complexity.

When the complexity of the offering is high, advertising and public relations cannot always convey benefits in the same way as personal selling. Personal selling allows the product to be demonstrated so that buyers can see and, if necessary, touch and taste it for themselves. Personal selling also allows explanations to be made about particular points that are of concern to the buyer or about the environment in which the buyer wishes to use the product.

Buyer significance

The significance of the product to the buyers in the target market is a very important factor in the decision on whether to use personal selling. Significance can be measured as a form of risk, and risk is associated with benefits and costs.

The significance of the product to the buyers in the target market is a very important factor in the decision on whether to use personal selling.

The absolute cost to the buyer will vary from organisation to organisation and from consumer to consumer. The significance of the purchase of an extra photocopier for a major multinational organisation may be low, but for a new start-up organisation or for an established organisation experiencing a dramatic turnaround, an extra photocopying machine may be highly significant and subject to high levels of resistance by a number of different internal stakeholders.

The timing of a product's introduction may well be crucial to the success of a wider plan or programme of activities. Only through personal selling can delivery be dovetailed into the client's scheme of events.

Communication effectiveness

There may be a number of ways to satisfy the communication objectives of a campaign, other than by using personal selling. Each of the other communication tools has strengths and weaknesses; consequently differing mixes provide different benefits. Have they all been considered?

One of the main reasons for using personal selling occurs when advertising alone, or any other medium, provides insufficient communications. The main reason for this inadequacy surfaces when advertising media cannot provide buyers with the information they require to make their decision. For example, someone buying a new car may well observe and read various magazine and newspaper advertisements. The decision to buy, however, requires information and data upon which a rational decision can be made. This rationality and experience of the car, through a test drive perhaps, balances the former, more emotional, elements that contributed to the earlier decision.

The decision to buy a car normally evokes high involvement, and motivation occurs through the central route of the ELM. Therefore, car manufacturers provide a rich balance of emotional and factual information in their literature, from which the prospective buyer seeks further information, experience and reassurance from car dealers, who provide a personal point of contact. Car buyers sign orders with the presence and encouragement of sales persons. Very few cars are bought on a mail order basis, although some are bought over the Internet.

Personal selling provides a number of characteristics that make it more effective than the other elements of the mix. As discussed, in business-to-business marketing the complexity of many products requires salespeople to be able to discuss with clients their specific needs; in other words, to be able to talk in the customer's own language, to build source credibility through expertise and hopefully trustworthiness, and build a relationship that corresponds with the psychographic profile of each member of the DMU. In this case, mass communications would be inappropriate.

Personal selling provides a number of characteristics that make it more effective than the other elements of the mix.

There are two further factors that influence the decision to use personal selling as part of the communications mix. When the customer base is small and dispersed across a wide geographic area it makes economic sense to use salespersons, as advertising in this situation is inadequate and ineffective.

Personal selling is the most expensive element of the communication mix. It may be that other elements of the mix may provide a more cost-effective way of delivering the message.

Channel network factors

If the communication strategy combines a larger amount of push rather than pull activities, then personal selling is required to provide the necessary communications for the other members of the performance network. Following on from this is the question regarding what information needs to be exchanged between members and what form and timing the information should be in. Handling objections, answering questions and overcoming misconceptions are also necessary information exchange skills.

When the number of members in a network is limited, the use of a sales force is advisable, as advertising is inefficient. Furthermore, the opportunity to build a close collaborative relationship with members may enable the development of a sustainable competitive advantage. Cravens (1987) has suggested that the factors in Table 29.1 are important and determine when the sales force is an important element of the communications mix.

The roles of personal selling and the sales force are altering because the environment in which organisations operate is changing dramatically.

The roles of personal selling and the sales force are altering because the environment in which organisations operate is changing dramatically. The repercussions of these changes will become evident following the discussion of the tasks that personal selling is expected to complete.

Tasks of personal selling

The tasks of those who undertake personal selling positions vary from organisation to organisation and in accord with the type of selling activities on which they focus. It is

Table 29.1   When personal selling is a major element of the communications mix

	Advertising relatively important	Personal selling relatively important
Number of customers	Large	Small
Buyers' information needs	Low	High
Size and importance of purchase	Small	Large
Post-purchase service required	Little	A lot
Product complexity	Low	High
Distribution strategy	Pull	Push
Pricing policy	Set	Negotiate
Resources available for promotion	Many	Few

Source: Adapted from Cravens (1987).

normally assumed that they collect and bring into the organisation orders from customers wishing to purchase the offering. In this sense the order aspect of the personal selling tool can be seen as one of four order-related tasks:

1. *Order takers* are salespersons to whom customers are drawn at the place of supply. Reception clerks at hotels and ticket desk personnel at theatres and cinemas typify this role.

2. *Order getters* are sales personnel who operate away from the organisation and who attempt to gain orders largely through the use of demonstration and persuasion.

3. *Order collectors* are those who attempt to gather orders over the telephone. The growth of telesales operations was discussed earlier (Chapter 28), but the time saved by both the buyer and the seller using the telephone to gather repeat and low-value orders frees valuable sales personnel to seek new customers and build relationships with current customers.

4. *Order supporters* are all those people who are secondary salespersons in that they are involved with the order once it has been secured, or are involved with the act of ordering, usually by supplying information. Order processing or financial advice services typify this role.

However, this perspective of personal selling is narrow and fails to set out the broader range of activities that a sales force can be required to achieve. Salespersons do more than get or take orders. The organisation should decide which tasks it expects its representatives to undertake. The tasks listed in Table 29.2 provide direction and purpose, and also help to establish the criteria by which the performance of members of the personal selling unit can be evaluated.

The organisation should decide which tasks it expects its representatives to undertake.

One view of personal selling is that the sales force is responsible for selling, installing and upgrading customer equipment and another is they are responsible for developing, selling and protecting accounts. The interesting point from both these examples is that responsibilities, or rather objectives, are extended either vertically upstream, into offer design, or vertically downstream, into the development and maintenance of long-term customer relationships, or both. It is the last point that is becoming increas-

In the business-to-business sector the sales activity mix is becoming more orientated to the need to build and sustain the relationships.

Table 29.2 Tasks of personal selling

Prospecting	Finding new customers
Communicating	Inform various stakeholders and feed back information about the market
Selling	The art of leading a prospect to a successful close
Information gathering	Reporting information about the market and reporting on individual activities
Servicing	Consulting, arranging, counselling, fixing and solving a multitude of customer 'problems'
Allocating	Placing scarce products and resources at times of shortage
Shaping	Building and sustaining relationships with major customers

ingly important. In the business-to-business sector the sales activity mix is becoming more orientated to the need to build and sustain the relationships that organisations have with their major customers. This will be discussed later.

How personal selling works: sales processes

A number of conceptual schemes have been proposed to explain the various stages in the sale process. These can be distilled into nine main stages, set out in Figure 29.1. The alignment and rigidity of the sequence should not be overstated, as the actual activities undertaken within each of these stages will vary not only from organisation to organisation but also between salespeople.

This rather simple approach to the sales process fails to explain how a salesperson should approach a customer or why some negotiations are successful and others are not. There have been many attempts to explain how *There have been many attempts to explain* the personal selling process works. One of the first *how the personal selling process works.* methods proposed was discussed in Chapter 20 when exploring the hierarchy of effects models. The AIDA sequence put forward by Strong (1925) says that prospects must be drawn along a continuum of mental states, from attention to interest, desire and finally stimulation to act in accordance with the vendor's wishes. This approach allows for a good deal of

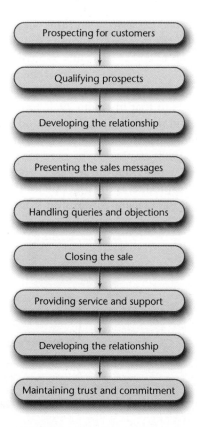

Figure 29.1   The main stages in the sales process.

flexibility in the salesperson's approach and permits movement around a central theme.

A further model, the stimulus–response model, suggests that if the salesperson can create the right set of circumstances then it is probable that the buyer will react in a particular way. Therefore, by controlling the circumstances of the sales process it is possible to induce the desired response. The salesperson is trained to deliver a particular stimulus (that is, what to say) and the buyer provides predictable responses, to which the salesperson has a number of expected responses. The sales presentation is therefore 'canned', ensuring that all aspects of the sale are covered in a logical order.

Jolson (1975) studied the results of such canned or prepared presentations with those that are personalised and determined more 'on the hoof'. His results indicated that buyers learned more through on-the-hoof presentations, but revealed that buyers had greater intentions to buy after the prepared presentation. This behavioural view is vendor led and discounts the cognitive processes of the buyer in its attempt to control the process and the differing needs of different buyers.

A third model focuses upon buyers and their needs. The role of the salesperson is to assist buyers to find solutions to their problems. According to Still *et al.* (1988), the salesperson needs to understand the cognitive processes of buyers in respect of their decision to buy or not to buy. This approach has been termed the 'buying formula' and is based upon the satisfactions that a buyer experiences when placing orders as a solution to perceived problems (from work based on Strong (1938)).

The sequence of the model, therefore, is that the buyer first recognises a problem or a need. A solution is then found, which is purchased and the buyer experiences a level of satisfaction. This formula can be seen in Figure 29.2. The solution contains two components, the product or service and the name of the organisation or the salesperson who facilitated the solution. When a buying habit is formed, the formula adjusts to that in Figure 29.3. To complete the formula, buyers must regard the product and the source as adequate and experience pleasant feelings when thinking of the components to the solution (Figure 29.4).

Buyers must regard the product and the source as adequate and experience pleasant feelings when thinking of the components to the solution.

Still *et al.* (1988) emphasise the need for salespersons to ensure that all the components of the buying habit are in place. For example, it is important that the buyer knows why the product is the best one for the identified problem and he or she must also have a pleasant feeling towards the source. This means that any competitor attack

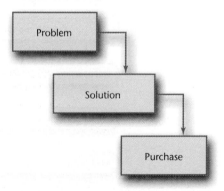

Figure 29.2 The mental stages involved in a purchase.

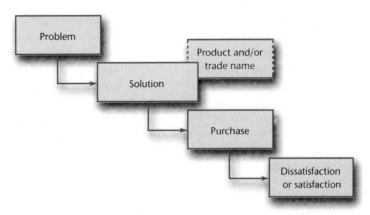

Figure 29.3   The buying formula. From Still *et al.* (1988); reproduced by kind permission of Prentice Hall Inc., Englewood Cliffs, NJ.

will be rebuffed because the current solution is deemed adequate. Reasons and pleasant feelings constitute the major elements of defence in a buying habit.

The essence of the buying formula approach is that a long-term relationship develops as a result of the satisfaction with the solutions offered by the salesperson.

While some people might reject this approach, the essence of the buying formula approach is that a long-term relationship develops as a result of the satisfaction with the solutions offered by the salesperson. If solutions are based upon knowledge and experience that the buyer can identify and empathise with, then the strength of the relationship is likely to be reinforced. It will come as no surprise that successful salespeople appear to hold high levels of interpersonal skills, are able to

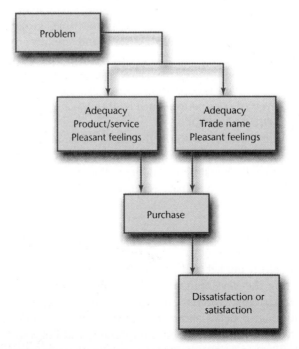

Figure 29.4   The complete buying formula. From Still *et al.* (1988); reproduced by kind permission of Prentice Hall Inc., Englewood Cliffs, NJ.

relate to customer problems, have solved similar problems and are experts at solving such problems (Rothschild, 1987).

A host of factors can influence the buying process, but one growing area of interest concerns the symbolic meaning of offerings and the communication aspects of products and services. This is referred to as semiotics, the science of signs and meaning. Through consumption, people communicate non-verbally who they are and the roles they are playing at a particular moment. Consumption allows people self-expression. This perspective is important to the salesperson, as the perception that buyers have of them can influence the sales process. Stuart and Fuller (1991) found that a buyer's initial perception of a salesperson, the products and the organisation he or she represents is strongly influenced by the clothing worn by the representative. Dress codes and uniforms, they conclude, can be used by an organisation to shape the desired customer perceptions of an organisation's size and ethics.

The way salespeople present themselves affects the perception of others and can influence the outcome of the sales process.

The implication is that marketing communications should not ignore issues about the dress code of an organisation, just as IBM always insisted that all its representatives wore a white shirt and plain tie, dark blue suit and black shoes. The way salespeople present themselves affects the perception of others and can influence the outcome of the sales process.

Communication apprehension refers to the degree to which an apprehension of communication will negatively affect a salesperson's performance. There appears to be a range of situations in which apprehension might be observed. McCroskey (1984) developed a framework depicting different apprehension levels. Essentially there are two main conditions. One is a condition which affects individuals in situations in which normal people would not consider threatening. The other is a state which refers to the normal apprehension felt by people when speaking in meetings, group situations, dyadic communications and public speaking situations. Generally speaking, it is not uncommon to find that above-average sales performance is achieved by individuals who have the lowest level of communication apprehension. Not surprisingly, those with low levels of sales performance tend to have high levels of communication apprehension (Pitt *et al.*, 2000).

Those with low levels of sales performance tend to have high levels of communication apprehension.

A further issue concerns the degree of ambiguity that both parties to a sales meeting might experience. Such ambiguity might refer to specific product-related information, failure to understand the problem that needs to be resolved, the time available to resolve it or the impact on other stakeholders related to the specific situation.

Sales force management and organisation

The target market and profile of the customer will have been established previously during the development of the communication plan. In particular, the communication strategy will have indicated the degree of push and pull to be used and will have illuminated detail about the nature of the channels in which the salesperson is to operate. Such information is important, as it helps to shape the sales strategy and the messages to be transmitted. Essentially, the salesperson acts as a link between a supplier and a customer, the primary role being to arrange matters so that the relationship can be continued and developed to the mutual benefit of both organisations and their participants.

In order to decide on an appropriate sales strategy, the nature of the desired communication needs to be examined. Are there to be salespersons negotiating with a single buyer or buying team? Is a sales team required in order to sell to buying teams or will conference and seminar selling achieve the desired goals? What is the degree of importance of the portfolio of accounts, and how should the organisations be contacted?

The answers to these questions and the range of issues associated with sales force management are so diverse that many of them are beyond the scope of this text. In particular, issues concerning the recruitment, selection, motivation and compensation of the sales force are not examined here. Attention is given to the way in which the sales force is organised and deployed, that is, where and in what numbers, in order that the organisation achieves its objectives. Attention is also given to the current trends in sales force management, to the new roles the sales force is expected to undertake in the new millennium and how different or multiple sales channels can improve the productivity of the sales department.

The primary and traditional sales channel is the field sales force. These are people who are recruited and trained to find prospective customers, to demonstrate or explain the organisation's products and services and to persuade prospects that they should buy the offering. Orders are then signed, and the salesperson reports the order to his or her organisation, which then fulfils the details of the customer's order, as agreed. However, while life is not this simple, this broad perspective is assumed to be the primary sales channel of many organisations, particularly those operating in the business-to-business sector.

Salespersons are like any other unit of resource in that they need to be deployed in a way that provides maximum benefit to the organisation.

Salespersons are like any other unit of resource in that they need to be deployed in a way that provides maximum benefit to the organisation. Grant and Cravens (1999) suggest that the effectiveness of the sales organisation (or unit) is determined as a result of two main antecedents: the sales manager and the sales force itself. These are shown in Figure 29.5.

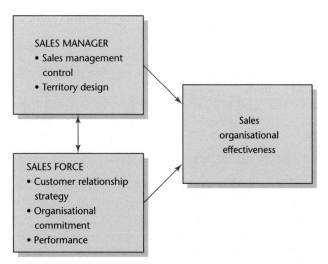

Figure 29.5 Antecedents of sales organisational effectiveness. From Grant and Cravens (1999); used with kind permission.

One of the first questions that needs to be addressed concerns the type of sales force to be used (assuming the decision has been made that some form of personal selling is required in the communications mix). Further questions are concerned with how many salespersons are required and where and how they should operate.

Decisions regarding the type, structure, size and territory of the sales force will be discussed on the basis that this is the only sales channel used by an organisation.

Sales force structure

There are a number of ways in which an organisation can structure the sales force, but there are three broad approaches (geographic, product and market/customer) which most organisations have used. The following examples are based upon Tgi PLC, which designs, manufactures and distributes loudspeaker products. These are purely examples of how it might organise its sales force and are not intended to represent the way in which Tgi approaches its markets.

Geographic-based sales force

The most common and straightforward method of organising a sales force is to assign individuals to separate geographic territories (Figure 29.6). In this type of sales force, the salesperson is responsible for all the activities necessary to sell all products to all potential customers in the region or area in which the territory is located. This method of assignment is used by new companies, in situations where customers tend to buy a range of products, where there is little difference in the geographic spread of the products or when resources are limited.

Strengths

This approach provides for the lowest cost, concentrates the selling effort throughout the territory and allows for a quick response to regional or local needs. This structure also ensures that customers only see one person from the selling organisation and are not at risk of becoming the recipient of multiple and conflicting messages.

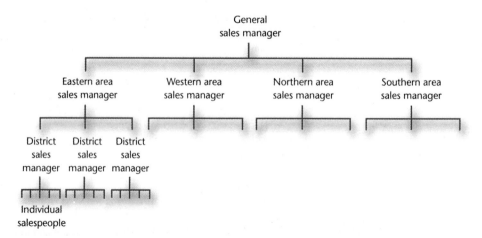

Figure 29.6 A geographically-based sales force structure.

Weaknesses

The level of specialised knowledge is reduced, as many products have to be promoted by each salesperson. Furthermore, salespeople under this structure tend to be allowed greater freedom in the design and execution of their working day. Consequently, the number of new customers is often low and the line of least resistance is usually pursued. This may also conflict with the objectives of the organisation, as, for example, call patterns may not be compatible with the overall goals of the sales force.

Call patterns may not be compatible with the overall goals of the sales force.

Product-based sales force

Under this type of structure, the organisation has different sales teams, each carrying a particular line of products (Figure 29.7). This is often used by organisations with large and diverse product lines. Also, organisations with highly technical and complex products, which require specialist knowledge and particular selling techniques, prefer this form of sales force structure.

Strengths

The most important advantage of this structural approach is that it allows the development of product knowledge and technical expertise. In business-to-business markets this factor can lead to improved source credibility, since the level of expertise,

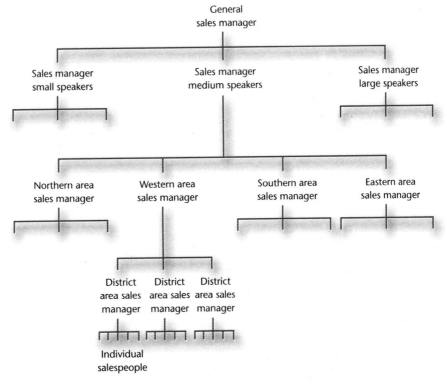

Figure 29.7   A product-based sales force structure.

and possibly trustworthiness, can be important if the messages are to be persuasive and effective. If the organisation's production facilities are organised by product (separate factories), each with a sales team operating out of the unit, then there can be increased cooperation, which in turn benefits the customer.

If greater focus is required upon a particular product, then more salespersons can be allocated appropriately.

Sales management is better able to control the allocation of the selling effort across all products under this type of structure. If greater focus is required upon a particular product, then more salespersons can be allocated appropriately.

Weaknesses

The major disadvantage is that there is a high probability that there will be duplication of sales effort. A customer could be called on by a number of different salespeople, all from the same organisation.

Selling expenses are driven higher and management time and costs rise as the company attempts to bring coordination.

Market-based sales force

Organising a sales force by market or customer type is an activity complementary to the marketing concept (Figure 29.8). This form of sales force organisation has increased in popularity, as it allows products with many applications to be sold into many different markets and hence to different customers.

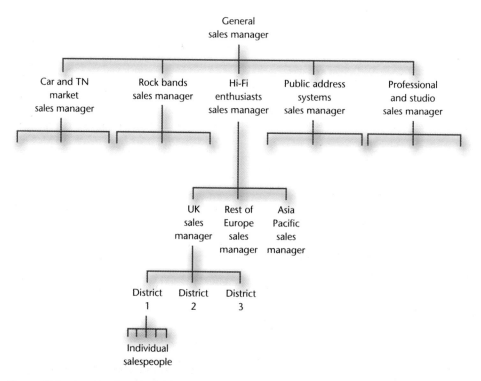

Figure 29.8   A market-based sales force structure.

Strengths

By calling on a single type of customer, a greater understanding of customer needs develops. Such customer specialisation can be used to foster specialist selling approaches for different markets. The size of the specialist sales forces can be varied by sales management in accordance with internal and external requirements. This is important for organisations operating in highly competitive and quickly changing environments.

Weaknesses

As with the product structure, duplication is a primary difficulty. The costs, however, of operating under this form of structure are higher than any of the others.

These three approaches to sales force design are not mutually exclusive, and most major organisations use a combination of them to meet the needs of their various stakeholders. As Still *et al.* (1988) state, the subdivision of the structure is usually related to primary and secondary needs for marketing success. Most organisations use geography as a subdivision, but whether this is a primary or secondary subdivision depends largely upon the importance of customer or product subdivisions for the achievement of competitive advantage. Such hybrid structures are not static and should evolve as the organisation and the environment in which it operates develop. Tgi uses the customer approach not only for the sales force but at an SBU level as well.

These three approaches to sales force design are not mutually exclusive, and most major organisations use a combination of them to meet the needs of their various stakeholders.

Sales force size and shape

The size of the sales force needs to be determined on a regular basis because the environments in which sales forces are operating are changing rapidly. The decision regarding the size of the sales force presents a dilemma. Increasing the size of the sales force will increase the sales revenue, but it will also increase costs. A balance needs to be achieved, and according to Govoni *et al.* (1986) the decision is a blend of the following factors: the number of potential customers, the sales potential of each of these accounts, the geographic concentration of the customers and the availability of financial resources.

There are many different approaches to the determination of the appropriate sales force size. Many of the more recent ones are based upon sophisticated software, but these are derived essentially from three main approaches: the *breakdown*, *workload* and *sales potential* methods.

The intuitive method is a label for all of the methods not based on reason, logic, market information or, in some cases, sense. At one extreme are the hunch and the 'I have been in this business for *x* years' approach, while at the other extreme there is the 'if it is good enough for the competition, then it is good enough for us' approach. These are to be rejected.

The breakdown method

This is the simplest method. Each salesperson is viewed as possessing the same sales productivity potential per period. Therefore, divide the total expected sales by the sales potential and the resultant figure equates to the number of salespeople required:

$$n = \frac{sv}{sp}$$

where n is the number of salespeople required, sv is the anticipated sales volume and sp is the estimated sales productivity of each salesperson/unit.

This technique is flawed in that it treats sales force size as a consequence of sales, yet the reverse is probably true. A further difficulty concerns the estimate of productivity used. It fails to account for different potentials, abilities and levels of compensation. Furthermore, there is no account of profitability as it treats sales as an end in itself.

This technique is flawed in that it treats sales force size as a consequence of sales, yet the reverse is probably true.

The workload method

Underlying this method is the premise that all salespeople should bear an equal amount of the work necessary to service the entire market. The example offered is based upon work by Govoni *et al.* (1986).

The first task is to classify customers into categories based on the level of sales to each account. The ABC rule of account classification holds that the first 15% of customers account for 65% of sales (A accounts), the next 20% will produce 20% of sales (B accounts) and the final 65% will yield only 15% (C accounts).

■ *Task 1*. Classify customers into categories:

Class A: large/very attractive	= 300
Class B: medium/moderately attractive	= 400
Class C: small/unattractive	= 1,300

■ *Task 2*. Determine the frequency and desired duration of each call for each type of account:

Class A: 15 times/pa 95 mins/call	= 23.75 hours
Class B: 10 times/pa 63 mins/call	= 10.50 hours
Class C: 6 times/pa 45 mins/call	= 4.50 hours

■ *Task 3*. Calculate the workload in covering the market:

Class A: 300 accounts 23.75 hours/account	= 7,125 hours
Class B: 400 accounts 10.50 hours/account	= 4,200 hours
Class C: 1,300 accounts 4.50 hours/account	= 5,850 hours
Total workload	= 17,175 hours

■ *Task 4*: Determine the time available per salesperson:

40 hours/week × 46 weeks/pa	= 1,840 hours

■ *Task 5*. Determine selling/contact time per salesperson:

Contact: 45%	= 828 hours
Travelling: 31%	= 570 hours
Non-selling: 24%	= 442 hours

■ *Task 6*. Calculate the number of salespersons required:

$$\text{number of salespersons} = \frac{\text{total work load}}{\text{contact hours}} \frac{17,175}{828} = 20.74$$

A total of 20 or 21 salespeople would be required using this method. While this technique is easy to calculate, it does not allow for differences in sales response among accounts that receive the same sales effort. It fails to account for servicing and assumes that all salespersons have the same contact time. This is simply not true. One further shortcoming is that the profitability per call is neglected.

The sales potential method

Semlow (1959) was one of the earliest to report the decreasing-returns principle when applied to sales force calculations. The principle recognises that there will be diminishing returns as extra salespeople are added to the sales force. For example, one extra salesperson may generate £120,000, but two more may only generate a total of £200,000 in new sales. Therefore, while the first generates £120,000, the other two only generate £100,000 each.

There will be diminishing returns as extra salespeople are added to the sales force.

Semlow found, for example, that sales in territories with 1% potential generated £160,000, whereas sales in territories with 5% averaged £200,000. Therefore 1% potential in the second territory equates to £40,000 (200,000/5) and £160,000 (160,000/1) in the first.

The conclusion reached was that a higher proportion of sales per 1% of potential could be realised if the territories were made smaller by adding salespeople. As asked above, what is the optimum number of salespersons, because costs rise as more salespeople are added?

Semlow's work provides the basis for some of the more sophisticated techniques and derivatives of the incremental or marginal approach. It is relatively simple in concept but exceedingly difficult to implement. The conclusion, that a salesperson in a low-potential territory is expected to achieve a greater proportion of the potential than a colleague in a high-potential territory is, as Churchill *et al.* (1990) say, 'intuitively appealing'.

Territory design

Having determined the number of salespeople that are necessary to achieve the set promotion objectives, attention must be given to the shape, potential and equality of the territories to be created. The decomposition of the total market into smaller units facilitates easier control of the sales strategy and operations. A sales territory is a grouping of customers and prospects assigned to an individual or team of salespeople. The reason for the establishment of sales territories is mainly orientated to aspects of planning and control. Sales territories enable the organisation to cover the designated market, to control costs, to assist the evaluation of salesperson performance, to contribute to sales force morale and to provide a bridge with other promotional activities, most notably advertising (Still *et al.*, 1988).

Attention must be given to the shape, potential and equality of the territories to be created.

Churchill *et al.* (1990) suggest that the steps depicted in Figure 29.9 are the most appropriate. The objective is to make all territories as equal as possible with respect to, firstly, sales potential, as this facilitates performance evaluation, and, secondly, work effort, as this tends to improve morale and reduce levels of conflict.

The most basic unit is a small geographic area. Small units permit easier adjustments to be made and allow for the reassignment of accounts from one salesperson to

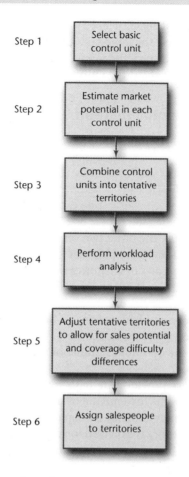

Step 1 — Select basic control unit

Step 2 — Estimate market potential in each control unit

Step 3 — Combine control units into tentative territories

Step 4 — Perform workload analysis

Step 5 — Adjust tentative territories to allow for sales potential and coverage difficulty differences

Step 6 — Assign salespeople to territories

Figure 29.9   Key steps in territory design. From Churchill *et al.* (1990); used with kind permission.

another. Units can be based on counties, local authority areas, postcodes (important in Greater London and other metropolitan areas), cities and regions.

Once the market potential in each unit has been established, approximate territories can be set up. From this point account analysis helps to determine the call frequency and duration necessary for the larger accounts. A matrix approach, based upon the attractiveness of the account and the ability of the organisation to exploit the opportunities presented, can help this part of the management process, as in Figure 29.10. The penultimate step is to make adjustments to the boundaries of the tentative territories established earlier. These adjustments are designed to equalise potential and workload in each area.

Once the market potential in each unit has been established, approximate territories can be set up.

It should be remembered that sales potential is never static, at the market, the territory or the account level. In particular, potential will vary with call frequency. It will be apparent that there is a relationship between account attractiveness (AA) and account effort (AE). While AA determines how hard the account should be worked, the frequency and duration will affect the sales derived from each account. There is a need to balance potentials and workloads if computer programs, such as Callplan, are not being used.

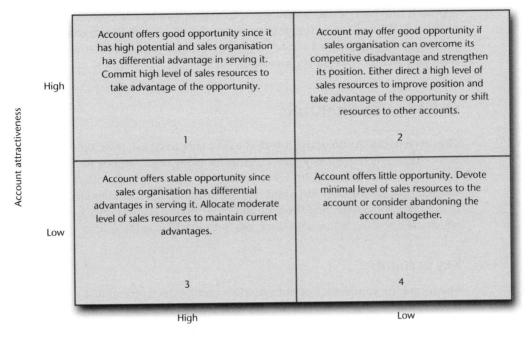

| | Account offers good opportunity since it has high potential and sales organisation has differential advantage in serving it. Commit high level of sales resources to take advantage of the opportunity. | Account may offer good opportunity if sales organisation can overcome its competitive disadvantage and strengthen its position. Either direct a high level of sales resources to improve position and take advantage of the opportunity or shift resources to other accounts. |

Account attractiveness

High

1

2

Account offers stable opportunity since sales organisation has differential advantages in serving it. Allocate moderate level of sales resources to maintain current advantages.

Account offers little opportunity. Devote minimal level of sales resources to the account or consider abandoning the account altogether.

Low

3

4

High   Low

Sales organisation competitive strength

Figure 29.10   Account planning matrix. From Churchill *et al.* (1990); used with kind permission.

There are several methods available. Empirically based methods use regression analysis to represent the relationship between sales and a number of key sales variables such as the number of calls, potential or workload. Judgement-based methods require the salesperson to estimate the sales/sales call ratio so that the optimum number of calls can be made on each account. The subjectively based method involves executives making changes in call frequency to reflect changes in the market or to achieve a specific objective.

The final task is to assign salespeople to territories. It should be remembered that salespeople have varying levels of ability. To overcome this disparity, the most able is allocated an index of 1.00 and all others rated relative to that individual. For example, an index of 0.75 means that a salesperson could achieve 75% of the business that a salesperson with an index of 1.0 could achieve in the same territory. Salespeople can then be allocated on a basis that maximises the return to the organisation.

It should be remembered that salespeople have varying levels of ability.

Grant and Cravens (1999) found that the effectiveness of a sales organisation is partly determined by the design of sales territories. For sales organisations that place high value on directing, evaluating, rewarding and monitoring, territory design and sales force commitment appear to be linked to sales unit effectiveness. From their research they state that territory design plays a 'pivotal role in sales unit effectiveness'. Decisions regarding the size, shape and form of the sales force need to made once a strategic decision has been made to employ a sales force. An alternative

An alternative approach is to hire or rent a sales force, by region, product or time, to suit the needs of the task at hand. These temporary sales forces are recruited from companies in the field marketing sector.

approach is to hire or rent a sales force, by region, product or time, to suit the needs of the task at hand. These temporary sales forces are recruited from companies in the field marketing sector. This sector has grown in significance and stature over the past few years, and more detail is provided in Chapter 30.

Other sales channels

The previous discussion of the role of the field sales force was pre-empted by the statement that this is the primary sales channel for many organisations in the business-to-business sector. There are, however, a growing number of organisations that see a different role for the sales force and that are introducing other sales channels in order to improve productivity and the bottom line. These are key accounts and team selling, which are discussed below, and direct marketing, which is the subject of Chapter 28.

Key accounts

The increasing complexity of both markets and products, combined with the trends towards purchasing centralisation and industrial concentration, means that a small number of major accounts have become essential for the survival of many organisations. The Pareto rule is often paramount: that 80% of sales are generated by just 20% of an organisation's customers. The growth in the significance of key account management is expected to continue and one of the results of this growth will be the change in expectations of buyers and sellers, in particular the demand for higher levels of expertise and integration and professionalism of sales forces.

The growth in the significance of key account management is expected to continue.

Who in the organisation should be responsible for these key accounts? Generally there are three main responses: to assign sales executives, to create a key account division or to create a key account sales force.

Assigning sales executives

This is common in smaller organisations who do not have the resources that are available to larger organisations. Normally senior executives would assume this role, and with it they bring the flexibility and responsive service that are required. They can make decisions about stock, price, distribution and levels of customisation.

There is a tendency for key accounts to receive a disproportionate level of attention, as the executives responsible for these major customers lose sight of their own organisation's marketing strategy.

Creating a key account division

The main advantage of this approach is that it offers close integration of production, finance, marketing and sales. The main disadvantage is that resources are duplicated and the organisation can become very inefficient. It is also a high-risk strategy, as the entire division is dependent upon a few customers.

Creating a key account sales force

Key account management allows sales executives to build a strong relationship with their customers and so provide a very high level of service. In mature and competitive

Key account management allows sales executives to build a strong relationship with their customers and so provide a very high level of service.

markets where there is little differentiation between the products, service may be the source of sustainable competitive advantage. The organisation is able to select its most experienced and able salespersons and so provide a career channel for those executives who prefer to stay in sales rather than move into management.

Administratively, this structure is inefficient as there is a level of duplication similar to that found in the customer-type structure discussed earlier. Furthermore, commission payable on these accounts is often a source of discontent, both for those within the key account sales force and those aspiring to join the select group. Issues concerning the management of key accounts are discussed in Chapter 15.

Team selling

It is becoming increasingly common for organisations to assign a team of salespeople to meet the needs of key account customers. A variety of different skills are thought necessary to meet the diversity of personnel making up the DMUs of the larger organisations. Consequently, a salesperson may gain access to an organisation, after which a stream of engineers, analysts, technicians, programmers, training executives and financial experts follow.

For example, when one of Goodman's (a division of Tgi discussed earlier) car-manufacturing clients plans a new model, a salesperson opens the door to provide a communication link between the two organisations. Soon, a project team evolves, consisting of engineering, manufacturing, purchasing, production and quality staff, all working to satisfy the needs of their client. Goodman even uses the same project code number as the client to provide for clarity and avoidance of confusion. It also helps to build the relationship and identification between the partners.

It also helps to build the relationship and identification between the partners.

Most leading IT-based organisations used to sell the hardware and then leave the customer to work out how to use it. Team selling is now used by Digital, Hewlett-Packard, IBM and others to provide customised combinations of hardware, software and technical support as solutions to their customer's business problems. This requires teams of salespeople and technical experts working closely with the customer's DMU throughout the sales/purchasing cycle and beyond (Hyatt Hills, 1992).

The sales team approach requires high levels of coordination and internal communication if it is to be successful and sell across product lines from various locations (Cespedes *et al.*, 1989). The costs associated with cross-functional team selling are large, which is one of the reasons this approach is restricted to key accounts.

The future role of the sales force

The performance networks of many markets are in transition; this in turn affects the structure and strategy of network members and has stimulated recognition that organisations should seek cooperative relationships (Jarillo, 1993) rather than be competitive in the manner which Porter (1985) and the Design School advocate.

Transition has also been brought about because of changing customer needs, the buoyancy of the European economy in the mid-1980s and its subsequent recession, and the shifting balance of key stakeholders. The expectations of organisational buyers and consumers have shifted so that new skills are required of a salesperson. Internally, organisations have moved their focus. For example, the manner in which performance is measured and resources are deployed has moved from a sales to a profit basis, while the sharp rise in costs of personal selling has required organisations to seek new ways of reaching and communicating with customers.

The manner in which performance is measured and resources are deployed has moved from a sales to a profit basis.

In consideration of the multiple sales channel approach and the factors that have brought significant change to the way in which field sales forces are organised, it is not surprising that the roles salespeople are expected to undertake are changing. Some of these roles are set out in Figure 29.11.

When these factors are brought together, the salesperson, who was seen earlier as working at the boundary of the organisation to generate sales, is now expected to act as a network coordinator and as a manager of customers (Wilson, 1993). In Chapter 15 it is identified that a collaborative communication strategy seeks to establish long-term relational transactions. The short-term market exchange perspective hinders the development of strategic advantage. Strong personal interaction with clients, based upon a problem–solution perspective to buyer needs, can provide a source of sustainable competitive advantage for organisations.

Integrating and coordinating the efforts of both the buying and the selling teams

Figure 29.11   New roles for the sales force. Adapted from Wilson (1993) and Anderson and Rosenbloom (1982).

will become an important role for the salesperson, particularly as the effects of concentration lead to even greater levels of centralisation of the buying function.

The integration of personal selling with the other elements of the promotional mix

Personal selling cannot work effectively in isolation from the other elements in the promotional mix. For example, members of the sales force are literally representative of the organisation for whom they work: they are mobile PR representatives. Stakeholders perceive them and partly shape their image of the selling organisation on the way in which, for example, the salesperson dresses, speaks and handles questions, the type of car driven and the level of courtesy displayed to the support staff.

The integration and compatibility of direct marketing with the sales force have been discussed and the degree of impact should not be underestimated. The sales force's role within sales promotions can be strong, especially with activities directed at members of the performance network. Members of the sales force are often used to distribute promotional merchandise to both consumers and the trade.

Advertising is more effective at the initial stages of the response hierarchy, but the later stages of inducing trial and closing for the order are more appropriate for personal selling.

It is with advertising that the strongest degree of integration with personal selling can be observed. As determined earlier, it would appear that these two elements of the communications mix complement each other in many ways. Advertising is more effective at the initial stages of the response hierarchy, but the later stages of inducing trial and closing for the order are more appropriate for personal selling.

Rothschild (1987) has reported Levitt's (1967) work which indicated that organisations that invest in advertising to create awareness are more likely to create a more favourable reception for their salespeople than those organisations which do not invest in awareness-building activities. However, those that had invested were also expected to have a better-trained sales force.

Morrill (1970) found that selling costs were as much as 28% lower if the customer had been made aware of the salesperson's organisation prior to the call. Swinyard and Ray (1977) determined that even if a sale was not made for reasons other than product quality then further use of advertising increased the probability of a future sale.

All these findings suggest that, by combining advertising with personal selling, costs will be reduced, reach extended and the probability of a sale considerably improved.

Summary

The role of personal selling in the promotional mix is changing. As organisations move to more relational exchanges, so the sales force will need to play a complementary role. This role will necessitate the execution of tasks such as managing customers and integrating the activities of the performance network.

The sales force will need to be deployed in a way that optimises the resources of the organisation and realises the greatest possible percentage of the available sales and profit potential that exists in the defined area of operation. This will result in a continuance of the growth of key accounts.

The use of the field sales force as the only means of personal selling is unlikely to remain. Technological advances and the need for increasing levels of promotional effectiveness and accountability, together with tighter cost constraints, indicate that the more progressive organisations will employ multiple sales channels. This may mean the use of telemarketing and direct mail to free the sales force from non-selling activities, which will allow management to focus the time of the sales force upon getting in front of customers and prospects, with a view to using their particular selling skills.

Review questions

1. What are the different types of personal selling?
2. Describe the role of personal selling and highlight its main strengths and weaknesses.
3. Which factors need to be considered when determining the significance of personal selling in the promotional mix?
4. What are the tasks that salespersons are normally expected to accomplish?
5. Describe two ways in which the personal selling process is thought to work.
6. Write a brief report highlighting the strengths and weaknesses of each of the main ways of structuring the sales force.
7. Identify the principal differences between the workload and the sales potential methods of determining sales force size.
8. Write brief notes outlining the way in which direct marketing might be used to assist personal selling activities.
9. Suggest four new roles that salespersons might be required to adopt in the future.
10. If an organisation seeks to establish relational exchanges with its partner organisations and customers, the size of the field sales force should be increased. Discuss.

MINI CASE

This mini case was written by Alan Moore of the Regent Business School, London.

Strategic deployment of the sales force at Hifzer

The sales director of the newly merged pharmaceutical company, Hifzer, was considering the role of the sales force in the new organisation. The view was quickly formed that there were target groups for whom the sales force could play a major role. These were general practitioners (GPs), hospital doctors, pharmacists and vets.

Many calls to GPs are made after the first surgery of the morning and the task is to introduce new products, to remind GPs of the portfolio of products which they might not be using or to discuss the role of some promotional activity. For example, Hifzer might offer the services of a nurse to attend the surgery once a week for three months to advise patients with a particular condition or need for a specific treatment.

Pharmacists could be fitted into the daily call pattern before or after visits to GPs but the task was to sell ethical drugs that needed a doctor's prescription before they could be 'sold' and over-the-counter (OTC) drugs. These OTC medicines do not require a doctor's prescription and can be supported by press and trade advertising. Hifzer had also acquired, through the merger activity, a range of food and beauty products that could also be sold through independent chemists.

The final segment of the business concerned the distribution of animal-related products. From a sales perspective, it was necessary to inform and remind vets of the company's veterinary product range. It had been a key part of the previous organisation's operations that this activity was managed separately from human medical products even though the actual products were similar to human treatments.

The sales director concluded that a number of different sales teams were required. One could be described as a consumer retailer team, selling to large multiple-outlet retailers. Another team was needed to sell specialised animal treatments to a customer base which did not have any really large customers but which had very sophisticated knowledgeable buyers. Another team specialising in ethical drug communications for a highly dispersed and knowledgeable base of buyers was also identified.

A few calculations showed that a lot of money was required to operate these teams of people and that the newly merged company had almost a complete duplication of two of these teams. Additionally, the sales director's previous company had developed schemes of communication which allowed individual members of sales staff to check, before each day's visit, the current position of each visited customer. Information on products delivered and on order, as well as a clear statement of any monies owed by the customer, was available. The data were rather less reliable where the customers received supplies from a wholesaler.

The next development was to make available information on products through a secure network of computer links. The worry for the sales director was about how likely busy people such as doctors, pharmacists and vets were to use such information. Could the provision of a Web site replace the information currently delivered through sales visits?

Pharmacists were used to placing orders through computer terminals to wholesalers but the facilities for receiving emails or longer text and diagram messages are uncommon in pharmacies.

Mini-case questions

1. What are the main factors that might shape the structure of the sales force at Hifzer?
2. Recommend a type of sales force structure that might best achieve Hifzer's objectives.
3. What are the different roles that each sales team will need to carry out?
4. Make recommendations concerning how Hifzer might best use technology. How might this vary across different markets?

References

Anderson, R.E. and Rosenbloom, B. (1982) Eclectic sales management: strategic responses to trends in the 1980s. *Journal of Personal Selling and Sales Management* (November), pp. 41–6.

Cespedes, F.V., Doyle, S.X. and Freedman, R.J. (1989) Teamwork for today's selling. *Harvard Business Review* (March/April), pp. 44–55.

Churchill, G.A., Ford, N.M. and Walker, C. (1990) *Sales Force Management*. Homewood, IL: Richard D. Irwin.

Cravens, D.W. (1987) *Strategic Marketing*. Homewood, IL: Richard D. Irwin.

Govoni, N., Eng, R. and Galper, M. (1986) *Promotional Management*. Englewood Cliffs, NJ: Prentice Hall.

Grant, K. and Cravens, D.W. (1999) Examining the antecedents of sales organisation effectiveness: an Australian study. *European Journal of Marketing*, **33**(9/10), pp. 945–57.

Hyatt Hills, C. (1992) Making the team. *Sales and Marketing Management* (February), pp. 54–7.

Jarillo, J.C. (1993) *Strategic Networks: Creating the Borderless Organisation*. Oxford: Butterworth-Heinemann.

Jolson, M.A. (1975) The underestimated potential of the canned sales presentation. *Journal of Marketing*, **39** (January), p. 75.

Levitt, T. (1967) Communications and industrial selling. *Journal of Marketing*, **31** (April), pp. 15–21.

Lloyd, J. (1997) Cut your rep free. *Pharmaceutical Marketing* (September), pp. 30–2.

McCroskey, J.C. (1984) The communication apprehension perspective. In *Avoiding Communication* (ed. J.A. Daley), pp. 13–38. Beverly Hills, CA: Sage.

Morrill, J.E. (1970) Industrial advertising pays off. *Harvard Business Review* (March/April), pp. 159–69.

Pitt, L.F., Berthon, P.R. and Robson, M.J. (2000) Communication apprehension and perceptions of salesperson performance: a multinational perspective. *Journal of Managerial Psychology*, **15**(1), pp. 68–97.

Porter, M. (1985) *Competitive Advantage*. New York: Free Press.

Rothschild, M.L. (1987) *Marketing Communications*. Lexington, MA: D.C. Heath.

Semlow, W.E. (1959) How many salesmen do you need? *Harvard Business Review* (May/June), pp. 126–32.

Still, R., Cundiff, E.W. and Govoni, N.A.P. (1988) *Sales Management*, 5th edn. Englewood Cliffs, NJ: Prentice Hall.

Strong, E.K. (1925) *The Psychology of Selling*. New York: McGraw-Hill.

Strong, E.K. (1938) *Psychological Aspects of Business*. New York: McGraw-Hill.

Stuart, E.W. and Fuller, B.K. (1991) Clothing as communication in two business-to-business sales settings. *Journal of Business Research*, **23**, pp. 269–90.

Swinyard, W.R. and Ray, M.L. (1977) Advertising–selling interactions: an attribution theory experiment. *Journal of Marketing Research*, **14** (November), pp. 509–16.

Wilson, K. (1993) Managing the industrial sales force of the 1990s. *Journal of Marketing Management*, **9**, pp. 123–39.

chapter **30**

Exhibitions, packaging and field marketing

The five major tools of the communications mix need supplementary activity for a message to be heard. Exhibitions are a significant part of b2b promotional work, packaging is vital to the fast-moving consumer goods sector as the majority of product decisions are made at the point of purchase while merchandising and supplementary activities are necessary to cut through the clutter of both b2bc and b2b messages.

▨ AIMS AND OBJECTIVES

The aims of this chapter are to consider a range of marketing communications activities which have no specific designation yet which can make a major contribution to a promotional campaign. These activities are applied to both the b2b and b2c markets.

The objectives of this chapter are:

1. To bring to attention the significance of exhibitions and trade shows.
2. To highlight the main advantages and disadvantages of using exhibitions as part of the promotional mix.
3. To understand the impact and characteristics of in-store promotional activities.
4. To explain the role and contribution of packaging.
5. To explore the range of ways in which packaging can contribute to marketing communications.
6. To consider the concept and role of product placement.
7. To introduce field marketing and explain the range of activities that it includes.

Introduction

The majority of marketing communications presented so far focus on the five primary tools. However, in order to provide a difference and to cut through the noise of competing brands it is necessary to provide additional resources and communications right up to the point that customers make decisions. Exhibitions fulfil a role for customers by enabling them to become familiar with new developments, new products and leading-edge brands.

Exhibitions fulfil a role for customers by enabling them to become familiar with new developments, new products and leading-edge brands.

Very often they will be opinion leaders and use word-of-mouth communications to convey their feelings and product experiences to others. In the b2b market exhibitions and trade shows are very often an integral and important component in the communications mix. Meeting friends, customers, suppliers, competitors and prospective customers is an important sociological and ritualistic event in the communication calendar for many companies.

In the consumer sector, and in particular the fast-moving consumer goods (FMCG) market, the need to provide a point of difference and to provide continuity for those people who make the brand choice decisions at the point of purchase is important. Packaging not only fulfils a role of protecting a product but also conveys associations and brand cues. Product placement enables a brand to be observed in a more natural environment than that achieved on a shelf. This part of marketing communications is growing and provides income for film producers, authenticity for brand managers and relief from advertising for consumers.

Finally, this chapter also considers the impact of field marketing and the needs of both b2c and b2b brands to be flexible and adaptive to changing market conditions and reducing internal resources.

Trade shows and exhibitions

The idea of many suppliers joining together at a particular location in order to set out their products and services so that customers may meet, make comparisons and place orders is far from new. Indeed, not only does this form of promotional activity stretch back many centuries, it has also been used to explain the way the Internet works (Bertheron *et al.*, 1996). They refer to the Internet as a virtual flea circus, a forum where buyers and sellers can meet, browse, discuss, find out more information and buy products and services if appropriate.

At a basic level, trade fairs can be orientated for industrial users or consumers and the content or purpose might be to consider general or specialised product/markets. According to Boukersi (2000), consumer-orientated general fairs tend to be larger and last longer than the more specialised industrial fairs and it is clear that this more highly segmented and focused approach is proving more successful, based upon the increasing number of these types of exhibitions.

Trade fairs can be orientated for industrial users or consumers and the content or purpose might be to consider general or specialised product/markets.

There are many reasons for their use, but the primary reasons appear not to be 'to make sales' or 'because the competition is there' but because these events provide opportunities to meet potential and established customers and to create and sustain a series of relational exchanges. The main aim, therefore, is to develop long-term partnerships with customers, to build upon or develop the corporate identity and to gather up-to-date market intelligence (Shipley and Wong, 1993). This implies that exhibitions should not be used as isolated events, but that they should be integrated into a series of activities. These activities serve to develop and sustain buyer relationships.

The main aim, therefore, is to develop long-term partnerships with customers, to build upon or develop the corporate identity and to gather up-to-date market intelligence.

After a tentative start to the 1990s, the exhibition industry is now experiencing real growth and with managers increasingly accountable for their promotional spend so a greater number of budgets was channelled into exhibitions and related events. In 1996 visitors attended 710 exhibitions in the UK and by 2000 the number had risen to 817 (exhibition venues over 2,000 square feet).

Costs can be further reduced by using private exhibitions, where the increased flexibility allows organisations to produce mini or private exhibitions for their clients at local venues (e.g. hotels). This can mean lower costs for the exhibitor and reduced time away from their businesses for those attending. The communication 'noise' and distraction associated with the larger public events can also be avoided by these private showings.

Characteristics

The main reasons for attending exhibitions and trade fairs are that it enables organisations to meet customers (potential) in an agreeable environment, one where both have independently volunteered their time to attend, to place/take orders, to generate leads and gather market information. The reasons for attending exhibitions are set out in Table 30.1.

From this it is possible to distinguish the following strengths and weaknesses of using exhibitions as part of the marketing communications programme.

■ *Strengths*

The costs associated with exhibitions, if controlled properly, can mean that this is an effective and efficient means of communicating with customers. The costs per enquiry need to be calculated, but care needs to be taken over who is classified as an enquirer, as the quality of the audience varies considerably. Costs per order taken are usually the prime means of evaluating the success of an exhibition. This can paint a false picture, as the true success can never really be determined in terms of orders because of the variety of other factors that impinge upon the placement and timing of orders.

Table 30.1 Reasons exhibitors chose to attend exhibitions

To meet existing customers
To take orders/make sales
To get leads and meet prospective new customers
To meet lapsed customers
To meet prospective members of the existing or new marketing channels
To provide market research opportunities and to collect marketing data

Products can be launched at exhibitions, and when integrated with a good PR campaign a powerful impact can be made. This can also be used to reinforce corporate identity.

Exhibitions are an important means of gaining information about competitors, buyers and technical and political developments in the market, and they often serve to facilitate the recruitment process. Above all else, exhibitions provide an opportunity to meet customers on relatively neutral ground and, through personal interaction, develop relationships. Products can be demonstrated, prices agreed, technical problems discussed and trust and credibility enhanced.

Exhibitions are an important means of gaining information about competitors, buyers and technical and political developments in the market.

■ *Weaknesses*

One of the main drawbacks associated with exhibition work is the vast and disproportionate amount of management time that can be tied up with the planning and implementation of exhibitions. However, good planning is essential if the full potential benefits of exhibition work are to be realised.

Taking members of the sales force 'off the road' can also incur large costs. Depending upon the nature of the business these opportunity costs can soar. Some pharmaceutical organisations estimate that it can cost approximately £5,000 per person per week to divert salespeople in this way.

The expected visitor profile must be analysed in order that the number of quality buyers visiting an exhibition can be determined. The variety of visitors attending an exhibition can be misleading, as the vast majority may not be serious buyers or indeed may not be directly related to the industry or the market in question.

Exhibitions as a form of marketing communications

As a form of marketing communications exhibitions enable products to be promoted, build brands and they can be an effective means of demonstrating products and building industry-wide credibility in a relatively short period of time. Attendance at exhibitions may also be regarded from a political dimension in that non-attendance may be seen as an opportunity by attendees to suggest weaknesses.

Attendance at exhibitions may also be regarded from a political dimension in that non-attendance may be seen as an opportunity by attendees to suggest weaknesses.

In the b2b sector new products and services are often introduced at exhibitions, especially if there are to be public relations activities and events that can be spun off the launch. In other words, exhibitions are not activities independent of the other parts of the promotional tools. Exhibitions, if used effectively, can be part of an integrated communications campaign. Advertising prior to, during and after a trade show can be dovetailed with public relations, sponsorship and personal selling. Sales promotions can also be incorporated through competitions among customers prior to the show to raise awareness, generate interest and to suggest customer involvement. Competitions during a show can be focused on the sales force to motivate and stimulate commercial activity and among visitors to generate interest in the stand, raise brand name attention and encourage focus upon particular products (new, revised or revolutionary) and generate sales leads and enquiries.

Above all else, exhibitions are an important way of building relationships and sig-

Smartcard 2001 – GEMPLUS

The Smartcard 2001 exhibition was held at the Excel Centre in London. It is the largest event in the UK sector and represents an opportunity for companies such as GEMPLUS to showcase their products, to network with customers and prospects and to build relationships with partners and other significant stakeholders.

In order to maximise the opportunities these events present, GEMPLUS plans the design of the stand, the logistics associated with the build of the stand and the way in which the stand is staffed, maintained and supported throughout the exhibition.

However, GEMPLUS also ensures that key customers receive suitable corporate hospitality. One example of this is the invitation to dinner on one night during the exhibition. Guests are often drawn from customers across the vertical markets in which GEMPLUS operates.

Just as on-line communications need the support of off-line communications, so exhibitions need a similar form of complementary activity. In order that the right stakeholders attend the exhibition and visit the GEMPLUS stand, usually as guests, direct mail is used to advise of the event, invitations are sent three weeks before the exhibition and a reminder is sent 10 days later. The GEMPLUS Web site has full information while, at the show, sales promotions and merchandise are used as give-aways to act as memory joggers and to create positive associations with the company. See Plate 30.1.

Material kindly supplied by Felicity Best and Sam Ullah at GEMPLUS

nalling corporate identity. Trade shows are an important means of providing corporate hospitality and showing gratitude to all its customers, but in particular to its key account customers and others of strategic interest. Positive relationships with customers, competitors and suppliers are often reinforced through face-to-face dialogue that happens both formally in the exhibition hall and informally through the variety of social activities that surround and support these events.

Positive relationships with customers, competitors and suppliers are often reinforced through face-to-face dialogue.

Packaging and in-store media

As an increasing number of brand choice decisions are made during the shopping experience, advertisers have become aware of the need to provide suitable in-store communications. The primary objective of using in-store media is to direct the attention of shoppers and to stimulate them to make purchases. The content of messages can be easily controlled by either the retailer or the manufacturer. In addition, the timing and the exact placement of in-store messages can be equally well controlled.

As mentioned previously, both retailers and manufacturers make use of in-store media, although, of the two main forms (point-of-purchase displays and packaging), retailers control the point-of-purchase displays and manufacturers the packaging.

In-store: point of purchase (POP)

There are a number of POP techniques, but the most used ones are window displays, floor and wall racks to display merchandise, posters and information cards, plus counter and check-out displays. The most obvious display a manufacturer has at the point of purchase is the packaging used to wrap and protect the product until it is ready for consumption. This particular element is discussed in detail later.

The most obvious display a manufacturer has at the point of purchase is the packaging used to wrap and protect the product until it is ready for consumption.

Supermarket trolleys with a video screen attached to them have been trialed by a number of stores. As soon as the trolley passes a particular infrared beam a short video is activated, promoting brands available in the immediate vicinity of the shopper. Other advances include electronic overhead signs, in-store videos at selected sites around the store and coupons for certain competitive products dispensed at the check-out once the purchased items have been scanned. Indirect messages can also play a role in in-store communications: for example, fresh bread smells can be circulated from the supermarket bakery at the furthest side of the store to the entrance area, enticing customers further into the supermarket. Some aroma systems allow for the smell to be restricted to just 45 cm (18 inches) of the display.

End-of-row bins and cards displaying special offers are POP media that aim to stimulate impulse buying. With over 75% of supermarket buying decisions made in store, a greater percentage of communication budgets will be allocated to POP items.

■ Strengths

Point-of-purchase media are good at attracting attention and providing information. Their ability to persuade is potentially strong, as these displays can highlight particular product attributes at a time when shoppers have devoted their attention to the purchase decision process. Any prior awareness a shopper might have can be reinforced.

Point-of-purchase media are good at attracting attention and providing information.

From management's point of view, the absolute and relative costs of POP advertisements are low. Furthermore, management can easily fine tune a POP advertisement to reflect changing conditions. For example, should stock levels be high and a promotion necessary to move stock out, POP displays can be introduced quickly.

■ Weaknesses

These messages are usually directed at customers who are already committed, at least partly, to purchasing the product or one from their evoked set. POP messages certainly fail to reach those not actively engaged in the shopping activity.

There can be difficulties maintaining message continuity across a large number of outlets. Signs and displays can also be damaged by customers, which can impact upon the status of a product. Shoppers can therefore be negatively influenced by the temporary inconvenience of damaged and confusing displays. Unless rigorously controlled by store management, the large amount of POP materials can lead to clutter and a deterioration in the perception shoppers have of a retail outlet.

Packaging

For a long time packaging has been considered a means of protecting and preserving products during transit and while they remain in store or on the shelf prior to purchase and consumption. In this sense, packaging can be regarded as an element of product strategy. To a certain extent this is still true, however, technology has progressed considerably and, with consumer choice continually widening, packaging has become a means by which buyers, particularly in consumer markets, can make significant brand choice decisions. To that extent, because packaging can be used to convey persuasive information and be part of the decision-making process, yet still protect the contents, it is an important means of marketing communications in particular markets, such as FMCG.

Low-involvement decision-making requires peripheral cues to stimulate buyers into action. It has already been noted that decisions made at the point of purchase, especially those in the FMCG sector, often require buyers to build awareness through recognition. The design of packages and wrappers is important, as continuity of design in combination with the power to attract and hold the attention of prospective buyers is a vital part of point-of-purchase activity.

Low-involvement decision-making requires peripheral cues to stimulate buyers into action.

The degree of importance that manufacturers place upon packaging and design was seen in 1994, when Sainsbury's introduced its own Cola. The reaction of the Coca-Cola company to the lookalike design of the own-label product is testimony to the value placed upon this aspect of brand personality.

There are a number of dimensions that can affect the power and utility of a package. Colour is influential, as the context of the product class can frame the purchase situation for a buyer. This means that colours should be appropriate to the product class, to the brand and to the prevailing culture if marketing overseas. For example, red is used to stimulate the appetite, white to symbolise purity and cleanliness, blue to signal freshness and green is increasingly being used to denote an environmental orientation and natural ingredients. From a cultural aspect, colours can be a problem. Buckley (1993) suggests that in Germany bright bold colours are regarded as appropriate for baby products, whereas in the United Kingdom pastel shades are more acceptable.

Red is used to stimulate the appetite, white to symbolise purity and cleanliness, blue to signal freshness and green is increasingly being used to denote an environmental orientation and natural ingredients.

Colour coding – Boots

Boots the Chemist uses colour to visually direct and help its customers. Its baby toiletries, for which it has 70% market share, are coded such that shampoo products are yellow, bath products green and lotions pink. When the scheme was introduced it was only the caps that were coloured; now the entire plastic bottle is coloured.

The shape of the package may reflect a physical attribute of the product itself and can be a strong from of persuasion. Verebelyi (2000) suggests that this influence may be due to the decorative impact of some brands. Various domestic lavatory cleaners have a twist in the neck or a trigger action, facilitating directable and easier application. See Exhibits 30.1 and 30.2 for examples of two such products. Research indicated that Lever Brothers should develop a product that was directable in order that it clean lavatories more effectively and economically. Domestos, a well-established brand, was redesigned, together with the other Lever European bleach brands, in a suc-

Exhibits 30.1 Dettox and Domestos cleaning fluid brands – packages designed for easier application. Pictures kindly supplied by Reckitt Benckiser and Lever Bros.

cessful attempt to harmonise packaging. The shape may also provide information about how to open and use the product, while some packages can be used after the product has been consumed for other purposes. For example, some jars can be reused as food containers, so providing a means of continual communication for the original brand in the home. Packaging can also be used as a means of brand identification, as a cue by which buyers recognise and differentiate a brand. The supreme example of this is the Coca-Cola contour bottle, with its unique shape and immediate power for brand recognition at the point of purchase. See Plate 30.2.

Some jars can be reused as food containers, so providing a means of continual communication for the original brand in the home.

Package size is important, as different target markets may consume varying amounts of product. Toothpaste is available in large-size family tubes and in smaller containers for those households that do not use so much.

Exhibit 30.2 Packaging for a new brand Bioform®. Picture reproduced with the kind permission of Charnos and Lewis Moberly.

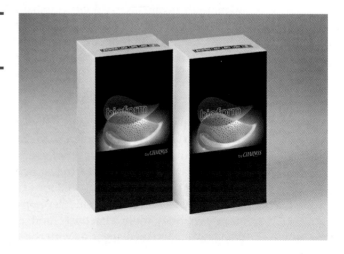

Washing and dishwasher powder manufacturers now provide plastic refill packs which are designed to provoke brand loyalty. These packs are cheaper than the original pack, partly because some of the packaging expense has been reduced as the customer has been introduced to the product at an earlier time. Purchase of the refill pack is dependent upon product quality and customer satisfaction and, as long as the brand name is prominent for identification and reminder purposes, the decision to select the refill is quicker, as most of the risk (financial, physical and social) has been removed through previous satisfactory usage.

All packages have to carry information concerning the ingredients, nutritional values and safety requirements, including sell-by and use-by dates. Non-food packages must also attempt to be sales agents and provide all the information that a prospective buyer might need and at the same time provide conviction that this product is the correct one to purchase. Labelling of products offers opportunities to manufacturers to harmonise the in-store presentation of their products in such a way that buyers from different countries can still identify the brand and remain brand loyal. For example, Buckley suggests that Unilever decided not to change the different brands of washing powder in favour of a pan-European brand. It decided instead to retain the existing names (Omo, Skip, Via, Persil and All) and to package them in a similar way, using similar visual devices, typography and colours. This not only allows customers to remain loyal but also presents opportunities to save on advertising and design costs and gain access to satellite and other cross-border media.

Packages carry tangible and intangible messages. The psychological impact that packages can have should not be underestimated. They convey information about the product but they also say something about the quality of the product (Hall, 1991) and how it differs from competitive offerings. In some cases, where there is little to differentiate products, buyers may use the packaging on its own for decision-making purposes.

Packages carry tangible and intangible messages.

Gordon (1996) argues that 'brand packaging communicates in the context of the competition and of related products'. This is achieved by using packaging that conforms to a design code that has been established for the category. This permits consumers to identify quickly the range of brands in the product field but does not necessarily allow for the identification of individual brands. She makes the important point that it is this process which allows own label brands to become part of a category without the support of advertising to establish credibility.

Packaging has been termed passive and active (Southgate, 1994). Passive packaging relies on vast amounts of advertising to infuse the design to create interest (e.g. Heinz). Active packaging is more demonstrative and tends to work with the other marketing and communication elements. Connolly and Davison (1996) quote Tango as an example of this type of packaging. Charnos Bioform® used packaging as an integral part of the overall brand. See Exhibit 30.2.

Passive packaging relies on vast amounts of advertising to infuse the design to create interest.

Product placement

One way of overcoming the irritation factor associated with advertisements screened in cinemas prior to a film showing is to incorporate the product in the film that is shown. This is referred to as product placement, which is the inclusion of products and services in films for deliberate promotional exposure, often, but not always, in return for an agreed financial sum. It is regarded by some as a form of sales promotion, but for the purposes of this text it is treated as an advertising medium because the 'advertiser' pays for the opportunity to present its product.

A wide variety of products can be placed in this way, including drinks (both soft and alcoholic), confectionery, newspapers, cars, airlines, perfume and even holiday destinations and sports equipment.

■ *Strengths*

By presenting the product as part of the film, not only is it possible to build awareness, but source credibility can be improved significantly and brand images reinforced. The audience are assisted to identify and associate themselves with the environment depicted in the film or with the celebrity who is using the product.

Levels of impact can be very high, as cinema audiences are very attentive to large-screen presentations.

Levels of impact can be very high, as cinema audiences are very attentive to large-screen presentations. Rates of exposure can be high, particularly now that cinema films are being released through video outlets and various new regional cable and satellite television organisations.

Perhaps the major advantage is that the majority of audiences appear to approve of this form of marketing communications, if only because it is unobtrusive and integral to the film (Nebenzahl and Secunda, 1993).

■ *Weaknesses*

Having achieved a placement in a film there is still a risk that the product will run unnoticed, especially if the placements coincide with distracting or action-orientated parts of the film. Associated with this is the lack of control the advertiser has over when, where and how the product will be presented. If the product is noticed, a small minority of audiences claim that this form of communication is unethical; it is even suggested that it is subliminal advertising, which is, of course, illegal. The

Product placement is not confined to cinema films. Music videos, television plays, dramas and soaps can also use this method to present advertisers' products.

absolute costs of product placement in films can be extremely high, counteracting the low relative costs or cost per contact. The final major drawback concerning this form of medium concerns its inability to provide explanation, detail, or indeed any substantive information about the product. The product is seen in use and is hopefully associated with an event, person(s) or objects which provide a source of pleasure, inspiration or aspiration for the individual viewer.

Product placement is not confined to cinema films. Music videos, television plays, dramas and soaps can also use this method to present advertisers' products.

Field marketing

Field marketing is a relatively new sector of the industry and seeks to provide support for the sales force and merchandising personnel along with data collection and research facilities for clients. The key to field marketing is the flexibility of services provided to clients. Sales forces can be hired on short-term contracts and promotional teams can be contracted to launch new prod-

It seeks to provide support for the sales force and merchandising personnel along with data collection and research facilities for clients.

Field marketing – Diet Pepsi

The Diet Pepsi brand was repositioned in 1997 to appeal to 18–24-year-old women. The brand was reformulated to overcome the aftertaste often associated with artificially sweetened drinks. By stressing the brand's different lifestyle positionings with 'Live life to the max' and 'Best tasting different' the campaign sought to present the brand with greater clarity and focus on the target audience.

Pepsi decided to undertake a nationwide sampling campaign entitled 'Tasting is Believing'. The goal was to reach 500,000 women in the target group, at venues such as shopping centres, parks, high streets, offices and beaches. The sampling was designed to build the brand identity and be relevant to the target audience: self-confident women. An all-female sampling team on rollerblades, clad in combat trousers and T-shirts, was chosen ahead of an all-male team, as 'the brand was require to talk *to* and *not at* [author's italics] women' (Campbell, 1997).

In contrast to this, the relaunch of Impulse, by Elida Gibbs, used an all-male team in order that the target audience be physically attracted to and motivated to move towards the sampling team and receive a spray of the new scent (Cobb, 1997).

ucts, provide samples (both in store and door to door) and undertake a range of other activities that are not part of an organisation's normal promotion endeavours.

The decision about whether to own or to hire a sales force has to be based on a variety of criteria, such as the degree of control required over not only the salesperson but also the message to be transmitted. A further criterion is flexibility. Ruckert *et al.* (1985) identified that in environments subject to rapid change, which brings uncertainty (for example, because of shortening product life cycles or large technological developments), the ability to adjust quickly the number of representatives in the distribution channel can be of major strategic importance. A further criterion is cost; for some the large fixed costs associated with a sales force can be avoided by using a commission-only team of representatives.

A number of pharmaceutical manufacturers use independent sales forces to supplement the activities of their own sales teams.

A large number of organisations choose to have their own their sales force, but of these many use the services of a manufacturer's agents to supplement their activities. A number of pharmaceutical manufacturers use independent sales forces to supplement the activities of their own sales teams.

Research undertaken by the Field Marketing Council found that there was a serious misunderstanding by clients and agencies of what field marketing activities encompass (McLuhan, 2000). Table 30.2 sets out the range of activities undertaken in the name of field marketing. To some extent it consists of tasks pulled from some of the five main promotional tools, repackaged and presented under a more contemporary title; for example, door-to-door and sales activities from personal selling, merchandising from both personal selling and sales promotion, sampling, which is a straight sales promotions task, and event marketing from public relations. Field marketing is a response to market needs and is a develop-

Field marketing is a response to market needs and is a development practitioners have pioneered to fulfil a range of customer need that presumably had not been adequately satisfied.

Table 30.2   Essential features of field marketing activities

Core activities	Essential features
Sales	Provides sales force personnel on either a temporary or a permanent basis. This is for business to business and direct to the public.
Merchandising	Generates awareness and brand visibility through point-of-purchase placement, in-store staff training, product displays and leaflets.
Sampling	Mainly to the public at shopping centres and station concourses but also for business-to-business purposes.
Auditing	Used for checking stock availability, pricing and positioning.
Mystery shopping	Provides feedback on the level and quality of service provided by retail staff and the promotion of special offers.
Event marketing	Used to create drama and to focus attention at sports events, open-air concerts and festivals. Essentially theatrical or entertainment based.
Door to door (home calls)	A form of selling where relatively uncomplex products and services can be sold through home visits. See illustration about Eastern Energy.

Source: Adapted from McLuhan (2000).

ment practitioners have pioneered to fulfil a range of customer need that presumably had not been adequately satisfied.

Field Marketing has undoubtedly expanded its role in recent years and in doing so has begun to establish itself as a core marketing support activity. Indeed, Moyies (2000) claims that field marketing should be cross-fertilised with direct marketing and sales promotion and in doing would not only benefit clients but add credibility to the industry.

Field marketing – Eastern Energy

CPM, a field marketing organisation, has been working with Eastern Energy to sign up new consumers to its services. Its targets have been existing and potential Eastern Energy customers at their homes to discuss their tariff options.

With a high level of competition there is an advantage to be able to explain benefits in person. As a result of the direct home sales approach, 160,000 new customers were signed up in 1998 alone. In 1999 the emphasis was on selling electricity accounts to its 3 million gas customers. Even if a visit fails to make a sale, CPM is able to collect demographic profile data and information on each household's use and a view of the competitors. This enables Eastern Energy to devise specific offers which can be highly targeted.

Eastern Energy, CPM and Ofgas (industry regulator) have worked together to formulate a working code of practice, and telephone audit checks are used to check on levels of customer satisfaction.

One of the essential tasks of field marketing is to continue to make brand signals available to consumers so that they can make the necessary brand associations that they have developed through advertising, and brand and category experience. It is a matter of keeping brand values alive at the point of purchase (Kemp, 2000).

Summary

As stated earlier, the use of exhibitions as a means of communicating with a variety of stakeholders has long been established. Organisations in both the consumer and the business-to-business markets use exhibitions as part of both pull and push strategies. Point-of-purchase communications are also seen to be an integral part of a coherent marketing communications a campaign. In sectors such as FMCG, packaging design is necessary to continue the brand associations that have been developed through above-the-line advertising and sales promotion work. Packaging plays an important role in terms of attracting attention, consolidating brand associations and conveying product category legitimacy.

Finally, the field marketing sector has grown as a reflection of the need of companies to be able to respond quickly to changing competitive conditions and customer needs. Field marketing companies provide a range of services, from merchandising and sampling to roadshows and personal selling.

Review questions

1. Evaluate the differences between consumer- and business-orientated trade shows.
2. As sales manager for a company making plastic mouldings for use in the manufacture of consumer durables, set out the reasons for and against attendance at trade shows and exhibitions.
3. Write brief notes explaining the role exhibitions might play in a company's integrated marketing communications strategy.
4. The development of interorganisational relationships is best undertaken through personal selling rather than through exhibitions and trade shows. Discuss.
5. Explain how packaging can be an integral part of a consumer's brand experience.
6. Find three brands where the shape of a package is an integral part of the product.
7. What is the difference between active and passive packaging?
8. Name two strengths and two weaknesses of product placement.
9. Identify four examples of product placement. Evaluate their effectiveness.
10. Name five core activities associated with field marketing and explain their essential features. Do not refer to Table 30.2 until you have attempted the exercise from memory.

MINI CASE

This mini case was written by Malcolm Kirkup, Lecturer at the University of Birmingham.

Halfords motor oil

Packaging in own-brand success

Halfords is the largest UK retailer of car parts and accessories. In 1996–97 Halfords achieved significant commercial success from their launch of a new range of own-brand motor oils. Success was partly achieved through an improvement in technical quality and competitive pricing, but innovation in packaging and marketing communication played a major role in substantially increasing Halfords' share of the motor oils market.

In 1995 Halfords' stores offered a mix of proprietary brands (Castrol, Duckhams and Mobil) alongside Halfords' limited own-brand range – Multigrade, XP7 and XP7i. Each brand range included different grades of oil to suit different types of engine, ages of engine, or different driving conditions. In 1995 Halfords' own-brand range achieved 6% brand share and, although perceived to offer good value for money, was not in the same quality league as the main proprietary brands. Following a review of the oil market in 1995, Halfords concluded there was significant potential to increase their own brand's share of the market as well as margins. They felt they could develop a serious alternative to the brand leaders, as well as extend the Halfords range into higher-margin diesel and synthetic oils.

Significantly, Halfords believed that innovation in *packaging* and *communication* could differentiate their brand. Research showed consumers were often confused when buying motor oil – many did not understand the difference between oil grades, terms such as 'viscosity' or which oil was correct for their car. Many chose their oil on price or out of habit. Furthermore, consumers were not satisfied with the handling or pouring qualities of existing oil containers. Halfords decided to deploy creative packaging design to overcome consumer concerns and creative communication to help consumers make a more informed choice of oil grade.

Halfords commissioned external agency Pentagram to design the containers, while agency Lippa Pearce developed the packaging graphics. The design brief stipulated that the cost of the new containers had to be kept in the same proportion to the cost of product as the existing containers, but the design also had to be differentiated from proprietary brands. The design had to produce shelf impact, communicate effectively, feature distinctive consumer benefits and reflect Halfords' brand values of quality, value for money, trust and confidence.

Pentagram's design process considered a host of factors – including aesthetics, handling, ease of filling, ease of manufacture, ease of transporting as well as uniqueness. Initial ideas included t-bar grips to help with pouring, hexagonal containers for ease of storage, churn-like containers to mimic old-fashioned oil jugs and even a shape that resembled a car wheel. Twelve designs were generated, and each was evaluated against 15 criteria. Halfords did not select the design that scored the highest on Pentagram's analysis but chose the most 'unique'. This design was later to pose significant challenges for manufacturing but it was also to prove a major factor in the product's success.

Features of the chosen design included ease of grip, the ability to lower the spout very near to the engine before oil begins to pour, a 'visi-strip' to indicate oil level and a leak- and tamper-proof cap. Different-coloured containers were proposed for each grade. The graphics took a visual direction from the type of information panels found in cars to give a feeling of technology and quality. Information on the front of the container was proposed to be simple and limited – viscosity, grade of oil, a description of cars for which that grade is suitable, and a quality statement. Information of secondary importance was on the reverse.

Consumer research was then commissioned to probe reactions to the design proposals. The classification system through colour coding was welcomed, and the metallic treatment enhanced the impression of quality. The proposed green and silver for Premium and Synthetic oils were well received, but not the yellow for Standard Plus (later changed to blue). Consumers immediately appreciated the visi-strip and ease of pouring and the containers were described as *modern, sculptured, expensive, different, impressive, eye catching* and *quality*. The consumer research demonstrated that the new packaging could successfully move Halfords Motor Oil up the hierarchy of brands. See Exhibit 30.3.

Before the packaging design was finalised, Halfords undertook further work to refine the 'quality' statement for the containers. They were keen to emphasise comparability with the leading brands and to maximise confidence, impact and understanding. Prior to launch the innovation in packaging was complemented by changes to in-store merchandising, and training programmes were also developed to help staff communicate the new range to consumers.

The new range was launched in May 1996. One year after launch Halfords were reporting average product prices across the range up 12%, a 19% increase in sales volume, 44% increase in sales value and 54% increase in margin. Halfords brand share in the UK motor oil market increased from 6% in 1996 to 12% in 1997.

Mini-case questions

1. Pentagram developed a list of 15 criteria against which their design proposals were evaluated. What might these criteria have been and what weighting would you have given to each criterion?

2. Develop recommendations for detailed labelling that should feature on Halfords' containers. Justify the information that should be included and decide how it should be worded and presented.

3. For the launch of the new range, the redesign and repositioning also required changes to merchandising within Halfords' stores. Considering Halfords' objectives for the new range, develop recommendations for merchandising (displays, shelf-space allocation, graphics, etc.) that will maximise impact, communicate the new classification system, convey the unique product benefits and encourage consumers to trade up. Bear in mind that Halfords wanted customers to appreciate that with the own-brand oil they could trade up to a higher grade but also save money.

4. When it came to the launch of the new range, Halfords decided that 'test marketing' would not be appropriate. They opted for a national launch on a set date. Consider the merits and disadvantages of this approach and develop a strategy for a national launch campaign.

Exhibit 30.3 New packaging of Halfords motor oils. Picture reproduced with the kind permission of Halfords.

References

Bertheron, P., Pitt, L.F. and Watson, R.T. (1996) The World Wide Web as an advertising medium. *Journal of Advertising Research,* **6**(1) (January/February), pp. 43–54.

Boukersi, L. (2000) The role of trade fairs and exhibitions in international marketing communications. In *The Handbook of International Marketing Communications* (ed. S. Moyne, pp. 117–35. London: Blackwell.

Buckley, N. (1993) More than just a pretty picture. *Financial Times,* 13 October, p. 23.

Campbell, L. (1997) Sampling with added sparkle. *Marketing,* 14 August, p. 25.

Cobb, R. (1997) Sweet smell of success. *Marketing,* 9 January, pp. 22–3.

Connolly, A. and Davison, L. (1996) How does design affect decisions at point of sale? *Journal of Brand Management,* **4**(2), pp. 100–7.

Gordon, W. and Valentine, V. (1996) *Buying the brand at point of choice.* MRS Conference, March.

Hall, J. (1991) Packaged good. *Campaign,* 18 October, pp. 21–3.

Kemp, G. (2000) Elastic brands. *Marketing Business* (October), pp. 40–1.

McLuhan, R. (2000) Fighting for a new view of field work. *Marketing,* 9 March, pp. 29–30.

Moyies, J. (2000) A healthier specimen. *Admap* (June), pp. 39–42.

Nebenzahl, I.D. and Secunda, E. (1993) Consumer attitudes toward product placement in movies. *International Journal of Advertising,* **12**, pp. 1–11.

Ruckert, R.W., Walker, O.C. and Roering, K.J. (1985) The organisation of marketing activities: a contingency theory of structure and performance. *Journal of Marketing* (Winter), pp. 13–25.

Shipley, D. and Wong, K.S. (1993) Exhibiting strategy and implementation. *International Journal of Advertising,* **12**(2), pp. 117–30.

Southgate, P. (1994) *Total Branding by Design.* London: Kogan Page.

Verebelyi, N. (2000) The power of the pack. *Marketing,* 27 April, p. 37.

31

Evaluating marketing communications

As part of the marketing communication process it is necessary to evaluate the overall impact and effect that a campaign has on a target audience. It needs to be reviewed in order that management can learn and better understand the impact of its communications and its audiences.

AIMS AND OBJECTIVES

The aim of this chapter is to review the ways in which marketing communications activities can be evaluated.

The objectives of this chapter are:

1. To discuss the role of evaluation as part of marketing communications.

2. To explore the value and methods of pre-testing and post-testing advertisements.

3. To provide an insight into the value of qualitative and quantitative testing techniques.

4. To appreciate the role technology plays in the assessment and evaluation of advertising.

5. To examine ways in which sales promotions can be evaluated.

6. To present the methods used to evaluate direct marketing.

7. To discuss the techniques and approaches used to measure and evaluate public relations.

8. To explore the ways in which personal selling activities can be measured.

9. To consider some of the issues associated with evaluating the effectiveness of on-line communications.

Introduction

All organisations review and evaluate the performance of their various activities. Many undertake formal mechanisms, while others review in an informal *ad hoc* manner, but the process of evaluation or reflection is a well-established management process. The objective is to monitor the often diverse activities of the organisation so that management can exercise control. It is through the process of review and evaluation that an organisation has the opportunity to learn and develop. In turn, this enables management to refine its competitive position and to provide for higher levels of customer satisfaction.

The process of evaluation or reflection is a well-established management process.

The use of marketing communications is a management activity, one that requires the use of rigorous research and testing procedures in addition to continual evaluation. This is necessary because planned communications involve a wide variety of stakeholders and have the potential to consume a vast amount of resources.

The evaluation of planned marketing communications consists of two distinct elements. The first element is concerned with the development and testing of individual messages. For example, a particular sales promotion (such as a sample pack) has individual characteristics that may or may not meet the objectives of a sales promotion event.

An advertising message has to achieve, among other things, a balance of emotion and information in order that the communication objectives and message strategy be achieved. To accomplish this, testing is required to ensure that the intended messages are encoded correctly and are capable of being decoded accurately by the target audience. The second element concerns the overall impact and effect that a campaign has on a target audience once a communications plan has been released. This post-test factor is critical, as it will either confirm or reject management's judgement about the viability of its communications strategy. The way in which the individual components of the communications mix work together needs to be understood so that strengths can be capitalised on and developed and weaknesses negated.

Testing is required to ensure that the intended messages are encoded correctly and are capable of being decoded accurately by the target audience.

This chapter examines the testing and evaluation methods that are appropriate to all the tools of the communications mix and introduces ideas relevant to the measurement of on-line communications.

The role of evaluation in planned communications

The evaluation process is a key part of marketing communications. The findings and results of the evaluative process feed back into the next campaign and provide indicators and benchmarks for further management decisions. The primary role of evaluating the performance of a communications strategy is to ensure that the communications objectives have been met and that the strategy has been effective. The secondary role is to ensure that the strategy has been executed efficiently, that the full potential of the individual promotional tools has been extracted and that resources have been used economically.

The evaluation process is a key part of marketing communications.

Research activity is undertaken for two main reasons. The first is guidance and development and the second is prediction and evaluation (Staverley, 1993). Guidance takes the form of shaping future strategies as a result of past experiences. Development is important in the context of determining whether the communications worked as they were intended to.

Prediction and evaluation require information about options and alternatives. For example, did sales presentation approach A prove to be more effective than B, and, if so, what would happen if A was used nationally? Predictably, the use of quantitative techniques is more prevalent with this set of reasons. This concluding chapter addresses the evaluation techniques appropriate for each of the promotional tools, in turn, before presenting a general summary of evaluation in marketing communications.

Advertising

An IPA report in 1998 stated that 23% of finance directors said that if business costs were under pressure they would cut marketing and advertising before anything else (Farrow, 1999). Among the reasons offered for this view was the feeling that advertising was extremely difficult to measure and thus problematic in terms of its overall contribution to the organisation. If in doubt, cut it. On a more optimistic note Fendwick (1996) suggests that there have been four main stages to the measurement of advertising effectiveness.

1. Direct response – coupon response.

2. Executions – measurement of consumer psychological responses to the way individual ads are executed. The recognition and recall techniques were developed and refined to reflect this approach.

3. Campaign evaluation (current age) – the evaluation of campaigns working over a period of time. The use of econometrics and modelling techniques to examine the influence of key variables typifies this approach.

4. Research nirvana (future age) – through the use of computers and vast data sets it will become possible to evaluate specific individual and panel data regarding various emotional and rational impacts of a variety of marketing communication messages. The effect will be to enable managers to adjust their communications messages and media quickly, efficiently and much more efficiently.

The techniques used to evaluate advertising are by far the most documented and, in view of the relative sizes of the promotional tools, it is not surprising that slightly more time is devoted to this tool. This is not to disregard or be disrespectful to the contribution each of the promotional tools can make to an integrated campaign. Indeed, it is the collective measure of success against the goals set at the outset that is the overriding imperative for measurement, as we shall see later.

Pre-testing

Advertisements can be researched prior to their release (pre-test) or after they have been released (post-test). Pre-tests, sometimes referred to as copy tests, have traditionally attracted more

Advertisements can be researched prior to their release (pre-test) or after they have been released (post-test).

attention, stimulated a greater variety of methods and generated much controversy, in comparison with post-tests.

Pre-testing, that is the practice of showing unfinished commercials to selected groups of the target audience with a view to refining the commercial to improve effectiveness, is still subject to debate about its effectiveness. It is argued that good pre-testing will support and seek to improve advertising performance, predictive in nature and positive in the way it sees the campaign developing (Reid, 2000)

The methods used to pre-test advertisements are based upon either qualitative or quantitative criteria.

The methods used to pre-test advertisements are based upon either qualitative or quantitative criteria. The most common methods used to pre-test advertisements are concept testing, focus groups, consumer juries, dummy vehicles, readability, theatre and physiological tests. Focus groups are the main qualitative method used and theatre or hall tests the main quantitative test. Each of these methods will be discussed later.

The primary purpose of testing advertisements during the developmental process is to ensure that the final creative will meet the advertising objectives. It is better to help shape the way an advertising message is formed, rather like potters continuously review their progress as they craft their vases, than to make a pot and then decide that it is not big enough or that the handle is the wrong shape. The practical objective of pre-testing unfinished and finished creative work is that it is more effective for an advertiser to terminate an advertisement before costs become so large and commitment too final. Changes to an advertisement that are made too late may be resisted partly because of the sunk costs and partly because of the political consequences that 'pulling' an advertisement might have.

Once a series of advertisements has been roughed or developed so that its messages can be clearly understood, advertisers seek reassurance and guidance regarding which of the alternatives should be developed further. Concept tests, in-depth interviews, focus groups and consumer juries can be used to determine which of the proposed advertisements are the better ones by using ranking and prioritisation procedures. Of those selected, further testing can be used to reveal the extent to which the intended message is accurately decoded. These comprehension and reaction tests are designed to prevent inappropriate advertisements reaching the finished stage.

Pre-testing unfinished advertisements

Concept testing

The concept test is an integral part of the developmental stage of advertising strategy.

The concept test is an integral part of the developmental stage of advertising strategy. The purpose is to reduce the number of alternative advertising ideas, to identify and build upon the good ideas and to reject those that the target audience feel are not suitable.

Concept testing can occur very early on in the development process, but is usually undertaken when the target audience can be presented with a *rough* outline or *storyboard* that represents the intended artwork and the messages to be used. See Exhibit 31.1. There are varying degrees of sophistication associated with concept testing, from the use of simple *cards* with no illustrations to *photomatics*, which are films of individual photographs shot in sequence, and *livematics*, which are films very close to the intended finished message. Their use will reflect the size of the advertiser's budget, the completion date of the campaign and the needs of the creative team.

Exhibit 31.1
Roughs for Kraft dressings prepared by Wayne Pashley and Nigel Pollard at J. Walter Thompson. Reproduced with kind permission.

Concept testing, by definition, has to be undertaken in artificial surroundings, but the main way of eliciting the target's views is essentially qualitatively orientated, based upon a group discussion. This group discussion is referred to as a focus group and is a technique used by most agencies.

Focus groups

When a small number (8–10) of target consumers are brought together and invited to discuss a particular topic, a focus group is formed. By using in-depth interviewing skills, a professional moderator can probe the thoughts and feelings held by the members of the group towards a product, media vehicles or advertising messages. One-way viewing rooms allow clients to observe the interaction without the focus group's behaviour being modified by external influences.

The advantage of focus groups is that they are relatively inexpensive to set up and run and they use members of the target audience. In this sense they are representative and allow true feelings and emotions to be uncovered in a way that other methods deny. They do not attempt to be quantitative and, in that sense, they lack objectivity. It is also suggested that the group dynamics may affect the responses in the 'artificial' environment. This means that there may be in-built bias to the responses and the interaction of the group members. Focus groups are very popular, but they should not be used on their own.

Consumer juries

A 'jury' of consumers, representative of the target market, is asked to judge which of a series of paste-ups and rough ideas would be their choice of a final advertisement. They are asked to rank in order of merit and provide reasons for their selections.

Emotional advertisements tend to receive higher scores than informational messages, even though the latter might do better in the marketplace.

There are difficulties associated with ranking and prioritisation tests. First, the consumers, realising the reason for their participation, may appoint themselves as 'experts', so they lose the objectivity that this process is intended to bring. Second, the 'halo' effect can occur, whereby an advertisement is rated excellent overall simply because one or two elements are good and the respondent overlooks the weaknesses. Finally, emotional advertisements tend to receive higher scores than informational messages, even though the latter might do better in the marketplace.

Pre-testing finished advertisements

When an advertisement is finished it can be subjected to a number of other tests before being released.

Dummy vehicles

Many of the pre-testing methods occur in an artificial environment such as a theatre, laboratory or meeting room. One way of testing so that the reader's natural environment is used is to produce a dummy or pretend magazine that can be consumed at home, work or wherever readers normally read magazines. Dummy magazines contain regular editorial matter with test advertisements inserted next to control advertisements. These pretend magazines are distributed to a random sample of households, that are asked to consume the magazine in their normal way. Readers are encouraged to observe the editorial and at a later date they are asked questions about both the editorial and the advertisements.

These pretend magazines are distributed to a random sample of households, that are asked to consume the magazine in their normal way.

The main advantage of using dummy vehicles is that the setting is natural, but, as with the focus group, the main disadvantage is that respondents are aware that they

Dummy vehicle – Flora

A test Flora advertisement comprising a central figure of a gingerbread man with copy above and below was inserted in *Woman* magazine and distributed on a complimentary basis to 150 housewives. Readers were asked to read the magazine in their normal manner over the course of a week, and they were not told what the purpose of the exercise was.

Three objectives were determined for the exercise:

■ The impact and branding of the advertisement.

■ The level of comprehension.

■ The generation of empathy toward the brand.

Results indicated that the gingerbread man provided a strong visual focus, which in turn generated empathy towards the brand. The copy line was also liked and read by an above average number of people.

However, by utilising the results, the size of the visual was increased and toned while the typestyle for the copyline was softened. The amount of copy was reduced and the Flora logo was repositioned for greater exit impact (Colinese, 1997).

are part of a test and may respond unnaturally. Research also suggests that recall may not be the best measure for low-involvement decisions or where motivation occurs through the peripheral route of the ELM. If awareness is required at the point of sale, then recognition may be a more reliable indicator of effectiveness than recall.

Readability tests

Rudolph Flesch (1974) developed a formula to assess the ease with which print copy could be read. The test involves, among other things, determining the average number of syllables per 100 words of copy, the average length of sentence and the percentage of personal words and sentences. By accounting for the educational level of the target audience and by comparing results with established norms, the tests suggest that comprehension is best when sentences are short, words are concrete and familiar, and personal references are used frequently.

Theatre tests

As a way of testing finished broadcast advertisements, target consumers are invited to a theatre (laboratory or hall) to preview television programmes. Before the programme commences, details regarding the respondents' demographic and attitudinal details are recorded and they are asked to nominate their product preferences from a list. At the end of the viewing their evaluation of the programme is sought and they are also requested to complete their product preferences a second time.

There are a number of variations on this theme: one is to telephone the respondents a few days after the viewing to measure recall and another is to provide joysticks, push buttons and pressure pads to measure reactions throughout the viewing. The main outcome of this process is a measure of the degree to which product preferences change as a result of exposure to the controlled viewing. This change is referred to as the *persuasion shift*. This approach provides for a quantitative dimension to be added to the testing process, as the scores recorded by respondents can be used to measure the effectiveness of advertisements and provide benchmarks for future testing.

It is argued that this form of testing is too artificial and that the measure of persuasion shift is too simple and unrealistic.

It is argued that this form of testing is too artificial and that the measure of persuasion shift is too simple and unrealistic. Furthermore, some believe that many respondents know what is happening and make changes because it is expected of them in the role of respondent. Those in favour of theatre testing state that the control is sound, that the value of established norms negates any 'role play' by respondents and that the actual sales data support the findings of the brand persuasion changes in the theatre.

A major evaluation of 400 individual advertising tests in the USA found, among many other things, that there is no clear relationship between measures of persuasion shift and eventual sales performance. This questions the use of an organisation's scarce resources and the viability of using these techniques (Lodish and Lubetkin, 1992).

This technique is used a great deal in the USA but has had limited use in the UK, until recently. However, Mazur (1993) reports that theatre testing is increasing in the UK. Agencies are concerned that the simplistic nature of recording scores as a means of testing advertisements ignores the complex imagery and emotional aspects of many messages. If likeability is an important aspect of eventual brand success, then it is unlikely that the quantitative approach to pre-testing will contribute any worthwhile information.

The increasing use of, or at least interest in, theatre tests and the movement towards greater utilisation of quantitative techniques in pre-testing procedures, runs concurrently with the increasing requirements of accountability, short-termism and periods of economic downturn. As no one method will ever be sufficient, a mix of qualitative and quantitative pre-test measures will, inevitably, always be required.

Physiological measures

A bank of physiological tests has been developed, partly as a response to advertisers' increasing interest in the emotional impact of advertising messages and partly because many other tests rely on the respondents' ability to interpret their reactions. Physiological tests have been designed to measure the involuntary responses to stimuli and so avoid the bias inherent in the other tests. There are substantial costs involved with the use of these techniques, and the validity of the results is questionable. Consequently, they are not used a great deal in practice, but, of them all, eye tracking is the most used and most reliable.

Eye tracking is the most used and most reliable.

Pupil dilation

Pupil dilation tests are designed to measure the respondent's reaction to a stimulus. Pupil dilation is associated with action and interest. If the pupil is constricted, then interest levels are low and energy is conserved. The level of arousal is used to determine the degree of interest and preference in a particular advertisement or package design.

On the surface, this method has a number of attractions, but it is not used very much as research has shown little evidence of success. The costs are high and the low number of respondents that can be processed limits the overall effectiveness.

Eye tracking

This technique requires the use of eye movement cameras which fire an infrared beam to track the movement of the eye as it scans an advertisement. The sequence in which the advertisement is read can be determined and particular areas which do or do not attract attention can be located; the layout of the advertisement can then be adjusted as necessary.

Galvanic skin response

This measures the resistance the skin offers to a small amount of current passed between two electrodes. Response to a stimulus will activate the sweat glands, which in turn will increase the resistance. Therefore, the greater the level of tension induced by an advertisement, the more effective it is as a form of communication.

When these deficiencies are combined with the high costs and low numbers of respondents that can be processed, it is not surprising that this method of pre-testing can have little but novelty value.

This simple premise is, however, misguided, as the

range of reactions and emotions, the degree of learning and recall, and aspects of preference and motivation are ignored. When these deficiencies are combined with the high costs and low numbers of respondents that can be processed, it is not surprising that this method of pre-testing can have little but novelty value.

Tachistoscopes

These measure the ability of an advertisement to attract attention. The speed at which an advertisement is flashed in front of a respondent is gradually slowed down until a point (about 1/100 second) is reached at which the respondent is able to identify components of the message. This can be used to identify those elements that respondents see first as a picture is exposed, and so facilitates the creation of impact-based messages.

Electroencephalographs

This approach involves the use of a scanner which monitors the electrical frequencies of the brain. There are essentially two ways of utilising this approach (Hansen, 1988). The first, hemispheric lateralisation, concerns the ability of the left-hand side of the brain to process rational, logical information. It tends to process verbal stimuli. In contrast, the right-hand side of the brain is thought to handle visual stimuli and respond more to emotional inputs. The right is best for recognition, the left is better for recall. Advertisements should be designed to appeal to each hemisphere, but recent research now appears to reject this once-popular notion.

The second approach involves measuring levels of brain activation. It is possible to measure the level of alpha wave activity, which indicates the degree to which the respondent is aroused and interested in a stimulus. Therefore, the lower the level of alpha activity, the greater the level of attention and cognitive processing. It would follow, therefore, that by measuring the alpha waves while a respondent is exposed to different advertisements, different levels of attention can be determined.

Both these approaches have been heavily criticised; indeed, the hemispheric lateralisation theory is rejected by many researchers.

Both these approaches have been heavily criticised; indeed, the hemispheric lateralisation theory is rejected by many researchers. Vaughn (1980) based part of his advertising planning grid (Chapter 12) on this theory, and it was regarded as an important breakthrough in our understanding of how advertising works. However, while the grid has been used extensively, there is little evidence of any commercial application of electroencephalographs.

Post-testing

Testing advertisements that have been released is generally more time consuming and involves greater expense than pre-testing. However, the big advantage with post-testing is that advertisements are evaluated in their proper environment, or at least the environment in which they are intended to be successful.

There are a number of methods used to evaluate the effectiveness of such advertisements, and of these inquiry, recall, recognition and sales-based tests predominate.

Inquiry tests

These tests are designed to measure the number of inquiries or direct responses stimulated by advertisements. Inquiries can take the form of returned coupons and response cards, requests for further literature or actual orders. They were originally used to test print messages, but some television advertisements now carry 0800 (free) telephone numbers. An increase in the use of direct response media will lead to an increase in the sales and leads generated by inquiry-stimulating messages, so this type of testing will become more prevalent.

Inquiry tests can be used to test single advertisements or a campaign in which responses are accumulated. Using a split run, an advertiser can use two different advertisements and run them in the same print vehicle. This allows measurement of the attention-getting properties of alternative messages. If identical messages are run in different media then the effect of the media vehicles can be tested.

Inquiry tests can be used to test single advertisements or a campaign in which responses are accumulated.

Care needs to be given to the interpretation of inquiry-based tests, as they may be misleading. An advertisement may not be efféctive simply because of the responses received. For example, people may respond because they have a strong need for the offering rather than the response being a reflection of the qualities of the advertisement. Likewise, other people may not respond despite the strong qualities of the advertisement, simply because they lack time, resources or need at that particular moment.

Recall tests

Recall tests are designed to assess the impression that particular advertisements have made on the memory of the target audience. Interviewers, therefore, do not use a copy of the advertisement as a stimulus, as the tests are intended to measure impressions and perception, not behaviour, opinions, attitudes or the advertising effect.

Normally, recall tests require the cooperation of several hundred respondents, all of whom were exposed to the advertisement. They are interviewed the day after an advertisement is screened, hence the reference to day-after-recall (DAR) tests. Once qualified by the interviewer, respondents are first asked if they remember a commercial for, say, air travel. If the respondent replies 'yes, Virgin', then this is recorded as *unaided recall* and is regarded as a strong measure of memory. If the respondent says 'no', the interviewer might ask the question 'did you see an advertisement for British Airways?' A positive answer to this prompt is recorded as *aided recall*.

These answers are then followed by questions such as 'What did the advertisement say about British Airways?', 'What did the commercial look like?' and 'What did it remind you of?' All the answers provided to this third group of questions are written down word for word and recorded as *verbatim* responses.

The reliability of recall scores is generally high. This means that each time the advertisement is tested, the same score is generated. Validity refers to the relationship or correlation between recall and the sales that ultimately result from an audience exposed to a particular advertisement. The

Recall tests have a number of other difficulties associated with them.

validity of recall tests is generally regarded by researchers as low (Gordon, 1992).

Recall tests have a number of other difficulties associated with them. First, they can be expensive, as a lot of resources can be consumed by looking for and qualifying respondents. Second, not only is interviewing time expensive, but the score may be rejected if, on examination of the verbatim responses, it appears that the respondent was guessing.

It has been suggested by Zielske (1982) that thinking/rational messages appear to be easier to recall than emotional/feeling ones. Therefore, it seems reasonable to assume that recall scores for emotional/feeling advertisements may be lower. It is possible that programme content may influence the memory and lead to different recall scores for the same offering. The use of a preselected group of respondents may reduce the costs associated with finding a qualified group, but they may increase their attention towards the commercials in the knowledge that they will be tested the following day. This will inevitably lead to higher levels of recall than actually exist.

On-the-air tests are a derivative of recall and theatre tests. By using advertisements that are run live in a test area, it is possible to measure the impact of these test advertisements with DAR. As recall tests reflect the degree of attention and interest in the advertisement, this is a way of controlling and predicting the outcome of a campaign when it is rolled out nationally.

Agencies accumulate vast amounts of recall data which can be used as benchmarks to judge whether an advertisement generated a score that was better or less than the average for the product class or brand.

Recall tests are used a great deal, even though their validity is low and their costs are high. Wells *et al.* (1992) argue that this is because recall scores provide an acceptable means by which decisions to invest heavily in advertising programmes can be made. Agencies accumulate vast amounts of recall data which can be used as benchmarks to judge whether an advertisement generated a score that was better or less than the average for the product class or brand. Having said that, and despite their popularity, they are adjudged to be poor predictors of sales (Lodish and Lubetkin, 1992).

Recognition tests

Recall tests are based upon the memory and the ability of respondents to reprocess information about an advertisement. A different way of determining advertising effectiveness is to ask respondents if they recognise an advertisement. This is the most common of the post-testing procedures for print advertisements. Of the many services available, perhaps the Starch Readership Report is the best known.

Recognition tests are normally conducted in the homes of approximately 200 respondents. Having agreed that the respondent has previously seen a copy of the magazine, it is opened at a predetermined page and the respondent is asked, for each advertisement, 'Did you see or read any part of the advertisement?' If the answer is yes, the respondent is asked to indicate exactly which parts of the copy or layout were seen or read.

Four principal readership scores are reported. The first is *noted*, that is the percentage of readers who remember seeing the advertisement. Second is *seen-associated*, the percentage of readers who recall seeing or reading any part of the advertisement identifying the offering. Third is *read most*, the percentage of readers who report reading at least 50% of the advertisement. Finally, signature is the percentage of readers who remember seeing the brand name or logo.

The reliability of recognition tests is very high, higher than recall scores.

The reliability of recognition tests is very high, higher than recall scores. Costs are lower, mainly because the questioning procedure is simpler and quicker. It is also possible to deconstruct an advertisement into its component parts and assess their individual effects on the reader. As with all interviewer-based research, bias is inevitable. Bias can also be introduced by the respondent or the research organisation through the instructions given or through fatigue of the interviewer.

The validity of recognition test scores is said to be high, especially after a number of insertions. However, there can be a problem of false claiming, where readers claim to have seen an advertisement but in fact have not. This, it is suggested, is because when readers confirm they have seen an advertisement, the underlying message is that they approve of and like that sort of advertisement. If they say that they have not seen an advertisement, the underlying message is that they do not usually look at that sort of advertisement. Krugman (1988), as reported by Wells *et al.* (1992), makes the important point that these readers are passing a 'consumer vote on whether the advertisement is worth more than a passing glance'. It might be that readers' memories are a reliable indicator of what the reader finds attractive in an advertisement and this could be a surrogate indicator for a level of likeability. This proposition has yet to be fully investigated, but it may be that the popularity of the recognition test is based on the validity rating and the approval that high scores give to advertisers.

Sales tests

If the effectiveness of advertisements could be measured by the level of sales that occurs during and after a campaign, then the usefulness of measuring sales as a testing procedure would not be in doubt. However, the practical difficulties associated with market tests are so large that these tests have little purpose. Only direct response counts and inquiry tests have any validity.

Practitioners have been reluctant to use market-based tests because they are not only expensive to conduct but they are also historical by definition.

Practitioners have been reluctant to use market-based tests because they are not only expensive to conduct but they are also historical by definition. Sales occur partly as a consequence of past actions, including past communication strategies, and the costs (production, agency and media) have already been sunk. There may be occasions where it makes little political and career sense to investigate an event unless it has been a success, or at the very least reached minimal acceptable expectations.

For these reasons and others, advertisers have used test markets to gauge the impact their campaigns have on representative samples of the national market.

Simulated market tests

This market representation is thought by some to provide an adequate measure of advertising effect.

By using control groups of matched consumers in particular geographic areas, the use of simulated test markets permits the effect of advertising on sales to be observed under controlled market conditions. These conditions are more realistic than those conducted within a theatre setting and are more representative of the national market than the limited in-house tests. This market representation is thought by some to provide an adequate measure of advertising effect. Other commentators, as discussed before, believe that unless advertising is the dominant element in the marketing mix, there are usually too many other factors which can affect sales. It is therefore unfair and unrealistic to place the sole responsibility for sales with advertising.

Single-source data

With the development and advances of technology it is now possible to correlate consumer purchases with the advertisements they have been exposed to. This is known as single-source data and involves the controlled transmission of advertisements to particular households whose every purchase is monitored through a scanner at supermarket checkouts. In other words, all the research data are derived from the same households.

The advent of cable television has facilitated this process. Consumers along one side of a street receive one set of control advertisements, while the others on the other side receive test advertisements. Single-source data provide exceptionally dependable results, but the technique is expensive, is inappropriate for testing single advertisements and tends to focus on the short-term effect, failing, for example, to cope with the concept of adstock.

In the UK many independent broadcasters have set up their own research facilities. Central TV first set up Adlab in the mid-1980s. This involved a panel of 1,000 housewives, each recording their media consumption and where, when and what they purchased. HTV introduced ScatScan, which requires the use of two panels each of 1,000 housewives, either side of the Bristol Channel. It was designed to help advertisers assess their advertising effectiveness in terms of copy testing, weight testing and even the use of mixed media. The use of split regions is very important, allowing comparisons to made of different strategies.

Other tests

There is a range of other measures that have been developed in an attempt to understand the effect of advertisements. Among these are tracking studies and financial analyses.

Tracking studies

A tracking study involves interviewing a large number of people on a regular basis, weekly or monthly, with the purpose of collecting data about buyers' perceptions of the advertisements and how these advertisements might be affecting the buyers' perceptions of the brand. By measuring and evaluating the impact of an advertising campaign when it is running, adjustments can be made quickly. The most common elements that are monitored, or tracked, are the awareness levels of an advertisement and the brand; image ratings of the brand and the focus organisation; and attributes and preferences.

By measuring and evaluating the impact of an advertising campaign when it is running, adjustments can be made quickly.

Tracking studies can be undertaken on a periodic or continuous basis. The latter is more expensive, but the information generated is more complete and absorbs the effect of competitor's actions, even if the effects are difficult to disaggregate. Sherwood *et al.* (1989) report that, in a general sense, continuous tracking appears more appropriate for new products and periodic tracking more appropriate for established products.

A further form of tracking study involves monitoring the stock held by retailers. Counts are usually undertaken each month, on a pre- and post-exposure basis. This method of measuring sales is used frequently. Audited sales data, market share figures and return on investment provide other measures of advertising effectiveness.

Financial analysis

The vast amount of resources that are directed at planned communications, and in particular advertising, requires that the organisation reviews, on a periodic basis, the amount and the manner in which its financial resources have been used. For some organisations the media spend alone constitutes one of the major items of expenditure. Pedigree Petfoods, according to Hazelhurst (1988), has three main areas of expenditure, other than staffing costs. These are the cans, the raw materials that go in them and the media spend to communicate the values of the brand. He regards it as imperative that the media spend be reviewed in just the same way as any other major item is bought on a forward basis, such as the cans, capital equipment or foreign exchange.

Variance analysis enables a continuous picture of the spend to be developed and acts as an early warning system should unexpected levels of expenditure be incurred.

Variance analysis enables a continuous picture of the spend to be developed and acts as an early warning system should unexpected levels of expenditure be incurred. In addition to this and other standard financial controls, the size of the discount obtained from media buying is becoming an important and vital part of the evaluation process.

Increasing levels of accountability and rapidly rising media costs have contributed to the development of centralised media buying. Under this arrangement, the promotion of an organisation's entire portfolio of brands, across all divisions, is contracted to a single media-buying organisation. Part of the reasoning is that the larger the account the greater the buying power an agency has, and this in turn should lead to greater discounts and value of advertising spend. For example, the high street retailer Boots has six major divisions, and each had traditionally been responsible for its own media spend (Izatt, 1993). In 1993 it was decided to centralise the buying under one media-buying centre. The deal, won by BMP DDB Needham, was reported to be worth £45 million a year and is intended to bring advertising economies of scale.

The point is that advertising economies of scale can be obtained by those organisations that spend a large amount of their resources on the media. To accommodate this, centralised buying has developed, which in turn creates higher entry and exit barriers, not only to and from the market but also from individual agencies.

Likeability

A major research study by the American Research Foundation investigated a range of different pre-testing methods with the objective of determining which were best at predicting sales success. The unexpected outcome was that, of all the measures and tests, the most powerful predictor was likeability: 'how much I liked the advertisement'.

From a research perspective, much work has been undertaken to clarify the term 'likeability', but it certainly cannot be measured in terms of a simple Likert scale of 'I liked the advertisement a lot', 'I liked the advertisement a little', etc. The term has a much deeper meaning and is concerned with the following issues (Gordon, 1992):

1. Personally meaningful, relevant, informative, true to life, believable, convincing.

2. Relevant, credible, clear product advantages, product usefulness, importance to 'me'.

3. Stimulates interest or curiosity about the brand; creates warm feelings through enjoyment of the advertisement.

The implication of these results is that post-testing should include a strong measure of how well an advertisement was liked at its deepest level of meaning.

The implication of these results is that post-testing should include a strong measure of how well an advertisement was liked at its deepest level of meaning.

Cognitive response analysis is an attempt to understand the internal dynamics of how an individual selects and processes messages, of how counter-arguing and message bolstering, for example, might be used to retain or reject an advertisement (see Chapter 21). Biel (1993) reports that there is a growing body of research evidence that links behaviour, attitude change and cognitive processing. He goes on to say that this approach, unlike many of the others, is not restricted to fast-moving consumer goods (FMCG) markets and can be deployed across service markets, durables and retailers.

One of the important points to be made from this understanding of likeability is the linkage with the concept of 'significant value' considered in Chapter 20. The degree to which advertising works is a measure of the impact a message makes with a buyer. This impact is mediated by the context in which messages are sent, received and personally managed. The main factors are that the product in question should be new or substantially different, interesting and stimulating, and personally significant. For advertising to be successful, it must be effective, and to be effective it should be of personally significant value to members of the target audience (those in the market to buy a product from the category in the near future).

The future use of technology will help the measurement and evaluation of advertising. The technology is now in place to meter what people are watching, by appending meters not to sets, but to people. Strapped on mobile people meters can pick up signals indicating which poster site, TV or radio programme is being walked past, seen or heard respectively.

Sales promotion

The measurement and evaluation of sales promotions are similar in principle to those conducted for advertising. The notion that some piloting should occur prior to launch in order that any wrinkles can be ironed out still holds strong, as does the need to balance qualitative with quantitative data. However, advertising seeks to influence awareness and image over the long term, whereas sales promotions seek to influence behaviour over the short term. As discussed earlier in this chapter, the evaluation of advertising can be imprecise and is subject to great debate. In the same way, the evaluation of sales promotions is subject to debate, but the means by which they are measured is not as ambiguous or as difficult as advertising (Shultz, 1987).

If the purpose of sales promotion is to influence purchasing behaviour, then a measure of sales performance is necessary in addition to the evaluation of individual promotions.

The use of quantitative methods as a testing tool leads to directly measurable and comparable outcomes, in comparison with the more subjective qualitative evaluations. Notionally, the balance in testing advertising is to use a greater proportion of qualitative than quantitative methods. The balance with sales promotions is shifted the other way. This is because the object being measured lends itself more to these kinds of measurement. If the purpose of sales promotion is to influence purchasing behaviour, then a measure of sales performance is necessary in addition to the evaluation of individual promotions.

In Chapter 24, the different types of sales promotion are discussed, and there it is identified that there are a number of different target audiences for sales promotions activities; these are resellers, consumers and the sales force.

Manufacturer to reseller

The main objectives are to stimulate the resellers to try new products and to encourage them to allocate increased shelf space for established products. If campaigns are devised to meet these objectives, then a pre- and post-test analysis of the amount of allocated shelf space and the number of new products taken into the reseller's portfolio needs to be completed. These processes are called retail audits (such as those undertaken by Nielsen Marketing Research), and although the information about changes in distribution and stock levels is not usually available until after the promotion has finished, it does provide accurate information concerning the effects that the event had on these variables.

Resellers to consumers

By generating higher levels of store traffic and moving stock from the store shelves to the consumers, sales promotions in this context require two main forms of evaluation. The first requires measures of the image held of the retailer, and this needs the use of tracking studies. The second requires measures of stock turnover per product category or brand against a predetermined planned level of turnover.

Manufacturers to consumers

The objectives are to encourage new users to try a product or to increase the amount that current users consume. Targets can be set for the number of coupons to be redeemed, sales generated during and after a price deal, the volume of bonus packs sold, the speed and volume of premiums disposed of and other direct measures of activity. Consumer audits reveal changes in the penetration and usage patterns of consumers.

Redemption levels give some indication of participation levels, but should not be considered as the sole method of evaluation.

Redemption levels give some indication of participation levels, but should not be considered as the sole method of evaluation, as there are many people who might be encouraged to purchase by the promotion but who then fail to participate for a variety of reasons.

Manufacturers to sales forces

The objectives of these activities are to build performance, morale and allegiance to the manufacturers and their products. Apart from measuring sales performance, the effectiveness of these activities can be expensive and difficult to measure. Attitude studies of the sales force can indicate the degree to which a contest has been influential, but it is hard to isolate the effects from those of other variables acting on them.

Through systematic tracking of sales and market share, products in mature markets can be evaluated in terms of their responsiveness to sales promotions. This type of information must be treated carefully, as the impact of other environmental factors has not been determined. Redemption rates allow for quantitative analysis, which, through time, leads to the establishment of a database from which benchmarks for promotional measurement and achievement can be obtained.

Using technology to evaluate sales promotions

It was noted in the previous section on advertising that advances in IT have radically altered the way in which advertising and product purchases can be evaluated. The same applies to sales promotions. It is now possible to predict with a high level of accuracy the impact on sales of different combinations of in-store promotions and price deals (Nielsen, 1993). This permits greater understanding of the way in which different sales promotions work and when they are most effective. This has two main benefits: the first is to focus promotions on activities that are effective; the second is to help to target the communication spend on periods of the year, month and week that consumers are most responsive.

Homescan is an electronic household panel offered by Nielsen, which tracks day-to-day shopping patterns. It measures the household penetration and the retail distribution of a product. Nielsen uses the system to analyse trial and repeat use. It can measure the number of households which use the product once and it can then determine how many of these trialists adopt a product through repeat purchase activity. It follows that test promotions can be used in particular stores or geographic areas, and control promotions can be used to test impact and effectiveness. What might work in one area might be unsuccessful elsewhere.

Coupons need not only be distributed via products and media. Technology has been developed which allows coupons of competitive brands to be automatically dispensed at the checkout once a product has been scanned.

Coupons need not only be distributed via products and media. Technology has been developed which allows coupons of competitive brands to be automatically dispensed at the checkout once a product has been scanned. This information, together with the demographics and psychographic details compiled for panel members, enables detailed profiles to be built up about the types, timing and value of sales promotions to which different consumers respond.

Sales promotions are a competitive tool that allows for swift reaction and placement. In that sense, they are not being used as part of an overall campaign, more as an *ad hoc* sales boost. This implies that the manageability of sales promotions is very high relative to the other elements of the promotions mix and that the opportunity to pre-test might not be as large in practice as is theoretically possible (Peattie and Peattie, 1993).

The evaluation of sales promotion is potentially fast, direct, precise and easily comprehended (Doyle and Saunders, 1985). However, evaluation is not necessarily that clear cut. The synergistic qualities of the promotion mix inevitably lead to cross-over effects where the impact of other communications influences responses to particular sales promotion events. Promotions may also bring about increased awareness in addition to the trial, use and switching activities. Peattie and Peattie suggest that not only might brand and product substitution result from promotions, but store loyalty patterns might also be affected.

Activities should be planned and research built into campaigns, but it is the availability of improved IT that will continue to improve and accelerate the quality of information that management has about its sales.

Of all the tools in the promotions mix, sales promotions lend themselves more easily to evaluation rather than to testing. Testing is not realistically possible in the time frames in which some organisations operate, particularly those in the FMCG sector. Activities should be planned and research built into campaigns, but it is the availability of improved IT that will continue to improve and accelerate the quality of information that management has about its sales.

Public relations

Each of the two main forms, corporate and marketing public relations, seeks to achieve different objectives and does so by employing different approaches and techniques. However, they are not mutually exclusive and the activities of one form of public relations impact upon the other; they are self-reinforcing.

Marketing public relations – Virgin Megastore

The launch of the Glasgow Virgin Megastore in December 1999 featured Richard Branson and Spice girl Mel C, abseiling down the building while Travis played a free gig in the street. All of this activity generated a great deal of exposure. *NME, Melody Maker, Big Breakfast, Channel Five News* and BBC Radio 1, *Financial Times, News of the World* and all of the Scottish Daily Press ran the feature. The stunt cost £94,000 the coverage was worth more than £1.2 million over three months.

Corporate public relations (CPR)

The objectives that are established at the beginning of a promotional campaign must form the basis of any evaluation and testing activity. However, much of the work of CPR is continuous, and therefore measurement should not be campaign orientated or time restricted but undertaken on a regular ongoing basis. CPR is mainly responsible for the identity cues that are presented to the organisation's various stakeholders as part of a planned programme of communications. These cues signal the visibility and profile of the organisation and are used by stakeholders to shape the image that each has of the focus organisation.

CPR is, therefore, focused upon communication activities, such as awareness, but there are others such as preference, interest and conviction. Evaluation should, in the first instance, measure levels of awareness of the organisation. Attention should then focus upon the levels of interest, goodwill and attitudes held towards the organisation as a result of all the planned and unplanned cues used by the organisation.

Traditionally these levels were assumed to have been generated by public relations activities. The main method of measuring their contribution to the communication programme was to collect press cuttings and to record the number of mentions the organisation received in the electronic media. These were then collated in a cuttings book which would be presented to the client. This would be similar to an explorer presenting an electric toaster to a tribe of warriors hitherto undisturbed by other civilisations. It looks nice, but what do you do with it and is it of any real use? Despite this slightly cynical interpretation, the cuttings book does provide an attempt to 'understand the level of opportunity to see' created by public relations activities (Parker, 1991).

The content of the cuttings book and the recorded media mentions can be converted into a different currency. The exchange rate used is the cost of the media that would have been incurred had this volume of communication or awareness been generated by advertising activity. For example, a 30-second news item about an organisation's contribution to a charity event may be exchanged for a 30-second advertisement at rate card cost. The temptation is clear, but the validity of the equation is not acceptable. By translating public relations into advertising currency, the client is expected not only to understand but also to approve of the enhanced credibility that advertising possesses. It is not surprising that the widely held notion that public relations is free advertising has grown so substantially when practitioners use this approach.

The content of the cuttings book and the recorded media mentions can be converted into a different currency.

A further refinement of the cuttings book is to analyse the material covered. The coverage may be positive or negative, approving or disapproving, so the quality of the cuttings needs to be reviewed in order that the client organisation can make an informed judgement about its next set of decisions. This survey of the material in the cuttings book is referred to as a content analysis. Traditionally, content analyses have had to be undertaken qualitatively and were therefore subject to poor interpretation and reviewer bias, however well they approached their task.

Increasingly sophisticated software is being used to produce a wealth of quantitative data reflecting the key variables that clients want evaluated.

Today, increasingly sophisticated software is being used to produce a wealth of quantitative data reflecting the key variables that clients want evaluated.

Hauss (1993) suggests that key variables could include the type of publication, the favourability of the article, the name of the journalist, the audiences being reached and the type of coverage. All these and others can be built into programmes. The results can then be cross-tabulated so that it is possible to see in which part of the country the most favourable comments are being generated or observe which opinion formers are positively or negatively disposed.

Corporate image

The approaches discussed so far are intended to evaluate specific media activity and comment about the focus organisation. Press releases are fed into the media and there is a response which is measured in terms of positive or negative, for or against. This quality of information, while useful, does not assist the management of the corporate identity. To do this requires an evaluation of the position that an organisation has in the eyes of key members of the performance network. In addition, the information is not specific enough to influence the strategic direction that an organisation has or the speed at which the organisation is changing. Indeed, most organisations now experience perpetual change; stability and continuity are terms related to an environment that is unlikely to be repeated.

The evaluation of the corporate image should be a regular exercise, supported by management. There are three main aspects. First, key stakeholders (including employees, as they are an important source of communications for external stakeholders), together with members of the performance network and customers, should be questioned regarding their perceptions of the important attributes of the focus organisation and the business they are in (Chapter 3). Second, how does the organisation perform against each of the attributes? Third, how does the organisation perform relative to its main competitors across these attributes?

The evaluation of the corporate image should be a regular exercise, supported by management.

The results of these perceptions can be evaluated so that corrective action can be directed at particular parts of the organisation and adjustments made to the strategies pursued at business and functional levels. For example, in the computer retailing business, prompt home delivery is a very important attribute. If company A had a rating of 90% on this attribute, but company B was believed to be so good that it was rated at 95%, regardless of actual performance levels, then although A was doing a superb job it would have to improve its delivery service and inform its stakeholders that it was particularly good at this part of the business.

Recruitment

Recruitment for some organisations can be a problem. In some sectors, where skills are in short supply, the best staff gravitate towards those organisations that are perceived to be better employers and provide better rewards and opportunities. Part of the task of CPR is to provide the necessary communications so that a target pool of employees is aware of the benefits of working with the focus organisation and develops a desire to work there.

Measurement of this aspect of CPR can be seductive. It is tempting just to measure the attitudes of the pool of talent prior to a campaign and then to measure it again at the end. This fails to account for the uncontrollable elements in CPR, for example, the actions of others in the market, but, even if this approach is simplistic and slightly erroneous, it does focus attention on an issue. ICI found that it was failing to attract the necessary number of talented undergraduates in the early and mid-1980s, partly because the organisation was perceived as unexciting, bureaucratic and lacking career opportunities. A coordinated marketing communications campaign was targeted at university students, partly at repositioning the organisation in such a way that they would want to work for ICI when they finished their degrees. The results indicated that students' approval of ICI as a future employer rose substantially in the period following the campaign.

Crisis management

During periods of high environmental turbulence and instability, organisations tend

When a crisis occurs, communications with stakeholders should increase to keep them informed and aware of developments.

to centralise their decision-making processes and their communications (Quinn and Mintzberg, 1992). When a crisis occurs, communications with stakeholders should increase to keep them informed and aware of developments. In Chapter 26, it was observed that crises normally follow a number of phases, during which different types of information must be communicated. When the crisis is over, the organisation enters a period of feedback and development for the organisation. 'What did we do?', 'How did it happen?', 'Why did we do that?' and 'What do we need to do in the future?' are typical questions that socially aware and mature organisations, that are concerned with quality and the needs of their stakeholders, should always ask themselves.

Pearson and Mitroff (1993) report that many organisations do not expose themselves to this learning process in fear of 'opening up old wounds'. Those organisations that do take action should communicate their actions to reassure all stakeholders that the organisation has done all it can do to prevent a recurrence, or at least to minimise the impact should the origin of the crisis be outside the control of management. A further question that needs to be addressed concerns the way the organisation was perceived during the different crisis phases. Was the image consistent? Did it change, and if so why? Management may believe that it did an excellent job in crisis containment, but what really matters is what stakeholders think; it is their attitudes and opinions that matter above all else.

The objective of crisis management is to limit the effect that a crisis might have on an organisation and its stakeholders, assuming the crisis cannot be prevented. The social system in which an organisation operates means that the image held of the organisation may well change as a result of the crisis event. The image does not necessarily become negative. On the contrary, it may be that the strategic credibility of the organisation could be considerably enhanced if the crisis is managed in an open and positive way. However, it is necessary for the image that stakeholders have of an organisation to be tracked on a regular basis. This means that the image and impact of the crisis can be monitored through each of the crisis phases. Sturges *et al.* (1991) argue that the objective of crisis management is to influence public opinion to the point that 'post-crisis opinions of any stakeholder group are at least positive, or more positive, or not more negative than before the crisis event'. This ties in with the need to monitor corporate image on a regular basis. The management process of scanning the environment for signals of change and change in the attitudes and the perception held by stakeholders towards the organisation make up a joint process which public relations activities have a major role in executing.

The objective of crisis management is to limit the effect that a crisis might have on an organisation and its stakeholders, assuming the crisis cannot be prevented.

The management process of scanning the environment for signals of change and change in the attitudes and the perception held by stakeholders towards the organisation make up a joint process which public relations activities have a major role in executing.

Marketing public relations (MPR)

It was identified earlier that there is evidence of the increasing use of MPR. There are many reasons for this growth, but some of the more important ones quoted by organisations are rising media costs, audience fragmentation, changing consumer attitudes and increasing educational needs (Kitchen, 1993). By using public relations to support the marketing effort in a direct way, organisations are acknowledging that the third-party endorsement provided by MPR delivers a high level of credibility and cost-effectiveness that the other elements of the promotions mix fail to provide.

As Kitchen rightly argues, MPR cannot exist in a vacuum; it must be integrated with the other elements of the mix and provide complementarity. It is through the use of MPR as a form of product support and as part of a planned communications mix that makes this a source of high-quality leads. However, evaluating the contribution of MPR is problematic.

Some practitioners believe that this can be overcome by coding press releases as a campaign, and with the use of particular software leads can be tracked and costed. Hauss (1993) quotes Obermayer of the Inquiry Handling Service, a US-based software house. If 25 press releases were generated and the client received 4,000 enquiries the analysis ends there. With the right software, the actual cost of a press release can be input and the number of leads that come back can be measured against sales on the database.

The software can not only estimate sales but also work out the number of leads required to make quota. The formula used is based on the rule that 45% of leads turn into sales for someone in the market within the year. The organisation's own conversion rate can be used to adjust the 45% and the quality of its lead conversion process can also be input.

The software can not only estimate sales but also work out the number of leads required to make quota.

One of the benefits of this approach is that quantitative outcomes provide a measure of effectiveness, but not necessarily the effectiveness of the MPR campaign.

Pre- and post-test measures of awareness, preference, comprehension and intentions are a better measure of the quality and impact that an MPR campaign might have on a target audience. Measuring the conversion ratio of leads to sales is not the only measure, as it fails to isolate the other forces that impact on market performance.

MPR in business-to-business markets is directly targeted at members of the performance network. The objectives are many and include building awareness, reducing costs, satisfying educational needs and enhancing image through improving credibility. The overriding need, however, is to improve the relationship between members of the network and to provide them with a reason to continue transactions with the focus organisation. The reasons are similar to those in the personal selling buying formula (Chapter 29), namely to associate product adequacy when the appropriate problem is surfaced and to create pleasant feelings when the name of the product or the organisation is mentioned in the same context. MPR in this situation is being used as a competitive tool to defend established positions. Measurement of the effectiveness of MPR, therefore, should be undertaken by evaluating the degree to which members support, like, endorse or prefer the focus organisation and the products it offers. This can be achieved through the use of tracking studies which plot attitudes and opinions, against which the timings of campaigns and MPR activities can be traced and evaluated.

Measurement of the effectiveness of MPR, therefore, should be undertaken by evaluating the degree to which members support, like, endorse or prefer the focus organisation and the products it offers.

Other measuring techniques – PR

Of all the tools available to practitioners, Goften (1999) reports the following as the most common approaches to measuring public relations:

Set objectives and agree the criteria in advance of a campaign.

Press cuttings, radio and TV tapes but this is a measure of volume and not quality of impact. A media equivalent value is then applied.

Media evaluation through commercial systems such as CAMMA, Impact, Precis. Under this approach, panels of readers judge whether a mention is positive or negative and whether the client's key message has been communicated. Computer programmes then cut through the data.

Tracking studies are expensive but are important when changing a perception of a brand etc.

Both CPR and MPR are difficult and elusive elements of the promotional mix to test, measure and evaluate. Practitioners use a variety of methods, but few of them provide the objectivity and validity that is necessary. For example, Comic Relief monitored the impact of media coverage on the organisation in the run up to Red Nose Day. It was able to track which initiatives were failing to attract attention and which issues were attracting negative coverage. It evaluated coverage over six key areas: TV initiatives, education, grants (Africa and UK), special projects, public fundraising and corporate fundraising.

Practitioners use a variety of methods, but few of them provide the objectivity and validity that is necessary.

The variety of measurement devices is increasing, especially as technology advances.

Technology and measuring PR – TeleTrax

TeleTrax is an electronic tagging system that can monitor broadcast use of its footage. Using an indelible code embedded within video tapes and through the use of approximately 100 listening posts across Europe, the company is alerted as soon as the tape is broadcast. Unfortunately it does not track the tone of the content. Monitoring the Internet for PR coverage is more taxing.

Net.Cut was set up originally to provide early warning of unfavourable corporate comment on the Internet. It can monitor comment in Internet publications, UK newsgroups and the WWW by searching the WWW at night and saving company mentions. The cuttings are then reviewed the following morning for key messages prior to warning the client as necessary. It costs about £50 a month and each alert costs an extra £1.

If, at the end of the process, evaluation and testing lack objectivity, then the method should not be used. As a greater number of organisations are beginning to recognise the impact that public relations can provide and establish a more credible balance to the promotional mix, so there is a greater requirement for planning and evaluation to be built into the process from the beginning (Watson, 1992).

Sponsorship

The measurement of sponsorship activities is problematic although the importance of doing so is accepted (Armstrong, 1998). The problem concerns the ability to separate the impact of the various elements of the promotional mix can be expensive and beyond the reach of smaller brands.

Many organisations attempt to measure the size of the media audience and then treat this as an indicator of effectiveness. This is misleading, as advertising and sponsorship are considered to work in different ways and cannot be measured in a similar way. Audiences consider events (a sports match, exhibition or TV programme) as their primary focus, not which organisation is sponsoring the activity, unlike advertising, where the message either dominates the screen or a page of a magazine and viewers attend according to their perceptual filters. The focus of attention is different, and so should be the means of evaluation.

Many organisations attempt to measure the size of the media audience and then treat this as an indicator of effectiveness.

Marshall and Cook (1992) found that sports sponsors preferred to use consumer surveys to examine customer (not audience) profiles, brand-related images, attitudes and purchasing activities. This was accomplished through the use of personal interviews and telephone and postal surveys. Because the level of funding in many of the smaller sponsorships is relatively low, few if any resources are allocating to evaluative practices.

Taylor Nelson *So*fres provides a single-source data panel (in collaboration with TSMS media sales house and Meridian Broadcasting). The viewing habits and purchase behaviour of a representative panel of consumers are monitored through a system called TVSpan. Unlike the similar competitive offering from TGI, TVSpan uses data from the AGB SuperPanel which collects data electronically. One of its prime tasks is to enable clients to monitor purchase behaviour and test advertisements at either pre- or post-test stage. Further uses are to test new creative ideas, to test the effects of advertising with or without below-the-line support and, interestingly, to test the interaction between advertising and sponsorship (Thorncroft, 1996).

The main way in which sponsorship activities should be measured is through the objectives set at the outset.

The main way in which sponsorship activities should be measured is through the objectives set at the outset.

By measuring performance rigorously against clearly defined sales and communication-based measures it is more likely that a reasonable process and outcome to the sponsorship activity will be established.

Personal selling

In contrast to the other elements of the promotional mix, personal selling requires different methods of evaluation. Pre- and post-testing the performance of each salesperson is impractical and inappropriate. What is more pertinent for evaluation are the inputs and the effectiveness (measured as outcomes) of the personal selling process. Oliver (1990) suggests that performance can be seen as a factor of the effort and costs (inputs) that an organisation contributes. Outputs can be regarded as sales and profits resulting from exchanges with customers, while productivity can be deemed to be the ratio of inputs to outputs (see Figure 31.1).

This is a useful approach because it focuses attention on aspects of the promotional process that can be measured with the use of quantitative tools. This contrasts with the other tools, where qualitative measures generally predominate. In addition to this framework, it is necessary to measure the effectiveness of the sales force as a unit and

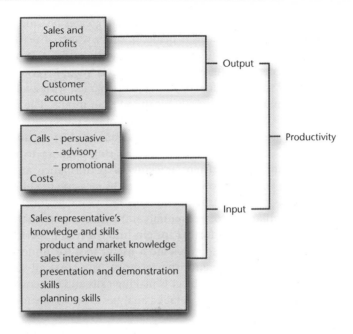

Figure 31.1   Methods for evaluating the performance of personal selling activities. From Oliver (1990); used with kind permission.

the degree to which interdepartmental cooperation is achieved in synchronising the activities of the mix.

Evaluating the performance of a salesperson

The performance of a salesperson requires the use of both qualitative and quantitative methods. There are two main types of inputs to the sales process. The first of these consists of the activities undertaken and the costs incurred as a result. The second type of input concerns the knowledge and skills necessary to achieve the required outputs. These will be examined in turn.

Measuring and then evaluating the activities of each salesperson, the inputs, is an important and frequently used measuring stick. The number of planned and unplanned sales calls, the number of presentations, the frequency with which the showroom has been used and the mix of accounts visited, plus the expenses, cost of samples used and time associated with these activities, can be measured and evaluated against organisational standards and expectations. These simple quantitative measures provide for objectivity and measurement; what they do not do is provide an insight into why the input and the ultimate performance rating did or did not achieve the required standard.

Measuring and evaluating the knowledge component of the input dimension require greater subjectivity and reliance on qualitative measures.

Measuring and evaluating the knowledge component of the input dimension require greater subjectivity and reliance on qualitative measures. How well a salesperson uses his or her selling skills and presents him- or herself to customers is vitally important. In addition, the depth of knowledge that the subject has of the products, customers, territory and market will probably have a greater bearing on the performance outcome than the number of visits made. In other words, it is the quality of the sales call that is important, not the number of sales calls made. As Churchill *et al.* (1990) claim, the measurement of these qualitative aspects 'must invariably rely on the personal judgement of the individual or individuals charged with evaluation'.

Outputs are more easily measured than inputs. The most common technique used is that of the ratings attached to the volume or value of sales generated in a particular period in a designated area. Using a quota to measure achievement can be important for consistent tracking of performance and for motivational purposes. Volume analysis allows management to measure the effectiveness of the sales process, as comparisons can be drawn with last year's performance, with other sales persons (with similar territory potential) and with the potential in the territory.

Outputs are more easily measured than inputs.

Ratios provide a further insight into the overall performance and productivity of a salesperson. Expense ratios are a useful tool for understanding the way in which a salesperson is managing the territory. The cost/call ratio, for example, reveals the extent to which the subject is making calls and the costs of supporting the individual in the territory. Further detailed analyses are possible, for example travel expenses/call:

$$\text{sales expense ratio} = \frac{\text{expenses}}{\text{sales}}$$

$$\text{cost per call ratio} = \frac{\text{total costs}}{\text{number of calls}}$$

Servicing ratios reveal the extent to which a territory's business potential has been acquired, for example, what percentage of a territory's accounts has been won, how many prospects become customers, how many customers are lost and what level of sales are achieved on average per customer or per call:

$$\text{account penetration ratio} = \frac{\text{accounts sold into}}{\text{total number of available accounts}}$$

$$\text{average order size ratio} = \frac{\text{total sales value}}{\text{total number of orders}}$$

$$\text{new account ratio} = \frac{\text{number of new accounts}}{\text{total number of accounts}}$$

The final group, activity ratios, determines the effort that is put into a territory. Calls/day, calls/account type and orders/call reveal the amount of planning and thought that is being put into an area:

$$\text{calls/accounts ratio} = \frac{\text{number of calls made}}{\text{total number of accounts}}$$

$$\text{orders/calls ratio} = \frac{\text{number of orders}}{\text{total number of calls}}$$

$$\text{calls/week ratio} = \frac{\text{number of calls}}{\text{number of weeks worked}}$$

In isolation these ratios provide some objectivity when attempting to measure the performance of a salesperson. Used in combination they become a more powerful tool, but only to the extent that they are an aid to decision-making. One major advantage of ratio analysis is the benchmarking effect. Comparisons become possible not only across the sales force but also across the industry, as norms become established through time.

While the traditional measure has been volume, increased emphasis is being placed upon measures of profitability, an efficiency measure (Burnett, 1993). The level of gross margin achieved by each salesperson and the contribution each makes to the overall profitability of the organisation are regarded by many organisations as more important than measures of volume. The approach requires the involvement of each salesperson not only in achieving the outcomes but also in the process of setting the appropriate performance targets in the first place. This requires different types of training and skills development, which in turn will affect the expectations held by each member of the sales force.

Evaluating the performance of a sales force

The methods looked at so far have been used to evaluate the performance of individual salespersons. An overall measure of the effectiveness of the larger unit, the sales force, is also necessary. The following constitute the main areas of evaluation: the objectives set in the promotion mix, the level of interaction with the other elements of the promotion mix, activity measures and achievement against quota, the effectiveness of the sales channels used and the quality of the relationships established with customers.

The sales force needs the support of the other elements of the mix.

The sales force, as a part of the promotion mix, has a responsibility to achieve the sales objectives set out in the promotion objectives. To do this the sales force needs the support of the other elements of the mix. Measuring this interdisciplinary factor is extremely difficult, but there is no doubt that each of the elements works more efficiently if they are coordinated with one another and the messages conveyed dovetail and reinforce each other.

Many of the measures used to evaluate the performance of individual salespersons can also be aggregated and used to evaluate the performance of the sales force as a whole. The sales force will have an overall sales budget, usually by volume and value, against which actual performance can be measured. The sales force will also be expected to open an agreed number of accounts each period and the value of business as a proportion of the potential will be watched closely.

There is no doubt that the role of the sales force is changing. If the expectations of the sales force are being adapted to new environmental conditions, it is probable that alternative measures will be required to determine the progress that a sales force is making. For example, in business-to-business markets, the traditional approach of the sales force is to manage products and their allocation to selected customers. The sales force of the future is going to be responsible, to a much greater degree, for the management of customer relationships (Wilson, 1993) and the maintenance of relational transactions that will provide organisations with strategic advantage. The use of simple quantitative techniques to measure the performance of the sales force will decline, the use of qualitative techniques will become more prevalent and the techniques themselves will become sophisticated. Measures will be required to evaluate the quality of the relationships developed by the sales force rather than the quantity of outputs achieved in a particular period. The traditional emphasis upon short-term quota achievement may well change to a focus upon long-term customer alliances and an evaluation of the strength of the relationship held between partners.

One further area of evaluation that is necessary is that of the sales channels themselves. The increased use of multiple sales channels and the contribution that direct marketing will make to the sales force cannot be ignored. Measures are required of the effectiveness of the field sales force, the key account selling team and the array of direct marketing techniques. Constant monitoring of the market is required to judge whether the classification of an account should be changed, and whether different combinations of selling approaches should be introduced.

One further area of evaluation that is necessary is that of the sales channels themselves.

Finally, customers need to be involved in the sales channel decision process and in the evaluation of the field sales force. If customers are happy with a sales channel, then they are more likely to continue using it. It is vital that the views of customers are monitored regularly and that they contribute to the evaluation process.

The evaluation of the sales force and its individual members has for a long time been orientated to quantitative measures of input and output productivity. These are useful, as they provide for comparison within the organisation and with the industry norms. However, in future, evaluation will move from revenue to a profit perspective and a much greater emphasis will be placed upon the quality of the relationships that the sales force develops with their customers. The current imbalance between the use of quantitative and qualitative measures will shift to a position where qualitative measures become more important in evaluating the performance of the sales force.

On-line communications

On-line research has grown as the Internet population has soared and the measures used have developed through trial and experience.

Banner ads

Not surprisingly there is disagreement about whether it is possible to measure effectively on-line advertising. Dreze and Zurfryden (1998) rightly point out that as a viable advertising media, Internet advertising must be subject to suitable measurement standards to gauge the effectiveness of the medium. Web servers can indicate how many pages have been requested, the time spent on each page and even the type of computers that were used to request the page. However, this type of information is largely superficial and fails to provide insight into the user, their motivation to visit the site or the behavioural or attitudinal outcomes as a result of the interaction. Traditional measurement techniques of reach, frequency and target audience impressions are not capable of being readily transferred to the Internet.

Internet advertising must be subject to suitable measurement standards to gauge the effectiveness of the medium.

Others argue that it is possible to measure on-line tools. For example, Briggs and Hollis (1997) point out that one of the more common measures used is the click-through rate. They indicate, however, that this normally only measures behaviour,

Table 31.1   On-line quantitative research

Strengths	Weaknesses
Relatively inexpensive	Respondent universe
Fast turnaround	Sampling issues: narrow target audience and difficult to identify
Automated data collection	Often self-completion, hence subject to self-selection
Can show graphics and video	Technical problems
No interviewer bias	
Quality of data	
Seamless international coordination	

whereas what is needed is an indicator of the user's attitudes. They claim to have developed a technique to measure attitudes (on-line) and show that banner advertising can be one of the most effective forms of advertising and brand development.

Web site effectiveness

Johnston cited by Gray (2000) reports that AC Nielsen offer a 9,000 strong panel in the UK. The panel consists of Internet users who have special software loaded on their PCs that records every web page they visit. The strengths and weaknesses of on-line qualitative and quantitative research are shown in Tables 31.1 and 31.2.

Good marketing management practice suggests that evaluation of any management activity should always include a consideration of the degree to which the objectives have been satisfied. However, the reasons organisations have for setting up a Web site are many and varied. For example, these might be to establish a Web presence, to move to new methods of commercial activity, to enter new markets, to adhere to parent company demands or to supplement current distribution channels. Consequently, it is not practicable to set up a definitive check list to use as a measure of Web site effectiveness, although certain principles need to be followed.

Table 31.2   On-line qualitative research

Strengths	Weaknesses
Slightly faster and cheaper than traditional focus group	Loss of non-verbal communications
Avoids the dominance of loud personalities	Less useful for emotional issues
More client control	On-line moderation requires new skills pattern
Can show concepts and/or Web sites	Slow keyboard skills can hamper some respondents
Allows for international coordination and permits mixed nationalities	Technical problems
	Sampling issues: difficult to identify a narrow target audience

Table 31.3 Criteria to assess Web site effectiveness

Visitor type	Cognitive state	Management action
All surfers	Level of awareness that a site exists: aware or not aware	Provide off-line and on-line information and directions
Those aware	Level of interest in the site: interested or not interested	Create interest and curiosity
Those interested	Known route to the site: determined or accidental	Enable greater opportunities for site hit
Determined visitors	Was the visit completed successfully? Transaction or no transaction	Encourage bookmarking and post-purchase communication to permit legitimate dialogue
Those who transacted	Will these visitors return to the site? Retained or not retained	Maintain and enhance top-of-mind site recall

Source: Adapted from Berthon *et al.* (1996). Used with kind permission.

One of the basic approaches is to develop profiles of Web site visitors built up by presenting every tenth visitor with a questionnaire. The next stage will be to provide media planners with these data to optimise banner ad placement. Based upon the work of Berthon *et al.* (1996), Table 31.3 suggests the criteria that might be used to test a site's effectiveness but that different criteria will have a different impact depending upon each organisation's situation.

There are difficulties associated with measuring the number of unique site visitors mainly because of various technology-related factors and the difficulties of isolating who is a unique visitor.

Dreze and Zufryden (1998) were apprehensive of the difficulties associated with measuring the number of unique site visitors mainly because of various technology-related factors and the difficulties of isolating who is a unique visitor.

Summary

The evaluation of a marketing communications plan, once implemented, is an essential part of the total system. The evaluation provides a potentially rich source of material for the next campaign and the ongoing communications that all organisations operate, either intentionally or not.

The degree to which the promotional objectives set for a campaign (Chapter 13) have been achieved has to be the focus of the evaluation process. The next important factor has to be the measurement of the contribution each part of the marketing communications mix may have made. Again, this can be determined from a holistic perspective or it can be usefully explored by employing some of the particular techniques and methodologies outlined in this chapter.

It would appear that, should resources be made available and should management appreciate the importance of measuring the effectiveness of their investment in marketing communications, then testing before and after exposure to each campaign activity is advisable, in order that a degree of change can be determined. While pre-

and post-testing is normally an advertising related approach the principle can be applied across all the tools of the mix, to some extent.

There are many issues involved with the assessment of each of the tools of the promotional mix, some associated with their individual characteristics. There is no perfect or ideal technique, but research must be undertaken if the communication performance of an offering is to be built or maintained. An important question is why so many managers choose not to measure effectiveness. The immediate answer is that all managers do measure the effectiveness as demonstrated through their observation of the sales results at the end of each period. However, proper testing and analysis is a practice rejected for many reasons. Some of the more prevalent ones are that research uses resources which some managers would prefer to sink into the product, to build sales or to building market awareness.

There can be disagreement about what is to be researched on the grounds that the many different people associated with a campaign have different needs, and as the budget is restricted the net result is that there is no research. Others argue that as it is very difficult, if not impossible, to isolate the effects of one particular tool, why waste resources on testing?

All these points can and should be refuted. Only by attempting to measure effectiveness will our understanding improve and lead to a more effective utilisation and more efficient use of marketing communications. Sales measurement is used most commonly because it is relatively cheap to administer and quick to implement, and to many managers sales and profits are derived from communications (and advertising in particular), so this constitutes the only meaningful measure.

Review questions

1. If the process is difficult and the outcomes imprecise, why should organisations evaluate and monitor their marketing communications?

2. What is pre- and post-testing?

3. Write a brief report comparing recall and recognition tests.

4. What are the principal dimensions of likeability as a measure of advertising effectiveness?

5. Identify four ways in which sales promotions can be evaluated.

6. Write brief notes explaining why the use of media comparison techniques are an insufficient when measuring the impact of public relations.

7. Why should the measurement of sales results be considered an inadequate measure of personal selling performance?

8. What are the techniques used to measure Web site effectiveness? Are they any good?

9. Many organisations fail to undertake suitable research to measure the success of their campaigns. Why is this and what can be done to change this situation?

10. Comment on the view that, if a method of evaluation and testing lacks objectivity and testing, then the method should not be used.

MINI CASE

This mini case was written by Julie Tinson, Marketing Lecturer at Bristol Business School.

East Coast Wireless

Background

East Coast Wireless, formally established in 1998, is a small family business which specialises in vintage and valve wireless repair, restoration and sales of restored wireless sets. The owners have, until recently, also been running a successful TV, VCR and audio repair and sales business called Vision Engineering, established in the late 1970s. However, because of the declining demand for this service, (most audio and visual products are now disposable and not repairable, especially with the advent of digital equipment, which even the manufacturers do not repair), it is planned that East Coast Wireless will become the principal focus of the business. East Coast Wireless (ECW), as the name suggests, is based in East Anglia.

Customers

The customers of ECW are perceived by the owners to be either over 50 or retired. However, lately several younger people have purchased a restored wireless to recapture their youth, or simply to match a 'period' look for a room. Some consumers are interested in the design content of the wireless and some in the technicalities of the 'innards'. There are also two types of customer – those wanting a restoration or supply of good-quality early transistor radios such as Hacker, Roberts, etc. and the valve radio owners or would-be owners.

Current communication

The type of products and service offered by ECW is increasingly in demand and the company has the appropriate skills and knowledge to exploit this need. However, it needs to develop its communication efforts and evaluate these to ensure that limited resources are effectively employed. It already has a Web site, although it is static at present, and further budget has been allocated to develop this marketing tool.

ECW has a stand at the National Vintage Wireless Show held at the NEC biannually. This is ECW's most successful selling venue and a relationship is developing with several regular customers.

A small amount of advertising and PR in the specialised press is undertaken (an advert in *Radio Bygones*, the magazine of the British Vintage Wireless Association). At present ECW advertises in *Saga Magazine*, expensive but effective, and in several specialist subscription magazines, mainly to maintain a presence rather than in expectation of direct work, although some work does result. As consumers contact ECW, they are asked how they heard of the company and most of its business seems to come from the Saga advertisement. No formal research or evaluation is conducted.

The outlook

ECW has the potential to be viable and successful. Future communication plans may include door drops, adverts in the local paper and PR on BBC Look East. Cross-selling and up-selling can also be utilised with little or no extra expense. Building the ECW brand is vital and can be facilitated by ensuring that plug stickers and leaflets go with every item leaving the shop.

Sponsorship, in kind, of local theatre productions to raise awareness among the local target audience has also been mooted as having potential.

Evaluation

Measuring the success of an integrated campaign, not merely the advertising effectiveness, is essential for the continuing success of this small but productive company.

More details can be found at www.East-Coast-Wireless.com.

Mini-case questions

1. Is there scope for evaluating and monitoring this organisation differently and, if so, in what ways would it make future communication both efficient and effective?

2. Which particular aspects would you monitor carefully and in what ways would this allow the integrated communications campaign to develop?

3. With the limited resources allocated for communication by small companies, is marketing research a realistic proposition?

References

Armstrong, C. (1998) Sport sponsorship: a case study approach to measuring its effectiveness. *European Research*, **16**(2), pp. 97–103.

Berthon, P., Pitt, L. and Watson, R. (1996) The world wide web as an advertising medium: toward an understanding of conversion efficiency. *Journal of Advertising Research*, **6**(1) (January/February), pp. 43–53.

Biel, A.L. (1993) Ad research in the US. *Admap* (May), pp. 27–9.

Briggs, R. and Hollis, N. (1997) Advertising on the Web: is there response before click-through? *Journal of Advertising Research*, **37**(2), pp. 33–46.

Burnett, J. (1993) *Promotion Management*. New York: Houghton Mifflin.

Churchill, G.A., Ford, N.M. and Walker, C. (1990) *Sales Force Management*. Homewood IL: Richard D. Irwin.

Colinese, R. (1997) Pretesting in the press. *Admap* (June), pp. 53–5.

Doyle, P. and Saunders, J. (1985) The lead effect of marketing decisions. *Journal of Marketing Research*, **22**(1), pp. 54–65.

Dreze, X. and Zurfryden, F. (1998) Is Internet advertising ready for prime time? *Journal of Advertising Research* (May/June), pp. 7–18.

Farrow, C. (1999) If it doesn't sell it isn't creative ... true or false? *Marketing News* (October/November), pp. 4–5.

Fendwick, P. (1996) The four ages of ad evaluation. *Admap*, (April), pp. 25–7.

Flesch, R. (1974) *The Art of Readable Writing*. New York: Harper & Row.

Goften, K. (1999) The measure of PR. *Campaign Report*, 2 April, p. 13.

Gordon, W. (1992) Ad pre-testing's hidden maps. *Admap* (June), pp. 23–7.

Gray, R. (2000) The relentless rise of online research. *Marketing*, 18 May, p. 41.

Hansen, F. (1988) Hemispheric lateralization: implications for understanding consumer behaviour. *Journal of Consumer Research*, **8**, pp. 23–36.

Hauss, D. (1993) Measuring the impact of public relations. *Public Relations Journal* (February), pp. 14–21.

Hazelhurst, L. (1988) How Pedigree Petfoods evaluate their advertising spend. *Admap* (June), pp. 29–31.

Izatt, J. (1993) Swayed Boots. *Media Week*, 1 October, pp. 20–1.

Kitchen, P.J. (1993) Public relations: a rationale for its development and usage within UK fast-moving consumer goods firms. *European Journal of Marketing*, **27**(7), pp. 53–75.

Krugman, H.E. (1988) Point of view: limits of attention to advertising. *Journal of Advertising Research*, **38**, pp. 47–50.

Lodish, L.M. and Lubetkin, B. (1992) General truths? *Admap* (February), pp. 9–15.

Marshall, D.W. and Cook, G. (1992) The corporate (sports) sponsor. *International Journal of Advertising*, **11**, pp. 307–24.

Mazur, L. (1993) Qualified for success? *Marketing*, 23 January, pp. 20–2.

Nielsen, A.C. (1993) Sales promotion and the information revolution. *Admap* (January), pp. 80–5.

Oliver, G. (1990) *Marketing Today*, 3rd edn. Hemel Hempstead: Prentice Hall.

Parker, K. (1991) Sponsorship: the research contribution. *European Journal of Marketing*, 25(11), pp. 22–30.

Peattie, K. and Peattie, S. (1993) Sales promotion – playing to win. *Journal of Marketing Management*, 9, pp. 255–69.

Pearson, C.M. and Mitroff, I. (1993) From crisis prone to crisis prepared: a framework for crisis management. *Academy of Management Executive*, 7(1), pp. 48–59.

Quinn, J.B. and Mintzberg, H. (1992) *The Strategy Process*, 2nd edn. Englewood Cliffs, NJ: Prentice Hall.

Reid, A. (2000) Testing Times. *Campaign*, 22 September, p. 40.

Sherwood, P.K., Stevens, R.E. and Warren, W.E. (1989) Periodic or continuous tracking studies: matching methodology with objectives. *Market Intelligence and Planning*, 7, pp. 11–13.

Shultz, D.E. (1987) Above or below the line? Growth of sales promotion in the United States. *International Journal of Advertising*, 6, pp. 17–27.

Staverley, N.T. (1993) Is it right ... will it work? *Admap* (May), pp. 23–6.

Sturges, D.L., Carrell, B.J., Newsom, D.A. and Barrera, M. (1991) Crisis communication management: the public opinion node and its relationship to environmental nimbus. *SAM Advanced Management Journal* (Summer), pp. 22–7.

Thorncroft, A. (1996) Business arts sponsorship: arts face a harsh set of realities. *Financial Times*, 4 July, p. 1.

Vaughn, R. (1980) How advertising works: a planning model. *Journal of Advertising Research* (October), pp. 27–33.

Watson, T. (1992) Evaluating PR effects. *Admap* (June), pp. 28–30.

Wells, W., Burnett, J. and Moriarty, S. (1992) *Advertising: Principles and Practice*, 2nd edn. Englewood Cliffs, NJ: Prentice Hall.

Wilson, K. (1993) Managing the industrial sales force of the 1990s. *Journal of Marketing Management*, 9, pp. 123–9.

Zielske, H.A. (1982) Does day-after recall penalise 'feeling' ads? *Journal of Advertising Research*, 22(1), pp. 19–22.

A

Suggested marketing communications plan for 'Porridge matters'

CONTENTS

Marketing communications plan for AHF:

Executive summary

The ambitious plan to increase market share by 50% over the next three years requires a communication strategy that repositions the Rainbow brand as a nutritious yet quick-to-prepare snack food. Using a push, pull and profile strategy, the Rainbow brand should have increased penetration through the independent sector and establish stronger brand values with a new market segment.

Contextual analysis

Business context

The organisation produces cereals under the Rainbow Foods brand (four products, of which three are muesli) and also produces many own-label products for the leading supermarket chains.

Established in the 1980s, AHF is relatively young in life cycle terms and might be most comfortably placed in the growth stage.

A growing turnover of £22 million, net profits of about 12% and market share at 8% rising to 12% over the next three years are indicative of an ambitious and well-managed organisation.

Distribution to over 2,300 independent retail outlets suggests wide geographic coverage and nationwide demand.

The marketing strategy requires that Rainbow be repositioned to meet the needs of the growing nutritious snack food market.

Customer context

The current target market is ABC1 women, aged 40–60, who have an active interest in healthy foods.

The emerging market, however, is characterised by people aged 18–35 who lead busy active lives and who perceive muesli products as a fast yet nutritious food which complements their lifestyle.

Positioned as a high-quality brand, premium pricing is sustained and the healthy food perception is a key factor in the brand's success to date.

Involvement in the purchase decision is relatively low, but the quality of the product and the health-based messages that have accompanied the brand to date have enabled buyers to reduce their functional risk and have used Rainbow to discriminate against competitor products. This has been a source of competitive advantage.

Internal context

Financially AHF seems well placed, but the promotional appropriation will be limited to approximately £1.7 million next year and £1.8 million the year after, assuming revenue growth of 10%.

Little is said about the internal marketing communication needs, but as a strong reputation is required, it will be necessary to develop good employee morale and identification with the aims and needs of the organisation. This means that resources must be diverted into good training programmes and good formal and informal communication systems.

Research activity appears limited, but the government report about nutrition presents an opportunity for the Rainbow brand to disassociate itself from the breakfast cereal market. This will allow for repositioning.

Awareness of the brand is 52% (current muesli users), but awareness among regular cereal buyers is much lower. Attitudes and perceptions are unknown and research in these areas is required.

External context

There appear to be trends towards healthier eating habits, but paradoxically working lives are becoming more demanding. A tension between the need to work and the need to live (eat) sensibly suggests opportunities for products that relieve the guilt associated with hard work and neglecting proper food intake.

Little is revealed about the stakeholders, but it is said that it is intended to grow the organisation and a combination of debt and equity will be sought from external financial sources to fund the policy. This means that it is necessary to develop suitable relationships with the financial markets and to communicate mission, strategies and performance results with these stakeholders.

It is necessary to communicate with the intermediaries on a regular basis to gain their cooperation and goodwill. In addition, it is important to communicate with the other organisations in the network and in the communities in which AHF operates, or is likely to operate, with a view to building the reputation of the organisation.

Promotional objectives and positioning

The promotional objectives are derived from the preceding analysis of the key communication factors facing AHF at the moment. In addition to the corporate objectives, two other sets of promotional objectives can be determined.

Corporate objectives

Over the next three years the corporate objectives are:

1. To increase turnover by 10% per annum. This level of performance for revenue and profits is justified on the basis of the increasing demand for health foods in many Western economies. This interest has recently received increased impetus from the media reports following the publication of the US report into health and cereal products.

2. To move into related markets with new products.

Marketing objectives

These are:

1. To double the Rainbow market share in the branded muesli market. This is justified by Rainbow's strong market position, positive perceptions held by independent grocery buyers towards AHF and the good levels of current buyer satisfaction.

2. To increase the purchase frequency of Rainbow muesli by current users from five to seven packets per year.

3. To increase the penetration level of independent stockists who sell Rainbow muesli from 2,300 to 3,000 over the next three years.

4. To improve ROI by 15% per annum.

This can be achieved by utilising a more efficient promotional mix and by driving other internal efficiency measures.

Marketing communication objectives

These are:

1. To raise levels of prompted awareness among current muesli consumers from 52% to 65% over the next 12 months.

2. To raise prompted and spontaneous awareness of Rainbow muesli among the emerging market of 18–35-year-old ABC1 males and females over the six months finishing 31 March next year.

3. To reposition Rainbow muesli among the current and emerging markets as a healthy, invigorating and life-enhancing all-purpose snack/food.

4. To achieve 60% of independent stockists preferring Rainbow as their first-choice muesli product.

Positioning

The market size for muesli and health foods is very likely to increase by anything from 12% to 16% per annum over each of the next five years, according to latest independent reports.

In order to compete and achieve the stated objectives, it will be necessary to reposition the brand and provide a stronger point of differentiation for consumers. This will be achieved by identifying the brand as a product that not only satisfies the health expectations of buyers but also is perceived as a snack food for anytime consumption. Key messages will require minimal copy, owing to the low level of involvement, but strong visual messages associating work and healthy food will be crucial.

The use of a strong spokesperson will be important for both internal and external audiences.

Promotional strategies

All three promotional strategies are required.

Pull strategy

A pull strategy will be required to achieve the awareness levels stated above and to reposition the brand as specified.

Such credibility can be enhanced with the use of suitable endorsers to assist cognitive processing, which is most likely to be via the peripheral route. A strategy to utilise significant opinion leaders will be necessary.

Messages should strengthen the position that Rainbow muesli is a healthy snack food that fits in with busy lifestyles. To assist in educating audiences, the use of recipes and innovative meals might be of assistance, together with sponsorship of appropriate events to which the 18–35-year-old market can relate.

The US report and other data will be used to substantiate benefit claims.

Fifty per cent of available resources are notionally allocated to pull.

Push strategy

A push strategy is necessary in order that the marketing objectives of an increased number of outlets can be achieved. Also, the communications objectives to achieve the required 60% preference rate among independent outlets need to be supported through consistent and high-quality communications.

Profitability targets are more likely to be achieved if margin does not have to be given away in the form of discounts to get shelf presence.

Thirty-five per cent of available resources are notionally allocated to a push strategy.

Profile

A profile strategy is necessary in order to build interest and understanding of AHF by various significant stakeholders, such as the financial sector, employees and the local community.

The key messages are that AHF is an environmentally aware, strategically credible and financially sound organisation which represents a good investment opportunity. In addition, the accent is to communicate high levels of service and deliver through positive employee identification.

While only 15% of available resources are to be allocated over the next 12 months, this figure will rise over the following two years.

The promotional mix

In the light of the desired strategies it is necessary to formulate three promotional mixes and allocate funds accordingly (Tables A.1–A.5). These costs are approximate

Table A1 The promotional mix to support the pull strategy

Advertising	Advertising is required to meet the awareness and repositioning goals. This is best achieved through an integrated approach. Television advertising is not possible because of the relatively small financial resources available. Radio, however, may provide suitable opportunities. Posters are to be used to build awareness (48 sheet and Adshel). To raise awareness in the emerging market of 18–35-year-olds, advertisements need to be placed in suitable general-interest magazines, such as *Cosmopolitan*, *Marie Claire*, *Loaded* and *FHM*. Celebrity opinion leaders need to be seen to use and endorse the brand. In order to reach current buyers, specialist consumer interest magazines should be used to convey the health and vitality message.
Sales promotion	Promotional leaflets available through health food and other independent high street outlets provide not only health information but also advice about diet and recipes using Rainbow oats. Sampling will be a major part of the repositioning exercise from which public relations opportunities will arise.
Sponsorship	Sponsorship opportunities to reinforce the positioning intentions need to be located.
Direct marketing	A database needs to be set up. Using a sales promotion (competition) to engage the new market will provide names and addresses for future mailings.
Public relations	Marketing public relations activities need to focus on the sponsorship opportunities and the celebrity opinion leaders.

Table A2 The promotional mix to support the push strategy

Personal selling	Personal selling will be important not only to achieve the sales output targets but also to reinforce the revised brand position. This will require training and a review of the skill requirements necessary to penetrate the sector and develop new relationships with significant accounts.
Sales promotion	High-quality sales literature will be used to reinforce the brand attributes and the positioning intentions. In an attempt to get strong self-presence, case discounts and advertising allowances should be offered to larger retailers and groups. Incentive schemes, such as competitions, are to be developed to encourage retailer involvement.
Advertising	Restricted use with most effort placed in leading trade journals (e.g. *The Grocer*). Promotional materials specific to the European markets will need to be prepared in order to support the Swiss agent. Independent retailers need to be supported with promotional materials including point-of-purchase materials.
Direct marketing	Direct mail facilities to be used to reach independent retailers and telemarketing to be used to service low-potential accounts.
Public relations	Marketing public relations are to be used to communicate the values and benefits of the Rainbow brand.

Table A3 The promotional mix to support the profile strategy

Public relations	The regular use of corporate public relations to reach all stakeholders is important. AHF should endeavour to understand the attitudes and disposition of significant stakeholders and should consider adjusting its stance as necessary. The use of press releases and events will be important.
Sponsorship	AHF should use sponsorship to develop awareness with potential investors and key stakeholders.
Newsletters	These are to be used to reach employees, intermediaries and others associated with the organisation.
Employee conferences	Employee conferences, as a reward, as a motivational factor and as a means of disseminating information, need to be held on a regular basis.
Training	Training for all employees in terms of providing high levels of customer service.

and the objective and task approach method will be required to determine actuals before implementation.

The schedule

Once the promotional mix is finalised, the next task is to schedule the activities so that resources can be allocated. In addition, it is necessary to manage the implementation so that there is consistency and integration. Indeed, an important aspect of IMC is the

Table A4   The schedule

	Year 1				Year 2			
	Q1	Q2	Q3	Q4	Q1	Q2	Q3	Q4
Pull strategy								
Advertising	✓	✓	✓	✓	✓	✓	✓	✓
Sales promotion		✓		✓		✓		✓
Sponsorship			✓	✓	✓	✓	✓	✓
Database	✓	✓	✓	✓	✓	✓	✓	✓
Public relations		✓			✓	✓	✓	
Push strategy								
Personal selling	✓	✓	✓	✓	✓	✓	✓	✓
Trade (sales) promotions	✓	✓		✓	✓		✓	✓
Advertising	✓		✓			✓	✓	
Direct marketing		✓	✓	✓		✓	✓	✓
Public relations	✓	✓	✓	✓	✓	✓	✓	✓
Profile strategy								
Public relations	✓	✓	✓	✓	✓	✓	✓	✓
Sponsorship			✓	✓	✓	✓	✓	✓
Newsletters		✓		✓		✓		✓
Employee conferences		✓		✓		✓		✓
Training	✓		✓		✓			✓

Table A5   The promotional budget (amounts in £000)

	Year 1	Year 2	Total
Pull strategy			
Advertising	480	330	810
Sales promotion	170	180	350
Sponsorship	nil	100	100
Direct marketing	75	150	225
Public relations	45	50	95
Research	80	90	170
Total pull cost	*850*	*900*	*1,750*
Push strategy			
Personal selling	(separate budget)		
Trade (sales) promotions	310	320	630
Advertising	110	90	200
Direct marketing	95	125	220
Public relations	35	40	75
Research	50	55	105
Total push cost	*600*	*630*	*1,230*
Profile strategy			
Public relations	40	45	85
Sponsorship	50	60	110
Newsletters	10	15	25
Employee conferences	50	55	105
Training	70	70	140
Research	30	25	55
Total profile cost	*250*	*270*	*520*
Total cost of promotional plan	£1.7 million	£1.8 million	£3.5 million

mutual reinforcement that the tools of the mix can provide. To help achieve the potential a Gantt chart can be developed. This can provide a quick visual interpretation of the sequence and timing of the promotional activities.

Control and evaluation

For the plan to remain on target, control procedures are required. These will be implemented partly by external agencies responsible for their own parts of the plan, but we will be responsible for the overall delivery and control.

Variance analysis will be used on a quarterly basis to monitor budgetary spend levels and a series of quantitative and qualitative measure will be used to evaluate the effectiveness of the individual elements as well as the overall impact of the promotional activities.

Focus groups, tracking studies (awareness and perception) and recall tests will be used to monitor the development of the Rainbow brand and the reputation of AHF.

In particular, the objectives set for both the marketing and the marketing communications components will be assessed regularly and will be the main form of evaluation of the campaign as an integrated marketing communications plan.

Author index

Subject index